S0-ADK-511

Sunset

MORE ideas for great DECORATING

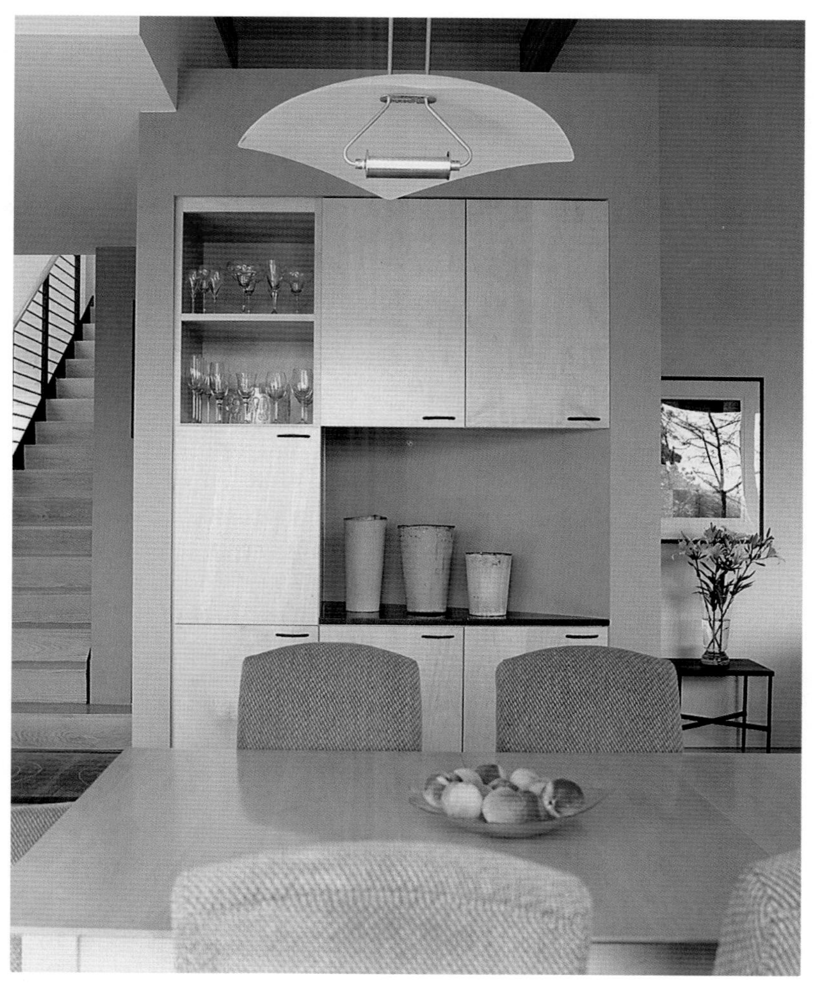

By Scott Atkinson, Cynthia Bix, Christine Olson Gedye,
Susan Lang, Marie Tupot Stock, and the Editors of Sunset Books

Menlo Park, California

Sunset Books
Vice President, General Manager:
Richard A. Smeby
Vice President, Editorial Director:
Bob Doyle
Production Director:
Lory Day
Director of Operations:
Rosann Sutherland
Retail Sales Development Manager:
Linda Barker
Executive Editor:
Bridget Biscotti Bradley
Art Director:
Vasken Guiragossian
Special Sales:
Brad Moses

Staff for this book:
Developmental Editors:
Kathryn Lescroart Detzer, Linda J. Selden
Editors:
Lynne Gilberg, Linda Hetzer
Copy Editors:
Barbara J. Braasch, Phyllis Elving, Marcia Williamson
Design:
Joe di Chiarro, Barbara Vick
Illustrations:
Beverley Bozarth Colgan, Susan Jaekel, Bill Oetinger, Eileen Whalen
Photo Director/Stylist:
JoAnn Masaoka Van Atta
Photo Research:
Toby Greenberg
Principal Photographers:
Jamie Hadley, Philip Harvey, Tom Haynes, E. Andrew McKinney
Prepress Coordinators:
Eligio Hernandez, Danielle Javier, Patricia S. Williams
Computer Production:
Kathy Avanzino Barone, Linda Bouchard, Areta Buk/Thumb Print, Susan Bryant Caron
Production Assistant:
Sara Newberry
Proof Reader:
Mary Roybal

10 9 8 7 6 5 4 3 2 1
First printing July 2004

ISBN 0-376-01267-6
Library of Congress Control Number: 2004106519
Printed in China.

More Great Ideas!

Following in the footsteps of our successful *Ideas for Great Decorating, More Ideas for Great Decorating* is a compilation of six previously published books: *Ideas for Great Wall Systems, Ideas for Great Home Lighting, Ideas for Great Baby Rooms, Ideas for Great Kids' Rooms, Ideas for Great Floors*, and *Ideas for Great Backyard Cottages.* With this new book as a guide, you will be able to create organized storage for your possessions; learn the latest techniques in home lighting—indoors and out; provide a special, very personal first environment for your baby; create a fun, inviting room for your child; select the floor covering of your dreams; and build your own backyard retreat. From a comfortable armchair you can examine scores of up-to-the-minute rooms in full color or explore the latest in beautiful designs and materials. When you're ready to dig in, you'll also find solid planning information as practiced by the pros.

Many individuals and firms assisted in the development of these Ideas for Great books. We'd especially like to thank Eurodesign Ltd. of Los Altos, CA; Galvins Workspace Furniture of Redwood City, CA; Häfele of San Francisco, CA; Southern Lumber Company of San Jose, CA; Ikea of Emeryville, CA; and Organized Living of San Mateo, CA for *Ideas for Great Wall Systems;* J. Art Hatley of Fiberstars, Inc. of Fremont, CA; Leslie Siegel of Cherish Gaines Lighting Systems of Berkeley, CA; Doug Ascher of Universal Light Source of San Francisco, CA; LIMN of San Francisco, CA; Stanford Electric Works of Palo Alto, CA; Coast Lighting of Redwood City, CA; and The Home Depot of East Palo Alto, CA for *Ideas for Great Home Lighting;* Sherri Peake of Bellini in Bellevue, WA; Go To Your Room of Seattle, WA; Cartan's Kids Stuff of San Ramon, CA; Ikea; Safety for Toddlers of Kirkland, WA; Barbara McQueen Interior Design; the Environmental Home Center; the Washington Toxics Coalition; the U.S. Consumer Products Safety Commission; and Lighting Design Lab of Seattle, WA for *Ideas for Great Baby Rooms;* Azrock Industries, Inc.; BetLar Products, Inc.; Calico Corners; California Kids; Circus Floors; Citation Carpet Mills; Eurodesign, Ltd.; Hold Everything; Imperial Wallcoverings; Jonathan Kaye; Juvenile Lifestyles, Inc.; Kids Furniture and Lullaby Lane; Lakeshore Learning Materials; Marin Designer Showcase; National Floor Products Co.; Palacek; Rubbermaid; Samson-McCann; San Francisco Decorator Showcase; Wallpapers to Go; Wroolie and LoPresti; Dr. Oscar L. Frick of the University of California at San Francisco; George Krall of Colgate Mattress Company; and Fox Elementary School in Belmont, CA for *Ideas for Great Kids' Rooms;* Hal Tupot of Custom Modern Tile & Construction; Bob Daniels of The Tile Council of America; Melissa Watkins; Cathy Gutkowski; Mark Frolich and Marge Ventura of the Expo Design Center in Union, NJ; Carol Swedlow of Aronson's; Jan MacLatchie of Artistic Tile; Brian J. Sakosits and Robert W. Sanzari of Hoboken Floors; Ray Wolf of Home Depot; and Halina Switzer of Nemo Tile for *Ideas for Great Floors;* and Karl Golden of Berkeley, CA; Keiko Takayama; San Francisco Decorator Showcase 2001; Roger Reynolds Nursery & Carriage Shop of Menlo Park, CA; and Jim and Cherylyn McCalligan for *Ideas for Great Backyard Cottages.*

Individual credits for design and photography are listed on pages 702–711.

contents

Ideas for Great Wall Systems **4**

Get Organized! **6**

A Planning Primer **9**

Great Wall Systems **29**

A Shopper's Guide **89**

Index **712**

Ideas for Great Home Lighting **128**

Paint It with Light **130**

A Planning Primer **133**

Great Lighting Ideas **153**

A Shopper's Guide **219**

Index **712**

Ideas for Great Baby Rooms **252**

A Dream Coming True **254**

A Planning Primer **257**

Great Baby Room Ideas **279**

A Shopper's Guide **333**

Index **712**

Ideas for Great Kids' Rooms **360**

Focusing on Kids **362**

A Planning Primer **365**

Great Kids' Rooms **395**

A Shopper's Guide **429**

Index **712**

Ideas for Great Floors **454**

On Which We Stand **456**

A Planning Primer **459**

Great Floor Ideas **481**

A Shopper's Guide **555**

Index **712**

Ideas for Great Backyard Cottages **578**

Cottage Pleasures **580**

Planning Your Cottage **583**

A Gallery of Cottages **609**

Cottage Elements **675**

Index **712**

Sunset

ideas for great wall systems

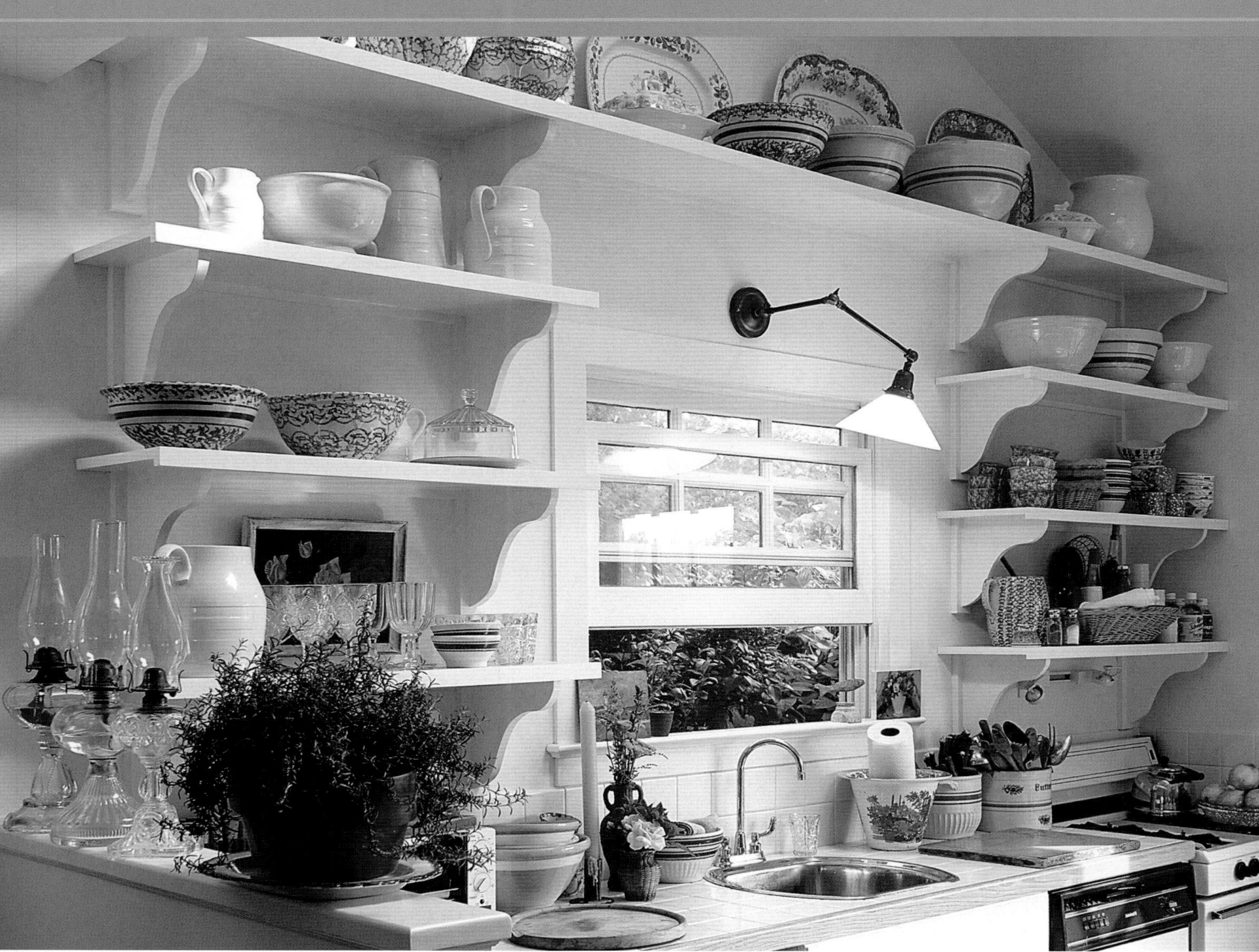

By Scott Atkinson and
the Editors of Sunset Books

Menlo Park, California

contents

6

Introduction

9

A Planning Primer

29

Great Wall Systems

89

A Shopper's Guide

712

Index

special features

Maximum Spans Between Supports **18**

Need Help? **19**

A Home Theater Overview **22**

Finding the Right Knobs & Pulls **99**

Tame Those Wires **113**

A Look at Finishing Products **125**

get organized!

BOOKS, TVs, COMPUTERS, compact discs, collectibles, sports gear—the piles of "stuff" that most people manage to accumulate over the years are staggering. Yet few homes provide enough space to stow all these goods in an orderly way.

When you can't stack your audio gear any higher, when your favorite collection is languishing in boxes in the basement, and when you can't wedge one more book onto your shelves, it's time to think about how to make better use of your present storage space or how to add to it without having to remodel your home or move to a new one.

One way to create a lasting solution to your organization and storage needs is to bring wall systems into the picture. What, you might ask, *is* a wall system? For an overview, see pages 10–11. A workable wall system can be as simple as an open shelf or as high-tech as a custom home-theater unit with drawers, doors, dividers, pullouts, and built-in speakers and lighting. Wall systems can stand alone or be built into a wall and finished to match the surroundings. They can hide messy storage items, showcase a prized collection, or perform both roles at once.

Deciding that you need a wall system is just the beginning. The next step is to evaluate your options. What items in your home need better organization? Where is the best place to put them? What approach works best? The first chapter of this book, "A Planning Primer," will guide you through the basics.

As you narrow down your choices, turn to the photos in the second chapter, "Great Wall Systems," for inspiration and ideas. You'll probably discover solutions you never thought of before.

Finally, you'll be ready to focus on the exact unit that's right for you. The third chapter, "A Shopper's Guide," will familiarize you with the myriad choices in shelves, cabinets, storage furnishings, and accessories on the market today.

In no time at all, you'll be enjoying the ease and convenience of a clutter-free home with a place for everything and everything in its place. Hopefully you've left some room for the *next* collection!

Manuel

A PLANNING PRIMER

READY TO JUMP IN? In the second chapter, "Great Wall Systems," you'll see photo after photo of open shelves; bold, multiuse storage walls; freestanding furniture pieces; and the latest in media glamour and gizmos. **BUT FIRST THINGS FIRST:** This chapter will help you identify your basic needs and explore your options in styles and materials of both freestanding furniture pieces and seamless, custom built-ins. Then it's time for some basic engineering—important details on shelf spans; shelf connections; sizes for books, CDs, and other media accessories; and ergonomic heights and depths. We'll also travel through the latest options in entertainment centers and home theater hookups. **FINALLY, WE TAKE A ROOM-BY-ROOM** tour, outlining ways you can get wall systems and shelves to work for you in almost any situation. For a more in-depth look at specific components and hardware choices, turn to "A Shopper's Guide," beginning on page 89.

what is a wall system?

The term *"wall system" is actually a catchall phrase that covers a broad sweep of furnishings used for display, organization, and storage. Wall systems range from simple open shelves to large component systems that include cabinets with doors, adjustable shelves, stacks of drawers, clothes rods, a desk, and even a drop-down bed. Traditional furniture pieces like armoires, hutches, and highboys may also fill the bill. These wall systems can go in virtually any room of the house and are used to store just about any household item.*

Shelves and boxes

Take a second to study the drawing on the facing page. You'll see horizontal shelves, vertical supports, drawer boxes, cabinet boxes, and doors that cover them. When it comes to wall systems, it all boils down to a matter of verticals, horizontals, and sometimes added boxes.

At its simplest, a wall system is a series of horizontal shelves hung on an open wall. Vertical sides or "uprights" support shelves inside a frame, like a shelving unit; shelves may be fixed or movable.

A bookcase is a frame that formalizes the relationship of both horizontals and verticals—in this example, a top, a bottom, and two sides. It often includes a back to keep the other elements firm and complete the box. A cabinet adds a door atop this open box. Drawers slide inside the box frame, too; think of them as "boxes within a box."

Bridge two boxes and you have a desk. Stack three tall boxes side-by-side and you have a media center. More elaborate systems add accessories such as hooks, sliding shelves, towers, racks, and other organizers.

Modularity is key

One feature characteristic of many wall systems is modularity. Components and accessories are often sized so that they can be interchanged and reconfigured as your needs change. Shelves can be raised or lowered, drawers refitted, and cabinet boxes stacked or ganged side by side. When you move, just break down the individual pieces and take them with you. It's this flexibility that makes modular systems so popular.

What makes all this possible? Uprights and components are all designed to fit a so-called "32-millimeter" grid. In other words, uprights, typically spaced about 24 or 32 inches apart, are drilled with double rows of holes every 32 millimeters (see facing page); shelf supports, drawer guides, door hinges, and even cabinet boxes plug right into these holes.

A LOOK AT CLASSIC COMPONENTS

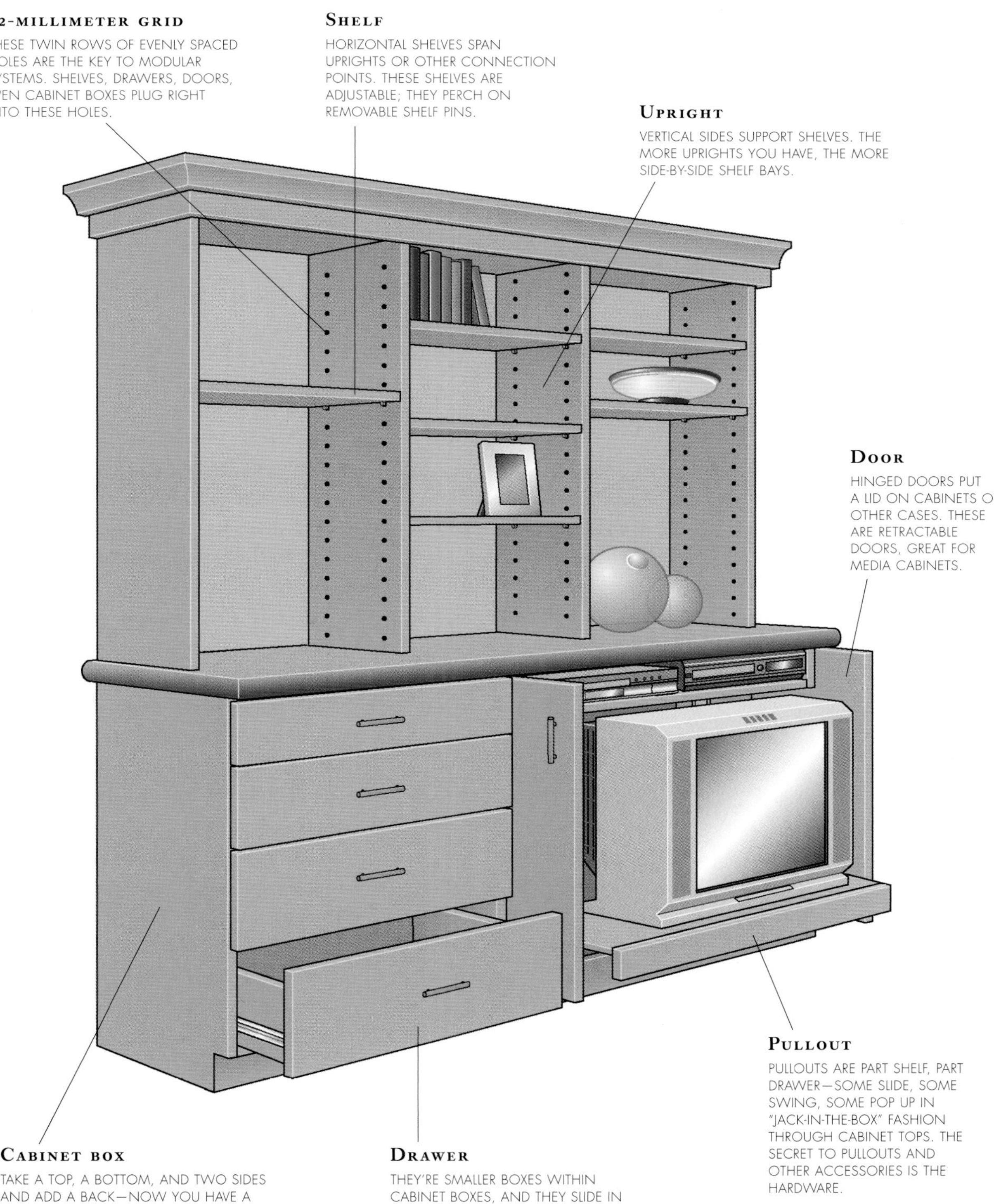

32-MILLIMETER GRID
THESE TWIN ROWS OF EVENLY SPACED HOLES ARE THE KEY TO MODULAR SYSTEMS. SHELVES, DRAWERS, DOORS, EVEN CABINET BOXES PLUG RIGHT INTO THESE HOLES.
SHELF
HORIZONTAL SHELVES SPAN UPRIGHTS OR OTHER CONNECTION POINTS. THESE SHELVES ARE ADJUSTABLE; THEY PERCH ON REMOVABLE SHELF PINS.
UPRIGHT
VERTICAL SIDES SUPPORT SHELVES. THE MORE UPRIGHTS YOU HAVE, THE MORE SIDE-BY-SIDE SHELF BAYS.
DOOR
HINGED DOORS PUT A LID ON CABINETS OR OTHER CASES. THESE ARE RETRACTABLE DOORS, GREAT FOR MEDIA CABINETS.
PULLOUT
PULLOUTS ARE PART SHELF, PART DRAWER—SOME SLIDE, SOME SWING, SOME POP UP IN "JACK-IN-THE-BOX" FASHION THROUGH CABINET TOPS. THE SECRET TO PULLOUTS AND OTHER ACCESSORIES IS THE HARDWARE.
CABINET BOX
TAKE A TOP, A BOTTOM, AND TWO SIDES AND ADD A BACK—NOW YOU HAVE A CABINET BOX OR "CARCASE."
DRAWER
THEY'RE SMALLER BOXES WITHIN CABINET BOXES, AND THEY SLIDE IN AND OUT ON SLEEK METAL GUIDES OR OTHER RUNNERS.

exploring your options

WALL SYSTEMS *come in an almost endless number of versions. You can buy budget pine shelving, fine hardwood cabinetry, a modern laminate library wall, a reproduction Shaker unit, high-end lacquered cabinetry, and scores of other styles. Your options span a wide range of sizes, shapes, and prices.*

Furniture or built-ins?

Broadly speaking, there are two different types of wall systems: furniture pieces and built-ins. To thicken the plot, furniture can be subdivided into traditional freestanding storage pieces and modern modular units. Here's a closer look at the pros and cons of each.

STORAGE FURNITURE. An obvious advantage of freestanding furniture is that it's movable. If it doesn't work in one location or is no longer needed there, you can move it somewhere else. And it goes along with you when you move. Moreover, you can see exactly what you're getting in the store and can usually, though not always, get quick delivery.

One drawback to buying ready-made storage pieces is that you may not always be able to get exactly the size and configuration you want.

MODULAR WALL SYSTEMS. As the name implies, modular components are designed to be mixed and matched—choose the look first, then the shelves, drawers, doors, and other accessories you need. Some modular systems are available "ready-to-assemble" or RTA, and can be broken down flat, moved, then reassembled elsewhere. You can rearrange them or buy additional components as your needs change.

Though buying modular components offers a great deal of flexibility, no system can meet every possible need. Modular systems complement modern room designs well, but if you're looking for a traditional or "unfitted" look, storage pieces or built-ins may be better options.

BUILT-INS. Perhaps the most favored feature of built-ins is that they can look almost seamless in a room. They also allow you to tailor the space precisely to your needs. Though some premade cabinetry can be fitted to look built-in, for the most part, built-ins are customized to your specifications by a cabinetmaker, finish carpenter, or other professional.

Built-ins are particularly well suited to odd-size spaces in your home where a piece of storage furniture can't fit—for example, within a thick wall, under a staircase, over a doorway, and around windows. When they're built into existing walls, they save valuable floor space.

An obvious drawback to built-ins is their expense. Like anything that is custom-made, a built-in unit can be very costly, though the price will vary depending on size, materials, and the complexity of the design. However, built-ins are considered permanent improvements that can return value when you sell your home.

Freestanding

Modular

What's your style?

Because of their sheer size, wall systems generally play a major role in a room's design. Do you want a mixed, open look, with shelves, display cubbies, and staggered lines? A quirky, one-of-a-kind painted piece? Or a monolithic wall where storage vanishes behind seamless, lacquered doors and drawer fronts?

Whether you buy premade furniture or build a custom unit, you can create a look that matches any decor. American country pieces, for example, typically have simple lines with sparse, unpretentious detailing. Contemporary pieces, while also characterized by simple, clean lines, are strong and sophisticated, with form often taking precedence over decoration. On the other hand, ornate moldings and carved door and drawer fronts lend old-world charm.

Color can be used to express style, too. For a sleek, sophisticated appearance, choose black, in either a matte or shiny finish. Wood tones, from light to dark, are characteristic of a more traditional style, but a unit painted white will also enhance a traditional living room. For a fresh, contemporary look, consider a bright color.

Built-in

Material matters

Most wall systems are made of a veneer of wood or laminate over a core of particleboard, medium-density fiberboard, or plywood. A few systems are made of solid wood. Glass is popular for formal display shelves, and some utility units are made from metals or molded plastics. For a closer look at materials not made from wood, see "A Shopper's Guide," beginning on page 89.

Sheet products. Wide panels are generally much more affordable than solid lumber because they require less handwork and utilize wood by-products for the panel cores. Options include particleboard, medium-density fiberboard, and hardwood-veneered plywood.

Workaday, unfinished particleboard is at the low end of the totem pole; choose it for utility cabinets or shelves. Particleboard is made from chips of waste wood—in fact, it's often called "chipboard." It has a roughly speckled appearance, as shown below. Particleboard tends to warp around moisture and can sag under its own weight, so keep shelf spans short (see page 18). Medium-density fiberboard (MDF)—a stronger, smoother cousin to particleboard—stays flatter, can be shaped, and takes paint very well. Both particleboard and MDF are commonly used as substrates for laminates (see below). They're both quite heavy.

Plywood is the most "woodlike" and, in most cases, the priciest sheet product. Plywood is built up from an odd number of thin layers, each peeled from a log and placed perpendicular to the layers above and below. This makes plywood panels more stable than solid lumber and also less likely to warp. Plywood used for wall systems and shelving is usually surfaced on front and back with attractive hardwood veneers, such as oak, maple, ash, or cherry. It comes in various qualities or grades, depending on appearance. The front edges of plywood panels need edge-banding or other trim to mask the raw inner layers.

Laminates. Because they're durable, easy to clean, and available in a wide range of colors and patterns, plastic laminates and films are popular surfacing materials for wall systems.

The laminate that covers the core (either particleboard or, for premium products, MDF) is applied in one of three ways. The cheapest and least durable method utilizes a vinyl or paper surface film. This film, available in a range of colors and simulated wood grains, is very thin and can peel away from the core panel.

The next grade of product is melamine, a layer of special paper impregnated with melamine resin. Because it's relatively durable and affordable, this material is quite common. It, too, is sold in many colors and patterns.

Thicker high-pressure laminates are the most durable and costly of the group. These materials come in many colors, patterns, textures, and finishes. Some are appropriate for flat (countertop) surfaces; others are specified only for vertical planes, such as cabinet doors or sides.

Solid lumber. Wood gives a warm, natural look that's hard to match with veneers. Solid wood is more durable, more elegant, and, not surprisingly, much more expensive than most laminates or wood veneer.

Hardwoods (deciduous trees) generally make more precise joints, hold fasteners better, and are more resistant to wear than softwoods (conifers). Hardwood species favored for furniture include light-toned woods, like oak, ash, maple, beech, and birch, and dark-toned species, like cherry, walnut, and mahogany. Alder, poplar, and aspen are budget-minded hardwoods, good for a stained or painted finish.

Most softwoods are less expensive, easier to tool, and more readily available than hardwoods. Pine and fir are the most common. Vertical-grained fir is a beautiful, relatively hard softwood that's normally clear-finished. Knotty pines are often chosen specifically for pickling or waxing when a casual or country look is desired. Otherwise, softwoods normally are painted.

a little engineering

Even the most *elaborate wall system won't work if it doesn't provide the right spaces in the right places for the items you need to corral. Plan to keep frequently used items readily accessible: on easily reached shelves, in shallow drawers, or at the front of cabinets. Seldom-used objects can be kept on very low or very high shelves or toward the back of cabinets.*

Remember to take into account objects' sizes and shapes and whether your needs are likely to change in the future. Particularly heavy objects demand strong shelves; for information, *see page 18.*

SOME IDEAL DIMENSIONS

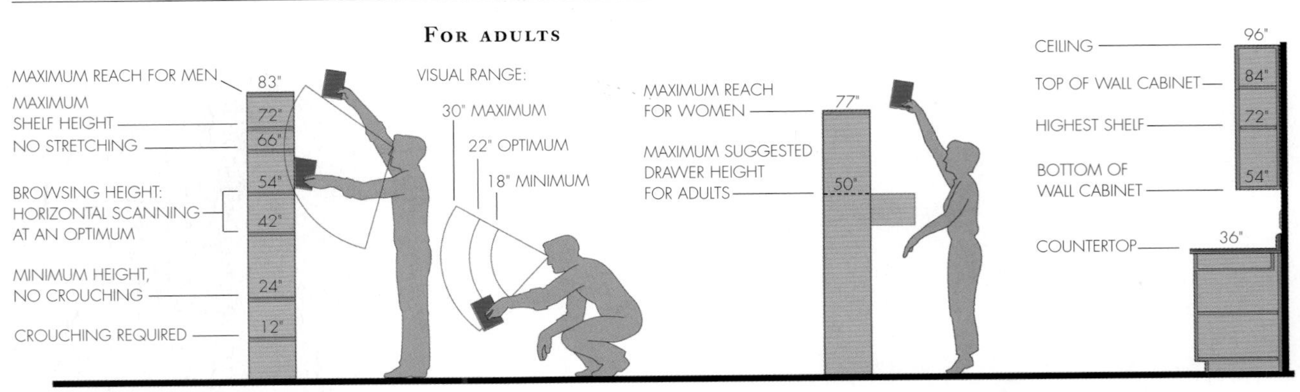

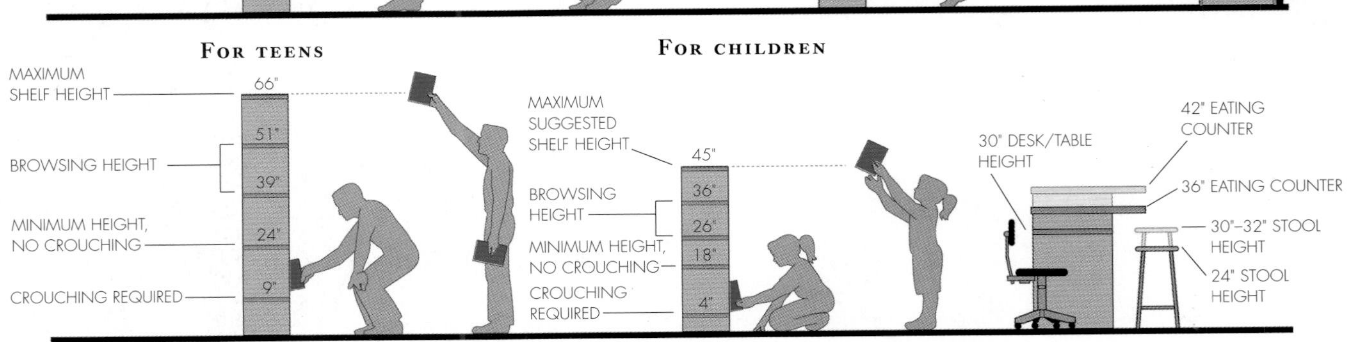

Design guidelines

The drawings on the facing page show norms for fitting wall systems to people. While they're not strict rules, they're good starting points when designing your system.

Don't place shelves out of reach—note that the recommended height for the highest shelf is 6 feet, unless you have a ladder or stool to help you reach its contents. On a similar theme, it's tough for the average adult to see inside a drawer that's over 50 inches off the ground. Also, be aware that accessing extra-low shelves and drawers can require uncomfortable crouching.

Usually, books are stored on open shelving where they can be easily seen and reached. In general, it's best to place heavy books and reference works on the lower tiers of a shelf system. Art books can go at eye level, and paperbacks can be arranged on higher shelves.

Bookshelf space should be a minimum of 9 inches high and 8 inches deep for books of average size. Larger volumes may require shelf space 12 inches high and deep. TV and A/V units usually need 16 to 24 inches of depth.

Though square footage is a good measure of floor space, think in terms of linear footage when figuring your shelving needs. A single shelf 6 feet long offers 6 linear feet of storage. A tall unit with six shelves, each 6 feet long, offers 36 linear feet of storage.

To get a rough idea of the linear footage of shelving you need, simply measure the linear footage of the books, collectibles, and other items you intend to store. If you're building bookshelves, figure 8 to 10 books per running foot of shelving. Allow extra room for expansion and open display space.

Shelf depth and height depend on the size of the objects you intend to put there. Adjustable shelves offer the most flexibility. To determine the right height for fixed shelves, measure the objects that will go there and add an inch or two for head space. The drawings below show the amount of space some common items require.

TYPICAL SIZES OF BOOKS, DISCS, RECORDS, AND TAPES

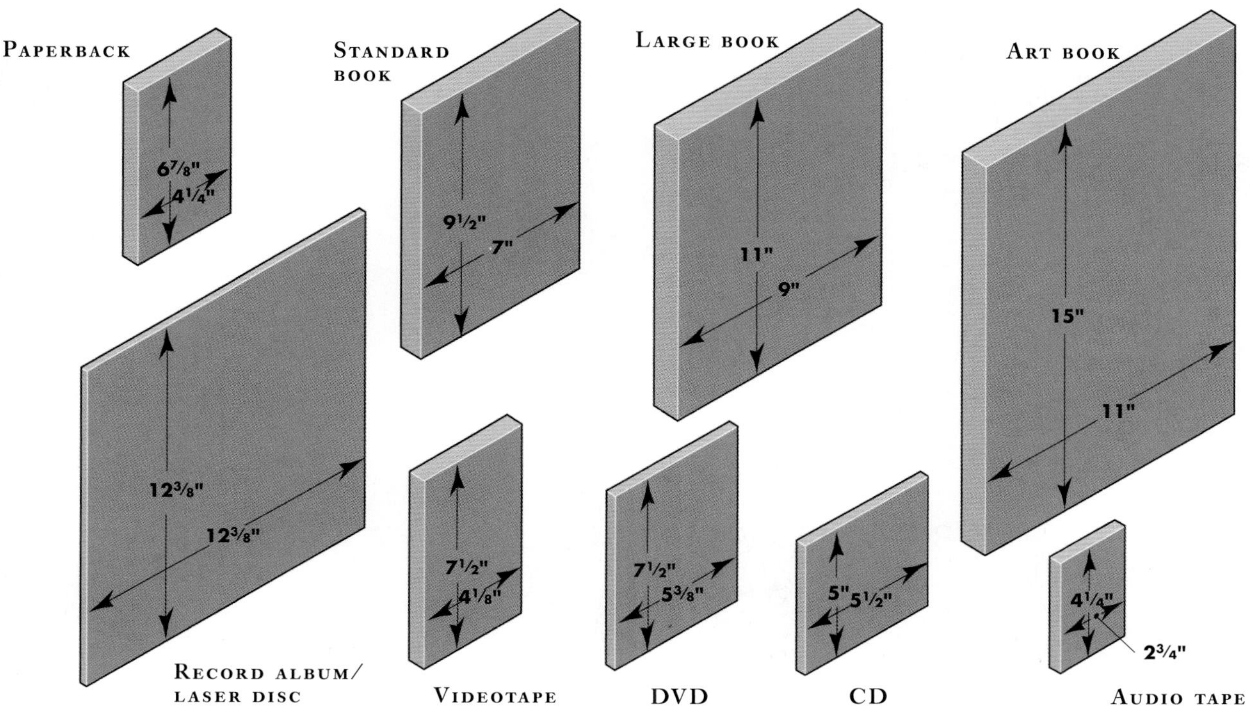

Shelf loads

You don't need to be a structural engineer to design and assemble your own shelves. Still, some fundamental principles should be observed.

The drawing below shows four basic ways to make a shelf; the one you should choose will depend on the expected load. To avoid a sagging shelf, always be conservative; use the stoutest construction you can.

For light loads (paperback books, small art objects, stemware), 1-by pine or fir (3/4-inch thick) or 3/4-inch sheet products up to 32 inches long work fine. For medium loads (art books, vases, some audio gear), you're better off going to thicker lumber. If you want to stick to 3/4-inch stock, shorten the shelf to 24 or even 16 inches; you can also reinforce the shelf edges, as shown.

Be especially cautious with heavy loads (wine racks, TVs, large audio rigs). Use 2-by lumber, two layers of plywood, or, even better, a solid-lumber web frame with plywood top and bottom.

Maximum Spans Between Supports

Note: Reduce all spans for heavy loads. Glass shelves are sized for lightweight loads only.

Material	**Span** (inches)
1-by (3/4-inch) pine or fir	32
2-by (1 1/2-inch) pine or fir	48
1-inch hardwood	48
3/4-inch plywood-core veneer or laminate	32
3/4-inch particleboard-core veneer or laminate	24
1/4-inch plate glass (12 inches deep)	36
3/8-inch plate glass (12 inches deep)	48
1/2-inch plate glass (12 inches deep)	60

FOUR WAYS TO MAKE A SHELF

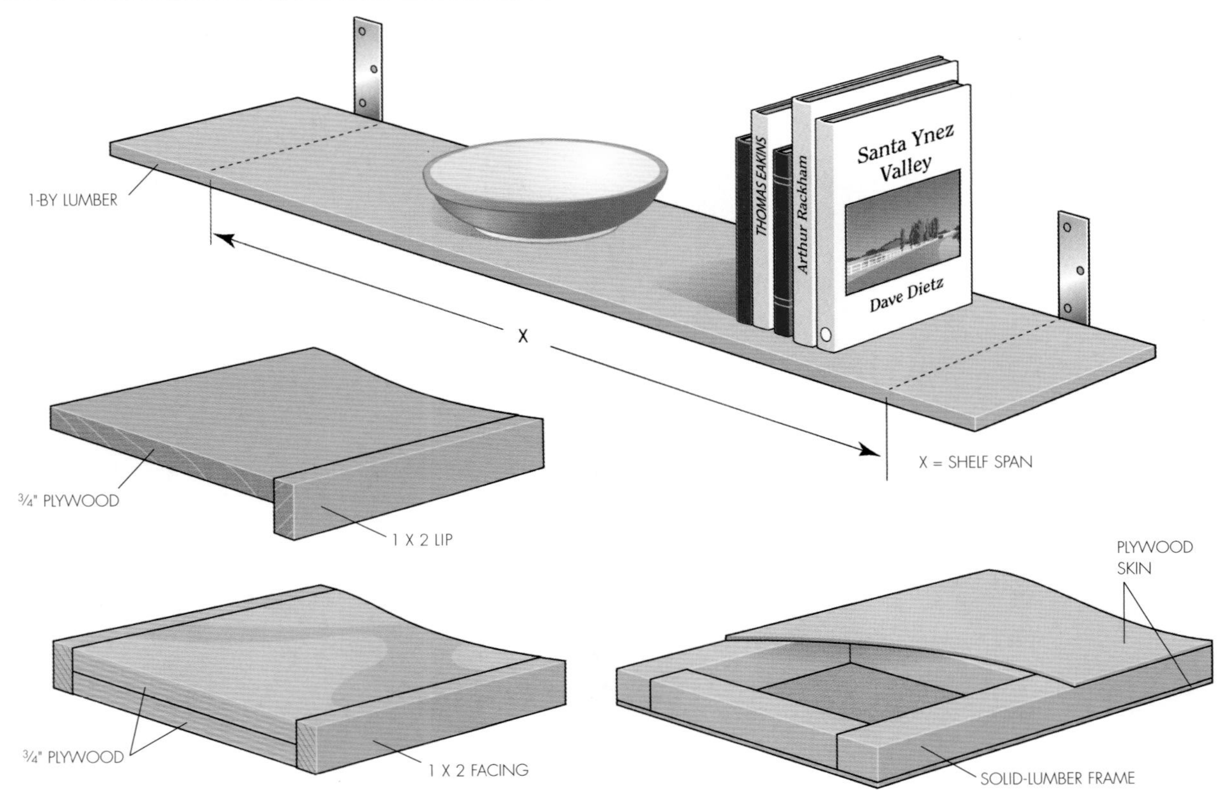

Make connections

Regardless of their appearance, remember that all wall systems consist at least of horizontals supported by verticals. Shelves can be supported from the floor, wall, or ceiling, but the basic geometry remains the same.

The simplest open shelves may require only wood or metal wall brackets, L-braces, or other "floating" hardware. For details, see pages 92–93.

Formal uprights can be made from ¾-inch sheet materials or 1-by or 2-by solid lumber. The load-carrying capacity depends more on the shelf-to-upright connection than on the thickness of the uprights.

Shelves may be fixed or adjustable, depending on your attachment method. Shown at right are four common fixed-shelf connections. Simple butt joints, glued and nailed or screwed, will suffice for light duty; biscuits or cleats add strength. Dadoed construction provides strong joints and adds rigidity to backless shelving units.

There are many different types of adjustable shelf connectors; the most popular are shown at right. Tracks and brackets are for open walls; tracks and clips, shelf pins, and other items connect shelves to uprights.

Need Help?

If you're uncertain about designing, building, and/or installing a wall system yourself, you may want to enlist the help of others who are experts at their trades. Here's a list of some professionals who can help:

- Architects
- Interior designers and decorators
- Furniture and wall system retailers
- Custom cabinetmakers
- Finish carpenters
- Media specialists

BASIC SHELF CONNECTIONS

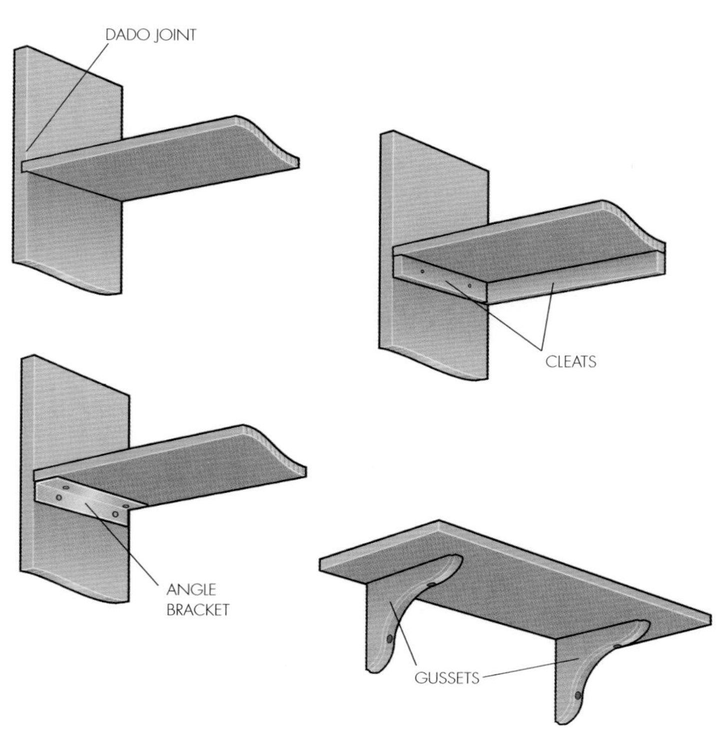

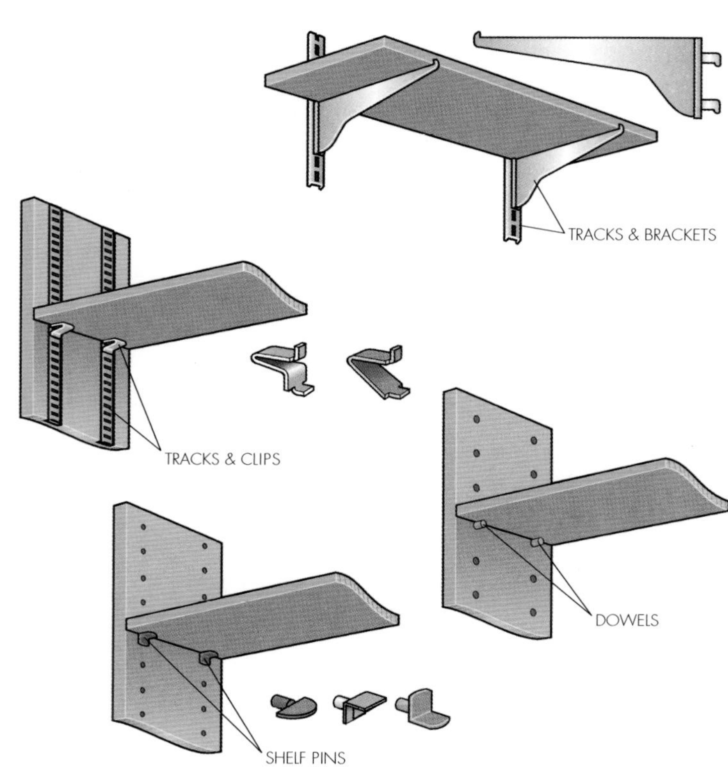

a home for electronics

WITH THE *surging tide of surround-sound, high-definition televisions, DVDs, and other digital innovations in our lives, organizing and storing audiovisual gear has become a high priority in many of today's homes. It's also one of the most popular uses for wall systems.*

Because the design of a large media center is critical to its function, you may want help. Be sure the designer you select has experience working with electronics or will consult with A/V experts.

Some basic checkpoints

"Home theater" might mean a DVD player and a large-screen television, or it could mean the real deal—projection screen, audiovisual receiver, and six or more speakers. Obviously, your storage strategy depends on which of these approaches you're leaning toward.

When it comes to organizing basic electronic equipment and accessories, nearly any type of unit will work, from a ready-made media cabinet to storage furniture, and from a modular system to custom cabinetry. For the most flexibility, look for a unit with adjustable shelving.

Shelving units with open backs provide the ventilation demanded by many electronic components. With adequate ventilation, cabinets work just as well as open shelving. They also help hide stacks of tapes, compact discs, vintage vinyl, and other paraphernalia, and keep them dust-free.

You'll need to decide whether to showcase your gear or hide it. Perhaps you want to recess the entire unit into the wall and cover it with speaker cloth. You can now buy infrared receiver units that allow you to use remote controls with cabinet doors closed.

Another consideration: flashy lines and colors can distract from the home-theater experience. When the lights go down, the unit should be merely background.

Whether you're buying ready-made furniture or designing your own built-in, remember that a television or other similar equipment can be very heavy. Be sure shelf and platform materials can support the weight (for information, see pages 18–19).

Choosing a location

Finding the right spot for your equipment isn't always easy. Though the family room may seem an obvious choice, especially for a television, audio components can go almost anywhere, as long as you can run wires from the equipment to speakers located in other parts of the house.

Often televisions are placed as afterthoughts when, in reality, they may be the room's main

feature. If space is limited, a corner wall unit for video and audio equipment can visually anchor it, gearing the area for both entertainment and conversation.

The shape, size, lighting, and acoustics of a room will all affect its performance. For a true home-theater environment, the room should be at least 10 by 14 feet. Also, take into account any glare from windows that could affect viewing. Subdued, neutral room colors are best for a home-theater environment.

Make sure there's sufficient lighting in the area to see titles on CDs and tapes and read equipment controls. If you're building a custom unit, consider including an interior lighting system. Because fluorescent light may cause interference, plan other light sources near a tuner or receiver. Some low-voltage dimmers and transformers may also cause buzzing. For more information on lighting, see page 126.

The epitome of a built-in wall system, this home theater setup boasts screen, projector, and surround-sound speakers (above). Moviegoers here are cushioned in comfort—with their feet up. The projector is suspended unobtrusively from the ceiling, and audiovisual gear is concealed in a nearby closet (left).

A Home Theater Overview

What transforms a TV, a VCR, and a bunch of other black boxes into a formal home theater? It's the systematic relationship between several key devices, all tied together with low-voltage wires and cables.

Typical home theater components are shown below. The television and speakers are the obvious stars, but it's the audiovisual receiver that's really "command central." A plethora of media signals may be routed to the A/V receiver from components both inside and outside the home: a cable box, satellite dish, off-the-air antenna, VCR, or DVD player. The receiver allows you to choose which of these input sources you want, and then encodes and outputs signals to the TV and speakers. Consider the A/V receiver as the axis of whatever scheme you're planning.

- **Video options.** Television monitors are available in a growing number of versions: direct view, rear projection, front projection, flat screen or plasma, and high definition. You'll need some showroom help unraveling your options; and, just as important, you'll need cable and wiring connections that are compatible with your A/V receiver.
- **Audio aspects.** Surround sound is the heart of the home theater experience. A battery of at least five and often six speakers is driven by digital encoding supplied by the A/V receiver. Matching speakers at front left and front right provide "stereo." A shielded center speaker, mounted above the TV or placed right on top, fills in the middle. (You could use the TV's built-in speaker, but a separate center speaker usually sounds better.) Left-rear and right-rear speakers create the surround-sound effect. In addition, a sixth speaker—a specialized subwoofer—is often placed at rear center (although technically it could be placed anywhere, as these low-frequency sounds have no clear "direction").

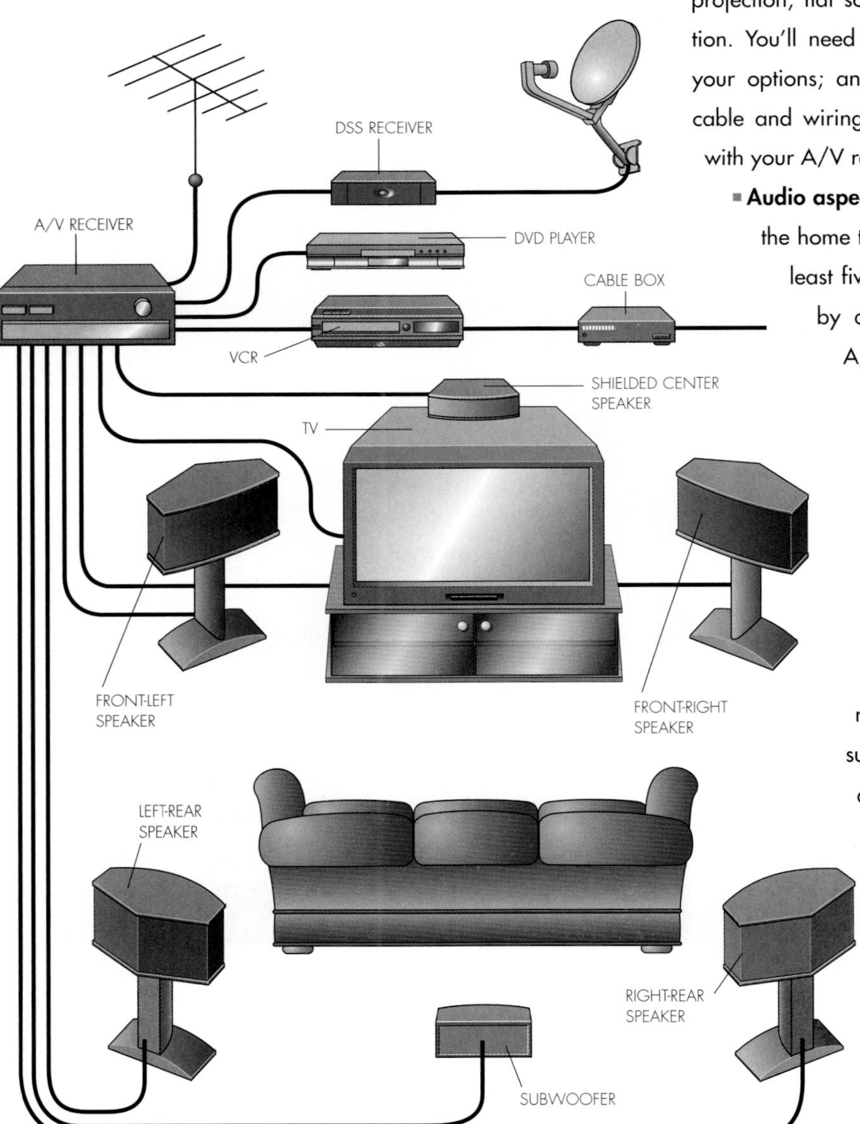

Equipment checklist

To plan your A/V setup, begin by making a list of the components you own and those you may want to add later, and note their measurements. Also count up your accoutrements, such as compact discs, vintage vinyl, and accessories. Decide what you'll house in the wall system and what components (speakers, for example) need to be nearby.

Televisions. Today's television sets can be tough to plan for—they're big, heavy, and most stick way out in back. The simplest large-screen storage solution is a low TV stand (shown below); some models roll on wheels, while others pivot.

Cabinet-housed TVs require sturdy shelves and extra depth. For a television that's not too heavy, consider a special TV shelf that pulls out of the cabinet and swivels for convenient viewing. A pullout shelf can also accommodate a lazy Susan or turntable (for details, see page 110). You can also buy TV lifts that pop up through a base cabinet.

Make sure that the doors on a television cabinet swing open far enough so they don't obstruct your view, or use retractable doors.

Components. Do you like the open-rack look or closed cabinets? You'll want components placed conveniently and accessibly, protected from overheating, and situated for optimal performance.

Pay strict attention to the manufacturer's recommendations, particularly in regard to ventilation. Though ventilation grilles (see page 112) at the back and top of a unit might suffice, you may need to install an exhaust fan if several pieces of equipment are grouped in one tight enclosure.

Tapes, records, and compact discs. For small items such as compact discs and cassette tapes, divided drawers offer the most efficient storage. You can get a lot of CDs in one drawer! For easy access, don't place drawers much higher than waist level. If you don't have room for drawers, commercial organizers can keep your tapes, compact discs, records, and accessories in order. Place tapes, compact discs, DVDs, laser discs, and vinyl away from direct sunlight and other heat sources.

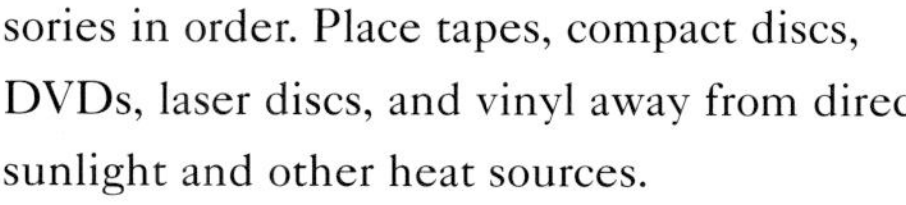

Speakers. Unless your speakers are the so-called "shielded" type, be sure they're located at least 12 inches from the television screen to prevent picture distortion. For optimum stereo separation, speakers need to be at least 5 feet away from each other.

Recessed wall speakers look neat and reduce clutter; other options include wall mounts, bookshelf mounts, and cabinet-housed speakers and components hidden behind larger sweeps of speaker cloth.

CD organizer

CD table racks

Component cabinet

TV stand

room-by-room solutions

WHEN IT COMES *to wall systems, every room in the house is fair game. Look carefully at each room's layout and the areas suitable for display and storage. Also browse through the scores of storage solutions in the next chapter, "Great Wall Systems," beginning on page 29. Ready to go? Here are some room-by-room guidelines to get you started.*

Living spaces

Whether you and your family congregate in an informal living room, a family room, a great room, or a den, that's the place where activities such as reading, watching television, game playing, and listening to music occur. Every one of those activities invites clutter.

The best living-room units are often a mixture of closed storage and open display niches. Lighting is important here—accent light for pictures and collectibles and ambient light to access storage items. A two-sided room divider can double your storage frontage and redefine a sprawling floor plan.

LIVING-ROOM MEDIA CENTER

Because they're so versatile, modular wall systems are popular in living areas. Equipped with adjustable shelving, cabinets, drawers, television bays, and other specialty options, these units can organize myriad objects.

But virtually any piece of storage furniture can help contain the clutter. How about a hand-painted pine bookcase? An antique armoire? Or, a deep central media unit with flanking side towers?

In more formal living areas, built-ins offer display and storage opportunities. A built-in that combines open shelving and cabinets can exhibit art objects and prized collectibles as well as conceal audio equipment and accessories.

Dining rooms

An armoire, hutch, or other freestanding cupboard or cabinet with glass or solid doors provides plenty of space for china and glassware and also helps keep them dust-free. Built-in units that include drawers, adjustable shelves, and cabinets are also good organizers. Stacks of dishes can be very heavy, so be sure shelves are strong and well-supported. When a low-profile unit is combined with a countertop, it also provides a buffet-style serving area.

If the dining area is part of a large kitchen or an extension of your living room, a wall system—floor to ceiling or just waist high—can effectively divide the space and create the effect of a separate dining room.

Where space is at a premium, a dining room that's used only part-time for meals can serve

Dining-room divider

other roles as well. A wall system outfitted with a fold-down desk, file drawers, and cabinets can provide efficient office space that's camouflaged when company arrives. Or how about a cabinet filled with audio equipment wired to speakers throughout the house?

Kitchens

Today, it's acknowledged that the kitchen is the hub of most homes, especially those with open or "great-room" floor plans. So it stands to reason that the concepts of kitchen storage and display are being stretched, too. Computers, video games, collections, and sewing centers are all part of the picture.

Display niches warm an otherwise blank stretch of cabinets. What about glass-fronted wall cabinets lit by built-in, low-voltage light fixtures? If you're worried about keeping things tidy, opt for translucent instead of clear glass. Or add a stand-alone display cabinet or recycled hutch. Don't overlook over-cabinet soffits, and consider glass shelves against a window. Flipper doors, fold-down doors, pullout shelves, and roll-around shelf units keep items tucked away when not in use.

Kitchen transition zones—spots between the main work triangle and other living spaces—are prime terrain for cubbyholes or a computer desk, an A/V rack, or a swiveling TV pullout.

Kitchen display soffit

Bedrooms and closets

Today's bedrooms are more than just rooms of repose. Master suites may include audio and video gear, fitness equipment, home office alcoves, reading nooks, sitting areas with fireplaces, and more.

Where space is limited in bedrooms, wall systems that store both clothing and other gear are particularly useful. For example, a large wall unit can stand in for conventional dressers. What about a built-in headboard with wraparound shelving? Or a freestanding room divider with headboard on one side and dresser drawers on the other?

Bedroom built-in

Guest bedrooms often double as offices or media rooms. A seamless, commercial wall system is a natural here, with built-in pullouts, fold-down worktable, and, perhaps, a Murphy bed.

Closets—especially those designated areas in master suites—can benefit from a wall system's organizing touch, too.

Bathrooms

Like bedrooms, bathrooms are dancing new steps, becoming bigger, multiuse retreats. Even small, traditional baths can benefit from fresh takes on storage and display.

Pedestal sinks are hot, but cost you the vanity storage below standard deck-mounted fixtures. So look to the walls: a mix of open and closed storage makes a bathroom seem less closed in and more energetic. Recessed storage is a good choice. Or stack up a storage tower with closed drawers, open shelves or ladders for colorful towels, and maybe some pantry pullouts.

When choosing commercial units, watch out for cheap laminates; they're easy to clean but susceptible to moisture damage. If you're using glass in the bath, make sure it's tempered safety glass. Whatever bathroom unit you opt for, good room ventilation is a must.

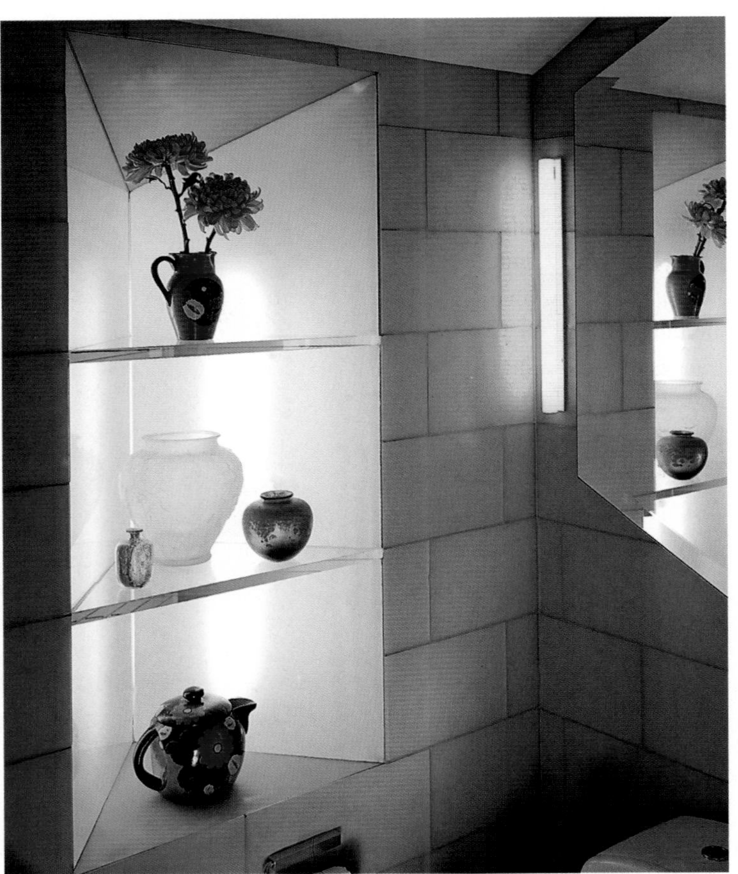

BATHROOM DISPLAY NICHE

KIDS' ROOM CORRAL

Kids' rooms

In children's rooms, flexibility is the key. Look for modular systems and accessories that can be raised or reconfigured as children grow. Units that bundle low bookshelves, a desk, and drawers together save space and encourage neatness. Some systems include the bed, too.

Bins, baskets, pegs, hooks, and stackable storage cubes are naturals for casual spaces. If you opt for open shelves, make them adjustable. Rolling carts and other mobile bins and shelving allow kids—and their parents—to custom-tailor space as projects and play require.

Home offices

Do you want closed storage or open display? It partially depends on whether you have a stand-alone space or are trying to tuck an office into another room. Often, a mix of open and closed storage is best. Remember that it's your home, not just an office, and choose styles and materials accordingly. Display niches and art pieces help personalize your workspace.

Commercial wall systems can create a seamless, efficient office area, fusing desk, credenza, shelves, computer and printer pullouts, and copious file drawers into one unit. Or select stand-alones like the classic rolltop desk, converted office armoire, and roll-around file cart. If you have the space and budget, built-in library cases can supply a traditional "study" style.

Hallways and stairs

Here it's all about found space; for colorful ideas, see pages 78–83. Stairways are prime targets: under-stair shelves, pullouts, and tansu drawers are classics. Look also to stair landings, where a little extra depth can make way for a built-in library. Recessed display niches add spark along the stairs' path.

Recessed built-ins are also good solutions for some hallways. To find space to add bookshelves or display niches, look up high or consider an end wall.

Think lighting when you're considering these found spaces. Most hallways and stairs are not as brightly lit as other living spaces, so you'll probably need to add some accent or task fixtures (see page 126).

Home office book wall

Under-stair cubbies

Utility areas

Laundry rooms, workrooms, garages, and other functional zones of the home can use shelving and cabinetry to keep tools and supplies organized. Because access is often more important than aesthetics in these areas, utility shelves and cabinets are usually sufficient for general storage.

Most home centers stock lines of modular utility units made from melamine or raw particleboard. Typical components include shelves, base cabinets, tall tool cabinets, drawers, worktables, and open shelves. Add a wall organizer, hooks, or an industrial shelving unit, and you're in business. Budget-priced wall cabinets from the kitchen department work here, too.

Vinyl-coated wire shelves, bins, and baskets are naturals for laundry rooms. For details, see pages 116–117.

Laundry shelves and bins

GREAT WALL SYSTEMS

NEED INSPIRATION? This chapter is packed with colorful examples of different wall systems, from basic movable shelves and shelf units to traditional furniture pieces and up-to-the-minute media centers. We've included great ideas for just about every storage and display need. All are designed to set you thinking about how to solve your own storage and styling challenges. AS YOU PERUSE THESE PAGES, study what materials were used and how the design relates to the room. Note also where the units are placed and how particular objects are displayed or stored in them. Though many of the wall systems shown were designed for a particular area and purpose, don't let that stop you—you can adapt them to nearly any situation. FOR SPECIFIC room-by-room guidelines, turn back to pages 24–27. See some hardware, component, or shelf lumber that piques your interest? Check out "A Shopper's Guide," beginning on page 89, for details.

simply shelves

Open shelves are handy and easy to install, and most have a certain wide-eyed charm. They don't dominate a room the way more complex wall units can.

Choose your shelves from solid wood, sheet products, glass, or metal in stock, custom, or homemade designs. For starters, you'll need to make sure the shelves and shelving hardware are strong enough for the weight you're piling on them. For guidelines, see pages 16–19. Besides providing extra strength, thicker shelves have a bolder profile that complements some styles.

Shelf connections are adjustable or fixed. Some hardware is standard in home centers: tracks and brackets, tracks and clips, and at least a few types of shelf pins that fit in drilled holes. Fixed hardware includes cleats, gussets, and angle brackets. Torsion boxes and other "floating" shelves are fixed and have no visible hardware. For a closer look at all these items, see pages 90–95.

A shelf unit requires side supports and maybe a back. Some designs are anchored to the wall; others aren't. The shelves may or may not be adjustable. Many systems are modular. You can even put a unit on wheels and roll it to the task.

Before you resolve to fill all your storage needs with shelves, be sure you want all that open storage. You'll be looking at those items all the time, even when they're dusty or disorganized. Sometimes, it's best to mix it up, choosing open shelves for display and things you use a lot, and drawers and cabinets for items you'd rather hide.

Dark-stained wood shelves float beside a kitchen pass-through, supporting both colorful, glazed 1950s pottery and working goods. The floating boxes are supported from behind by invisible, cantilevered hardware.

Why not roll the shelves to the task? This movable cart features industrial-strength steel shelves—plus a quartet of heavy-duty casters.

SUGAR
COFFEE
TEA
FLOUR
SUGAR

Simple and traditional, the kitchen scheme above features curved wood gussets and wall cleats that prop up 1-by shelves lipped with stronger 1 by 2s. All components are painted a clean, classic white.

Some shelves do double duty: this one organizes children's clothes and offers a secure perch for a household frog. The traditional design—called a peg rail—is comprised of wall ledger, inset wooden pegs (you could also use metal hooks), top shelf, and side gussets.

Clear, curved shelving displays a collection of art glass in bright hues from around the color ring. Barely noticeable supporting hardware hangs from a metal-laminate soffit.

Simple flat shelves bridge commercial track-and-bracket hardware. You can buy the pieces at a home center. Anchor vertical tracks to wall framing, insert brackets, lay a commercial shelf—or one of your own—across them, and you're done.

Maybe you don't even need a shelf. These floating perches, with formal crown molding profiles, are just deep enough for pictures and paintings—much like a classic picture rail.

Magazines are always hard to keep a handle on, but the open rack shown at right can help. This home office space also sports a bookcase on wheels; just give a tug and pull it where you want.

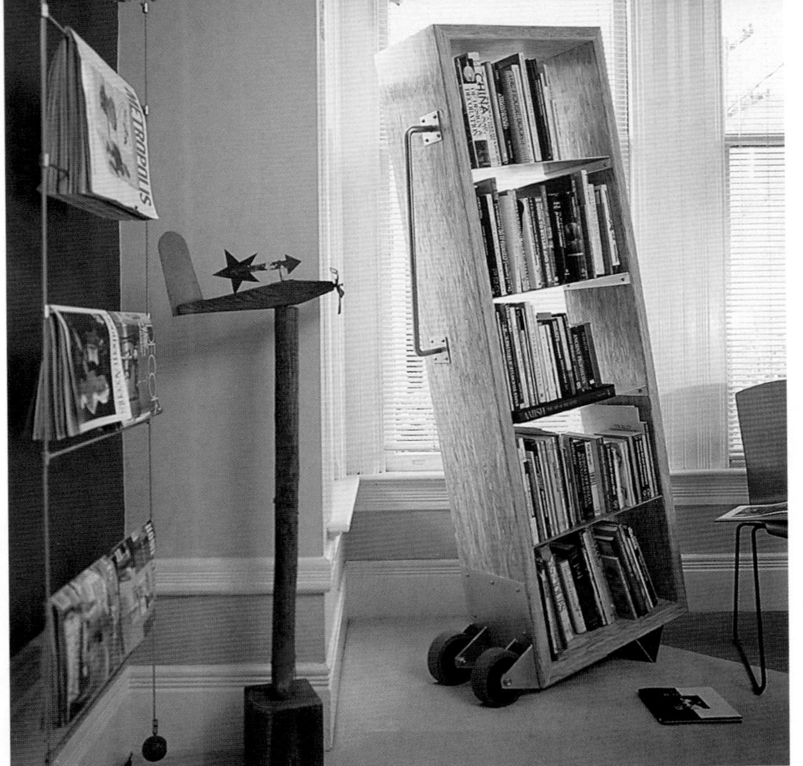

Serious cooking requires serious shelving, and this all-steel gourmet unit is ready for the work-load. Part display and part industrial, many of these strong, stylish units offer modular components that can be mixed and matched to fit your needs.

Anything you can stably stack becomes a shelving unit. At left, a set of matching wooden benches was covered with multiple paint layers, then sanded and abraded for an antique, distressed look.

Freestanding shelf ladders made of soldered copper pipe and fittings create a vivid, contemporary display wall with a whimsical space for the television set right in the middle.

Curving glass shelves lend a bright, open feel to this combination pass-through/display niche. The clear glass allows the halogen accent light to shine down unhindered from shelf to shelf.

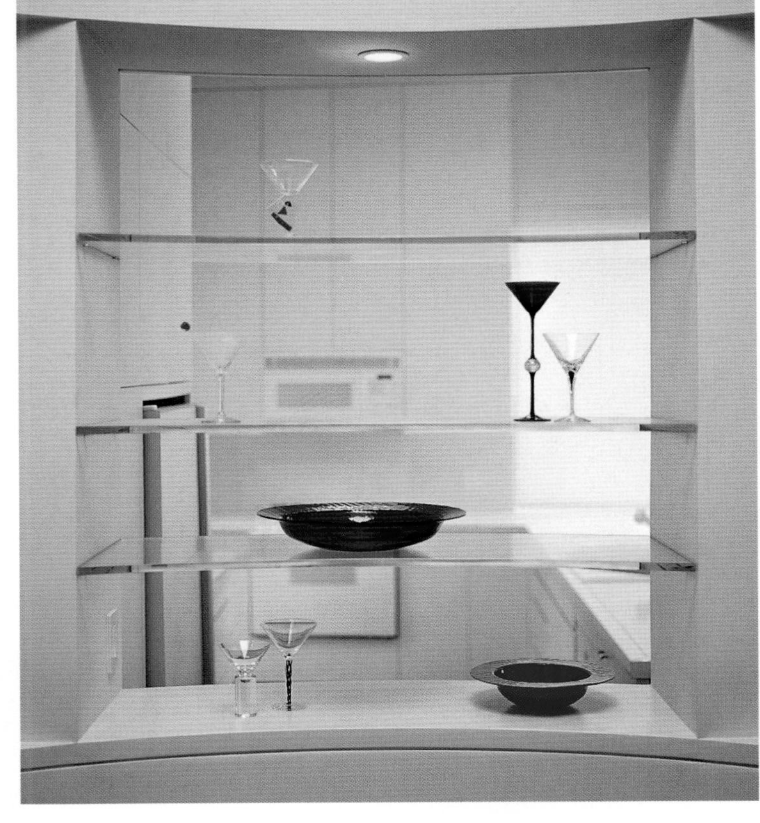

A fir bookcase sits on a bright blue wall above the piano. The wall unit, with trim strips on front of shelves and vertical pilasters to match, has no visible hanging hardware to mar the clean lines.

Serenity comes to the master bath in the form of these clean, simple display shelves, which are wall-mounted to float like the bench. Honey-toned hemlock adds a warm glow.

hardworking walls

THE JUMP from open shelves to wall systems is one of both style and function. Although wall systems may simply formalize shelves, such as in the case of a large wall of books, they may also incorporate cabinet frames, doors, drawers, pullouts, and other add-on accessories. These latter components vary the look of shelves and make them more useful.

What if you own stacks and stacks of books? It's no problem to go higher if you have the headroom—plus a solid library ladder to scale those heights.

Some wall systems shown here are freestanding pieces, while others are built-ins (for more on built-ins, see pages 50–55). Book walls can be positioned as high as you like, but remember that you'll need access to the upper levels; note the library ladders shown on these two pages. Modular systems abound, as do your choices in furniture components, kitchen cabinets, and media units. All of these options are addressed in the chapter "A Shopper's Guide," beginning on page 89.

To reach a happy ending, it's usually best to think of a large wall system as an integral part of your room's design, not just an add-on. Strive to keep the look uncluttered, but also vary components to break the monotony of a potentially blank wall. Display niches (see pages 56–61), staggered lines, and choices of both materials and finishes make huge differences in the visual weight of your hardworking wall.

Add doors to a set of bookshelves and you have a wall system of cabinets. The key architectural feature of this family room is an enlarged, built-in, stepped tansu surrounding the fireplace. The sandalwood-finished maple cabinets house the entertainment system and provide tidy storage for discs, tapes, and books.

White, formal surroundings call for a built-in book wall to match. In this case, the entire wall is built out into the room, and the shelf bays are recessed in the resulting space. Wide, flat trim frames the space, echoing the arched entry door and the built-up ceiling bays.

Boxlike cherry wall cabinets, some open for display, establish this family room's rectilinear frame. With a vivid palette of purple, raspberry, emerald, and teal sprinkled throughout, the cabinets offer plenty of room for storage, display, and a computer desk.

This combination sitting room, media space, and display gallery is all tied together with wall systems. The open knee-wall shelf curves to follow the window bay, leading the eye toward the fireplace-flanking open shelves and closed, Euro-style cabinets.

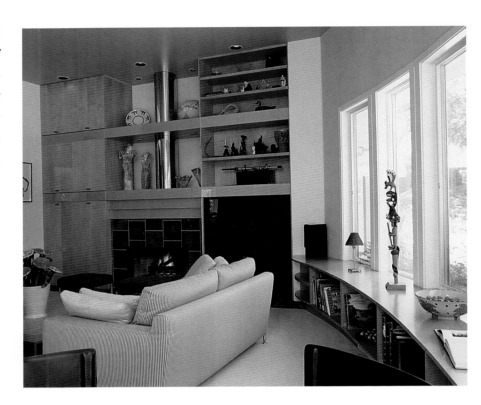

Handsome, vertical veneers wrap around seamless home office built-ins, integrating bookshelves, display spaces, and an extra-tall soffit area above window level. Note the floating kickspace below the units, which are anchored to the wall, not the floor.

Part room, part wall system, this walk-in window seat alcove has built-ins throughout. Shelves flank the doorway and ring the window, and drawers pull out below the cushion. Black backs on shelf bays add depth and contrast to display items.

LINDBERGH
THE HILL TOWNS OF ITALY
TUSCANY

As the focal point of an open, comfortable master suite, this striking cedar storage wall divides bedroom from bath and also functions as a headboard.

A unit of walnut cubes forms this built-in headboard. Cubes are solid in the actual headboard section, form square display cubbies elsewhere, and blend right in with the adjacent doors and door trim. The unit is wired with phone jacks and electrical outlets.

Furniture-grade cherry forms a hardworking but great-looking storage wall in a transition zone between kitchen and living room. Cabinets combine open shelves, soffit niches, and closed pantry doors below with textured glass above—a striking mix of open, closed, and partially veiled storage and display space.

Hardworking walls are a big plus in the bathroom, where space is always lacking. This storage wall combines plenty of drawer space with amenities like glass display shelves, arched soffit trim, fluted vertical pilasters, and the traditional touch of beaded boards in the open case back.

unfitted furnishings

THE SEAMLESS LOOK is one option; the other time-honored approach is to use individual, freestanding pieces. This unfitted style is especially apt in casual, eclectic, or period settings—or anywhere a looser look or floor plan is desired. It also makes it much easier to mix and match storage pieces you might find along the way.

An antique pine hutch makes the perfect backdrop for an antique dining table. The hutch shows off a fine collection of majolica—distinctly glazed earthenware featuring shapes and motifs from nature.

Furniture stores stock many freestanding designs. For shopping tips, see pages 102–105. Home-improvement warehouses, retail shops, and mail-order catalogs offer an increasing number of storage and display units.

There are other possibilities, too. What about an antique hutch, armoire, or credenza? Or a stack of recycled straw baskets, wire bins, or storage cubes? Scour thrift stores and garage sales for storage subjects in a broad range of colors and textures. Or look for pieces to decorate yourself.

It's your basic freestanding bookcase, but with some personalized touches: floating vertical dividers, a swirling decorative finish, and a swimming fish medallion at the top.

Unfinished freestanding pieces—typically built from pine or budget hardwoods like alder or poplar—offer an almost blank canvas for personal expression. Stain a bookcase, paint it white, or paint each shelf a different hue. Pickle that armoire, apply a crackle finish, or "age" and distress the doors with sandpaper, file, or even a hammer. You could also strip and refinish an old flea-market find—who knows what lies underneath?

Freestanding boxes and cubes—including colorful doors, drawer fronts, and open, see-through shelf bays—can be stacked and rotated atop one another. Flat, matching countertops float atop the unit. This assemblage doubles as a kids' room divider and personal "fortress."

Bright red barrister cases with glass-front doors are stacked to form a lively mix of storage and display. The individual boxes sit atop an integral base with decorative legs.

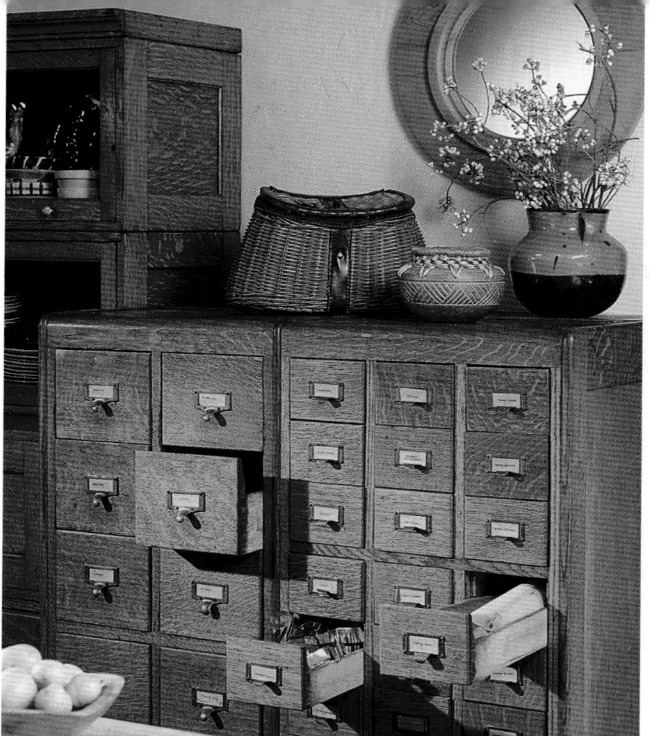

A lot of "found" items can be stacked or recycled as wall systems. At left, a former library card catalog is now labeled for kitchen utensils.

The ornamental, ladderlike shelf unit above houses pullout rattan baskets.

Corners are often prime space wasters, so why not tailor a wall unit to use this area? This trim, triangular dining-room piece was finished with pickled white paint, which was then partially rubbed away for an aged effect.

beautiful built-ins

A contemporary room design is highlighted by fireside built-ins. Recessed plaster niches on top have spotlights to accent display pieces. Downlights embedded in plaster soffits shine down and through glass shelves, washing collectibles below.

ON THE FAR SIDE of the fence from freestanding pieces are so-called built-ins. A built-in unit that forms an integral part of the room's architecture can save a lot of space. It can also look like it belongs in the room in a way that more casual pieces may not—especially in formal or modern settings.

A shallow recessed niche at one end of the kitchen counter displays earthenware pottery in all of the home's palette colors. The tile-lined alcove sports a single, distressed wood shelf.

As you thumb through the following pages, note how both the materials and the trimmings interact with the room designs. Baseboards that ring a room continue on below built-in units; integral ceiling or crown moldings likewise tie areas together. Some units are clearly made of wood, while others seem to blend with the wall materials: wallboard, plaster, or tile.

While many so-called "built-ins" are actually built into the wall, others are really built out from the wall. Schemes range from simple, between-stud wall recesses to those that entail reframing the entire wall to surround the built-in. Most built-ins are custom-fitted, but you could take stock units and either recess them or fill in around them with new wall coverings. In either case, moldings surrounding the opening blend the new and old.

Custom units allow great flexibility in terms of both materials and details like doors, drawers, or glass-shelved display "windows." You can also purchase specialty accessories (see pages 120–123) to plug into custom or commercial built-ins. Light fixtures (see page 126) and A/V wires are much simpler to incorporate into built-ins than into some stand-alone pieces.

A decorative glass window is framed by warm-toned wood built-ins. Note how heavy-profiled baseboards and crown moldings tie all the components together.

A hardworking storage cube is lined with brightly painted beaded paneling, and accented with decorative wrought-iron hinges and hardware. The box houses adjustable bookshelves, an open phone niche, and ample closed storage to the right.

An amply sized foyer can do double duty as a family library or home office when outfitted with built-ins. These shelves frame an interior passage, creating an extra-thick wall or tunnel.

Square, recessed display niches and other custom touches, usually reserved for formal living rooms, dress up this master bedroom's conversation space. Collectibles are accented by tiny strip lights tucked behind the top front of each niche.

Burly, fixed timber shelves are the perfect counterpart to a plastered wall alcove. Note how the matching baseboards weave in and out of the recessed space, augmenting the built-in effect.

on display

Bowls and vases seem to hover within this elegant display cabinet. Recessed downlights shine from the top; additional light on a separate switch comes from fiber optics behind the translucent back.

BOOKSHELVES ARE the perfect vehicle, of course, for storing books. But a wall of solid books can rob a room of interest, visual texture, and decorative focal points. That's why it's often important to break up the monotony with objects worthy of display.

Gather the items you want to display, grouping objects that have something in common, such as color, form, or function. Position adjustable shelves so that they align in an attractive, organized way or form an interesting pattern. You can remove a shelf or two to create spaces for larger objects.

If you need to devote a lot of shelf space to books, avoid placing them wall-to-wall. Instead, shorten the rows, propping books with bookends, and display art objects or other items in the remaining space.

Special pieces may need protection, security, and lighting. A ready-made or built-in unit with glass shelves, sliding glass doors, and interior lighting allows you to enjoy your collection and, at the same time, keep it safe, secure, and clean. Some collectibles can be kept on open shelves; others should be stored in dust-free cabinets or drawers.

Good lighting is critical to many displays. Ceiling-mounted downlights or tracks can highlight any display; built-in options include low-voltage downlights, strip lights, and other discreet fixtures (see page 126).

If you live in an area prone to earthquakes, you might opt for a cabinet with doors that can be locked or latched closed.

Railed, recessed shelving in a colonial-style kitchen holds a collection of blue-patterned chargers and cups from different design traditions.

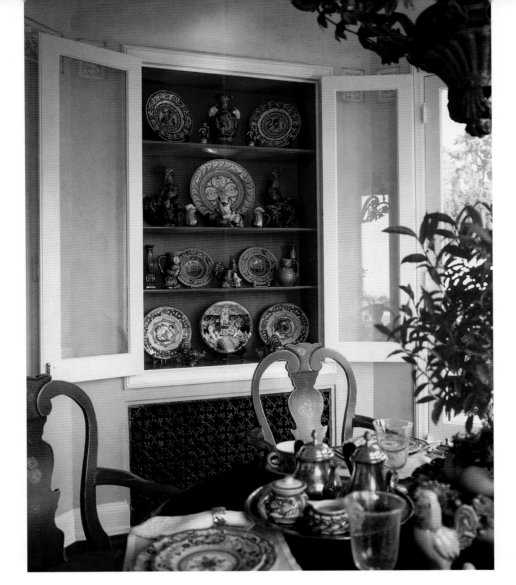

Seamless floor-to-ceiling maple cabinets include velvet-lined display niches. Built-in, low-voltage downlights in each niche highlight collectibles, which seem to leap out of their flat-black backgrounds.

Rich red shelving showcases a collection of majolica plates, pitchers, candlesticks, and pewter accent pieces in a recessed corner cabinet. Glass-paneled doors showcase the contents while keeping them secure and dust-free.

Glass shelves, glass interior doors, and a matching courtyard window in back—this see-through display cabinet is illuminated not only by recessed downlights from above, but also by daylight shining through the windows behind.

Rough, knife-applied plaster dresses up the display niche above and even covers the wood shelves, forming a colorful, casual frame for the collection within.

Discreet metal angle brackets lend support to narrow, scooped shelves, which in turn cradle a collection of classic rolling pins in this gourmet chef's kitchen.

The shelves above float on invisible hardware. Their clean lines are matched by pinpoint lighting, courtesy of low-voltage fixtures with aimable slot apertures.

At left, African art pieces are "framed" behind glass in recessed niches that step down in tandem with the nearby stairs.

media stars

The sleek, modern lines of this family room center on both the traditional fireplace and the up-to-the-minute home entertainment system. The floor-to-ceiling media unit that joins the black wraparound hearth includes shelf space and display niches, along with a heavy-duty TV and components.

ONE OF THE hottest arenas for wall systems is the media unit or home entertainment center. Besides contemplating cost and looks, you'll need to decide whether you want to feature all those gleaming gizmos or hide them. Do you want freestanding separates, a coordinated modular system, or custom built-ins with handy doors, drawers, and pullouts? Some setups are modest; others, like full-blown home theaters, are dazzlingly complex. Regardless of your specific case, the basic question remains: how do you keep all this stuff from taking over?

First, decide if the system is to be a focal point in your room. The media center often takes the place of the fireplace/hearth as a living-room's focus. If this is your desire, make sure to plan accordingly; if not, then take steps to hide it. You'll see both approaches on these pages.

Popular large-screen televisions can be a major design challenge. How do you house that big rear end or that blank, boring screen? Corner built-ins are one prime option, utilizing an oft-wasted space; pullouts, pop-ups, and turntables can also accommodate a TV's depth. Flipper doors or tambour doors cover the screen when it's not in use. For a closer look at all these items, see pages 110–113.

Remember that it's not just the electronics that need housing, but the CDs, DVDs, cassettes, vintage vinyl, and other media that go along with them. For sizing guidelines, see page 17.

Armoires take up less floor space than some media-center alternatives because they use vertical, rather than horizontal, space. The armoire below conceals a TV.

This major, wall-to-wall media system discloses a massive large-screen television when the sliding doors are open (top of page). When it's movie time, the doors slide closed and a projection screen descends (above). A sliding library ladder helps access the lofty regions of the sturdy wood shelves.

A pair of purple bi-fold doors, hinged vertically with a piano hinge, open to expose a serious collection of rack-mounted A/V components—everything from classic turntable to surround-sound receiver.

A wide, plasma-screen TV becomes part of the display, too, as it floats amidst an open shelf grid.

CD storage can be boring, but not with this unit. The free-form metal "wave" and "bookends" complement the modern color scheme perfectly. You can stack up all the CDs you want—at least until gravity kicks in.

The media center on the facing page could have been overly dominant, but careful detailing helps the design blend in with its surroundings. Made of pine, with hand-pegged doors, the cabinetry features dentil detailing beneath crown molding; the speaker cloth matches the TV screen.

Sometimes television viewing and formal entertaining don't coincide. In this case, however, a corner location not only moved the TV to the side, but also allowed extra cabinet depth to accommodate it. The built-in unit features pocket doors; the TV sits on a swivel mount.

Tucked into a corner below existing beams, this 10- by 14-foot structure sports a simple, serene façade that's covered mostly by sliding shoji screens. A walk-in closet fits behind the entertainment center; its sliding panel allows access to the stereo components.

room dividers

NOT ALL WALL SYSTEMS stand against a wall. Islands and peninsulas that float alone in a room can stretch available wall space, redirect traffic patterns, or even define different areas. Storage-wise, room dividers help you get rid of clutter by consolidating open and closed shelves and cabinets. They also make great media centers.

A soaring maple built-in dramatically divides the dining room from the entryway; at the same time, it adds lots of display and storage space. Base cabinets are joined by a glass-doored, glass-shelved wall unit. High soffit lighting shines down on the maple counter below.

Room dividers may be short, tall, narrow, or deep. They can be used in any space from great room and dining room to breakfast nook, bedroom, and bath. Short units may be freestanding; taller ones should be firmly anchored to the floor, wall, and/or ceiling. They can be single- or double-sided. For even more storage, pack the protruding end with display niches.

Decide whether your room divider should blend with its surroundings or add some contrasting energy. Should it appear to be built into the room or to be a brash, brightly-stained, furniture piece? Should you tie it in with integral baseboards or crown molding? Consider capping a short base unit with a granite countertop; add a library ladder to a floor-to-ceiling tower.

This cherry-and-marble built-in, housed in a pass-through space, does triple duty as room divider, display shelf, and dining room buffet.

A bank of blank, closed cabinets can be oppressive, so it's important to mix things up, perhaps by adding see-through windows, glass-paneled doors, display niches, and built-in accent lighting to your storage wall. Or stagger the sizes and shapes of shelves, drawer fronts, and doors.

A 30-inch-wide "storage spine" (below) runs nearly the length of the house and acts as a divider between public and private spaces. All storage closets, cabinets, and drawers are located here. Turn the corner (left) and you'll find a CD collection on short shelves. Freeing perimeter walls of cabinets gave the owners much more room for furniture and art.

This remodeled storage wall is clean, simple, and colorful—all done on a budget. The cabinets are basic plywood. By painting them in bright colors, the owners made them special. In the living room, they created a built-in display case to showcase art and conceal audio equipment.

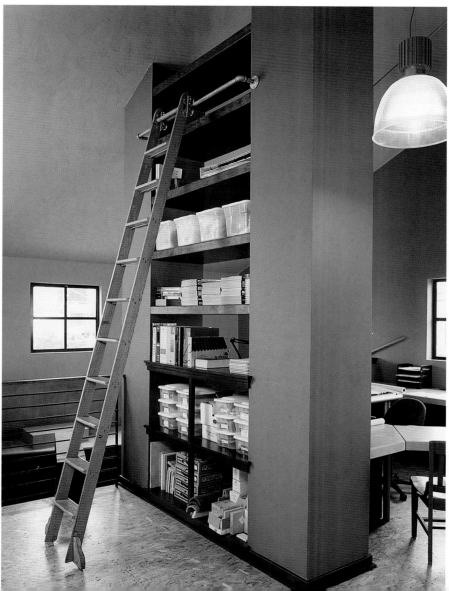

A two-sided divider that's part wall, part tower defines an office area and provides a home for office literature and sample products. The ladder slides on its plumbing-pipe top rail, offering access to the unit's upper nooks and crannies.

office ideas

A tall, gable-end wall is meticulously fitted with built-in office shelves and cabinets in elegant, dark-stained wood. Traditional cabinetry steps down to the lowered desk surface and back up to tall, shallow bookcases. A sliding ladder (the rail is visible toward the top of the shelves) allows access to upper shelves.

AS HOME-OFFICE USE mushrooms, so do new wall-system solutions. Phones, computers, printers, files, bookcases, binder and magazine racks, and big bunches of tangled wires are common parts of the puzzle. But these spaces aren't always just for work; display and even media-center needs are being folded in. Both commercial and custom designs and materials are getting more sophisticated. As they say, it's not just an office; it's your home, too.

Modular systems (pages 106–109) are one popular way to go. You can buy work counters, file cabinets, overhead bins, and platforms for printers, then mix and match them to fit your space. On the other hand, built-ins offer an unmatched opportunity for formal and traditional looks. Either way, you'll find a growing number of high-tech pullouts and computer accessories to choose from; for starters, see pages 120–123. Some office storage is totally open, some totally closed. As usual, a mix of both styles seems to work best, allowing you to camouflage storage chaos while allowing for some custom touches.

Remember that an office can be located anywhere: in a guest room or kitchen alcove, on a stair landing, or inside a former closet. For other "found-space" options, see pages 78–81. An office can also stand alone—for example, consider an armoire (see page 77) or another freestanding furniture piece with doors and drawers.

An upstairs hall can be more than just a passageway, as this 4-foot-wide homework station shows.

AFRICA
FREEDOM FROM FEAR
CARRY ME HOME
MALCOLM
RHAPSODIES IN BLACK
PETER J. GOMES
THE GOOD BOOK

Two drawer units and a file cabinet are bridged by a granite countertop to make a handsome desk. The shallow, white, wall-mounted uppers include recycled windows as glass doors. Integral ceiling moldings link wall unit to room.

A compact office on an upper landing includes sleek, clean-lined wall units that mix open storage and display with sliding doors on discreet hardware. Frosted doors allow a glimpse of what's inside, but hide clutter.

Recessed, glass-doored library cases, crafted in hardwood with brass accents, form a classic backdrop for a formal, wood-paneled study.

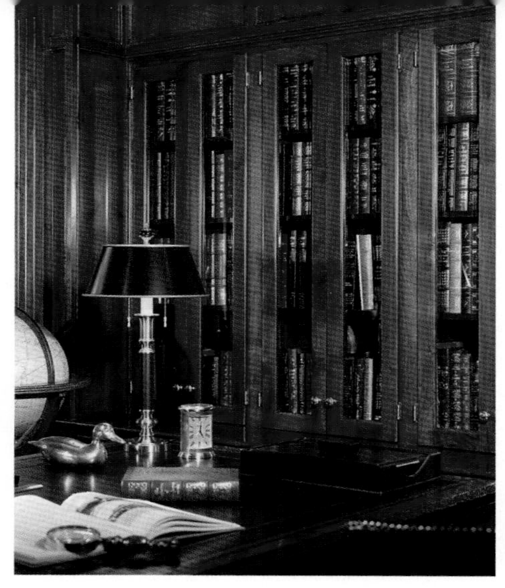

Tailored fir built-ins wrap this home office in style. Floor-to-ceiling units, tied together with integral crown and base moldings, include plenty of closed storage below and adjustable shelving above. Along the way there's an efficient built-in desk, plus a comfy looking couch for napping until inspiration strikes.

Tucked in beside the refrigerator, this compact command center includes maple storage niches, black-stained ash drawers, and a cantilevered, angled maple work surface reminiscent of a country school desk.

A recessed wall cabinet or pantry door can provide bonus space for a message center. The unit shown below packs lower drawers, central cubbies, a writing surface, and an upper compartment with a door into one super-slim package.

A kitchen storage wall includes a mini-office, shown above, plus pantry, washer and dryer, and water heater—all tucked behind a series of sliding doors.

What do you do when a home office meets a media center? The handsome cabinetry above features low pullout drawers for heavy vinyl LPs, solid doors for the TV, a countertop for a turntable that needs a lot of vertical space, and glass-fronted uppers for other components.

This efficient armoire adds work space to a bedroom while allowing its owner and designer to put a lid on the workday when it's over. The laminate-lined piece houses a computer, TV, audio gear, work counter, task lights, and storage files—and it's fully wired for action.

found-space solutions

LOOKING FOR STORAGE spaces in all the wrong places? Try some of the following spots: hallways and stairs, entries and exits, unused room corners, closets, and odd nooks and crannies both high and low.

Stairways are prime targets for both storage and display built-ins. The space below stairs is often just waiting to be used; other possibilities include landings as well as stairside shelves or display niches along the way.

In hallways, try between-stud spaces, an open end wall, or look overhead. While you're looking up, check out the soffit areas above kitchen wall cabinets, or kneel down and add drawers or display cubbies below a window seat or island. An angled corner unit can transform any unused corner into a brand-new focal point.

Underutilized closets, if there is such a thing, make ready-made recesses for wall systems; just remove the doors and add shelves. Or borrow the space from a closet in an adjacent room for a built-in unit on the other side.

Some great ideas are even smaller in scale: think pullouts and pantry packs. Modular showrooms and specialty firms have lots of clever accessories you can build in; for shopping tips, see pages 120–123. The ultimate pullout—the Murphy bed—is perfect for guest-room/office multitasking.

If your book collection outgrows its allotted space, try breaking it up. This library spreads around a remodeled stair landing leading to the master bedroom. Built-ins along the landing form an intimate book nook where one can study, browse, or simply gaze out through the peaked window wall to greenery beyond.

Display space is where you find it: in this case, it's tucked into one end of a central kitchen island that is framed in the room's entry.

Perhaps the ultimate found-space retreat, this is more than a window seat: it's a self-contained nook that functions as a mini-library (note the bookshelves), a cozy reading nook, a storage chest, and even a guest bed.

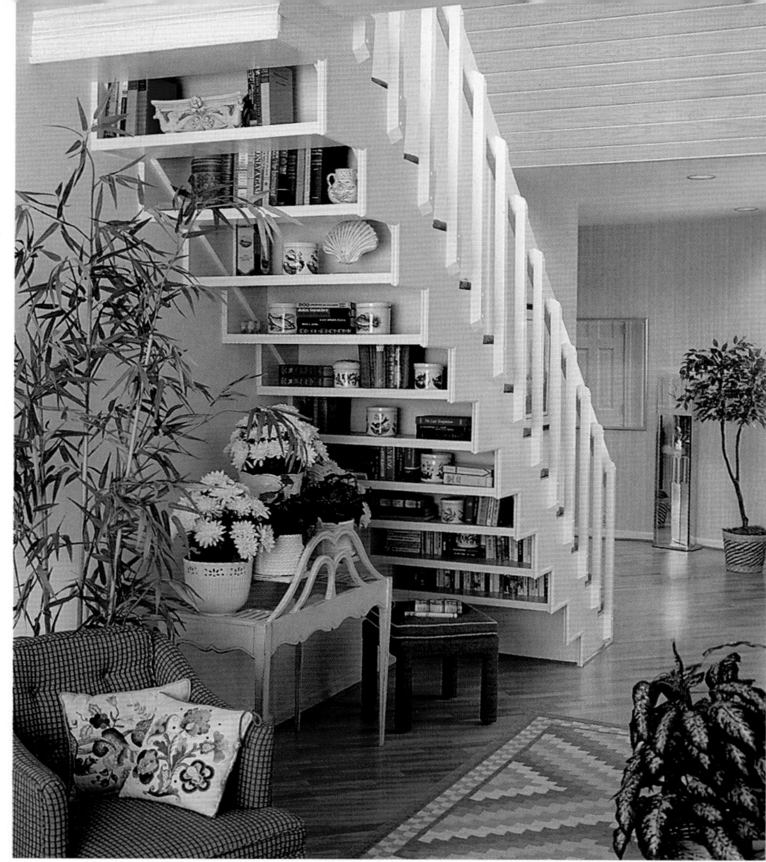

While the wedge below the stairs is one way to go, what about the bottoms of the stairs themselves? In this case, the space remains open, but a clever set of ascending shelf niches mirrors the course of the stairs above.

Frustrated by a lack of closets, the owner found space under the staircase in the entry. Two small storage units slide out like drawers, making items immediately and fully accessible. One unit has a seating area for removing shoes; the other holds coats and boots.

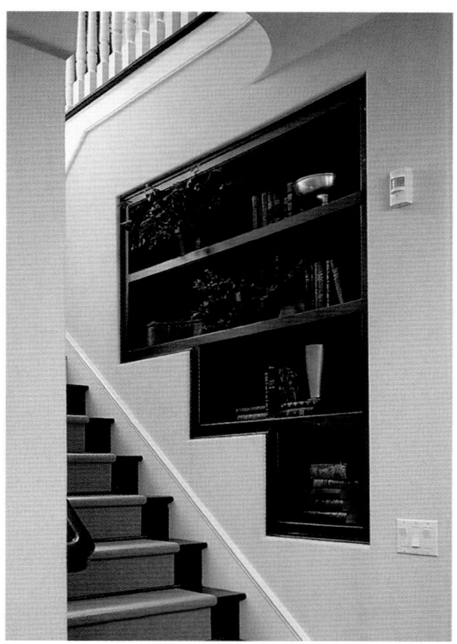

Another stairside spot to consider is the wall flanking the stairs' run, often a good opportunity for shallow or recessed shelves. Note how neatly this dark-stained bookcase meets the surrounding plaster.

What appear to be two simple white cabinet doors (above) are actually part of a single panel that hides a Murphy bed (right). These disappearing acts work particularly well in rooms that serve multiple functions, such as guest room/home office combinations.

A freestanding armoire not only invades the kitchen, but the dishwasher is cleverly tucked into its lower left-hand reaches. Most dishwashers accommodate removable, replaceable door panels; in this case, the panel blends seamlessly with the armoire.

One classic spot to tuck display shelves is in the space between vertical wall studs. This narrow, shallow space—typically about 14½ inches wide by 4 inches deep—may be all you need in a hallway, entryway, or bath. As an added benefit, you won't waste any floor space.

Stumped for shelf space? Look up! The kitchen at left did a high-wire act in the so-called "soffit area" atop the door and window trim, which is usually wasted space.

utility players

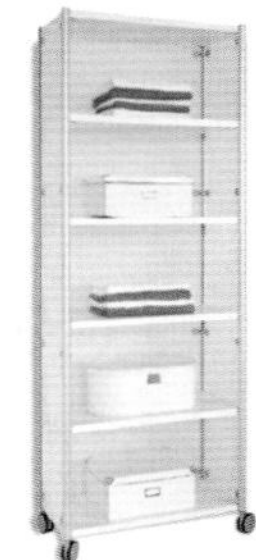

LAST, BUT NOT LEAST, come those sometimes no-frills wall systems designed for combat duty in places like mudrooms, basements, laundry rooms, workshops, and garages. Typically, these units aren't glamorous, but they're nevertheless important. Think strong materials, easy cleaning, and durability. Also be sure there's good ventilation for stored items.

Modular units range from modest to high-end. This stylish, beautifully made closet system takes the prize for both looks and efficiency. Plenty of drawers, pullouts, clothes rods, and even a swing-down rack at center can allow you to mix and match the system of your dreams.

Bins and baskets may be all you need. For easier access, put them on rollers. Modular budget units abound, with many systems combining closed cabinets, utility shelves, drawers, hooks and rods, and even work counters in one. Sturdy warehouse shelves are another option; combine them with garage pegboard hangers and you're in business. Heavy-duty "ventilated" shelves—typically washable, vinyl-coated steel—perch atop oversize track-and-bracket hardware (see page 92) specially designed for this use. They're great for laundry areas.

A built-in wall unit is one of the best ways to organize a family's sports gear, hats, jackets, shoes, pool towels, and the like.

Don't forget closets. There's an exploding array of stock, custom, and modular units now available. As you'll see, some of these custom or commercial units are not only amazingly efficient; they're also quite stylish.

Store items that are seldom used or dangerous to children on high shelves or inside locked cabinets, small items that are hard to spot at eye level, and light but large items on bottom shelves. Pullouts or pantry packs can help you avoid stooping and can maximize your usable space.

The mud room shown above, an entry alcove located near both laundry room and kitchen, has plenty of nooks and crannies for clothes, ski boots, artwork, and messages. Each family member has his or her own "zone."

In this garage, storage is open—the workhorses are "ventilated" wire shelves on a heavy-duty track-and-bracket system that's designed for utility use and abuse. Another star performer is the wire-basket system that rolls around the space as needed.

The linen closet pictured at left hides maximum shelf space behind a pair of stylish bi-fold doors. The kick base keeps dust from rolling right into the closet and makes cleaning easier.

Located off the basement hall, this ultimate laundry room contains built-in cabinetry that camouflages storage—as well as both the washer and dryer.

Wine storage calls not only for stable temperatures, but also for stable shelves and bins. The reason for both notched rails and diamond-shaped bins: wine bottles are expensive, fragile, and—most importantly—round.

A SHOPPER'S GUIDE

IT'S TIME FOR A SHOPPING SPREE. Whether you're looking for track-and-bracket shelf hardware, an unfinished armoire, or an ultra-smooth TV pullout, we'll show you shopping options from A to Z (actually, from shelves to moldings) on the following pages. **WE BEGIN WITH THE BASICS**—prefab shelves, shelf materials, and both fixed and adjustable hardware. **THEN IT'S ON TO CABINETS,** doors and drawers, freestanding furniture pieces, and the latest looks in both budget-minded and high-end modular systems. Along the way you'll find lots of specialized pullouts and hardware to make your hardworking wall system work even harder. **FINISHING TOUCHES** include built-in light fixtures; stains, paints, and clear finishes; and stylish moldings that will turn your new unit into an integral part of your home's design.

Shelves

FROM BOARDS AND BRACKETS TO BOOKCASES

Of all storage and display components, shelves are the most basic. They're installed in cabinets, built into all types of wall units, or simply mounted by themselves on brackets or other supports. Some are fixed in place; others are adjustable; still others pull out, swivel, or lift up.

Shelf materials

When you shop, you'll discover shelves made of a variety of materials, including numerous kinds of solid wood, sheet products, and glass. Which is best? That depends on the appearance and strength you want the shelving to have.

Some materials can span farther than others without bowing or breaking under a given load; guidelines are given in the chart on page 18. Use the maximum spans for lightweight to medium-weight loads, such as art objects, most books, pictures, and relatively lightweight electronic gear. For heavier loads, such as televisions, wine racks, heavy books, and magazine stacks, shorten the spans or use stronger materials. Place only lightweight objects on glass shelving.

PINE, FIR, AND OTHER SOFTWOODS. Sold as boards through home centers and lumber dealers, these softwoods are favored for relatively inexpensive, do-it-yourself shelving.

Several grades are available. For most shelving, the appearance grades of Select (sometimes called Clear) and Common are preferred. Look for C-and-better Selects if you want flawless, knotless wood. Other less-expensive choices for shelving are No. 2 and No. 3 Common "knotty" pine. Whatever the grade, let your eyes be the final judge.

Boards are sold by the foot, usually in "1-by" (or 3/4-inch) thickness, although thicker boards are sometimes available. Lumberyards will sometimes cut them to length for you. If your boards require finishing, see pages 124–125 for information.

SOLID HARDWOODS. Hardwoods such as oak, cherry, and maple are available through hardwood lumber dealers and some home centers. They're typically available in 4/4, 5/4, 6/4, and 8/4 thicknesses—about 3/4-inch to 1½ inches. Hardwoods tend to be expensive, particularly in the rare, wide boards required for shelving. (Several widths are often glued together by cabinetmakers—or some home-improvement centers—to form wider boards.)

SHEET PRODUCTS. Hardwood-veneered plywood is more commonly used for shelving than solid hardwood. Plywood is considerably less expen-

CLEAR FIR

"KNOTTY" PINE

RED OAK

sive, comes in wide (4- by 8-foot) sheets, and won't warp or twist as readily as solid wood. In shelf construction, the plywood is usually edged with hardwood veneer tape (see below) or trimmed with solid hardwood. Other edge treatments are also available.

Particleboard shelves are serviceable but fairly weak; don't pick them for heavy loads. Medium-density fiberboard, or MDF, is stronger than standard fiberboard and is sometimes available in thicker 1-inch pieces.

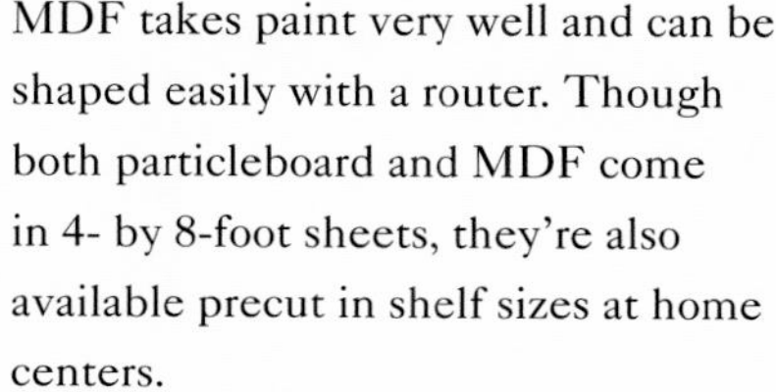

Glass shelf kit

Veneer tape

MDF takes paint very well and can be shaped easily with a router. Though both particleboard and MDF come in 4- by 8-foot sheets, they're also available precut in shelf sizes at home centers.

Shelves covered with vinyl, melamine, plastic laminate, or related films are easy to maintain and relatively inexpensive. Of the three surfacing materials, plastic laminate is by far the most durable. Melamine, a surface layer of resin-impregnated paper, is very serviceable and considerably less expensive than plastic laminate. Vinyl-wrapped shelves are the lowest grade.

Glass. Plate glass with ground edges is a popular shelf material for displays because it allows you to view objects more fully and doesn't block the light. Choose ¼-, ⅜-, or ½-inch thickness, depending on the span.

Some glass suppliers offer a range of colors and surface textures. Though pricier, it's best to opt for tempered safety glass.

Vinyl wrap

Particleboard

Paint-grade poplar

Melamine

Shelf hardware

Hardware for open shelves supports the undersides of shelves. Do you need adjustable hardware, or extra-strong support? Here's a look at your choices.

TRACKS AND BRACKETS. This popular adjustable hardware (shown at right) allows you to tailor a complex shelving system to fit your specific needs. The tracks need to be screwed into wall studs to support the weight of the shelves and the items stored on them. Then the tabs on the ends of the brackets slip into the tracks' slots. If you opt to change things later, just pop the bracket out of the slots and reposition it.

Both tracks and brackets come in a variety of finishes, including chrome, gold, bronze, white, and sometimes other painted finishes. Track lengths run from about 24 to 72 inches; brackets range from 6 to 12 inches long. You'll also find heavy-duty tracks and brackets (shown at far right), with beefier construction and double slots, designed for heavy utility loads.

Because tracks need to be fastened to wall studs, which are usually 16 inches apart, your tracks will be about 16, 32, or 48 inches apart, depending on your design and the load the shelves will bear. Attach the tracks with screws that penetrate the wood for at least two-thirds their length.

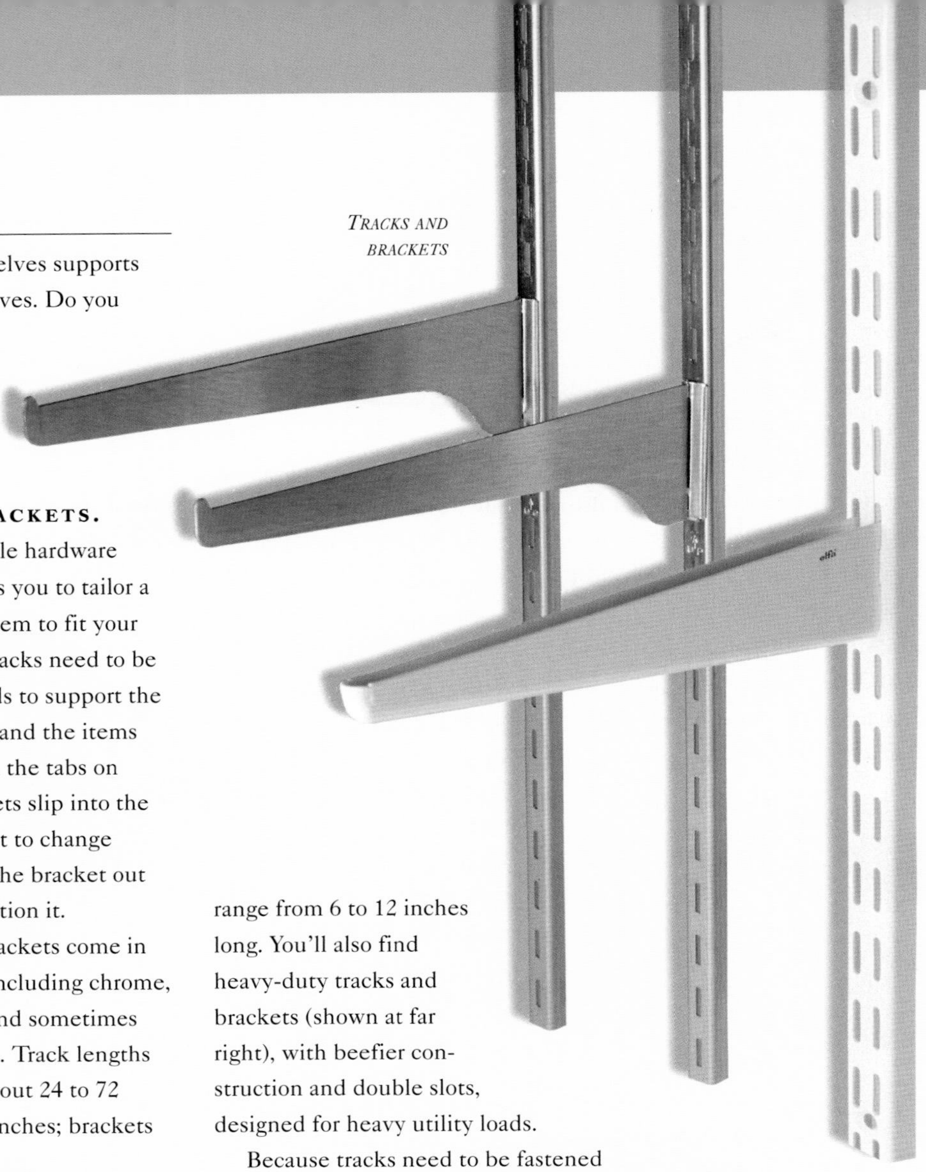

TRACKS AND BRACKETS

HEAVY-DUTY TRACK AND BRACKET

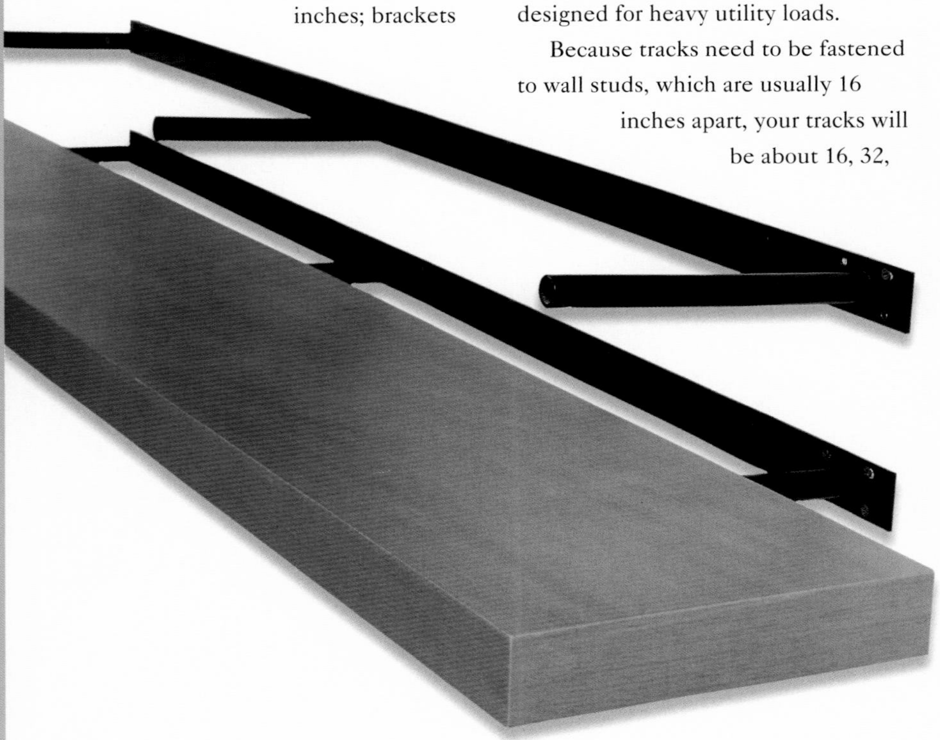

TORSION-BOX SHELF

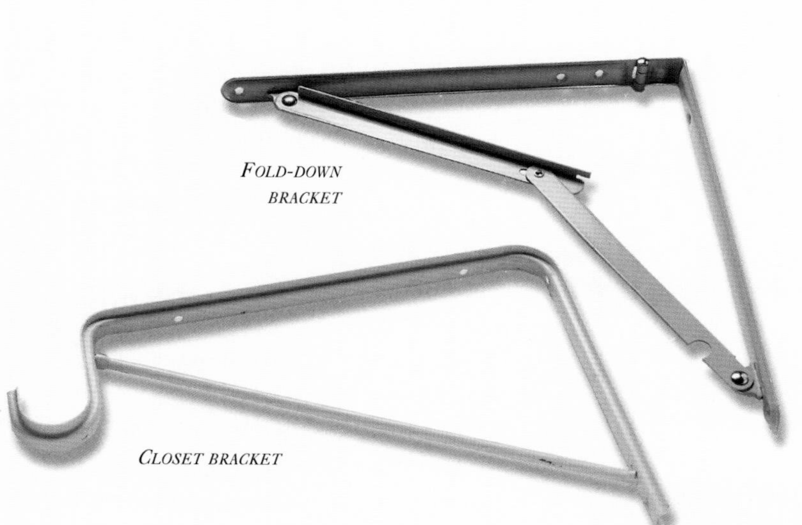
Fold-down bracket

Closet bracket

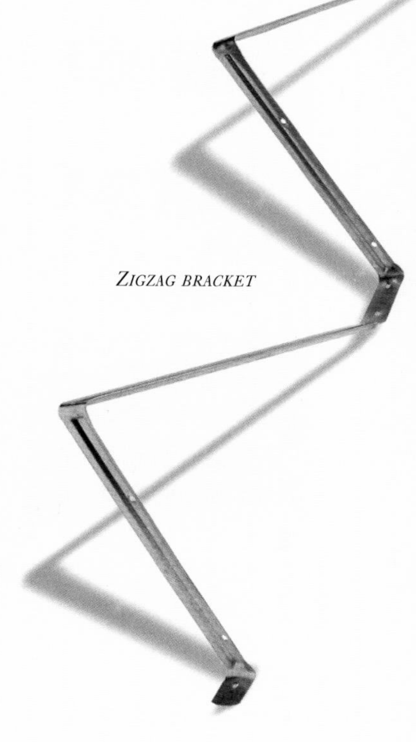
Zigzag bracket

Fixed brackets and gussets. Decorative brackets and gussets are more attractive but less flexible than adjustable tracks and brackets. Here, you screw the brackets themselves to the studs. If you have a choice, buy a size that's just slightly smaller than your shelf depth.

Options include ornate pine or oak and a range of metal brackets, from harshly utilitarian to highly decorative. Zigzag and fold-down metal brackets are for heavy utility uses. Closet brackets include a curved cradle at the end that supports a standard closet dowel below the shelf support.

You'll also find prefab kits that contain both shelf and brackets. Some are pretty pedestrian; others, including hollow torsion-box shelves (see facing page) and other "floating" units, are more stylish.

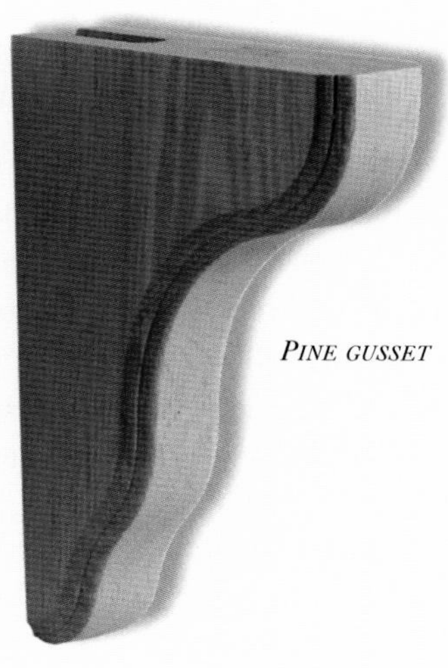
Pine gusset

Metal brackets

Modular shelving unit

Movable box modules

Shelving units

Support the ends, not the midspans, of your shelves with cross-rungs or uprights, and you've suddenly created a shelving unit. Add a top, a bottom, and maybe a back, and you're looking at a bookcase.

You'll find all sorts of variations on these themes at home centers, home-improvement warehouses, furniture retailers, office supply stores, and the like. Or take advantage of some specialized hardware and build your own project.

Stack it up. At its most basic, a shelving unit is a pair of ladderlike uprights and, hopefully, some sturdy shelves that span them. Cross-braces or a wire X-brace at the back can help strengthen the structure. This scheme lends itself to modularity: just buy taller uprights for more vertical height or more uprights or bays for horizontal expansion. Add more shelves for books or kitchen goods; omit some shelves for larger items or to create display niches.

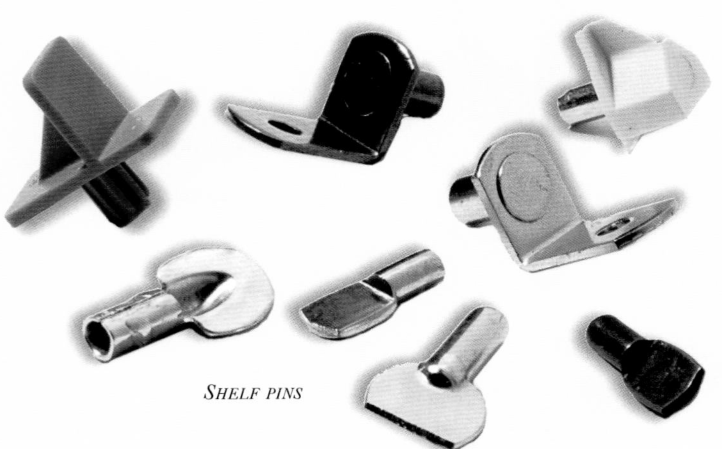

Shelf pins

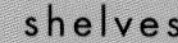

Track-and-clip hardware

Swiveling shelves

Predrilled melamine upright

Other units are basically boxes designed to be stacked on top of each other. Sometimes, box modules are available in single-, double-, and even triple-length versions, allowing you to nest pieces together to form the size and shape you want.

Hardware. Like free-floating shelves, shelving units and bookcases have their own adjustable hardware options.

Spade pins and bracket pins (facing page), made of metal or plastic, fit in drilled holes in cabinet sides and allow you to change and adjust shelf heights.

Track-and-clip hardware (above) is designed for installation in cabinet frames, simplifying the building of bookcases and making it possible to adjust the shelves. Simply cut tracks to length, as needed, and then tack them in place along the case sides; for a more finished look, recess tracks in grooves so they are flush with the wood.

Uprights to go. Some well-stocked home centers now carry prefabricated bookcase sides, or uprights, in pine, melamine, or both. As shown at right, some sides come predrilled for shelf pins; others are grooved for 1-by shelving boards, tracks, clips, and/or a ¼-inch-thick back.

Grooved pine uprights

Doors and Drawers

LIDS, BOXES, HINGES, AND OTHER HARDWARE

Doors hide clutter, seal out dust, and enliven the appearance of both bookcases and cabinets. Drawers are essentially boxes, that slide in and out. Add doors, drawers, or both to your shelving unit, and you have a full-fledged wall system.

Door details

Cabinet doors can hinge, slide, drop down, fold up, or retract. The type that works best on a particular unit depends on the purpose.

Hinged doors, by far the most common, open easily and allow total access to a cabinet's contents. Sliding doors always look tidy and don't require room to swing, but they allow access into only half the cabinet at a time.

Drop-down doors, which swing down rather than to the side, can double as a work surface.

Folding and tambour (roll-away) doors open the cabinet completely; they require little or no swinging room, but they are sometimes awkward to operate.

Retractable (or "flipper") doors hinge open and then slide back into a cabinet. These doors are particularly effective where hinged doors would be an obstruction. They can be installed either vertically or horizontally.

Sliding doors

Retractable doors

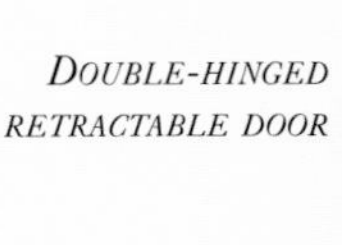

Double-hinged retractable door

Drop-down door

Study cabinet doors and you'll notice that there are several ways to mount a door with respect to the cabinet face. A *recessed* door is mounted inside the opening, with its face flush with the front of the cabinet or face frame. On a *lipped* door, a rabbet (notch) is cut around the inside edges of the door so that half its thickness projects beyond the face frame. An *overlay* door overlaps the edges of the opening and is mounted with its inside face against the cabinet frame.

How doors are made

Cabinet doors are constructed either as flat pieces or as a panel surrounded by a frame. The flat type (shown above) is normally wood veneer or laminate over a core of plywood, particleboard, or medium-density fiberboard (MDF). A frame-and-panel door may be made of solid hardwood or a combination of hardwood frame and veneered panels. The best frames have mortise-and-tenon or doweled joints. Panels may be flat, veneered sheet products, or shaped or "raised" from solid wood or MDF.

Glass doors, especially those made of etched, beveled, or leaded glass, may utilize a hardwood frame, much like a frame-and-panel door, except that glass replaces the panel. Or glass sheets can be fitted into tracks to serve as sliders. Still other glass doors are hinged; some hinges clamp in place, while others are secured through holes bored in the glass.

Hinges and hardware

Shown on this page is a sampling of the many hinges available to hang different types of doors.

European cup hinges, which are hidden behind the door, are by far the most popular for frameless cabinets and modular wall systems. The best of these are adjustable and allow a door to open completely—110°, 120°, or even 170°—rather than restricting it to a 90° swing. Good European hinges can be aligned simply with a screwdriver; clip-on versions allow you to take the door off and on without touching a screw.

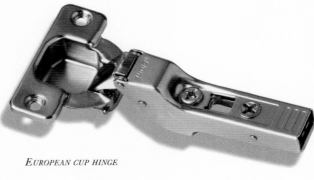

European cup hinge

Concealed hinge

These hinges come in full-overlay, half-overlay, and recessed versions.

Use other hinges for visual impact or special effects. Small butt hinges are traditional for standard face-frame cabinets (see page 114) or other period styles. Other options for standard doors include pin hinges, concealed hinges, and offset hinges (the last for lipped doors only). All these hinges are harder to install and adjust than cup hinges.

Specialty doors have their own hinge styles. Lightweight sliding doors run in wood, metal, or vinyl tracks; heavy sliding doors hang from overhead tracks and runners. Drop-down doors use piano hinges, butterfly hinges, or stay supports to keep them in check; retractable or "flipper" hinges (see page 110) allow doors to fold back completely out of the way.

So-called "snap-closing" cup hinges are enough to keep doors closed, but other hinges may call for catches and latches (see the facing page). Magnetic catches are generally your best bet; they are less dependent on strict alignment than other types and don't wear out. Other alternatives include friction catches, touch latches, and security latches. All these styles are shown on the facing page.

Glass door hinge

Butt hinge

Offset hinge

Decorative brass hinge

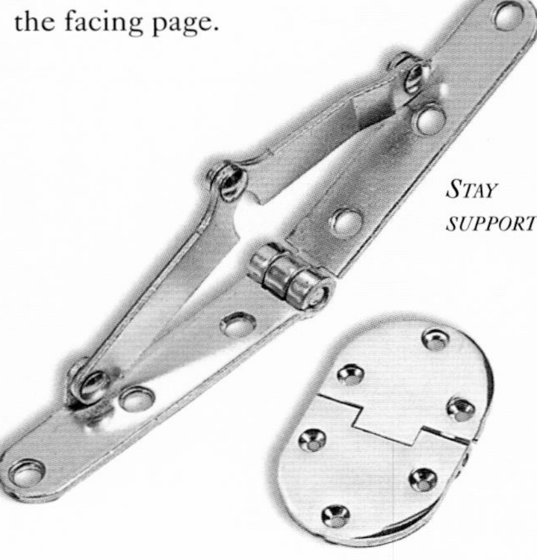

Stay support

Butterfly hinge

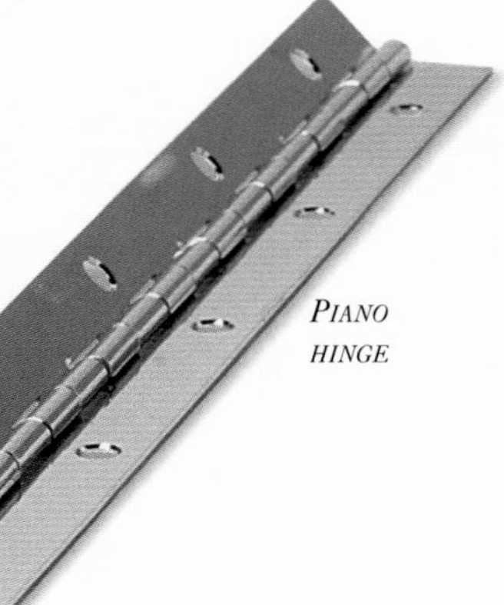

Piano hinge

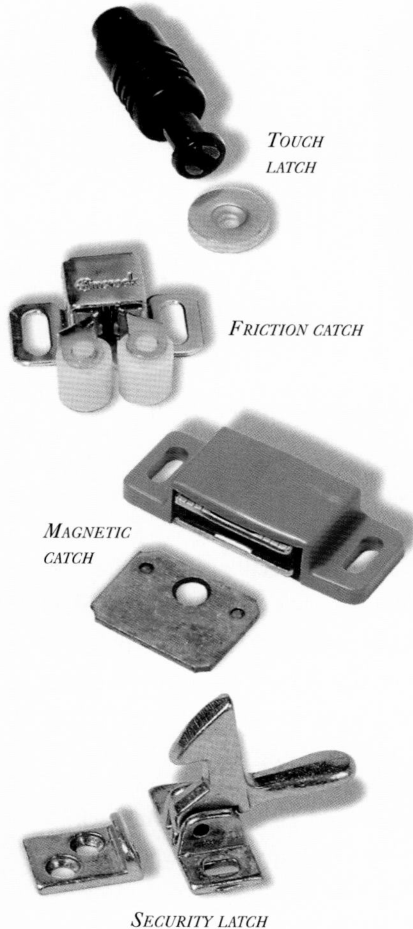

Touch latch

Friction catch

Magnetic catch

Security latch

Locks can be used on display cabinets to keep valuables visible but safe. Traditional mortise lock assemblies include a bolt, a strike plate, and an escutcheon, which encircles the keyhole. Cam locks are trimmer, but less secure. If you have more than one lock, you can buy them keyed alike.

Cam lock

Finding the Right Knobs and Pulls

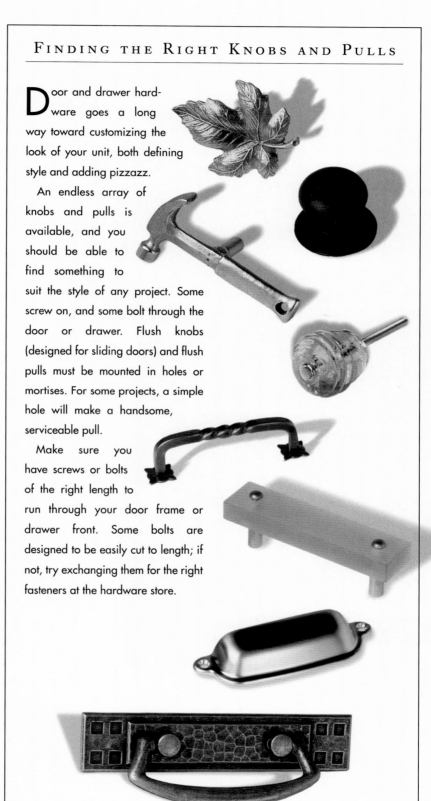

Door and drawer hardware goes a long way toward customizing the look of your unit, both defining style and adding pizzazz.

An endless array of knobs and pulls is available, and you should be able to find something to suit the style of any project. Some screw on, and some bolt through the door or drawer. Flush knobs (designed for sliding doors) and flush pulls must be mounted in holes or mortises. For some projects, a simple hole will make a handsome, serviceable pull.

Make sure you have screws or bolts of the right length to run through your door frame or drawer front. Some bolts are designed to be easily cut to length; if not, try exchanging them for the right fasteners at the hardware store.

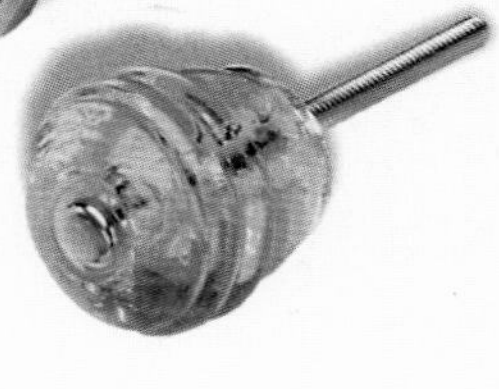

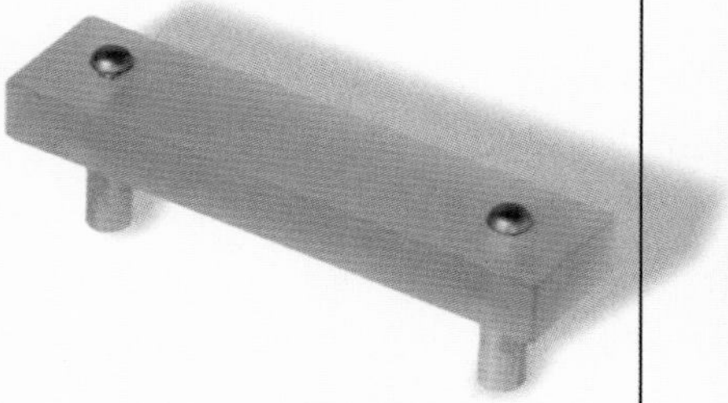

Drawer construction

A drawer is essentially a box with four sides and a bottom. The manner in which the box is built is a good way to judge the overall quality of the system. Traditionally, the best drawers have hardwood sides dovetailed to a front panel that is separate from the drawer's face (see above left). A sturdy ¼-inch plywood bottom is set into dadoes, or grooves, in the sides and front, and sometimes in the back. Other high-quality drawers feature void-free marine plywood—called Finnish ply or Apply ply—which has handsome edge detailing and is actually more stable than hardwood.

Medium-grade drawers may have sides built of hardwood, standard hardwood plywood, or melamine-surfaced plywood or particleboard. Sides may be doweled and glued, biscuit-joined, secured with knock-down fasteners, or rabbeted (notched) and nailed to front panels.

Other medium-grade drawers are molded completely from rigid plastics and given a front panel that matches the cabinet system. These drawers are sturdy and maintenance-free.

Lowest-quality drawers are built of particleboard wrapped with vinyl paper. Some are "folded" together from a single piece and mitered at the corners. Sides are attached directly to the finish front with hot-melt glue and staples, an unreliable method that may result in the drawer's falling apart with time. The bottom is often made of thin, 3⁄16-inch hardboard.

Like doors, drawer faces can overlay the front frame, sit partially inside the frame, or they can be recessed fully inside the frame.

All about drawer guides

Traditional furniture drawers were simply friction-fit or operated on waxed runners. But furniture aesthetics aside, adding a sturdy set of drawer guides is the best way to go. Side-mounted guides generally handle more weight and operate more smoothly than center guides. These guides require about ½-inch clearance between each drawer side and the cabinet frame.

Epoxy-coated, side-mounted, steel slides with nylon rollers (below right) are industry standards, combining easy operation with modest cost. When rollers are rimmed with a rubber ring, action will be smoothest. One nice feature with some of these rollers is that they are self-closing; as the drawer face approaches the cabinet front, it automatically slides "downhill" into a closed position.

Heavy-duty, steel ball-bearing guides (below left) are stronger and run more smoothly, but they are significantly more expensive. When you push the drawer closed, these guides will seat the drawer firmly against the cabinet front.

Center guides are most appropriate for lightweight, narrow drawers. Some new center guides, though, are stronger, and because they're "invisible," they allow you to combine a guideless, furniture-like appearance with the practicality of a smooth slide. (These guides do require substantial bottom clearance.)

The length that guides extend is important to consider, particularly if you'll need full access to the backs of drawers. Most drawer guides extend only three-quarters of their length; high-quality ball-bearing guides extend completely. Most good guide designs allow the drawer to be disconnected and removed from the cabinet.

Drawer organizer

Epoxy-coated slide

Heavy-duty ball-bearing guide

Custom corner drawer

Storage Furniture

THESE STAND-ALONES WERE THE FIRST WALL SYSTEMS

Loosely speaking, the term "furniture" means movable—a unit that's either freestanding or attached to a wall for support. Beyond that, furniture implies "tradition," although not all furniture-like wall systems look traditional. These days they range from country casual to formal elegance. In general, furniture units are ready-made and available on short notice. You'll wait longer to have custom furniture designed and/or built by a woodworking professional.

Unfinished bookcase

Unfinished armoire

With a few exceptions, furniture designs are not as flexible as modular wall systems (see pages 106–109). Still, a visit to a retail furniture showroom will unveil a surprising range of ready-made storage and display options. You'll discover budget bookcases, Shaker-style media centers, French etageres, and many styles of chests and cabinets that can be used individually or in groupings to meet your display and storage needs.

Storage pieces

Stand-alone furniture pieces are fun to find and are especially apt for eclectic or country-style decorating schemes. Buy them new, buy them as antiques, or rescue them from thrift shops. Or look for unfinished pieces and put your personal stamp on them, saving money in the process.

Bookcases run the gamut from particleboard and pine boards to fine hardwoods like walnut and cherry. Some have bare-bones styling; others sport ornate moldings and face frames (see page 114). Do you need adjustable shelves or extra-deep or extra-strong spans? You're sure to find a bookcase to meet any budget.

Armoires are tall, capacious cupboards with doors and sometimes drawers. Depending on how you outfit them inside, they can fulfill their traditional purpose as clothes closets or house anything from office supplies to your audiovisual equipment.

Hutches and other wood cabinets have been made in a seemingly limitless variety of sizes and types, from wall and corner cupboards to dry sinks, pie safes, and chests of drawers. The classic choice for storing dishes and glassware, a hutch can just as easily become a display case for sculpture or a collection.

Also be on the lookout for roll-top desks, trunks, chests, china cabinets, and buffets.

Antique hutch

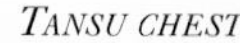

Tansu chest

Custom contemporary piece

Handpainted cupboard

Furniture collections

Many large furniture manufacturers offer collections of furniture—as many as twenty or so pieces—designed to coordinate in style and finish. Most collections include specialized pieces such as media centers, china cabinets, and storage units.

Some storage furnishings come as a single piece, such as the tall armoire. Others consist of cabinets or units that you stack up or join side by side. Perhaps the oldest example of the stacked type is the lowboy with a highboy deck. Another example is the china deck that sits on top of a credenza.

Side-by-side groupings generally include different types of tall cabinets. For example, you can buy a tall curio cabinet as a center piece, add matching pier cabinets on either side of it, and finish off the ends with angled corner units. The result is a coordinated wall of cabinetry suited to a variety of purposes. These ensembles were, in fact, the original "wall systems."

Where can you buy it?

You can buy storage furniture at many outlets, including furniture stores, department stores, and designer showrooms. Some single pieces are sold through mail-order catalogs. For complete media centers or furniture to organize electronic gear, visit quality home-electronics stores. And if you look around a bit, you can find ready-made storage solutions in many other places, among them antique stores, unfinished furniture stores, and office-supply outlets.

As a rule, furniture stores excel in service. Many offer design help, financing, and, if needed, assembly.

Desk grouping (open and closed)

Kitchen hutch with "distressed" finish

Most department stores sell from floor models or catalogs. They offer the same services as furniture stores, but, because floor space is limited, you may not find as large a selection. Department stores buy mostly from large, established manufacturers.

Designer showrooms sell ready-made and custom storage furniture and wall systems at wholesale prices to designers and architects. To view products in these showrooms and to make purchases, you may need to be accompanied by a professional.

Judging quality

As with any furniture, quality is often self-evident in the appearance and materials of a product. The best pieces are made of durable, high-grade materials such as solid hardwood and/or hardwood plywood. The quality of the piece is generally reflected in the joinery and detailing of doors, drawers, and similar parts (see pages 96–101).

Of course, the higher the quality, the higher the price.

Modular Wall Systems

MIX AND MATCH YOUR FAVORITE PIECES

Born in Scandinavia, modular wall systems have over the years gained favor worldwide as sensible, practical, and sometimes beautiful display and storage units.

It's easy to understand the appeal of a modular system. The keys to its success are modular design, functional flexibility, and ease of installation. You can combine shelves, cabinets, doors, drawers, and other components to fit your exact needs and space requirements. And, when you move, you simply pack up the pieces and take them with you and rearrange them for your new situation.

32-MILLIMETER HOLES

Most manufacturers offer scores of components, accessories, and finishes. One company produces more than 200 different components and accessories in three kinds of wood and more than two dozen finishes, with seven kinds of hardware. At the very least, nearly all systems are sold in a range of heights, widths, and depths.

Components often include several types of cabinets, a variety of shelves, several different doors, desk units, drawers, integral bases, light fixtures, even fold-up beds. In addition, many systems offer a range of special accessories, such as CD racks, swiveling pullout television shelves, wine racks, and other helpful organizers. (For more about these special components and accessories, see pages 120–123.)

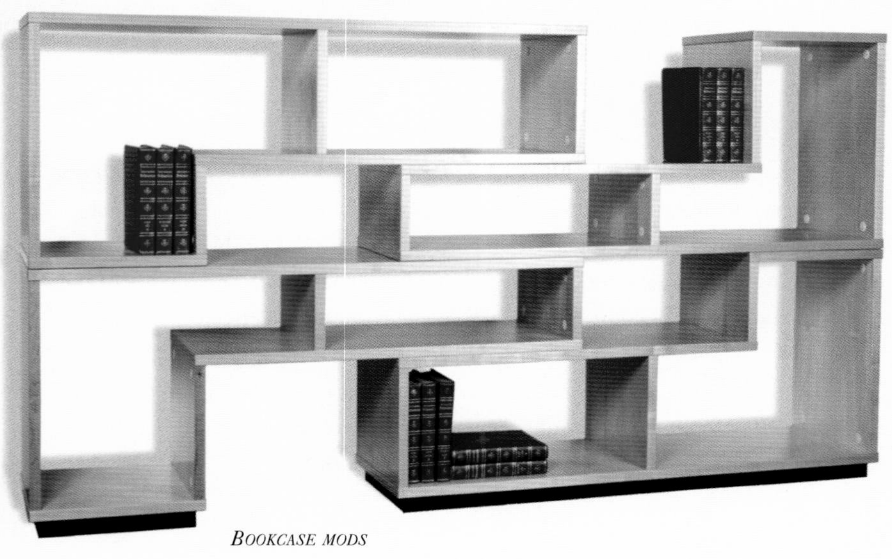

BOOKCASE MODS

Despite this diversity, practically all systems allow you to combine differing components and accessories into one integrated unit, enabling you to create custom-looking pieces of furniture at stock prices. One way manufacturers do this is by configuring their components on a 32-millimeter grid, meaning that uprights are drilled every 32 millimeters to receive hinges, shelf pegs, drawer guides, fasteners, and other hardware.

Preassembled or RTA?

Some modular systems are largely preassembled; all you need to do is mount the components on supports. With other systems, you may need to install door fronts on cabinets; still others require that you assemble everything, even the drawers.

This last type (units that come completely disassembled and packed flat in boxes) is referred to as "ready-to-assemble," or RTA. Manufacturers of such systems avoid assembly labor costs and high shipping expenses, passing the savings along to you in exchange for (hopefully!) only a few hours of your time.

Most RTA storage systems are made of melamine, laminate, or wood-

Stackable mods

Modular office unit

veneered panels that are connected with special "knockdown" (KD) hardware. Two types of knockdown hardware are available. One type allows you to disassemble the components for storage or transport; the other joins pieces permanently. Some common KD fittings are shown at right.

Assembly is usually a straightforward job, requiring a few basic hand tools, sometimes included in the package.

Remember, however, that modules can be extremely heavy when they're fully assembled; you may need a helper or two. Also, some finished units are so large that they will need to be constructed on-site, in the room where they'll be located.

Knockdown (KD) hardware

Where to buy them

These days, modular wall systems are showing up in lots of places at a variety of prices. You'll still find many of the best-quality, most flexible, and most attractive units at high-end specialty stores. Showroom personnel in these stores, as well as the people at retailers featuring European designs, work with you to figure your exact needs.

What's new is that there's a rapidly expanding, wider range of less expensive furniture shown at home warehouses and office-supply stores or on the pages of mail-order storage catalogs. You won't find top materials or styles here—or much service—but if your needs are modest and well defined, these sources might be just the ticket.

The modular idea is even migrating to home-improvement centers in the form of budget-minded utility units. For a closer look, see pages 116–117.

Judging quality

Wall system quality is partly a matter of materials, fit, and available components. It's also a matter of looks. You could spend \$100 to \$10,000; the trick is to buy what's appropriate for your needs and your budget.

Most lower-end units are built from particleboard covered with vinyl-wrapped veneers or laminate. Sometimes you'll find solid pine or relatively soft, less-desirable hardwoods like alder or aspen.

Better lines feature stronger MDF (medium-density fiberboard) cores,

EUROPEAN WALL SYSTEM (OPEN AND CLOSED)

DISPLAY WALL WITH SLIDING DOORS AND LIBRARY LADDER

either ¾-inch or 1-inch thick, and better veneers—real wood or high-quality laminates with woodlike texture. Some lines offer solid-wood doors and drawer faces in classic hardwood species like maple and cherry. Wood units are finished with subtle, durable layers of penetrating oil, lacquer, or varnish (see pages 124–125).

When shopping, keep the following questions in mind:

- What components, widths, depths, and heights are available? What finishes? What accessories?
- How much design help can you expect?
- Is installation included or available for a fee?
- What sort of guarantee comes with the unit?
- How easy is the system to assemble (if necessary), and how easy to move and reassemble? Are the joints strong enough, and/or are knockdown fasteners up to the task of repeated use?
- How is the unit secured to the wall? Are leveling feet included?

Media Centers

CORRAL TVS, CDS, AND SURROUND-SOUND SYSTEMS

Televisions, audiovisual receivers, DVD players, surround-sound speakers, compact disc collections—where does it all go? Fortunately, wall system manufacturers are becoming attentive to this problem, and there's an entire new generation of media cabinets and organizers out there. We'll outline your options below. Need help planning for electronics? See pages 20–22.

When shopping for media cabinets, some general questions to ask include: Can the unit handle the size and weight of all your components? Is there room for expansion? How will wires enter and exit? What about ventilation and air circulation? Do you need protection from dust?

TV solutions

They're big, they're wide, and they're bulky. Large-screen televisions are posing new challenges for both wall systems and stand-alone storage units.

Television stands come in solid pine, metal, melamine, and laminate; with or without wheels; and with or without a swiveling top. Many have drawers and DVD compartments behind glass doors. Some electronics companies make integral bases that echo the design of their television sets. These bare-bones, mundane-looking platforms sit on the floor, with the TV perching on top.

You'll also discover a growing number of pullouts and turntables for TVs (some products include both), and even lifts that raise the television up from a wall cabinet below. Order these from a wall-system dealer or buy the hardware and fit it to your own cabinetry. For a closer look at cabinet accessories, see pages 120–123.

RETRACTABLE "FLIPPER" DOOR HARDWARE

HEAVY-DUTY TV PULLOUT WITH SWIVELING TOP

BALL-BEARING TURNTABLE

Rack 'em up

The now-traditional solution for audio components, so-called "racks," allows you to stack components vertically and access them from either the front or back. Most racks resemble vertical shelving units, with frames and shelves built from laminate or metal. For dust protection, most have fronts (and sometimes tops) of hinged glass or acrylic. Some units have backs as well. Many racks roll on wheels, a handy feature unless you have plush carpeting.

Make sure your components will fit side to side and front to back. (Remember that you don't simply need room for the components, you need extra depth—at least 2 inches—for the wire connections behind them.)

There's also a trend toward low-lying, horizontal A/V units, featuring side-by-side dividers or a series of stackable, modular cubbyholes. Some TV stands include lower compartments for these units.

Thinking low-tech? Simple solutions include open shelves and shelving units (see pages 90–95)—just be sure they're deep enough for the task at hand.

Shop for racks at mass-market electronics stores or see audio specialists. Or check out home-furnishing and storage catalogs.

Entertainment armoire

Mobile TV cart

Modular entertainment unit

Integral home theater system

Moving up to home theater

Some home theater setups are basically a large-screen TV and a DVD player. Others include an A/V receiver, six or more speakers, the audio components discussed above, and more. If all of these components are grouped together, the big systems obviously call for different setups than we've talked about so far.

Small-scale media cabinets, capable of housing television and audio gear and related items, are available as preassembled furniture or knockdown, ready-to-assemble kits. Materials range from solid pine, oak, and alder to veneered particleboard and MDF panels.

Entertainment armoires are also available in a number of styles and finishes. Look for retractable "flipper" doors or those that fold back on double hinges. Be sure TV pullouts or turntables can handle the weight of your equipment. Drawers are a must for organizing the small stuff.

On a slightly larger scale, say enough room for a large TV, A/V receiver, and three front surround-sound speakers, look to furniture stores, mass-market electronics stores, or wall system specialists. Or assemble stock base and wall cabinets (pages 114–115) under a countertop.

For full-blown media centers, your best bets are furniture ensembles, large modular wall systems, or custom cabinetry from a cabinetmaker or fabricator who works with audiovisual consultants. Materials for custom units typically are hardwood plywood, solid hardwood, or MDF. As to price, the sky's the limit.

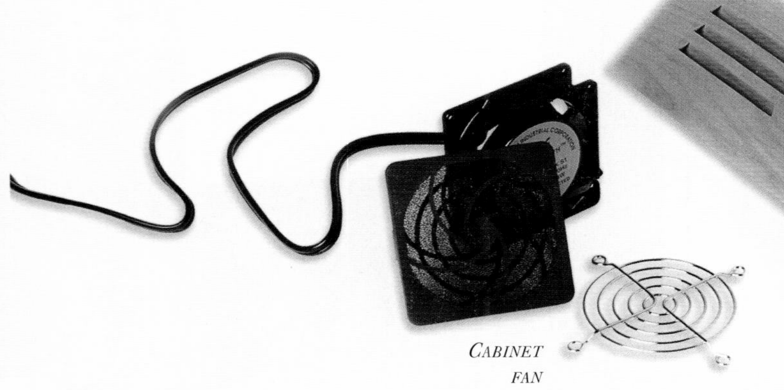

Cabinet fan

Hardwood vent grille

CD ORGANIZER

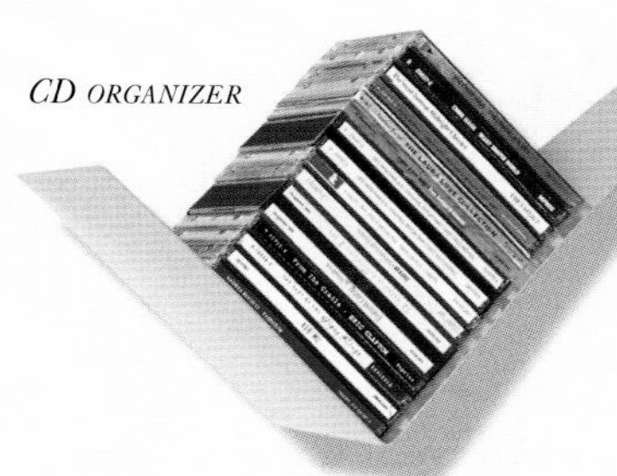

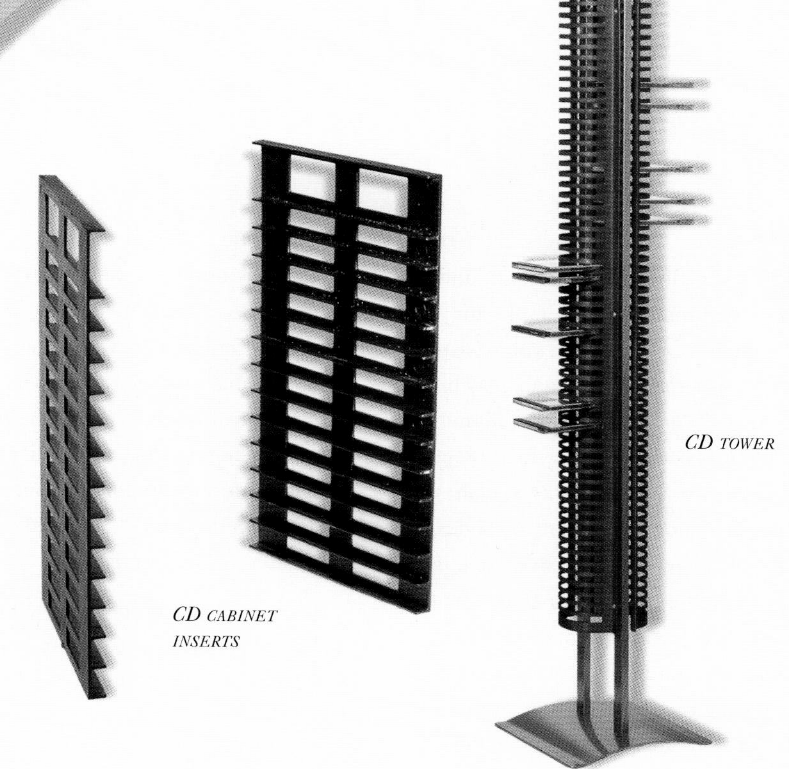

CD CABINET INSERTS

CD TOWER

Combating chaos

Compact discs, DVDs, vintage vinyl, and other media collections get out of hand quickly, but there's help available. Prefabricated cubes, towers, and wall units are one solution. Or buy grooved CD inserts, shown at right, and use them to line a bookcase or drawer.

Snarls of electrical wires and cables are another form of creeping chaos. To control the snarl, see "Tame Those Wires," below.

TAME THOSE WIRES

Forget the paper-free revolution—how about a cord-free revolution? Between TVs, DVD players, surround-sound speakers, computers, and a swarm of phone lines, wires can create a real Gordian knot around and behind your wall system.

Fortunately, a new generation of wire-management devices, several of which are pictured at right, now comes to the rescue.

Desktop grommets, round or oblong and available in numerous sizes and finishes, are probably the easiest aids to find. Troughs direct cords along the back of a desk to a point where they can all exit. Vertical channels direct wires to the floor and match some troughs. Friction clips hold wires tight to the desk like brooms in a broom closet. Raceways mount to desk, wall, or floor and direct wires anywhere. Surge protectors not only guard against power spikes but help organize your cords.

Grommets, raceways, and troughs are showing up at some office-supply, computer, and hardware stores; otherwise, try office outlets or woodworking mail-order sources. You'll find wire ties, wire staples, plastic conduit, and other hardware at electrical-supply houses and in the electrical departments of some home-improvement centers and hardware stores.

Stock Cabinets

KITCHEN AND BATH UNITS DANCE NEW STEPS

Factory-made cabinets, the type typically used in kitchens and bathrooms, are an important option to consider when you're planning permanent, built-in display or storage for any room in your home.

Sold through cabinet dealers and home-improvement centers, manufactured cabinets come in many styles, from relatively inexpensive stock models to high-end, semi-custom creations. The three main configurations are base, wall, and specialty cabinets. You can gang them side by side or stack them to create storage walls, room dividers, buffets, entertainment centers, and much more.

Traditional or European-style?

First, you'll need to decide whether you want framed or frameless cabinets.

Traditional American cabinets mask the raw front edges of each box with a 1-by-2 "face frame." Doors and drawers then fit in one of three ways: inset within the frame; partially offset, with a lip; or completely overlaying the frame.

Since the face frame covers up the basic box, thinner or lower-quality wood can be used in its sides, somewhat decreasing the cost. But the frame takes up space and reduces the size of the openings, so drawers or slide-out accessories must be significantly smaller than the full width of the cabinet, slightly decreasing storage capacity.

Europeans, when faced with postwar lumber shortages, came up with "frameless" cabinets. A simple trim strip covers raw edges, which butt directly against one another. Doors and drawers often fit to within ⅛-inch of each other, revealing a thin sliver of the trim. Interior components, such as drawers, can be sized almost to the full dimensions of the box.

Another big difference: frameless cabinets typically have a separate toespace pedestal, or plinth, below them. This allows you to set counter heights specifically to your liking, stack base units, or make use of space at floor level.

Basic size options

Cabinets typically are manufactured in sizes from 9 to 48 inches wide, in 3-inch increments.

Base cabinets, typically 34½ inches tall and 24 inches deep, are made to fit under kitchen counters, so they probably won't have a top panel. Wall cabinets measure 12, 18, 24, 30, 48, and 60 inches high; 30 inches wide, and 12 inches deep is standard.

Tall cabinets—often some of the best components for general storage—come 84, 90, and 96 inches high. Wardrobe and hutch-style accessories vary from 30 to 96 inches tall and from 18 to 24 inches deep.

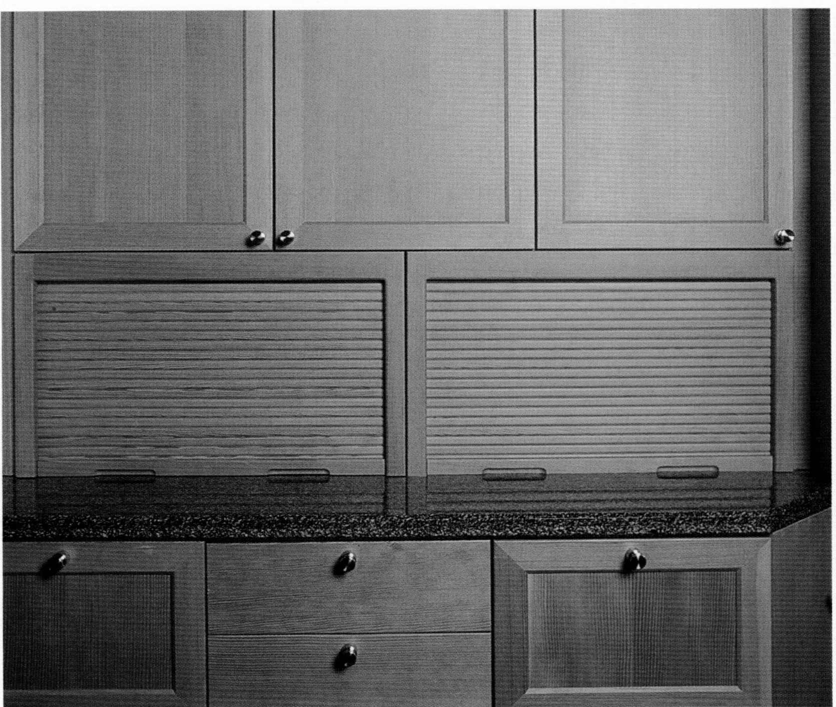

Overlay doors and drawers

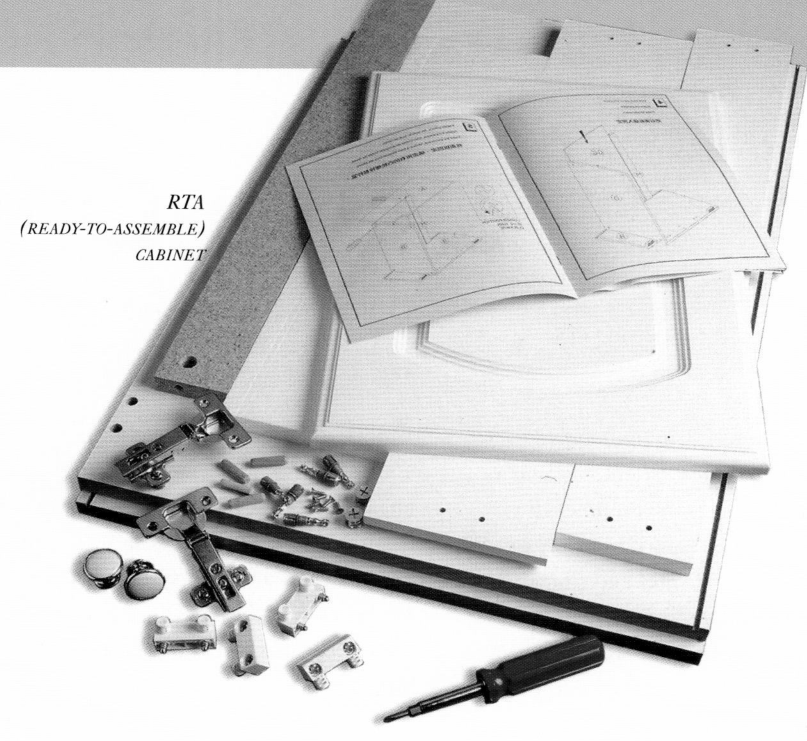
RTA (READY-TO-ASSEMBLE) CABINET

You can specify door styles, direction of door swing, and whether side panels are finished; sometimes you get other options and add-ons (see pages 120–123).

So-called semi-custom systems come in a wide range of sizes, with many options for each size. If necessary, heights, widths, and depths can be modified to fit almost any design.

Because semi-custom cabinets are configured to order and many are imported from abroad, it may take longer to receive them than it would to order custom units from a local cabinetmaker. Order either type of cabinet as far ahead as possible.

Judging quality

To determine the quality of a stock cabinet, first look at the drawers. They take more of a beating than any other part. Several designs are shown on page 100.

Door hinges are also critical hardware elements. European cup hinges (page 98) are the most trouble free type of hinge. They are the best choices unless you want the period look of surface hardware.

Most cabinet boxes are made from sheet products like hardwood plywood, particleboard (plain or laminated), or medium-density fiberboard. If solid lumber is used, it's usually reserved for doors and drawer faces. For a rundown on these products, see pages 14–15.

A recent development, the so-called RTA (ready-to-assemble) cabinet, costs even less than other stock units, but requires some basic tools and elbow grease to put together. An RTA stock cabinet is shown above.

FACE FRAME CABINETS

FRAMELESS CABINETS

Utility Units

THEY'RE STURDY—AND EVEN STYLISH

Closets, laundry rooms, pantries, basements, and garages—sometimes these spaces get no respect, but they can still gain valuable display and storage space via wall systems and shelving. These specialized offerings, which we might call utility units, range from the truly prosaic to those that rival the looks of a living room's most stylish displays.

Buying the basics

Some utility units are beautiful, others simply inexpensive. You'll find a selection of serviceable, budget-minded closet and garage lines at home centers. These systems follow the same modular principle as the more stylized European wall systems (see pages 106–109). A certain number of interchangeable boxes, rods, shelves, drawer units, and countertops can be mixed and matched to form a system that works for you. Most of these units are made from particleboard, some with melamine (a better choice) or vinyl veneers on top. Both painted and plastic versions are available.

The home-center units are typically packed flat, RTA-style. You load the boxes (which can be heavy), take them home, and assemble them. Some dealers will deliver and install for a fee.

In addition to modular boxes, you'll also find open-wire or "ventilated" shelf systems. These systems are popular for use in closets, dressing rooms, laundries, and pantry areas. Some wire systems are chrome-plated, some are galvanized, and others have a white or black vinyl coating on the wire. Some manufacturers also make pullout wire baskets, wall hooks, and other accessories that can be used alone or mixed with the shelf modules. Support for all this comes from a backing grid (see the facing page), a ladder frame, or some variation on the track-and-bracket scheme (see page 92).

On the garage front, you also have a number of industrial-type options, including pegboard, steel, and plastic shelving units, bare particleboard modules, and units that are built from resin-coated MDF.

When it comes to utility shelves, pay attention to the spans; manufacturers may be overly optimistic about the weights their designs carry. Particleboard, the substratum for most budget units, is unreliable for even medium loads and spans. For more details on shelf spans and reinforcement, see page 18.

Ventilated utility shelves

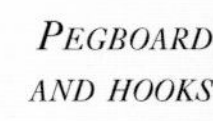

Pegboard and hooks

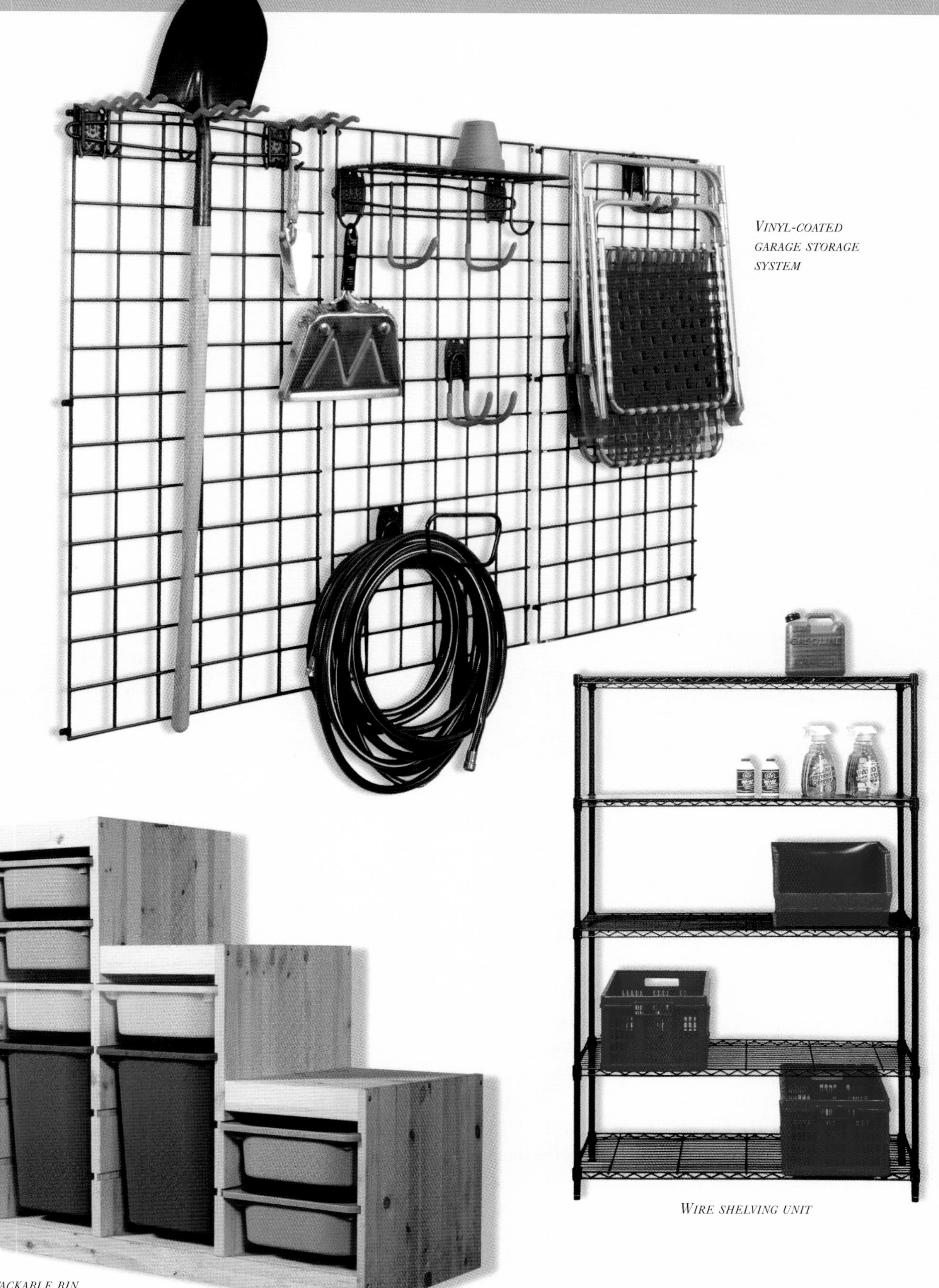

Vinyl-coated garage storage system

Wire shelving unit

Stackable bin modules

"Built-in" closet with integral room divider

A step up

Specialty firms offer better looks, better materials, and complete design services—all for a price. To shop, look in the yellow pages under "Closets & Closet Accessories"; most offerings are designed for closets and home offices. Some companies mix and match stock sizes; others will make any size unit you need. Typically, you fill out a questionnaire and provide overall measurements.

Most systems are based on the now-classic 32-millimeter design concept that allows you to plug in doors, drawers, adjustable shelves, closet rods, and other offerings. Units are usually built from particleboard and melamine. Some firms offer laminate veneers and choices of door and drawer styles. Expect prices to rise with options.

Basically, the best units are extensions of higher-end modular systems. Look for MDF or plywood cores, hardwood or laminate veneers, and a range of door and drawer shapes and styles (see pages 96–101), many in solid hardwood. For more shopping pointers, see pages 106–109.

Movable closet cart

Modular closet components

Accessories

ADD CUSTOM EFFICIENCY WITH STOCK HARDWARE

Nearly all wall system manufacturers, and a growing number of other companies, offer at least a few special components and accessories that stretch the capabilities of the units. These choices allow you to turn an ordinary wall system into a multifunctional machine by day and then to fold it all up at night.

For example, what appears to be a waist-high drawer may be a drop-down door that reveals a pullout ironing board. Deep drawer fronts can hide roomy hanging-file systems. A breakfast table or desktop can pull straight out of a wall system or fold down into place. A television can magically rise from the top of a cabinet.

You'll find specialty add-ons for every imaginable use: home theater, home office, kitchen, bath, guest room, closet, and garage.

Wire pullout bins

Fold-down cabinet shelves

Cabinet insert organizers

Fold-down table

Media pullout

Wire office organizers

Triple-extension work counter

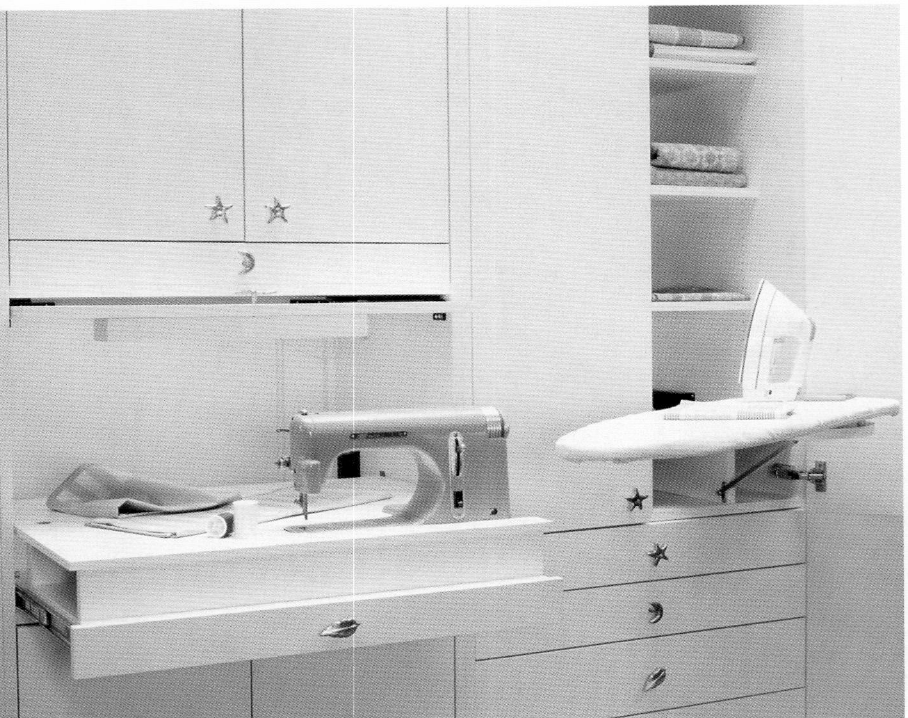

Modular sewing center

Fold-down ironing board

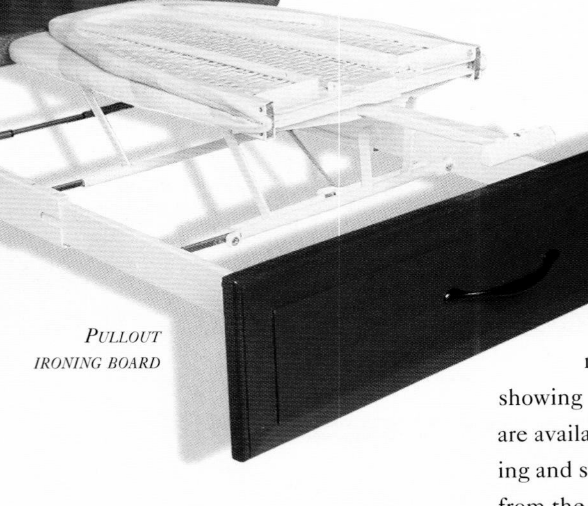

Pullout ironing board

Most fittings for these specialized pieces are produced by European hardware manufacturers. The products are sold directly through catalogs and distributors to cabinet manufacturers, custom woodworking shops, and some well-stocked builder's-hardware retailers. Some lines are now showing up in home centers; others are available via mail-order woodworking and specialty home catalogs and from the Internet.

If you're outfitting a preexisting cabinet or one bought from another source, be sure to check the sizes and clearances required for add-ons; they usually have clearly prescribed tolerances.

Pullout bins

Modular Murphy bed (open and closed)

Modular home gym

Finishing Touches

STAINS, TOP COATS, LIGHTS, AND MOLDINGS

Details make the difference between a mundane wall system and a handsome one. To make both room and wall unit appear as an integrated setting, consider three main areas: finish, auxiliary lighting, and moldings.

Gel stain

Water-base varnish

A fine finish

A wood's finish dramatically affects its impact. But a good finish also keeps dirt and moisture out of wood pores, wards off dents, and protects the wood from abrasion, heat, and chemicals.

Solid wood or wood-veneered wall systems can be treated with any of several types of stains, paints, and clear coatings. The chart on the facing page outlines the characteristics of common wood-finishing products. For additional help, consult your paint dealer.

Both stains and finishes come in traditional oil-base and newer water-base versions. All things being equal, choose the water-base products—they're easier to use, clean up with water, and produce far fewer noxious fumes than the oil-base products.

Stains. In most cases, stains are not final finishes; they are used for color or accent only. You still need to seal the surface with a clear finish. If your pieces are made of unfinished pine, apply a sealer before staining to achieve even coloring.

Though you may encounter many stain names and brands, products fall into two general types: pigmented stains and dyes. Pigmented stains, sold as oil stain, wood stain, and pigmented wiping stain, are composed of finely ground particles of color held in suspension in oil solvent.

Penetrating oil

Dyes are mostly aniline (a coal-tar derivative), dissolved in either water or alcohol. Because they are actually absorbed by the wood fibers, dye stains allow the grain to show through. If you can't find dyes at retail stores, look for them in wood-finishing specialty stores or woodworking catalogs.

Clear finishes. Generally, clear finishing products fall into two basic types: penetrating finishes and surface coatings.

Penetrating finishes soak into the pores of the wood to give it a natural look and feel. Though a penetrating finish sinks below the wood's surface, it's still fairly durable—without the "dipped-in-plastic" appearance of some of the more protective coatings.

Surface finishes lie on top of the wood and provide protection in the form of a thin, durable shield. This kind of coating, often available in a number of sheens, may be glasslike in appearance, but it can be dulled down, if desired, by rubbing.

Enamels. Water-base (latex) and oil-base (alkyd) enamels are both used for interior surfaces. Latex paints are easier to use because water is their solvent, but alkyds are more durable.

Paint finishes range from flat, or matte, to high gloss. Since there's no industry standard for sheens, a medium gloss may be called pearl, semi-gloss, or some other name, and it can range from moderately to very shiny, depending on the manufacturer. The glossier the finish, the more durable and washable it is.

A Look at Finishing Products

STAINS

Pigmented oil stain

Simple to apply; won't fade or bleed. Useful for making one wood species look like another. Heavy pigments tend to obscure grain and gum up pores in hardwoods such as oak and walnut. Not compatible with shellac or lacquer.

Penetrating oil stain

One-step product stains with dyes rather than pigments, so pores and grain show through. Similar to penetrating resin, but with color added. Produces irregular results on softwoods and plywoods. Handy for repairs, touch-up jobs.

Gel stain

May contain both pigments and dyes. Very easy to apply (just wipe on, buff out, and let dry), but results may be uneven on large surfaces.

Aniline dye (water base)

Colors are brilliant, clear, and permanent. Since water raises wood grain, light resanding may be necessary. Very slow drying. Sold in powdered form; can be hard to find.

Aniline dye (alcohol base)

Quick-drying alcohol stains won't raise grain, but they aren't very light-fast; they're best reserved for small touch-up jobs. Should be sprayed on to avoid lap marks.

Non-grain-raising stain

Bright, transparent colors; won't raise wood grain. Available premixed by mail. Very short drying time; best when sprayed. Not for use on softwoods.

PENETRATING FINISHES

Boiled linseed oil

Lends warm, slightly dull patina to wood. Dries very slowly and requires many coats. Moderate resistance to heat, water, and chemicals. Easily renewable.

Tung oil

Natural oil finish that's hard and highly resistant to abrasion, moisture, heat, acid, and mildew. Requires several thin, hand-rubbed applications (heavy coats wrinkle badly). Best with polymer resins added.

Penetrating resin (Danish oil, antique oil)

Use on hard, open-grain woods. Leaves wood looking and feeling "natural." Easy to apply and retouch, but doesn't protect against heat or abrasion. May darken some woods.

Rub-on varnish

Penetrating resin and varnish combination that builds up sheen as coats are applied; dries fairly quickly. Moderately resistant to water and alcohol. Darkens wood.

SURFACE FINISHES

Shellac

Lends warm luster to wood. Lays down in thin, quick-drying coats that can be rubbed to a high sheen. Little resistance to heat, alcohol, and moisture. Comes in white (blonde), orange, and brownish (button) versions. Available in flake form or premixed.

Lacquer (nitrocellulose)

Strong, clear, quick-drying finish in both spraying and brushing form. Very durable, though vulnerable to moisture. Requires 3 or more coats; can be polished to a high gloss. Noxious fumes; highly flammable.

Lacquer (water base)

Easier to clean, less toxic, and much less flammable than nitrocellulose lacquer—more practical spray product for do-it-yourselfer. Raises grain; use sanding sealer. May dry more slowly than nitrocellulose lacquer. Can smell strongly of ammonia.

Varnish (oil base)

Widely compatible oil-base interior varnish that produces a thick coating with good overall resistance. Comes in numerous sheens. Dries slowly and darkens with time. Brush marks and dust can be a problem.

Varnish (water base)

Easy cleanup. Dries quickly; nontoxic when dry. Though early versions lacked durability, new products are greatly improved. Finish goes on milky, but dries clear and won't yellow. Raises wood grain. May require numerous coats. Expensive.

Polyurethane varnish

Thick, plastic, irreversible coating that's nearly impervious to water, heat, and alcohol. Dries overnight. Incompatible with some stains and sealers. Follow instructions to ensure good bonding between coats.

Enamel

Available in flat, semigloss, and gloss sheens, and in a wide range of colors. May have lacquer or varnish (alkyd, water, or polyurethane) base; each shares same qualities as clear finish of the same type.

Wax

Occasionally used as a finish, especially on antiques or "aged" pine. More often applied over harder top coats. Increases luster of wood. Not very durable, but offers some protection against liquids when renewed frequently. Available in various shades.

Lighting for shelves

Whether you use wall systems to conceal clutter or display treasures, you should pay attention to one other ingredient—light. With the proper lighting, your wall system becomes not only more functional but also more aesthetically pleasing.

You can light shelves from either inside or outside the unit. If you're building a custom unit, consider adding recessed or indirect lighting during construction. Your basic options include recessed downlights, canisters, track lights, strip lights, and under-cabinet task lights. Commercial wall systems often include light "bridges" (soffits with downlights) or built-ins as accessory options.

Recessed downlights and tracks can be located either at the top of the unit or in the ceiling with light directed down to the unit. Most built-in canisters are low-voltage, meaning they require a transformer to "step down" power from standard household current to a more manageable 12 volts. Why go low voltage? The fixtures are much smaller and they use less energy. Most low-voltage fixtures house either halogen or xenon (a cooler-burning cousin) bulbs.

For high-lighting wall systems, it's usually best to buy swiveling lights or lights that can be aimed at a unit.

Strip lights resemble Christmas tree lights. Some are housed on a flexible backing strip; others, called rope lights, are tucked inside clear or colored plastic tubing. Put strip lights out of sight inside the unit or above the top, shining up to outline the unit. You shouldn't see the bulbs, just the glow.

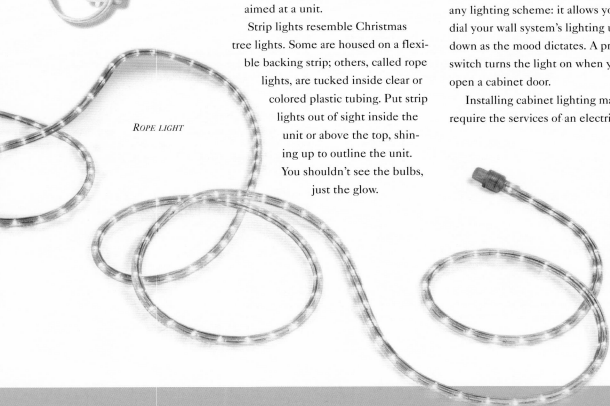

Cable light

Transformer

Low-voltage xenon downlight

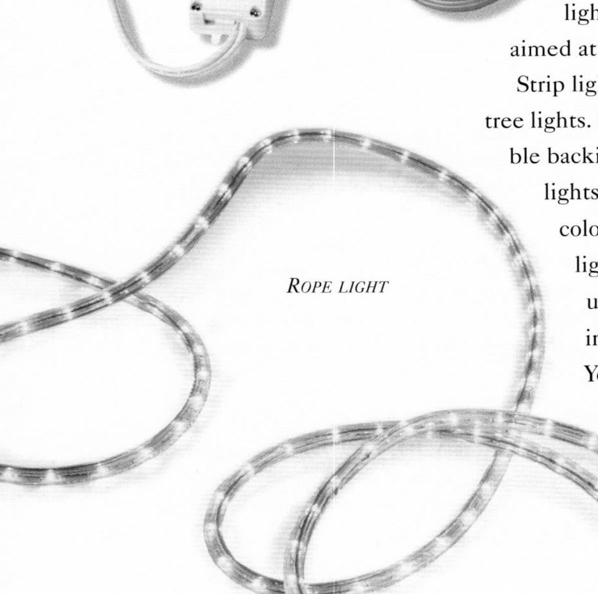

Rope light

Several kinds of under-cabinet fixtures are available: halogen, incandescent, and fluorescent. Most are compatible with standard household current and are available in switched (plug-in) and wire-in (direct-wired) versions. Designed for kitchen counters, they can light a wall system's work surface from above, or they can be mounted inside the top of the cabinet so that light washes down.

A dimmer switch is a big plus for any lighting scheme: it allows you to dial your wall system's lighting up and down as the mood dictates. A pressure switch turns the light on when you open a cabinet door.

Installing cabinet lighting may require the services of an electrician.

Moldings and trim

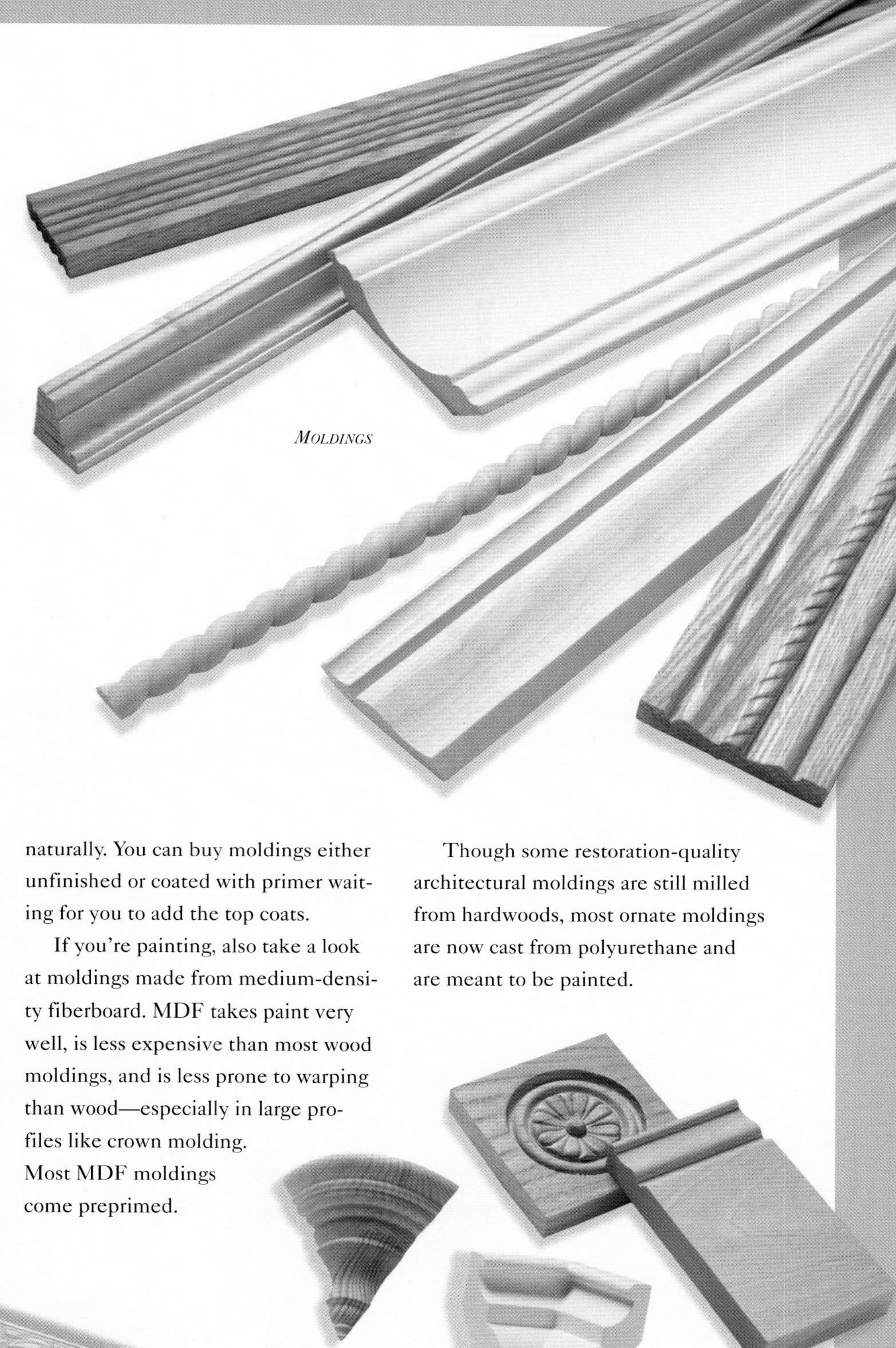

Moldings

Even the most basic shelving unit can be dressed up by the addition of moldings. Whether applied to the face of the unit or to the surrounding wall, moldings can add classic detailing and visually integrate the wall system with the rest of the room.

Moldings come in a wide range of standard profiles, including crown molding, baseboard, and window and door casing. You can also buy reproductions of architectural details, such as pediments, mantels, and pilasters. Before you shop, collect ideas by studying how moldings have been used in the wall systems shown in this book. Then browse through a molding dealer's selection to see how different moldings can be combined to form interesting profiles.

You can buy stock moldings from lumberyards or home centers, and special or custom patterns from molding and millwork shops. Priced by the linear foot, they vary widely, from about 15 cents per foot for small, simple patterns to more than $15 per foot for ornate architectural styles. "Paint-grade" pine moldings, which have visible finger joints along their length, are much less expensive than "stain-grade" oak or other hardwoods that can be finished naturally. You can buy moldings either unfinished or coated with primer waiting for you to add the top coats.

If you're painting, also take a look at moldings made from medium-density fiberboard. MDF takes paint very well, is less expensive than most wood moldings, and is less prone to warping than wood—especially in large profiles like crown molding. Most MDF moldings come preprimed.

Though some restoration-quality architectural moldings are still milled from hardwoods, most ornate moldings are now cast from polyurethane and are meant to be painted.

Sunset

ideas for great HOME LIGHTING

By Scott Atkinson
and the Editors of Sunset Books

Sunset Books ■ Menlo Park, California

contents

130

Paint It with Light

133

A Planning Primer

153

Great Lighting Ideas

219

A Shopper's Guide

712

Index

special features

Testing Your Ideas **143**

Energy-saving Options **145**

What about Low-voltage? **147**

Technical Talk **151**

Speaking in Code **221**

Handling Halogens **225**

Bulb Comparisons at a Glance **228**

Night-lights, Moonlights **233**

Make Your Mark **237**

Low-voltage Logistics **241**

Going Wireless **245**

Harness the Sun **251**

paint it with light

Flexible, efficient, and a little bit fun—that's the plan for today's home lighting. Take your pick: crisp highlights or moody shadows; bold strokes or a soft, flattering wash. Or mix them together. Indoors or out, you'll discover lighting products and techniques that deliver comfort, safety, and style.

Flexibility is the new byword; glare is the big bad wolf in lighting lingo. Flexibility means multiple light sources or *layers* operated by multiple controls, allowing you to dial in your mood; dimmer switches provide fine-tuning options. Motion sensors, timers, and daylight sensors abound. Computerized control panels are gaining steam.

Light sources are more energy-efficient and more adaptable than ever before. Fluorescent bulbs and tubes are much improved—just in time, given energy codes requiring ambient fluorescent light in some locales. Once available only in "cool-white" (read "ghoulish blue-green"), fluorescents now come in about 200 colors; fixture choices are expanding, too, with the advent of compact fluorescent bulbs. Long-lasting halogen bulbs are another option, delivering punch and focus. Also up-and-coming are decorative fiber optics, cold cathode, and an "industrial" source: metal halide.

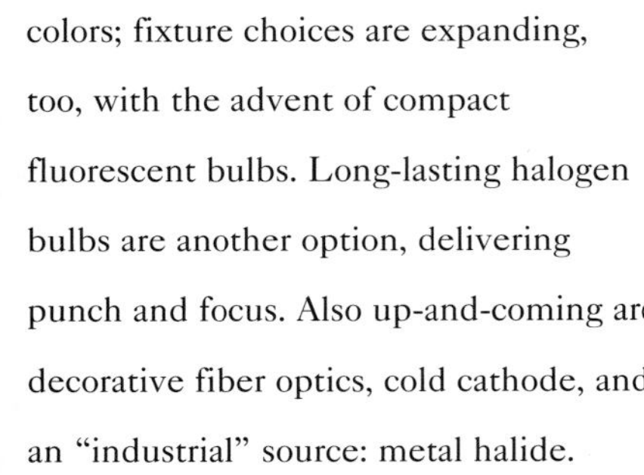

Fixtures are shrinking in size. In today's lighting philosophy, unless you want to feature it, it should be invisible. What if you *do* want to feature your fixtures? You'll find endless new designs, from halogen pendants and contemporary wall sconces to tiny, jazzy low-voltage tracks and rope lights.

Outdoors, good lighting provides safety and security, but lighting pros also speak of increased curb value and the way exterior lighting expands interior space. Today's outdoor lighting designs are subtle, even those incorporating sophisticated security options. Like indoor schemes, new outdoor installations tend to be multilayered and flexible.

Ready to light it up? This book takes a three-phase approach. The first section, "A Planning Primer," paints the basic terms and techniques you'll need to know. Next, "Great Lighting Ideas" makes a colorful, room-by-room house tour—and then heads outdoors. Want to shop? Turn to "A Shopper's Guide" for the scoop on bulbs, fixtures, and controls.

A PLANNING PRIMER

THE PLEASURES of good lighting have an elusive quality. When you walk into a room with a successful lighting design, you don't remark "What fantastic lighting!" But your eyes sense that everything is comfortably visible, and you feel somehow both stimulated and at ease. In fact, our eyes don't observe the light itself, but rather the things on which it shines; a great lighting scheme serves as a silent partner in enhancing the surroundings. **THIS CHAPTER GIVES YOU** a good start toward bringing this partner into your home. In these pages we identify the properties of effective lighting and explain them in clear terms to help you achieve the best lighting design for your own situation. **FOR INSPIRATION AND IDEAS** to use both indoors and out, browse through "Great Lighting Ideas," beginning on page 153. And for guidance in choosing bulbs, fixtures, and innovative controls, see "A Shopper's Guide," pages 219–251.

designing with light

HOME LIGHTING *is the art of painting light and shadow onto a dark canvas. The best lighting designer is a problem solver, determining where light is needed and then directing it there with economy and flair. Professionals approach lighting with the following arsenal of terms and tools; you can, too.*

Four types of light

Lighting designers have traditionally split lighting into three basic categories: task, accent, and ambient. But as a counterpoint to the current trend of making basic fixtures unobtrusive, a fourth type is emerging: decorative light, using fixtures that are deliberately featured. Here are definitions of all four categories.

TASK LIGHTING. This bright light illuminates a particular area where a visual activity takes place—reading, sewing, or preparing food, for example. Task lighting is often achieved by means of individual fixtures that direct a tight pattern of light onto the work surface.

Adjustability is important for task lighting. So is shielding—hiding the bulb from direct sight. It's best to aim task lighting at an angle so it won't cause "hot spots" or throw shadows onto the work area. Where possible, two sources are better than one.

ACCENT LIGHTING. Similar to task lighting in that it consists largely of directional light, accent lighting is used to focus attention on artwork, to highlight architectural features, to set a mood, or to provide a sense of drama.

Beam spread, intensity, and color are often critical considerations for accent light. Low-voltage halogen bulbs (pages 224–225) produce especially clean white accent light, and they are available in a wide variety of intensities and beam patterns.

AMBIENT LIGHTING. With ambient lighting, the undefined areas of a room are filled with a soft level of general light—say, enough for someone to watch television by or to navigate safely through the room. An ambient glow not only makes a room more inviting, it helps

TASK LIGHTING

Ambient lighting

Decorative lighting

people look their best, filling in harsh shadows created by stronger point sources.

Ambient lighting usually comes from indirect fixtures that provide diffuse illumination. Directional fixtures aimed at a wall can also produce a wash of soft light. Or consider built-in lighting coves, cornices, valances, and soffits. These simple architectural devices ensure that light sources are shielded from view, allowing light to spill out around the shields.

Decorative lighting. These fixtures draw attention to themselves as objects. The classic chandelier is an example; newer options include zoomy low-voltage pendant fixtures, neon, and fiber optics. Decorative strip lights (pages 236–237) can add sparkle and warmth to a room while highlighting architectural lines. And don't forget candles, either the traditional kind or electric ones.

Accent lighting

This multiuse dining space has flexible, multilayered light sources to match. Discreet downlights shine down on dining table, artwork, and collectibles. Striking wall sconces add decorative style and ambient fill light.

The art of layering

One basic rule of efficient lighting is to put light where you need it. But to ensure an attractive, comfortable lighting scheme, you must also think about balancing light—that is, creating an effective spread of dim and strong light throughout a room. A laundry room, hallway, or guest bedroom may not need more than one set of fixtures, but multiple-use areas such as living rooms, great rooms, and kitchens present more of a challenge.

The key to balancing light is layering. That's where the four different lighting types come in. Lighting designers first identify the main activity areas, or the room's focal point or points (having two or three is often best). This is where they direct the brightest layer of light. Next, a middle layer provides interest in specific areas without detracting from the focal points. The last layer fills in the background.

The first two layers are supplied by task or accent lighting, depending on what is being lit. The lower-level "fill" or ambient light is usually indirect (like that provided by wall sconces, for example). The ratio of the brightest light in the room to the fill light usually should be about 3

to 1—at most 5 to 1. Ratios of 10 or even 100 to 1 are great for high drama but uncomfortable for everyday living. To learn how to check light ratios, read "Testing Your Ideas" on page 143.

Once the essential layers are in place, you can add decorative fixtures, if you like. General light will appear to emanate from these sources, but since you've already set up levels of task, accent, and ambient layers, this light isn't necessary in the overall scheme. When chandeliers are used as primary light givers, they can produce harsh glare; dimmed to a comfortable glow, they become inviting decorative additions.

Getting control

Dimmers and control panels (see pages 244–245) can help you custom-tailor light for multiple uses and decorative effects. Dimmers—also called rheostats—enable you to set a fixture or group of fixtures at any brightness level, from soft glow to full throttle. They're also energy savers. Be aware, though, that some light sources—notably fluorescents—can be difficult or unduly expensive to dim; bone up on your options when you go shopping.

Control panels allow you to monitor a number of functions or "scenes" from one spot. Originally designed for commercial use, they're now showing up in residential lighting, too. And as the world of computers meets that of residential design, software-programmed lighting and/or "smart house" systems have become a reality. These allow an almost infinite degree of lighting control and flexibility—for a price.

Beware of glare

One of the most important considerations in the placement of light fixtures is the glare they produce. Direct glare—as from a bare light bulb—is the worst kind. Deeply recessed fixtures or fixtures with black baffles or small apertures (see page 241) can remedy the problem. Clip-on louvers and shutters also cut glare. Silvered-bowl bulbs (page 221) help tame the glare from traditional lamps and fixtures, as do diffusing shades or covers.

Also watch out for reflected glare—light bouncing off an object into your eyes. Light reflects off an object at the same angle as it strikes it (as shown at right); if the angle is too steep, the light produces a hot spot. The safety range is about 30 to 45 degrees from vertical.

A fixture located directly over a flat, shiny surface—a dining room table, for instance—can create "veiling" glare. Objects placed on the table can help deflect this glare; a dimmer can also reduce the reflected light to a comfortable level.

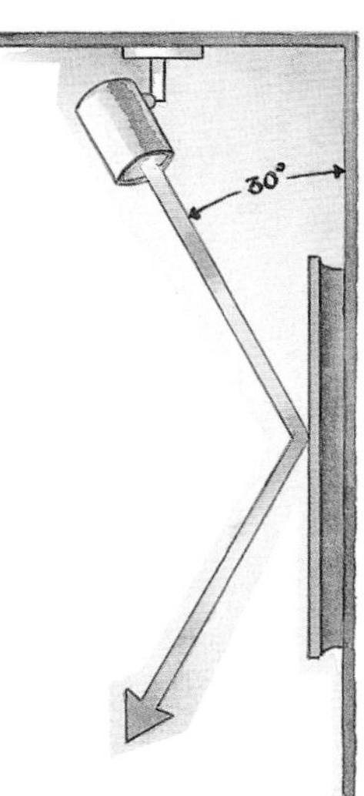

To minimize reflected glare, light artwork from a 30- to 45-degree angle.

Tricks of the trade

You can use light both to draw the eye to the architectural features and decor in your house and to help disguise any aspects you'd like to play down. Designers mix and match the basic lighting tricks shown below. In addition, consider the following time-tested techniques.

- **Ceilings** can pose problems, or they can become special features. If your ceilings seem too low, bounced light from uplights can visually "raise" them. Cathedral or beamed ceilings can take on new importance with uplighting. Many designers also use beams to hold track lighting (see pages 238–239), taking advantage of architectural lines to disguise the track.

  A common problem in older homes is rough or patchy plaster. For dealing with this and also with ceilings that seem too high, the solution is the same: keep light off the ceiling by using downlighting. The darker surface will seem lower, and imperfections will go unnoticed.

- **Room dimensions** can be altered visually with lighting tricks. Small rooms can look open and airy with the right lighting, and large rooms can be made to appear cozy and inviting.

  Washing the walls of a small room with an even layer of light seems to push them outward, expanding the perceived sense of space. When the wall is a light color, the effect is even more pronounced.

  Illuminating a large room with a few soft pools of light concentrated on important objects or areas makes it seem smaller and more intimate; the lighted areas absorb more attention than the room as a whole.

  Narrow rooms benefit from lighting trickery, too. Placing lights along shorter walls draws the eye away from the long ones, resulting in a "wider" space.

- **Windows,** sources of daylight, can seem like dark mirrors or black holes if left uncovered at night. One way to avoid reflections is to light

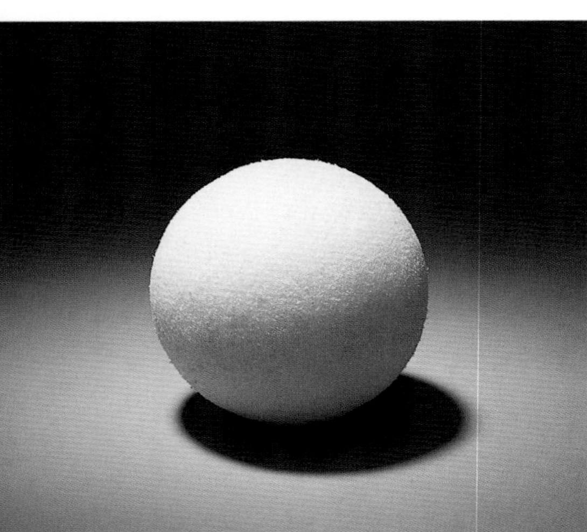

◄ Downlighting

This look is probably familiar—after all, sunlight is downlighting. The degree of focus determines the effect. The tighter the beam, the more drama and the heavier the shadows.

Silhouetting ►

Like backlighting (above right), the light here comes from behind—but in this case it faces the background, dropping the cube into dark relief. In daylight, cube and background are similar colors; it's the lighting that makes one appear bright and the other near-black.

Uplighting ►

The opposite of downlighting (above left), this technique makes objects seem to "float" from below. Uplighting can create strong light contrasts; for a softer look, add fill light from above.

the area outside a window or patio door to a high enough level that lights inside balance those outside. Another solution is to use opaque pendant fixtures or recessed downlights, so that only the lighted areas reflect, not the light sources themselves.

- **MASONRY SURFACES** such as brick walls or a stone fireplace take on new beauty when lighted at an acute angle, a technique called "grazing." You can play up the textures of fabric walls and window coverings in a similar way.
- **ARTWORK** can be lit in a variety of ways. For the most dramatic effect, spotlight works of art from above or below: a 30-degree angle off the vertical is best—even less if you wish to play up the surface texture of a particular piece.

 Frame-mounted picture lights are also available (see pages 232–233, though these may not illuminate a large painting evenly.

 Sculpture and other three-dimensional objects usually call for lighting from two sides to minimize shadows. Or you can emphasize shadows or a silhouette by aiming a single spot from behind or below. Don't hesitate to experiment with uplighting, downlighting, grazing, or backlighting.
- **INDOOR PLANTS** need light to help them look their best—and to help them grow. Try silhouetting plants with concealed uplights or backlighting them against a luminous screen or lighted wall. Or bounce light down through the foliage with a fixture recessed in the ceiling or suspended from it.
- **COLLECTIONS** can be lit evenly overall, or spotlights can be focused on individual pieces. Downlighting shelves or display cabinets may make upper shelves cast shadows on shelves below. Backlighting, lighting vertically from the sides, or attaching lights under the front edges of shelves will eliminate this problem. Concealing fixtures will help keep down glare and lend a clean look to your display.

◄ BACKLIGHTING

The light comes from behind, aimed toward the object. Backlighting makes translucent objects—like this glass vase—glow with light. Note the "rim-lighting" effect where light rays bend around the vase's outline.

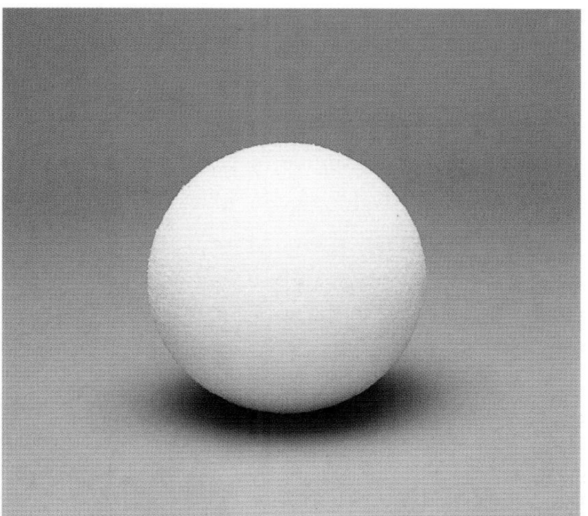

◄ BOUNCE LIGHTING

Also called indirect lighting, this is the softest light form, often used for ambient fill. Light hits a wall or ceiling, then bounces back to the subject. Compare this to downlighting on the facing page: it's the same ball, but here highlights and shadows are much softer.

GRAZING ►

Use this technique to emphasize textures—such as masonry, fabric, a plastered wall—or even an oil painting. Place the light source near the surface and "skim" light across it. If the light spread is broader and a little less steep, it's called "wall washing."

color and reflectance

BEFORE CHOOSING *light sources for a room, it helps to know some basic theory about the nature of light and color. The interaction between a light source and a room's colors and surfaces creates two additional subjects to consider: color rendition and reflectance.*

What is light?

What our retinas perceive as "light" is just part of a wider range of electromagnetic radiation produced in the form of waves. The intensity of light waves creates their color. Infrared rays, ultraviolet rays, X-rays, radio waves, and heat are part of the spectrum that we can't see.

We think of midday sunlight as the standard for pure white light color. When daylight is passed through a prism, however, it is actually rendered as equal parts of a continuous spectrum including red, orange, yellow, green, blue, and violet (see the drawing below).

In contrast, artificial light sources give off varying amounts of color. Incandescent light includes most of the spectrum but has a large proportion of yellow and red. When dimmed, incandescent light becomes even redder.

Many people think of fluorescent light as being low in red and high in green and blue light waves, but in fact fluorescent tubes now come in more than 200 colors. Quartz halogen produces brighter, "whiter" light than either incandescent or fluorescent sources; it's popular for commercial display and museum lighting as well as for residential accenting.

THE COLOR SPECTRUM

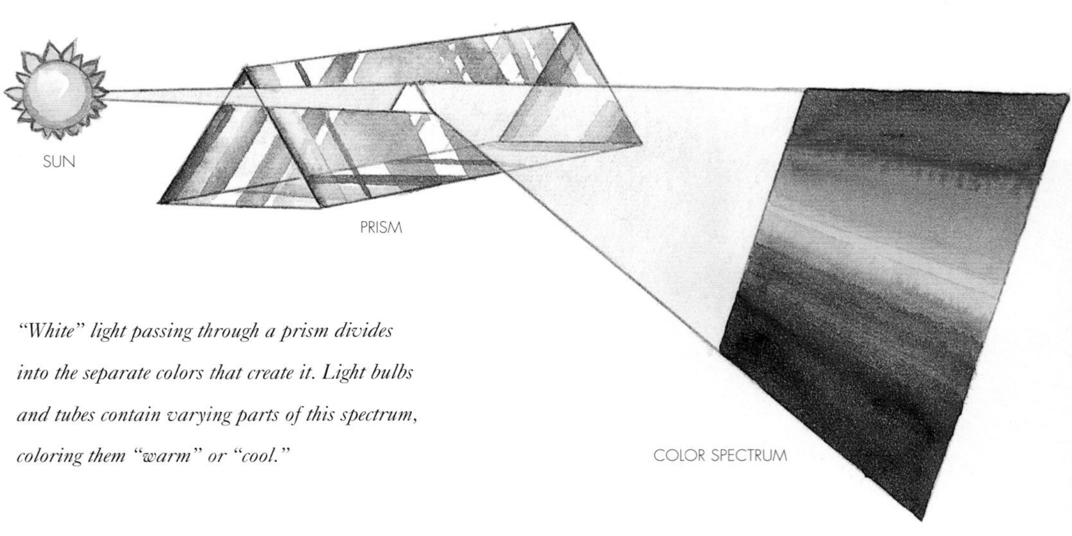

"White" light passing through a prism divides into the separate colors that create it. Light bulbs and tubes contain varying parts of this spectrum, coloring them "warm" or "cool."

Light bulbs are formally rated by color temperature, measured in degrees Kelvin (K). Temperatures below 3,500°K are warm-toned; higher temperatures are increasingly blue, or cool. The chart at right shows the position of several standard light sources on such a "thermometer."

Color rendition

How we perceive the color of an object is determined by two things: the surface color of the object itself and the color in the light that shines on it. The color of a blue vase under a blue light will be heightened, because the color of the light intensifies the blue of the vase. Under a red light, the same blue vase will appear dull and grayish, because the red light waves are absorbed and there are no blue waves to be reflected by the vase.

Because lighting can affect the apparent color of fabrics and wallpaper, it's always a good idea to choose furnishings and decorating materials under the same type of light you'll be using at home. If possible, bring home a swatch of material or a paint sample, or take sample materials to a lighting store. Today's "light labs"—showrooms where you can directly compare light sources—make this evaluation a lot easier.

Reflectance

The colors and textures of a room's walls, ceiling, and floor not only affect the room's decor but also contribute to the general light level according to their reflectance—that is, the degree to which they reflect light. Colors and textures of furnishings and display objects can affect overall light levels, too.

Colors that contain a lot of white reflect a large amount of light, of course, while darker colors absorb more light. A white object reflects 80 percent of the light that strikes it, while a black object reflects 5 percent or less. The illumination in a room with light-colored walls is distributed farther and more evenly as it is reflected from surface to surface until it gradually diminishes. For this reason, if you were to redecorate your living room by covering creamy white walls with a rich blue wallpaper, you'd find that you needed more light sources and bulbs of higher wattage to reach the same light levels as before.

Texture plays a part in reflectance, too. Matte finishes diffuse light; glossy finishes bounce light onto other surfaces. Thus, a room with fabric-covered walls requires more fixtures or brighter bulbs than a room with painted walls in order to achieve the same level of light.

A COLOR THERMOMETER

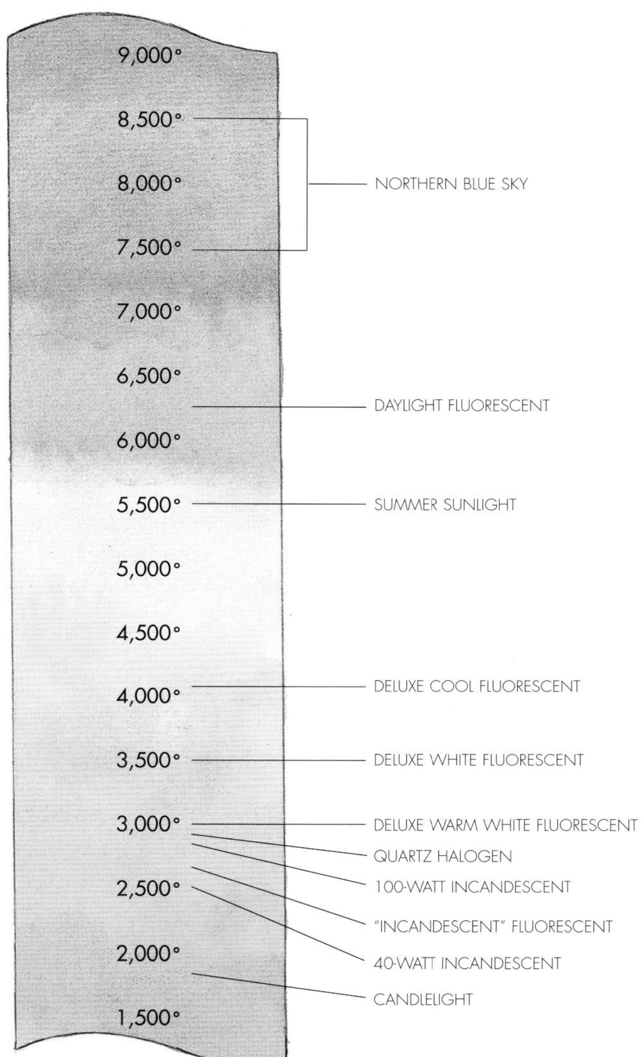

how much is enough?

LIGHT LEVELS *are partly a matter of individual preference. Some people grow accustomed to brightly lit offices and want similar uniform illumination in their homes. Others feel more relaxed and secure with relatively low light levels, preferring to focus on the area where they're reading, working, or dining. The current thinking is toward bright, efficient lighting in task areas, with surroundings more softly lit.*

Taking stock

So how much task light is "enough?" When planning, consider these factors:

- How difficult is the task to be performed?
- How much speed and accuracy does the task require?
- How much color contrast is there among materials involved in the task?
- How good is the eyesight of the person who will be engaged in the activity?

If an older person will be doing embroidery on a dark cloth with richly colored thread, lots of light will probably be required; the task calls for a high degree of accuracy, and the weak contrast between the fabric and the thread is hard on older eyes. For less demanding visual activities, such as reading the newspaper or watching television, light levels can be much lower.

Measuring lumens

One method for measuring and planning light levels involves adding up the amount of light—measured in lumens—emitted by all the bulbs in a certain area. If you look at the sleeve around a light bulb, you'll see that it states both the bulb's wattage (the amount of electricity used by the bulb) and the number of lumens (amount of light) that the bulb produces. Lumen outputs vary from one manufacturer to another, and they diminish as bulbs age.

As a rule of thumb, the most difficult visual tasks, such as embroidery, require a total of at least 2,500 lumens in an average-size room, with the greatest number of lumens concentrated at the work location. A casual task, such as watching television, requires from 1,500 to 2,000 lumens. To figure total lumens, just add up the lumen outputs of all the bulbs in the room.

For reference purposes, a standard 40-watt incandescent A-bulb (the familiar pear shape) puts out about 455 lumens, a 75-watt bulb casts 1,190 lumens, and a 150-watt bulb produces 2,880 lumens.

Measuring footcandles

A second and more precise method of measuring light levels uses the footcandle, the amount of illumination provided by a single lumen distributed over a foot-square surface.

Lighting designers and engineers have determined standard footcandle levels needed to perform ordinary household tasks. The chart below includes both a high and a low number of footcandles; the higher level is recommended for older people, the lower level for younger eyes. While these are recommended levels, individuals may prefer more or less light. Remember that dimmers (page 244) allow you to dial light up for one use, and down for another.

Experts measure footcandles with a special footcandle meter, but you can use the light meter built into a 35mm camera; for directions, see "Testing Your Ideas" at right.

Providing enough light for task areas is of primary importance, but care should also be taken to provide the surrounding areas with ambient light. In rooms with task lighting, the recommended ambient light level is 20 footcandles or about a third of the task area's footcandle value, whichever is less. For rooms where the main activity is entertaining or relaxing, a level of 5 to 10 footcandles is recommended. Entries, stairs, and passageways should also have a general light level of 5 to 10 footcandles.

Recommended Minimum Footcandles

Activity	Footcandles
Entertaining	10–20
Dining	10–20
Casual reading	20–50
Grooming	20–50
Kitchen, laundry—general light	20–50
Kitchen—food preparation	50–100
Prolonged reading or studying	50–100
Workshop activities	50–100
Sewing, medium-colored fabrics	50–100
Sewing, dark fabrics	100–200
Hobbies involving fine detail	100–200

Testing Your Ideas

It pays to know what kind of light you want and where it should be placed before you invest in fixtures for a room. But how can you find out? For basic experimenting you won't need much: a standard utility lamp or trouble light, a 1- or 2-pound coffee can, a homemade paper shade, a few bulbs, perhaps a table lamp borrowed from another room, and one or more extension cords. You'll also need a stepladder if you're planning to test ceiling fixtures. The coffee can, with its bottom cut out, gives you a kind of directional spotlight; the utility lamp's reflector produces a broader-beamed, more general light; and a paper shade casts a soft, diffuse glow.

Experts use a special meter to measure footcandles, but you can use the light meter built into a 35mm camera that has manually adjustable settings. To determine the number of footcandles of light reaching your kitchen counter, for example, prop a large sheet of white paper or cardboard on the counter at a 45-degree angle. Set the camera's ASA dial at 100 and the shutter speed at 1⁄15 of a second. The f-stop reading you get can then be translated into the approximate footcandle level, as listed below.

At ASA 100 and 1⁄15 second:

f4 = 10 footcandles
f5.6 = 20 footcandles
f8 = 40 footcandles
f11 = 80 footcandles
f16 = 160 footcandles
f19 (between f16 and f22) = 240 footcandles

The camera also lets you preview light ratios. From a central vantage point, aim the camera at both brightly lit objects and shadowy areas, then compare readings. A 3-to-1 light ratio equals a 1⁄2 f-stop difference between the highest and lowest reading; a 4-to-1 ratio equals a difference of 2 f-stops, and a 10-to-1 ratio equals a difference of 3½ f-stops.

choosing light sources

DO YOU WANT *warm light or cool light? Spotlights or broad beams? Discreet downlights or futuristic halogen pendants? You'd think fixtures would be the first thing to come up in any lighting discussion, but professional designers first pick the bulbs—which they call "lamps"—and only then the appropriate fixtures to shape the light and add style.*

Light bulbs and tubes

Bulbs and tubes can be grouped in general categories according to how they produce light. The following is a brief breakdown. Photos and charts in "A Shopper's Guide," starting on page 219, present the broad spectrum of available bulbs and tubes, with information about wattages, light outputs, efficiency, and color rendition.

INCANDESCENT BULBS. A tungsten filament burning inside a glass bulb filled with inert gas, usually argon, produces the warm incandescent light that we're all familiar with. The most common incandescent bulb is the pear-shaped A-bulb, but many other shapes and sizes are available (see pages 220–221). Most incandescents are designed for standard 120-volt household current, but low-voltage versions (see page 147) are also available.

INCANDESCENT BULB

Incandescent bulbs have excellent color rendering properties but, in general, are not very efficient. While A-bulbs are inexpensive to buy, they don't last nearly as long as other bulb types. Use a more efficient source (such as fluorescent light) when the warmth and excellent color-rendering properties of incandescent light are not crucial.

FLUORESCENT TUBES. When electricity passes through a fluorescent tube, it burns the mercury vapor there, producing ultraviolet light that is reradiated as visible light by the phosphors coating the inside of the tube. Because the light comes evenly from the entire tube surface, it spreads in all directions, creating a steady, shadowless light. Tubes require a ballast to ignite and maintain the electrical flow. You can also get energy-saving compact fluorescents that screw into a socket; these can be used to replace incandescent bulbs in regular fixtures. For details, see pages 222–223.

Fluorescent tubes are unrivaled for energy efficiency, and they last far longer than incandescent bulbs. In some energy-conscious places, ambient lighting in kitchens and bathrooms *must* be fluorescent.

FLUORESCENT TUBE

Older fluorescent tubes have been criticized for noise, flicker, and poor color rendition. Electronic ballasts and better fixture shielding against glare have remedied the first two problems; as for color, manufacturers have developed fluorescents in a wide spectrum of hues, from very warm (about 2,700°K) to very cool (about 6,300°K).

HALOGEN BULBS. Containing a tiny quartz filament and a chemical coating (halogens), these bulbs produce a brighter beam and last longer than incandescent sources. They're excellent for task lighting, pinpoint accenting, and other dramatic effects. Many halogen fixtures use tube-shaped halogen bulbs, but there are a variety of shapes on the market (see pages 224–225), including bulbs shaped to replace common incandescent A-bulbs, and various reflectors. Halogen is usually low-voltage but may be standard 120-volt household current.

Halogen's one disadvantage, besides the initial cost, is that it's very hot. To be used safely, halogen bulbs must be used in halogen fixtures. Shop carefully; some fixtures on the market are not UL-approved.

HALOGEN BULB

OTHER SOURCES. *High-intensity discharge (HID)* bulbs produce light when electricity excites specific gases in pressurized bulbs. Requiring special fixtures and ballasts, these lights may take several minutes to ignite after being switched on. The color emitted by most HID bulbs is rather unflattering, but they offer long life and efficiency. One HID source—mercury vapor—is commonly used for outdoor security lighting. For details, see page 229.

Neon light is also generated by electricity passing through a gas; neon gas glows orange-red, while other gases give off a variety of colors. Neon (page 226) is almost strictly decorative. *Cold cathode*, a close cousin of neon, puts out more light and is useful for ambient or indirect lighting as well as decoration. *Fiber optics* (pages 226–227) allow for exciting installations but at present are quite pricey.

HIGH-INTENSITY DISCHARGE BULB

ENERGY-SAVING OPTIONS

In the average household, lighting accounts for 15 to 20 percent of all electrical power consumed. By carefully planning new lighting or making a few changes in your present habits, you can trim your energy consumption and costs. Here's a checklist of 16 energy-saving tips to get you started:

- Switch off lights when you leave a room
- Paint your walls light colors
- Take advantage of daylight
- Emphasize task lighting
- Buy compact fluorescent bulbs
- Dust light bulbs regularly
- Buy three-way bulbs
- Use energy-saving night-lights
- Use the lowest-wattage light bulbs possible
- Move lamps toward the corners of rooms
- Add dimmers to your lamps and light circuits
- Install timer switches
- Opt for low-voltage garden lights
- Install motion detectors and photocells outdoors
- Make security lights fluorescent or mercury vapor
- Go solar to power garden lighting

Light fixtures

TORCHÈRE

Once you've formed some ideas about the kinds of light sources you need, selecting fixtures would appear to be easy. But given the great variety available today, finding the right fixtures can be confusing and downright complicated. Here are some points to keep in mind.

PENDANT

FIXTURE TYPES. Your basic fixture options include movable lamps, surface-mounted ceiling and wall lights, track systems, and recessed downlights. Each of these is discussed in detail in "A Shopper's Guide," pages 230–241.

In addition, built-in coves, cornices, valances, and soffits can be used when indirect lighting is desired. Architectural in design, these devices shield light sources from view, allowing light to spill out around the shields. You'll find these built-in fixtures in action throughout the following section, "Great Lighting Ideas."

WALL SCONCE

TASK LIGHT

BEAM PATTERN. One of the primary considerations for any fixture is how it directs light. Does it create a narrow, focused beam of light, a broad, diffuse spread—or something in between, like the torchère shown at left? For greatest efficiency, match the fixture's light distribution pattern to the lighting need.

SIZE. Fixtures often seem smaller in the store than they will in your home. Take measurements of your top choices; then hold bowls or boxes of the same sizes in place back at home to evaluate the scale. Manufacturers often produce fixtures in graded sizes, so ask about other possibilities.

DESIGN. Personal taste will be your guide, leading you to whatever suits your decor. Professionals have found that a sense of decorative continuity can be created by using similar fixtures throughout a home. In response, manufacturers offer "families" of fixtures that include spotlights, pendants, track lights, and ceiling fixtures.

COST. When calculating costs, there's more to consider than the price of the fixture. The energy consumption of the bulbs or tubes that will be used in the fixture is a significant factor; for a comparative look at light bulbs, turn to pages 228–229. Also, be aware that some fixtures are more efficient than others, transmitting a higher percentage of the light produced by the bulbs or

Built-in cove lighting

Track

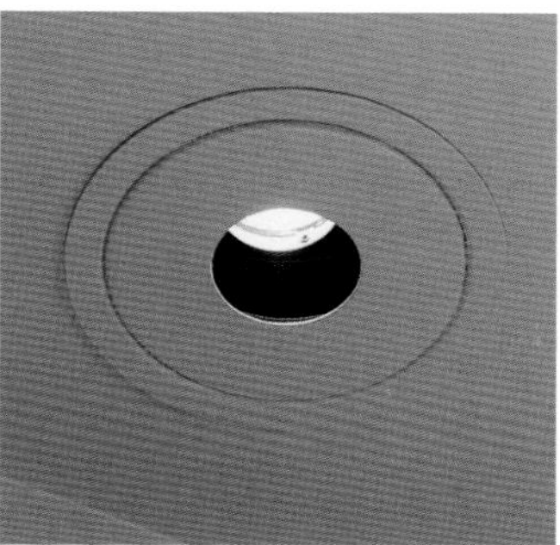

Recessed downlight

tubes they contain and, therefore, providing more light for the amount of electricity consumed.

Flexibility. Tastes, habits, and styles change over the years. Your lighting system should be flexible enough to accommodate such changes. Movable or adjustable lamps, of course, are flexible by design. But track systems and even recessed downlights can be changed, too. You can move fixtures along a track or readjust the way they're aimed. A regular built-in downlight can be transformed into an accent light or a wall-washing light.

Maintenance. To operate efficiently, all fixtures need to be cleaned regularly. Kitchens, bathrooms, and work areas in particular demand fixtures that are easy to reach and clean. For hard-to-reach areas, such as above stairs, a fixture with a long-lived fluorescent or halogen bulb is a good choice.

What about Low-voltage?

Low-voltage lighting for indoor use has become common on the residential scene. Operating on 12 or 24 volts, low-voltage lights require transformers (sometimes built into the fixtures) to step down the voltage from standard 120-volt household circuits. The small bulbs are especially useful for accent lighting, where light must be baffled or precisely directed onto a small area. The compact fixtures that house the bulbs are decorative in their own right.

Low-voltage fixtures and bulbs are relatively expensive to buy, but this kind of lighting can be energy-efficient if carefully planned. To learn more about your options, see "A Shopper's Guide," beginning on page 219.

Cable light

moving outdoors

PLAN OUTDOOR LIGHTING, *either low-voltage or 120-volt, much as you would indoor lighting. Begin by deciding where you'll need light at night for safety, activity, and security. Then you can add decorative or festive accents—though in many cases functional lighting can also be decorative.*

Less is best

Because the contrast between darkness and a light source is so great, glare can be a big problem at night. Solve the problem by following these three rules of thumb:

- Choose shielded fixtures.
- Place fixtures out of sight lines.
- Lower the overall light levels.

With a shielded fixture, the bulb area is protected by an opaque covering that directs light away from the viewer's eyes. Instead of a hot spot of light, the eye sees the warm glow of the lighted object.

Place shielded fixtures either low (as along a walk) or very high. By doing this properly, you can direct fixtures so that only the light playing in the tree branches is noticed—not a bright glare from the source.

Reduce light levels by using several softer lights, strategically placed around the patio and yard, rather than a single high-wattage bulb.

A little light goes a long way at night. Twenty watts is considered strong, and even 12 watts can be very bright. If a bulb is clearly visible (a porch light in a clear housing, for example), you may find that even a 12-watt refrigerator bulb is adequate for welcoming guests.

Low-voltage or standard current?

Because low-voltage lighting is safer, more energy-efficient, and easier to install than standard 120-volt systems, it is often used outdoors. Low-voltage systems use a transformer to step down household current to 12 volts.

Installing a low-voltage system is relatively simple. Cable can lie on top of the ground, perhaps hidden by mulch or foliage; most fixtures connect easily to cables, and no grounding hookups are required. For more about components, see pages 248–249.

The standard 120-volt system does have some advantages outdoors. The buried cable and metallic fixtures of such an installation give it a look of permanence. Also, light can be projected a great distance, especially useful for increasing security and for lighting trees from ground level. An additional advantage is that power tools and patio heaters can be plugged into 120-volt outdoor outlets.

Setting the stage

Night lighting lets you edit your views; basically, the garden stops where the light stops. Whether your garden is large or small, you should always start by determining how much of it you want to light. It's important to be aware of how your

This garden looks great in daylight (left), but when the sun goes down it really comes alive. Effects include dramatic uplighting below palm and olive trees, downlighting to brighten patio and table, ground-level lighting to highlight planting beds, backlighting behind the potted trees, and wall washing on the end wall and fireplace.

lights might affect the neighbors, too (some communities even have ordinances regulating "light trespass").

If you view your garden as a large outdoor room, you'll see that hedges and fences can act as walls, and trees and arbors as ceilings. The same lighting techniques and tricks that work for a room indoors can help you design the lighting for this outdoor space.

Light can help you create a sense of perspective within your outdoor canvas. Lighting designers do this by dividing a garden into three zones: a foreground, which has relatively mid-level brightness; a middle ground, with low-level light and an interplay of shadows; and a background, often given the brightest light of all in order to draw the eye through the garden.

Lighting for safety and security

Ideally, outdoor lighting should combine safety, security, and style. Safety comes first. With this in mind, examine the driveway, the front walk and steps, the front door, the back door and other house approaches, and the swimming pool or spa, if you have one.

The trick to lighting these areas is to combine efficient light with both adequate shielding and a sense of subtlety. You'll find numerous examples in "Great Lighting Ideas," pages 206–217. For a look at some outdoor fixtures and security lights, see "A Shopper's Guide," pages 246–251.

Photocells, timers, and outdoor motion sensors all save energy by switching security lights on and off automatically. Photocells turn lights on at dusk and back off at dawn; with timers, you set the times. Motion-sensor fixtures stay on for a preset interval after being triggered. For shopping pointers, see pages 250–251.

These decorative garden fixtures not only mark the path; they're stylish, too. Semi-opaque glass shades cut glare to a warm glow.

Decorative techniques

You can use a number of lighting techniques to tie a garden's elements together. The two basic mounting positions are downlighting and uplighting. Of the two, downlighting looks more natural—light comes from above and accents or gently washes areas below—though it can also have a dramatic impact. Uplighting, placing the light source beneath what it's illuminating, is more theatrical. It can be especially useful in new gardens lacking mature trees.

A single, direct source sometimes flattens a lighted object unnaturally, making it look like a billboard. Multiple sources give it dimension. For a dappled, "moonlight" effect, use both uplights and downlights to light a large tree. Decorative rope lights used to outline trees, steps, and railings can lend sparkle to your landscape.

You can create interesting garden effects by placing uplights, downlights, and accent lights on separate switches. Install dimmers (page 244) for even greater flexibility.

What does it take to install new lighting? Replacing an outdated fixture or dimmer with a new one can be a simple half-hour matter of screws, wire nuts, and a screwdriver. When adding a new fixture, though, things get messier: you need to run new electrical cable (shown below) from an existing source to the new location, mount a new fixture box, and then wire in the new fixture and secure it to the box.

- **Mapping.** Before you add lighting—as opposed to replacing an existing fixture—it's important to know which circuits control which existing fixtures, plug-in outlets, and switches. Some circuits may already be carrying the maximum current allowed by law.

To chart circuits, you'll need a small table lamp or night-light that you can carry around to test plug-in outlets. After turning the first circuit breaker to the OFF position or removing the first fuse, go through the house and check all appliances, switches, and outlets; on a rough map of your house, label those that are now dead with the circuit number.

Repeat the process with each circuit, making sure that you've turned the previous circuit breaker back on or replaced the previous fuse.

Once you've mapped your circuits, you can plan to add fixtures or plug-in outlets to circuits controlled by 15-amp circuit breakers or fuses.

ELECTRICAL CABLE (TYPE NM)

Technical Talk

As a rule, a 15-amp circuit can handle a maximum of 1,440 watts. Add up the watts marked on the appliances and bulbs fed by the circuit to which you want to add. Subtract this sum from 1,440 to find out how many watts you can add to the circuit.

If you're confused by load calculations or want to know whether you can tap into a circuit rated at more than 15 amps, call on your local building department's electrical inspector.

- **Wiring.** Thinking of doing the wiring yourself? The trick is to find a route for new electrical cable. If walls and/or floors and ceilings are exposed, you're in luck. Otherwise, you'll almost certainly need to cut into—then patch and paint—wall and ceiling materials to gain access for cable. For step-by-step planning and wiring details, see the Sunset book *Complete Home Wiring*.

Where cutting into walls, ceilings, and floors to route new wire is too difficult, surface wiring may be the answer—especially if you're comfortable with the somewhat "industrial" look that results. Surface wiring systems are safe and neat, usually consisting of protective channels and housing boxes (shown at left below) that allow you to mount wiring on practically any wall or ceiling material.

If you do plan to tackle a home wiring project yourself, there's one firm rule: Never work on a "live" circuit. Always remove the fuse or switch the circuit breaker to the OFF position before beginning work.

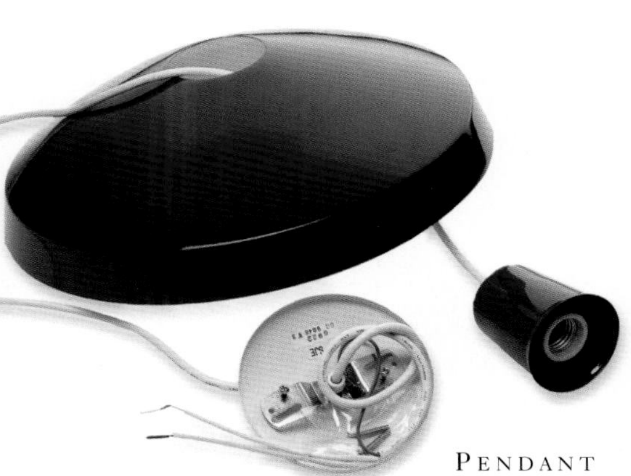

Pendant

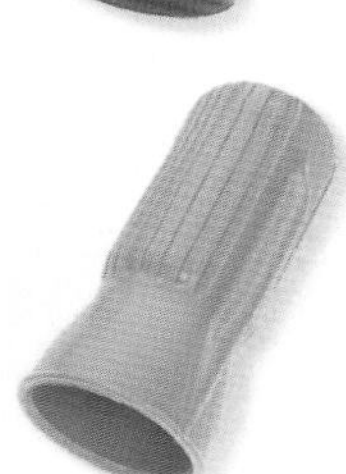

Wire nuts

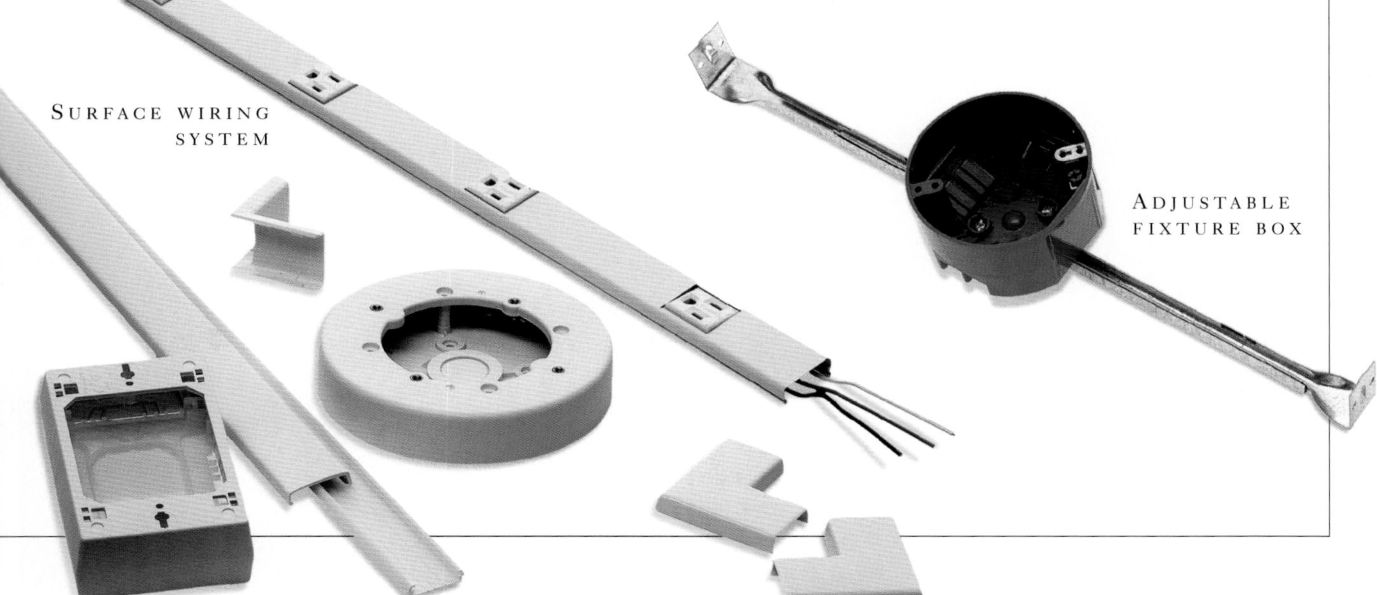

Surface wiring system

Adjustable fixture box

GREAT LIGHTING IDEAS

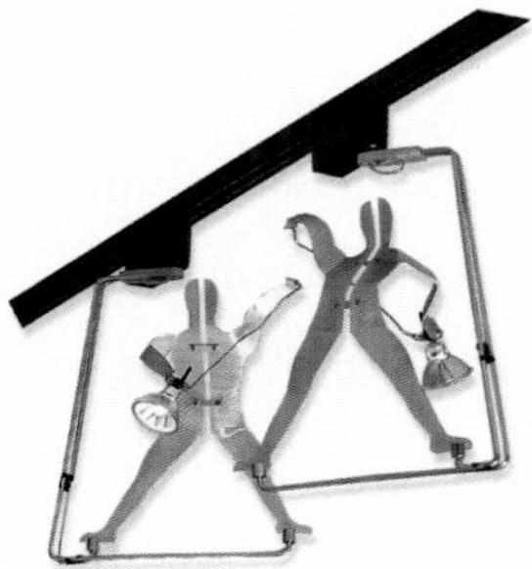

YOU'VE LEARNED THE BASICS—now it's time to get creative. In this chapter we take you on a photo tour of great home lighting ideas, traveling room by room. Along the way you're sure to find styles as well as strategies that will work for you. **WE BEGIN AT THE FRONT DOOR,** wind our way through the living room, kitchen, and dining area, and then move on down the hall to the bedroom, bath, and home office. Finally, it's off to the great outdoors, where we show how good lighting blends sparkle with both safety and security. **BROWSE AT YOUR LEISURE,** perhaps marking your favorite pictures to show to a lighting designer or supplier. If you run across unfamiliar terms, you should be able to find explanations of them in the previous section of this book, "A Planning Primer." See some fixtures or controls you'd like to learn more about? Turn to "A Shopper's Guide," beginning on page 219.

entries

ENTRIES MAKE first impressions. Light them warmly and you allow your guests to look their best as you invite them to come on in. Don't overlight: the contrast to the outdoors can be disorienting. Both porch and entry fixtures should be well shielded to minimize glare.

An entry's lighting sets the tone for what lies beyond in your home. The rule for both lighting style and fixtures: *keep it simple.* If you opt for an eye-catching chandelier or pendant, don't add competing focal points. The same goes for accenting display objects and plantings. Add soft fill light, controlled by dimmers, by means of built-in cove lighting, light-diffusing wall sconces, or even an antique table lamp with an opaque shade.

What's the view down the hall? Entry light levels and fixture style should complement the areas that are visible beyond the entry. A focal point or points down a long entryway can lead guests on into the living spaces.

Lighting can make your entry seem bigger or smaller. Stretch an entry's perceived size by uplighting a light-colored ceiling or by spacing fixtures horizontally down a hallway. To make a large space seem more intimate, try spare down-lighting, higher-contrast lighting, pinpoint accenting, or light-diffusing wall sconces positioned low to effectively lower the ceiling line. Mirrors also spread light and create the illusion of more space.

A light for the coat closet and another near a mirror for that last-minute check make entry lighting complete.

There's no glare-producing ceiling fixture here. Instead, the glowing, faux-painted walls are softly lit by indirect ceiling cove lighting, aided by a modern wall sconce. Pinpoint accenting adds punch, courtesy of ceiling-mounted down-lights with aimable eyeball trim.

A bold entry sports twin cast-metal lamps that flank a stylish mirror and sit atop a demilune table.

A streamlined entry previews the ultramodern home design beyond. Lighting is correspondingly clean: hidden downlights accent the framed photos, and a warm glow comes from strip lighting tucked beneath the floating shelf's lip.

Entry mirrors can stretch apparent space and spread available light. This narrow, windowless entry in an urban row house achieves both effects. Wall sconces positioned on the mirror add a warm glow and echo fixtures found throughout the house.

Effective lighting pulls the eye into this entry and down an open hallway that doubles as an art gallery. The zoomy entry sconce sets the tone; paintings are lit by ceiling-mounted downlights with slot apertures. A built-in soffit bounces soft fill light off the ceiling.

living rooms

Pinpoint downlights handle both ambient and accent lighting needs. These fixtures are meant to be in the background, allowing the decorative neon wall art to take center stage.

Living spaces present prime opportunities for flexible, multilayered lighting schemes. You'll want to include well-shielded task lighting for reading or handiwork as well as accent lighting for artwork, collections, or architectural features. Soft, adjustable levels of ambient light set a congenial mood for entertaining or watching television.

Built-in architectural fixtures such as valances, soffits, and coves are effective ambient sources. So are wall sconces, movable torchères, and wall washers. Traditional floor and table lamps are enjoying a renaissance, too, with many new design options on the market and in the works. Remember, though, that these and other decorative fixtures shouldn't carry the lighting load: if turned up high, they're big glare producers. Pharmacy lamps with adjustable necks and built-in dimmers are tops for efficient task lighting.

Discreet downlights can complement both contemporary and traditional styles of decor, but they're best reserved for accenting or for lighting casual tasks. Art and furnishings change over time; choose adjustable downlights that can be adapted for future needs. If you're retrofitting, consider whimsical cable lights or other low-voltage tracks.

Dimmers, panels that control individual lighting scenes, or computer controls let you adjust multiple light sources for varied living-room uses and moods. Floor outlets enable lamp cords to follow furnishings; three- and four-way switches let you access lights as you enter one way and exit another.

Collectibles seem to float within this elegant display cabinet. Recessed downlights shine from the top; backlighting, separately switched, comes from fiber optics behind the translucent back.

VENETIAN VILLAS

Understated colors and accessories are underscored by a matte-black pharmacy lamp—a particularly apt choice for living-room task lighting (especially when supplied with a dimmer).

A beautifully spare living room and the bedroom beyond are highlighted by low-voltage MR-16 downlights with aimable slot apertures. The hallway's smooth, indirect light comes from two dimmable 250-watt quartz wall washers tucked up in the skylight well.

ATLAS OF THE WORLD
VAN GOGH

Comfortable and eclectic, this TV room has seemingly casual but highly efficient lighting. The overhead pendant casts diffuse light down and bounce light up, avoiding the glare of a standard ceiling fixture. Discreet downlights with pinhole apertures add "invisible" accents. A paper-shaded corner fixture supplies fun and fill light. Light from an adjacent space is shared through glass blocks.

Lined up along a pedestal shelf surrounding the sunken room, a marching row of tall torchères extends style and ambient light into an otherwise dark area. Torchères are handy, movable alternatives to sconces or other ambient built-ins.

Tall walls—especially those below vaulted ceilings—are made for built-in uplighting. The wall sconces at left, mounted in the high "clerestory" area, shine light up and off the white, angled ceiling, creating lots of soft ambient fill for the living space below.

Soft fill light, harder accenting, and a warm candlelight glow combine in this inviting living room. The design takes advantage of open ceiling trusses to hide rows of adjustable track fixtures. High-mounted wall sconces supply the fill.

Formal but flexible, twin table lamps atop a library desk serve both desk and sofa. Classic candelabra sconces above the fireplace mantel add ambient light as well as decorative sparkle.

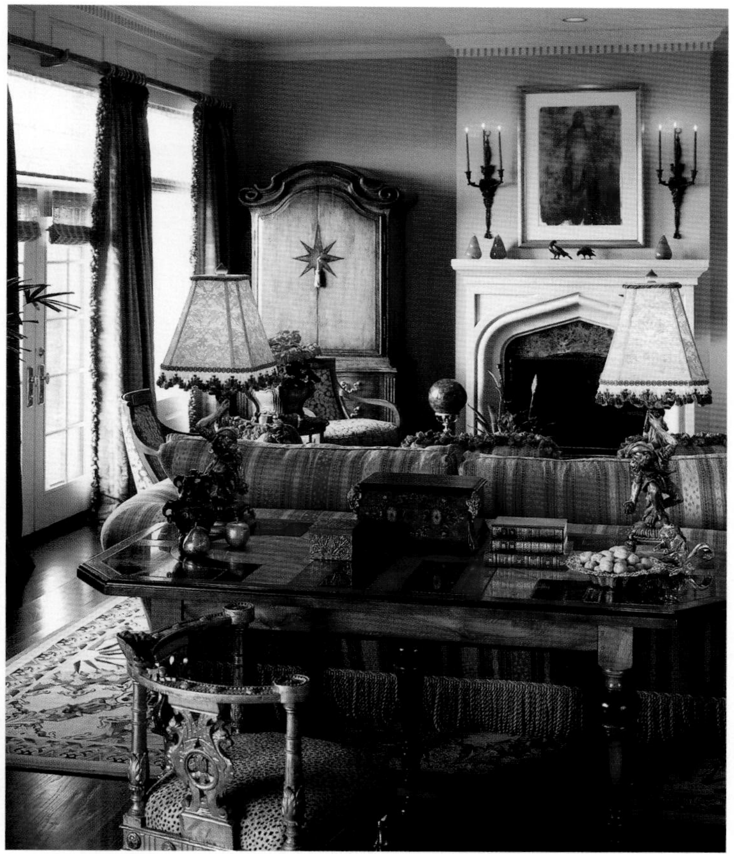

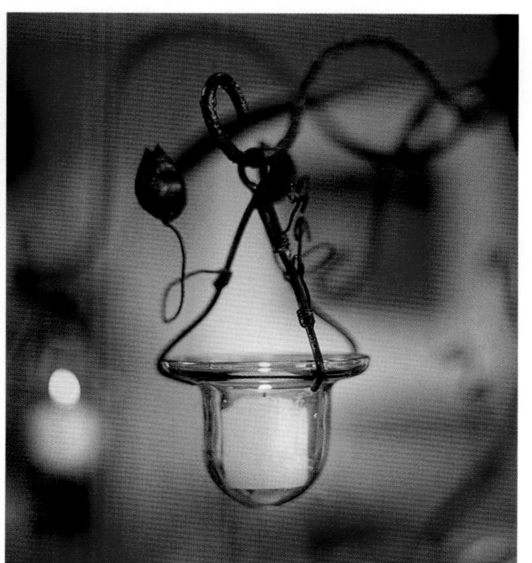

Votives in glass holders dance from decorative wrought-iron fixtures, bringing soft light to a garden-room scene.

This retro decor is brought to life by integral banks of fluorescent fixtures that send ample light both up and down. Light shines down through mesh-screen covers that serve as louvers, softening the output and cutting glare. Open above, these fixtures bounce additional fill light up and off the ceiling.

A curving cable system is an updated alternative to traditional track fixtures. Here, the mini–reflector bulbs handle accenting and wall-washing tasks. Cable systems make easy retrofits for existing ceiling fixtures and can help "liven up" a tall, potentially cold-looking room.

It's not illegal to have fun with light fixtures! This inventive "chandelier," straight from the hardware store, forms the perfect counterpoint to a wall display of junkyard car emblems and a parking-lot mirror. The fixture is fashioned from standard work lights or "clamp lamps" hard-wired into several junction boxes above.

You can accent artwork in many ways. One of the simplest—and least expensive—is with an add-on picture light. The fixture shown here looks traditional and helps artwork appear bolder and shine brighter.

A portable, easy-to-add uplight silhouettes a tall indoor plant and highlights the textures of rough-hewn walls and moldings.

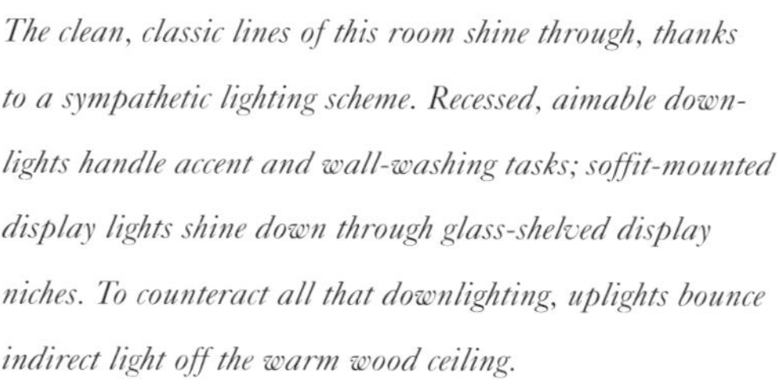

The clean, classic lines of this room shine through, thanks to a sympathetic lighting scheme. Recessed, aimable down-lights handle accent and wall-washing tasks; soffit-mounted display lights shine down through glass-shelved display niches. To counteract all that downlighting, uplights bounce indirect light off the warm wood ceiling.

kitchens

TODAY'S KITCHEN is the household hub or "command center." As a gathering place, a kitchen needs flexible lighting for both late-night snacks and full-scale entertaining. And whether there's one cook or a crew of kitchen helpers at work, task lighting for the sink, countertops, and cooktop is essential. Multiple sources and dimmer controls let you turn light up full-throttle when you're working or down to a warm glow after hours.

You'll want strong, shadowless light right over each kitchen work area. In most cases, shielded strip lights under the cabinets—hidden behind a trim strip or valance—are the best way to light counter areas. Downlights effectively illuminate the sink and work islands.

Surface-mounted fixtures, once a kitchen mainstay, are now used specifically to draw attention to themselves. Hanging pendants are especially popular; place them over a breakfast nook or an island—or anywhere they won't present a traffic hazard.

Fluorescent tubes are unrivaled for energy efficiency; they also last far longer than incandescent bulbs. In some energy-conscious areas, general lighting for new kitchens *must* be fluorescent. Though fixture options for fluorescent bulbs and tubes are limited, indirect treatments using them are popular: the tubes are placed in soffits atop cabinets or in overhead coves.

Kitchen task lighting is often delivered by means of under-cabinet strip lights. Here they're sealed and softened within frosted acrylic panels on cabinet bottoms.

The owner of this kitchen, part of a remodeled winery, wanted lots of light, but the raised ceiling made it a tough task. Stylish red Italian pendants housing tiny but efficient quartz bulbs solved the problem and defined the space. Electrical conduit, painted white, leads from the roofline down to the fixtures, which were designed to be ceiling-mounted.

Drink
MOXIE
DISTINCTIVELY DIFFERENT
feast of eden

An eclectic, casual kitchen sports casual, "unfitted" lighting to match, including two chain-hung glass pendants, table lamps, and even a jaunty string of Christmas lights. Sure, it's less efficient than some schemes, but it's more fun.

Three glass-and-chrome pendants follow the line of the butcher-block prep island. Downlights mark the rear countertop; decorative uplights in high cabinet soffits add background fill.

While many designers chafe against energy requirements that demand fluorescents in kitchens, the architect of this space reveled in the look—finding them the perfect touch for a retro 50s design. Overhead lighting is flaunted, courtesy of a 36-inch, soffit-mounted ceiling globe. Tubes behind wall cabinets graze the concrete-block wall, and more tubes bounce light off the painted wood ceiling. The lighting is classic "cool" fluorescent throughout.

Need to add light where there's limited overhead access? These surface-mounted, low-voltage track fixtures include integral transformers and add a gleaming look to a high-tech kitchen. Just be sure your cabinet doors will clear the tracks you choose!

No, it's not the War of the Worlds, just fluorescents meeting the future. Except for the trio of tiny pendants hovering near the eating counter, all ceiling fixtures here house space-saving PL-fluorescent tubes.

A hollow central "beam" houses recessed downlights and follows the work surfaces of a hard-working island, shining strong quartz lighting where it's most needed. Track fixtures supply the general lighting; tucked along open ceiling beams, they were custom-colored to blend with the surroundings.

Kitchen schemes rarely feature purely decorative effects, but this one fills the bill. Incandescent mini-tracks run through the soffit area above the wall cabinets, backlighting bundled dried twigs. This provides enough ambient light to negotiate the kitchen at night when other sources are switched off.

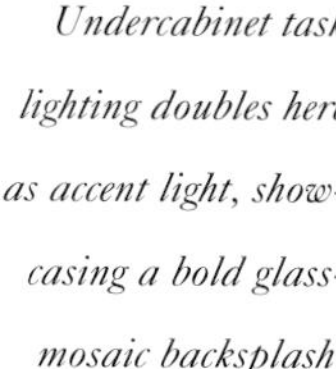

Undercabinet task lighting doubles here as accent light, showcasing a bold glass-mosaic backsplash.

dining areas

Dimmable eyeball MR-16s are the workhorses here, recessed in hollow box beams above the large dining table. Wall sconces flank a built-in buffet, supplying glare-free ambient wash. Candles add decorative glow for formal occasions.

THE FOCUS HERE is the dining table, which can be lit by a traditional chandelier, modern pendants, recessed downlights—or, even better, some combination of these.

The proportions of a dining-table light fixture in relation to its surroundings are critical. To keep diners or passersby from bumping into it, a hanging fixture should be at least 12 inches narrower than the table. Hanging it about 30 inches above the table surface will help cut down on reflected glare from the tabletop.

A decorative fixture like a chandelier should *not* be the only light source—it's sure to cause discomfort from glare when turned up. Instead, augment a decorative fixture with one or more adjustable downlights that really do the work. Dimmers can be a real plus—turned up high, the light aids in the task of setting the table or directing guests; turned low, the gentle beam creates a festive atmosphere and minimizes glare. In order to dispel harsh glare and shadows, augment your table lighting with softer fill light on the walls or ceiling. Ambient options include built-in cove lighting, wall sconces, and movable torchères. Accent light on paintings or inside display niches can double as ambient fill, too.

A separate set of fixtures over a buffet will supply light for serving as well as providing background light at mealtimes. Traditional candelabra-style fixtures and modern wall sconces are both popular choices, depending on the room's decor.

Good things can come in threes—like these blown-glass pendants, a decorative departure from the traditional chandelier.

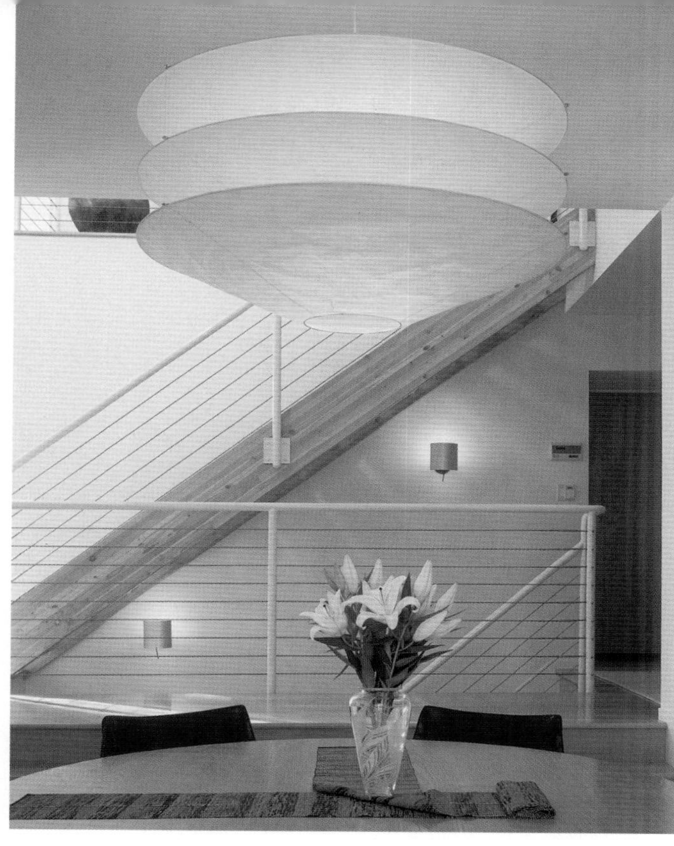

A three-tiered paper shade makes a handsome dining-room accent, doubling as a centerpiece while cutting a hanging pendant's glare-prone output. Staggered wall sconces add fill light while echoing the angle formed by the nearby staircase.

A classic chandelier provides sparkle, not glare; most light comes from the hard-working cove overhead. Four eyeball-trimmed downlights add even accent across the wall screen.

Three beaded pendants hang from low-voltage cables, marking the line of a sturdy waxed-pine dining table. Fixed table lamps are mounted in window alcoves flanking the far fireplace; MR-16 monospots wash fir-paneled walls, lending ambient fill to middle zones. Display cabinets are backlit with strip lights tucked behind rear valances.

A row of modern glass pendants follows the dining-room table; each halogen fixture includes a frosted diffusing ring to minimize glare. The sculptural room divider beyond houses sparkling, end-lit fiber optics inside each niche.

Candles form the focal point (above), while more modern sources—tucked away—contribute accent lighting. Beam-housed fixtures (right) bounce warm light down off the wood ceiling.

hallways and stairs

HALLWAYS MAY BE slim passageways, art galleries, or even glassed-in open areas. But as routes for human traffic, they should be neither much dimmer nor much brighter than adjoining rooms so that your eyes don't have to make big adjustments as you move from room to room.

When planning hall lighting, keep it simple. Downlights are popular here, as are tracks and opaque pendants. If the hall is wide enough, consider spaced wall sconces. A hallway can make an exciting gallery for art, but be sure the light is dimmable—or consider a second set of fixtures for soft illumination, or night-lights for late-night path lighting.

If you have a full staircase—or even just two steps to another level—it's important to provide adequate light for safety. The edge of each tread and the depth of each step should be clearly defined. One way to achieve this is to combine a downlight over the stairs (to light edges) with a softer light projected from the landing below (to define the depth). Another option is to build low-voltage fixtures into the wall just above every third or fourth step. Lights hidden in a handrail can also illuminate treads. For a main landing or entry stairs, consider decorative and accent options as well.

For either halls or stairs, plan to install three- or four-way switches at each end or hallway opening; a dimmer can replace one switch for decorative lighting control.

Lighting a nonlinear central hallway required something new in tracks: a curved, custom statement. The elegant pewter track blends well with the softly faux-painted walls, while the "lily" shades, each with its own MR-16 spot, accent ranks of framed prints.

Part warehouse, part nautical in mood, these recessed wall lights help mark the way down concrete stair risers. Downlights fill in from overhead.

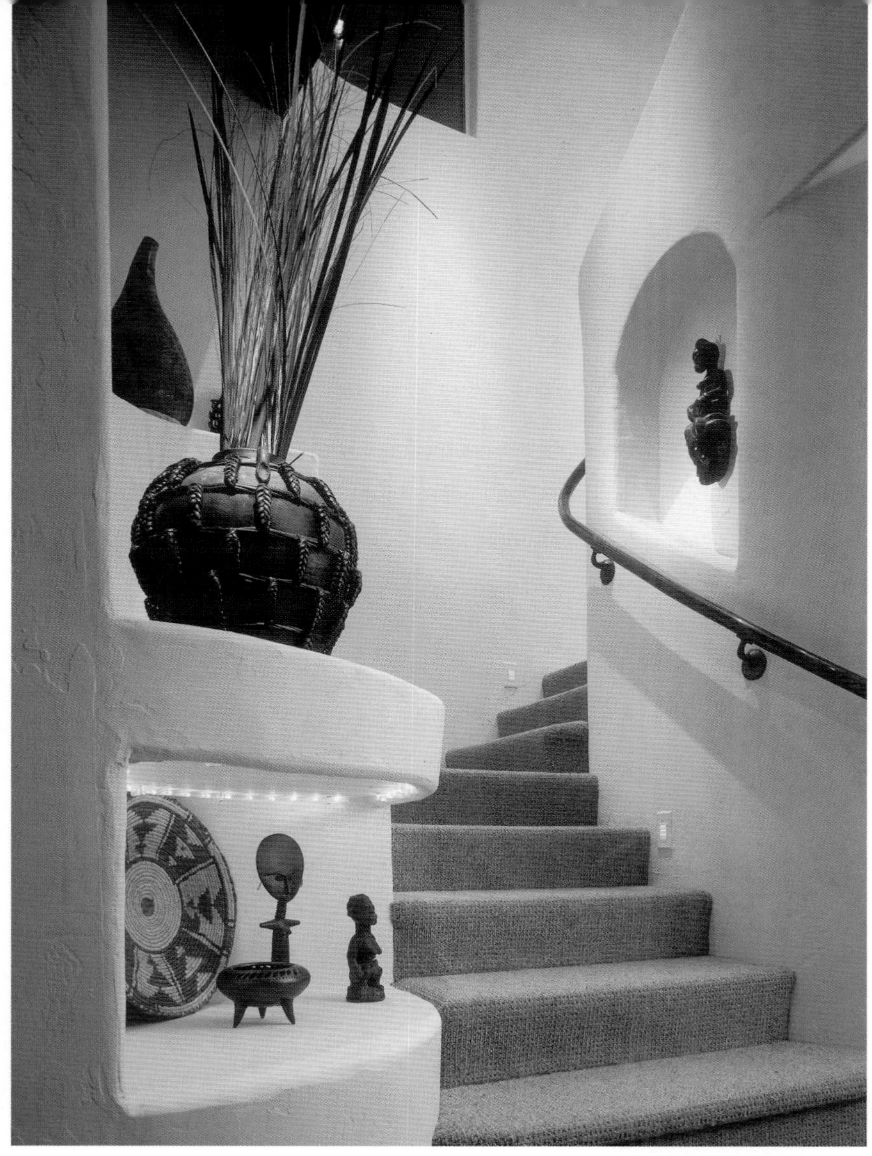

Glowing mini-lights on a remote transformer light the display niche in the foreground, while an MR-16 monospot illuminates the stair-side niche. Adjustable downlights wash the walls with light.

A curving, low-voltage cable system follows the ins and outs of an upstairs art collection. All that accent light adds ambient hallway light, too, as it bounces off the art and the white walls. A track-mounted globe pendant dives down the stair-well, brightening the space below.

Translucent glass stair treads, shown here from below, seem to glow. The light really comes from MR-16 bulbs tucked inside the built-in, recessed wall rectangles.

bedrooms

ONCE THE REALM of a glare-producing ceiling globe and clunky plug-in table lamps, the bedroom is now the setting for major news in lighting design. Multiple, dimmable light sources can add welcome flexibility—especially useful for today's open master-suite schemes.

On the subtle end of the bedroom lighting scale, soft ambient levels create a quiet aura. Decorative sconces, torchères, or built-in cove lighting can provide soft, glare-free fill light. If you're replacing an existing ceiling globe, consider an opaque pendant that directs light up and off the ceiling. Check to ensure that glare won't be a problem for someone reclining in bed: overhead fixtures should be carefully aimed and fitted, as needed, with tight trim covers and baffles or louvers. And be sure the bedroom fixtures and bulbs you choose produce minimal noise or "hum."

Bright, directional reading lights on either side of a bed allow one person to sleep while the other reads into the wee hours. Such fixtures should be adjustable and well shielded. Or use a pair of dimmable low-voltage downlights, cross-aimed like overhead airline lights to prevent shadows.

A bedside switch to turn off main room lights is handy. A second switch can control night-lights. A recent innovation is a bedside master switch to control computerized security lights both indoors and out.

There's a soft look overall here—appropriate for a master bedroom—but it's built up from several flexible sources. Recessed downlights with aimable slot apertures direct ambient wall-wash to the headboard area. Monospots with honeycombed louvers create tight, low-glare accents on paintings. A pair of bedside task lamps provides adjustable light for reading.

The pewter bedside light in this guest room has been custom-fitted to a mounting block; it rides up and down the post of a steel canopy bed, tightening with the turn of a brass knob.

A multilayered lighting scheme, usually reserved for formal living rooms, comes to this master-suite conversation space. Punchy PAR downlights wash the fireplace; low-voltage downlights pinpoint mirror and mantel. Strip lights tucked behind a ceiling cove furnish ambient fill. There's more accent lighting inside the display cases. A table lamp lends a cozy, traditional feel and ample reading light.

"Classic but clean" was the plan, and recessed downlights helped carry it out. General lighting is via dimmable PAR lights with polished reflectors; smaller MR-16s with louvers spotlight planters. When it's time for relaxing, the downlights are turned off, leaving the soft indirect glow from strip lights in the coved ceiling (they're hidden behind classic crown moldings).

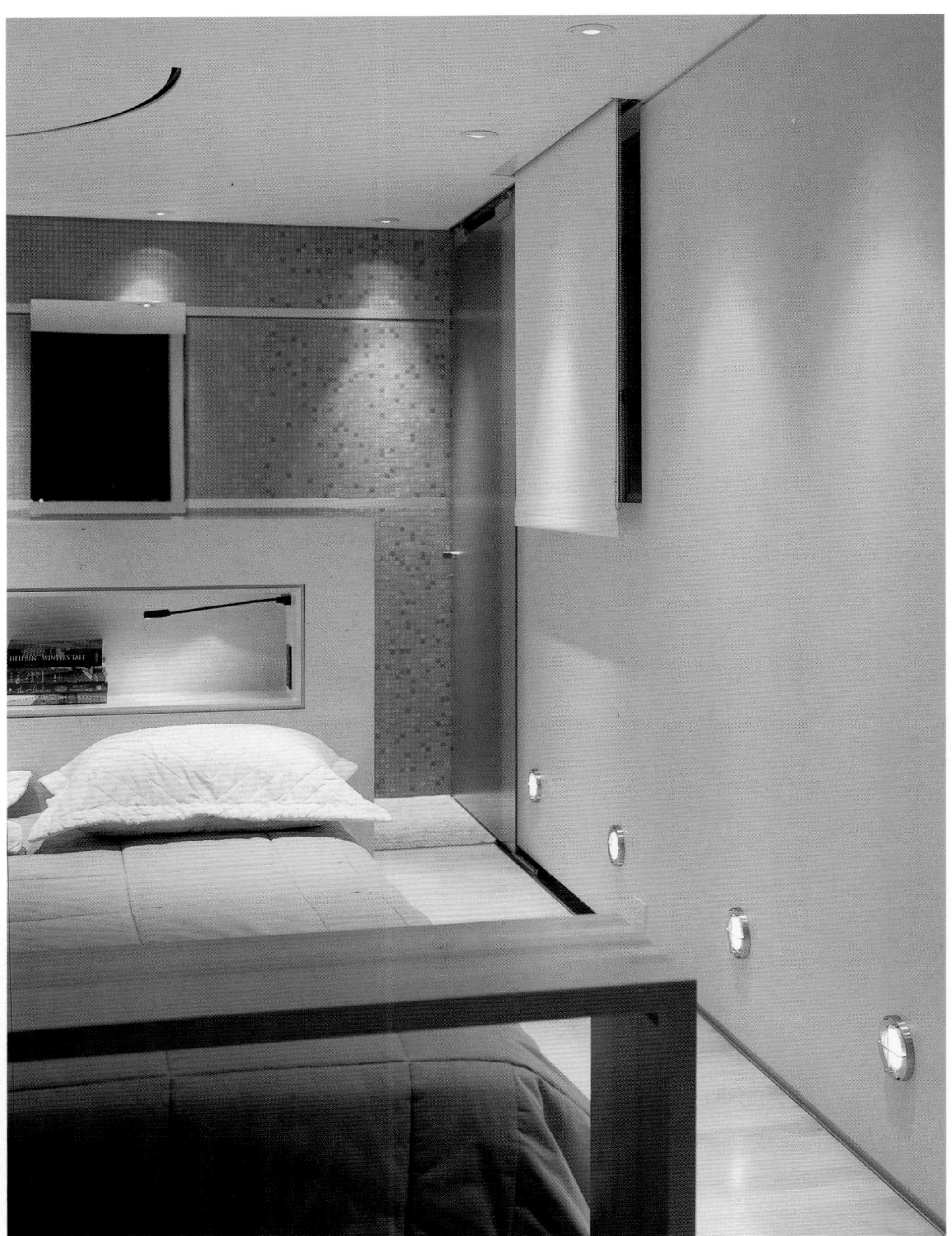

It doesn't need to be complicated! The spare design at right keeps the light—and the overall bedroom look—simple, shapely, and colorful. Matching reading lamps offer bedside task light; a pair of wall sconces adds style and fill light. Fixture shapes and colors are echoed in the wall art.

This minimalist bedroom scheme includes no night table, so it features an articulating reading lamp (with its own switch) housed inside the recessed headboard. Low, wall-recessed lights mark the path from bed to bath; they can be turned on separately for soft fill or to guide a late-night bed-to-bath stroll.

The closets in this basement bedroom are faced with translucent, sliding shoji panels that match an overall Oriental theme—and add soft ambient light. The glowing panels are lit from behind and are washed from the front by downlights fitted with slot apertures.

bathrooms

THE NUMBER ONE TRICK to lighting bathrooms effectively is to provide task light that's gently flattering yet strong enough for grooming. Lights around a mirror used for shaving or applying makeup should spread light over a person's face rather than onto the mirror surface. To avoid heavy shadows, place lights at the sides rather than only at the top of the bathroom mirror.

Popular solutions include theater makeup bars, wall sconces, and tubes mounted vertically. Some mirror units have integral tubes, inset light diffusers, or swing-out makeup mirrors with their own light source. Choose warm-toned tubes or bulbs for accurate makeup light and good skin tones.

Because they are the most energy-efficient choice, fluorescent lights are required for general bathroom lighting in some locales. Indirect sources work well here: consider cove and soffit lighting, translucent diffusers, and other "bounce" lighting to spread a soft, even level of illumination.

Tub, shower, and toilet compartments may need their own light fixtures. Bath and shower lights must be sealed and approved for wet locations. Any light fixture within reach of water should be protected by a GFCI (ground fault circuit interrupter) to prevent electrical shock.

Multiple light sources and multiple controls allow you to alternate between morning efficiency and nighttime serenity. Consider dimmers here. Also plan to provide low-energy night lighting for safety and convenience.

A fluorescent ring surrounds the mirror above a stylish pedestal sink. The fixture supplies even grooming light from all directions.

During daylight hours, decorative glass is a source of discreet ambient light; at night, one wall is washed by a bank of angled downlights with slot apertures. At the mirror, a glareproof frosted wall sconce provides efficient side light for grooming; a downlight fills in from above. The undercounter glow is just for fun.

This master bath features a long vanity with hand-tooled marble top and a matching mirror cabinet broken by flush-mounted, vertical incandescent tubes for even make-up lighting. The backsplash and counter are washed by additional light from the cabinet's bottom edge.

While lighting was kept intentionally spare in the modern bath shown below, it maximizes both task and decorative opportunities. At the mirror, a diffused inset fixture gives just the right amount of makeup light. The lighted niche at right glows with warm fluorescent light that passes through the diffusing panel between open and closed storage areas. Through another opening, the niche glows as a decorative "night-light" for the hallway beyond.

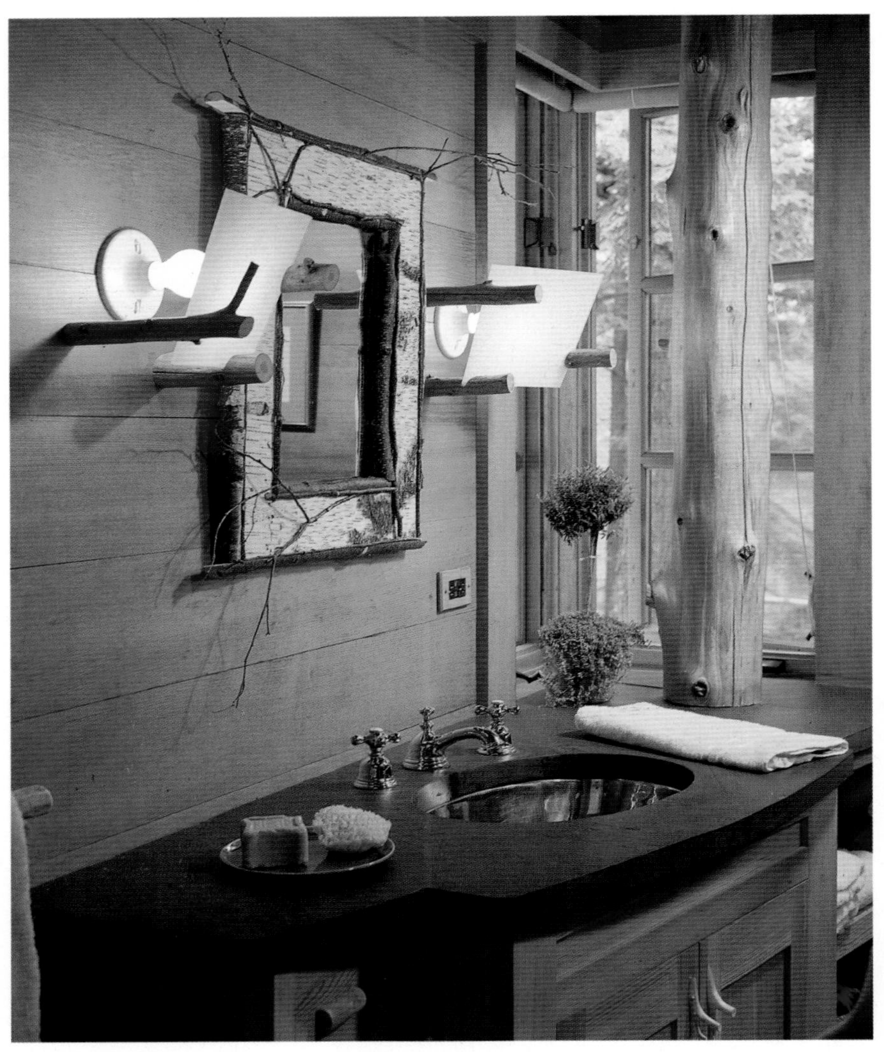

Twin wall sconces flank the chestlike wood mirror frame, providing warm, welcoming grooming light in a small powder room. The glass-block wall passes available light around the windowless space, adding decoration and a mottled, shimmering light.

Workaday, sinkside porcelain wall sockets retain some of their down-home feel but are dressed up and shielded by "lodge-style" twigs supporting translucent diffusers.

A powder room showcases a handpainted pedestal sink, brash black-and-white marble, and—embedded in diamond-shaped floor accents—a decorative flourish of fiber-optic lighting. A garage below yielded a home for the lighting tubes, which shine up through glass inserts in the subfloor.

work spaces

THE FIRST DESIGN RULE for today's home office is this: *don't* make it look like an office. In other words, choose both your interior decor and your light fixtures to complement the surrounding living spaces within your home.

When arranging light fixtures and choosing bulbs, make sure that your work surface will be free of heavy shadows, which can cause eyestrain. By combining diffuse ambient lighting and adjustable task lighting, you can avoid overly strong contrasts between a work area and the rest of a room.

Fluorescent built-ins, wall washers, and wall sconces are effective for fill lighting. A PL-fluorescent or halogen task lamp—or a fixture that combines the two—is effective for close work.

Glare is a potential problem, especially around a computer screen. A screen shade or glare guard can help shield your monitor. Adjust screen illumination to match the room lighting level, and turn up the contrast. It's best if lighting—including natural light—comes from the side; light behind the monitor can cause eyestrain, while light in front can bounce glare off the screen.

Light-colored blotters on dark-finished desks and light-hued walls and ceiling will reflect light back onto your work. But a wall or ceiling that's too bright may throw glare onto your computer screen. One solution: place ambient lights on dimmers, then dial them up or down as needed, depending on the task at hand.

Unlike standard track fixtures, some cable lights can follow curves—in this case, the line of a custom-built desk. A wall sconce creates ambient fill and reinforces the idea that this is a home, not just an office. The little halogen fixture on the desk is primarily decorative.

A rustic home office sports two pharmacy lamps mounted on bookcase walls; recessed downlights with slot apertures; and larger, open-trim downlights and uplights in bookcase soffits.

A dark attic office has a pair of traditional, movable desk lamps to match its impeccable Craftsman detailing. When you need close, shadow-free task light, two sources are better than one.

The lighting here was designed to look "soft," in contrast to the hard, industrial concrete and stone. A low-voltage cable system follows the curve of the desk alcove above floating maple shelves; aluminum louvers control light spill and add style. For ambient fill, the stone wall is grazed by light from a string of reflector lamps hidden inside a light well.

Subtle, multilayered lighting comes to the home office. It begins here with a traditional ceiling fixture, but this one diffuses light for more ambient ceiling bounce and less glare. Strip lights above and below the bookcase illuminate the counter and add a decorative glow on top; downlights over the window shine onto the counter there and wash window coverings. Primary task lighting comes from a tabletop lamp.

When was the last time you saw a laundry room with good lighting? This one has plenty of general light for moving around and seeing inside cabinets, thanks to recessed downlights with diffusing lenses. They're coupled with efficient fluorescent undercabinet task lighting.

You wouldn't call this just a home office. For starters, there's the eye-popping ceiling pendant—and then there's accent light from inside the glass-fronted cabinets and from tracks partly hidden by a ceiling valance. A compact lamp takes over for desktop tasks.

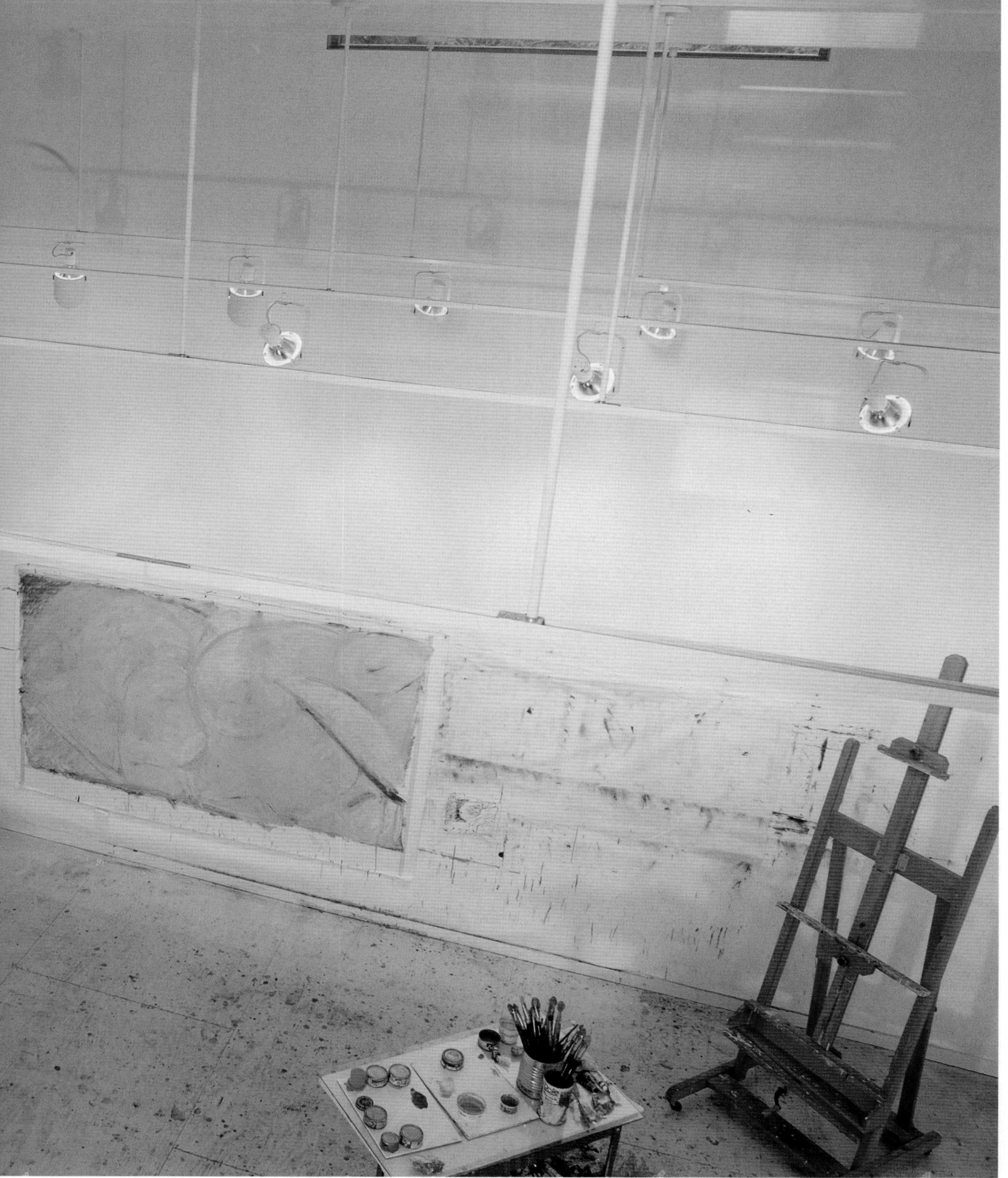

How do you light a tall, open studio space? One way is to effectively lower the ceiling by lowering the fixtures—in this case, sturdy traditional tracks suspended from vertical feeds off overhead ceiling boxes.

outdoor ideas

Safety and security are the starting points for outdoor lighting schemes, but new designs fold these into subtle, decorative landscaping plans. Glare and harsh point sources are outdoor bugaboos. Be sure that light sources are shielded; it's best if they're not seen at all. Multiple light sources are much better than a single glaring flood or clear-glass point source. Basic techniques for successful outdoor lighting are outlined on pages 148–151.

Driveways—especially if they're long and wooded—should have some kind of low, soft lights to define their boundaries. The garage area needs security lighting, preferably controlled by switches both inside and out. Motion-sensitive fixtures mounted on a garage are also useful; for details, see page 250.

Viewed through the open gate, this inviting entry corridor has equally inviting lighting. Shielded eye-level lights shine both up and down off arbor and stone columns, while arbor eaves house uplighting and some well-placed downlights. At the far end, the interior entry light glows warmly through decorative glass doors.

Garden path lights can be garden decor, too—day or night. This fixture has a handblown glass shade "flower" and a patinaed copper "stem."

Front walks and steps are easiest to light if their surfaces are a light, reflective color. Low fixtures that spread soft pools of light can guide guests and at the same time highlight your garden's virtues along the walkway. If your house has deep eaves or an overhang that extends the length of your walk, consider installing weatherproof downlights. Even single steps should be illuminated if they're any distance from the door.

At the front door, you'll want light to serve several purposes. Besides illuminating your house number and welcoming guests, it should provide sufficient brightness for you to see a caller's face. If you choose decorative fixtures of clear glass at the front door, keep low-wattage bulbs in them to avoid uncomfortable brightness.

(Continued on page 208)

On decks and patios, a low level of light is often enough for quiet conversation or alfresco dining. By lighting steps, railings, or benches from underneath—or directly, with strip lights—you can outline the edges of your structure for safety. Don't forget to add stronger light wherever you do your serving or barbecuing. Downlights are a popular choice for this, but indirect lighting—diffused through plastic or another translucent material—is also useful.

Light swimming pools and spas for safety and also to make them attractive from inside the house. To avoid glare off the water, consider putting pool lights on a dimmer. For relaxing and entertaining, all the light that's needed is a soft glow to outline the water's edges, but the light should be at full brightness when children are swimming. A spa or garden pool can be illuminated with low-voltage strip lights that will subtly outline its perimeter or steps. Water and electricity don't mix—when planning these systems, it's best to get professional help.

Uplighting, downlighting, and backlighting (see pages 138–139) are all effective ways to light foliage. Decorative mini-lights lend sparkle to trees, shrubs, and outdoor structures. Be aware that plant species and type (deciduous or evergreen) will affect the spread of light. Translucent foliage transmits light; dense leaves drink it up. And keep in mind that unless you prune regularly, your lighting effects will change significantly as plantings mature. Conversely, fixture and bulb spread can dramatically alter landscaping effects; so can the use of colored filters.

Here's an easy and subtle way to add night light to a patio fence: a hollow wood sleeve with a low-voltage light built into the top. The unit slips over any tall 4-by-4 post, leaving enough room for the power cord.

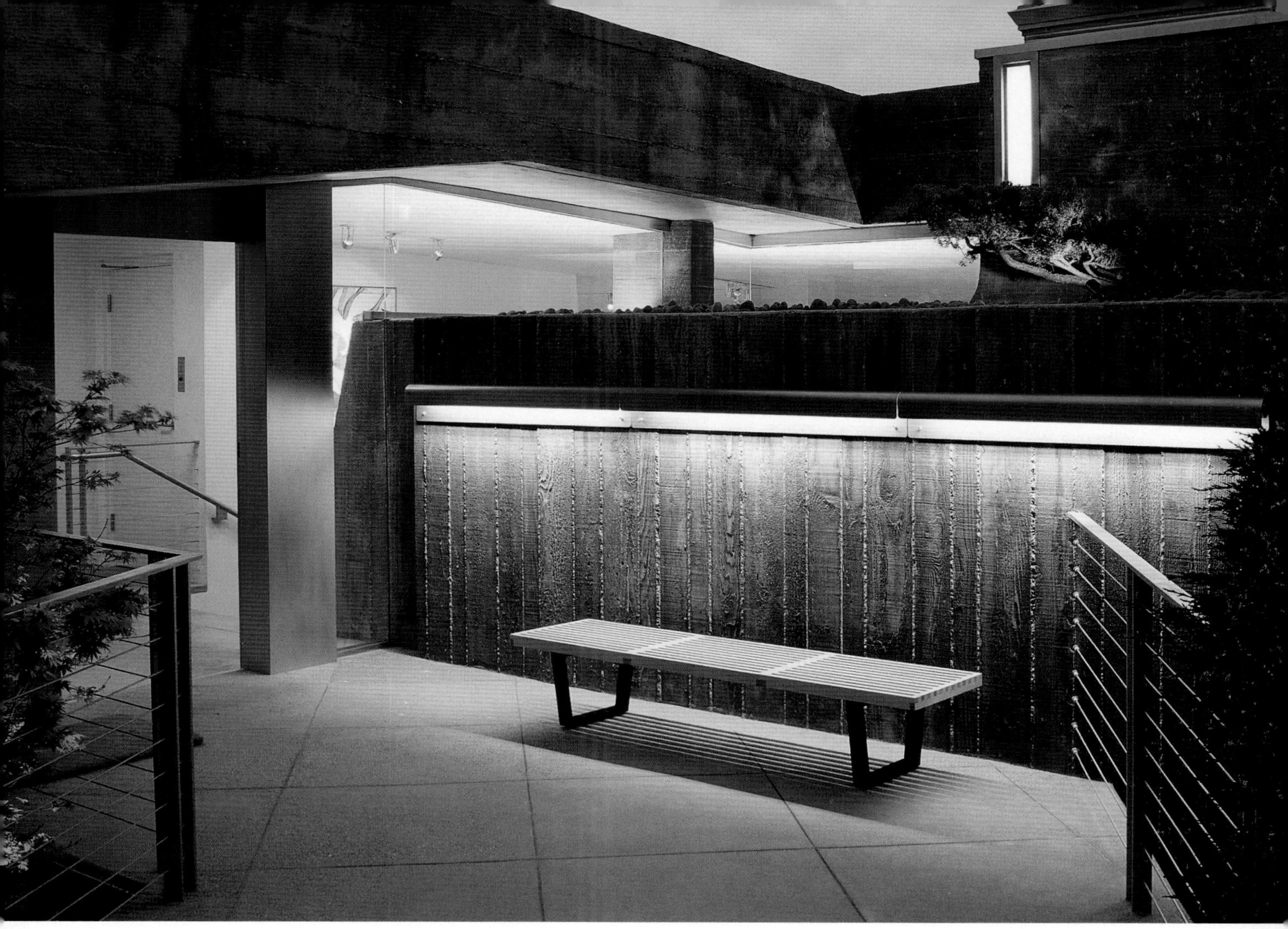

The house itself can be a glowing light source, both decorative and welcoming. This translucent overhead marks the front entry; it's lit by wall-mounted downlights from above, casting a warm glow across the entry deck below.

A long, shielded fluorescent fixture safely lights the entry walkway while highlighting a garden bench and the rough concrete wall behind. Large windows and skylights add light from inside the house.

A wide-open house plan that intentionally bridges inside and outside living areas calls for good outdoor lighting, too. Living-space lighting here features efficient monospots and floor lamps. Outside the telescoping French doors, a sitting area is highlighted by crisp halogen downlighting and accented, for fun, with low-voltage rope lights tied to the copper-clad arbor.

Outdoor grazing highlights stone and wood textures here, adding ambient light and minimizing glare. Post-mounted arbor lights shine both up and down but are shielded at eye level.

In a whimsically splayed lineup, classic candle lanterns tilt to and fro along winding garden steps; they're both functional and festive.

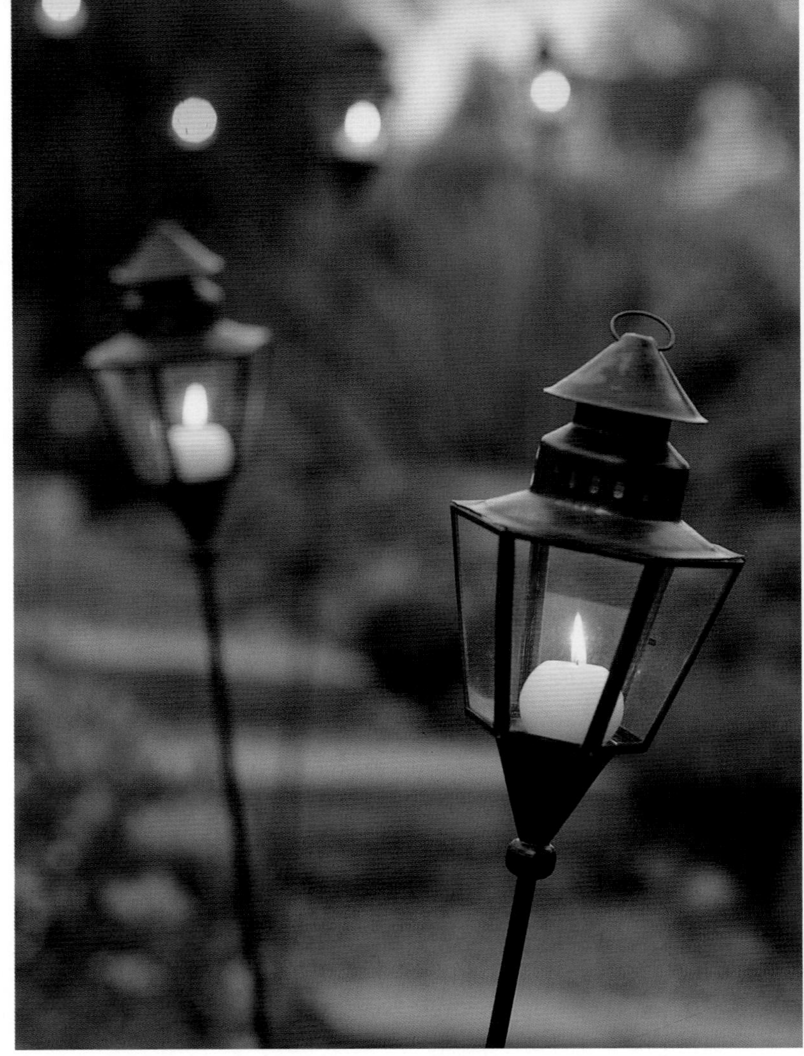

Special occasions such as holidays or outdoor parties may call for temporary lighting. Classic Mexican luminarias—open paper bags that contain votive candles set in sand—have now been electrified. A broad range of lanterns is also available, from hurricane lamps that burn oil to glass-sided lanterns that house candles.

Path lights to mark direction and distance at night can look great, too—witness the unusual fixtures above. Choose between bold, bright standard-voltage fixtures and smaller, low-voltage options; the latter can be repositioned until you get things just right.

This octagonal umbrella casts cooling shade by day and warm, reflected light by night. Four bulbs nestle at the top of the center pole, bouncing a soft glow off the umbrella and back down below.

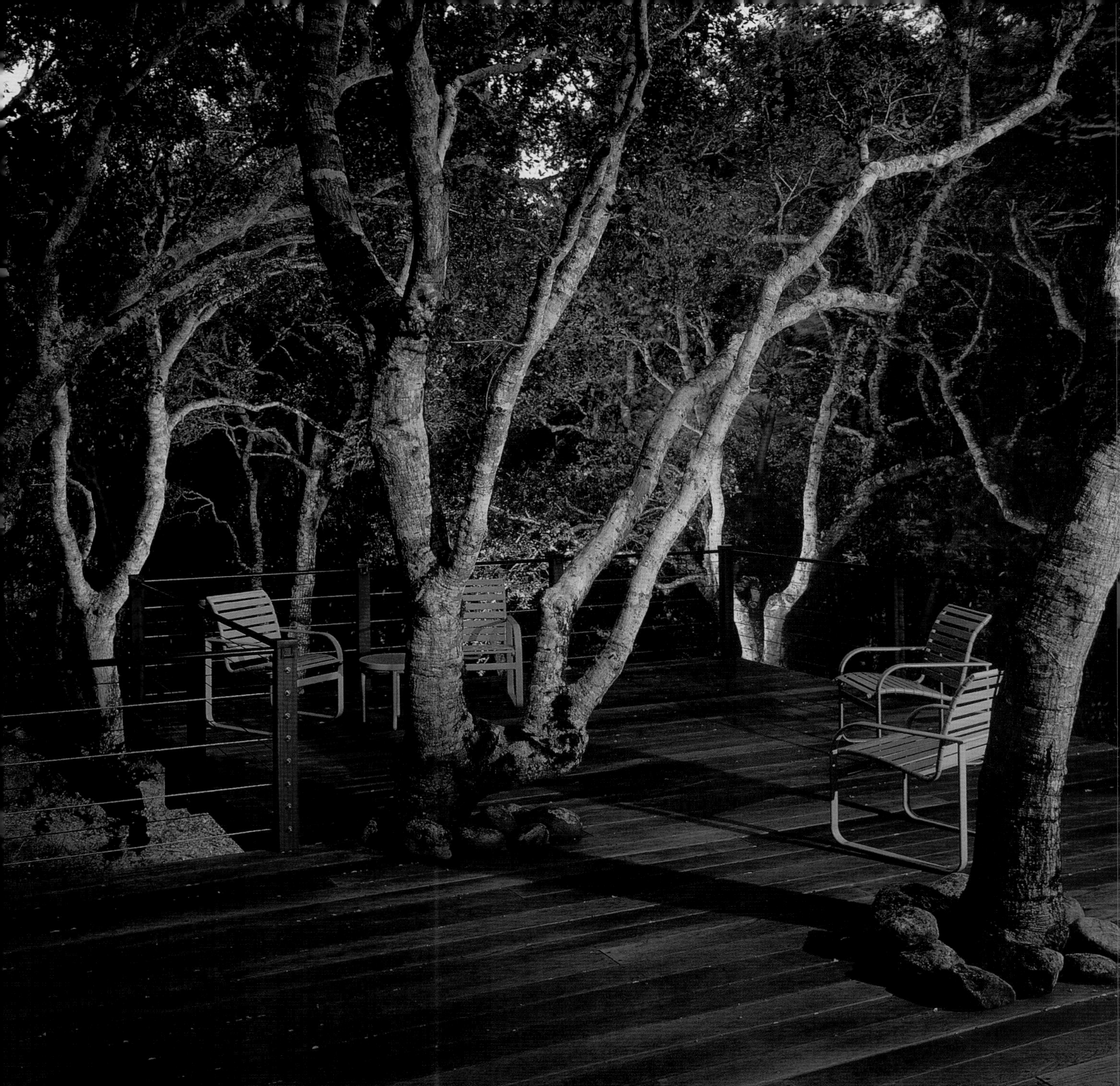

At night, the view ends where the light ends, but this forest of oaks and madrones presents a multilayered drama, thanks to careful fixture placement. The 150-watt, standard-voltage uplights are mounted to deck fascias; softer downlights for foot traffic are attached to house siding and fitted with glare-reducing louvers. The strong light penetrates tinted windows, allowing the owners to view the trees from inside the house.

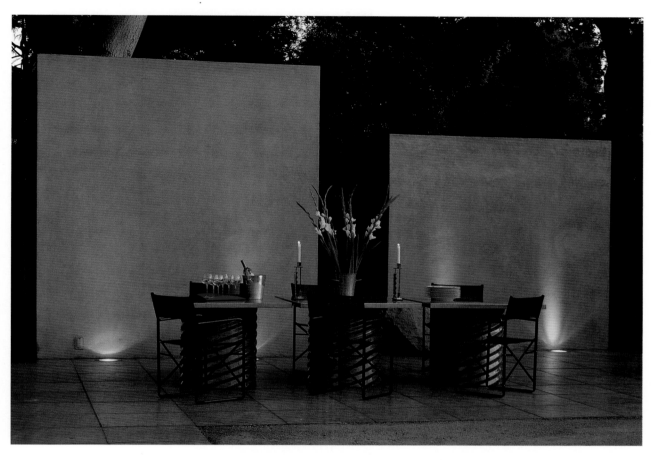

Recessed, sealed well lights graze colorful concrete walls, forming a soft, textured backdrop for alfresco dining. Candles add their warm, decorative glow atop the table.

The homeowners stretched their indoor space by fashioning this outdoor "living room," complete with a lighting scheme that echoes indoor lighting. Fluorescent wall sconces provide ambient light; plantings are accented with buried halogen uplights. Each colorful tile cube is backlit by its own step light; safety lights mark stair risers. Pool and waterfall are highlighted by two submersible pool lights.

This naturalistic garden pond features a combination of subtle light sources. Uplights tucked into rocks accent water plants, while submerged pool lights create the water's glow and show off the waterfall shelf.

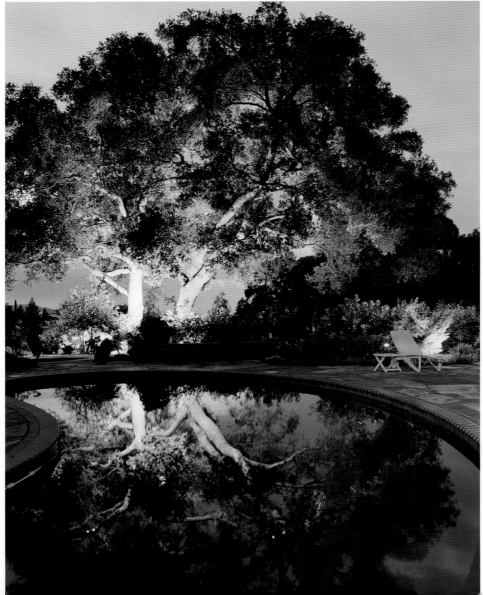

Punchy uplights accent massive oaks, reflected in a quiet, shimmering swimming pool; other discreet fixtures paint surrounding plantings. The pool should have its own lights, separately controlled, for safe swimming.

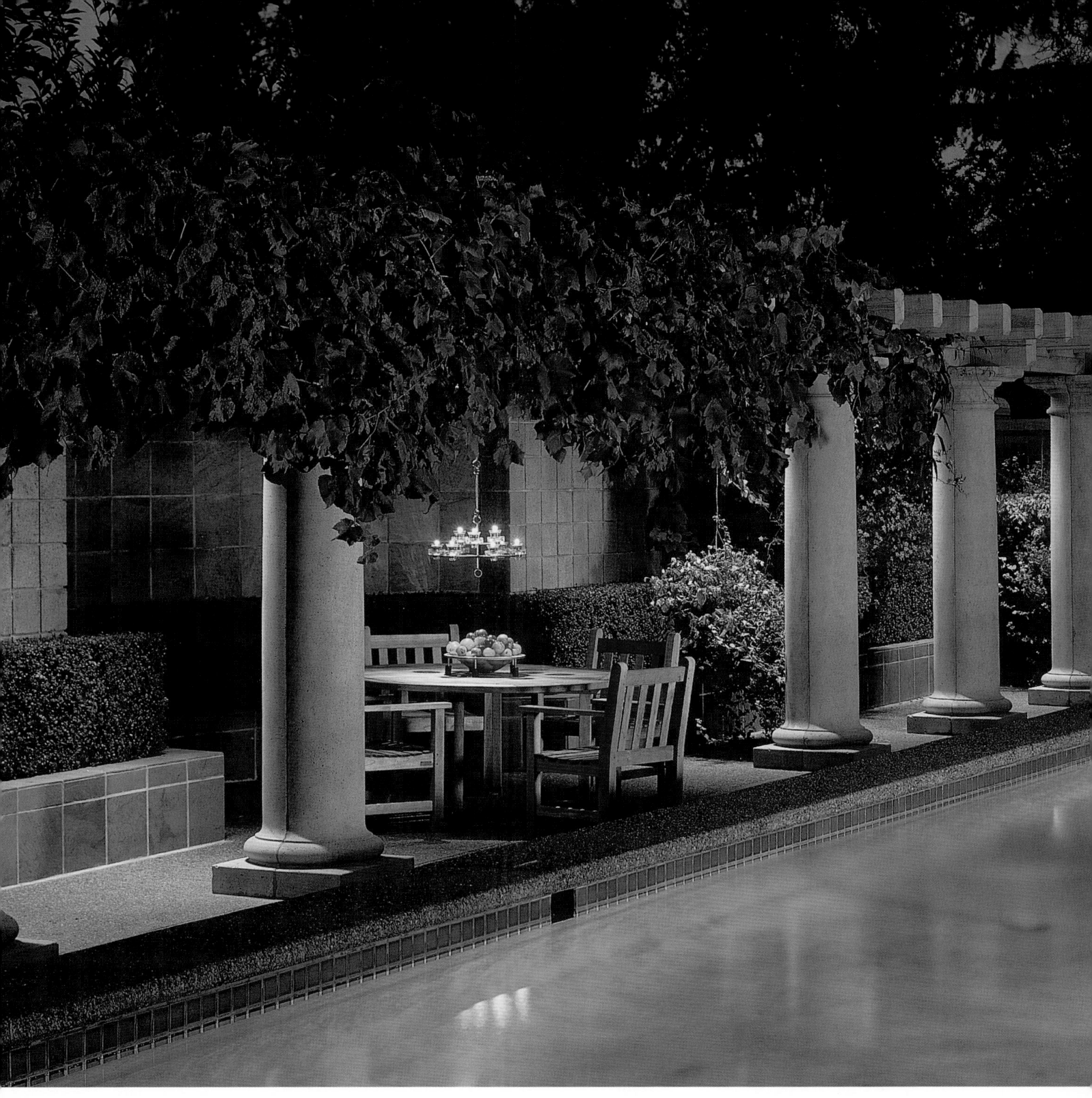

A classical poolside loggia is ready for a quiet summer evening's repose. Above the dining table, a hanging candelabra with votive candles produces a soft glow; it's augmented with a central downlight above. Accent light comes from 75-watt reflector bulbs housed in arbor-mounted downlights; two flank the back of each column, backlighting them dramatically. The water's glow is the result of two wall-mounted pool fixtures.

A SHOPPER'S GUIDE

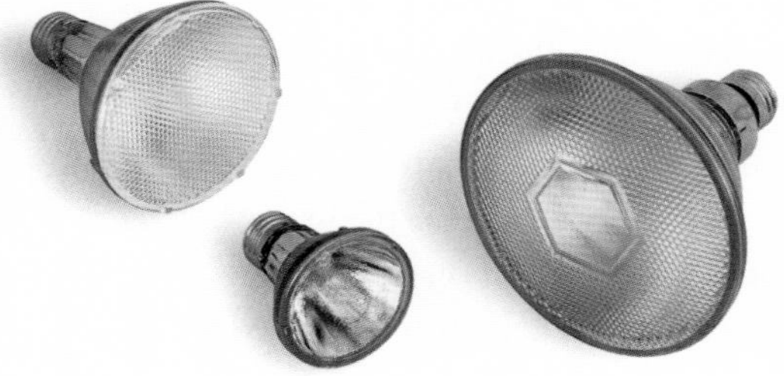

You've seen what great lighting can do. Now it's time to take a closer look at the hardware that makes it happen. Some devices stay quietly in the background, while some just beg to be noticed. Bulbs come first, then the fixtures that house them and shape the light. Controls—a catchall phrase for a slew of switches, dimmers, and timers—are also a big part of today's flexible schemes. **And lighting technology** doesn't stop indoors. For gardens, patios, and pools, choose from punchy 120-volt or sparkling low-voltage effects. Outdoor controls like photocells, timers, and motion sensors add both convenience and security. **Where do you get** all these products? Increasingly, you'll find a sizable selection at home improvement centers; for outdoor products, check garden centers and landscape suppliers. Lighting showrooms and "light labs" handle the zoomier styles and let you see your options in action. Lighting professionals and electricians can help with the fine points, such as low-voltage logistics, wiring practicalities, high-end controls, and "smart-house" strategies.

Incandescent Bulbs

THE OLD STANDBYS

Incandescent light, the kind we're most familiar with, is produced by a tungsten filament that burns slowly inside a glass bulb (shown on page 144). Incandescent light has a warm, comfortable glow that gets even warmer when it's dimmed.

Incandescent bulbs are inexpensive and easy to find; they fit a wide variety of fixture types and styles. They're also easy to dim using standard dimmers (see page 244).

On the minus side, incandescent is the least energy-efficient light source now available, and it tends not to last as long as other sources. For a closer look at how various light types stack up, see "Bulb Comparisons at a Glance" on pages 228–229.

A-BULBS are the old incandescent standbys; they actually date back to the 1800s. As shown below, A-bulbs come in clear, frosted, and colored versions (including skin-flattering pink and a new blue-coated "daylight" bulb). The light emitted from an A-bulb spreads in all directions—it's the fixture or shade that shapes the light.

A-bulb sizes include A15, A17, A19, A21, and A23. (For a translation, see "Speaking in Code" on the facing page.) Common wattages range from 15 to 250 watts.

R-BULB

Three-way bulbs, which fit special floor and table lamps, have twin filaments that combine to produce switchable spreads from 30/70/100 to 100/200/300 watts.

R (REFLECTOR) BULBS brought directional accent lighting to the residential scene when they were first introduced in the 1950s. Internal aluminized reflectors allowed them to project light forward, paving the way for two now-classic fixtures: tracks and recessed downlights. By today's standards, though, R-bulbs are big and bulky; more important, they're now considered energy hogs—so much so that they're being phased out. The similarly shaped PAR bulb is generally much more efficient, and while there are incandescent PAR bulbs out there, most are now halogen (for details, see page 225).

A-BULBS

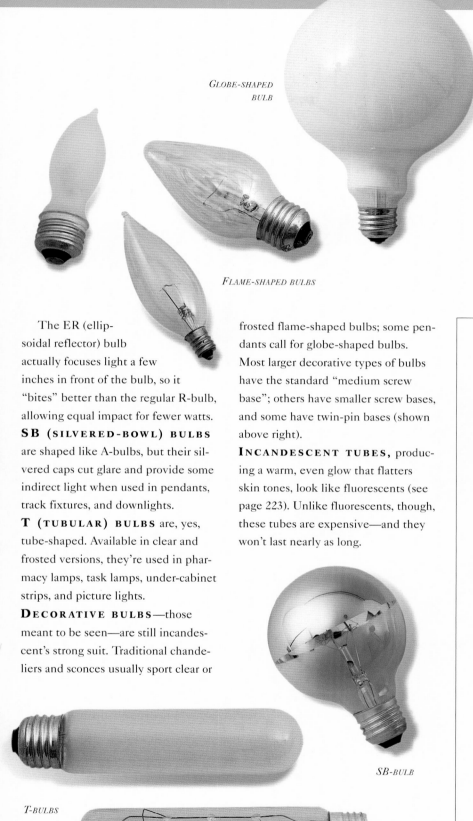

Globe-shaped bulb

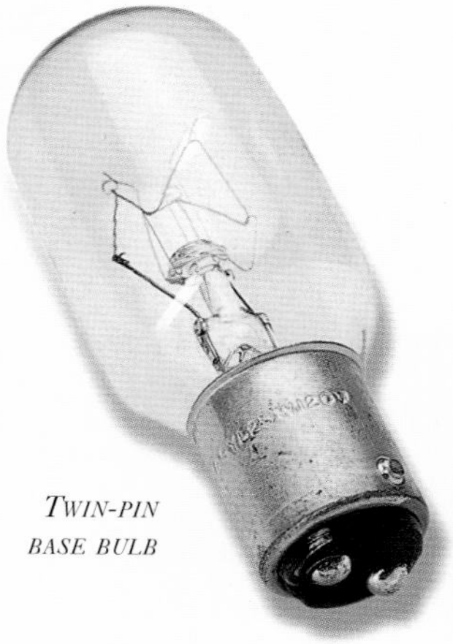

Twin-pin base bulb

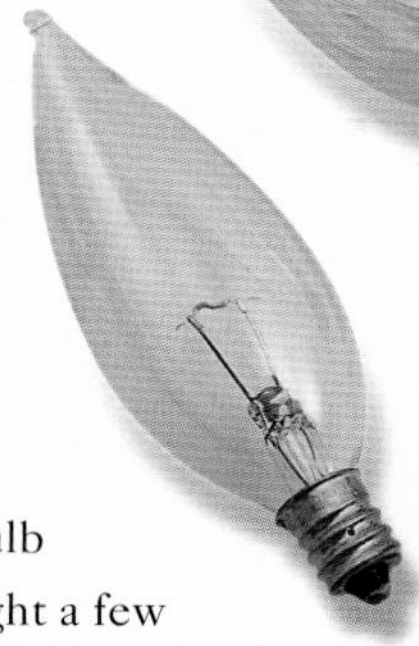

Flame-shaped bulbs

The ER (ellipsoidal reflector) bulb actually focuses light a few inches in front of the bulb, so it "bites" better than the regular R-bulb, allowing equal impact for fewer watts.

SB (silvered-bowl) bulbs are shaped like A-bulbs, but their silvered caps cut glare and provide some indirect light when used in pendants, track fixtures, and downlights.

T (tubular) bulbs are, yes, tube-shaped. Available in clear and frosted versions, they're used in pharmacy lamps, task lamps, under-cabinet strips, and picture lights.

Decorative bulbs—those meant to be seen—are still incandescent's strong suit. Traditional chandeliers and sconces usually sport clear or frosted flame-shaped bulbs; some pendants call for globe-shaped bulbs. Most larger decorative types of bulbs have the standard "medium screw base"; others have smaller screw bases, and some have twin-pin bases (shown above right).

Incandescent tubes, producing a warm, even glow that flatters skin tones, look like fluorescents (see page 223). Unlike fluorescents, though, these tubes are expensive—and they won't last nearly as long.

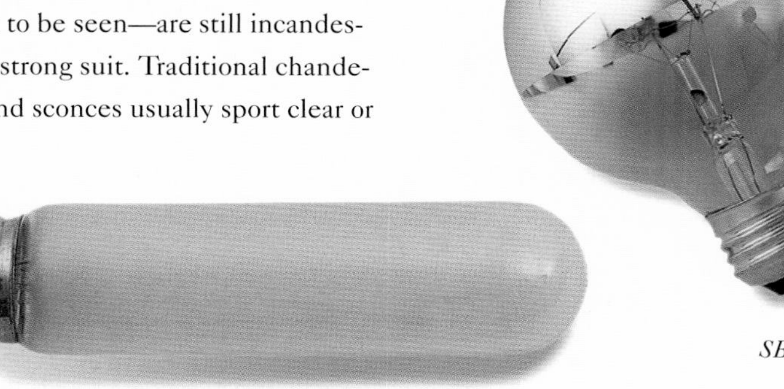

SB-bulb

T-bulbs

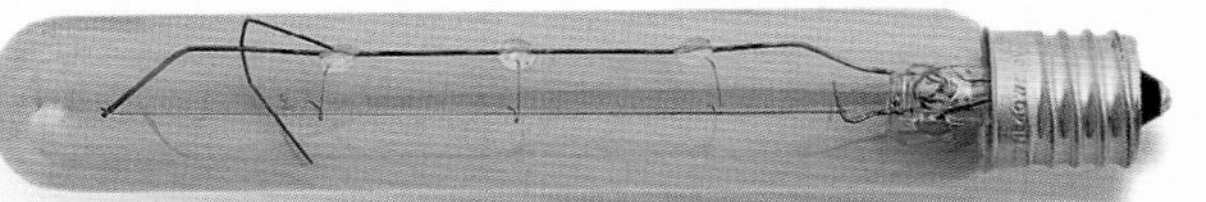

Speaking in Code

Light bulbs are sometimes identified with a terse numbering system that seems obscure, but it's actually simple to crack. Here's an example:

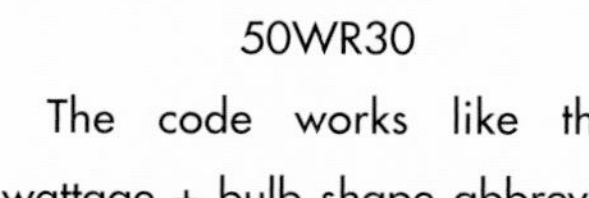

50WR30

The code works like this: wattage + bulb shape abbreviation + diameter. In this case, it's a 50-watt R-bulb that's $\frac{30}{8}$ inches in diameter.

It's $\frac{30}{8}$ inches in diameter? Yes, the numbers given for size are in $\frac{1}{8}$-inch increments, so a size 30 is about $3\frac{3}{4}$ inches across. An A19 A-bulb measures about $2\frac{3}{8}$ inches across.

Sometimes a code for beam spread or pattern is tagged onto the end. If the listing says "50WR30FL," the FL stands for "flood." VNSP means "very narrow spot."

Fluorescent Tubes and Bulbs

GREAT NEW SHAPES AND COLORS

Though renowned for both energy efficiency and long life, fluorescent light still got no respect—until recently.

Early fluorescents were notorious for hum, flicker, and unpleasant color rendering. Better fixtures and fixture ballasts (integral voltage regulators) have largely remedied the first two problems; new tube technology has vastly expanded color options. And while fixture designs for traditional tubes are still limited, new compact fluorescent bulbs are impacting fixture styling.

Fluorescents diffuse light evenly in all directions, so they're great for broad, ambient light or for close-at-hand tasks. Cool operating temperatures and long life make them excellent for hard-to-vent, hard-to-reach soffits, coves, and other architectural built-ins. Fluorescents won't, however, provide much accent punch. And they're trickier to dim than both halogen (see pages 224–225) and incandescent, requiring a dimmable fixture ballast and a matching fluorescent dimmer.

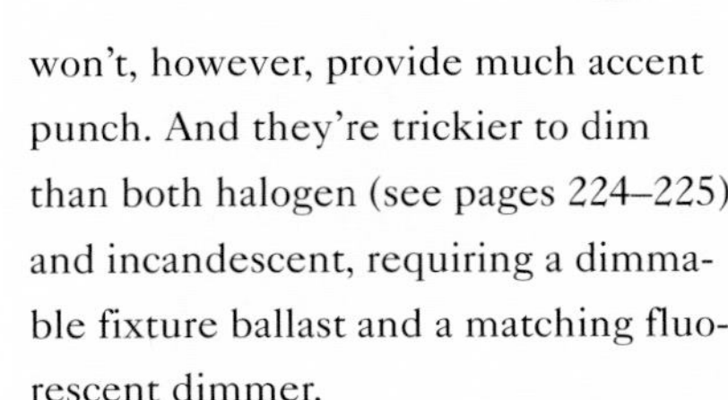

Compact fluorescents

Fluorescent tubes (pictured on facing page) come in four basic diameters: T-2, T-5, T-8, and T-12. Remember that bulb/tube diameters are usually specified in ⅛-inch increments; thus the popular T-12 size is about 1½ inches across. Tubes commonly come in lengths from about 12 inches to 6 feet. You'll need to buy the right pin configuration for your fixture: for example, single-pin, recessed pin, or twin-pin, as shown on the facing page. You'll also need to match the tube to your fixture's ballast—either preheat or rapid-start.

Besides energy-conscious improvements to fluorescent tubes (especially in the T-8 size), the big news is color temperature. Once limited basically to cool white or warm white, fluorescents now come in a dizzying spectrum of colors from very warm (2,700°K) to distinctly cool (6,300°K)—allowing you to match other lights and to choose the effect that suits your taste

COMPARING ENERGY REQUIREMENTS

Incandescent Bulbs (watts)	Compact Fluorescents (watts)
40	10
60	15
75	20
100	25

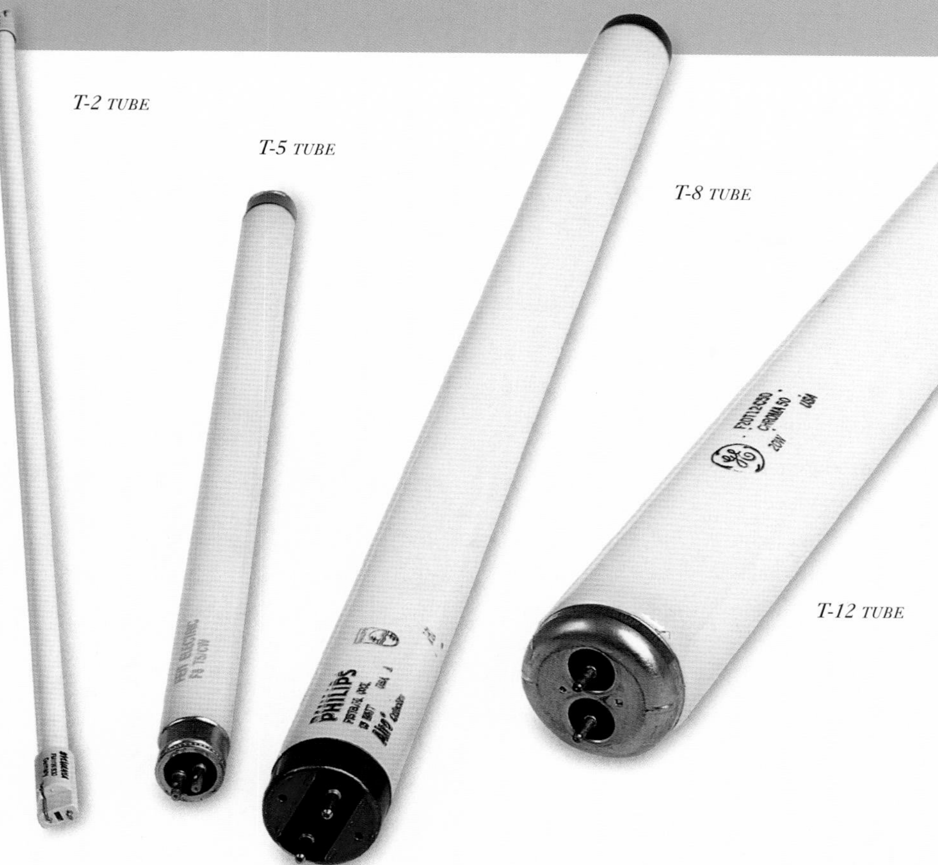

T-2 TUBE

T-5 TUBE

T-8 TUBE

T-12 TUBE

and your decor. For a closer look at the color spectrum, see pages 140–141. **PL-FLUORESCENTS** look like small traditional tubes that have been bent back on themselves, allowing fluorescent light to be used in smaller, trimmer fixtures—recessed downlights, for instance. PL-fluorescents come in both twin-tube and quad-tube versions, in a variety of wattages and color temperatures.

PL-FLUORESCENTS

CIRCLINE TUBE

CIRCLINE TUBES fit rounded ceiling fixtures and pendants, providing an energy-efficient, ambient alternative to incandescent A-bulbs. Older circline tubes had pin connections, but newer versions screw right into standard light sockets. The circline tube shown above is suitable for any fixture big enough to accept it.

COMPACT FLUORESCENTS (CFLs) directly replace incandescent A-bulbs: they have built-in ballasts and screw bases, so you simply screw a CFL's medium-size base into a standard fixture socket. Some CFLs resemble ordinary A-bulbs or globes; others have exposed tubes bent into a U shape or a coil. CFLs may be too big for some ceiling fixtures. For these, you can use the flatter circline tube.

The table on the facing page shows the energy requirements (watts) of incandescent bulbs and CFLs that produce comparable brightness (usually expressed in lumens). CFLs produce 40 to 60 lumens per watt compared with 8 to 18 lumens for incandescent bulbs.

Halogen Bulbs

BRIGHT WHITE LIGHT

Quartz halogen bulbs, also called tungsten, contain a halogen gas that produces a brighter, whiter beam than other light sources. This recipe also enables halogen bulbs to dramatically outlast their incandescent cousins. Though they don't rival fluorescents for longevity, halogens are unmatched for intensive task lighting, pinpoint accenting, and other dramatic effects. Often they are low voltage, but some halogens use standard line current.

Is there a down side? A halogen bulb gets very hot, and it must be used in fixtures specifically designed and approved for it. The bulbs can be pricey and awkward to handle (see sidebar, facing page), and specialized bulbs used in some fixtures can be hard to find. And even though halogen bulbs burn "white" at full throttle, they still turn a warmish yellow, like incandescents, when dimmed.

MR-16 BULB

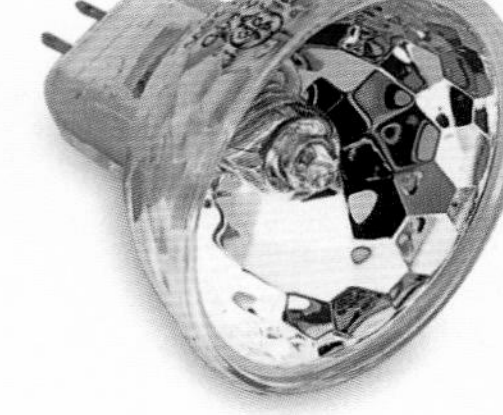

MR-11 BULB

MR-16 AND MR-11 (MULTI-REFLECTOR) BULBS create the tightest beams. Originally made for movie projectors, these tiny bulbs journeyed to residential use via museum and display lighting, allowing fixture sizes to shrink dramatically. These halogens are used extensively in today's discreet low-voltage downlights, low-voltage tracks, modern pendants, and whimsical cable lights.

MR-16 and MR-11 bulbs come in a wattage range from 20 to 75 and also in a broad spread of beam patterns, including very narrow spot, narrow spot, narrow flood, flood, and wide flood.

Perhaps in a nod to their original use, these bulbs tend to be given their own three-letter abbreviation system instead of the standard wattage/shape/size/spread code of other bulbs. For example, an EZX bulb is a 20-watt MR-16 with a 7-degree spot pattern. The same bulb with a 40-degree flood pattern is called a BAB!

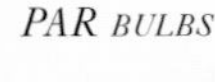

PAR BULBS

Halogen specialty bulbs

Handling Halogens

The oils on our hands don't agree with the coatings on halogen bulbs, so it's important to not touch these bulbs directly. Dirty bulbs can crack—or even explode!

Instead, grip new halogen bulbs gently with gloves or a clean rag while installing them. If you do come in contact with the glass, try cleaning the spot with alcohol. Remember that halogen burns very hot, so use care when replacing a newly blown bulb.

PAR (parabolic aluminized reflector) bulbs are bigger and punchier than MR-16s; choose them when you need a longer reach and wider coverage. Sizes range from PAR-20 to PAR-38 and wattages from 35 to 250. The large sweep in available wattage reflects the fact that some PAR bulbs are low voltage, while other, larger ones are standard line voltage. The popular PAR-36 bulbs are low voltage only, while PAR-38s are standard voltage.

Like MR-11s and MR-16s, PAR bulbs come in a variety of beam patterns, from very narrow spot through very wide flood. Oblong- or ovoid-shaped patterns are also available.

Some PAR bulbs, particularly low-voltage PAR-36 bulbs, can produce a hum—especially when dimmed. One solution is to install low-voltage fixtures with remote external rather than integral transformers (see page 241) and place the transformers outside the actual living space.

Halogen specialty bulbs, from tube shapes to tiny Christmas lights, complete a host of halogen fixtures from torchères and pendants to high-intensity task lamps and under-cabinet strips. Heat buildup can be a problem here, so be sure to use the exact bulb specified for the fixture.

Xenon bulbs are new, cooler-burning spin-offs of halogen. Their tiny size and extra-long life span make them naturals for strip-light applications (see pages 236-237). They're great for small, recessed display lights and under-cabinet task fixtures. Also look for xenon in hard-to-reach built-ins such as coves and soffits.

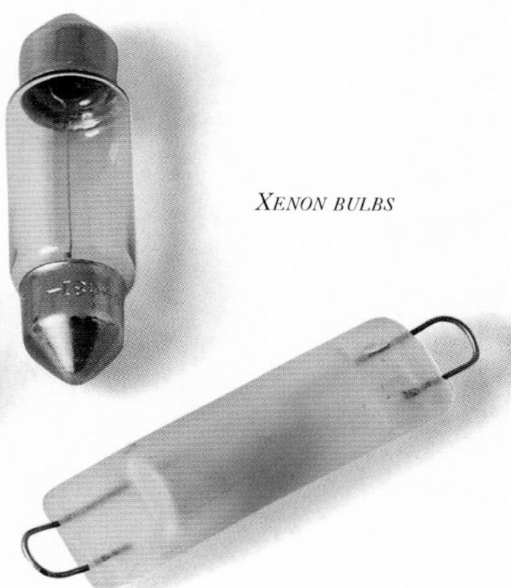

Xenon bulbs

Specialty Sources

PART ART, PART INDUSTRY

Though incandescents, fluorescents, and halogen bulbs are the workhorses of home lighting, several other light sources are gaining a foothold, too. Some, like neon and HID, have been around for a while; others, notably fiber optics, are up-and-coming stars. Look for improved, updated versions of all these sources in the coming years.

Neon

This zoomy light source, bringing to mind 1950s casino and bar signs, is generated when electricity passes through a gas. Neon gas, to be specific, glows orange-red (other gases give off a variety of colors). Neon's low light output makes it undesirable as a functional light source, but it can be bent into all sorts of decorative, sculptural shapes.

Requiring a 24-volt transformer, neon fixtures can be expensive to buy, though they don't use much energy and may last for years. Newer transformers have reduced the sometimes objectionable buzz emitted from older neon sources.

Neon for home lighting is sold primarily as freestanding pieces through individual artisans or lighting showrooms.

Cold cathode

Long-lasting cold cathode shines in contoured, confined quarters where other sources fear to tread. Its typical white light is brighter than neon, making it more useful for ambient lighting, and its custom-shaping capability offers decorative flourish.

Cold cathode is often the high-end light of choice for indirect, architectural use and for inaccessible coves and valances where changing shorter-lived bulbs or tubes presents a major challenge.

Think of it as fluorescent that can follow a curve.

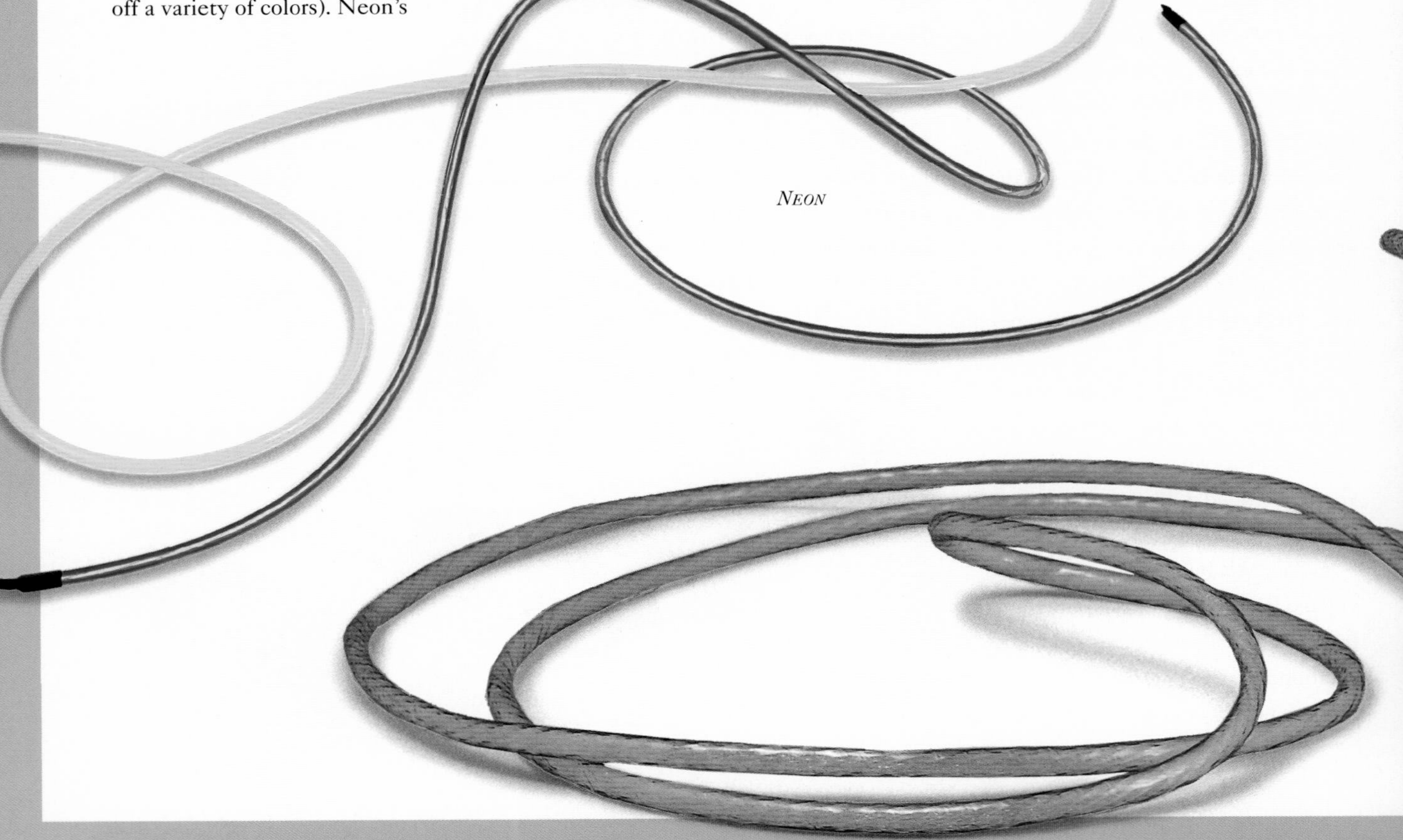

Neon

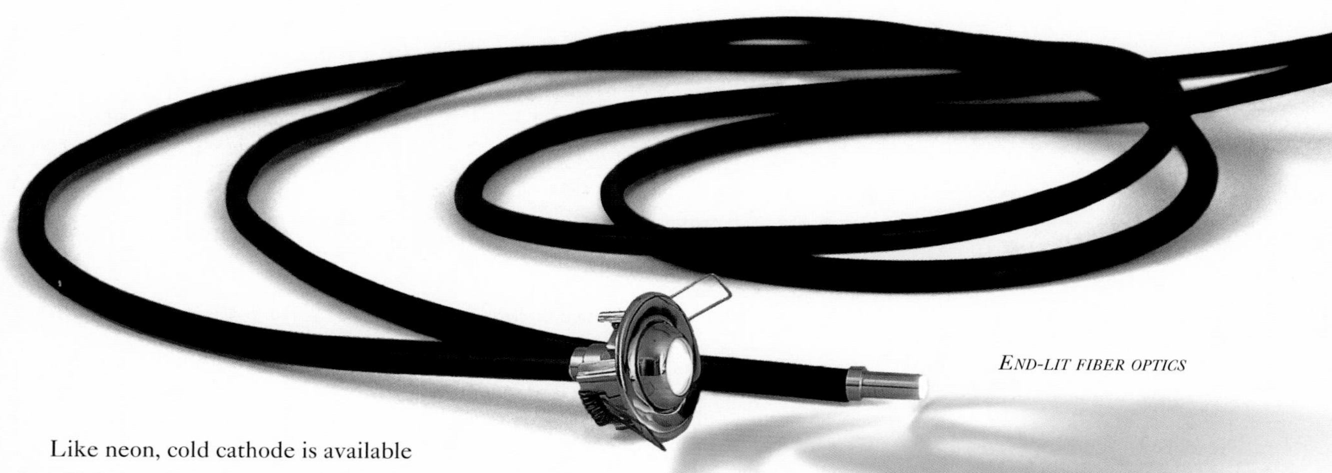

End-lit fiber optics

Like neon, cold cathode is available from lighting showrooms and lighting designers.

Fiber optics

Really a vehicle rather than a light source, fiber optics carry light or other media (such as data signals) as if through a tunnel. Put a light source such as halogen or metal halide at one end, and the glass or plastic fiber tubing will beam it efficiently toward the other. End-lit fiber optics shine bright light out the end of opaque fiber cable; edge-lit versions shine all the way along transparent tubing. On one hand, fiber optics function as a decorative alternative to neon or cold cathode, following contoured shapes at will. Unlike neon or cold cathode, however, fiber optics will transmit any color, by shining the light through colored filters. Fiber optics excel in several other ways, too: the end-lit fiber cable can go places ordinary electrical cable can't, and it can be covered over; and because there's no electrical current passing through the cable itself, it's a natural to use around water, indoors and out.

On the down side, fiber optics are still quite expensive, and they can be tricky to connect.

Cold cathode

Edge-lit fiber optics

Bulb Comparisons at a Glance

INCANDESCENT	Description	Common Wattages	Efficiency (lumens per watt)
A-bulb	Familiar pear shape; frosted or clear.	15 to 250	13.5 to 18.5
Three-way	A-bulb shape; frosted; two filaments provide three light levels.	30/70/100 to 100/200/300	10 to 15
T—Tubular	Tube-shaped, from 5" long. Frosted or clear.	15 to 40	7.5 to 10
R—Reflector	White or silvered coating directs light out end of funnel-shaped bulb.	30 to 120	8 to 12.5
Silvered bowl	Same shape as A-bulb, with silvered cap to cut glare and produce indirect light.	25 to 60	8
G—Globe	Ball-shaped bulb, 2" to 6" in diameter; frosted or clear.	25 to 100	6 to 12
Flame-shaped (candle)	Decorative; specially coated; frosted or clear.	15 to 60	8 to 11
FLUORESCENT			
Tube	Tube-shaped, 5" to 96" long. Needs special fixture and ballast.	8 to 95	35 to 48
PL—Compact tube	U-shaped with base; 5¼" to 7½" long.	7 to 27	70 to 78
Circline	Circular, 6" to 16" in diameter; may replace A-bulbs or require special fixtures.	22 to 40	50 to 66
Compact bulb	Many shapes and sizes, replacing incandescent bulbs without needing special sockets.	11 to 42	41 to 58
QUARTZ HALOGEN			
Low-voltage MR-16 (mini-reflector)	Tiny (2" diameter) projector bulb; gives small circle of light from a distance.	20 to 75	14 to 19
PAR—Parabolic aluminized reflector	Similar to auto headlamps; special shape and coating project light and control beam.	50 to 120	8 to 13
Specialty	Small, clear bulb with consistently high light output; used in halogen fixtures only.	50 to 500	18 to 22
HIGH-INTENSITY DISCHARGE (HID)			
Mercury vapor	Bulb-within-a-bulb, shaped like an oversize A-bulb; needs special ballast.	100 to 250	63
Metal halide	Almost twice as efficient as old mercury vapor; needs special ballast and fixture.	175 to 400	71 to 100
High-pressure sodium	Orange-hued light; needs special ballast and fixture.	50 to 400	64 to 95

Color Temperature (K)	Bulb Life (hours)
2,800	750 to 2,500
2,800	1,000 to 1,600
2,800	1,000 to 1,500
2,800	1,000 to 2,000
2,700 to 3,000	1,000
2,800	1,500 to 2,500
2,800	1,500
2,700 to 6,300	7,500 to 20,000
2,700 to 6,300	9,000 to 10,000
2,700 to 4,200	12,000
2,700 to 6,300	9,000 to 10,000
2,925 to 3,050	2,000 to 4,000
3,050	2,000 to 6,000
3,050	2,000
3,300 to 3,900	16,000 to 24,000
3,700 to 4,000	7,500 to 20,000
2,100	16,000 to 24,000

High-intensity discharge (HID)

HID bulbs produce a lot of light while using a relatively small amount of power. You've seen them, but it's probably been in street lighting or public places. Requiring special fixtures and ballasts, these largish lights may take up to 7 minutes to ignite once switched on. The color emitted by most HID bulbs ranges from mildly to extremely unflattering; metal halide is a notable exception.

Mercury vapor light is produced by a bulb-within-a-bulb shaped much like an oversize A-bulb. Fixtures are available for garden and security lighting. While color rendering is a ghoulish blue-green, it's usually acceptable for outdoor uses.

High-pressure sodium, a distinctively orangish source, is the number one choice for street lighting. It's also used indoors commercially and industrially. Like mercury vapor, high-pressure sodium bulbs require a special ballast and fixture.

Low-pressure sodium sports a U-shaped tube within a larger bulb. An even duller orange than its high-pressure counterpart, low-pressure sodium is even more efficient. Thus it's used extensively for highway and security lighting.

Metal halide is the HID source most likely to come in from the cold in coming years. Why? Its color temperature is far more pleasant than most HIDs, ranging from 3,000°K to 4,000°K. The technology is similar to mercury vapor but almost twice as efficient.

In addition, metal halide bulbs can be made smaller than other HID sources, allowing for more attractive fixtures. While it's used primarily for outdoor security lighting, metal halide is now also available in table lamp wattages with integral ballasts.

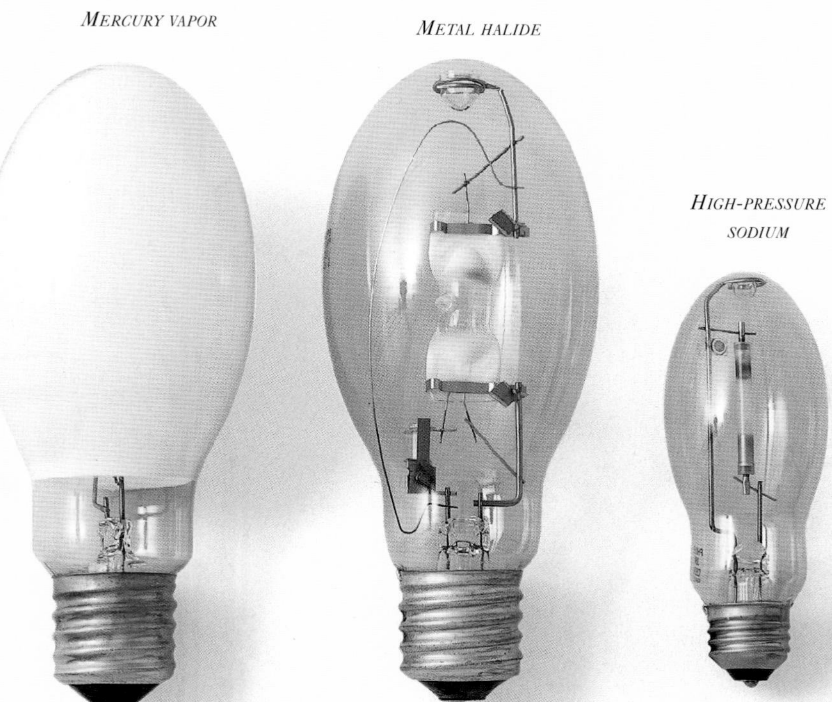

Mercury vapor

Metal halide

High-pressure sodium

Movable Fixtures

EXPRESS YOURSELF

Table lamps, floor lamps, and small specialty lamps are easy to buy, easy to change, and easy to take along when you move. Within this category you'll find fixtures that will provide any quality of light you need. Be careful, though: while they can go a long way toward setting a design style, movable fixtures can look jumbled and busy if overused or mismatched. One solution is to think of them as either primarily decorative or task-specific and to use other, more discreet sources for ambient light.

TABLE LAMPS show individuality and style at the same time that they mark space or provide task light. Variety, mobility, and ease of installation add to their appeal. Styles range from quietly traditional to brashly avant-garde. Three-way and dimmable table lamps offer the most flexibility, letting you dial from an unobtrusive background glow to bright task levels instantly.

TRADITIONAL TABLE LAMP

The choice of a lampshade is crucial to the effectiveness of a table lamp. A difference of only 2 inches in the diameter of the shade's lower edge can make a significant difference in the spread of light. How opaque or translucent is the lampshade? Will it produce a warm, soft glow—or unwelcome glare?

The height of the bulb within a shade also affects the circle of illumination: light will spread farther when the bulb is set low in the shade. To adjust the shade height, you can use small extension screws on the lamp harp. Look for these screws at home centers and lighting supply stores.

FLOOR LAMPS offer great flexibility. A traditional floor lamp often provides a combination of light levels, serving either as a reading light or as a source of soft ambient light. Unobtru-

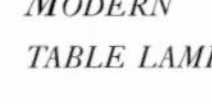

MODERN TABLE LAMP

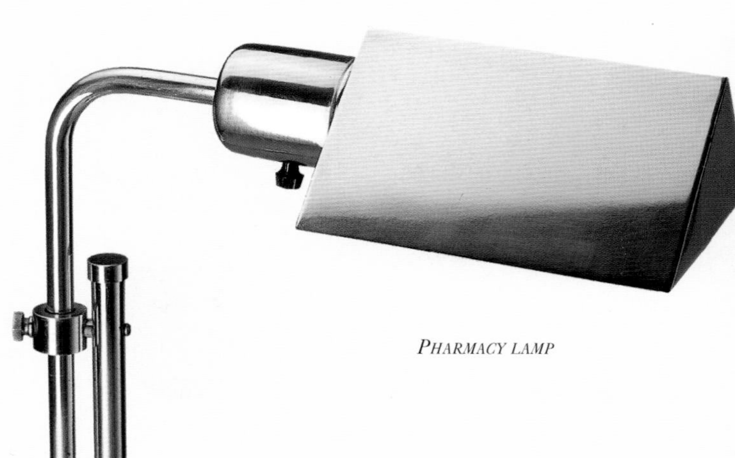

PHARMACY LAMP

sive pharmacy lamps, especially those with built-in dimmers, offer a range of options, particularly for tasks such as reading or sewing. Lamps with adjustable directional shades, such as two- or three-source lamps ("tree lamps"), are a practical choice for task lighting—but beware of glare.

TORCHÈRES—available in halogen, incandescent, and now compact fluorescent versions—bounce bright light onto the ceiling for a dramatic form of indirect lighting. However, the standard 8-foot ceiling often is too low for the typical 6- to 6½-foot-high torchère; in this case, look for one with a built-in diffuser to avoid creating a hot spot.

Some torchères include a dimmer unit for controlling light output. Fluorescent models tend to produce softer, more diffuse light than incandescent or halogen fixtures. They're energy-savers, too.

Traditional floor lamp

Torchères

Paper lamp

Tree lamp

TASK LAMPS are sometimes just smaller, focused versions of traditional table lamps. *Adjustable-neck task lamps* supply a small, bright pool of light while leaving your immediate work area uncluttered. Halogen lamps produce the cleanest, tightest beam, while fluorescent models are tops for reducing glare and shadows. Some drafting lamps include both types of light, providing perhaps the best of both worlds. Easily adjusted *clip-on lights* are practical for providing task lighting over beds, desks, and shelves.

SPECIALTY LAMPS in new varieties are constantly appearing on the market. Some lamps—like the traditional picture light—can fill a specific need while remaining movable, and they require no special wiring.

Uplight cans highlight indoor plants or wash walls with light for instant decorating touches. *Aimable spotlights* are handy for pinpointing plants, paintings, or sculpture from nearby. *Picture lights* are inexpensive, easy-to-add options for accenting individual paintings or wall art. Available in several shapes and finishes, the lights simply screw to the back of the picture frame.

T-2 FLUORESCENT TASK LAMP

UPLIGHT CAN

CLIP-ON LIGHT

HALOGEN TASK LAMP

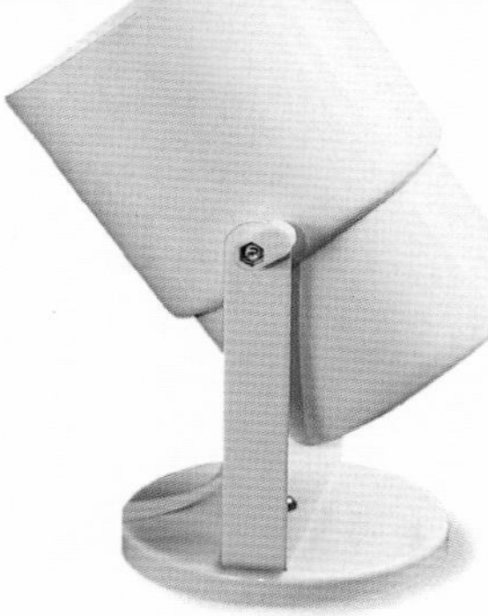

AIMABLE SPOTLIGHT

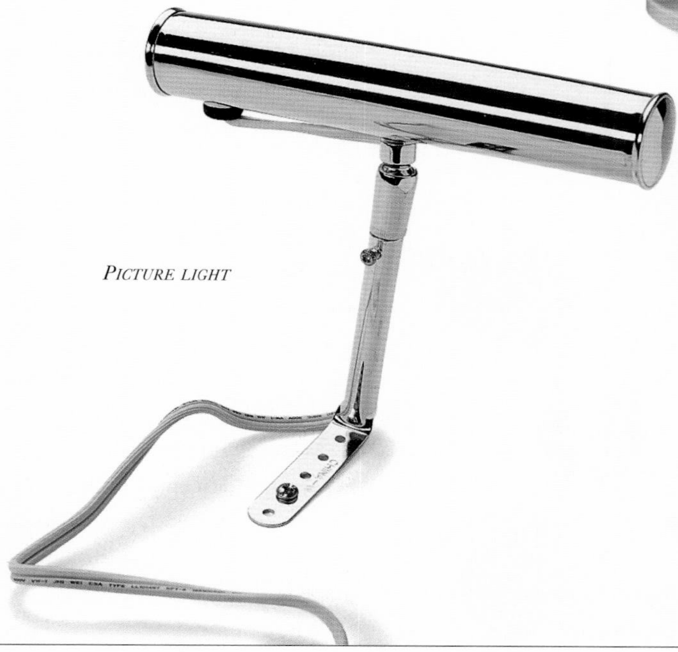

PICTURE LIGHT

AIMABLE TABLE LAMP

NIGHT-LIGHTS, MOONLIGHTS

Plug-in night-lights consume only a few watts a night while scaring away bedroom goblins and aiding navigation through a darkened house. Neon plug-ins that glow in a variety of colors and electroluminescent panels that gleam with a bluish or greenish tint use the merest trickle of electricity. Or you can opt for a pivoting plug-in light with a photocell—it turns on automatically at night and can be aimed along a hallway.

Then there are battery-operated lights, the ultimate movable fixture. A battery-powered "moonlight" turns on when you slap the globe, so there's no fumbling for a switch. Battery-driven fluorescent strips can supply handy, low-temperature light in closets and tight utility spaces where it's hard or awkward to run wires or find heat clearance for a standard fixture.

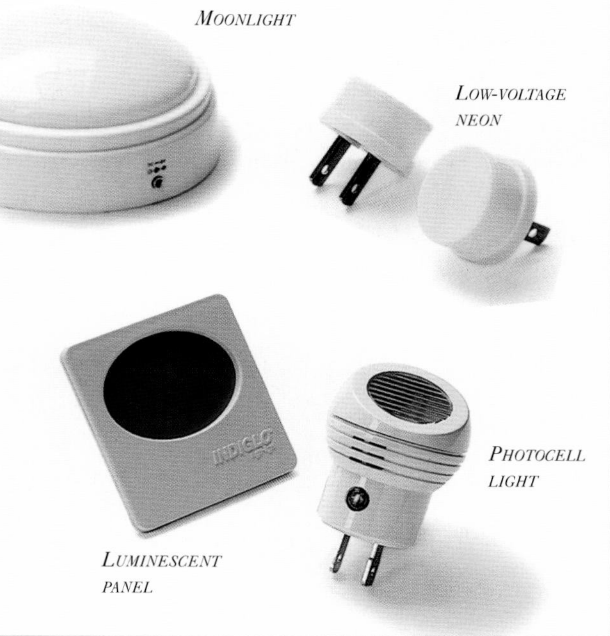

MOONLIGHT

LOW-VOLTAGE NEON

PHOTOCELL LIGHT

LUMINESCENT PANEL

Surface-mounted Fixtures

FOR WALLS, CEILINGS, OR CABINETS

Installed on either walls or ceilings, surface-mounted fixtures are integral to most home lighting designs. They're especially good at providing diffuse ambient light, though some fixtures are highly decorative, too. Under-cabinet strips can supply effective task lighting in kitchens and workshops.

Most surface fixtures come with their own mounting hardware, adaptable to any standard fixture box. Heavier types—such as ceiling fan/light combinations or large chandeliers—may require beefier support, such as a mounting bar, hickey, or J-hook. Some pendants, wall sconces, and under-cabinet lights plug into a nearby receptacle.

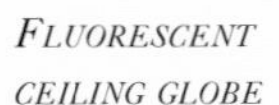

FLUORESCENT CEILING GLOBE

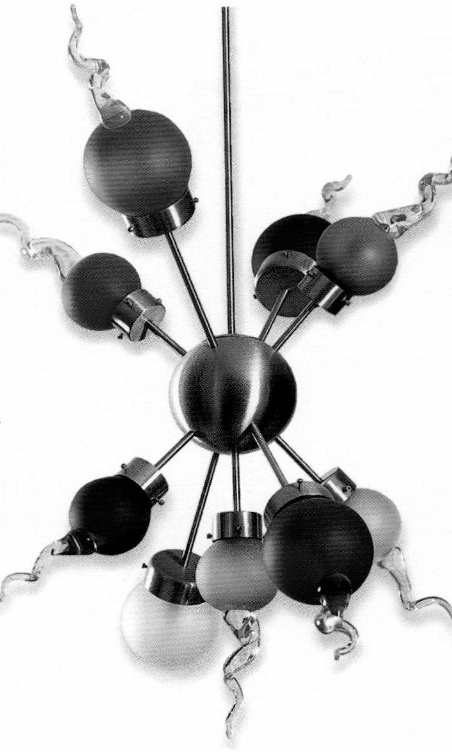

AVANT-GARDE PENDANT

FLUSH-MOUNTED FIXTURES, which mount directly to a housing box, provide general illumination in traffic areas such as landings, entries, and hallways. Kitchens, bathrooms, and workshops often benefit from the added light of surface fixtures used in conjunction with task lighting on work surfaces.

Models in this category range from functional frosted glass globes to delicate, decorative wall fixtures. When considering a fixture, look closely at how light bounces off the wall or ceiling to make sure it will be directed where you want it.

Most traditional flush fixtures house incandescent A-bulbs, but new fluorescent globes with trim circline tubes (see page 223) are becoming more common.

When fluorescent panels sit against the ceiling, they're loosely named *shoplights;* when they're flush—as within a suspended ceiling—they're called *troffers.* The only real difference is that troffers aren't finished on the sides. Except in utility spaces, the tubes these fixtures house are usually covered with acrylic diffusing panels. Multiple panels may be grouped or "ganged," end-to-end or side-by-side, to make one large light source.

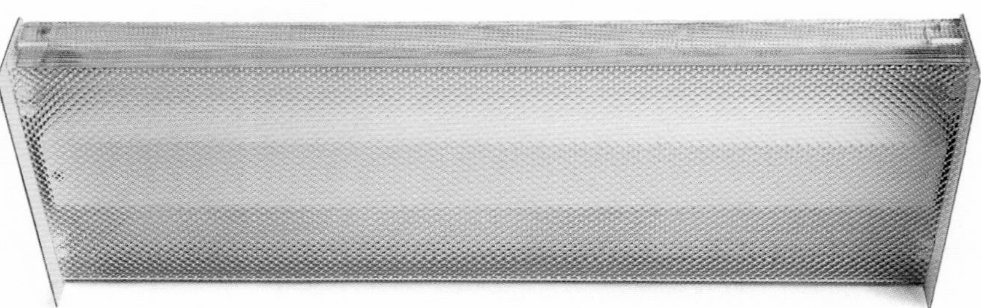

FLUORESCENT SHOPLIGHT

Ceiling fan/light

Chandeliers and pendants add sparkle and style in high-ceilinged entries and above dining tables and breakfast nooks. Depending on your needs, these decorative fixtures can give direct or diffused light—or a combination of the two. It's always a good idea to wire such fixtures to a dimmer, allowing you to fine-tune their output. Swags—chain-suspended pendants with cords and plugs—offer a movable alternative.

The size of a fixture relative to its surroundings is critical. A pendant used over a table should be at least 12 inches narrower than the table to keep diners or passersby from colliding with it. In an entry, be sure to allow enough room below a chandelier to guarantee safe passage for tall people.

Chandelier

Wall sconces, available in a huge array of styles, are great for hallways (providing they don't impede traffic) and for indirect lighting in living spaces. From the photos in the previous section, "Great Lighting Ideas," you can see that sconces often travel in pairs, flanking windows, doorways, fireplaces, or furniture groupings.

Place sconces about 5½ feet up from the floor, and keep them away from corners—otherwise, they'll create hot spots.

Ceiling fan/light combinations can reduce your dependence on an air conditioner when the fan is used regularly. Or you can use one only as needed to improve the comfort of a room.

Wall sconces

UNDER-CABINET "PUCK" LIGHTS

UNDER-CABINET FLUORESCENT LIGHT

HALOGEN STRIP LIGHT

ROPE LIGHT

ROPE LIGHT CONNECTORS

BATHROOM MAKEUP LIGHTS should fulfill two basic requirements: provide shadow-free task lighting and offer warm, smooth-toned color temperature. The classic choice is so-called "theater lighting"—strings of

Bathroom makeup light

incandescent globes on a striplike base; you'll find several versions at most home centers. Other options abound, including vertically mounted fluorescent tubes, incandescent tubes (see page 221), and wall sconces flanking either side of a mirror.

Under-cabinet task lights come thin and narrow to fit the space below a kitchen's wall cabinets and shine on the countertop below. Fluorescents are popular here, in both plug-in and wire-in versions. These units, as thin as 1³⁄₁₆ inches, screw to the bottom of the cabinets. Lengths from 12 inches on up are available; some can be "ganged" together to make longer runs.

Incandescent and halogen strips (see following) also make sense for under-cabinet use—particularly if you wish to be able to dim the lights.

Strip lights are partly for fun, partly for effective task lighting. They add a splash of light and color to display niches, kitchen soffits, stair railings, architectural columns, or just about anywhere.

You'll find both rigid and flexible versions. Rigid strips, equipped with tiny incandescent or halogen bulbs, are wired into a line with a semirigid metal or plastic backing; often they can be joined end-to-end to make longer strips. Fixtures with larger bulbs are also available; these are essentially miniature track systems (see pages 238–239).

Flexible versions called *rope lights* feature tiny bulbs encased in flexible plastic tubes. Rope lights are finding their way into home improvement centers, along with a full line of connectors to install them and splice runs into whatever shapes you choose.

Make Your Mark

Have you ever wanted to resurrect a favorite old fixture—or build your own from scratch? Prowl around most home improvement centers and you'll discover a sizable collection of table-lamp components: lamp harps, shades, cords, sockets, switches, bases—even complete kits containing all these pieces.

You'll also find a mix-and-match group of ceiling fixture parts and retrofits, such as canopies, globes, mounting hardware, even traditional plaster-of-paris escutcheons for chandeliers and ceiling fans.

Many lamp parts and kits come with assembly instructions. For details on fixture-wiring tools and techniques, see the Sunset book *Complete Home Wiring*.

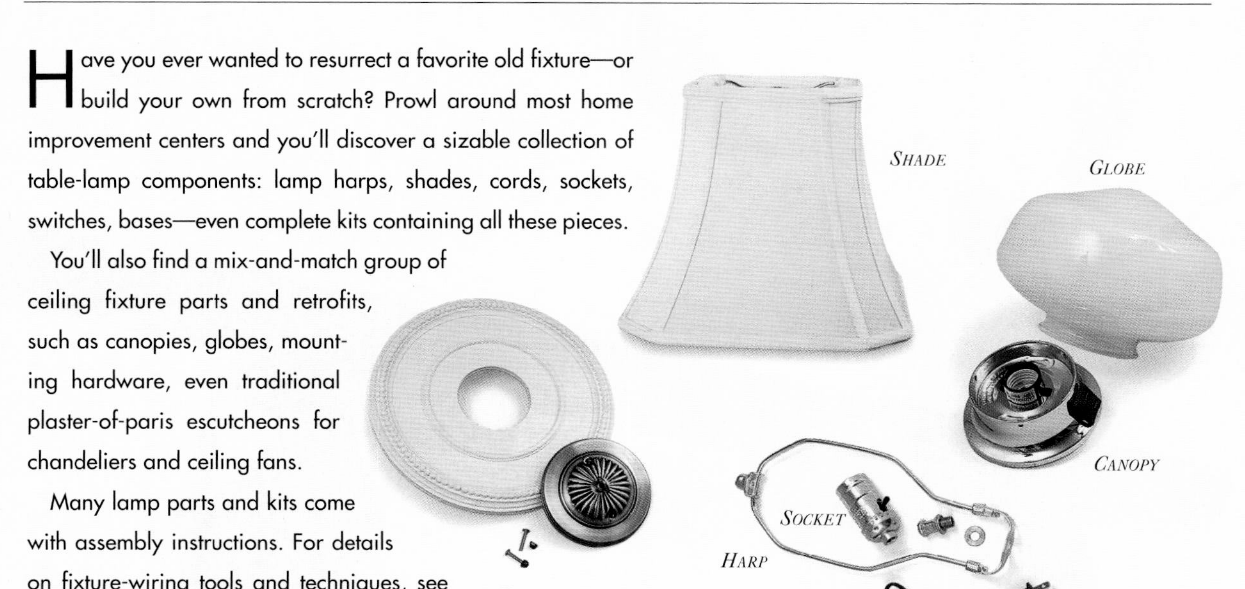

Track Fixtures

EASY TO ADD, EASY TO AIM

Track lighting offers both versatility and ease of installation. Available in varying lengths, tracks are really electrical lines extended from the housing box they tie into (or the wall outlet they plug into); matching fixtures can be mounted anywhere along each line.

Early track fixtures were large and clunky, since they needed to house R (reflector) and PAR bulbs. Now they're becoming smaller and more stylish, especially those designed for low-voltage halogen bulbs. New cable lights (see facing page) are the latest development—even the "track" is getting smaller!

Tracks can accommodate pendant fixtures, clip-on lamps, and low-voltage spotlights as well as a large selection of standard spots. Some low-voltage fixtures have an integral transformer (which can sometimes be big and buzzy), while some fit a standard track by means of an adapter. Other tracks require an external transformer mounted away from the track (which can serve several tracks and lights). For details, see page 241.

For safety, avoid track lighting in damp areas such as bathrooms or laundry rooms.

Making connections. Standard track systems are mounted to the wall or ceiling either directly or with mounting clips. Power typically is provided by a wire-in saddle mounted to a housing box (plug-in units or adapters are also available). A "floating" saddle lets you tie in anywhere along the track, not just at one end.

Track connectors make it possible to extend some systems indefinitely—in a straight line, at an angle, or even in a rectangular pattern. Most systems offer a host of connector options.

Tracks come in one- and multi-circuit varieties; the multi-circuit type allows you to operate two or more sets of lights independently.

Accessories. You can modify light output or direct it away from people's sight lines with track fixture accessories. Lenses

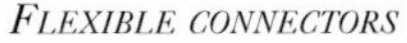

Flexible connectors

Plug-in adapters

Low-voltage fixture with integral transformer

120-volt fixture

Track connectors

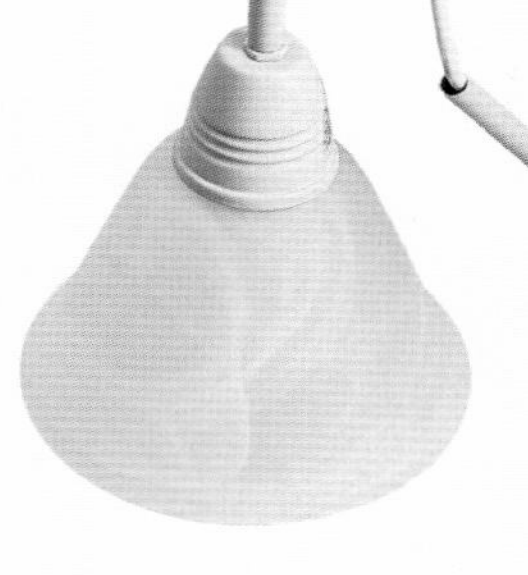

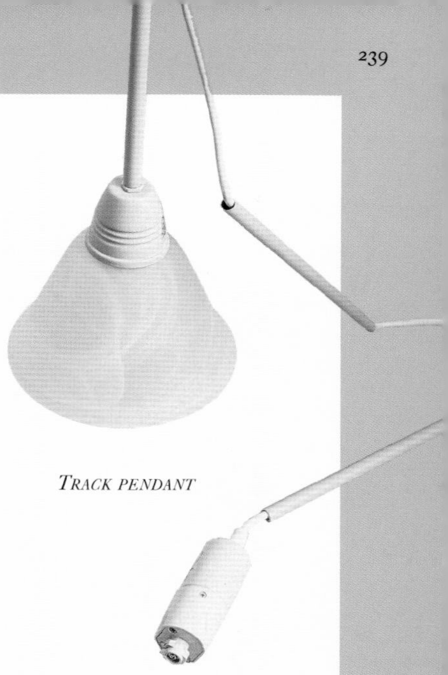

Track pendant

focus or diffuse light, louvers cut glare, and baffles and barndoors cut or shape light output. Filters can add subtle or not-so-subtle color accents.

Cable lights. After illuminating shops and showrooms for years, these low-voltage lights are now gaining popularity with homeowners. Minimalist, futuristic, fantastic, or whimsical, the diminutive fixtures are designed to be at once notable and discreet.

A cable light system has four basic components: power source, cables, lights, and mounting hardware. Some manufacturers offer basic kits that can be installed by homeowners; more elaborate systems may require professional installation.

At the heart of each fixture is the exposed light: a tiny halogen MR-11 or MR-16 bulb (see page 224). Transformers can simply be plugged into a wall outlet or wired into a ceiling box, in some cases, or be located remotely, with wires run to the room. The cables run in parallel pairs spaced from 1 inch to more than 6 inches apart, depending on the fixtures used. Support brackets, cable anchors, and turnbuckles complete the picture; how much of this hardware you need depends on the complexity of your installation.

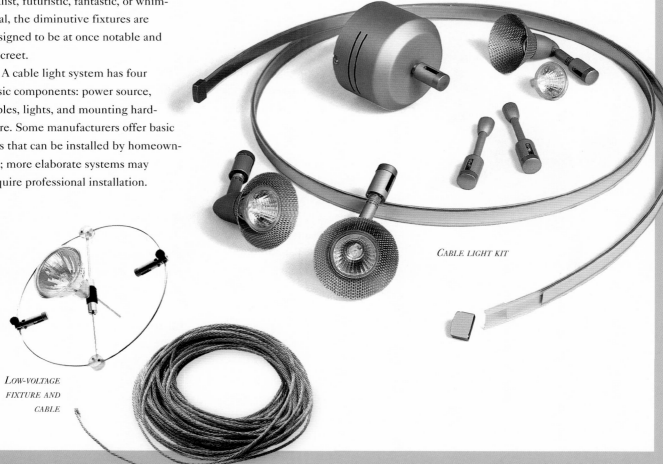

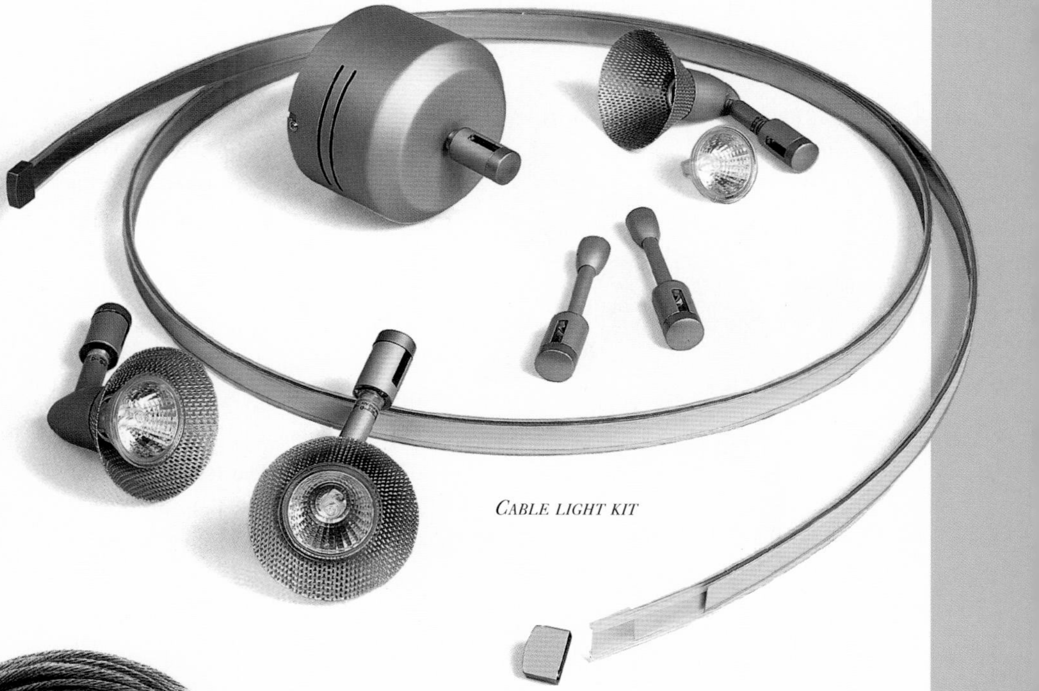

Cable light kit

Low-voltage fixture and cable

Recessed Fixtures

MIX AND MATCH

Recessed downlights offer effective light without the intrusion of a visible fixture. Basically domes with light bulbs set into their tops, most fixtures can be fitted with any of a number of bulb types and sizes, trims, and accessories that shape the light to the desired function. When installed, only the trim is visible, not the fixture itself.

New-work housing

Low-voltage downlights—particularly those with MR-16 bulbs—are especially popular for tight accent lighting. For a longer throw or more impact, choose low- or standard-voltage PAR bulbs in aimable fixture housings rather than MR-16s. Like their track counterparts, many low-voltage downlights include an integral transformer; or you can use a single remote transformer (see facing page) to serve a number of fixtures.

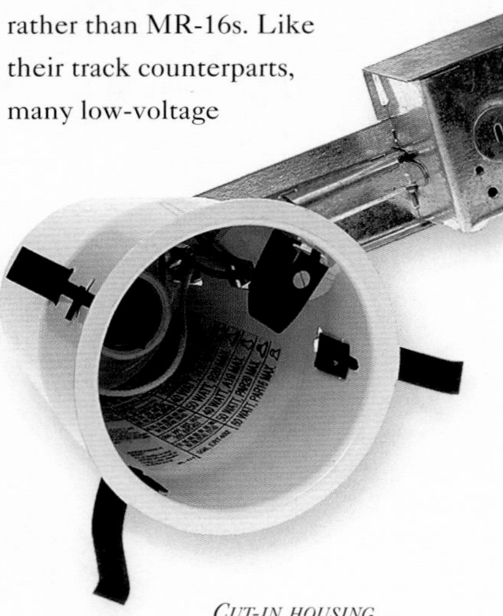

Cut-in housing

Downlights make good ambient sources, too, and some can now be fitted with energy-saving fluorescent bulbs (see pages 222–223). However, designers have learned not to trust downlights for task lighting—one's head tends to block the light from the task at hand!

START WITH THE HOUSING. Downlights are usually prewired and grounded to their own junction boxes. These fixtures need several inches of clearance above the ceiling, so they're most easily installed below an unfinished attic or crawl space. If space is tight, you can purchase low-clearance fixtures.

So-called "new-work" units, used in new construction, are easy to secure between exposed ceiling members. Cut-in or remodeling models are also available—they slip into, then clip onto, a hole cut in the existing ceiling.

Many downlights produce a lot of heat, so you must either remove insulation within 3 inches of the fixture or buy an "IC" fixture rated for direct contact with surrounding materials.

CHOOSE THE TRIM. Trim rings, baffles, lenses, and louvers are modular accessories in most downlight lines: pick the one you want and snap it in place. Besides shaping the light, the

Slot aperture

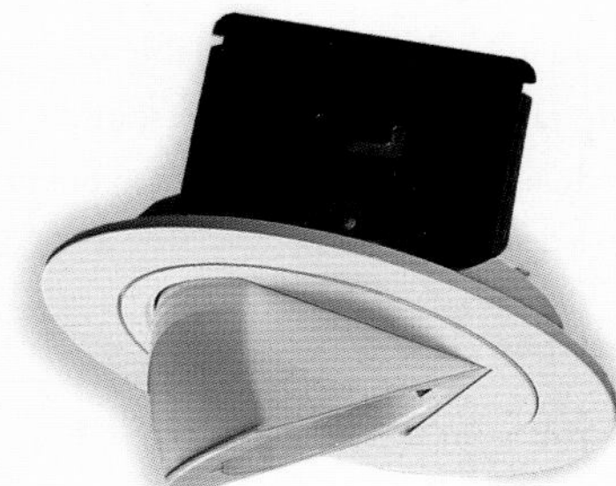

Aimable aperture

trim ring covers the rough edges of the fixture housing and ceiling hole, providing an attractive integral look.

A sampling of trim rings and other accessories is shown on this page. Brass and chrome reflector rings bounce extra light; black baffles cut it off. Slot apertures shape tight accent patterns; aimable eyeballs allow wider patterns. Acrylic lenses soften light and cut glare, as do honeycomb louvers.

Low-voltage Logistics

Smaller, safer, and more energy-efficient than standard 120-volt systems, low-voltage light fixtures have become popular indoors as well as out. Low-voltage lights use a transformer to step down household current to 12 or 24 volts; you can buy prepackaged systems or create your own with individual fixtures.

Low-voltage tracks or downlights may include an integral transformer, or you can use a remote external transformer to serve a number of fixtures. Both options are shown.

Which arrangement is best? Both have pluses and minuses. Integral transformers are convenient, especially when only one or two fixtures are involved. But the built-in unit makes the fixture bulkier and more expensive; some integral units may also hum, especially when coupled with dimmers. A remote transformer housed in a nearby closet, basement, or ceiling can serve a number of fixtures; but you will have to hassle with more routing and calculate what wire size you'll need. The size of the transformer limits the total wattage of lamps that can be hooked up to it.

Integral transformer

External transformer

Trim rings

Controls

TURN IT ON—BY HAND OR COMPUTER

Switches, timers, and dimmers—collectively called controls—provide the key to fine-tuning a layered, flexible lighting scheme.

Besides the classic two-way toggle, you'll also find three- and four-way switches, pilot switches, motion sensors, timers, and a wide range of dimmer designs (see page 244). New offerings appear constantly.

Standard switches

The classic single-pole switch controls a light or an outlet from one location only. It comes in 15- and 20-amp models—pick the switch that matches your circuit rating. Modern versions include a grounding connection; older switches have two hot terminals only.

Three-way switches operate in pairs to control lights or receptacles from two locations—such as the opposite ends of a hallway. Four-way switches are used only in combination with three-way switches to control lights or receptacles from more than two locations.

A pilot switch has a toggle that glows when the fixture is on. Pilot switches often are used for lights that may be out of sight and mind—as in the basement, the attic, or outdoors.

Basic switches often come in several grades: the cheapest grade is "residential" or "contractor"; higher-quality models are called "heavy-duty," "commercial," or "spec." "Designer" switches may be so named for their looks only, not for the grade of construction.

Unlike the lowly plug-in receptacle, switches are now available in a wide range of colors, finishes, and toggle designs—even night-light versions that glow in the dark.

Receptacles

What if your fixture has a plug? For walls, choose a standard duplex (two-outlet) receptacle or—in potentially wet areas—a shockproof GFCI (ground fault circuit interrupter). Depending on how it's wired, the standard receptacle may have both of its outlets "hot," both outlets switch-controlled, or one outlet hot and the other switch-controlled. This last option is handy in living rooms and bedrooms where movable lamps and other electronics mingle.

THREE-WAY SWITCH

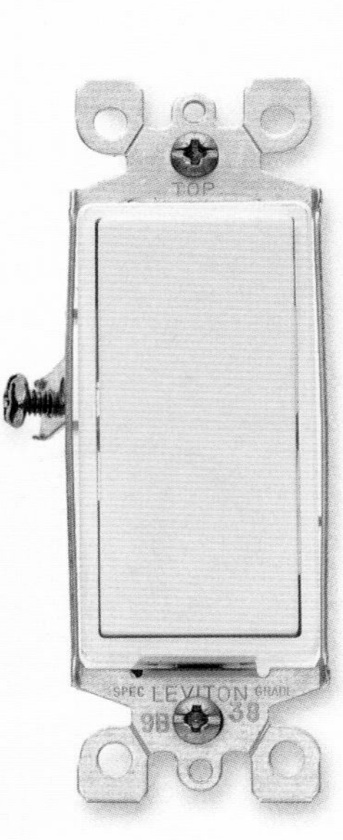

SINGLE-POLE DESIGNER SWITCH

FOUR-WAY SWITCH

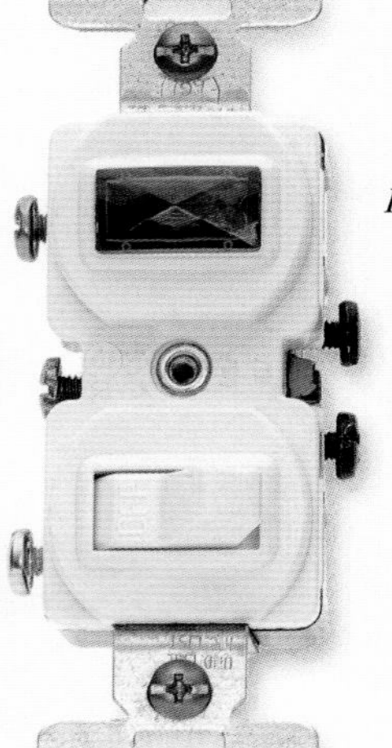

PILOT SWITCH

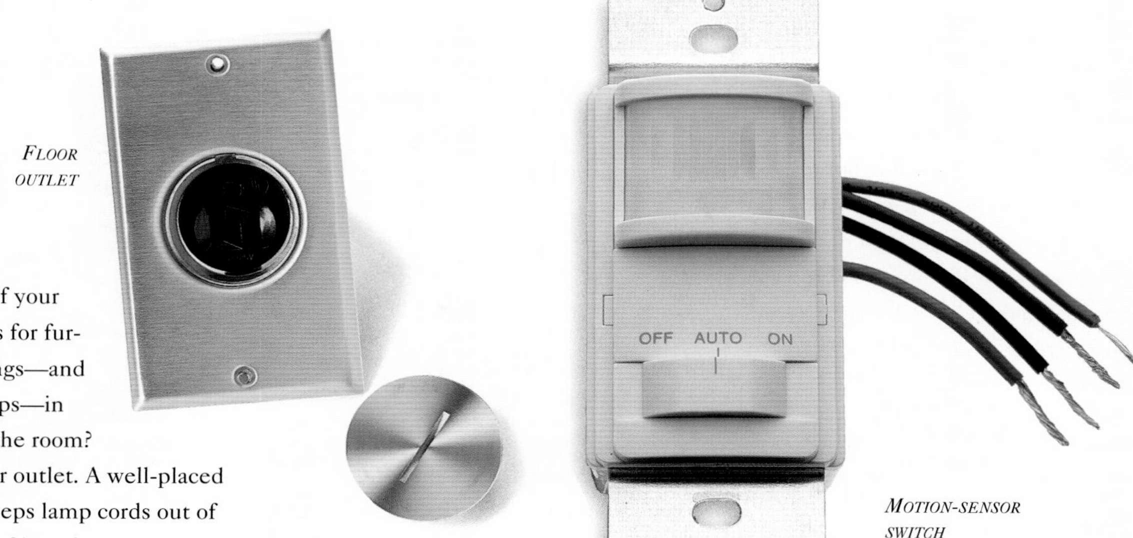

FLOOR OUTLET

MOTION-SENSOR SWITCH

And what if your floor plan calls for furniture groupings—and attendant lamps—in the center of the room? Enter the floor outlet. A well-placed floor outlet keeps lamp cords out of sight and out of harm's way.

Motion-sensor switches

Used for security, convenience, or energy savings, a motion-sensor switch turns on a light (or lights) when it detects movement in a room, then shuts it off after a predetermined interval. Both single-pole and three-way versions are available. Better designs allow you to adjust for sensitivity and time interval and include a manual ON/OFF lever.

For motion sensors used in outdoor lighting, see page 250.

Timers

Timers come in wire-in and plug-in versions. The former replaces a standard wall switch; the latter plugs into a receptacle, and movable lamps are then plugged into the timer.

Standard wire-in timer switches allow you to set a light or other device to turn on at preset time intervals. Programmable timer switches take things one step further, providing multiple daily settings or even weekly cycles for security lights, a fan, even the television. If a fixture is controlled by two different switches, purchase a three-way timer; otherwise, buy a single-pole timer.

Unlike most other switches, some timer switches require a neutral wire as well as the hot wires—so you may need to wire these in from scratch rather than simply replacing your existing switches.

A plug-in timer can turn a lamp on several times a day and for several days in a row, depending on how fancy the version is and where you position the tabs around the dial.

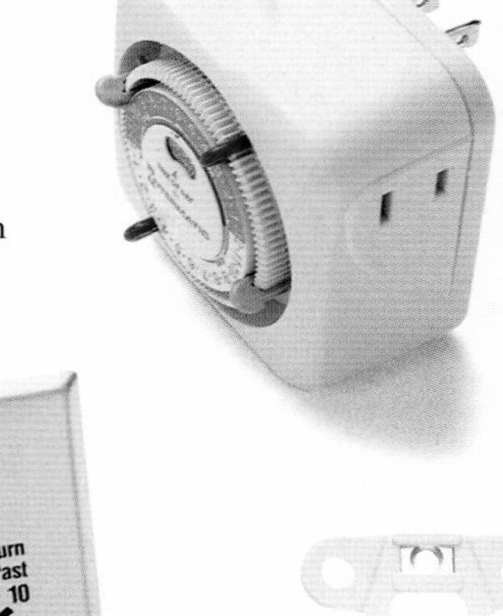

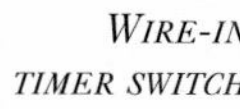

WIRE-IN TIMER SWITCH

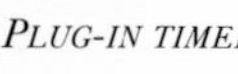

PLUG-IN TIMER

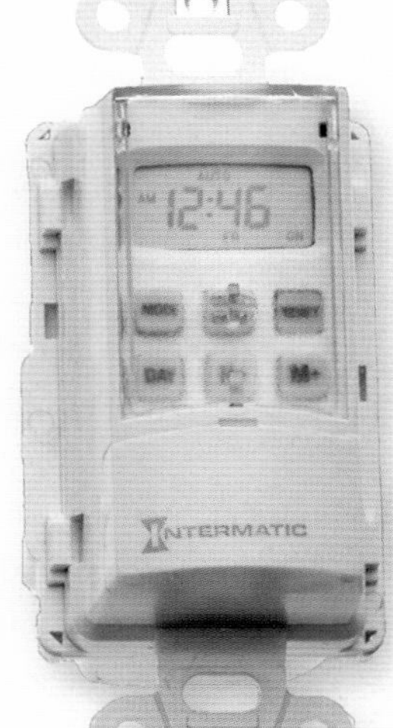

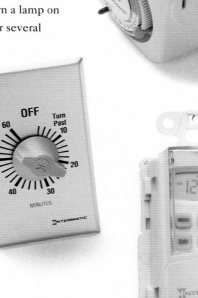

PROGRAMMABLE TIMER SWITCH

Dimmer switches

Originally called rheostats, dimmers take the place of standard switches in wall-mounted housing boxes. When dialed down, a dimmer essentially "clips off" part of the electrical current flowing to the light. Numerous styles are available, some with presets and fade controls.

Get a dimmer that matches your voltage and the bulb type. Standard-voltage incandescents and halogens are relatively easy to dim. You'll want a low-voltage dimmer for low-voltage lights. To minimize humming or potential interference (as from radio or television), match the dimmer type to the low-voltage transformer in use—either magnetic (older) or solid-state (better).

Dimmers are rated for maximum wattage. For line-voltage models, 600 watts is the standard; you can also find 1,000-watt versions. Some low-voltage dimmers may handle only 300 watts.

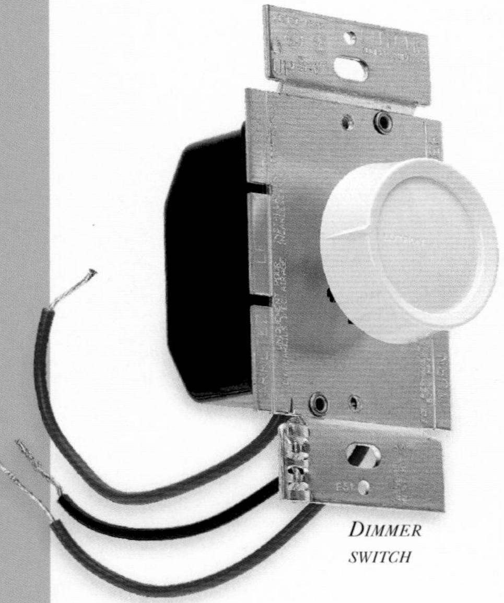

Dimmer switch

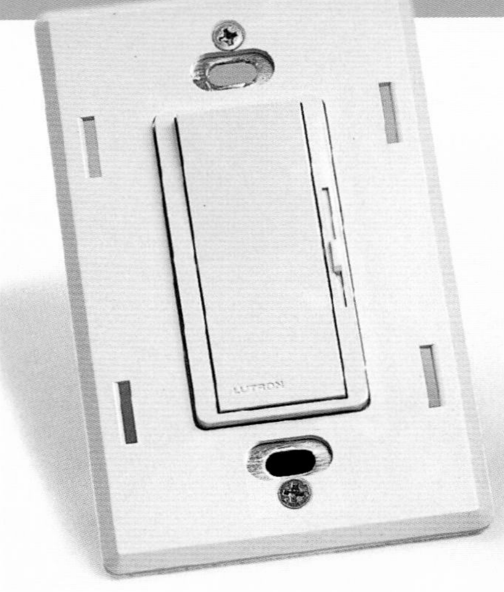

Preset dimmer switches

Fluorescent lights require fluorescent dimmers and, just as important, a dimming ballast in the fixture itself. This can be a problematic retrofit—it may be easier to simply replace an existing fixture with one that's dimmable. Solid-state dimmers and ballasts work best.

If you have a three-way setup—a light controlled by two switches that do not have ON and OFF printed on their toggles—only one of the switches can be a dimmer. Replace the three-way switch most often used with a three-way dimmer, and leave the second three-way switch in place. For a fixture controlled by a single switch, purchase a single-pole dimmer.

In-line dimmers

A number of devices can be used to convert an ordinary lamp into one that dims. You can plug a table lamp or a floor lamp into a dimmer that in turn plugs into a wall outlet. Or you can screw a light bulb into a lamp-base dimmer, then screw the assembly into a lamp's light bulb socket. With a little more work, you can add an in-line dimmer to a lamp cord. All three devices are shown below.

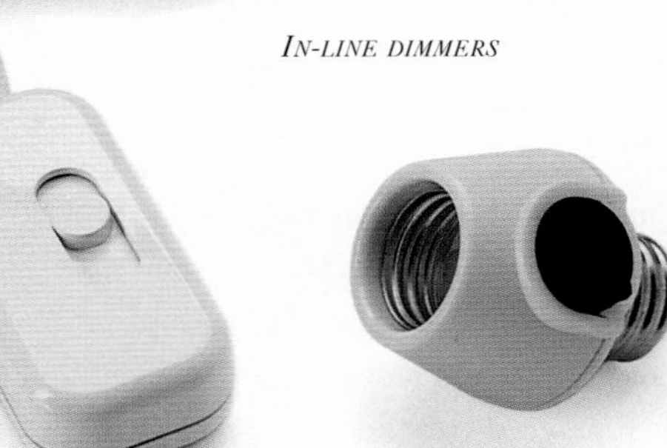

In-line dimmers

Control panels

More controls mean extra clutter from ganged switches and dimmers. New multiscene control panels do away with all this and allow you to quickly dial in a preset number of lighting "scenes." Panels controlling six or so scenes can fit into a standard housing box; larger panels require a special box and more involved wiring.

Look for control panels that have gentle fades between scenes and manual ON/OFF overrides. A panel with a "panic button" lets you dial every light to full strength instantly.

Centralized control systems—those that consolidate the lights for an entire house—require a dedicated closet or crawl space area. Increasingly, these sophisticated systems are controlled by a computer with the potential to link indoor lights to a household alarm system, outdoor security lighting, audio-visual wiring, and telecommunications. The "smart house" is here—for a price, of course.

Wiring integrated systems can be quite involved, so they're difficult to retrofit in existing spaces. But if you're building or remodeling, many experts recommend that you install a wiring "chase" and run Cat-5 communications cable, coaxial cable, A/V wires, and even fiber optics from room to room, awaiting future technologies.

Cat-5 cable

Going Wireless

New technology might be a lot easier to install if it weren't for all those wires! In fact, radio-controlled switches and dimmers that can control a lamp, a chandelier, or a ceiling fan/light combination are widely available. These push-button transmitters have ON/OFF and dimming capabilities. Besides the handheld remote, you need just a small receiver unit, which usually tucks into an existing fixture canopy or housing box. You'll need to wire the receiver to the fixture.

More ambitious "X-10" technology includes not only keychain button transmitters but larger keypads that control up to 16 lights. The transmitter powers a receiver on each fixture, light socket, dimmer, or wall outlet. How well do these systems work? The jury is still out.

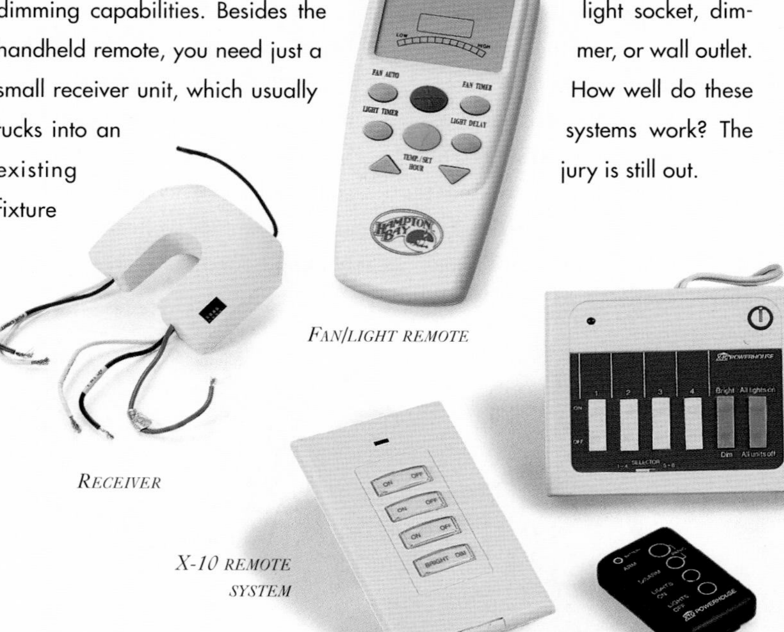

Fan/light remote

Receiver

X-10 remote system

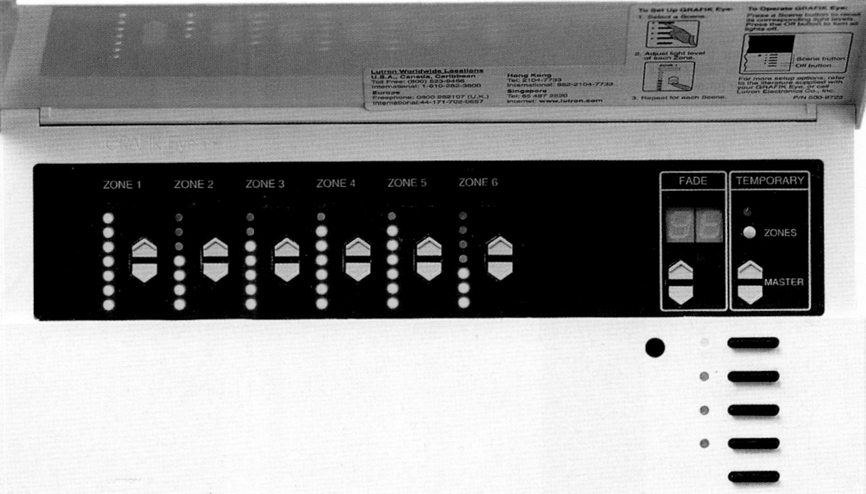

Control panel

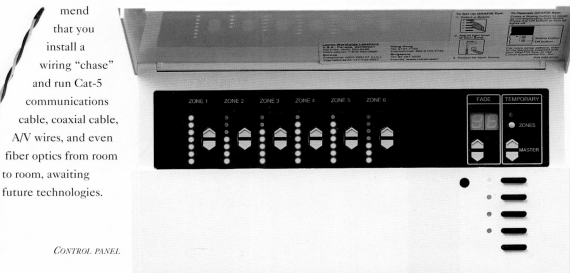

Outdoor Lighting

MAKE IT SUBTLE, BRIGHT, OR BOTH

What's your preference: line-voltage fixtures, low-voltage fixtures, or both?

A 120-volt outdoor lighting system offers several advantages over a 12-volt system (see pages 248–249)—especially when security, not aesthetics, is the issue. For starters, 120-volt fixtures usually illuminate larger areas than 12-volt fixtures can—useful both for security and for lighting trees from the ground. The bigger fixtures are also sturdier, and their buried cables and connections provide a look of permanence lacking in some low-voltage systems.

On the other hand, 12-volt systems are simpler to install—especially for homeowners. And the cable and smaller fixtures can snake just about anywhere you need them.

Confused? It helps to choose the bulbs you want first (see pages 220–229) and then the appropriate fixtures. For instance, low-voltage halogen MR-16 bulbs are popular for accenting; PAR spots and floods, available in both standard and low voltage, are best for lighting trees or wide areas.

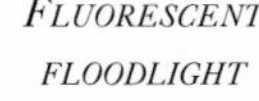

FLUORESCENT FLOODLIGHT

POST LIGHT

120-volt systems

A 120-volt outdoor system consists of a set of light fixtures and either type UF (underground feeder) cable, if allowed by local code, or individual wires run inside rigid metal or PVC conduit. (All three materials are shown on the facing page.)

Keep in mind that 120-volt wire splices and fixture connections must always occur inside a housing box. Boxes for exterior use come in two types: so-called driptight boxes that deflect vertically falling water and watertight boxes that keep out water coming from any direction. For anyplace likely to get wet, a watertight box is best. All covers for watertight boxes are sealed with gaskets. The outdoor fixture box shown on the facing page is typical.

PATH LIGHT

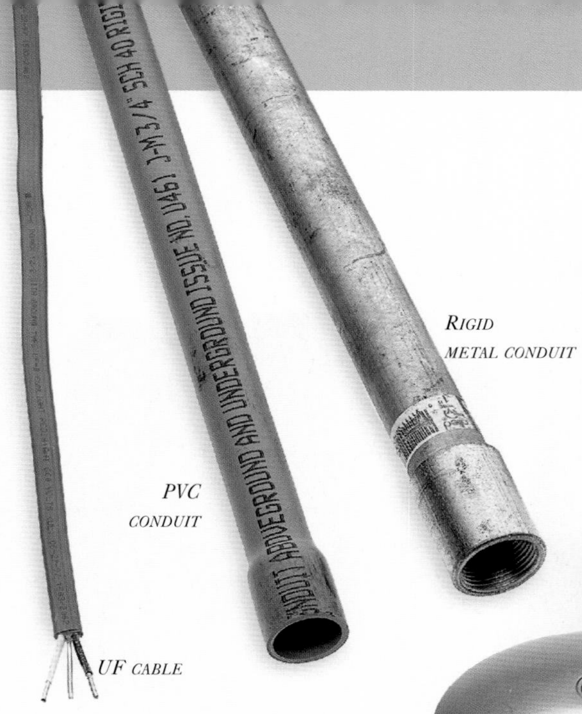

RIGID METAL CONDUIT

PVC CONDUIT

UF CABLE

OUTDOOR FIXTURE BOX

OUTDOOR DOWNLIGHT

Fixtures for 120-volt outdoor systems range from well lights and other portable uplights to post lights that mark front walks, spread lights that illuminate paths or bridges, and downlights designed to be anchored to the house wall, eaves, or trees.

Outdoor fixtures come in various sizes, mostly made of bronze, cast or extruded aluminum, copper, or plastic. But you can also find decorative fixtures in stone, concrete, porcelain, and wood (redwood, cedar, and teak weather best). When evaluating fixtures, look for gaskets, high-quality components at joints and pivot points, and locking devices for aiming the fixtures.

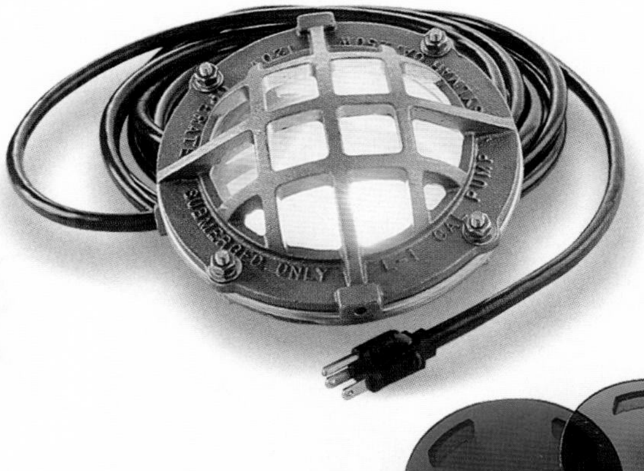

SUBMERSIBLE POOL LIGHT

WELL LIGHT

COLORED FILTERS

Low-voltage systems

Although low-voltage fixtures lack the punch of standard-current fixtures, their output is sufficient for most outdoor applications. Since it carries only 12 volts, low-voltage wiring doesn't present the dangers of 120 volts, nor does it require the special conduit and boxes of other outdoor wiring. All you need is a plug-in transformer, 12-volt cable, and low-voltage fixtures. To make things even easier, you'll find kits containing all these components at home and garden centers.

Nuts and bolts. The transformer, usually housed in an integral driptight box, steps down 120-volt household current to 12 volts. Plug it into a nearby receptacle, then run the 12-volt cable from the low-voltage side of the transformer to where you want your lights. The cable can be buried a few inches deep or simply covered with mulch in a planting area; but to avoid accidentally spading through it, consider running the cable alongside structures, walks, and fences where you won't be likely to cultivate.

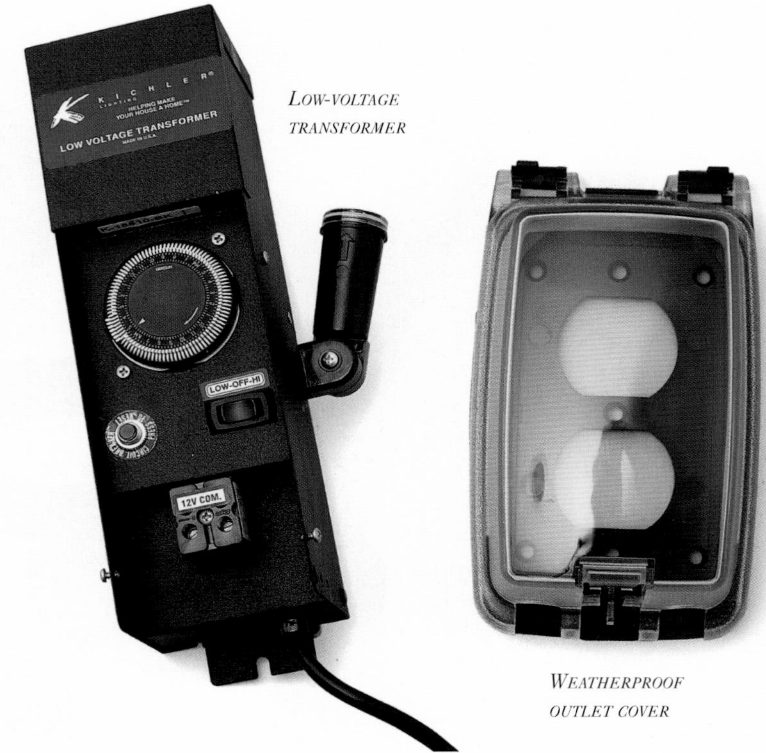

Low-voltage transformer

Weatherproof outlet cover

Some low-voltage light fixtures clip right onto the wire, while others require a clamp connector and still others must be spliced into the system and connected with wire nuts. Be sure to use the wire and connections specified in the instructions. If you don't already have a receptacle to plug the transformer into, install a GFCI-protected outlet and weatherproof cover (shown above).

Sizing your system. Most 12-volt transformers are rated for loads of 100 to 300 watts. In most cases, you simply add up the wattages of all the fixtures you wish to install, then choose a transformer and cable size that can handle the load.

Portable "rock" lights

Movable uplight

Outdoor step lights

Outdoor party lights

For long cable runs, however, you must "de-rate" the circuit to account for "voltage drop"—the accumulated resistance in all that wire. The solution? Drop a fixture or two or beef up the cable size. Your kit or cable will probably come with guidelines.

Low-voltage light and cable

Low-voltage bollard light

Outdoor Controls

THESE DEVICES DO ALL THE WORK

How can you set up landscape or security lights to take care of themselves? A timer is one solution. Two other options are daylight-sensitive photocells and motion-sensor fixtures or add-ons.

DAYLIGHT SENSORS. These are simply photocells that react to daylight. When it's dark, the photocell sends power to the light fixture it's connected to; come dawn, the sensor opens the circuit, shutting down the fixture. You can install fixtures with built-in photocells or buy sensors separately.

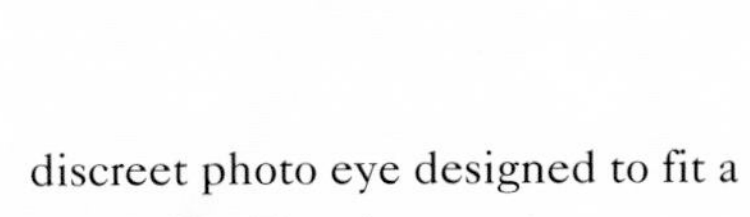

MOTION-SENSOR FIXTURE

Several retrofits are shown on the facing page. The most common type is a large photocell mounted directly onto a knockout in an outdoor fixture box. You can also buy a simple screw-base adapter with built-in sensor that fits a standard bulb socket; the bulb screws into the adapter. Or opt for a discreet photo eye designed to fit a hole drilled in a lamppost.

MOTION SENSORS. Handy both for security and for unloading a batch of groceries after dark, these "remote eyes" come in two basic versions: infrared and microwave. Some units combine both wave types. Like daylight sensors, motion sensors can be purchased alone or integrated into a fixture that houses one or more floodlights (as shown at left and above).

MOTION-SENSOR ADD-ONS

Plan to install the motion sensor on a house wall, eaves, or a freestanding post, no higher than about 12 feet off the ground. The trick is aiming the sensor's detection lobes or waves. Don't align them so they're parallel to the most likely traffic path (for example, a front walkway); there are "dead spots" between the parallel detection bands. Instead, place the sensor so the lobes will cut across the traffic area.

Some motion sensors have adjustable ranges of sensitivity and can be set to remain on for varying lengths of time. Achieving just the right combination of aim, response level, and duration will probably take some trial and error.

TIMERS. If your outdoor lighting circuit begins indoors, you can control it with the same switches and timers shown on pages 242–243. But if your system connects outdoors, choose one of the hardier outdoor timers shown at right.

There's nothing fancy about the gunmetal gray timer shown at far right—it turns lights and other electrical devices on and off once a day. But it can handle heavy loads (up to 4,100 watts); it has a rugged, driptight housing that withstands abuse; and you can lock the cover.

If you have a string of plug-in outdoor lights (such as Christmas lights, decorative patio lights, or rope lights), attach the digital sensor/timer combo shown above left to the side of your house, plug it into an outlet, and then plug the lights into the unit. You can control the lights with the daylight sensor, the timer, or the manual ON/OFF switch.

HEAVY-DUTY OUTDOOR TIMER

DIGITAL SENSOR/TIMER

SECURITY LIGHT WITH BUILT-IN PHOTOCELL

DAYLIGHT SENSORS

HARNESS THE SUN

Costing nothing at all to operate, solar-powered garden lights collect all the energy they need from the sun by means of solar cells mounted atop each light. Such fixtures, though not exceptionally bright, can adequately mark a pathway or decorate a planting bed.

Just stick the stake-mounted lights into the ground and wait. It may take them a few days to achieve full strength, but when they do they'll go on automatically when darkness falls and recharge again during the daylight hours.

SOLAR FIXTURES

Sunset

ideas for great BABY ROOMS

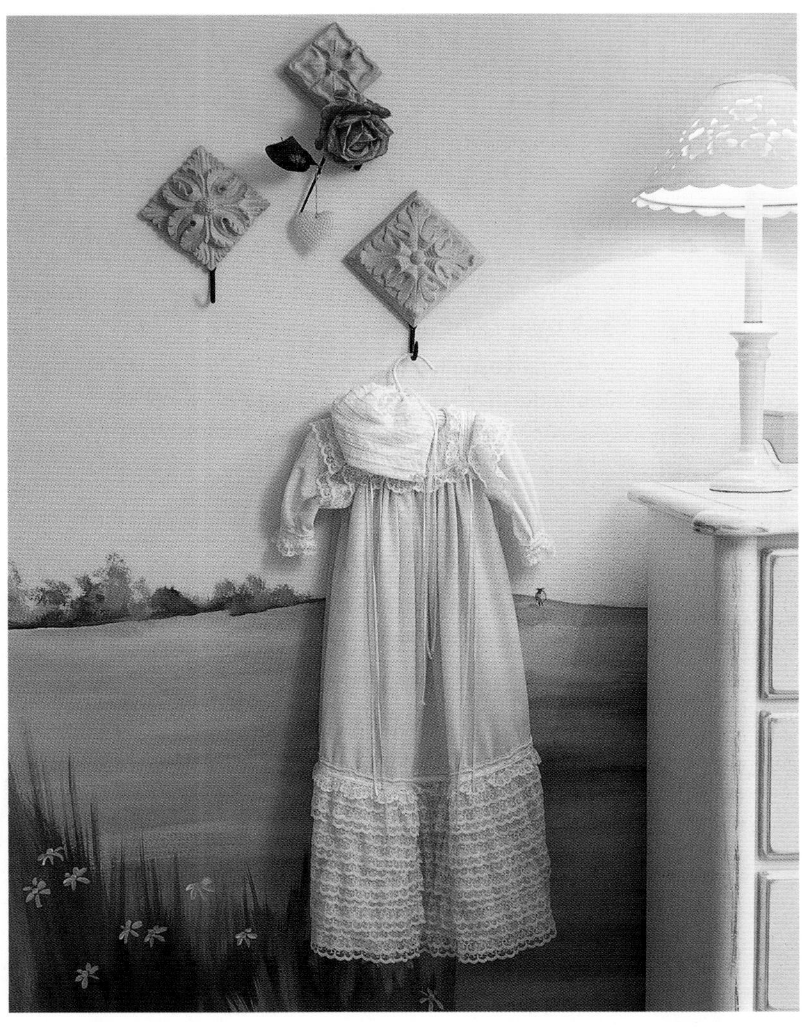

By Christine Olson Gedye and
the Editors of Sunset Books

Sunset Books ■ Menlo Park, California

contents

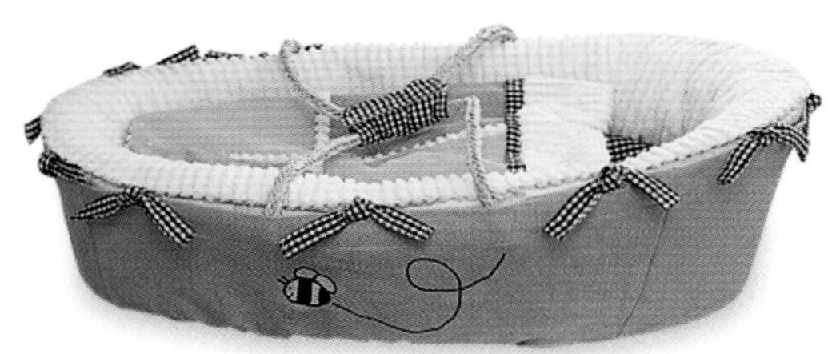

254
A Dream Coming True

257
A Planning Primer

279
Great Baby Room Ideas

333
A Shopper's Guide

712
Index

special features

Nursery Essentials **263**
Creating a Layout **266**
A Warning for Pregnant Women **269**
From the Baby's Perspective **277**
Diaper Duty **341**
Shopping for Furniture: Where to Go, What to Ask, How to Save **343**
A Word on Children and Environmental Toxins **351**

a dream coming true

WILL IT BE an undersea motif, complete with a coral-reef mural and tropical-fish curtains? Or perhaps a soft, vintage look with an heirloom bassinet, chenille cushions, and a stenciled floral border? If you're like most parents-to-be, you start fantasizing about the nursery well before you settle on a name for the baby.

The famous "nesting" instinct that kicks in during those months of anticipation has a lot to do with it. Every parent wants the newest member of the family to be cozy and comfortable, and it seems prudent to take care of as many preparations as possible before there's an actual baby to tend.

But there are other reasons the nursery awakens the interior designer in everyone. Decorating this room is more fun than decorating any other room in the house, and usually much less stressful. You can make a splash with colors and patterns you probably wouldn't consider using in other rooms, or try your hand at painting a mural or stitching some decorative pillow covers. For some parents, this is the chance to realize their own fantasies of a child's dream room. After all, it may be the last time the room's occupant isn't going to whine about your choices.

On the practical side, outfitting a nursery can be relatively inexpensive compared to redoing a kitchen, bath, or living room. Many parents start with a borrowed crib, secondhand toy shelves, and a simple bureau that doubles as a changing table.

However, well-chosen top-of-the-line furniture can last through high school, making the investment worthwhile.

Whether you're a novice on the decorating front or a practiced hand, you'll appreciate this book's step-by-step process. Use "A Planning Primer" (pages 257 to 277) to take stock of what you have, decide what you'll need (before baby arrives and later on), and put it together in a space that will be able to serve a growing child. The photo gallery in "Great Baby Room Ideas" (pages 279 to 331) offers pictures of dozens of finished rooms that will inspire you. Finally, "A Shopper's Guide" (pages 333 to 359) is a reference to help you choose everything from cribs and changing tables to lighting and floor coverings. The pros and cons of all the options are spelled out clearly—you need only decide which pattern or style or color will make your baby's room a dream come true.

EXPRESS

A PLANNING PRIMER

If your baby is still on the way, it might be hard to see much past delivery day. But it's important to think about the future as you plan the nursery. **Where will the baby sleep** in those first weeks of night wakings? Will the room function as both play space and sleeping quarters, or do you have a family room where most of the toys will be kept? Will the room eventually be shared? Or might the baby later move out of the nursery to make room for a new sibling? **Consider your budget and timetable** as you work out the room's ideal layout and look. "A Shopper's Guide" (pages 333 to 359) can help you estimate the costs. **Plan for safety** as you use this chapter to develop your design. The in-depth checklist on pages 270 to 271 will help you make sure the nursery is hazard-free from floor to ceiling. **How will the baby respond?** On page 277, we provide a glimpse into what babies would like to see in a nursery—as well as what they actually can and cannot see.

the master plan

The excitement *of impending parenthood brings with it not only a strong nesting instinct, but also an extra measure of impulsiveness and, inevitably, a little forgetfulness. Here a well-thought-out plan comes to the rescue. So pull out a notebook, a pencil, and a tape measure, and get ready to lay the foundation for a great nursery.*

Once the rocking-horse fabric was chosen for this baby boy's room, the rest came together easily. A matching wall border banded with trim gives the architecturally plain room more character; the window valance lifts the pattern higher. Sponge-painted walls will disguise the inevitable smudges and dings.

How feathered a nest?

Your child's room will serve many functions over the next few months and years: changing station, sleeping quarters, scribble art gallery, and center stage for a developing imagination. The more you think through its likely uses and incarnations now, the less likely you'll have to revamp the room at each of your child's developmental stages.

Though baby stores would have you believe otherwise, a newborn's real needs are few: soft clothing, breast milk or formula, diapers, a car safety seat, and a snug place to sleep.

For many new parents, the sleeping place ends up being in or near their own bed—at least for the first few months, when the baby is waking up several times a night. If the baby is close at hand, Mom or Dad can respond to his cries before they escalate to a panic, and the whole

This nursery is situated just off a Tuscan-inspired living area, so the parents opted for sophisticated earth colors. The garden border is a washable wallpaper framed with strips of trim for an illusion of greater depth. The fabrics used are tied together with a sage, cream, and terra-cotta color scheme.

feeding goes more smoothly. (It's not surprising that many seasoned parents say the best furniture investment they could have made prebaby was a king-size bed!)

Why go to the trouble of putting together a nursery? First, the "co-sleeping" arrangement doesn't work for every family. Some parents decide to put a daybed in the nursery so that one can spend feedings in comfort in the baby's room while the other gets a good night's sleep. Other families find that a comfortable rocking chair or armchair in the nursery is sufficient to handle an infant's night wakings.

Of course, regardless of how the night routine is worked out (and most won't settle on a solution until weeks after the baby is born), the baby will still need a place to sleep during the day, a place for diaper changing, and a place to store clothes, bedding, and a few simple toys. And keep in mind that, while you might be content to buy only a few special outfits and playthings, between shower gifts and packages from well-meaning friends and relatives, your baby will almost certainly amass a generous wardrobe and toy collection in need of homes.

Looking down the road a few months, the nursery will need to accommodate the delicate knees and hands of a crawler, a developing brain that thrives on change and stimulation, and—all too soon—the wobbly gait of a toddler. Safety, cleanliness, functionality, and comfort (for both baby and parent) must come together as in no one other room.

For some expectant parents, that means buying a full suite of furniture, painting an elaborate mural on the walls, and acquiring curtains, crib linens, and lamp shades to match. For the Shabby-Chic inclined, it may mean combing antique stores for a vintage rocking chair and a beautiful old braided rug to complement a distressed-finish crib. Another couple might opt simply to roll a fresh coat of paint on the walls, borrow a crib from a friend, and move in a set of drawers and a bookshelf from other parts of the house. Both the baby's and the parents' needs can be met with any of these treatments, and with a whole range in between.

To arrive at the plan that suits your family best, take a close look at the three factors that will become the parameters of your nursery project: budget, time, and space.

A little ingenuity brought eclectic charm to this budget nursery. Mom's childhood bookshelf showcases books and toys; ceramic knobs become a fanciful hanging rack. An old chifforobe (above) displays treasures safely out of reach. Decorative paper plates above the crib (above, right) catch the baby's eye without compromising safety.

Decide on a budget

Babies are expensive. The essentials—food, medical attention, child care, clothing, and education—add up quickly. With those expenditures on the horizon, it's wise to sit down and decide how much you want to spend on the nursery.

First, know that you can put together a fine room on a bare-bones budget—as long as you have plenty of time (to visit garage sales and to comparison-shop) and creativity (with painting or sewing) and an eye for pulling together disparate elements. Luck figures in, too. If you have friends who can lend you baby furniture and trimmings, consider yourself charmed.

If you are on a budget, be sure to let your fingers do some walking—through the phone book, through catalogs, and over your computer keyboard. The Internet is increasingly useful as a source of baby goods. For more on the pros and cons of various shopping options, see "A Shopper's Guide," page 333.

Even if your motto is "the sky's the limit," try to come up with a ballpark figure of what you'd like to spend. You'd be surprised how quickly the different elements can add up. It's not hard to walk into a high-end baby store and drop $6,000 on furniture and bedding alone. Tack on another $2,000 for a rug, window coverings, fresh paint, a mural, and accessories. And that's just the room. You'll also be buying a stroller, a highchair, and a car seat. The list will grow, and so will the bottom line.

So, as you read through the rest of this chapter, keep running lists, preferably in a notebook you can refer to while you're shopping. One list is "To Do" and the other "To Buy." As you flip through catalogs, visit stores and garage sales, and consult with contractors, you'll get a sense of how much you can expect to spend on each item. Juggle the dollar amounts so that the total stays within your budget. And don't forget, you won't need everything right away, and sometimes it helps to spread out the expenses. The crib, for instance, can wait until the baby is three or four months old if necessary (and you might decide to skip it if co-sleeping works for your family).

Nursery Essentials

Not sure what you'll need for Junior? The good news is, not everything right away. Following is a list of the basic necessities, an overview of must-haves. "A Shopper's Guide," pages 333 to 359, goes into more detail on each of these subjects. (Keep in mind that this list does not include non-nursery essentials, such as a car seat, a front-pack carrier, clothes, diapers, bottles, blankets, and so on; consult a baby-care manual for a complete list of accessories.)

A place to sleep. Unless you want the baby to sleep with you, for the first few months this will probably be a bassinet, cradle, Moses basket, or large pram. Some people simply cushion a drawer or clothes basket with towels and blankets, and let the baby snooze there until it's time to move to a crib—at around three months, or whenever the baby starts rolling over.

Storage for small clothes, toys and books. "Small" is the key word here. All those little onesies, booties, and blankets will become a jumbled mess in typical large bureau drawers and closets. Miniature board books will be swallowed up by most bookshelves. Stuffed animals, on the other hand, are often large, and they multiply on every birthday and holiday. Consult pages 344 to 346 for smart storage strategies.

A place for diaper changing. A contoured pad snapped onto a hip-height dresser or desk is a sensible solution; the pad can be removed once the diaper phase is past (by two to three years for most children), and you'll be left with a perfectly usable piece of furniture. Or you can bypass furniture altogether and simply fill a basket with wipes, diapers, creams, and a foldable waterproof changing pad that can be used on a bed, floor, or couch in any part of the house.

A diaper bin. If you opt for a cloth-diaper service, it will probably provide this, so hold off on purchasing one until you know. If you choose disposable diapers, you'll need a bin with a sealable top (more on this on page 341).

A nursing chair. It might be an old family rocking chair or your favorite old overstuffed armchair. Whatever you choose, make sure it will be comfortable to sit in for long periods and the arms are generously padded. Many mothers opt to do their feedings lying down on a daybed in the nursery instead; it gets passed along to Junior when he graduates from the crib.

An electronic monitor. These listening devices allow you to go about your business in the rest of the house (or even the garden) without losing touch while the baby snoozes in his room.

A crib mobile. Brightly colored objects hanging in baby's view are a prime diversion in the pre-sitting, pre-toy-grasping months. Make sure you choose one that captivates baby from his point of view: looking up from below. Also, the bolder the contrast, the greater the appeal will be in the early weeks; black and white or primary colors are popular with babies for a reason.

Which room is right?

This nursery can still function as the guest room it once was—and also let a parent recline in comfort during night feedings. Masterful painting effects tie it all together: the wooden crib is finished to match the wrought-iron bed, and trellis murals echo the bed's headboard design.

When you select a room in your house to be the nursery, there are several factors to consider. You'll find it's convenient to be near a bathroom, especially if the baby's room is diaper-changing central and lacks a sink. If you choose a room that's close to your bedroom, you will be able to respond quickly to your newborn's nighttime cries. Of course, if you plan to have your baby sleep in your room at night, this is less of an issue; you might prefer the convenience of having the daytime napping place and changing table closer to wherever you spend most of your waking hours.

While it may seem obvious to choose the smallest room in the house for this tiny occupant, that's not necessarily the best long-term solution. Children end up spending much more time in their bedrooms than most adults do; their rooms become a play space, a study, and a place for entertaining friends and hosting sleepovers. Make sure there is space for your child to grow, unless your plan is to use the smallest room as a nursery for the babies and graduate them into bigger rooms as siblings come along.

Another set of considerations involves noise. Excessive street noise can disrupt sleep, and soundproof windows or storm windows are a help only if you don't need fresh air to circulate in the room. While you don't want to have the room so quiet that your baby becomes oversensitive to sound, it may be better to choose the bedroom farthest from the street. It's also wise to have the nursery away from the living and dining rooms if you're likely to entertain during evening hours.

Another question to consider: Will the room be warm enough in the colder months? If there are drafts, consider storm windows. You may also want to install an adjustable-speed ceiling fan, which can moderate extreme temperatures at

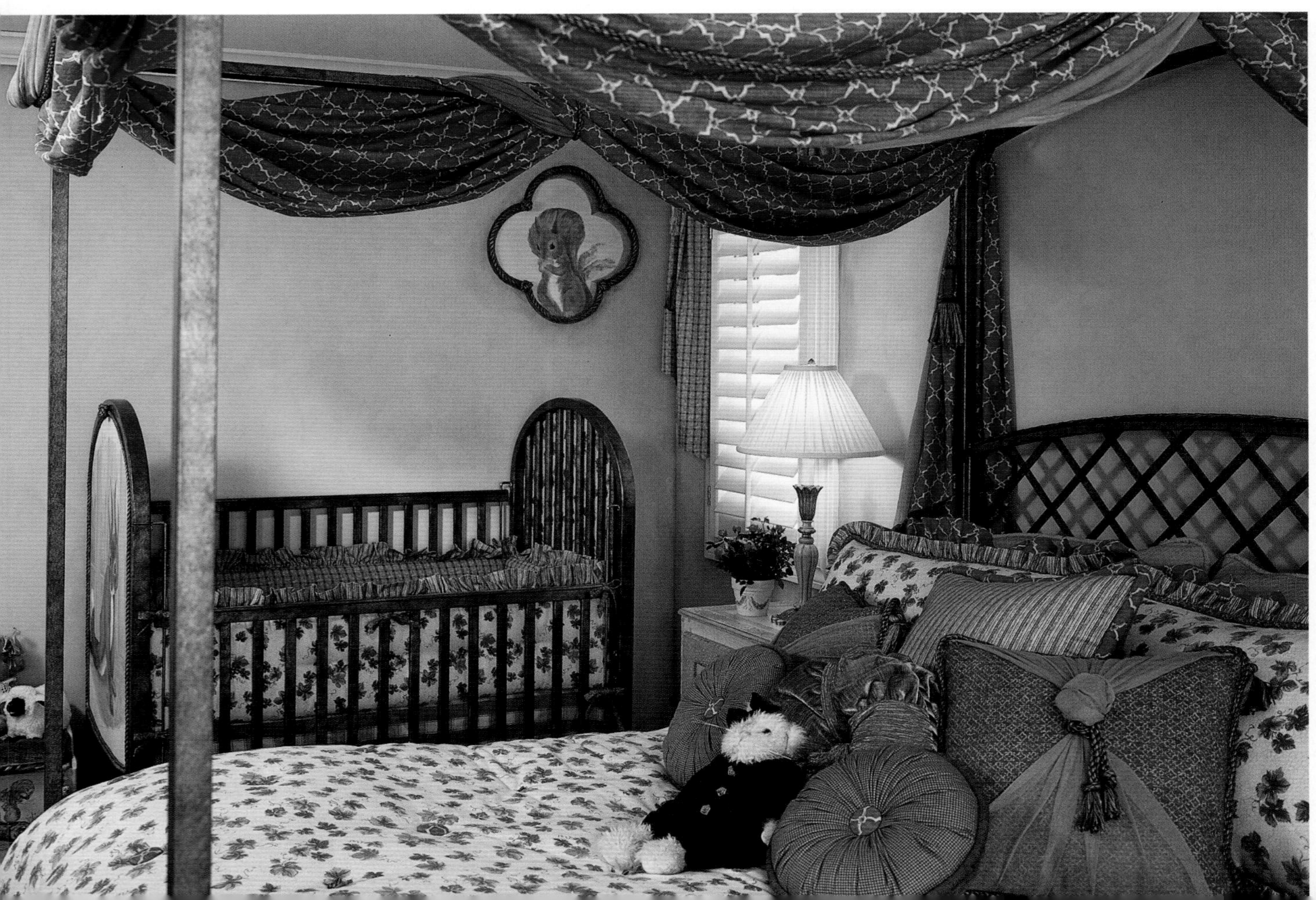

any time of year, depending on how the blades are turning, and is safely out of a child's reach. (A bonus here: babies are easily transfixed and calmed by the sight of slowly rotating fans.) While you're at it, check how many electrical outlets the room has. It's ideal to have at least one on each wall, since you won't want extension cords trailing around a toddler's room.

If you can, choose a room with plenty of natural light. South-facing is ideal. Don't worry about the room being too bright for daytime sleep: blackout blinds are always an option. The advantages of having a cheerful, naturally lit room will far outweigh the cost of any window coverings you may find necessary.

Overcoming fundamental flaws

If you are fortunate enough to have a large, regularly shaped room with plenty of light, and walls and floors that are in good shape, congratulations. You can easily fit in a crib, dresser, rocking chair or daybed, toy shelf, and maybe even some extras like a chifforobe or toy chest.

On the other hand, if you have a small or awkwardly shaped room or windows that open to an oppressive scene or let in little natural light, you'll have to be more selective. Fortunately, most architectural deficiencies can be overcome with clever decorating techniques.

Small rooms. Paint the walls, trim, and furniture in the same light color to create the illusion of more space. Minimize clutter. Can the child's toys live in the family room? Can "diaper central" be in the bathroom? Use small-scale furnishings and a small print in wallpaper and fabrics. Built-in furniture takes up the least amount of floor space. Use wall or ceiling light fixtures rather than floor or table lamps; they take up less space, and they're safer, too.

Dark rooms. Use warm, pale colors, such as yellow and pink, to brighten rooms that face north or east. Position mirrors to reflect as much

A large closet with charmingly painted sliding doors conceals a built-in changing table and plenty of storage for clothes and toys; cupboards on top store items not currently in use. The faux window on the right is framed with painted rope for an added sense of dimension.

Creating a Layout

Well before you go nursery-furniture shopping, draw a plan of the room on graph paper. Using a ¼" = 1' scale, map out the outer dimensions of the room, noting doors (and their direction of swing), windows, closets, and so on. Be sure to indicate the placement of outlets, light fixtures, wall switches, heaters, and vents. Note window dimensions, as well as their height from the floor, plus the measurements of any door frames, window trim, baseboards, or chair rails that might affect furniture placement, window treatments, or wall-covering purchases.

Once you've done the basic floor plan, play around with furniture placement. One initially time-consuming but worthwhile way to do this is to cut out pieces of paper representing the size and shape of the furniture you will be using in the room. The following standard measurements should give you a place to start in cutting out these scaled furniture templates.

Crib: 30" x 54"

Changing table: 15" x 34"

Chest of drawers: 18" deep x 42"–60" high x 31"–36" wide

Rocking chair/glider: 24"x 30" (plus rocking space)

Bookcase: 9"–12"deep x 2'–6' wide

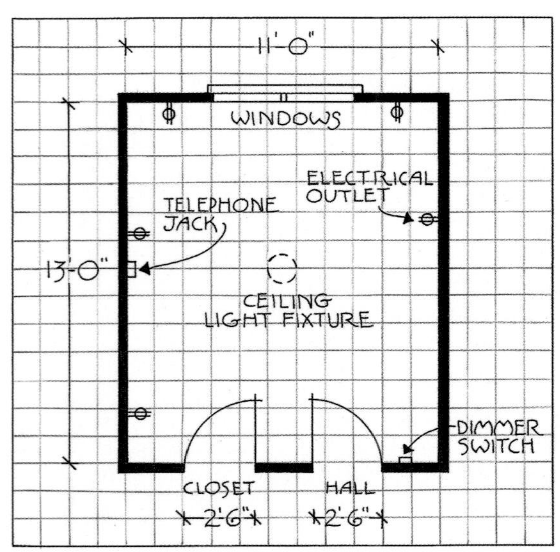

Some furniture arrangement tips:

- Place the crib first, as it is likely to be the largest item. If you have the space (and your crib that has two drop-down sides), it's handy to have the crib approachable from either side. Otherwise, a corner placement is both safe and space-saving.
- Place the dresser/changing table close to the closet so that everything is handy at changing time.
- Both the crib and the changing table should be away from windows, radiators, heat or air-conditioning ducts, and any pull cords or draperies.
- Maximize open floor space so your baby will have plenty of room to crawl and later play. Think train sets, somersaults and roughhousing.
- Utilize vertical space for storage by choosing tall bookcases or high wall-mounted shelves. A bracket shelf mounted a foot below the ceiling is a great spot to stash growing collections of soft toys (see page 316 for an example).
- Place electrical devices (monitor, music player) near outlets to avoid the use of extension cords.
- Children love to look out the window; make one accessible with a bench or window seat. Be sure the child cannot open the window, and consider using reinforced glass or a safety gate in front of the window.
- If you are planning on a mural, make sure your layout takes it into consideration (you won't want furniture to block it). Whether you have a hardwood floor or wall-to-wall carpet, you can use throw rugs to define areas: Use one in front of the changing area, one near the toy and book shelf, and one at the base of the crib. A round or oval rug can soften a room with lots of angular furniture and corners. Be sure to use nonskid pads under all area rugs; you may even want to use several pieces of double-stick tape if your floor is especially slippery.

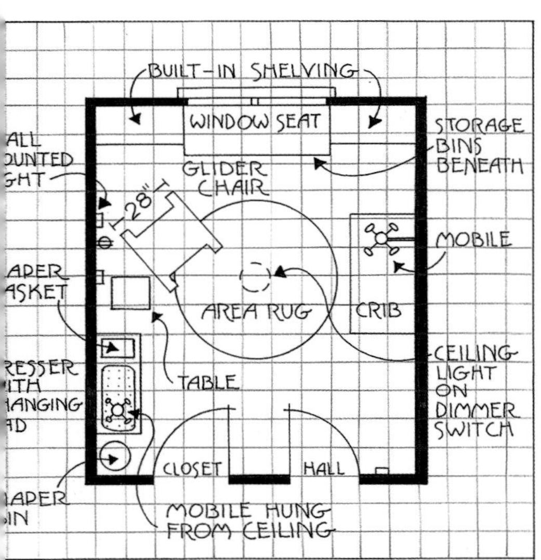

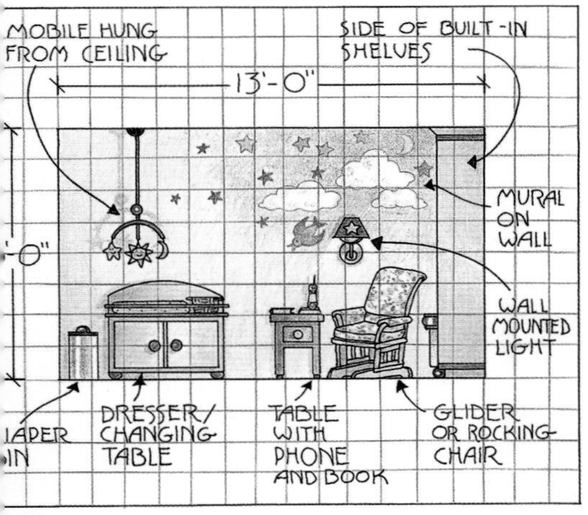

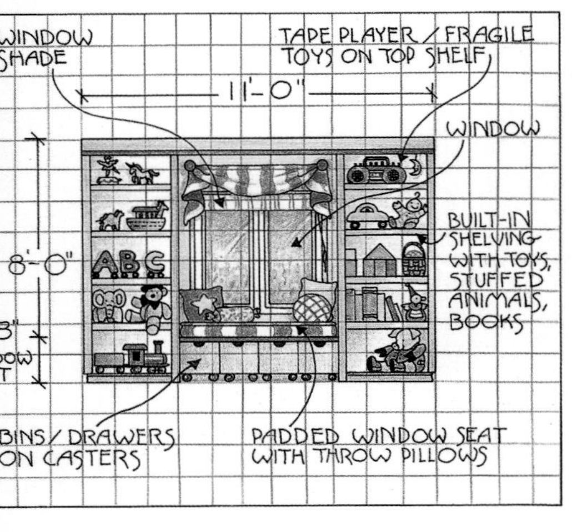

light as possible. Cover the windows with simple sheer panels that provide privacy without sacrificing natural light. And, of course, install a high-powered ceiling fixture (on a dimmer switch) for general lighting, and wall lamps for the changing table and rocking chair.

Overly large rooms. Make a big nursery seem snugger with warm, rich tones. Bold and/or large-print wallpaper will have a shrinking effect. Use a darker shade to visually lower the ceiling, and bring this color down to a picture-hanging rail or border high on the wall.

Awkwardly shaped rooms. For disproportionate rooms, remember the magic of stripes: Vertical lines have a heightening effect in short areas, whereas horizontal lines will make the room seem wider or longer. If the room has a dormer ceiling along one wall, put the crib there; as long as the baby isn't standing, there's no risk of his bumping his head on the sloping wall. If the dormer slopes all the way to the floor, build in low toy shelves for the bottom two feet and deem it a "get down and play" area; put the changing table in the middle of the room where the ceiling is highest.

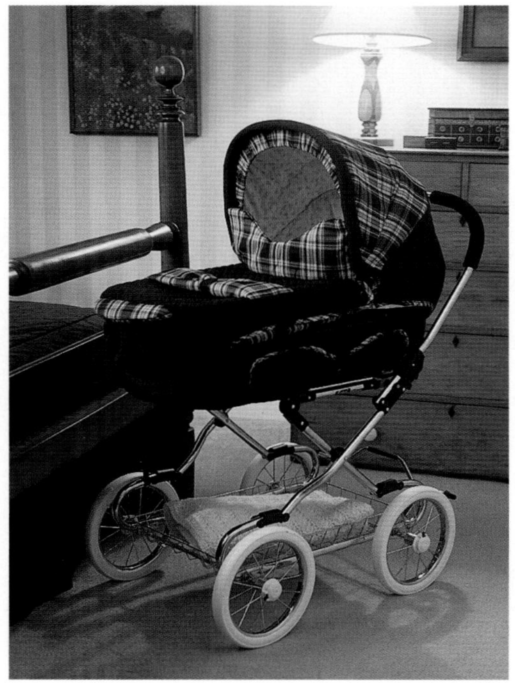

An old-fashioned baby carriage with a bassinet attachment makes a convenient first bed, as it can be wheeled indoors or out without disturbing the baby. The bassinet can be lifted from the base and replaced with a seat when the baby is sitting up.

Sharing a room

Though this family was willing to give up their guest room for a nursery, the older sister insisted on sharing her room with the new baby. The striped wallpaper has a traditional look, but with a whimsical watercolor touch. A braided chenille rug softens the old fir floor.

Sometimes sharing a room is the only option: there simply isn't another bedroom to offer a new baby, or the extra bedroom has to be used as an office for a work-at-home parent. But sometimes sharing a room is the option of choice, either for an older sibling who wants the baby's company at night (yes, it really does happen!) or for parents who wouldn't dream of separating their twins or triplets.

With multiples, the challenge is mostly a space issue: how to fit in two or more cribs and enough storage space for all their belongings. Consider some of the layout tips outlined in the "Small Wonders" section (pages 308 to 313), and take a close look at "Clutter Control" (pages 326 to 331) for clever storage ideas. Unless you have help, you'll rarely be changing more than one baby's diaper at a time, so one changing table is probably sufficient. If you don't insist that the babies wear matching outfits, they can swap clothes, giving you more flexibility and requiring less clothes storage space.

Making space for a baby in an older sibling's room may seem more daunting. Won't the baby wake up the older child? What about all those toys that are choking hazards for a crawling baby? And if one is a boy and one a girl, how do you handle the decor?

First, your child may be a deeper sleeper than you suspect; many preschoolers surprise

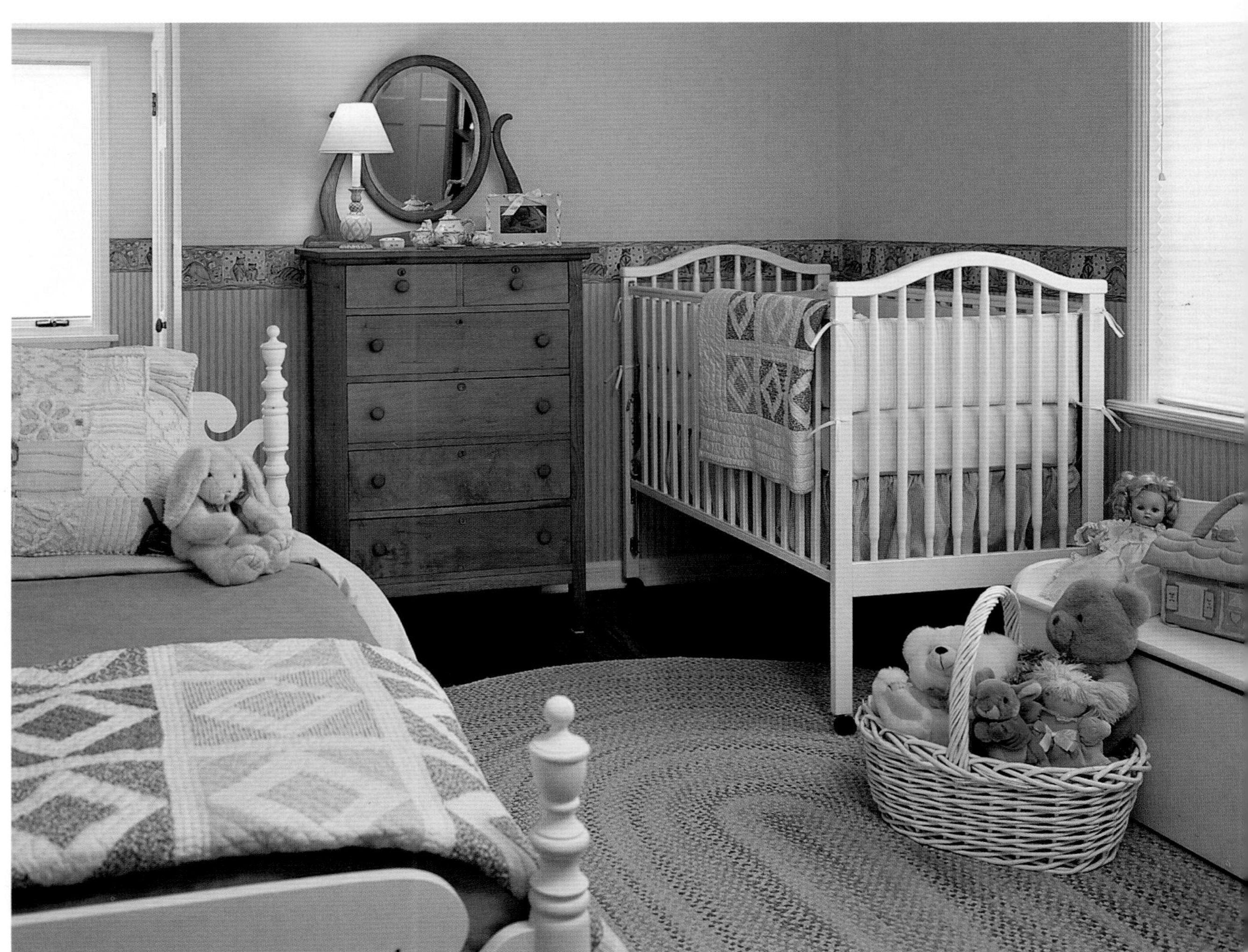

their parents by sleeping right through most of a baby's night awakenings. If that isn't the case for you, have your newborn sleep in a bassinet or portable crib in your own bedroom or another nearby room for the first few months, or until he no longer needs to eat at night. This is handier for you anyway, and will help the older sibling ease into life with a baby. Or set up a camping pad and sleeping bag at the foot of your bed or in another room for those nights when the baby's cries wake your older child.

On the toy front, some parents simply move all too-small-for-baby toys into a family room, where it is easier to monitor play. Another solution is to restrict small toys to the shared bedroom, but never allow the baby to be there unsupervised. A gate on the bedroom door that only parents and the older sibling can operate will achieve this once baby is moving around the house on his own. The advantage to this strategy is that the older child has a greater feeling of keeping his "turf" and has a place to go if he doesn't want to be bothered by the baby.

As for the boy/girl decor dilemma, think of it as incentive to create a room that lets kids be kids instead of macho boys or dainty girls. Primary colors help achieve this, although soft blue and yellow are gender-neutral colors in a subtler palette. Or choose ivory or white walls with wood floors and furniture, and let the children's toys and bedding be the accents.

Finally when it comes to compromises, the best way to preserve the peace at this stage is to go with the older child's preferences, as long as they don't pose a safety hazard.

Even a small room can be shared with a newborn. In this Minnie Mouse-inspired room, a cradle fits in at the base of big sister's bed.

A Warning for Pregnant Women

The nesting instinct might give you a hankering to repaint the nursery walls or strip an old toy chest down to the original wood, but expectant mothers should channel that energy in other decorating directions.

While today's latex paints are safer than the arsenic-, lead-, and mercury-containing paints of yore, it's safest to leave painting projects to a spouse or good friend and vacate the house while the work is being done. Choose low-toxin, not just low-VOC (volatile organic compounds) paints. Also, make sure there is plenty of ventilation both during and after the job; ideally, let the house air out for a few days after painting before the mother-to-be returns. Have any painting done as far in advance of the baby's arrival as possible so residual fumes and gases have time to dissipate. The same goes for installing new carpets with backings or pads that could give off harmful toxins.

If refinishing furniture or stripping wood is in your plans, that, too, should be left to someone other than the mother. Most chemical paint removers are highly toxic, and the chance of absorbing harmful additives from the paints you are removing is too great a risk for a pregnant woman to take.

a safe haven

CREATING A HAZARD-FREE *environment is a top priority in nursery planning. Well before you're expecting it, your baby will be rolling and reaching, then pulling up and climbing. Sometime before your baby is six months old, look at his room from a safety perspective.*

A custom-made gate swings open easily for adults, but keeps triplets from wandering into trouble.

GET DOWN ON YOUR HANDS AND KNEES. Look around. You'll probably see outlets, electrical cords, dangling curtain cords, and a host of other obvious hazards. There are dozens of others that aren't nearly as obvious. Use this section as a checklist for baby-proofing the nursery.

Some parents turn over this job to professional baby-safety experts. To find a pro in your area, contact the International Association for Child Safety at 1-888-677-IACS. Remember: no matter how many safety devices you install, there is no substitute for vigilant supervision, especially in the first two years of life.

CRADLES, BASSINETS, AND CRIBS. Make sure cradle and bassinet stands are sturdy and stable. Read the crib safety specifications on page 85. For maximum security, place the crib in a corner, away from windows and window cords. As soon as the baby can sit up, lower the mattress to the bottom level and remove all bumpers, pillows, and soft toys that could possibly be used for climbing. Toy bars should be attached to the middle of the back wall of the crib so they can't be used like rungs in a ladder. Any fitted crib sheet should have elastic all the way around and should be generously cut to allow for shrinkage; fitted sheets that come loose present a choking hazard. Pillows, quilts, and thick comforters pose a suffocation risk and shouldn't be used in the baby's first year.

WINDOWS. Put locks on windows and remove all furniture and potential "step stools" from under windows, or add bars or a shatterproof film. Imported vinyl miniblinds may

contain lead, so be sure to buy those labeled lead-free. Keep long curtain and blind cords out of reach by wrapping them around cleats high on the window frame; on blinds, choose wands instead of cords when possible.

Furniture. Make sure all furniture is sturdy and splinter-free, with rounded edges and no protrusions or loose screws. Assume it will be climbed on: bolt any tall or tippy pieces to the wall. Toy chests should have safety hinges and air holes.

Changing table. Buy a changing pad with a concave shape to nestle the baby and discourage rolling over while you're changing him. Many changing pads come with straps; even if your baby submits to wearing the uncomfortable things, it is not a permission slip to turn away from the table for even one moment while the baby is on it. The changing table is second only to the bathtub in terms of required vigilance. Keep all creams and baby-care items out of the baby's reach. Overhead mobiles must be beyond grabbing distance, and the diaper pail should have a child-proof lid.

Electrical and heating. Push furniture in front of as many outlets as possible; install self-closing outlet covers (see page 359) on the others—outlet plugs can become choking hazards. Keep electrical cords out of reach by fastening them to the wall with cord sleeves or colored duct tape. Simple winders can take up excess cord. Use overhead fixtures instead of tip-prone lamps. Cover radiators and baseboard heaters with screens.

Also:

- Steer clear of toys and objects with small parts or ribbons, cords, or loops that could choke a baby. Keep siblings' toys out of reach and pay attention to age recommendations on toys, especially those marked for children over three.
- Use safety mirrors or treat mirror backs with safety film to prevent shards of glass from forming during breakage. Do not hang mirrors or heavy pictures above a child's crib.
- Do not leave a night-light on all night: preliminary studies show a relationship between myopia and excessive exposure to nighttime light during the first two years of life.
- Discard all plastic bags and packing materials, and keep them out of baby's reach.
- Install smoke and carbon monoxide detectors in or just outside the nursery.

From left: A discreetly placed video camera helps parents monitor kids in cribs. A cleat wraps excess window-covering cord, which otherwise might be a choking hazard. An out-of-reach door latch makes the closet a safe storage place.

a look that will last

ONCE YOU'VE ASSESSED BASIC NEEDS, *it's time to think about the look and feel you want to create for your baby's first environment. This is where color, pattern, texture, furniture style, and all the decorative details come together.*

CHANCES ARE, you already have a starting point for the look of your baby's nursery. Maybe you've chosen country pine furniture that would work with a farmyard mural and chambray bedding. Or perhaps the view out the nursery window suggests a nautical theme or a garden scene. You may have found a charming bedding set, wallpaper border, or area rug that can be a foundation for other choices. Or perhaps you've always known you wanted a sunny yellow nursery with a sky blue ceiling, and all the details will flow from that color scheme.

Some families take a cue from the other rooms in the house and build from there. Whether you favor traditional furniture or contemporary, coordinated decor or a more eclec-

The warm, rich colors in this nursery-in-waiting will work for a boy or girl. The Old English alphabet border is at once sophisticated and playful, appealing to both baby and parents. The animal-print lithographs on the wall come from an old book; an antique rocking horse was reconfigured into a lamp.

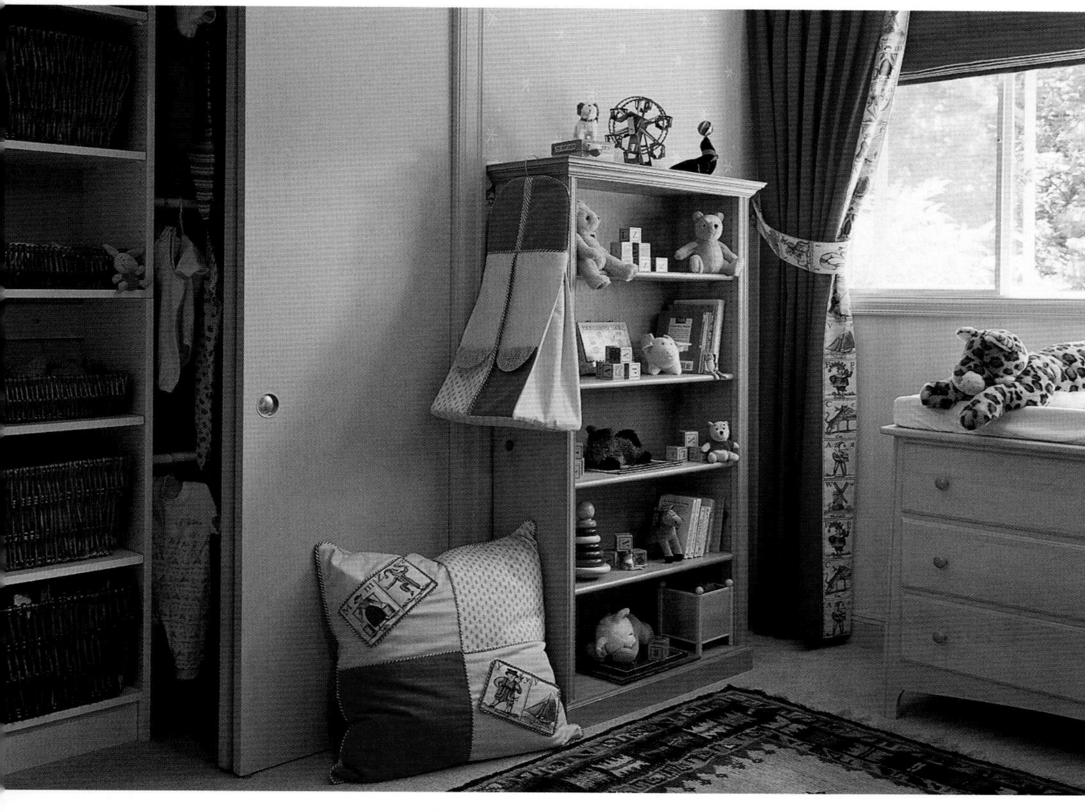

The closet was cleverly refitted with shelves and baskets on one side, three poles on the other. A bookcase's top shelf keeps antique toys out of jeopardy. A soft wool rug adds to the room's richness. Roman shades and curtains are hung at ceiling level to "heighten" the room.

tic look, you will be able to find baby furnishings that echo the style you've already established.

If, however, you are truly starting from scratch, look for visual ideas everywhere. The handiest place to start is this book's photo gallery, "Great Baby Room Ideas" (pages 279 to 331). Each room pictured is filled with ideas you can borrow. Then peruse catalogs and magazines and visit stores, collecting photos, swatches of fabric, and paint chips or wallpaper samples that are pleasing to your eye. Most likely, a pattern will emerge—a color scheme, a theme, a look, a feel. Continue to build on it.

Later, when you're ready to make some decisions, go through your collection of swatches and photos and narrow your choices down to the pieces that work well together, or to the design or color scheme you've settled on. Glue or staple these items to the inside of a manila folder, and put your room layout inside. Carry this "room collage" with you whenever you shop so you can avoid costly mistakes and mismatches.

Many parents decide that a nursery—more than any other room in the house—beckons for a full-fledged mural.

What could be more cheerful and evocative than a storybook scene painted on the walls? A word of caution before you plunge into this potentially expensive pursuit. A one-note, four-wall mural throws to the wind the cardinal rule of nurseries: flexibility. Furniture is harder to arrange when the wall decor is permanent. Curtains and bedding can be trickier to select, unless you choose those first and get the muralist to work with them. Finally, you will be much more hesitant to paint over a mural that you or your child grows tired of than you would be to hang a new poster.

If, however, you decide that now is the time and the nursery is the place, an experienced muralist can help you work through some of these issues.

Referrals from friends are the best bet; boutique-like nursery-furnishing stores are a safe alternative. Whomever you hire, be sure to look at examples of previous work—ideally the originals, or, if that's not possible, a wide range of photos. Is it the style you had envisioned? Ask what type of paint was used, and how nontoxic and washable it is. If your child takes a permanent marker to it, will the artist come out and fix it? Finally, have postcards, a book, or other visual references to give the artist a sense of what you're looking for, and ask to see sketches or a scale drawing before he begins.

Boy or girl?

Many expectant parents like to take a wait-and-see approach on finding out the sex of their baby. Does that mean the nursery decor has to be put on hold as well? Not at all.

In fact, many thoughtfully designed rooms these days are fairly gender-neutral, as parents try not to foster traditional boy–girl stereotypes. Many color schemes work for either a boy or a girl: yellow, green, bold primaries, and neutrals like earth tones and whites. Even blue, once thought to be the province of boys' rooms, has become a familiar background color in girls' nurseries. And with so many gender-neutral themes to choose from—nature, animals, the alphabet, and so on—there's no reason to limit your baby's room to something overly boyish or girlish.

In praise of simplicity

The final consideration to keep in mind as you dream up your baby's nursery is this: you will have to take care of it. Crib linens will have to be washed—often—and the delicate cycle won't do it. There will be spills and spit-ups on the floor, the rocking chair cushion, and just about every piece of furniture. The walls will suffer fingerprints and errant scribbles. So, as you're making purchasing decisions on everything from sheets to wallpaper to window coverings, think in terms of what can be easily cleaned and maintained and what will be able to hide stains, bumps, bite marks, and scratches. After all, you'll want to spend as much of those first years playing with baby—not cleaning his room.

This room's decorative painting complements the themed crib bedding, but its bold colors and stripes will easily transition to different motifs over the years. A wavy line dances around the room, echoing the scalloped edge on the crib quilt (used as a wall hanging). Natural-finish furniture with rounded lines softens an otherwise vivid room.

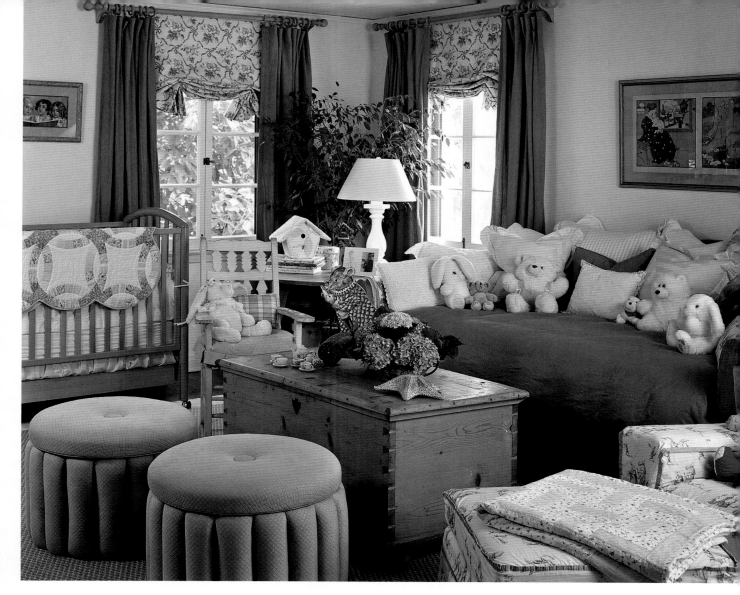

The challenge in this spacious nursery was making it cozy. Creating a sitting area made the room an intimate gathering spot for the whole family, and ficus and ivy leaves invite the outside in. The full-size daybed with trundle was ideal for the baby nurse in the early months, and later will make slumber parties a breeze. The round ottomans shift around the room easily for seating, and store toys as well. The handsome wooden trunk provides more storage, and serves as both coffee table and play surface. A built-in bookcase is ideal for toy and book storage; the top shelf displays family collectibles. French doors open onto a sunny patio.

Turquoise, orange, and red are sure to brighten any child's room. Equally gender-neutral are the plaids, stripes, and swirls on the cushions for the built-in bench. Padded fabric cornices jazz up easy-care louvered shutters and bring the lively colors higher.

From the Baby's Perspective

Just how much your baby appreciates his new environment is directly correlated with his age. Up until two months, he sees clearly only what's within 8 to 12 inches of his face, and even then he doesn't see in color. Bold, high-contrast patterns and simple shapes are the most eye-catching, followed closely by anything in motion. That's why you'll find lots of black-and-white toys and mobiles in the infant section of toy stores. Not until a baby is six to nine months old will he be able to clearly see and focus on things both near and far, and in a full range of colors.

Does that mean a black-and-white-striped crib set is the best choice? Not necessarily. A baby's vision and interests change so rapidly in the first six months that such bedding would quickly become a bore. Also, the crib isn't the best place for intense stimulation. A few well-chosen toys and pictures against a tranquil backdrop are all a newborn really needs.

If you have a collection that's easy to rotate, so much the better; your baby will appreciate a change of scenery every so often. Hang a mobile with changeable attachments above the diaper area—a great place to have some distraction. Or attach a few bulldog clips to a clothes hanger over that area and attach a changing array of soft, colorful toys. Don't forget, the baby will be gazing at these from below; position them accordingly.

THIS POPULAR MOBILE COMES WITH HIGH CONTRAST CARDS THAT CAN REVERSE TO MORE DETAILED DESIGNS, AND THEN CAN BE REPLACED WITH COLOR DESIGNS, AS THE CHILD'S VISUAL ACUITY SHARPENS.

Wall hangings and other decorative elements can both give the baby something to look at and lend the room a finished quality. Here are some ideas.

- Look in school-supply stores for colorful borders and laminated posters. Use a temporary adhesive to mount them on the wall.
- Hang a pair of clear plastic box frames on a wall, and change the contents frequently. Use enlarged family or baby photos, illustrations from old children's picture books, or an older sibling's drawings.
- Hang a kite or wind sock from the ceiling.

Finally, remember that vision is only one of your baby's senses; be aware of the textures, noises, and scents in his environment as well. Are the sheets soft to the touch? Have you made a space on a high shelf for a portable stereo to provide cheerful tunes during the daytime or lullabies at night? And what about a safely elevated bud vase containing a single flower—for sweet scent and for color?

GREAT BABY ROOM IDEAS

In "A Planning Primer," we laid the practical groundwork for your baby's nursery. Now it's time to picture the room's look and feel. This photo gallery will provide ideas and inspiration to help you do just that. From folk art to French provincial, from pastel pink to bold primaries, you'll see dozens of different approaches. The first two sections of this chapter focus on rooms as a whole—what qualities unify each space and make it work both aesthetically and practically. Subsequent sections focus on special challenges: small rooms, sharing a room with a sibling, making the room comfortable for all who use it, and, finally, solving the storage problem. As you browse through these pages, look not necessarily for entire plans you can duplicate, but for pleasing color combinations, creative ways with paint or fabric, interesting uses of furniture. Take notes and flag pictures as you go; chances are, you'll take away several ideas you can use wholesale, and dozens of others you can personalize.

tying it all together

MOST NURSERIES have the basics: a crib, a place to change diapers, storage for toys and clothes, and a light overhead. But every once in a while you come across a room that has an extra quality that makes you say "Ahhh, yes." In some cases, it's a beautiful but unexpected color scheme. In others, it's a feeling of family history. In many rooms, what evokes that response is a certain harmony, a common theme that unifies the elements.

Spring-loaded hinges on this toy chest keep fingers pinch-free. Mural details are brought below the chair rail, where a darker background color will camouflage smudges.

That's not to say that one character dances across everything from the sheets to the wallpaper to the lamp shades. While this is perhaps the simplest and surest way to achieve a cohesive look, these rooms can actually look too pulled together, and lack interest. Rather, rooms with high "ahhh" factors have a freshness about them that is decidedly free of most of the media-hyped images. In the examples here, the visual themes are more along the lines of American folk art, a sunny garden, French country design. They are playful. Imaginative. The elements in the room blend, rather than match. There's just the right amount of contrast. And the magic, by and large, is in the details: a lavish light fixture, a vintage toy collection, handpainted dresser knobs, a beautifully hung print.

The happy side effect is that these nurseries are as soothing and pleasing and joyful to the parents as to the babies. And given the amount of time Mom and Dad are likely to spend in the room, that is definitely a goal worth pursuing.

The folk-fanciful birds that decorate these walls were inspired by a pattern on the mother's own baby blanket; garage-sale furniture was handpainted with complementary motifs. The wardrobe's pole and shelves hold all the baby's clothing and blankets, freeing the room's closet for grown-up storage.

MR. LUNCH
PLANE RIDE

An inviting sitting room off the sleeping area houses an armoire for clothes, a window seat with storage space under the bench, and (out of view) a television cabinet, toy shelves, and a walk-in closet.

Topiary wallpaper with a picket-fence border, white wicker furniture, and airy toile fabric throughout create a sunporch feeling that will grow with the child. The wicker bed can sleep a nanny or older sibling—and eventually the crib's graduate. Shallow bracket shelves and a rolling cart keep essentials handy at diaper-changing time. When the diapering stage is over, the dresser top's elevated sides can be removed.

BoNNe Nuit

There's nothing babyish about the folk-art motif in this small nursery. All the furniture (except the crib) was designed by the baby's mother. Wall shelves display collectibles. A tray on the changing table holds three lidded boxes with ointments, cotton balls, and other necessities. The handmade lidded hamper and trash bin keep little hands (and the family dog's paws) out of trouble.

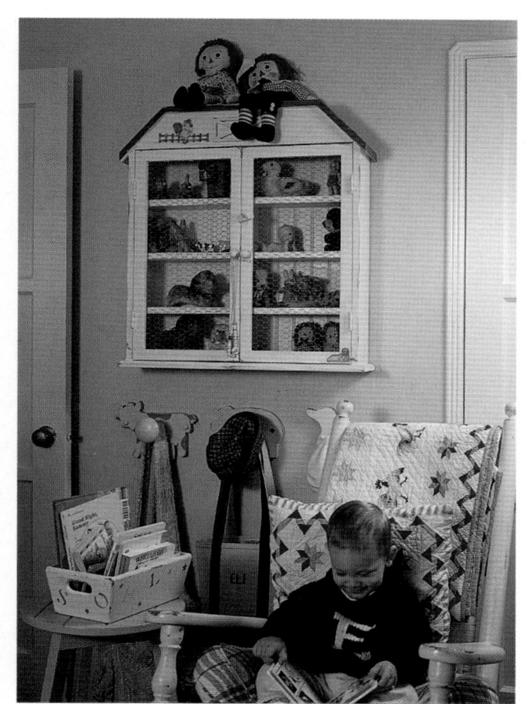

The mustard, sage, and burgundy quilt inspired the room's gender-neutral color scheme. Behind the chicken-wire doors of a barn-shaped wall cupboard is a collection of antique toys. Farmyard-animal pegs keep hats and other essentials within easy reach, while a stool functions as a small-scale side table.

Toys are stored in open crates with handles that make it easy for a toddler to tote them around. A rolling cart provides mobile storage. The crib's bumper was co-quilted by the baby's mother and grandma.

In the changing area, painted-on clotheslines are "strung" with tacked-on clothespins holding fabric scraps and antique linens. The changing table itself was new, but its distressed finish gives it a softer, more farmhouse-like look. A real clothesline and more pins lift fabric remnants to form a soft valance for the wood slat blinds.

Trompe l'oeil painting, inventive furnishing details, and vintage fabrics combine to create a sunny, country feeling. Real birdhouses—one hanging, one on a stand—blend humorously with two-dimensional versions. An old baby scale has been converted to a low occasional table, at perfect height for the mini-armchair next to it.

The inside of this old corner cabinet was painted pink, and the glass on the doors was replaced with chicken wire, also pink. On the right, a painting by the artist-mother bears the child's nickname. The doll bed and footstool are heirlooms, contributing to the room's warm sense of family history.

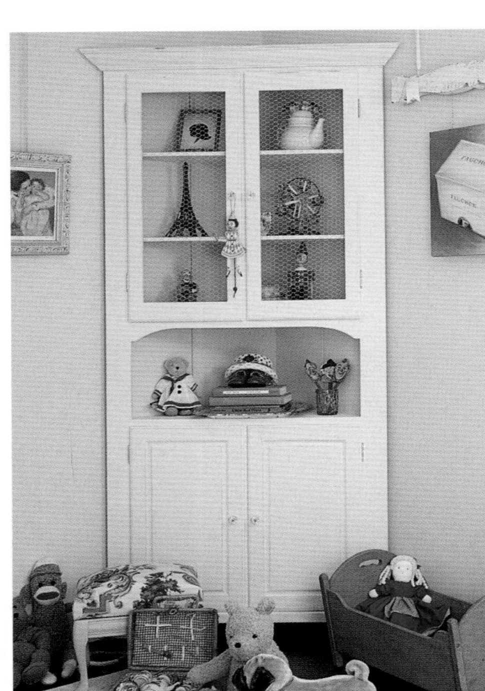

The antique crystal chandelier, purchased in Paris, was the inspiration for this French country room. A linen veil hangs with hook-and-loop fastener from a crown painted by the artist-mother. A Manet print in an elegant little frame is hung with upholstery cording and a silk tassel from the picture rail.

Simple but grand toile curtains hang from wrought-iron rods set well above the window tops to accentuate the high ceiling. The dresser, a family piece, was stripped, whitewashed, distressed by heavy sanding, monogrammed, and then protected with wax. Generations of family memorabilia decorate the dresser top, along with a jug of fragrant lavender. The small rocker was crafted by an uncle.

murals and color

Perhaps the simplest way to transform a room is with a coat or two of paint. Even a subtle color change will provide an appreciated freshness. But with a little extra effort, paint can create a magical transformation. Consider using two colors sponged or ragged on for added depth. Or add a thin pinstripe border just below the ceiling, or a contrasting color on a chair or picture rail.

Start by choosing a color you're naturally attracted to, rather than one that seems baby-appropriate. Test it out on a large piece of primed cardboard and move the sample around from wall to wall at different times of day. Consider it with the flooring, trim, bedding, and curtains you have. If your favorite color packs too much punch for all four walls, use it on just one or two, with a more subdued tone on the remaining walls.

Colorful Mexican fabrics are attuned to the vibrantly painted furniture. A swan-shaped rocking toy was redesigned into a rocking gecko.

Stencils and rubber stamps can yield beautiful decorative touches even for beginners. Try out your design on paper first. And color need not be limited to paint on the walls. Consider the furniture in the room as an extension of your canvas.

If a mural holds strong appeal for you, consider limiting it to one wall. Also, the less babyish a mural is, the longer it will be appreciated. The themes with the most longevity are general ones, such as nature, animals, sports, or transportation, as opposed to those that revolve around one particular character. Unless you possess confidence with a paintbrush, you'll probably want to hire a muralist. See page 274 for some hiring tips.

A midpregnancy dream of "happy geckos" inspired this color- and critter-filled nursery. The mother hoped the bright hues and playfully abundant use of pattern would encourage her child's creative side.

Babies appreciate vivid colors at least as much as older kids. The view from this crib includes sea creatures peeking in through portholes on one wall and a jungle scene on the other. Bright yellow paint frames each painting. (Stuffed toys and pillows, which can be suffocation hazards, are removed when the baby is sleeping.)

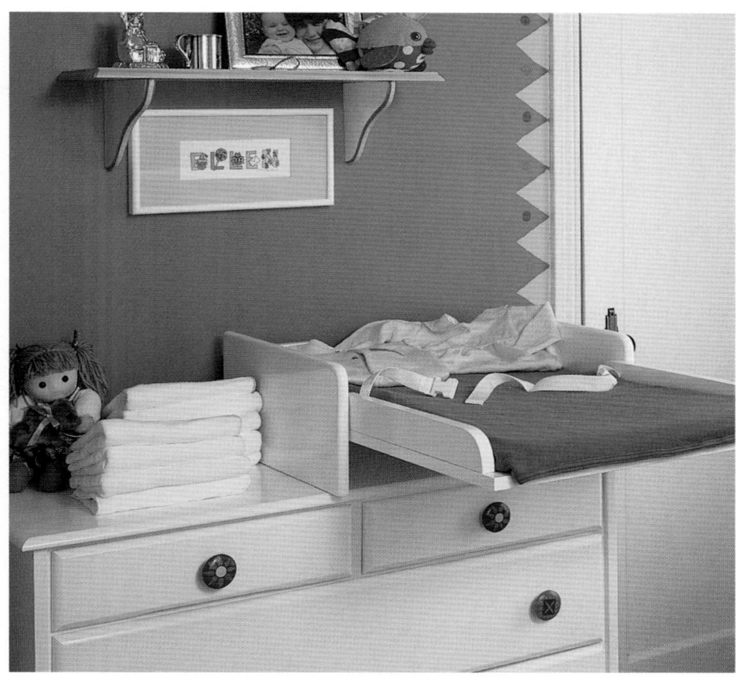

In this space-saving unit, the changing top flips closed when not in use; it will lift off when no longer needed. Handpainted knobs customize the piece in the style of the wall treatment. Baby treasures sit out of reach on a bracket-supported shelf.

A recycled glider got a face-lift with a hand-sewn slipcover; buttons were painted to match mural colors. A baby book is kept handy for quick scribbles while nursing, and the telephone is within convenient reach. The small round table is free of potentially hazardous corners.

A child's toys blend right in with the bright hues in this room. The crib and the melamine corner dresser unit, formerly white and gray for an older sister's room, were painted in bold planes of gold and purple. The rounded cabinets are streamlined as well as corner-free. The area rug was made to order by a craftsperson spotted at an art fair.

A tall storage cabinet ties in all the room's colors. Playful-looking, delicate lamps are set safely high. The floor lamp, placed out of reach behind a chair, illuminates bedtime stories.

Here the walls get a lift not from paint, but from a canopy of striped fabric hung to create a circus-tent look. The theme was chosen because it's playful, colorful, not strictly feminine, and leaves lots of room for the imagination. Crib bedding was sewn from a reissue of vintage fabric, while the circus prints came from an old "Bozo the Clown" record album. To the left of the crib, a child's armoire (a flea-market find) has hanging space and drawers to store clothes and bedding.

An old storekeeper's chest with glass-fronted drawers holds diaper supplies near the top and a collection of older sisters' shoes, which lies in wait for the youngest.

A tiger appears on the wall at child's-eye level; the child-sized chair and stuffed menagerie reiterate the jungle theme.

High ceilings give headroom when a giraffe strides across the wall. Dark colors on the mural's lower half will hide inevitable fingerprints. Animal-print fabric ties the furniture into the mural's theme.

Though primarily yellow and blue, the room has mural-related accents of barn red on the lamp, the edge of the dresser top, knobs, chair buttons, ball pillows, and pull-out bins under the window seat. The left compartment under the bench is open for a heat vent.

A huge storybook moon looming in the corner creates a floating-through-space feeling in this hey-diddle-diddle nursery. Delicate metal "aircraft" hanging above the crib spring up and down with a parent's gentle pull—an artistic alternative to the more familiar crib mobile.

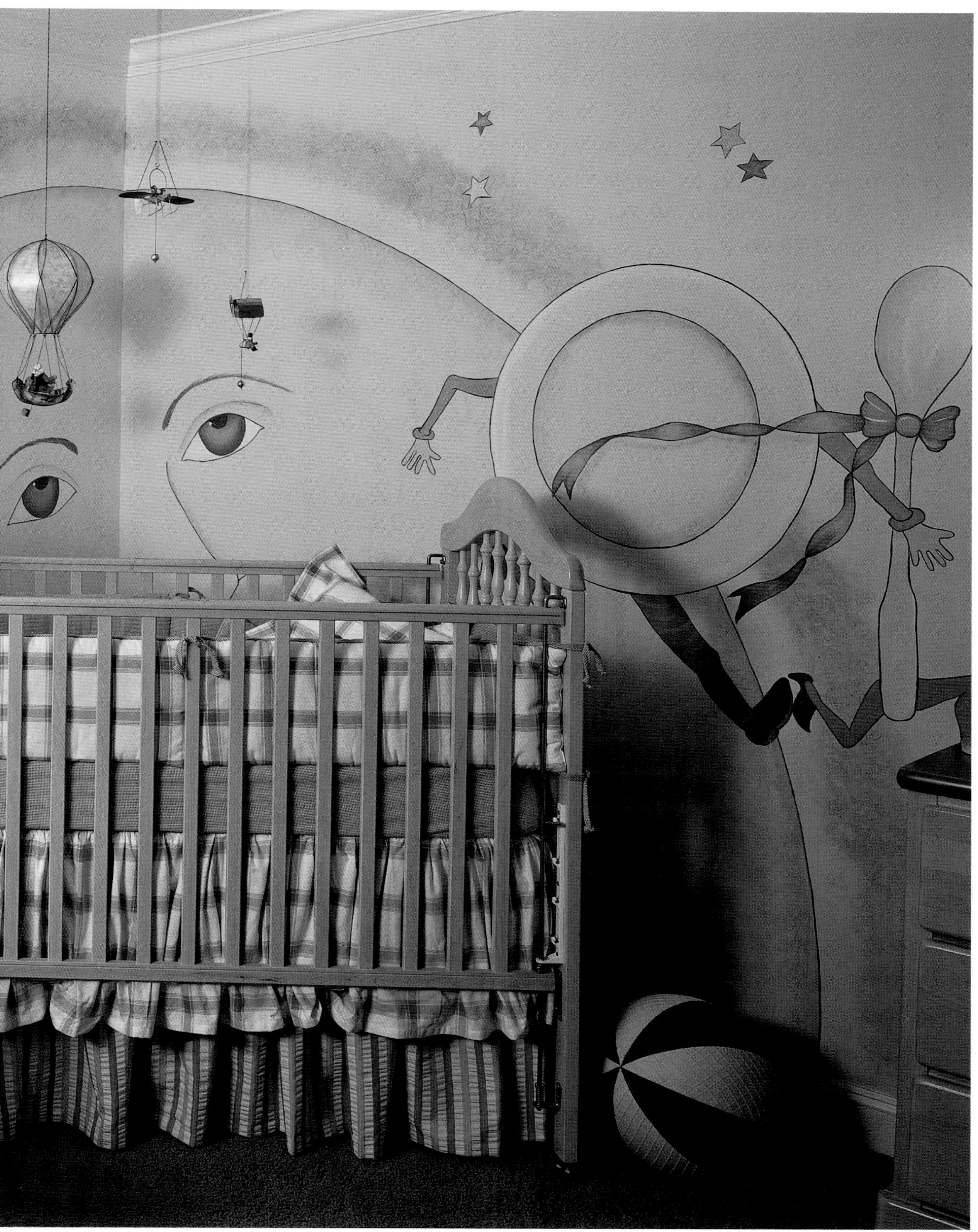

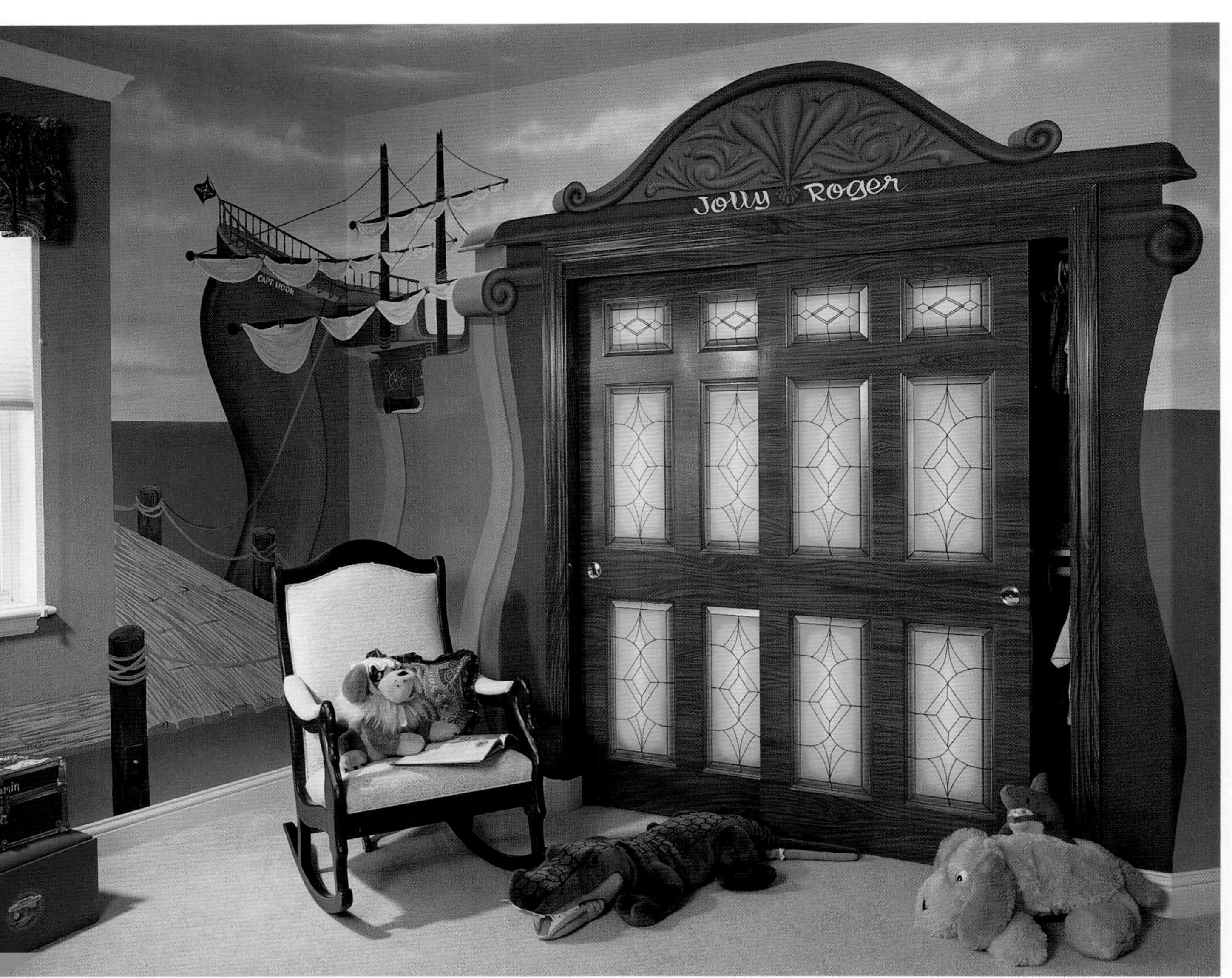

This whole-room mural sets the stage for high-seas adventures. The closet's sliding doors were finished with automotive paint so they can take many years of opening and closing.

Manipulating perspective in the mural makes this room seem larger than it is. The receding pier was personalized with names of businesses of family friends.

FREMONT BANK
LONDON HARBOUR
Darling Building
BENNY'S SPRINKLERS
MASSIMO'S
OF LONDON
Massimo's of London
OPEN

HUGGIES

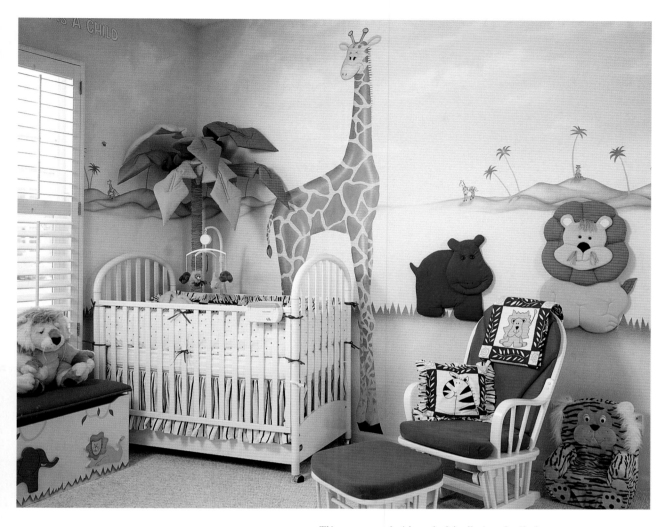

This room started with a colorful collection of quilted animal wall hangings, the toy chest, and the cloth palm tree. The muralist created a safari environment in the same cartoonish style, then added the amiable-looking giraffe. With a little imagination, the shapes of the painted clouds also read as animals.

A combination of drawers and shelves in the changing area concentrates most of the storage at one end of the room, freeing up floor space for play. The mural was painted with this furniture placement in mind.

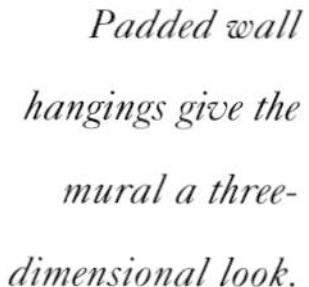

Padded wall hangings give the mural a three-dimensional look.

Curtain fabric with a "Mary, Mary, Quite Contrary" motif inspired the mural here. Three-dimensional gateposts and the path winding toward a distant cottage give the small room an appealing sense of depth. The lattice-trimmed, built-in corner cabinet provides storage while taking up little floor space.

The muralist watered her paint significantly to achieve the soft, almost translucent colors; the previously faux-finished wall made a complementary background. Real fence pickets were sanded down and nailed onto the wall before painting to provide a realistic touch.

The Italian countryside, long a favorite destination of the parents, set the tone for this fresh-air mural. The painting also incorporates a few details from the mother's favorite childhood nursery rhymes—such as the Jack-be-nimble candlestick on the trompe l'oeil shelf, which also displays painted alphabet blocks representing the family names.

The mural is carried onto the toy chest, across the ceiling, and into an adjacent bathroom (not shown). This continuity, along with the openness of the sky and the diminutive size of villages on a distant horizon, visually expands the small room. Though the colors are soft, they are stronger than babyish pastels, and will easily "grow" with the child.

Friendly pairs in a Noah's-ark mural give this nursery a cheerful quality. By limiting the mural to one wall, the parents gained more options for rearranging the furniture. A wall unit makes efficient use of space; eventually, the changing surface will be replaced by a shelf.

The starry fabric of the bedding, chair, table covering, and window relate to the mural in color but not content. The parents made a conscious effort to limit the ark theme to the mural and remain open to other patterns and motifs throughout the rest of the room.

small wonders

THINK OF IT THIS WAY: a small room is cozy, which is ideal for a baby. That doesn't mean that small spaces don't have their challenges, but most of them can be overcome.

First, clutter is a big no-no: keep a give-away bin handy for all the little clothes and toys your baby doesn't really need. Can most of the toys and books be stored in the family room? A rocking chair or glider is a true space hog; consider putting it in the master bedroom or living room.

The muted, monochromatic color scheme simplifies the small room. An armoire keeps clothes used on a day-to-day basis handy; the closet stores items the child will grow into.

Always choose the most efficient option when you're looking at furniture: a dresser that doubles as a changing table, a bookcase with adjustable shelves. Also, make sure the piece is simple in design and small in scale. Before you order anything, measure the furniture and the room very carefully, and prepare a to-scale layout of the room (see pages 266 to 267). By pushing furniture against the walls, you'll maximize open floor space. Draw in as much natural light as possible with a strategically placed mirror.

Simplify your color scheme: choose one pale and subtle color to use on walls, furniture, window coverings, and bedding. Perk things up with a wall hanging here, a pillow there. When choosing fabrics, use small-scale prints (checks and dots are good) or rich textures.

Finally, don't forget to go vertical. Draw the eyes up with stripes on the walls or curtains. Bring window coverings right up to the ceiling, even if the windows stop well short of it (see photo on page 273). High-mounted shelves will achieve the same purpose.

This room's coastal theme was inspired by the mother's childhood; natural light floods the room, contributing to the outdoor atmosphere. Floor space was maximized by placing furniture against the walls; vertical stripes and the stencil detail near the ceiling draw the eye up. The dresser and the toy chest were handpainted to picture both the family dog and the room's current occupant.

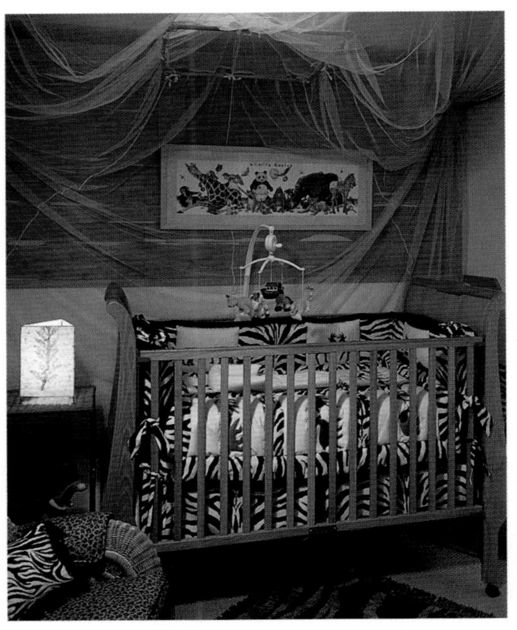

Situated in one of the master bedroom's already ventilated walk-in closets, this nursery is handy not only to the parents but also to the bathroom. (The extra bedroom is freed up for use as a home office.) Built-in shelves store toys; bamboo trim glued onto their edges maintains the safari motif. The animal-print fabrics and rug, handpainted drawer pulls, and a folding screen develop the theme further. "Mosquito netting" softens the closet's cedar lining.

Here, a limited palette of colors and complementary patterns keep the room simple without being bland. The French provincial bunny print on the wallpaper and balloon valance is playful but not childish. Highboy drawers provide abundant storage for a baby's small things without taking up a great deal of floor space. A white-painted cupboard, to be used as a changing table for the baby, will display childhood treasures in just a few years.

A small corner in any room can become a big source of entertainment. Two shatter-proof mirrors are bolted to the wall at crawl-right-up level. A colorful pad on the floor makes it a comfy place for the baby to keep herself company.

A small-scale room calls for appropriately scaled furniture. The birdhouse-inspired shelf holds small books and mementos. The tall but shallow table provides display space without blocking the wall's mural; a picket-trimmed box holds diapers, wipes, and a pad for on-the-floor changes.

Having a place for everything minimizes clutter in a small room. Books are stowed in the rattan drawers on the left, clothes in the dresser under the changing table. The chifforobe holds shoes, blankets, and extra lotions; its low mirror has a space-expanding effect, and thrills the baby at playtime.

peas in a pod

Sharing a room may seem like second-best from a parent's point of view. But ask most young children, and they'll rate it tops. Oh, sure, there will be tough moments—like when the baby wakes up crying and rouses the other—but these issues can always be worked out with a bit of inventiveness (see pages 268 and 269 for ideas).

For now, there's the challenge of creating a room that works for all involved. If you have multiple babies, the task is easier: the occupants are less opinionated than an older sibling would be. From a practical standpoint, which items do you really need two of? Two cribs definitely. But one changing table, one diaper bin (emptied frequently) and one well-organized dresser should suffice initially if space is limited.

When it comes to the nursery's decor, do you want a "matched set" look, with identical cribs, bedding, and toys? Or do you want to take a mix-and-match approach? Several factors may figure in: Are the babies the same gender? Identical or fraternal? Do you prefer an organized look, or a more eclectic setting?

When the shared room involves an older sibling and a new arrival, it's more a matter of carving out space for the newcomer. Take cues from the one who is old enough to speak his mind. Rearrange to accommodate a crib, a changing table and some baby toys and books. If he's reluctant to welcome baby into his room, choose the least intrusive corner for the crib, and have the changing area in the bathroom.

Sisters share this small room done on a tight budget. The baby's crib and dresser were previously used by her older sister.

Paint perks up the walls, closet doors, and a consignment wicker chair; the soft colors are tied together in the curtains made from sheets that match the twin bedding. Until sleep routines were established, the baby slept in a portable crib in the family room, closer to the parents' room.

SISTERS
ARE SPECIAL
EMILY

Fabrics were chosen in advance of the babies' birth to suit whatever gender combination arrived (two boys and a girl). The awning-style window toppers complement the garden picnic theme of the mural and accommodate the arched windows; the scalloped lines are repeated on the cribs and changing units. A full-length couch at the end of the room allows the whole family to enjoy story time together.

With triplets, organization is the name of the game. This custom wall unit, designed and fabricated by the father, makes simultaneous diaper changes a snap for Mom, Dad, and nanny. The vertical cabinets below store a diaper bin and laundry hamper for each child, while drawers store all their clothes (the room has no closet).

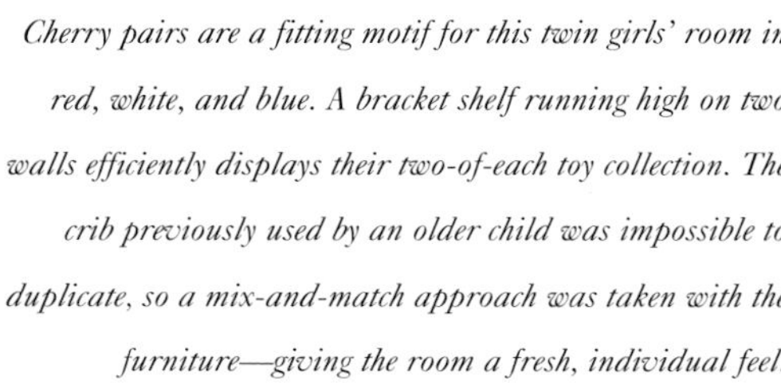

Cherry pairs are a fitting motif for this twin girls' room in red, white, and blue. A bracket shelf running high on two walls efficiently displays their two-of-each toy collection. The crib previously used by an older child was impossible to duplicate, so a mix-and-match approach was taken with the furniture—giving the room a fresh, individual feel.

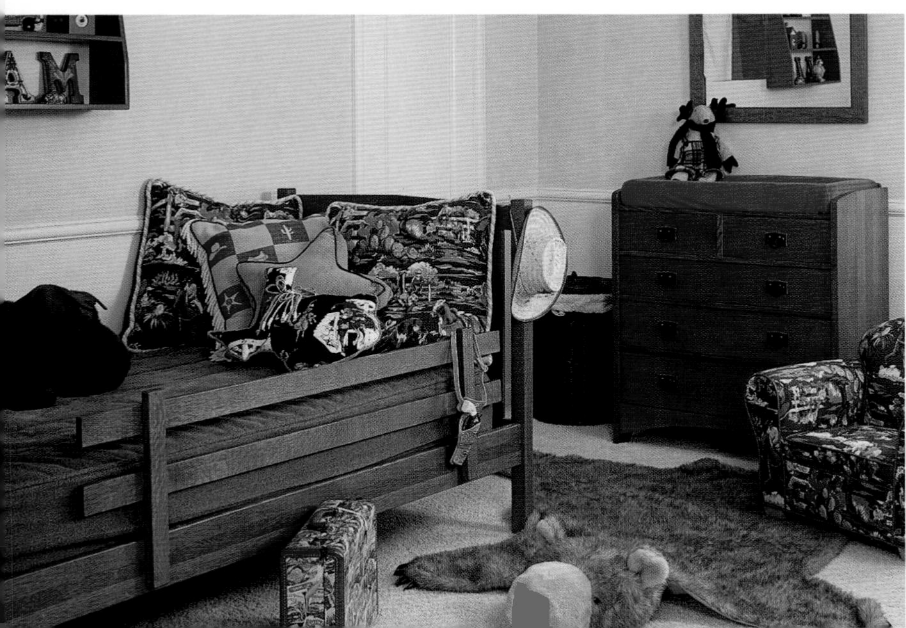

A sepia-toned Western scene, inspired by a similar painting in the father's childhood room, captivates the two boys who share this room. The bandana-like bumper ties, the footstool's retro fabric and other decorative details continue the idea. The masculine-looking Arts-and-Crafts-style furniture carries out the Western motif, and will last well into the next generation. When the younger boy outgrows his crib, a matching twin bed will become the lower unit of a set of bunk beds.

Twin girls share a room that, though feminine, is not babyish. Romantic balloon shades are lined with blackout fabric for nap time. A slipcovered chair and ottoman, previously used in another room of the house, are comfy enough for mom to snooze on at night. The floral-motif rug was discovered at a flea market. An open closet displays the girls' clothes, hats, and shoes.

comfort counts

IN THE BABY'S FIRST YEAR especially, most parents' top priority is sleep—for everyone in the family. For the baby, that usually happens in a crib or, early on, in a bassinet, pram, or cradle. Some families find co-sleeping in the parents' bed is what best assures a restful night's sleep. Whatever you decide, be sure the sheets on the bed are extra soft and securely tucked under, and that only thin blankets are used—or better yet, a warm sleeper and no blanket at all. Thick comforters pose a suffocation risk in the first year of life and are best used as decorative wall hangings or as floor blankets.

Placing a cradle right next to the parents' bed was to make midnight feedings easier; the tiny newborn still prefers the coziness of a Moses basket, so it is set inside the cradle.

Just as important is the parents' comfort in the nursery. Where will you recline during those middle-of-the-night feedings? Do you have somewhere to sit while the baby plays on the floor? Yes, you'll want to be down on the floor with him as much as possible, but there will be times when you just want to sit in a comfortable chair or rest on a soft bed or couch.

A rocker-glider is as comfortable as a medium-size chair can get, especially for nursing while sitting. But if space allows, consider putting a daybed in the nursery. It can provide a great way for both parents to get a better night's sleep: the one who is up to feed can lay down while feeding the baby, and the other is hardly disturbed at all. During the day it's a cozy place for story time. (For more information on cribs, bedding, and rocker-gliders, see those sections in "A Shopper's Guide.")

For something altogether different: a round crib with a high canopy draped in white eyelet is a feminine fantasy. The nearby bench doubles as a toy chest.

Originally brought in for the baby nurse, this twin bed waits for its future occupant. Meanwhile, caregivers lounge there while the baby plays on the floor. A unique frog-shaped toy chest complements the sea-creature theme.

Once the centerpiece of a guest room, the elegant queen-size wrought-iron bed stayed on in the room's nursery incarnation and set the tone for the decor. Though sometimes still used for visitors, the bed is mostly a luxurious comfort zone for nights when the baby needs company.

With closet doors removed, a double-size daybed fits nicely in the closet space and doesn't crowd the room. Most of the baby's clothes are in a dresser (not shown), but some hang from a pole above the bed. There is more storage under the bed and on a closet shelf obscured by the swag, made from sheets that match the bedding. Bumble-bee napkin rings decorate the curtain tiebacks.

Draping a mosquito tent over a newborn's crib ties into the mural's outdoor theme (it will be removed once the baby is rolling over). The painting's most engaging elements are low on the wall, where the baby can appreciate them. Simple linen bedding suits the room's restrained nature theme.

A crescent moon cradle rocks the baby to sleep in this dreamy, star-studded nursery. A child-size wing chair welcomes an older sibling at story time, while a matching parent-size chair is more than adequate for nursing sessions. Wall-to-wall lapis blue carpet is inlaid with gold stars.

clutter control

NOTHING DETRACTS from a room's potential as quickly as clutter. A baby's belongings, though small, are many: tiny socks, dozens of diapers, an armload of blankets, and toys, toys, toys. A messy space is inefficient and can be hazardous.

The best solution, of course, is to start by getting rid of any excess. At the very least, get it out of the nursery, or at least out of sight. If the clothes or toys are outgrown, give them away or store them on a high shelf in the baby's closet or in the basement. Also, keep a large, clear plastic bin in the closet for toys that you "rotate" off the shelves in your baby's room every month or so.

An open closet means no doors to pinch fingers, and allows the twin girls to help pick out their own outfits. Shelves, drawers, and an extra pole were built in for added efficiency.

Design solutions can make a big difference on the neatness front as well. Start with a thoughtfully planned closet—one that has child-scale hanging space, plus extra drawers, bins, or shelves. A shoe holder with clear pockets hanging on the back of the closet door is a great place for booties, socks, hats and other items likely to get lost in a big drawer. A changing table with drawers underneath keeps diapers, wipes, and creams handy but out of sight.

Be creative in solving your storage dilemmas. Can it be hung from wall pegs? Do you have an armoire in the house that can be relocated to the nursery? Can you mount shelves into a recess in a wall or across a corner? Consider open baskets and bins for storing toys—they make it easier for you and your child to identify what goes where and to get it there with ease. For more storage ideas, see pages 344 to 346.

A custom-built unit houses a cabinet complete with mini-fridge and microwave for storing and heating bottles. Baskets are mounted on drawer-like glides that keep them from falling out. The unit will eventually move to the playroom, where it will keep snacks handy.

SHARP Carousel

A family-heirloom washstand was treated to a coat of paint to match the walls, then topped with a snap-on contoured changing pad. The drawer keeps diapering supplies close at hand, while toys above entertain the baby during changes.

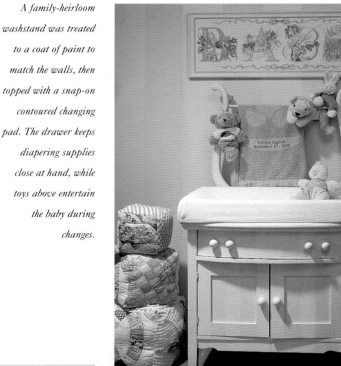

Walls can provide valuable storage and display space when shelves with pegs are hung. The out-of-reach space is ideal for precious mementos.

A distressed-finished armoire houses books, toys, and framed photos, as well as shoes, hats, and other accessories. Tall and narrow, it makes good use of vertical space in this small room. The doors can be closed for an even tidier look.

It's A Boy!
ANIMALS
BIG RED BARN

my first

A sturdy wall unit bolted to studs in the wall and painted a vivid red holds small toys and books now, and is large and versatile enough to house evolving collections throughout childhood.

A narrow wall space between closet and bathroom doors is efficiently used with a toy chest/bench below and wall-mounted shelves above. It's also an eye-catching place for a pony parade.

A flea-market-find cabinet was spruced up with fresh paint and flower details; it holds the mother's collection of glass animals and other delicate items. The cabinet has safety latches and is bolted to the wall. The arched doors on the right open to a deeply recessed cabinet with pullout drawers for toys not currently in use.

A SHOPPER'S GUIDE

BY NOW you've probably established an idea of the overall look you want your baby's room to have. But how do you pull it together? From bassinets and dressers to lighting and flooring, this chapter will provide the information you need. THE OPTIONS today are much more varied—often more sensible and, in most cases, much safer—than they were a generation ago. Traditional changing tables have been replaced by longer-lasting dressers with removable changing tops; cribs now meet strict safety guidelines; and old-style rocking chairs have evolved into comfy rocker-gliders. Also, there are as many different prices for any given item as there are places to buy it; being a savvy shopper can pay. LAST BUT NOT LEAST, health and safety concerns are ever more important in parents' buying decisions. We hear more each year about the effects of hazardous products and materials on small children, and we must make fully informed choices. Let this chapter be your guide.

Cribs and Cradles

COZY, SAFE BEDS FOR LITTLE SLEEPYHEADS

When it comes to the nighttime routine, not all families start with a crib. Most babies spend their first months sleeping in something smaller and cozier, such as a cradle or bassinet, that can be set up in the master bedroom for convenience during night feedings. And some parents take their baby into bed with them from the start and find the closeness both convenient and rewarding for them and comforting for the baby (if you're considering this arrangement, called "co-sleeping," discuss it with your pediatrician as there are risks associated with it). By the time a baby is rolling over, it's time to move to a crib.

Beds for newborns

While smaller beds aren't really necessary, many parents find they are easier to move from room to room during the first sleep-heavy months. Others buy or borrow a cradle or bassinet so they can put off the purchase of an expensive crib until they find out whether or not co-sleeping works for their family. Unlike cribs, these little beds are not regulated for safety features, so check them over carefully before you buy.

CRADLES are like miniature cribs on rockers. They're usually made of wood, measuring about 18" × 36", and are too heavy to move around easily. Because they're larger than most bassinets, they can be used longer—until just before a child begins to sit up, at about five months (which is why you'll want a substantial mattress—at least 2 inches thick). They are also the most expensive of the four types of newborn beds, ranging in price from $120 to $350, including bedding. Many families have an heirloom cradle that has been passed from generation to generation; sometimes parents buy a new one, intending to start a tradition.

A BASSINET is a stiff, woven basket that sits on a stand. (Ideally, you can lift it out of the stand to carry it downstairs.) Most come with a hood, which is handy for shading the baby from light during outdoor or daytime rests. Bassinets are lighter and slightly smaller than cradles, and can be less expensive; prices range from $40 to $550. Make sure the stand is sturdy and locks securely into position to prevent folding while in use. If the stand has casters, you can push the unit back and forth to lull the baby to sleep; check that the wheels are substantial and roll and swivel smoothly. As with cribs and cradles, the mattress should be firm and fit snugly in the basket. A shelf in the lower part of the stand is handy for storing extra blankets.

A cradle's side-to-side motion soothes the baby into slumber; a rocker lock stabilizes the cradle once the baby's asleep.

The bassinet usually ends up in the parents' room for convenience sake; consider choosing a fabric to match your room rather than the baby's.

A Moses basket (see top photo on page 336) is the least expensive of the newborn beds ($40 to $250), but by no means the least desirable. It's woven of corn husks and has relatively soft sides; it can even be packed into a large suitcase for travel to Grandma's house. While not likely to last generations, a decent-quality Moses basket will last for the first few months for several babies.

Sidecar sleepers (see bottom photo on page 336) are a response to the growing number of families who want to keep their baby close to them at night. These devices look like playpens (and, indeed, many of them convert to playpens), but with only three walls and a mattress elevated to the same height as the parents' bed. The unit attaches to the bed securely so the baby won't fall through the cracks (literally) but can rest within handy distance to the nursing mom. Models range in price from $150 to $300. Some parents achieve the sidecar effect by removing the drop side of a crib and wedging the crib between their bed and a wall.

Cribs

Once the baby has outgrown his cradle, bassinet, or basket, it's time to move to a crib. Cribs have been under strict safety regulations since the 1980s, so you can rest assured that any new crib you buy in the United States will be safe. Here are the basic safety requirements, as stated by the U.S. Consumer Product Safety Commission.

- Crib slats should be no more than 2 ⅜" apart; make sure none is missing, loose, or cracked.
- The mattress should fit snugly (no more than two adult finger-widths should fit between the mattress and the crib's side).
- The mattress support should be firmly attached to both head and foot boards.
- Corner posts should be no more than 1⁄16" high.
- The head and foot boards should not have cutouts, which allow entrapment.
- The side-release latches should not be operable by the baby, and should securely hold the sides in the raised position.
- All hardware should be present and tight.
- No soft bedding—comforters, pillows, sheepskins—should be placed in the crib.
- The baby should be put to sleep on his back.

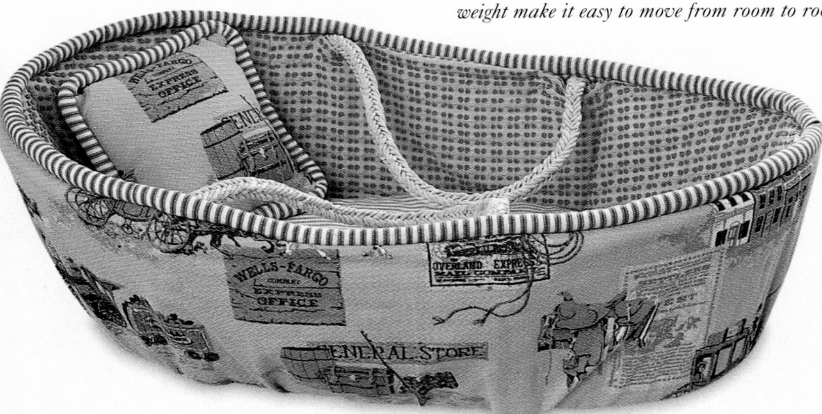

A Moses basket's manageable handles and light weight make it easy to move from room to room.

A few other things to look for: Is the crib sturdy or wobbly? Give it a few good pushes. If you are buying a metal bed, examine the welding closely, and run your hand over it—any sharp edges? Are the casters sturdy, and do they lock in place—or are they removable? (Active toddlers sometimes like to make their cribs "walk" across the room.)

Is the mattress support sturdy, and does it allow for air circulation? Some cribs have only vinyl straps or even cardboard supports; wood slats are sturdy, but offer little give; spring coils are a nice choice, and will be appreciated during the years of jumping on the bed.

Look at and ask about the finish. Luckily, lead paint was phased out in the late '70s (you shouldn't even consider using a crib of that vintage or earlier, even if it is a family heirloom). Still, the finish should be nontoxic and not prone to chipping. The more coats of nontoxic lacquer a crib has, the more gracefully it will take its inevitable beating.

Next, how does the side-release mechanism work? Some require the use of two hands spread an adult's arm-span apart, making it impossible for a baby or child to release. The downside to this type is that you can't operate it with a baby in your arms. Many cribs are moving to the lift-with-one-hand, push-with-knee action. This keeps one arm free for holding the baby, and the hardware is either invisible or minimally visible. The potential downside: a good-size sibling could open this without too much trouble.

Popular for years, and still found on some models, is the foot-release bar, which you press down with one foot while lowering the crib rail with one arm. This mechanism is falling out of favor, as the spring-loaded hardware is both visible and sometimes noisy, and too easy for even small kids to trigger. Less safe is the fold-down crib railing, which can pinch fingers (even limbs),

A sidecar sleeper keeps the newborn within arm's reach, making nighttime feedings less disruptive for everyone. Later, it converts to a playpen or travel bed.

and provide a foothold for babies to launch themselves out of the crib.

What about crib-mattress levels? While different models have as many as four levels, a practical, safety-minded parent would say only two are needed: a high position for before the baby is sitting or pulling up, and a very low position to last until the toddler reaches 35 inches in height or can climb or fall over the sides (signs that it's time to move to a regular bed). Also assess the frustration factor for the height-adjustment mechanism; lowering the mattress is one chore you won't want to procrastinate about.

Some cribs boast "convertibility." Remove one side and lower the mattress one last notch, and you have a so-called "junior" bed that uses the same crib bedding and looks like a little daybed. On others you unstack a dresser off the end, put on a longer mattress or mattress extension and have a "youth" bed, which requires sheets in a size that can be hard to find. In the end, most toddlers are quite ready to move directly from a crib to a new and exciting twin-size bed, and anything between is little more than a marketing gimmick.

The only other factors that separate the hundreds of cribs on the market are style, price, and quality. You can buy a crib for as little as $100 at a baby superstore, or pay up to $700 at a high-end shop. Styles range as much as in adult furniture. As this piece will probably be used the shortest length of time of any furniture in the nursery (except the cradle or bassinet), you may want to choose the style of dresser or armoire you like first, and pick the crib to coordinate with it (rather than the other way around). If you plan on using the crib for more than one child, it is probably worth spending a little more for extra sturdiness and a stronger finish. A word to the wise: Buy plastic teething covers for both side rails when you purchase the crib—babies start gnawing sooner than you think.

This crib's distressed finish will make it look less violated by the bangs and bumps baby furniture must endure.

Crib mattresses

There are generally two types of crib mattresses to choose from: innerspring and foam, with a wide range of quality and firmness in both types. Prices run from $40 to $150, and you can pay upwards of $600 for an organic-cotton crib mattress. Some higher-end furniture stores sell only innersprings, claiming foam mattresses break down too quickly. But a quality foam mattress will last a long time and can give better value than a cheap innerspring.

Whichever you choose, be certain it fits snugly in the crib you've chosen. Also, babies need good, firm support to prevent suffocation. If the mattress is foam, press your hand on it, and then see how quickly it regains its original shape. The heavier (denser) the foam, the longer the mattress should last. On an innerspring, check not only the number of steel coils but the thickness of the coils, and look for a border rod to give the edges support.

If you want the advantages of both foam and innerspring, seek out one of the new combination mattresses with dense foam on one side, for the baby months, and springs on the other side, for the toddler period.

Dressers and Changing Tables

WHEN IT'S TIME FOR A CHANGE, YOU'LL BE READY

While a tiny baby doesn't need a lot of furniture in those first months, you will definitely want a convenient, comfortable place to change diapers up to a dozen times a day. And even the tiniest clothes need to be stashed somewhere. Blankets, sheets, waterproof pads, and diapers need a home, too. Unless your nursery closet is spacious and outfitted with drawers or shelves, you'll probably need some sort of a dresser or armoire.

Diaper-changing surfaces

A changing table can lead a very short life. Even though some children wear diapers well into their fourth year, few parents bother hoisting them up onto a changing table beyond age two.

Luckily, the trend on the furniture side is away from short-use, stand-alone changing tables toward dual-purpose items—dressers whose tops start as changing tables and convert to hutches (or just plain dresser tops). You can pay as little as $100 for an assemble-it-yourself unit at a baby superstore, or as much as $700 for a high-end European model. Or you can create this effect yourself by simply using any hip-height dresser and fastening a contoured changing pad on top (they snap onto the back of the dresser with included hardware). Be sure that the dresser/pad combination is at a comfortable height for the person who will be changing the most diapers; bending over can be especially painful for new mothers who have had a cesarean-section delivery or epidural anesthetic.

The most important safety feature of a changing table is not straps or a raised side, as you might think; these features may lull you into a false sense of security when, in fact, you should never leave the changing table's side while your baby is on it. No, the most important precaution you can take is to have everything you need for the change within arm's reach—waterproof pads, clean diapers, a dirty-diaper bin, wipes or water, diaper creams, clean clothes. Be sure you arrange the space in and around the changing area to accommodate these supplies.

An option for families with a large bathroom counter is simply to make part of that room "diaper central." The surfaces are probably easier to clean, disposing of the diaper contents could not be handier, and warm water (a cheap, healthy cleanser for the baby's bottom) is in plentiful supply.

Finally, when you choose your changing pad, look for raised sides to keep your baby from rolling over in mid-change. Also, check on the availability of cloth covers. Do they come in colors that work for your nursery? Are they a standard size or by special order only? You'll want to have two or three covers, as well as a dozen or so small waterproof pads so you can place a fresh one on top for each change.

If the dresser you've chosen isn't at a comfortable changing height, you can buy a "deck" that will raise the pad and provide space for diapers and other change essentials underneath.

Once the changing-table surface on this wall unit is no longer necessary, a second hutch can be added to the dresser. Here, corner shelves hold baby-soft gear. They can be added at any time.

Dressers and armoires

When deciding on a dresser style, think not only about how much space you have but also about what you will put in it and how a child will use it. It will be used much longer than the crib, so choose with an eye to the future. You may even want to buy this piece at an "adult" furniture store. You can also get an inexpensive dresser at an unfinished furniture store, then paint or stain it to match your crib or other furniture you may already have chosen. Spend a little extra on unique knobs, and you'll have a custom piece for a fraction of the price.

A low, double-wide bureau is a wise choice, as all the drawers are easy-access by age three (with the aid of a small step stool), when most kids start wanting to dress themselves. A highboy makes sense only if you are short on floor space and want to store things out of your child's reach; make sure any tall dresser is securely anchored to the wall.

An armoire can function as a closet while the baby's hanging clothes are few and small. In later years, it can be used as a media cabinet or for collection display and storage.

Think about how the dresser will function in the future. Some models are part of a set that allows you to add a hutch on top or a corner shelf unit (also called a "radius shelf") on either side. Your child's storage needs will only grow, so plan accordingly.

Armoires are an increasingly popular choice; in the baby years, the top cupboard is outfitted with a pole to hang small dresses or jackets, while the lower drawers store the rest of the clothes and blankets. Some parents start out with shelves in the top portion, leave the doors open, and use it as a display area for the baby's treasures. Later, the cupboard can store collections, books, or even a television.

Safety considerations include the obvious—is it sturdy and free of sharp edges?—and the not so obvious—are the drawer knobs or handles easy for small hands to get a grip on? Gliders or center guides will make drawers slide in and out more smoothly, making it easier for preschoolers to dress themselves and put away their clothes. Drawers that are heavy and quick to shut, however, are a recipe for pinched fingers. If your toddler is a climber, put safety locks on the drawers, or they may be used as steps (another reason to anchor the dresser to the wall). Finally, ensure that the drawers can't be removed altogether, or a toddler may end up pulling one out on top of himself.

Other items you may want to save space for in your child's room: a small table and chair set (it will be appreciated by 18 months of age), a miniature armchair for "reading" (even one-year-olds love to imitate Mom and Dad), and a nightstand for next to the rocking chair (until the "big bed" comes along).

Toddlers enjoy having a small table and chair. Be sure to buy the smallest-scale version available so a little guy can get on and off the chair himself with ease. Some sets come with interchangeable legs that allow the table to "grow" as the child does.

Diaper Duty

If you are using a cloth-diaper service, it will provide you with a diaper bin; for safety's sake, use only nontoxic deodorizer cakes to keep it smelling fresh. For those who use disposable diapers, one kind of bin actually seals each used diaper into a plastic sheath to cut down on odor. The device's downsides: Some parents find it complicated to use, the sheath refills are an ongoing expense (on top of the cost of diapers and the bin itself, about $30), and the sheaths add even more plastic to landfills. A lined deodorized pail with a childproof lid, emptied daily, is kind enough on most parents' noses.

Rocking Chairs

A COMFY ROOST FOR WEE-HOUR FEEDINGS

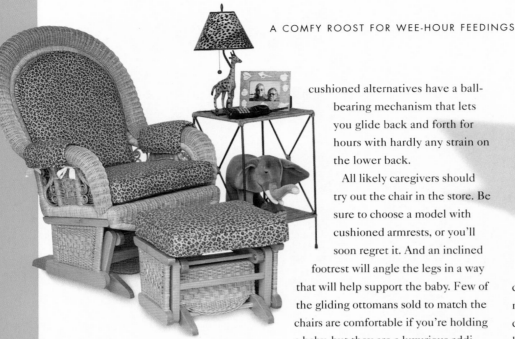

Rocker-gliders are available in hundreds of styles and upholstery choices. A nearby table keeps a reading light and telephone handy.

The baby's comfort quotient isn't the only one that matters—moms and dads will spend many hours throughout the day and night feeding and soothing their newborn, and a supportive, cozy chair makes everyone happier. Traditionally, rockers were the answer. But while their spindle back and wooden seat and arms look great, they're hardly what you want to sink into when you crawl out of bed for a middle-of-the-night feeding. Rocking chairs also have a tendency to travel across the floor as you rock them.

Step into any nursery furniture store and you'll see that some clever (or bone-weary) soul has come to the rescue with rocker-gliders. These heavily cushioned alternatives have a ball-bearing mechanism that lets you glide back and forth for hours with hardly any strain on the lower back.

All likely caregivers should try out the chair in the store. Be sure to choose a model with cushioned armrests, or you'll soon regret it. And an inclined footrest will angle the legs in a way that will help support the baby. Few of the gliding ottomans sold to match the chairs are comfortable if you're holding a baby, but they are a luxurious addition for future use.

Rocker-gliders are available in hundreds of styles, finishes, and upholstery choices to match any decor, from Shaker to contemporary. Rather than coordinating it with the nursery, many parents select a model that fits in with the master bedroom or whatever room the chair might be moved to later.

Not only is the chair likely to be the most comfortable seat in the house, it can also represent a significant investment: prices range from $100 for discount-store models to $1,000 for high-end, leather versions with swivel options, recline positions, even heated massage. Matching gliding ottomans can cost up to $430. As with cribs and other nursery furnishings, high-end gliders offer the best selection of styles and upholstery, but cost the most and require special ordering.

Some people prefer a simpler rocker. Luckily, more easy chairs are being "rocker-ized," like the two shown here. Again, look for good back support, a comfortable size, and an easy rocking motion.

Don't forget the most comfortable option of all (provided you have the space)—a daybed set up in the nursery to accommodate middle-of-the-night feedings.

Newer rocking chairs are both stylish and comfortable.

Shopping for Furniture: Where to Go, What to Ask, How to Save

The baby boom has created an enormous market for all things baby. But the level of service, quality of merchandise, and prices will vary depending on where you shop.

Baby specialty retailers, for instance, range in size from independent mom-and-pop stores to small chains to high-end, national franchises. These stores usually carry mid- to high-quality brands—and relatively high prices. On the plus side, they are also more likely to offer a higher level of customer service.

You'll find more competitive prices, but less in the way of helpful advice, at baby superstores; these tend to carry not only furniture and bedding but also baby clothes, diapers, and accessories.

Many department stores—discount and traditional—are quite likely to have baby departments these days. The furniture selection is often more limited and the staff less knowledgeable than in specialty stores; price ranges vary, depending on the store. And don't forget regular furniture stores—the crib is the only item you'll really need that you won't find there.

Web sites and catalogs are popping up all over. Prices can be very reasonable, though bedding and accessories may be better buys than furniture, for which shipping costs can be prohibitive. You can't see and touch the merchandise before you buy, so find out as much as possible about the brand and quality by asking detailed questions of the customer-service representative before you place your order. Some companies will even send out fabric or finish samples for a refundable fee.

Another popular option for bargain hunters is secondhand furniture. While you can find good dressers, rockers, and smaller items this way, buying a used crib is risky business as it's very difficult to know if it meets current safety standards (see page 335). To find out if there have been any safety complaints about secondhand items you've been given or have found at garage sales or consignment stores, contact the U.S. Consumer Product Safety Commission at (800) 638-2772.

Wherever you shop, evaluate baby furniture as you would any other major purchase. First, find out what it is made of. Solid wood is most durable, but also most expensive; a good veneer can often match it in appearance and beat it in price. Composition board is less expensive, but more prone to chipping. Finally, laminates are very sturdy, colorful, easy to care for, and reasonably priced.

Ask yourself these questions: Is the piece solid and sturdy? Is it free of sharp edges and splinters? Is the hardware secure, and are the corners rounded? Do all the moving parts work well? Always inquire about the item's warranty and the store's return procedure. For expensive items, you may want to think twice about a store-credit-only policy.

Storage

WHERE TO STASH, STACK, AND STORE ALL THAT STUFF

A baby's belongings grow exponentially, so storage space is always at a premium. Closets, floor space, and wall space can all be used very efficiently, thanks to the boom in storage devices and planning services. Most of the items mentioned here can be found at specialty storage shops, home centers, and large discount outlets.

Closets

Chances are, your nursery closet was designed for an adult's clothes and has one long pole hanging about five feet above the floor, with perhaps one shelf above that. Whether you do it yourself or hire a closet-organizing service (look under Closet Accessories in the yellow pages), you can make the space work more efficiently for your baby.

Early on you will need only one small pole for hanging clothes, and then only if you have a little girl with dresses. The pole's height should be adjustable, so that once your child is old enough to put clothes on a hanger (two to three years) she can reach to put them away herself.

Install shelves or sliding wire drawers on glider tracks below or next to the pole. Hang a clear shoe-storage bag over the back of the closet door for shoes, socks, hats, and other small items that are easily lost.

Save some space in the closet to store clothes, equipment, or toys that the child has outgrown (if you are sav-

One side of a double-wide closet has been fitted with an efficient combination of pull-out wire bins (for toys), drawers (for clothes), and shelves. A hanging mesh bag catches the baby's laundry items. The other side of the closet has more shelves, as well as two levels of hanging space.

ing them for another baby) as well as the clothes he has yet to grow into. Also, keep a large, clear plastic bin in the closet for toys that you "rotate" off the shelves in your baby's room every month or so; when you bring them back out, they'll shine like new again.

Shelves and bookcases

Bookcases, though one of the most practical furniture items a parent can invest in, are seldom sold as part of nursery furniture sets—yet another reason to shop at adult or unfinished furniture stores. The longer you intend to keep the shelves, the more durable you'll want them, and the more you may have to pay. Solid hardwood will hold up better in the long run than less expensive laminates or veneers.

As with dressers, if floor space is at a minimum, go for height (and be sure to anchor the bookcase to the wall). You'll want easily adjustable shelves, as toys and books range and change in size over the years. A 12- to 14-inch depth will accommodate most toys and books, yet is not so deep that things get lost.

Built-in shelving allows you to maximize space from floor to ceiling, and from wall to wall. Modular units—combinations of shelves, cupboards, and drawers—are often available in a wide enough range of sizes to offer the look and function of built-ins at a fraction of the cost and with much more flexibility. They are sold at many value-oriented furniture stores.

While closed cupboards may keep clutter out of sight, they make it harder for a toddler to see, get out, and put away his toys easily. Open baskets, bins, or clear shoe- or sweater-storage

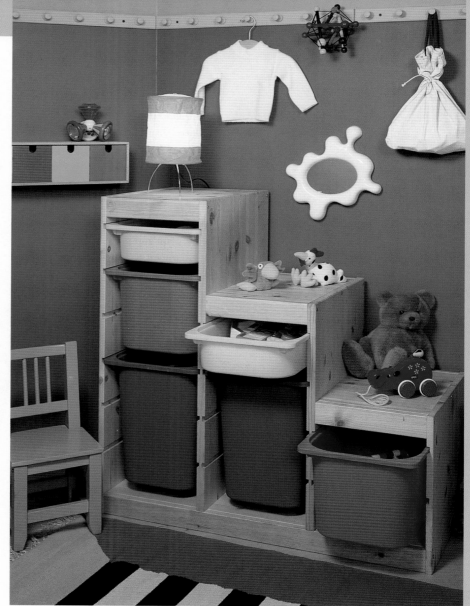

Lightweight plastic bins of varying sizes can slide out and be set on the floor; small, wall-mounted drawers are painted in colors to coordinate. The strip of wall-mounted peg rack acts as a dado molding, separating zones of contrasting wall color.

Peg racks can be simple or decorative; use them to hang clothes, hats, or toys. Mount them at least 36 inches off the ground to be above eye-injury height.

CD shelves are the perfect size for a baby's board books and small toys.

boxes on low shelves are easy to find and actually make maintaining order easier. Label containers with a picture of their contents to make them even more child-legible.

On the walls

Wall space can provide another dimension to your storage solutions. In addition to being practical, a variety of wall shelves, peg racks, and display cupboards add a decorative element. Small, high shelves are ideal for displaying framed photos, and glass-fronted display cupboards are a dust-free way to show off precious collectibles and mementos. Peg racks can be purchased everywhere from hardware outlet stores to baby-furniture boutiques, depending on whether you want plain and practical or cute and decorative. Use them to hang sweaters, bonnets, and christening gowns, or to hang drawstring bags full of toys.

Toy chests

While many parents-to-be think a toy chest is a nursery essential, this notion is mostly nostalgia. In fact, toy chests are more like toy "black holes": They are deep and big, and encourage disorder. They are great, however, for storing baby blankets or linens.

An important safety note: Heirloom toy chests and chests not designed for children's use can actually be hazardous, as the lids can slam down on fingers (and heads) and can entrap children. As you evaluate toy chests, look for ventilation holes, lids that are free of latches, and hinges that are spring-loaded to support the lid open in any position. Corner risers that create a finger space between the lid and the box are also recommended.

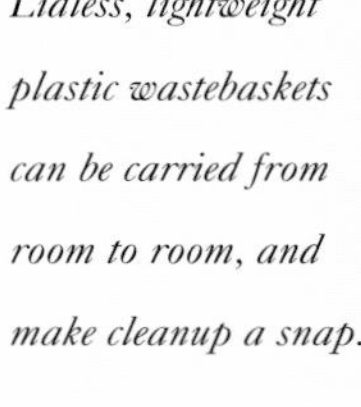

Lidless, lightweight plastic wastebaskets can be carried from room to room, and make cleanup a snap.

A handpainted toy chest is a beautiful addition to the nursery, and brings visual storytelling to a crawler's eye level.

Crib Bedding

PRACTICAL CONSIDERATIONS FOR THIS FABRIC FOCAL POINT

Translucent plastic in this space-theme crib mobile plays with light, casting rainbows around the room.

The linens available for cribs today are so lively and appealing that they can easily serve as the foundation for a nursery's decor. In fact, many companies offer everything from lamp shades to height-measuring sticks to stencil patterns that coordinate with their bedding lines. The trick is to rein yourself in and be sure your choices are safe and sensible.

The basics

What exactly do you need, and what should you look for? On the minimalist end, you will need three or four crib sheets and a few light crib blankets. A bumper isn't really necessary, and should be taken out of the crib as soon as the baby is sitting or pulling up, usually by around five or six months. Sheets should be generously cut to allow for shrinkage, as too-small sheets can slip off the mattress and entangle the baby. For the same reason, they should have good-quality elastic all around, not just on the corners. Make sure the sheet fits snugly and remains tucked under at all times. Cotton, knit, or flannel—it's up to you, but put baby's safety and comfort first.

The best crib blankets aren't the fluffy comforters sold in many bedding sets. In fact, because of the more than 1,000 crib deaths per year associated with suffocation, the U.S. Consumer Product Safety Commission recommends keeping fluffy bedding,

There's no rule saying infant bedding must be in pastels; babies also appreciate bold, high-contrast colors and patterns.

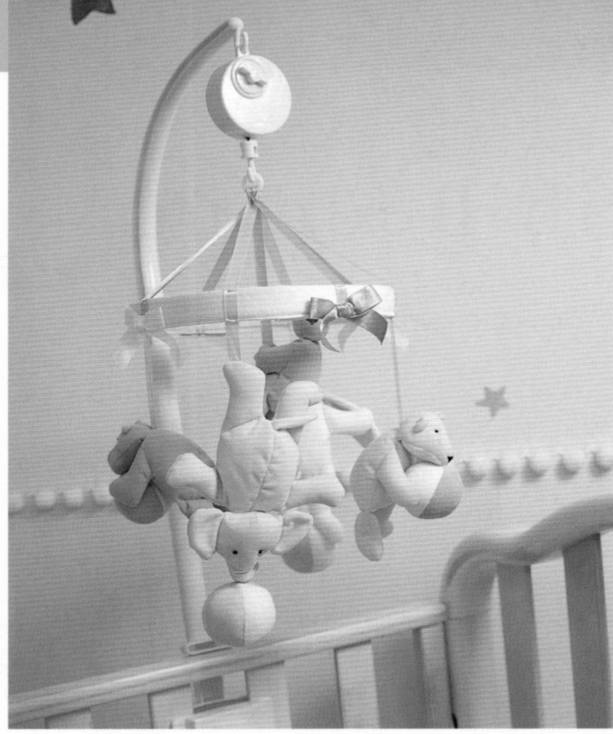

Soft, friendly creatures gaze downward at the baby from a wind-up musical mobile.

pillows, and stuffed animals, out of the crib altogether for the first year. (Comforters often end up being used on the floor or hung on the wall as decoration.) Temperature-appropriate pajamas or sleepers are the best covering, but if you must use a blanket, choose one that is lightweight and loosely woven, and tuck it under the mattress so that it covers only up to the infant's chest. Make sure your baby's head remains uncovered while sleeping.

Bedding sets

Most coordinated bedding sets come with a fitted sheet, a bumper, a bed skirt, and a blanket, coverlet, comforter, or duvet cover. (Remember, soft bedding is not to be used in the crib during the first year.) Most juvenile-furnishings stores charge from $150 to $250 for these sets, though they can be found for less at cut-rate department stores and baby superstores. Inspect each of the items individually, and be sure you can buy extra fitted sheets that will look attractive with the set. Also, keep an eye out for bedding sets with so-called "summer blankets"—these match the set but have no filling, so they pose less risk of suffocation.

You can also buy sets by the piece from linen catalogs, children's furnishings catalogs, and the increasing number of home stores offering baby lines. There is also the special-order option, available at most juvenile furniture stores, which will net you the greatest range of styles and, in many cases, better quality than off-the-shelf sets. Expect to pay between $300 and $700 for special-order or custom bedding.

Some quality checkpoints: Is the fabric prewashed for shrinkage and softness? Is the pattern printed on or stamped on? (If the latter, it will fade more quickly.) How tight is the stitching? If there are appliqués, are they secure? Are the bumper ties sewn on tightly, and on both the top and bottom of the bumper (and are there at least 12 bumper ties)? Is the bumper washable, or does it have to be dry-cleaned? Some high-end bumpers and comforters come with removable covers for easy washing.

Chances are, if you pay a little more for a higher-quality product, it will look better and last longer. Remember, you will launder this bedding more than most, and may use it for more than one baby (one reason to choose a gender-neutral set you really love).

Mobiles

Hung above nearly every crib (and most changing tables) is a twirling, cheerful, and sometimes musical mobile to entertain the baby. While these are often sold to match bedding sets, a mobile is more than just a nursery accessory. It's the baby's first toy and should be at least as functional as it is attractive.

The primary consideration should be: How will this look to the occupant of the crib? View it from underneath. The best mobile designs have the decorations angled downward so the baby gets the full visual impact. A musical option is nice too.

A versatile, C-shaped cushion is an ideal nursing pillow, as well as a supportive first chair and prop for the baby.

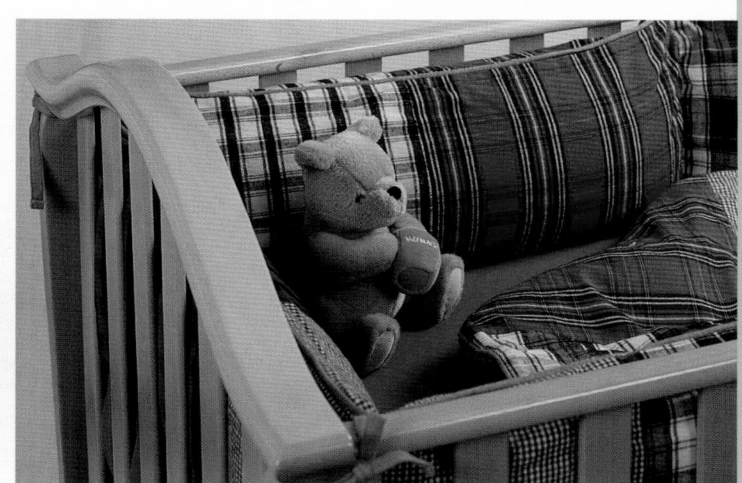

Crib sets come in every pattern and palette imaginable. And if you can't find what you want in a store or catalog, it can always be custom-made in the fabric of your choice.

Wall Treatments

TURN A BLANK CANVAS INTO A COLORFUL BACKDROP

Walls can be a simple background for the nursery's other highlights. Or they can be the room's focal point, setting the theme with an elaborate mural or whimsical wallpaper. Whichever you choose, the finish should be nontoxic and easy to clean.

Yellow and white stripes below are separated from the stars and swirls above by a glued-on strip of ball fringe.

Paint

A fresh coat of paint in just the right shade can change a room's look overnight. While color is the main paint question parents ponder, there are important safety issues to consider, too. First, if your house was built before 1978, when lead-base paint was banned in this country, have the walls and trim checked for lead by a professional or by using a home test kit. Lead poisoning is a serious danger for adults, children, and even a fetus. If lead is detected, call the Lead Information Center and Clearinghouse at (800) 532-3394 for information on how to proceed.

Next, which finish and type of paint should you choose? Most parents select a water-base latex in a wipeable eggshell finish for the walls, and a durable, easy-to-wash semigloss finish for the trim. Water-base paints are not only less smelly than their oil-base counterparts, they are also quick and easy to apply, and they dry faster.

Because of increased awareness about the harmful effects of solvents, more and more parents are choosing not only paints that are water-base latex (which have less solvent in them than oil-base formulations) but also those labeled "Low VOC" or "No VOC" (for volatile organic compounds). Most paint stores carry these health- and environment-friendly products in the same range of colors as regular paints. Whatever product you choose, paint the nursery at least a month before the baby is due, and allow plenty of ventilation during and after painting.

Rubber stamps dipped in colorful acrylic paints are easy enough for the most amateur decorator to create effective designs.

Decorative painting

A baby's room seems the perfect place for a mural or stencil treatment. An increasing number of professional muralists are offering their services; word of mouth is the best source, followed by references from baby-furnishings stores. College art students are a less expensive alternative. There are also paint-by-number mural transfer kits that give professional-looking results to the most amateur painter. Rubber stamps dipped in acrylic craft paints are perhaps the simplest and quickest way to give walls an individualized treatment.

One money-saving approach that will make changes easier down the road: Limit the mural to one wall, and paint the other walls in the background color or a complementary shade.

Wallpaper

Another way to jazz up nursery walls is with colorful wallpapers or borders. If you've already selected the bedding, window coverings, or trim paint, be

Crawlers appreciate it when an engaging mural comes down to their level.

sure to bring samples or swatches with you when you go to the wallpaper store. Bring along room measurements, too, so you can get an accurate estimate of how much paper you'll need.

Vinyl wallpaper is most durable and the easiest to clean, but it can harbor mildew in hot, humid climates with air conditioning. Coated paper is also wipeable, but be sure to ask about recommended cleaning procedures. Uncoated paper wallpaper isn't practical for a nursery or child's room. If you haven't wallpapered before and/or your walls are uneven (as they are in many older houses), you may want professional installation.

Wallpaper borders are an even simpler way to bring pattern to nursery walls. Though often applied where the walls meet the ceiling, mounting them lower on the wall provides more fun for the baby. Some parents apply the border about 30 inches from the floor, or about where a chair rail would be, and either use different colors above and below it or apply an easy-to-clean paint below and wallpaper above.

As with paints, ask store salespeople or your installation expert about using low-VOC adhesives, and allow at least a few days for the room to air out after application.

Wall accessories

Plain walls can be dressed up easily with all manner of pictures, framed photos, and cloth wall hangings (here's your chance to display the quilt or comforter that can't be used in the baby's crib). Make sure whatever you hang is secured to the wall firmly; anything hung above the crib should be extremely lightweight (consider decorative paper plates or printed fabric). Posters or fancy sheets of gift wrap laminated on pressboard give a finished, easy-to-wipe look without glass; most frame shops offer this service—and charge less for it than for regular framing.

Nursery no-nos

While chalkboard paint and corkboard walls are great choices for older children, they're unsafe for babies. Chalk and chalk dust are too likely to be ingested, and the tacks used to attach things to cork walls are a hazard.

Borders and wallpaper can be mixed and matched or used on their own to bring life to dull walls.

A Word on Children and Environmental Toxins

More and more research is being done on the potential effects of toxins in everything from paint to wallpaper adhesives to carpet backing to new furniture. While the verdict is still out on many issues, it is clear that babies are the most vulnerable population for adverse reactions, for a number of reasons. Their organs and systems are not yet fully developed; they take in more air in proportion to their body weight than do adults; they spend more time close to the ground where toxicants in dust and carpets settle; and their hand-to-mouth behavior creates pathways for exposure to toxicants, especially lead in paint chips or pesticide residues.

If you are interested in learning more about making healthy choices consult the resources on Children's Environmental Health Network's Web site, www.cehn.org, contact Mothers and Others for a Livable Planet at www.mothers.org, or check the Washington Toxics Coalition at www.accessone.com/~watoxics.

Flooring

THE LOWDOWN ON WHAT'S UNDERFOOT

Babies spend a lot of their first two years on the floor—crawling, playing, and yes, falling. You'll want a surface that's hospitable to the little one's various activities but also easy to keep clean. While carpeting is soft for crawlers, most types are not suitable for, say, building block towers. It also stains easily and traps dust mites and residues tracked in on shoes. Wood floors and resilient surfaces, such as vinyl and cork, are better for play and far easier to keep clean, but offer little cushion for a fall. That's why most experts recommend a combination of hard or resilient surfacing with one or two small rugs or a carpeted area.

Resilient surfaces

Though often associated with kitchens and bathrooms, vinyl, linoleum, cork, and rubber are also good choices for the nursery, as they are hard-wearing, easy to clean, and softer than wood. Sealed cork is especially practical, as it is sound-absorbing as well as soft underfoot. Available in tiles or sheets, it is relatively easy to install.

Stenciled numbers and letters add a playful element to Douglas fir flooring, above. The primary colors blend well with children's toys and bedding, and the random pattern provides flexibility in arranging the furniture. Resilient flooring (below, left) can be cut and fit together seamlessly into playful patterns and color combinations, either wall to wall or as an area "rug." Playful interlocking rubber "puzzle" tiles cushion falls (below, right). The tiles come up easily and can be configured to fit any room shape. Edging pieces are available.

Vinyl is another resilient flooring, especially appealing for the array of colors and patterns available. Cushion-backed vinyl is softer underfoot but may dent under heavy furniture or with a child's playful abuse. Inlaid patterns wear longer than photographically printed patterns. Be sure to ask about the protective finish on any vinyl you consider, as well as cleaning requirements (some have to be waxed, while others have an easy-care finish). Some vinyls must be professionally installed; others you can install yourself. Costs vary from about $4 to $40 per yard, not including installation.

Wood floors

Warm and appealing in its look, wood is a natural choice. Though a bare wood floor can be noisy, an area rug here and there will quiet things down, as well as add color and softness. If the nursery already has wood floors, make

sure they are splinter-free. Fill any cracks or spaces between boards, or they will attract crumbs, dirt, beads, and siblings' other very small toys.

If the floors are in rough shape and you'd like to refinish them, again look for low VOC-content products. Alternatively, you could sand the rough spots and paint the floor in a geometric pattern, or add a stenciled border. Be sure to apply a top coat of sealer for easier cleaning.

Sculpted carpet can be made into area rugs, as shown here, or be designed for wall-to-wall installation.

Carpet

While wall-to-wall carpet seems like a soft, quiet solution for the nursery, spills and spit-ups create hard-to-remove stains, and dust settles in too deeply for most vacuums to extract. The latter is especially problematic for babies with allergies or asthma. If you are nevertheless set on wall-to-wall carpeting, choose a very low pile, a loop carpet, or commercial-grade carpet. Consider a border of a different color and texture to appeal to a baby's developing tactile and visual senses; composing a pattern from an array of carpet squares can also add interest.

When choosing carpets, inquire about which is most stain resistant and easiest to clean, and least allergenic. Nylon often fits that bill, in addition to being less prone to pilling and static electricity. Be sure to use padding under it, not only to cushion falls but also to protect the carpet itself and the flooring.

As with paint and wallpaper, the backing, foam, dyes, insecticides, and adhesives used in carpet and installation often off-gas VOCs (volatile organic compounds). If this is a concern for you, shop for environmental and health-friendly natural floor coverings and pads. Install carpet with tacks rather than glue, do the job as far in advance of the baby's arrival as possible, and let the nursery air out with open windows for at least 72 hours.

Area rugs

Throw rugs and larger area rugs are available in many nursery-appropriate colors and designs. Look not only in baby furnishings stores but also in home-furnishing and bed-linen catalogs and stores.

Hooked rugs offer the most detail and wonderful colors, and even come in whimsical shapes; most of them are made of cotton or nylon. Check with the manufacturer about cleaning procedures. The old braided rugs are back, in brighter colors, in wonderfully soft chenille; they come in a wide range of sizes, in both oval and round shapes. And don't forget thick bathroom throw mats that come in every color towels do and couldn't be easier to clean.

Whichever rug you choose to soften up an area of the floor, be sure to leave some hard surfacing for racing cars, floor puzzles, and the like. Also, use a nonslip pad to keep the rug in place.

Low-pile or looped carpet in patterns (left) adds visual interest underfoot and helps mask stains. Hooked rugs (right) come in a fanciful array of motifs and colors. Be sure to use nonslip pads underneath them.

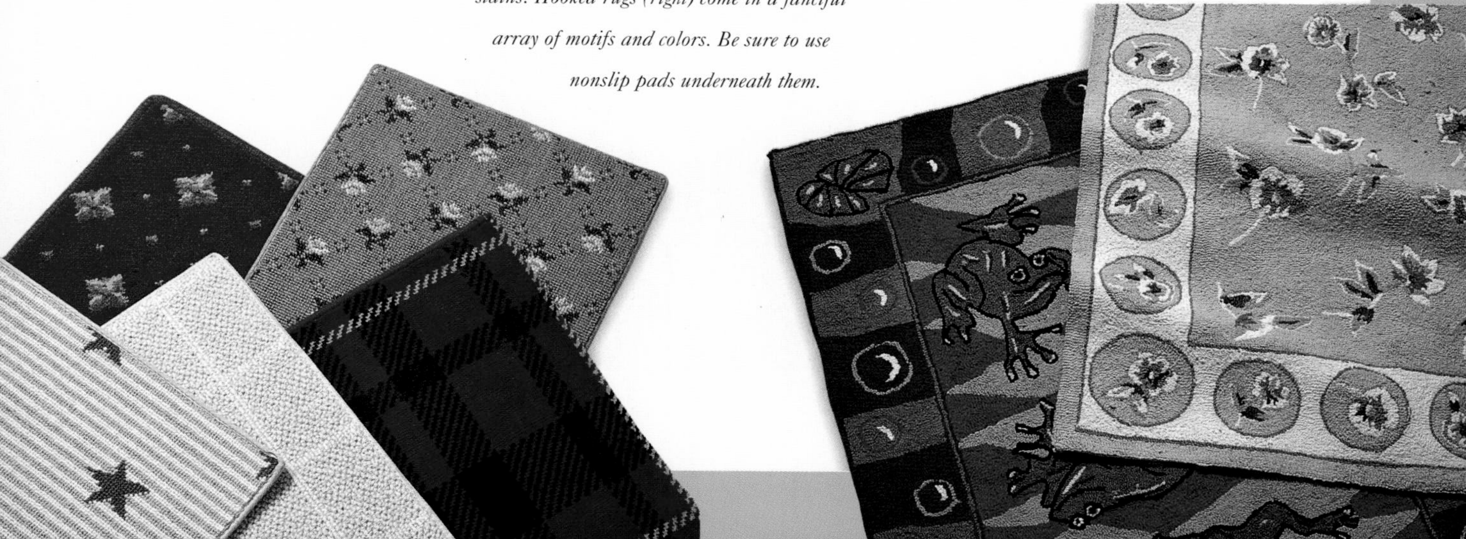

Window Treatments

FANCIFUL WAYS TO DARKEN A ROOM DURING THE DAY

Window coverings in the nursery not only help modulate the light (important for those early afternoon naps) but add a decorative element, too. Balancing the two jobs is easy, given the abundance of choices and their mix- and match-ability. As always, safety is a top concern, especially when it comes to the cords and pulls associated with many window coverings. Also think about ease of cleaning, as you will have less time but more messes on your hands once you become a parent.

When you head to the store, be sure to bring detailed measurements of your nursery windows; photos will help when it comes to describing exactly where the coverings will be installed, and which measurements apply to what areas. If climate control is an issue where you live, ask about the window covering's R-value, which indicates a product's resistance to heat loss (the higher the R-value, the more complete the insulation).

Blinds

Wooden-slat blinds are more traditional and and give better insulation, while metal and plastic look crisp and contemporary and are less expensive. All types are relatively easy to keep clean. One caution: Replace any imported vinyl miniblinds made before the summer of 1996, as these have been found to contain lead.

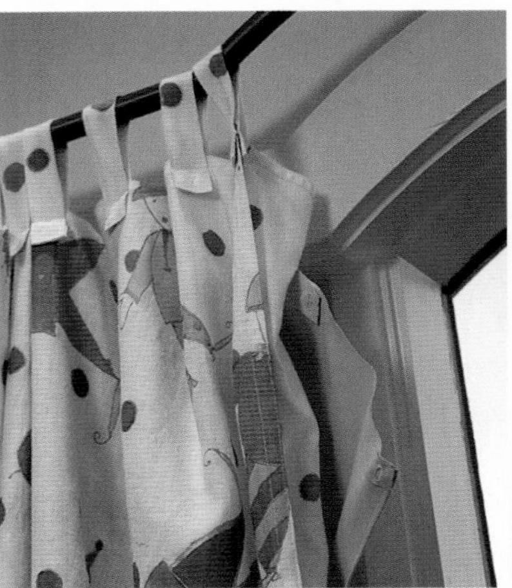

An odd-shaped window gets special treatment with a custom wrought-iron curtain rod and custom painted-linen curtains that follow the window's curve. A button-out blackout lining blocks strong eastern light and is removed easily when it's time to launder the curtains.

A valance is accented with painted letters spelling out the child's name (top). Traditional wood-slat blinds (above) make it easy to modulate light; their clean lines are softened with a button-trimmed valance.

If you have standard-size windows, you may find off-the-shelf blinds to fit; otherwise, you'll have to special-order them (delivery rarely takes more than a week or two). While blinds come in a wide range of colors, the most sensible choice is to match the window trim. You can hide the hardware for the blinds and add color and pattern with a cloth valance or boxlike, fabric-covered cornice.

Remember, blinds' cords present a choking hazard: wrap excess cord tightly around a cord cleat fixed as high on the window frame as the shortest adult can reach.

Shades

Choices here range from a simple roller shade to custom-made Roman or balloon shades to the newer cellular shades. Roller shades are the least expensive, and can be dressed up with iron-on fabric, wallpaper, or even painted designs (use fabric paints). Kids may be tempted to toy with the auto-release mechanism on some shades; choosing a pulley system will make this less attractive. On a pulley system, though, be sure to have the continuous-loop chain cut short enough so it can't be reached by children.

Blackout shades have an inner layer that keeps light from penetrating, giving a nightlike feel to a room for daytime sleeping. Be sure these shades are cut generously enough so rays don't sneak in from the sides or bottom of the shade.

Curtains

While curtains and draperies can really dress up a window, they are the least practical option in a nursery. They tend to be harder to clean than blinds or shades; and because they gather more dust, they can be especially aggravating for allergy- or asthma-prone children. They are also tempting for little ones to play with and hang on.

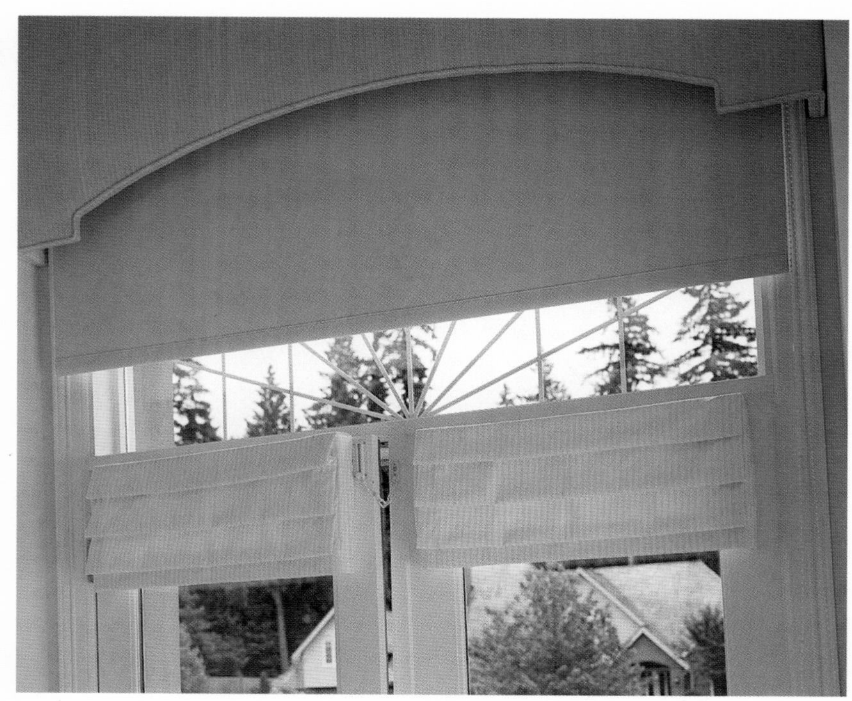

Blackout blinds hang behind the Roman shade-like valance on the terrace door and also behind the cornice on the arched window above the terrace door.

Lighting

BRIGHT IDEAS FOR ILLUMINATING THE ROOM

For your sake as well as your baby's, think carefully about the nursery's lighting. You will want to be able to check on your sleepyhead without waking him, as well as have adequate light for story reading and playtime. Because lights involve both hot bulbs and electricity, safety is, again, a primary concern.

You'll find suitable light fixtures at a range of suppliers. Juvenile-furnishings boutiques will have the widest array of child-oriented lamps, while general lighting stores will offer a wider range of ceiling fixtures in simple styles that would be fine for a nursery and would adapt well to a child's room. Specialty lighting and juvenile-furnishings catalogs are another source of lamps and light fixtures.

When choosing lights for the nursery, stick with those that accept regular incandescent bulbs. Halogen bulbs, while long-lasting, burn dangerously hot and produce too bright a light for babies. Also consider the light switch: Will it be easy for a small hand to operate? While initially you may not appreciate a toddler's frequent on-and-off-with-the-lights games (a product of their fascination with cause and effect), there will soon come a day when you appreciate their independence in such small tasks.

Ceiling fixtures

Overhead fixtures are the safest light source in a nursery since the wiring is behind walls and the fixture itself is well out of the baby's reach. Choose a fixture style with a shade that covers the bulb and softens the light; babies spend a lot of time staring at the ceiling, and untamed bulbs can be harsh on young eyes. Some shades have glow-in-the-dark designs that linger long after lights-out, giving the baby something to gaze at.

If you are having several recessed lights installed, consider having several switches so that the lights can be operated independently. And whether you have one overhead light or several, be sure to install a dimmer switch to make it easy to check on the baby at night without rousing him.

Wall fixtures

Sconces and wall fixtures provide more localized lighting than an overhead fixture. They are safer than table lamps because they aren't easily knocked over, but chances are they are reachable by a determined toddler, so teach your child a healthy respect for hot bulbs early on.

Ideally, wall lights are hard-wired into the wall so there are no cords hanging loose. If that's not possible, hang the fixture as close to the outlet as possible and secure the cords in

Table lamps can be dressed up with shades hand-decorated to reflect the room's look.

This low-wattage lamp's colored insert rotates slowly, creating moving pictures on darkened walls.

Lamps like this one are often sold as part of a bedding collection.

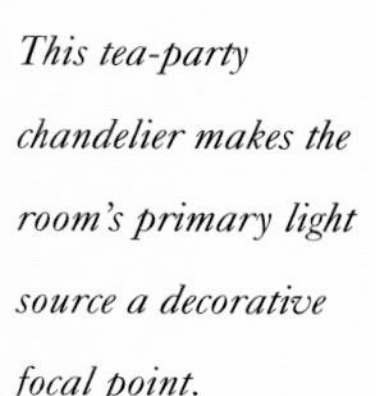

This tea-party chandelier makes the room's primary light source a decorative focal point.

A ceramic ceiling fixture features star cutouts—a subtle, gender-neutral touch.

covers adhered to the wall (some people use duct tape or masking tape painted the color of the wall).

Freestanding lamps

Table lamps come in a wide range of nursery-appropriate styles; many are designed to match bedding sets or have juvenile themes. Some are made of ceramic, others of painted wood, and still others are crafted from antique toys. In some cases, the lamp base is the decorative centerpiece, while other lamps feature a clever shade.

While nursery table lamps are decorative, they can also be dangerous. Ideally, they sit out of reach on a table that blocks the outlet they are plugged into; excess cord should be gathered on a cord winder. For extra safety, consider screwing the lamp onto the table or dresser.

Floor lamps are an option only for older children.

Nightlights

Recent studies suggest that a nightlight (or any dim light) left on all night in a room occupied by a baby under two may be related to later myopia (nearsightedness). While the research still needs follow-up, the evidence is compelling enough to suggest that a nightlight is appropriate for the hallway, but not the nursery (unless it is turned off once the baby falls asleep). All the more reason to put the main light on a dimmer that you can regulate as you enter and leave the room. If you do use a nightlight, be sure to locate it well away from any flammable materials, and consider using nightlights that have cooler neon minibulbs, rather than 4- or 7-watt bulbs.

Wall-mounted lamps can provide soft indirect light (sailboat) or act as reading lights (gooseneck and beaded hat).

Safety

HOW TO KEEP THE NURSERY HAZARD-FREE

The good news about home safety is that most childhood injuries are actually preventable through a combination of good sense, safety devices, and supervision. While you can hire "baby proofers" to come into your home and secure it Fort Knox-style, you can probably accomplish the same thing yourself for a fraction of the cost and find most of the products at home centers, drugstores, mail-order catalogs, and baby-oriented Web sites.

When evaluating safety equipment, remember that in order to be effective it must be used. Is installation relatively simple? Will the device work on the intended door, cabinet, or drawer? Is it easy enough for older siblings to use and resecure? Assume your toddler will test the device: Will it withstand these assaults? If the answer to any of these questions is no, choose another model. And keep your receipts: Safety devices are notorious for working in a limited range of situations.

The gear recommended on these pages is limited in scope to nursery safety; consult baby-care books or the U.S. Consumer Product Safety Commission's Web site (www.cpsc.gov) for information on the rest of the house.

With a safety gate mounted on the outside, a terrace door can be opened for fresh air without any worry that the terrace's wrought-iron railing will be climbed. The knob cover provides an extra measure of security.

Safety latches and locks are for cabinets, closets, and drawers, or anywhere you keep items that could be hazardous to babies, including medicines, scissors, fire ladders, and so on. Doorknob covers are another way to keep small children out of closets.

An adjustable bracket secures a bookshelf to the wall, but allows some movement in case of earthquake.

Safety gates can be used to keep a baby from wandering during a play period or after a nap (if the crib no longer does the job). They can also be installed in window frames above the first floor to prevent dangerous falls (or look for special window guards). When evaluating a safety gate, be sure slats are vertical so they can't become toeholds. Those that are mounted onto the walls are safer than pressure gates, especially in windows and at the tops of stairs. The latch should be easy for an adult to operate. Look for a seal of approval from the Juvenile Products Manufacturers Association (JPMA).

A smoke detector should be installed just outside the nursery (in fact, outside every sleeping area in the home). Be sure to check the battery monthly and replace it annually, or use a 10-year battery.

A carbon monoxide alarm should be placed outside the baby's room if you have gas or oil heat or an attached garage. Be sure the device meets requirements of the most recent UL standard 2034 or International Approval Services standard 696.

Outlet covers are a must to prevent shock and electrocution. If you use outlet plugs, make sure they are UL-listed and cannot be easily removed or choked on. Because it is so

Smoke and fire detectors (far left) should be mounted either inside or just outside of the nursery. A sliding safety latch mounted on the bifold closet door (top left) keeps the doors closed and fingers from being pinched. Mounted sliding outlet covers (bottom left) are easy for parents to use, but keep paper clips and small fingertips out.

easy to misuse these plugs (take one out to plug something in, then never replace it), a better choice might be to install outlet plates that require a left-sliding motion to plug in a cord. If you won't need the outlet, replace the face with a blank plate. If you are concerned about your child pulling a cord out of the outlet, look for outlet and plug hoods that prevent this.

Window-blind cords should be cut if they are looped, to prevent strangulation (remove the buckle as well); put safety tassels on the cut ends. Use cord cleats high on the window frame to take up excess cord. If you are buying new window coverings, inform the salesperson that you would like to have safety options on the cords.

L-brackets, available at hardware stores, will secure tall or tip-prone dressers and bookcases to the wall—essential if you have a "climber." If you live in an area prone to earthquakes, look for a hinged model.

A baby monitor will alert you when a sleeping baby awakens or otherwise needs you. Monitors in which both the base unit and the receiver can be powered by either household current or a battery give you the most flexibility.

A cordless phone is an invaluable safety device, as it allows you to supervise your child even when callers beckon.

If you are concerned about a product's safety—especially if you are buying a used item—the U.S. Consumer Product Safety Commission lists all product recalls since 1994 on their Web site at www.cpsc.gov; or call (800) 638-2772 for recorded messages or a live operator.

IDEAS FOR GREAT

KIDS' ROOMS

DESIGN: JEANESE ROWELL INTERIORS

A Western ranch was the inspiration for this theme room featuring rough-hewn pine bunk beds, a leather easy chair, a rustic clothes pole, Indian-design pillows, and outdoor gear including a lasso and fishing creel.

contents

362

Focusing on Kids

365

A Planning Primer

395

Great Kids' Rooms

429

A Shopper's Guide

712

Index

special features

Safety Tips **369**

Dealing with Allergies **370**

Partners in Planning **374**

A Room Fit to Live in **384**

Space Savers **387**

Displaying Collections **391**

Buying a Mattress **433**

Shopping for Furniture **438**

FOCUSING ON KIDS

In the past, a child's room tended to be treated like any other bedroom in the house. The room was outfitted with standard furniture, and frequently bore the same color scheme as the rest of the home. Only the belongings revealed that the occupant was not an adult.

Sometimes stereotypes took over the decor, resulting in frilly pink furnishings in a girl's room and what were generally regarded as "masculine" colors and accessories in a boy's.

Now there's a growing recognition that a child's room should be designed to suit one particular child, and that the space is not only a place to sleep but also a personal environment that needs to fulfill many roles—play area, study hall, hobby center, meeting site, and storage locker.

It's not enough just to create a functional, comfortable room. Kids today are more style conscious than ever, about everything from running shoes to pillow covers. They want their rooms to look cool. That means getting the right colors, the right furniture, and the right accessories.

(Even if your child isn't yet old enough to have strong opinions about room decor, it's only a matter of time

Harlequin-motif puppet theater occupies a corner play area. The young puppeteer can hang belongings on the whimsical clothes pole.

DESIGN: CROWORKS AND JOYCE BOHLMAN DESIGNS

before individual preference and peer pressure kick in.)

Although you'd like to please your child, you certainly don't want a room so trendy that you have to overhaul it repeatedly to keep pace with changing fads. This book shows you how to create a room with long-lasting appeal that's also open to adaptation.

In the following pages, you'll find all the nuts-and-bolts information necessary to devise a workable plan. For inspiration, thumb through the gallery of photographs. Then turn to the shopping guide for product information and buying tips.

Coordinating bedding, window treatment, and wallpaper border establish a nautical theme.

DESIGN: LANDS' END

A cozy sleigh bed and a building-shaped cupboard are prominent features in this blue and white room. Checks and plaids tie together the decor and convey a homey feeling.

DESIGN: NANCY RUBINSTEIN AND JEANNE WHITE INTERIORS

K A N D I N S K Y

DESIGN: SAMSON McCANN

A PLANNING PRIMER

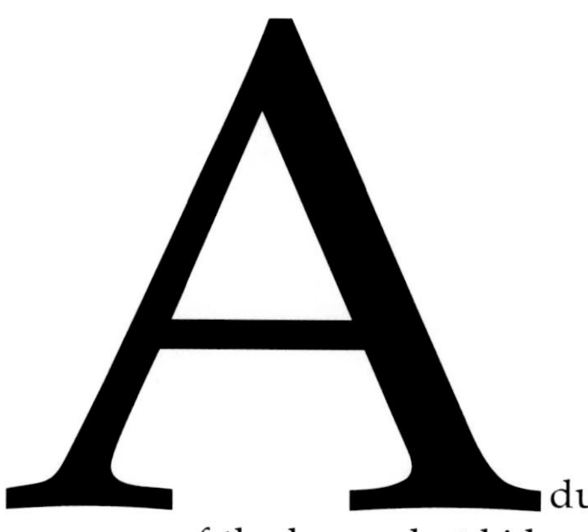

Adults use many rooms of the house, but kids pack most of their living into a single room. A bedroom may be a sleeping chamber to a grown-up, but to a kid it's also a place to listen to music, play games, sprawl on the floor, roughhouse, read, study, build models, daydream, visit with friends, and stash innumerable possessions. That's asking a lot from four walls!

You'll need to plan carefully to create a room that serves all those functions, yet is comfortable and inviting—and has enough staying power so you don't have to redecorate every few years. This chapter guides you through the process, starting with some general observations about children's needs and seeing you through to a specific plan for your own child.

Bright colors create a cheery atmosphere for the occupant of this compact but well-organized space. The low sleeping loft, accessible by scarlet ladder rungs, contains plenty of storage below. A desk extends from one side.

DECORATING CONSIDERATIONS

In the case of any room, including your child's, the physical layout—not only the dimensions but also the locations of windows, doors, electrical outlets, telephone jacks, and heating vents—dictates many decorating decisions. Of these "givens," electrical outlets and telephone jacks are usually the easiest and least expensive to change, so don't feel boxed in if they are inconveniently placed.

Budget is another important constraint. If there are no limitations, you can do whatever you like—buy a roomful of coordinated furniture or hire a designer to create a fantasy-satisfying refuge. Otherwise, you'll have to prioritize your needs. You may want to invest most substantially in a few good pieces, such as a solidly constructed bed and dresser, and spend less on the rest of the furnishings. Or you may want to buy modular pieces that can be added to or reconfigured over the years.

You don't have to buy everything new. There's a large market for used furnishings for kids. Just make sure that any secondhand items you acquire are safe and sturdy.

Beyond physical and budgetary limitations are other considerations more directly related to your child. A nicely decorated room may look great to parents and friends, but unless the style and contents suit the child, he or she won't fully enjoy the room. Here are some observations to help you start defining your own child's requirements.

WINDOW TREATMENTS & ACCESSORIES: MUFFY HOOK

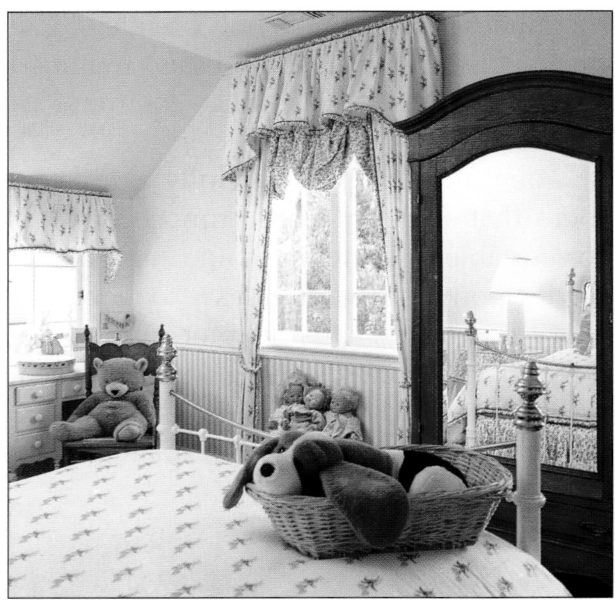

This pretty room was designed for a young girl who likes feminine things. Remove the dolls and stuffed animals, and the decor is sophisticated enough to take the resident into her teen years.

Age

Obviously, the arrangement should be appropriate for your child's age. A toddler feels comfortable in a room with a low bed, small-scaled chairs, pictures of nursery-rhyme characters, lots of stuffed animals, and brightly colored accessories—whereas a budding teenager would be mortified to bring friends home to such a room. Kids develop so quickly that you have to be on your toes to keep up with their evolving needs and tastes; see pages 371-373 for basic room requirements at various ages.

You'll also have to consider the desired life span of the decor. If you intend to redecorate frequently, you can indulge in furnishings that appeal to a limited age group and change the look when it's obvious that your child has outgrown it. But if you want the decor to last longer, more planning is required. You'll have to think ahead if you want the same basic furnishings to serve your child from infancy to young adulthood, with only slight modifications over the years. Many parents take a middle road, opting to redecorate every six or seven years.

Personality & Interests

Like adults, children feel more at home in rooms that reflect their personalities and interests. There is no generic kid's room, just as there is no standard room that will appeal to all adults. If you're fixing up a nursery, the decor will reflect your own preferences. But it doesn't take much time for youngsters to exhibit traits and tastes that can be expressed in the decorating process. If they're old enough, include them in the planning; such involvement may also motivate them to take better care of their things.

Rather than build the decor around a specific person with specific likes and dislikes, you may be tempted to let gender guide you. But be aware that your child might not be happy with the results. Your young daughter may love a room filled with pink ruffles—or she may prefer a play loft that allows her to jump and climb. Don't count on your young son relishing a sports theme just because he's a boy. He may be more interested in astronomy.

DESIGN: SARA OLESKER, LTD.

A child's zeal for computer games suggested a room's decor (top)—easily altered with a change of bedding and window treatments. These young girls (at right) enjoy furniture their own size.

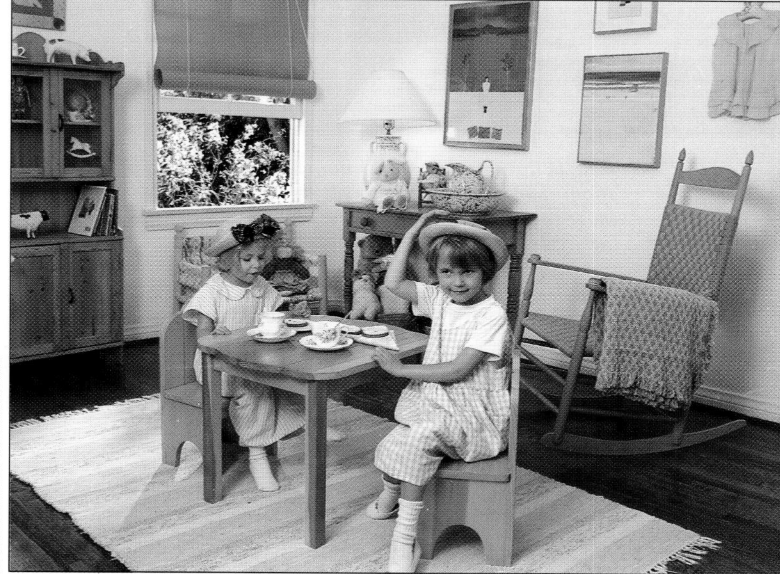

DESIGN: SUNDAY HENDRICKSON

Planned Activities

Since kids really *live* in their rooms, allow space for the many activities that will take place there: playing, studying, reading, pet care, painting, listening to music, and entertaining friends. If there's a separate playroom, some of these activities can be accommodated there.

Unless there's a permanent place elsewhere in the house for your child to build model ships or conduct science experiments, plan a hobby area in the bedroom even if it's a tight squeeze. That way, you won't have to keep clearing the kitchen table or living-room floor, and your child's efforts won't be repeatedly disrupted.

Scale

Homes are designed and furnished for the comfort and convenience of adults. At least in their own rooms, kids should have a sense of control over their environment. They should be able to hang up clothes, reach toys or books, sit in chairs their own size, and look at pictures without having to crane their necks.

Placement of furnishings is important from the start, since children discover much of the world by touch. Toy shelves, drawers, and pictures should be placed low in baby years. "Out of sight, out of mind," so keep possessions visible and within easy reach of little kids. Also, if children can't reach their belongings, they have to rely on adults to get what they need—or they may endanger themselves by trying to climb up and grab what they want.

When planning a room for a young child, think small—imagine that you've shrunk to less than half your height. The real challenge is to arrange the room so that it stays in scale with a youngster who grows bigger each year. Adjustable furniture—shelves that can be rearranged or a table with a top that can be raised—is a wise investment.

DESIGN: SARA OLESKER, LTD.

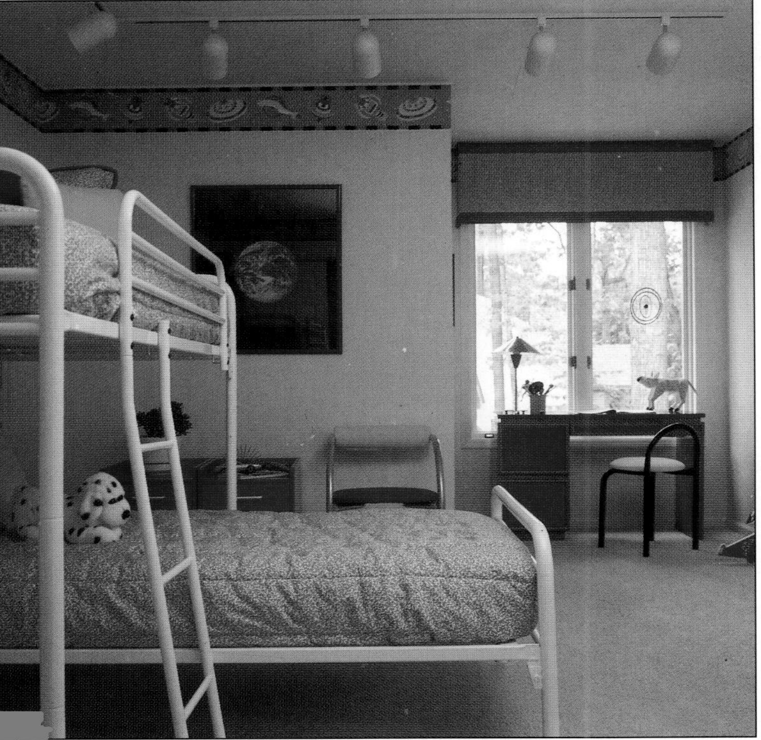

Red, yellow, and green combine in a fresh way in this room. The color scheme is all the more striking set against beige walls and carpeting.

Furnishings should also be in scale with the surrounding space. It's jarring to have a tall canopy bed in a tiny room with a low ceiling, or a diminutive dresser in a cavernous room. Having a lot of large furniture in close quarters can overwhelm a child, just as too-sparse decor can engender a sense of loneliness.

Colors

You might prefer a fairly neutral palette in the rest of the house, but no such inhibitions apply in a kid's room. Here, anything goes—including bold, brassy colors and wild combinations. In fact, a committed color scheme helps you choose coordinated furnishings. You can use color to set a mood, unify disparate elements in the room, or define territory in shared quarters. Color can even have a coding function, helping children know where to return playthings, books, or clothes after use.

The color wheel, at right, provides some basic information. Among the pure hues, the most powerful are the primaries—yellow, blue, and red, the source of all other colors. Secondary colors (green, orange, and violet, formed by combining primary colors) are a little weaker, although still vivid. Intermediate colors, created by mixing a primary with an adjacent secondary color, have less impact.

Most kids love bright, unadulterated colors until they're about 10. Avoid an all-white, sterile-looking room, since young children need visual stimulus. Also refrain from using a lot of very dark or deep colors for fear of creating a dreary or oppressive atmosphere. Extended colors—those to which a little black, white, or gray have been added—are a great choice for teens, since they produce a more sophisticated look than pure colors do.

There are two schools of thought about choosing colors for kids' rooms. Some experts advocate letting even toddlers pick their own colors, on the theory that they will be drawn to ones that fulfill some psychological need. Others advise parents to make the aesthetic decisions until the child develops a good sense of color preference, which can happen as early as age three or four. Even when youngsters can't verbally express their feelings

Color Wheel

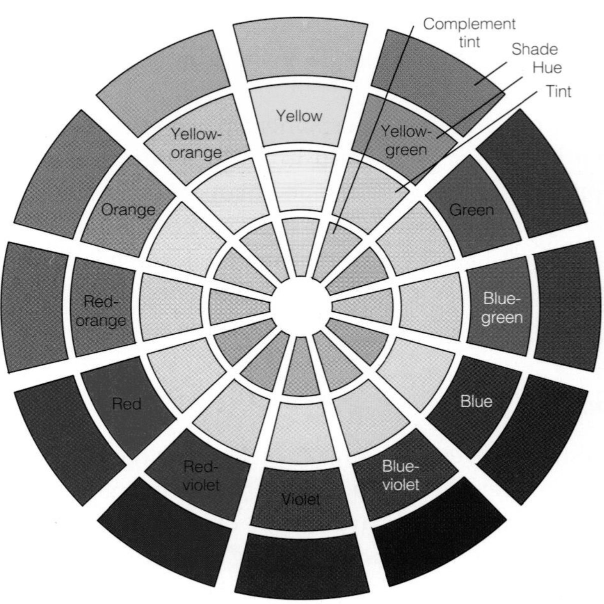

The color wheel locates primary colors (yellow, blue, and red) at equidistant intervals around a circle; transitional colors connect them. Each pure hue is labeled. Adding black to a color makes a "shade"; adding white makes a "tint." A "complement tint" is formed by adding a bit of the color opposite on the wheel.

SAFETY TIPS

A safe environment is important at all stages of life, but it's critical for young kids. Here are some simple measures to make your child's room safe.

Cribs & Beds

■ Make sure the crib conforms to current safety standards; see page 431. For tips on buying cradles and bassinets, see page 430.

■ Keep an infant's bed free of long ribbons, cords, and hanging toys that the baby might reach. Remove crib gyms and mobiles when the baby is able to push up onto hands and knees.

■ When your child leaves the crib for a bed, attach a low guardrail if the sleeping surface is more than a foot off the floor. Placing the bed in a corner, fenced by walls on two sides, adds a measure of safety.

■ Reserve the top level of a bunk bed and other elevated beds for kids at least six years of age.

Electrical & Heating

■ Keep lamp and appliance cords out of reach so the baby can't tug or chew on them.

■ As soon as your baby begins to crawl, cover unused outlets with safety caps and replace broken or missing receptacle cover plates.

■ Use a wire reel to keep excess lamp cord neatly stored.

■ Eliminate extension cords whenever possible by rearranging furniture. If you must use an extension cord, unplug it when not in use.

■ Screen off any unguarded heating register, radiator, or other heat source.

Windows

■ Keep crib and playpen far enough from windows so your child can't yank on curtains, break glass, or climb out the window.

■ Don't put climbable objects under windows.

■ Install window locks that allow only partial opening so a small child can't fall out.

■ Keep drapery, shade, and blind cords out of reach of young children. Shortened cords and wands are available by special order. If you don't want to cut a long cord, wrap it around a cleat mounted high on the wall.

Furnishings & Storage

■ Use a changing table or mat with raised sides and a safety strap.

■ Arrange furniture to make sure your child won't climb to dangerous heights.

■ Store toys and games low to the ground, and keep potentially dangerous items such as lotions or scissors high and out of reach.

■ Make sure a lidded toy chest has safety hinges to prevent the lid from slamming shut. Safer choices for toy storage include open chests, plastic bins, and low shelves.

■ Position storage hooks either above or below your child's eye level.

■ Get sturdy, well-constructed furniture, since you can't predict how a child will use it. Look for smooth or rounded edges, not sharp ones.

■ Anchor tall or unstable furniture to the wall.

Miscellaneous

■ Get rid of small objects that could find their way into a crawling baby's mouth. Also avoid decorating a toddler's room with accessories small enough to be swallowed.

■ Keep baby care products well beyond a tot's reach. Use a diaper pail with a childproof lid.

■ Use throw rugs with skidproof backing.

■ Install smoke detectors to comply with local codes.

■ Make sure that walls, furniture, and toys are free of lead-based or other toxic finishes. This might be a danger with any surface painted before 1978, when regulations outlawing lead in paint went into effect. If you find lead (special swabs for detecting it are available), remove it while wearing an approved breathing device, eye protection, and old clothing that you can throw away; don't sand the finish, or you'll fill the air with lead dust. Apply a new, nontoxic finish specified for children's products.

■ For the latest information on warnings and recalls on children's products, call the Consumer Product Safety Commission hotline at (800) 638-2772.

about color, they often provide clues—for example, in the colors of crayons or construction paper they most frequently choose. Some kids favor toys of certain colors.

If you consider your child's taste extreme, limit the preferred color to wall paint—it's far easier to repaint than to replace all the furnishings. Or highlight that color in the bedding, which you will probably need to replace in a few years anyway.

Maintenance

A child's living space isn't a showroom—it's a place where a real kid spends a lot of time working and playing as well as sleeping. Filling the room with fragile, easily marred furnishings or ones that absorb dirt and stains is asking for trouble.

Even generally tidy kids aren't saints (and neither are their friends), so don't expect too much of them. Not only do accidents happen, but also kids can be expected to let loose from time to time. Choose materials that make it easy to maintain the room, no matter who's in charge of tidying up—you or the child.

The younger or more careless your child, the more durable and easy to clean the materials should be. Look for hard-wearing, spillproof, dirt-resistant surfaces for the floor, walls, and furniture. Good choices include scrubbable vinyl wallpaper, wood with a waterproof finish, and laminate tabletops. And washable fabrics are more practical than those that must be dry cleaned.

Noise Control

Controlling noise may be an important factor, depending on the type of activities taking place in your child's room and the room's location relative to other living areas in the house. The sound of incessant music or boisterous play may drive you crazy if your child's quarters are near a room where you or other family members spend a lot of time.

If your house is large, consider moving the noisemaker to a more remote part of it. But if you're stuck with the current setup, choose materials that deaden sound. Cover the floor with wall-to-wall carpeting or a large area rug, and use cork or another bulletin-board surface on the walls and ceiling.

DEALING WITH ALLERGIES

You can take steps to minimize your child's suffering from allergies without going to the extreme of stripping the room so bare that it looks like a monk's cell.

Reducing the amount of dust in the bedroom, since that's where your child spends so much time, will improve the problem dramatically. A significant allergen is the house dust mite, a microscopic creature that lives in house dust and feeds on natural fibers and on skin and dandruff shed by humans. The mites are prevalent in bedding, natural-fiber carpeting, and cotton-linters (the stuffing in mattresses and upholstered furniture).

Cut down on exposure to mites by encasing the mattress and box spring in dustproof plastic protectors that zip shut; get the kind sold by companies specializing in allergy products (allergists usually provide order forms). Some plastic mattress cases sold through mass merchandisers tend to sweat and crinkle.

When furnishing the room, avoid upholstered furniture and choose synthetic materials rather than natural fibers. Instead of feather-filled pillows, use polyester-filled ones. Cotton sheets and blankets are all right, as long as they're washed frequently. Choose washable rather than dry-cleanable window treatments. Stuffed animals should also be washable.

Hardwood or resilient floors are preferable, but if you must have wall-to-wall carpeting in your child's room, make sure it's made of nylon or another synthetic material and not wool. Throw rugs that can be laundered frequently are fine.

Avoid dust catchers. Anything that isn't moved regularly, such as the contents of a bookcase, accumulates dust. Keep surfaces as clear as possible so they can be dusted or vacuumed two or three times a week.

Filters will prevent forced-air heating systems from spreading dust through the house. You can get filtering units for individual vents or a single filter for the whole furnace.

Ban any pets with hair, fur, or feathers from your child's room. You don't have to deprive a pet lover, though—cold-blooded animals, such as fish and turtles, won't cause any harm.

AGES & STAGES

A room that suits your child perfectly at one stage of development can be pretty hard to live with at another. Kids change so much in such a short time that you need to be alert.

The following are basic requirements for different age groups. They're generalizations that may or may not apply to a particular child, but they can give you a rough idea of what to expect. If your child doesn't fit the mold, forget about generalities and pay attention to what he or she is telling you verbally or through behavior cues.

Infancy

An infant needs only a safe place to sleep and to be changed. Plan to provide convenient storage for diapers, toiletries, and clothing and a comfortable chair where you can feed and cuddle the baby. You'll also want to have an overhead light on a dimmer, a nightlight, and a window covering that allows the room to be darkened. Once you take care of these basics, you can decorate the room however you please—but realize that you're doing it more for yourself than baby.

Newborns can't see well enough to appreciate a nursery decked out in frills or peopled with storybook characters. Even though their eyesight gradually improves (by the age of six months, they can focus on details across the room), babies appear happiest with a limited amount of stimulation.

Babies are interested in sights and sounds close to them. Until they're about six to nine months old, they see black and white and other sharply contrasting colors the best. Simple patterns seem to elicit the most pleasurable response—for example, three dots representing the eyes and mouth of a human face, a bull's eye, or a checkerboard.

An infant's senses of touch and hearing are almost up to adult standards. Babies like a variety of textures and soft, melodic sounds. They're more interested in tactile objects and in crib toys that move or play music than they are in a static wallpaper pattern or furniture with a juvenile theme.

Once a child starts to crawl and then to walk, safety becomes even more vital; for measures to protect tots, see page 369. Even though toddlers have senses that are more finely developed, they still aren't old enough to appreciate nursery decoration.

If you want to keep things simple, you can satisfy your baby's requirements and yet create a room pleasing to the adult eye. The style of the furniture along with the color of the crib bumpers and bedding can give the room personality. You might like to round out the decor with details such as a wallpaper border or a shelf of stuffed animals.

Two to Five

This is a time of great exploration, as youngsters climb on furniture, take things apart, and poke into everything they can reach. Keeping safety in mind, stock the room with sturdy, spillproof furnishings and keep breakables out of reach. Walls should be washable and floors hard-wearing and easy to clean.

Children appreciate decoration now, especially images of favorite storybook or cartoon characters, and they love bright colors. A chalkboard, bulletin board, artist's easel, or continuous roll of paper will provide a safe outlet for creative urges.

Your toddler can go directly from the crib to an adult-size bed, or you can opt for a smaller bed that will last until about age five. Some kids will kick up a fuss about an intermediate bed, demanding a standard-size one like the other kids have.

At this stage, youngsters need lots of toy storage. Keep it low so they can reach items and put them away easily. A toy chest or several color-coordinated bins can handle this job. Toys could also go on low shelves or in drawers under the bed.

DESIGN: LEWIS OF LONDON

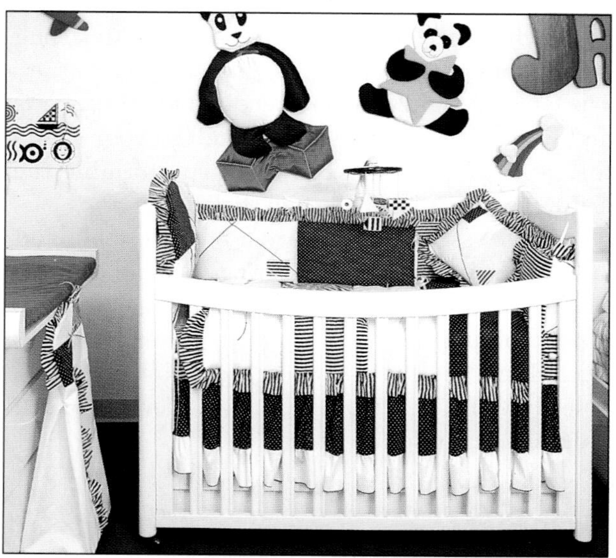

Infants seem to appreciate simple black-and-white patterns within close view, such as the designs on this crib mobile and bedding.

DESIGN: LITTLE ONE'S HAND PAINTED FURNITURE

Propped in a corner, a fancifully painted folding screen with door and window cutouts creates an enchanting hideaway for two- to five-year-olds.

Ample play space is also important. Younger kids like to play wherever parents are, so toys usually end up all over the house. Older kids are more comfortable playing in their rooms by themselves. The floor is the favored place for play, so you'll want to keep a good portion cleared. If the room has a wood or resilient floor, add cozy throw rugs or an area rug to create soft places to sit.

A child-size table and chair set provides snug seating for crafts, painting, puzzles, and tea parties. The tabletop should be large enough for art projects and the chair should be low enough so your child's feet rest on the floor. The more comfortable the child, the longer he or she will stick to the task.

Other essential items are a bedside table and lamp. Choose a window covering that can dim the room if you want your child to sleep when it's light outside. Young kids don't usually have many articles of clothing that need hanging, so a dresser, stackable drawers, or a wardrobe with plenty of shelf space is usually sufficient.

Six to Eight

At this stage, kids are developing strong opinions about decor and can participate more in choosing furnishings or rearranging the room. Listen to your young ones and take them shopping with you, but be prepared to help them compromise, since their choices may not be sufficiently practical.

Despite how grown-up they may seem at times, they're still kids. Even though they attend school full time, they also spend many hours in their rooms and so need plenty of play space. Your child is now old enough for a high platform or climbing structure, if you want to incorporate one.

Kids this age are mature enough for elevated sleeping, in a loft bed or the top level of a bunk bed. This is about the time they begin to ask for sleepovers, so think about providing a trundle bed or some other guest accommodation.

It's time to replace child-size tables and chairs with larger furniture that can be used for homework. Add lighting to illuminate study, reading, and other specialized task areas in the room.

The need for storage only seems to grow as kids get older. To make room, you may want to stow seldom-used toys and games elsewhere in the house or give them away. Modular storage units will allow you to add capacity as your child needs it.

DESIGN: KATHERINE WALDEN. DECORATIVE PAINTING: AUDREY P. RABY

Six- to eight-year-olds need plenty of places to stash toys and ample floor space for play. The decor here is playful, but not too juvenile.

DESIGN: EURODESIGN, LTD.

The well-organized study area in this preteen's room incorporates a pop-up dressing table. The wreath over the bed provides another grown-up touch.

Nine to Twelve

Decor assumes new importance at this stage, and many kids like to take charge of fixing up their rooms. Give them a good surface for tacking up posters and other doodads if you want to preserve the walls.

Although kids in this age group still play, they now engage more seriously in sports and hobbies. They begin collecting things in earnest—rocks, baseball cards, books, animal figurines, whatever strikes their fancy.

As they approach the teenage years, youngsters become increasingly intolerant of anything that seems babyish. They no longer want to be associated with a climbing or other play structure or items with a juvenile theme. They may ask for more grown-up belongings—for example, your daughter may want a dressing table with a mirror.

Storage is a major consideration, since kids need room for collections, games, books, and assorted possessions. Now is also when they begin needing space for more—and longer—clothes.

Youngsters have more homework now and need good study areas. Your child may be ready for a computer in the room. If you've been holding off on purchasing good carpeting and window treatments, your child may now be responsible enough to justify installing them.

Teens

At this stage, kids become increasingly independent. They spend more time away from home and when at home, especially in their own rooms, privacy is paramount. A teen feels that his or her room is a personal domain, to be run without interference.

Relics of early childhood are an embarrassment. Your teen may even consider bunk beds too childish, so you may want to unstack them to use as twin beds. Other easy ways to give the room teen appeal are to swap old bedding and window treatments for more sophisticated ones, and to trade small throw rugs for a larger area rug. Toning down bright primary colors on the walls and ceiling can also make the room seem more grown-up.

There's more homework now than ever before, so your teen needs a good study space with plenty of room to spread out books. Another requirement is an area for listening to music. Seating for friends is also a must—it can be in the form of a day bed, folding chairs, or floor pillows.

A teenager wants to be able to accommodate a growing wardrobe. Storage areas previously used for toys can now house hobby materials, collections, books, sports gear, a stereo system, and electronics equipment. Since your teen's reach has increased, you can install higher shelving.

DESIGN: EURODESIGN LTD. & LILY T. SACHS INTERIOR DESIGN

Teenager's room features sophisticated accessories and a modular wall system that stores study and hobby gear.

PARTNERS IN PLANNING

The ultimate experts on what kids like best are kids themselves. It makes sense to bring your child into the planning process since he or she has to live in the room. Helping to plan the room and pick out items for it also instills a feeling of self-worth and pride.

Don't expect young kids to understand the concept of room coordination. They may want furnishings with colors and patterns that clash wildly. You may have to inject some order into the process—but don't modify your child's concept so much that you deal it a deathblow.

Don't expect every desire expressed to be realistic—not many parents have the budget or space to install a swimming pool or jacuzzi in a kid's room. But keep an open mind. Some of the ideas may be workable just as they are, others may need a little refinement, and still others may spark more practical inspirations.

For fun, we asked a group of fifth graders in Belmont, California, to describe their dream rooms. Here is a sampling of their responses in words and pictures.

After I watch my big-screen TV, I can relax and read a good book. In my reading nook there are a lot of soft pillows and warm blankets. There is also a big green beanbag chair that squishes when I sit on it.

—Allison

My dream room has a gorgeous canopy bed and closets full from shopping. My bed has a peach comforter and satin pillows of every color. The high canopy has pink flowers and pretty peach drapes that I can close at night.

—Meghan

My dream room has a secret area in the wall where you can hide money, a diary, or anything else personal. You open it by pushing on one side of my green-and-black bed.

—Jason

Wouldn't it be fun to have a computer with all sorts of games and a window that can change its scenery just by pressing a button?

—Mina

My dream room has a beautiful aquarium and a refreshing slurpy machine. The aquarium serves as my wall and has many tropical and unknown fish in it.

—Renee

ROOM TO GROW

You can rightly expect a newly decorated living room or master bedroom to stay pretty much unchanged for many years. But a kid's room shouldn't be static. You can't fix up a room for a young child and think your decorating chores are finished until your offspring leaves for college.

You can choose to redo the room completely every time your youngster outgrows or tires of the decor—but that's unnecessary, not to mention expensive. If you plan well and decorate with an eye toward the future, you'll be able to modify the room periodically to meet the needs and tastes of a developing child.

The key is to build flexibility into the decor. One of the best ways to do that is with adaptable furnishings—pieces that can be added onto, reconfigured, raised, or converted to another purpose as your child grows.

DESIGN: CHILD CRAFT

This crib converts from sleeping quarters for a baby to an intermediate bed for an active young boy or girl. Just detach the side rails, add a mattress extender, and move the chest of drawers to the side.

DESIGN: TARA RYAN, L.A.I. DESIGN

Here, the crib can be moved out and an adult bed slipped in without rearranging all the furniture. The crown molding will create a canopy effect over the bed.

Modular Furnishings

Many manufacturers offer modular room groupings that include beds, dressers, work surfaces, bookcases, and other components. The modules can be configured to your child's requirements and then rearranged as needed. Make sure that what you choose now will be usable later on. Bookcases may hold stuffed animals today, but they should be suitable for school texts or encyclopedia volumes tomorrow.

A modular closet system is also practical over the long haul. The shelves, drawers, poles, and other components can be rearranged as your child grows.

Although often considered part of a closet system, sturdy stacking drawers and bins can have other uses. For example, drawers can be stacked to create a low dresser for a small child. When your child outgrows the dresser, restack the drawers to support a plywood or laminated desktop. Stacking bins make wonderful storage containers: start low and stack higher as your child gets taller.

Convertible Furnishings

Convertible furniture offers flexibility. Many kids' stores sell dressers with a top that serves as a changing table, then later flips over to become a toy or knickknack shelf. You can also buy cribs that convert into day beds and toddler beds, or toddler beds that convert into adult-size beds. A sturdy cart that you use for baby supplies can support a television set or a stereo system later on.

Infancy

Ages 6-8

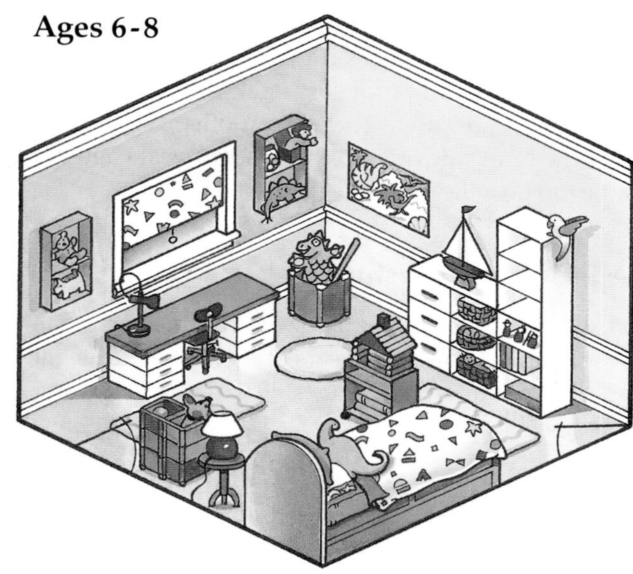

Ages 2-5

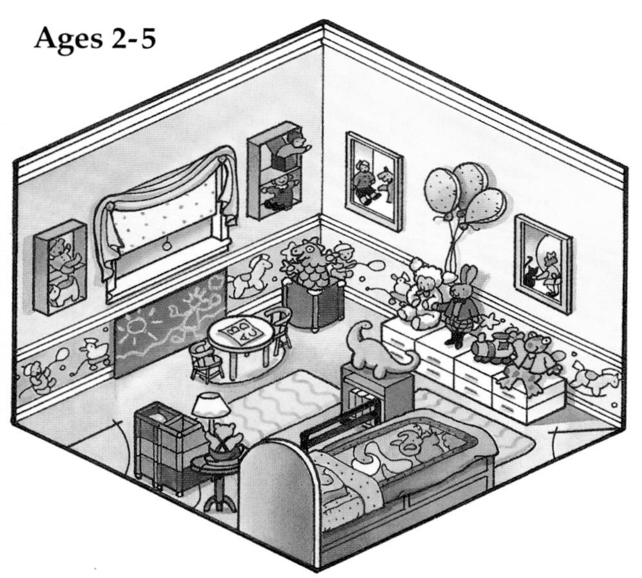

Ages 9-12

Teens

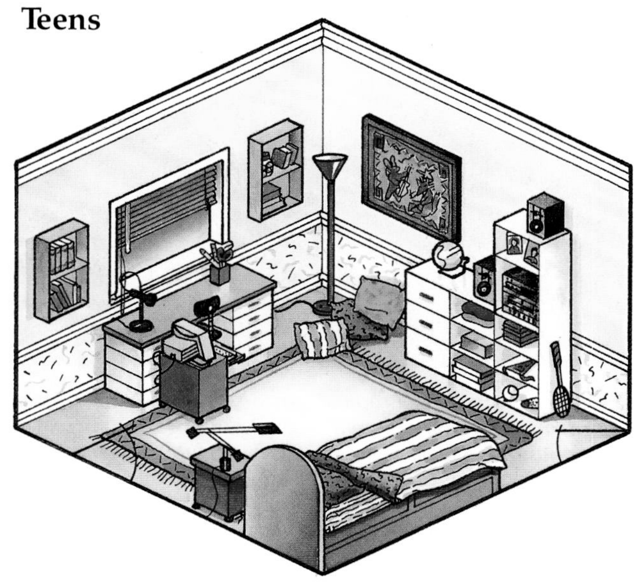

If planned well, a child's room can serve admirably from infancy to young adulthood with relatively few changes over the years. Stacking drawers, a rolling cart, and wall-hung shelves are constants in this room. The drawers start out as a storage unit and base for a portable baby changer, then restack at different stages into a low dresser, a low desk, and, finally, a standard-height desk.

At appropriate stages, the cart holds baby supplies, toys, a radio, and then a computer. The shelves house stuffed animals during the early years, schoolbooks later on. Periodically switching to more sophisticated styles of bedding, lamps, pictures, and window treatment ensures that the room keeps pace with the child's development.

Most bunk beds are versatile. Some accommodate either a mattress or a desktop insert in the lower bunk. Many types unstack to become twin beds—a wonderful feature if your offspring decides that the bunks he or she craved a few years ago are now too juvenile.

Adjustable Furnishings

Pieces that can be raised or lowered are also practical. A secretarial chair gives years of use, since the height and back support are adjustable. One manufacturer makes a table and bench set that adjusts to three different heights for toddlers to preteens. Various mechanisms for adjusting furniture can be built into custom pieces. For example, a desktop might slide into a series of notches or slots at different heights so the work surface can be raised as the child grows.

In the same way, position pictures and other wall decorations low when your child is young, then move them up. Wallpaper borders, moldings, and storage hooks are other wall items that little children appreciate placed low but older kids prefer higher up.

DESIGN: SETTERLUND INTERIORS

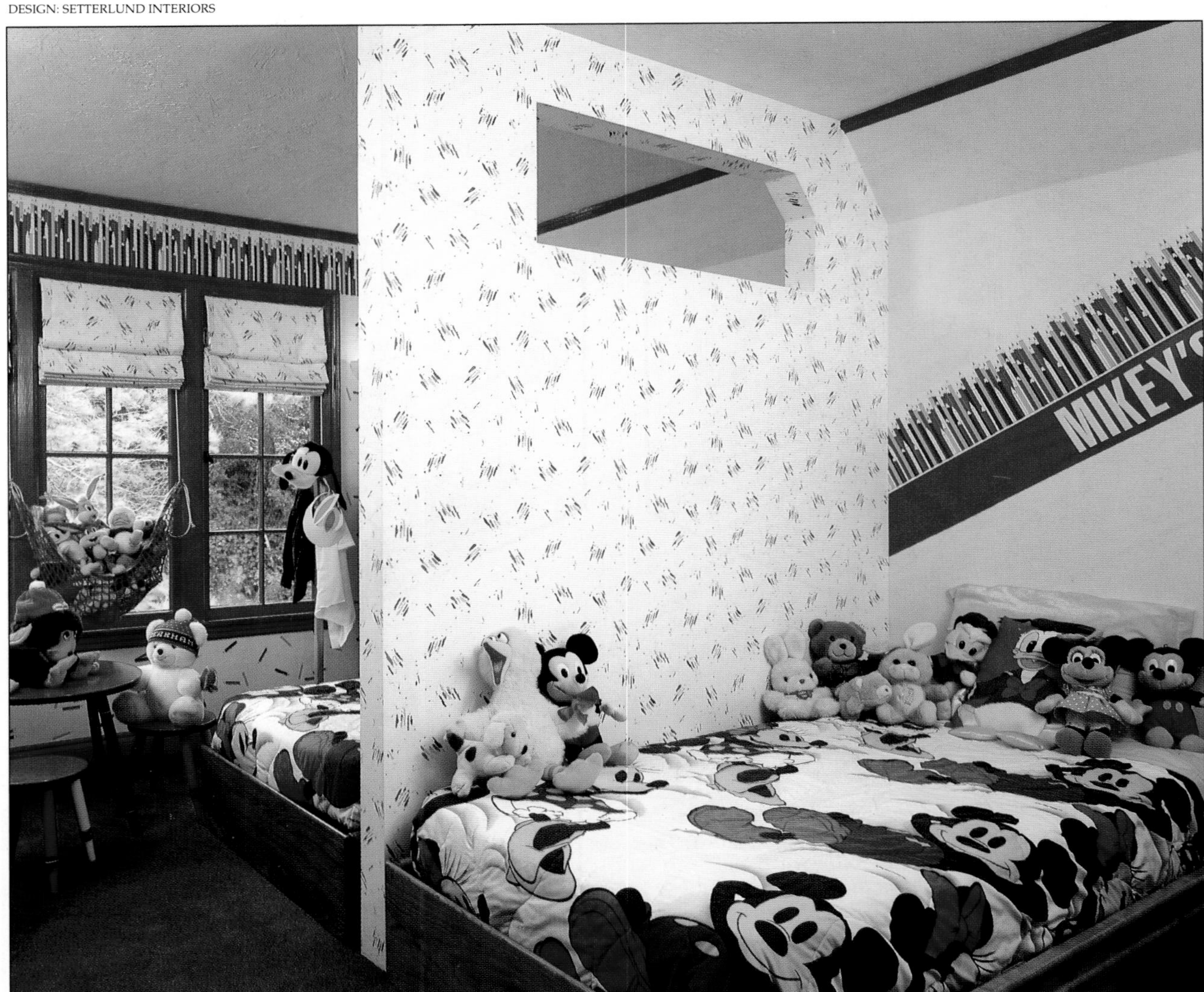

An irregularly shaped room partition, covered in an abstract wallpaper pattern to match the window shade fabric, provides young siblings with privacy. A personalized wallpaper border placed diagonally over the beds identifies each child's territory. A consistent use of red, white, blue, and yellow throughout the room helps unify the separate spaces, as do the identical bedding and the repetition of the pencil-motif border above the window.

ROOM FOR TWO OR MORE

Planning a room that will be shared by brothers or sisters is much more challenging than arranging one for a sole occupant. That's because the shared room must meet the needs of each resident for space, individuality, and privacy. The ideas offered below will help you make the best of togetherness.

Even if the room has only one regular occupant, you'll be wise to plan for overnight guests. That way, you won't throw the room into a shambles every time you try to put up a visitor.

Sharing with a Sibling

Sharing a room has a positive side—companionship—but it also has a negative aspect—lack of privacy. With two or more kids in close quarters, it's inevitable that they'll get on each other's nerves now and then. However, if you plan well, you can create a room that keeps its residents happy most of the time.

Remember that a shared room must accommodate kids with different personalities and interests. Forsake the idea of a theme room or other highly specific decor unless both kids fancy the concept. A less precisely defined decor, such as one based on a color scheme or built around a modular furniture grouping, will give the kids more freedom to express their individuality.

Because roommates are forced to spend so much time together, it's important to give each child personal space. Assign the kids their own drawers and closet space, and provide each with a place for hobby equipment and displays. The children should also have their own desks or study areas, preferably apart from each other.

Separate play areas are important if the kids are far enough apart in age to need different toys and games. Individual areas will discourage the younger sibling from grabbing the older one's possessions and deter the older sibling from carelessly stepping all over the younger one's belongings.

The bed often serves as a private retreat in a shared room, so arrange the sleeping quarters to maximize privacy. Bunk beds are a good choice, since the kids can't see each other when they're in bed. Other solutions include arranging twin beds on each side of a painted plywood panel or placing the beds at right angles with a table between them.

Physical dividers (like the plywood panel) are a clear way to define territory and provide privacy. Many other kinds of dividers can be used: a two-sided shelving unit or bookcase, a wallboard partition that goes partway up, a row of stacking storage units, a folding screen, or curtains hung from the ceiling.

Sometimes psychological divisions are just as effective as physical ones in marking territory. For example, color coding each child's area makes it perfectly clear who has the rightful claim on what furnishings.

If you want to keep squabbles to a minimum, be fair when allocating space. Try to divide it so that each occupant has access to desirable features, such as windows and closets.

It's easier to design a room with the possibility of a second child in mind than to try to cram in an extra bed after the fact. You can always use a spare bed for a visiting child, even when the room has only one real occupant.

Making Room for Friends

Children enjoy sleepovers, so plan a place for young visitors to sleep. No one will get any rest if the kids are piled into one bed without room to stretch out.

You may want to get bunk beds for a single child so the extra bunk can accommodate a guest. A trundle under your child's bed is another good solu-

DESIGN: JAMES STEWART POLSHEK & PARTNERS

An extra bed serves as a comfortable couch for one or extra seating for friends during the day and at-the-ready sleeping quarters for an overnight guest.

DESIGN: McMILLEN, INC.

DESIGN: NOEL JEFFREY

In both rooms above, the sleeping area is well defined without being the most prominent feature. In the top photo, a valance and curtains hung from crown molding produce a canopy effect that is light and airy, even though the bed is placed in a corner against two walls. In the bottom photo, the bed is nestled in a corner alcove away from other room elements.

tion. So is either a day bed or a futon, either of which can also serve as a comfortable lounging place. If the room is large enough, you might want to put in twin beds.

A child-size couch that converts into a guest bed is suitable for little kids. Stow-away options that can work for children of all ages include sleeping bags, air mattresses, and folding cots.

ROOM ELEMENTS

Besides providing sleep and play areas, accommodating hobbies and collections, and storing belongings, the room should be a pleasant place for your child to live. Achieving this will be easier if you break the room into its separate functions and figure out how you want to handle each one.

The following section discusses the room elements generally; for more information about furnishings, see the shopping guide on pages 429-453.

Sleeping Space

When planning the sleep area, start with the obvious: don't block doors, windows, or heating vents. Avoid putting a young child's bed under a window—but if there's no other option, install a lock so the window can't open wide enough for the child to fall out. A more secure location is a corner of the room, where two sides of the bed will be protected. (For more about safety considerations, see page 369.)

For the first few months of life, your baby can sleep in a bassinet, cradle, crib, or even a padded drawer or basket. A crib is the best choice from about three months to when the youngster begins to climb out regularly or attains a height of 35 inches. At that point, the child can move to an intermediate bed, suitable until about age five, or take the big step to an adult-size bed. If you're worried about the child rolling out, you can start by using the mattress alone on the floor, without a frame.

Generally, manufacturers recommend that top bunks and loft beds remain off-limits to kids under six. But you'll have to judge the abilities of your own child. Some six-year-olds aren't ready for high living, while some younger kids are adept at scampering up and down ladders and can be trusted in an elevated environment.

Your child's preference is important, but other factors enter into the choice of a bed, such as its cost, how long you want it to last, and how much space it requires. And some beds may suit your decorating scheme better than others: a wooden four-poster bed will seem more at home in an old-fashioned room, while one with a tubular metal frame will look better in a contemporary scheme.

If saving floor space is important, think about such options as loft beds, wall beds, and trundles. A loft bed gives your child more than just a place to sleep—it incorporates storage and study or play

Each youngster has his own toy storage and display space in a shared room (top), where carpet and bare floor provide surfaces for different types of play. A corner play area (bottom) features a child-size sofa and chair, plus a coffee table with a painted-on chalkboard surface.

areas. A chest bed or captain's bed, with its built-in drawers, is a good choice for a small room with limited storage space. Many other bed designs offer the option of under-bed drawers.

Perhaps your child craves a fantasy bed, but your budget won't allow it or you don't want to invest in a piece of furniture that will last only a few years. With a little imagination, you can satisfy both your needs and your child's. Transform an ordinary bed by attaching a plywood headboard cut in the shape of a castle, tree, animal, or other object. Paint the headboard or cover it with fabric. When the child outgrows the illusion, unbolt the headboard and replace it with something more conventional.

Play Areas

Most of the floor space in a young child's room should be allocated for play. Although little kids will sit at a low table, they really like to sprawl out on the floor with toys and games. Some playthings require a smooth, level surface, while others are fine on carpet-

ing. You can plan for a hard surface through most of the room, with a few throw rugs to provide comfortable places to sit or lie.

In a small room, maximize floor space by arranging the furnishings against the walls. A bed that folds up or slides away is a great space saver. One that has built-in compartments or under-bed drawers provides lots of storage room without taking up extra floor space.

Kids love cozy nooks. If your child doesn't need all the available closet space for storage, you could turn the closet into a hideaway or puppet theater. If the closet is large enough, you may be able to build a loft—anchor a sheet of sturdy plywood to the inside closet wall at any height and affix a ladder to the loft surface. Cover the plywood with a thin foam mattress and pile it with pillows. To create a simple theater, remove the closet door and put up a curtain with a cutout area for puppets. Remember, you'll need lighting inside the closet if it's to serve as a play area.

If you buy bunk beds for one child, the extra bunk can be used as a play area when it's not serving an overnight visitor. Attach curtains to the sides to create a private retreat or secret clubhouse. (Bunks are often sold with optional curtains or tents.)

ARCHITECT: FRED FISHER, AIA

A child-size table and chair set, like this one made of molded plastic (top), is an ideal place for a tot to do puzzles and artwork. Compact study center (bottom) features a drafting table, a filing cabinet, a bulletin board, and shelving.

Study Areas

A well-designed study area will foster good study habits and neatness. Your child will be better organized and more likely to consult reference books if bookshelves are within easy reach above or to the side of the desk. Handy shelves and drawers will also encourage your youngster to keep the desk clear. If supplies must be hauled back and forth from across the room, they'll tend to stay piled on the desk.

A little table or desk will do as a homework area for a kid just starting school, but a well-organized study area becomes important later. The basic requirements are a work surface (at least 2 feet deep and 4 feet wide), a comfortable chair, and good lighting. Computer equipment requires extra space. If the study area is to double as a craft or hobby center, you'll need to make sure the work surface is extra-large.

A modular study center allows you to add components, including extra work surface, as needed. If you opt for a loft or bunk unit that incorporates a desk, be sure the desk is big enough to serve your child throughout school. Having to add more work surface later defeats the purpose of buying such a space-saving structure.

Some children are easily distracted if the study area is in front of a window or if the desk chair can swivel. You have to know your child when you plan the study setup.

Hobby Areas

If your child has a hobby that can be conducted in the room, then plan a place for it. For example, a plant lover could use deep windowsills for container gardening. An astronomy buff could set up a telescope in front of a window that offers a good view of the night sky. For an avid reader, a comfortable armchair in a well-lighted corner near a bookcase is heaven.

Combining the hobby and study areas is fine if it's easy to stash away schoolbooks and hobby gear between uses. For some hobbies, such as sewing, it's much more convenient to leave equipment out until a project is finished. In such cases, you'll want to plan a separate hobby area if the room is large enough.

If your child wants to keep fish, hamsters, mice, or some other creatures in the room, you'll need to plan an area for them. Allow enough space so that the aquarium or cage isn't in danger of being knocked over, but is still accessible for easy cleaning. You'll also have to take the animals' needs into account—for example, whether they should be kept away from heating vents or direct sunlight.

DESIGN: LITTLE ONE'S HAND PAINTED FURNITURE

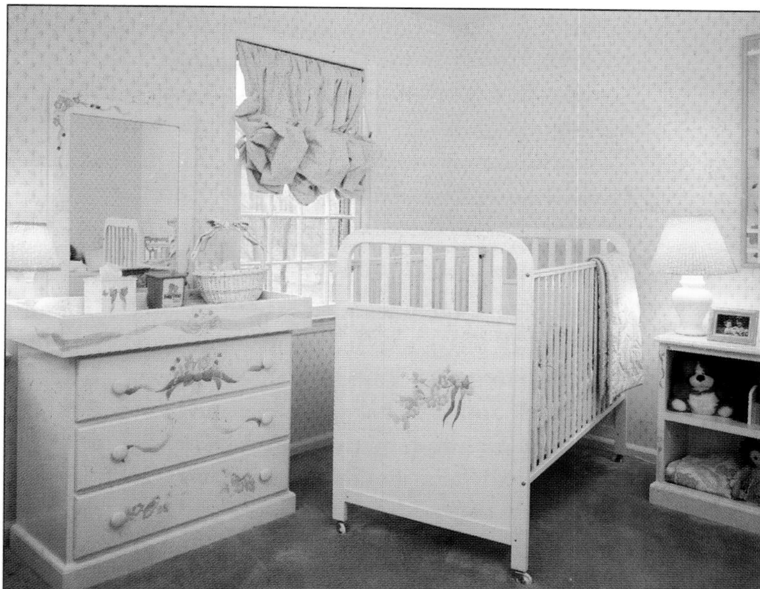

These prettily painted pieces are part of a furniture collection. Later, the changer top can be removed and a coordinating bed can substitute for the crib.

Furniture

You have many options when shopping for a child's room. Your choices will depend largely on your budget and on how much flexibility you want. You can order from stock or have a piece custom-built. Ready-made furniture can be stand-alone, modular, or part of a furniture collection; custom pieces are often built-in. To stretch a budget, you can buy unfinished pieces or tap the large market of used furniture. The pros and cons of the various options are discussed below.

ARCHITECT: LES WALKER

A youngster with many interests stocks his hobby area with a microscope, tools, and paints. Shelves are specially designed to store specific items.

No matter what kind of furniture you choose, make sure it is sturdy and has no sharp or protruding edges. Easy-to-maintain surfaces are important—for example, sealed wood, laminates, or metal. For tips on shopping for furniture, see page 438.

Stand-alone. This furniture is movable: you can rearrange it, shunt it into another room if your child no longer needs it, or take it with you when you move. But unless the piece is custom-made, it comes in standard dimensions—so you may not be able to get the exact size and configuration you want.

Modular. Modular furniture offers great flexibility, allowing you to combine components—such as a bed, headboard, shelves, drawers, cabinets, and work surfaces—to fit your child's exact needs. Many of the units stack or abut to form larger composites. You can add components (if the manufacturer still makes the item when you're ready to buy) and reconfigure the whole arrangement as needed in the future. The components can be packed up when you move and rearranged in a new room. Some modular systems require assembly.

Furniture Collections. Many manufacturers offer collections of furniture—often as many as a few dozen pieces that coordinate in style and finish. A collection designed for a kid's room may include several different choices among stylistically coordinated beds, headboards, bedside tables, dressers, armoires, bookcases, hutches, desks, chairs, and framed mirrors.

Built-in. Ready-made furniture that fits an area precisely can sometimes give a built-in look, but more often such pieces are custom-made. You can build furniture into nooks or under windows, creating a seamless look and utilizing space that might otherwise be wasted. A custom built-in can be expensive, and you can't usually take it with you when you move.

Unfinished. Well-constructed unfinished furniture is usually a good value. Pieces made from soft white pine are the least expensive—and also the least durable. Sturdy pieces made of knotty pine, maple, or birch are a step up in quality and price. The best-quality and costliest items are usually made of solid oak or cherry. You can customize unfinished furniture with hardware and a painted, stained, or clear finish.

Used. You can often get a good deal on used furniture, but pay close attention to safety. Make sure the piece is sturdy and well made. A secondhand crib should conform to current safety standards (see page 431). Be wary of old paint, which may contain lead; for information on removing a suspect finish, see page 369.

A ROOM FIT TO LIVE IN

Children enjoy their rooms more when they can sit comfortably at the table or desk, and when many of their possessions are at eye level or within easy reach. This chart containing average measurements will help you create a safe, livable environment for your child.

AGE	HEIGHT	EYE LEVEL	HIGH REACH	TABLE HEIGHT	CHAIR HEIGHT
3	37	33	41	15	8
5	39-47	35-43	43-52	18	10
7	44-52	40-48	49-59	19	11
9	47-57	43-53	53-65	21	12
12	53-64	49-60	61-73	23	13
15	61-71	57-66	70-82	26	15
Adult women	61-70	57-66	70-81	29	18
Adult men	65-75	61-70	74-86	29	18

Measurements are in inches.

Ideal Shelving Dimensions

For children

Maximum suggested shelf height 45"
36"
Browsing height 26"
Minimum height for no crouching 18"
Crouching required 4"
Child: 45" tall

For teens

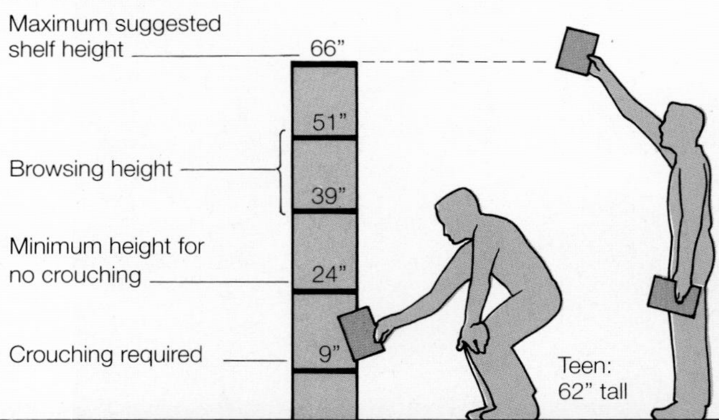

Regularly used items should be placed at less than maximum reach so kids can get them without straining or standing on tiptoes. Put often-used objects on higher shelves when kids grow taller.

Storage

Adults usually want to keep items that aren't in constant use hidden in cabinets or behind closed doors, but that's not always the best kind of storage for kids' rooms.

The idea is to organize the clutter so that the room looks neat, yet the child knows where to find things. It's perfectly fine to keep articles in sight, but arranged on open shelves or stuffed into boxes, bins, and other receptacles. Clear, covered containers are a good solution if you want to keep possessions free of dust.

Even clothes can be kept in plain sight. Removing a closet door for a year or two reminds youngsters who are learning to dress themselves that they can enter the closet and select an outfit for the day. Remember, little kids can hang up their own clothes only if the pole or hooks are placed low enough for them to reach.

Storage needs change over the years. At first, you'll need containers for diapers and baby supplies. Then your young child will need places to stow toys and games, stuffed animals, art materials, storybooks, and clothes. Next, space will be required for schoolwork, hobbies, collections, electronic equipment, and sports gear. The same units you start out with can continue to serve your growing child—if you plan carefully and don't lock yourself into juvenile themes.

If the room is small, look for units that use space efficiently. Under-bed drawers provide handy storage—and indulge a child's love for throwing things under the bed. Other space savers include storage units that stack on the floor, attach to the wall, or hang from hooks. A built-in storage area, such as a window seat with storage inside, utilizes space well, although you can't take it with you when you move.

Many types of bins and boxes are sold expressly for storage, but you can press into service any number of other containers, some of them found around the house. The myriad possibilities include shoe boxes, empty coffee cans (check for sharp edges), plastic jars, cutlery trays, and fishing tackle

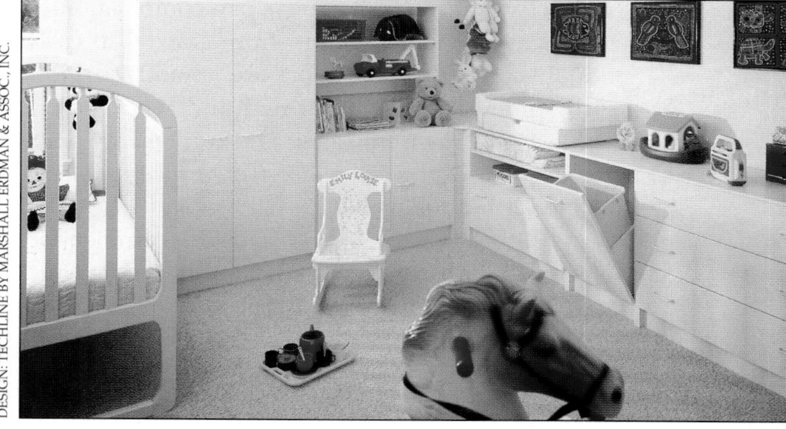

DESIGN: TECHLINE BY MARSHALL ERDMAN & ASSOC., INC.

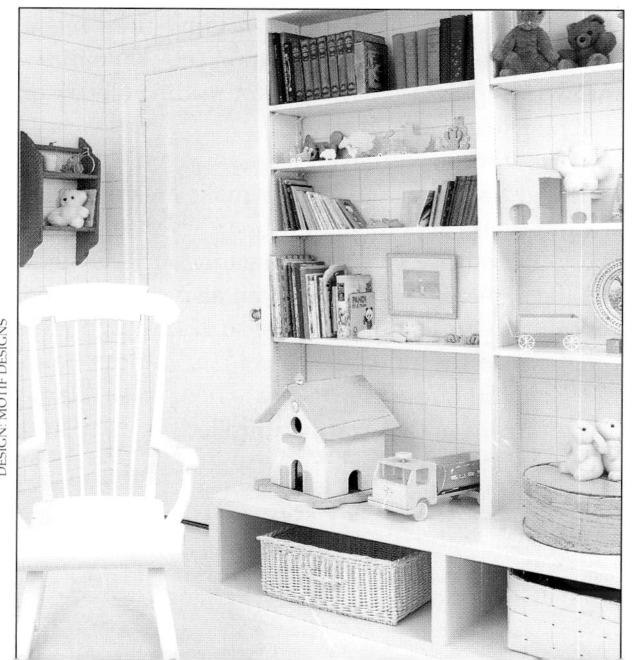

DESIGN: MOTIF DESIGNS

Tower of tubs (top) makes order out of chaos and is fun to climb. Modular wall unit (middle) contains lots of storage room and even a clothes hamper. Shelf unit (bottom) stores larger items at the base and smaller items higher up.

boxes. Color coding or using symbols on the containers will help your child remember what goes where. Don't forget a "lost-and-found bin" for unidentified odds and ends.

If you want to promote neatness, locate storage near the activity area. This may not be where you think your child should be conducting the activity, but be realistic. Art supplies should be stored near where your child draws or paints. Toys should be stored near where your child tends to play.

Flooring

The flooring in a youngster's room does more than just provide passage from one point to another. Children spend much of their time on the floor, at first crawling and then playing and drawing. Even older kids often read or listen to music while lounging on the floor. So the floor should be comfortable, safe for play, and easy to maintain.

You can choose a smooth, level surface (wood or a resilient flooring such as vinyl), a soft surface (wall-to-wall carpeting or rugs), or a combination.

For a very young child—from crawler to early school years—the best floors are smooth surfaces with some give. Both resilient and wood floors cushion falls, clean up easily, and can be kept dust-free. They also provide a nice flat surface for stacking blocks and rolling balls.

Wall-to-wall carpeting is usually recommended for older kids, since it's harder to keep clean and doesn't work well for toys that need a perfectly level surface. But a low-pile industrial-grade or indoor/outdoor carpet is an inexpensive option that stands up to little kids and is fairly flat.

A combination of hard and soft surfaces can be very successful. For example, a vinyl floor has a smooth, level surface for a toy train set, while fluffy throw rugs provide cozy areas for reading a book or watching television.

The flooring can even be a source of fun and learning. Several manufacturers make area rugs and wall-to-wall carpeting with boards for checkers, chess, and other games printed on the surface—they sell the game pieces, too. You can also get rugs and carpeting with learning motifs, such as how to tell time or read the alphabet. Of course, you can paint the same sort of designs on a bare floor or on a large piece of canvas that can be unrolled for play and then stowed away.

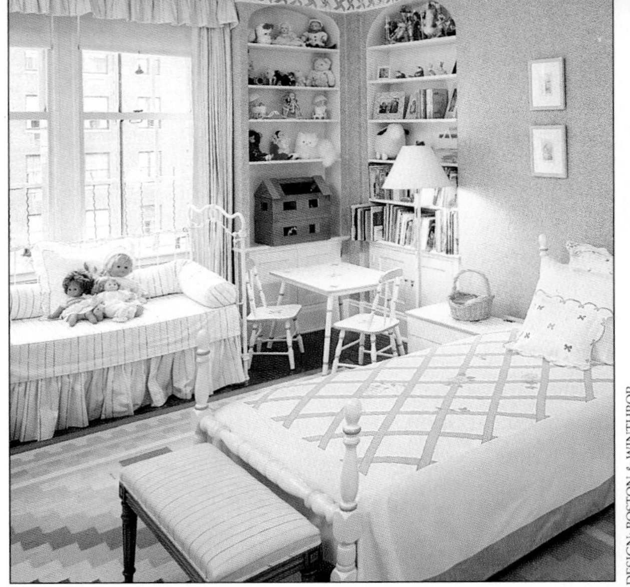

DESIGN: BOSTON & WINTHROP

Young girl's room features built-in cabinets for storage and display. The flat-woven, decorative dhurrie rug makes a cozy play surface.

Walls & Ceiling

The walls and ceiling in a child's room offer great decorating potential, more so than in other rooms of the house. That's because kids' rooms invite a playful, sky's-the-limit approach.

A little paint will transform the room. You can keep it simple—solid colors on the walls and ceiling,

DESIGN: KIM KEYWAN ETHERTON, ASID

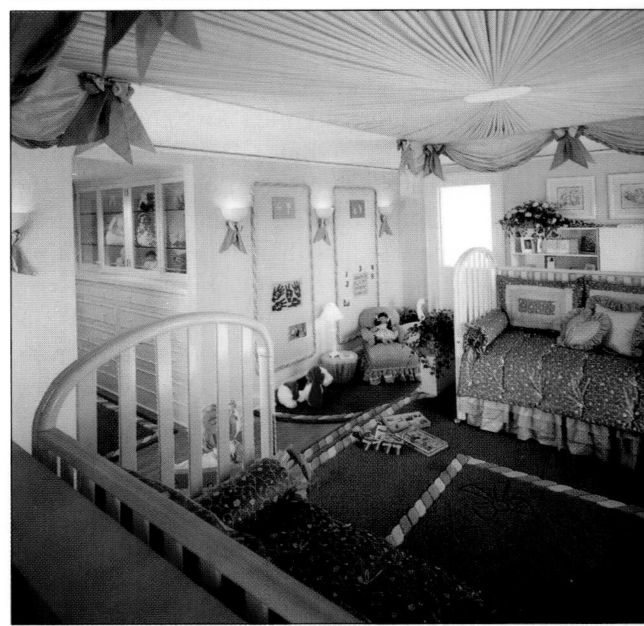

The fabric braiding on the walls echoes the rug border and cabinet molding. The ceiling features shirred fabric with a center rosette.

SPACE SAVERS

Coping with skimpy space is a common problem in today's small-scale bedrooms. Here are some ways to maximize your child's territory.

- A loft bed makes optimum use of floor space because so many functions are served within the footprint of the bed. The sleeping area is on top, with storage and a play or study area beneath.
- Stacking bunk beds take up the space of a single bed, yet accommodate two kids. If there's only one child, the extra bunk serves as both play space and guest accommodation.
- A disappearing bed, such as a wall bed, clears the decks for play or hobbies.
- Under-bed drawers, offered as accessories for many types of beds, utilize what would otherwise be wasted space. Bins, boxes, and other portable storage units that fit underneath the bed are just as useful.
- Hooks, shoe bags, and pouches hung on chair-rail molding or on the backs of closet or room doors provide off-the-floor storage.
- A hinged work surface or table folds against the wall when not in use, liberating floor space for other activities.
- Shelving units that hang on the wall instead of sitting on the floor free up floor space.
- An organized closet with shelves, stacking baskets, and other modules holds much more than a standard one.
- A minimum of furniture makes the room seem more spacious. Look for multipurpose pieces, such as a toy box with a bench top or a bed with built-in storage.

and a contrasting trim. If you want something more creative but don't want to hire a professional, here are some simple ideas: paint clouds or stencil stars onto the ceiling, brush a rainbow onto the wall, or let your child help you spatterpaint the walls with bright colors. Another simple technique: buy sponges in the shape of fish, letters, numbers, or other objects (or cut them out yourself if you can't find the design you want), dip them into paint, and print the walls or ceiling with them. If you opt for a professional, then you can choose from many decorative techniques, including murals and trompe l'oeil.

Wallpaper offers additional options. You can use a single pattern or coordinate two or more—and cover all the walls or just one. You can even cover the ceiling with such patterns as a starry sky or fluttering birds. Be just as creative with wallpaper borders: circle the ceiling, ring the walls at your child's eye level, or outline the windows and doorway.

Although paneling may seem more appropriate for a den or study, it can be used imaginatively in a kid's room. For a casual look, choose a light wood or paintable finish, and install the paneling only partway up the wall; add a decorative wood molding and coat with a protective sealer.

Other practical wall treatments include chalkboards and bulletin boards. Create an art area by applying special chalkboard paint on a section of wall—it can be a plain rectangle or a whimsical shape, such as the silhouette of a whale or a boat. You can wall-mount a store-bought bulletin board or create your own pinup surface by covering a wall with cork or fabric-wrapped fiberboard.

DESIGN: KATHERINE WALDEN. DECORATIVE PAINTNG: AUDREY P. RABY

A balloon valance made of plywood partially covers a towering window, bringing it down a little and making it less intimidating to a small child.

DESIGN: LAUREN ELIA. DECORATIVE PAINTING: PATRICK SHEEHEE

A mural of a fox den (at left) camouflages the entrance to a storage area. Recessed lights over the headboard and in the ceiling slope augment natural light in a teen's bedroom (above). Table lamps provide additional illumination.

You can give walls additional interest with pictures, posters, wall hangings, moldings, and decorative shelves. Some manufacturers sell decorating kits in various motifs. Designed to be used by children, the kits come with repositionable borders and appliqués. Keep track of your child's growth by attaching a decorative tape measure to the wall.

You can buy glow-in-the-dark ceiling appliqués in the shape of stars. Suspending objects, such as model airplanes or kites, is another great way to decorate the ceiling. If you're handy with a sewing machine, make some plump, white pillows in amorphous shapes; hung from the ceiling, they'll look like clouds.

Windows & Doors

Since kids spend many daylight hours in their rooms, choose a window treatment that lets in plenty of natural light. The treatment should also be capable of dimming the room if you want your child to sleep when the sun's shining.

Options include curtains, blinds, shades, and shutters. If you're buying for the long term, choose a treatment that's durable, easy-care, and no trouble for your child to operate.

The color or pattern of the window treatment can provide much of the visual appeal. Some companies offer ready-made curtains and shades to match bedding, or you can sew them yourself from sheets. You'll also find coordinating fabrics available with many wallpaper patterns. Shutters will take on new life when painted a lively color. Plain shades or curtains can be customized with fabric paints or glue-on designs.

Other ways to decorate a window include outlining it with a wallpaper border, stenciling a design around it, dangling a mobile in front of it, or building a window seat underneath it.

Don't forget the door when you're decorating a kid's room. You might outline it with paint or wallpaper, paint your child's name on it in decorative stencil-on letters, or incorporate it into a wall mural. You can put the back of the door to practical use by building a storage unit on it or turning it into a bulletin board. Delight a young child by removing the closet door and replacing it with a curtain for a puppet theater or a secret clubhouse.

Lighting

There's more to illuminating a child's room than just choosing decorative fixtures. You must also consider function and safety.

Designers divide lighting into three categories: ambient, task, and accent. The first two are the most important in kids' rooms. Ambient lighting provides a soft level of general light, while task lighting focuses stronger light on an area where a visual activity, such as reading or homework, takes place. Primarily decorative, accent lighting is less commonly found in a child's room, although you might decide to install some to highlight a trophy case or doll collection.

Babies are most comfortable with soft, diffused light from an overhead fixture on a dimmer or a table lamp with a low-wattage bulb. The soft glow from a night-light will reassure the baby, as well as guide you into the room late at night. Parents may want to have a stronger light available near the changing area.

Ceiling fixtures are the safest type of lighting for very young kids, since they're out of reach. They provide general illumination needed for play and make the room less scary. Also plan on having a table lamp within easy reach of your child's bed.

As your child grows, add task lighting for art projects and puzzles and later for homework and other activities requiring concentrated light. A task light shouldn't cast a shadow or create glare. Too much contrast between the illuminated area and the adjacent area can strain eyes. Experts recommend keeping the surrounding area at least a third as bright as the lighted area.

Task lighting should be positioned at the proper height for your child, so that the work area is illuminated but the child isn't able to see the light bulb when seated next to the fixture. Lighting for a computer should come from overhead; if it comes from the side or from behind, it creates glare on the screen.

If an opaque shade doesn't provide enough light, replace it with a translucent shade, which will diffuse light to a larger area. You can also install dimmers to control the amount of light.

For specifics about the types of lighting fixtures and bulbs or tubes appropriate for kids' rooms, see pages 452-453.

TYPES & STYLES

There's no need to choose a particular style or type of room when you decorate. The room can be eclectic, or it can be a one-of-a-kind creation that defies pigeonholing. But in case you do opt for a specific type of room, here's some information about a few of the most common ones.

Theme Rooms

Living in a room that looks just like a scene from the Old West, a jungle, the deep sea, or the interior of a spaceship may appeal to your child—but think carefully before you decide to implement such a theme.

Some child specialists argue against theme rooms that are so realistic they resemble movie sets, so detailed they leave nothing to the imagination. These experts recommend treatments that give kids the chance to exercise their own imaginations.

For a circus theme, for example, there's no need to set up three rings with a life-size figure of a ringmaster, a bed in the shape of an elephant, and a mural of acrobats and performing animals. Instead, you could find thematic bedding and a wallpaper border. Complete the fantasy with three-dimensional fabric balloons on the walls, a tentlike canopy over the bed, and rows of stuffed animals that your child can orchestrate in pretend performances. You've gotten across the feeling of a circus without cramping your child's creativity.

Another reason not to invest too much time and money in creating a truly authentic-looking scene is that kids' interests are apt to change rapidly. Recognizing that, restrict the theme to items that can easily be replaced, such as a comforter, curtains, posters, a wallpaper border, or a headboard that can be unbolted.

A theme based on a child's serious, long-standing interest or hobby—such as ballet, astronomy, football, or horseback riding—is likelier to stay the

DESIGN: 3M

A decorating kit offers a fast, simple way to create a theme room. Available in many thematic designs, the kits contain borders and precut appliqués that can be moved around repeatedly without damaging the walls.

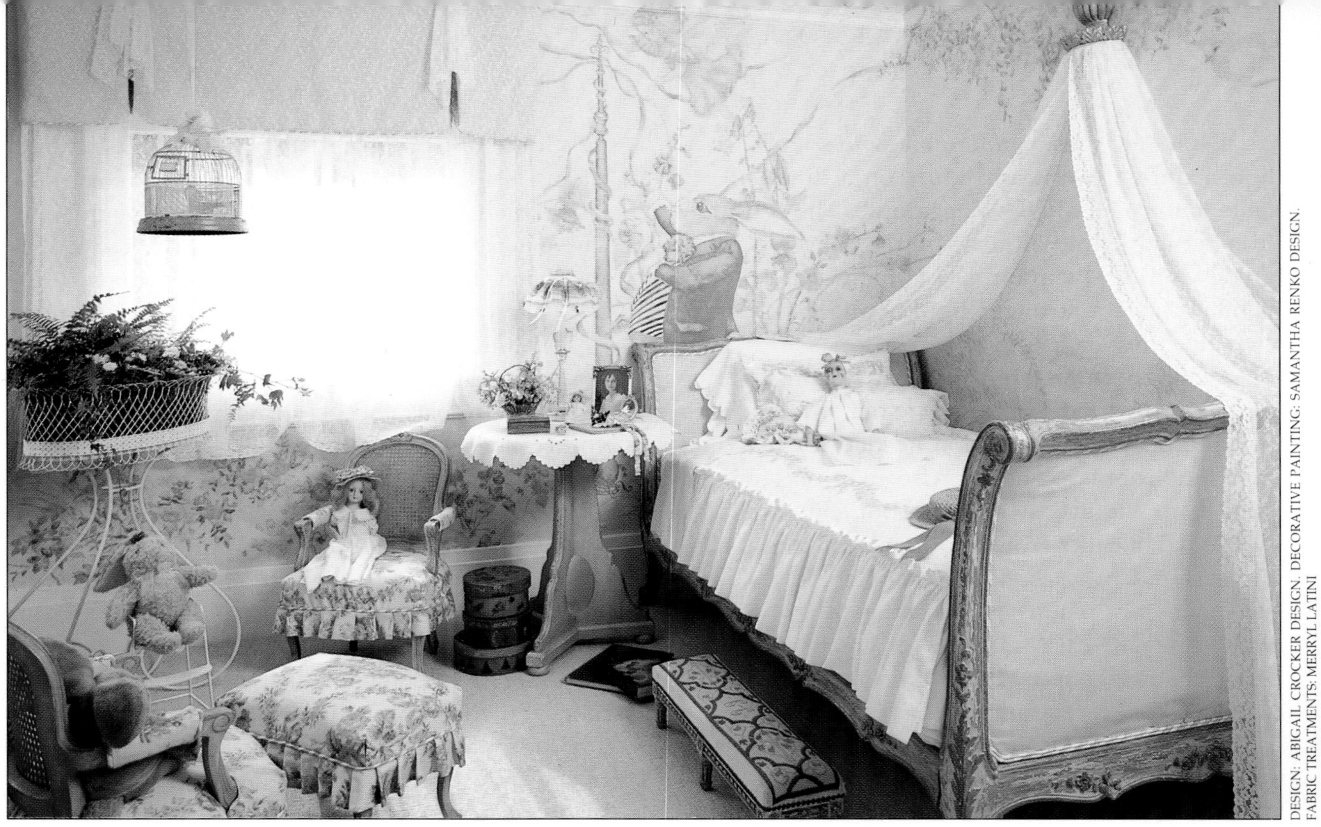

DESIGN: ABIGAIL CROCKER DESIGN. DECORATIVE PAINTING: SAMANTHA RENKO DESIGN. FABRIC TREATMENTS: MERRYL LATINI

The delicate frills and flourishes in this room evoke a romantic period in history, without being true in every detail to a particular era.

course than a standard theme picked at random. As your child learns or achieves more in the chosen field, he or she can augment the decor with newly acquired paraphernalia or with ribbons or trophies.

Period Rooms

The use of certain colors, details, and materials will help you create a room reminiscent of a particular historical period, such as Early American or Victorian.

Early American is a simple, unpretentious style. Its hallmarks are quilts, rag rugs, plain curtains, crude wooden toys, and simple stencil decorations on the walls, floors, and furniture—the latter usually made of pine, maple, cherry, or hickory. Low-post beds and trundles were typical of the period. And the colors most often used by the colonists were off-white and earthy shades of brown, green, and blue.

If the Early American style celebrated simplicity, Victorian decor reveled in ornateness. The telltale signs are overstuffed furniture, rich dark colors, busy patterns, layered window treatments, cornices, wainscoting, and a profusion of knickknacks. The wallpaper designs and room ornaments often related to discoveries of the period, such as automobiles and steam trains, and it was common to combine several patterns. Mahogany was a popular furniture material, as were wicker and rattan.

A room needn't be faithful to its style in every aspect. For example, if traditional Victoriana seems too oppressive for a child, feel free to lighten the colors, simplify the window treatments, and avoid some of the clutter. For an Early American motif, there's nothing wrong with introducing a modern quilt pattern or colors the colonists didn't use.

Contemporary Rooms

Another option is a room with clean lines and sleek, modern furniture. Don't worry about the room being too sterile or stark for a youngster. Visual appeal can come from the color scheme or from the decoration.

Such a room often displays artifacts of pop culture—for example, it might boast neon lights, posters of celebrities, logos of trendy companies, or high-tech images.

The decor can easily become dated if it relies too heavily on current culture. To avoid that problem, limit the number of images so that they can be easily replaced, or use only classic ones.

Several materials are suitable for furniture in a contemporary room: wood, tubular metal, plastic, glass (but avoid the latter in a young child's room). Laminates also work extremely well.

PUTTING IT ALL TOGETHER

Where do you start? A good beginning is your child, if he or she is old enough to voice decorating preferences. (For a sample of what happens when you ask for opinions, see pages 374-375.) Your offspring may have definite ideas for the room—and, if you're lucky, these may be easy to implement. If not, they may suggest other, more workable notions that appeal just as strongly to your youngster. If the gap between your taste and your child's is wide, you may have to reconcile some differences before proceeding.

One of the attractions of a theme room is that it offers clear direction: once you have the theme, you just look for elements that fit it. For example, you would choose such items as a captain's bed, a sea chest, cargo netting, and wooden crates for a nautical theme. A period room offers just as plain a path: you look for furnishings that recall the chosen era in history.

DECORATIVE PAINTING: JASON FOTOS

This contemporary room, with its flamboyant and flashy mural, exhibits the energy and vitality of its young sports-loving occupant. Rollerblading and skateboarding are among favored activities.

Pulling together the decor for other types of rooms may not be as obvious. One tactic is to start with a centerpiece—for example, an appealing wallpaper pattern, colorful bedding, or a special piece of furniture, such as a loft bed or an antique wardrobe—and build the decor around it. Then coordinate other furnishings with the central item.

Another approach is to start with a color scheme. If you and your child decide on a green, yellow, and white room, look for furnishings that fit the color scheme—and pretty soon the room will take shape.

Unfortunately, ideas don't always spring forth full blown and complete in every detail, so you may be looking for help. This book is designed to spark ideas. Other good sources of inspiration include friends' houses, kids' stores, furniture showrooms, catalogs that sell children's products, decorating magazines, fabric shops, and wallpaper stores.

If you see a concept you like, you don't have to use it intact. You can borrow parts of it, or reinter-

DISPLAYING COLLECTIONS

Kids love collecting objects—including ones that have no intrinsic value but are important to them. They're proud of these items and enjoy looking at them and showing them off to friends.

The type of collection will often suggest the method of display. Objects that sit on a flat surface—for instance, rocks, dolls, stuffed animals, and albums—can be arranged on shelves. Some collections can be affixed to the wall—an assortment of hats hung from hooks screwed into picture molding, or autographed pictures of sports celebrities on a bulletin-board surface. Prize ribbons for sporting events can be arranged in acrylic plastic frames and hung on the wall. Model airplanes can be suspended from the ceiling. Small, round, or colorful objects like marbles can be stored in transparent containers on a dresser or bookcase.

You may want to install a glass-fronted cabinet to show off an attractive collection and keep it dust-free. Wait until your child is old enough to treat breakables with respect. A young child is better off with open shelving—it's safer, and the displayed objects are more accessible.

A visually appealing collection may merit accent lighting. Place directional lights above the collection and focus them on the objects.

Plan Drawings

If you were designing a room for a nine-year-old boy who needed a place for an aquarium, a cozy reading nook, a study area, and lots of storage, you might come up with one of these basic plans.

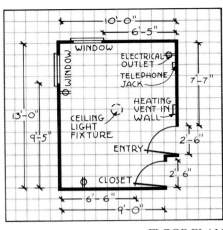

10'-0"
6'-5"
WINDOW
WINDOW
ELECTRICAL OUTLET
TELEPHONE JACK
7'-7"
13'-0"
9'-5"
HEATING VENT IN WALL
CEILING LIGHT FIXTURE
2'-6"
ENTRY
2'-6"
CLOSET
6'-6"
9'-0"

FLOOR PLAN

PLAN A

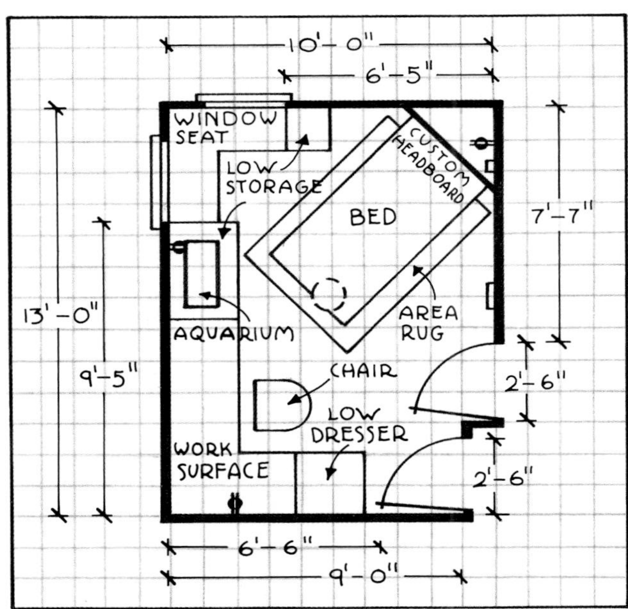

PLAN A ELEVATION

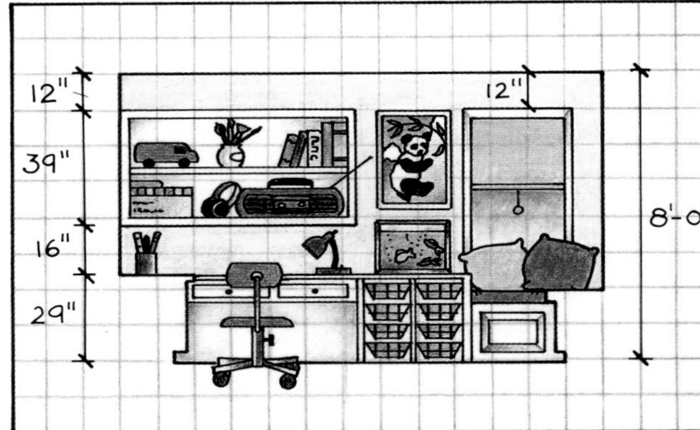

Plan A features a built-in window seat, modular furniture, and wall-hung bookshelves.

PLAN B

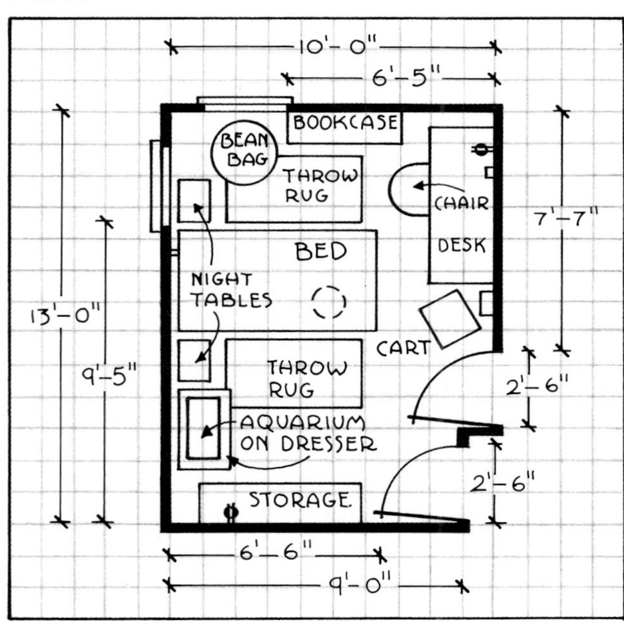

PLAN B ELEVATION

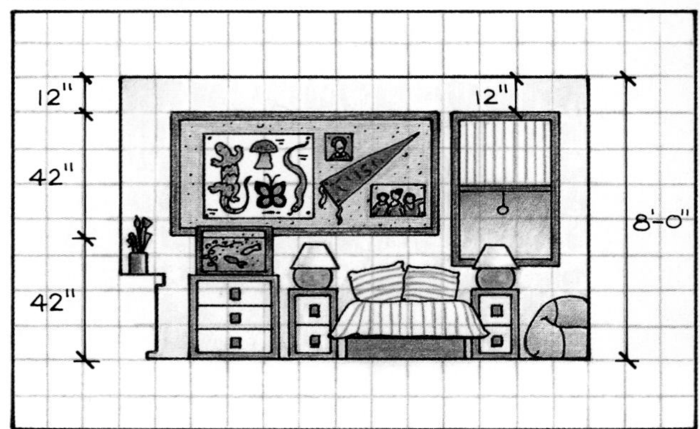

Plan B provides a beanbag for the reading nook and uses stand-alone furniture.

pret it. If you decide to replicate a room, remember that real rooms rarely look as picture-perfect as ones in magazines and showrooms. To avoid disappointment, try to envisage the room occupied by your child and a clutch of belongings.

Resolving Differences

What if you just can't go along with your child's wishes for the room? Your youngster may want to plaster the whole room with images of a popular cartoon or movie character whose appeal may take a nosedive the next year. Or the desire may be for a luminous purple and orange room, when the rest of the house is decorated in neutral tones.

You'll have to judge the depth of your child's yearning and whether vetoing the expressed preference outright will cause problems. Compromise may be in order. If your child won't be happy without the cartoon character, you could limit the image to posters or pieces of memorabilia that don't dominate the room and can be easily replaced when the attraction fades.

In the case of a color scheme that you find offensive, you could swallow your revulsion and use the colors your child likes. But you could tone them down just enough so that they become more acceptable to you without losing their magic for your child. You could also restrict the colors to wall paint so that the scheme could be easily changed in the future.

Planning on Paper

Before becoming committed to a particular decor or actually purchasing any furniture, experiment with your ideas on paper to be sure they will work. If the furnishings you want to use don't fit the space well, you may have to rethink your design. And if you're short on ideas, the process of mapping out the room may inspire you.

Measure the room, including the closet, then draw it to scale on graph paper. With the appropriate program, you could lay out the room on a computer. Either way, be sure to mark the windows and doors, and draw an arc to show which way the doors and any casement windows swing. Indicate all electrical outlets, light switches, permanent lighting fixtures, telephone jacks, and heating vents. Show all the dimensions on the plan.

Next, you can start on the room design. If you're working manually, develop your ideas on photocopies or on tracing paper laid over the graph paper. If you're using a computer, save the original, and work on a copy of the file.

Unless you plan to change the locations of outlets, switches, jacks, or vents, work around them as you place furniture. Also be sure to leave enough room to open doors fully, pull back chairs, extend drawers, and make the bed.

Having lots of open floor space doesn't matter in an adult's bedroom, but it's critical in a young child's. Leave as much floor area clear as possible for playing and spreading out toys.

Function should win over aesthetics when the two clash. Your child should be able to travel directly from one key area to another. Clothes are more likely to be hung up if your child can move easily from the bed to the closet, and toys are more apt to be put away after use if toy storage is convenient to the play area. A well-planned room doesn't guarantee neatness, but does encourage it.

Drawing a floor plan will help you see how everything fits, but don't stop there. Elevation drawings, which show the furnishings against the walls, can give you an even better idea of how the room will look. If you like, use marking pens or crayons to approximate the color scheme.

DESIGN: SARA OLESKER, LTD.

Clear passage from one functional area to another was designed into this room.

ax
fan
flag

DESIGN: CYNTHIA BRIAN OF STARSTYLE INTERIORS

GREAT KIDS' ROOMS

Need ideas to get your creative juices flowing? The following pages are filled with innovative ways to treat whole rooms as well as individual room elements, such as sleeping nooks and storage areas.

As you thumb through the gallery, notice novel ways to allocate space and to use colors and furnishings. There are ideas for saving space and for sharing it, as well as ways to bring fantasies to life and fashion kid-pleasing hideaways. Pay particular attention to all the little touches that turn an ordinary space into a special one.

Treatments range from whimsical to worldly, and from old-fashioned to sleekly modern. There are even rooms cool enough to merit a kid's stamp of approval.

Camping under the stars (and stripes) is an everyday adventure when the bed is a mattress with a tent canopy. Three different wallpaper patterns are cleverly combined to carry through the patriotic theme, established by flags and red, white, and blue bedding. A bright red ceiling fan keeps things cool during hot weather.

FOR BABIES ONLY

DESIGN: CARYL HALL STUDIOS

DECORATIVE PAINTING: ANN BLAIR DAVISON

The charming flower-filled wall mural will be cherished for many years after baby outgrows the white-enameled iron, four-poster crib. The most detailed sections of the garden were positioned at a young child's eye level.

This whimsical scene of clowns and other circus favorites can be moved or stowed away when baby outgrows it. That's because the characters were painted on canvas rather than directly on the wall.

If baby gets bored while being ch
she can admire snapshots of h
arranged in a humorous mo
The fanciful, hand-painted ch
table holds nursery supplies
open shelf and in a cabinet ca
flaged by a scene of a fruit or

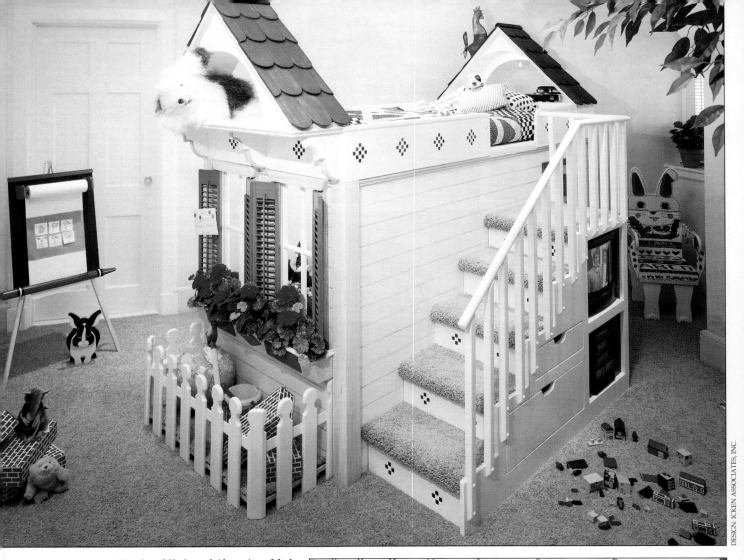

DESIGN: ICKEN ASSOCIATES, INC.

This fun-filled, multifunctional loft unit (above) contains a rooftop bed, an entertainment center built into the stairway, fenced-in toy storage under the window box, and a playhouse at the back (at right). A birthday party is in progress in the playhouse, which features a spacious built-in couch and desk.

SPACE SAVERS

This one-of-a-kind bench is more than just a comfortable place to lounge and read—the cutouts turn the base into a dollhouse. In later years, the recesses can hold other decorative items.

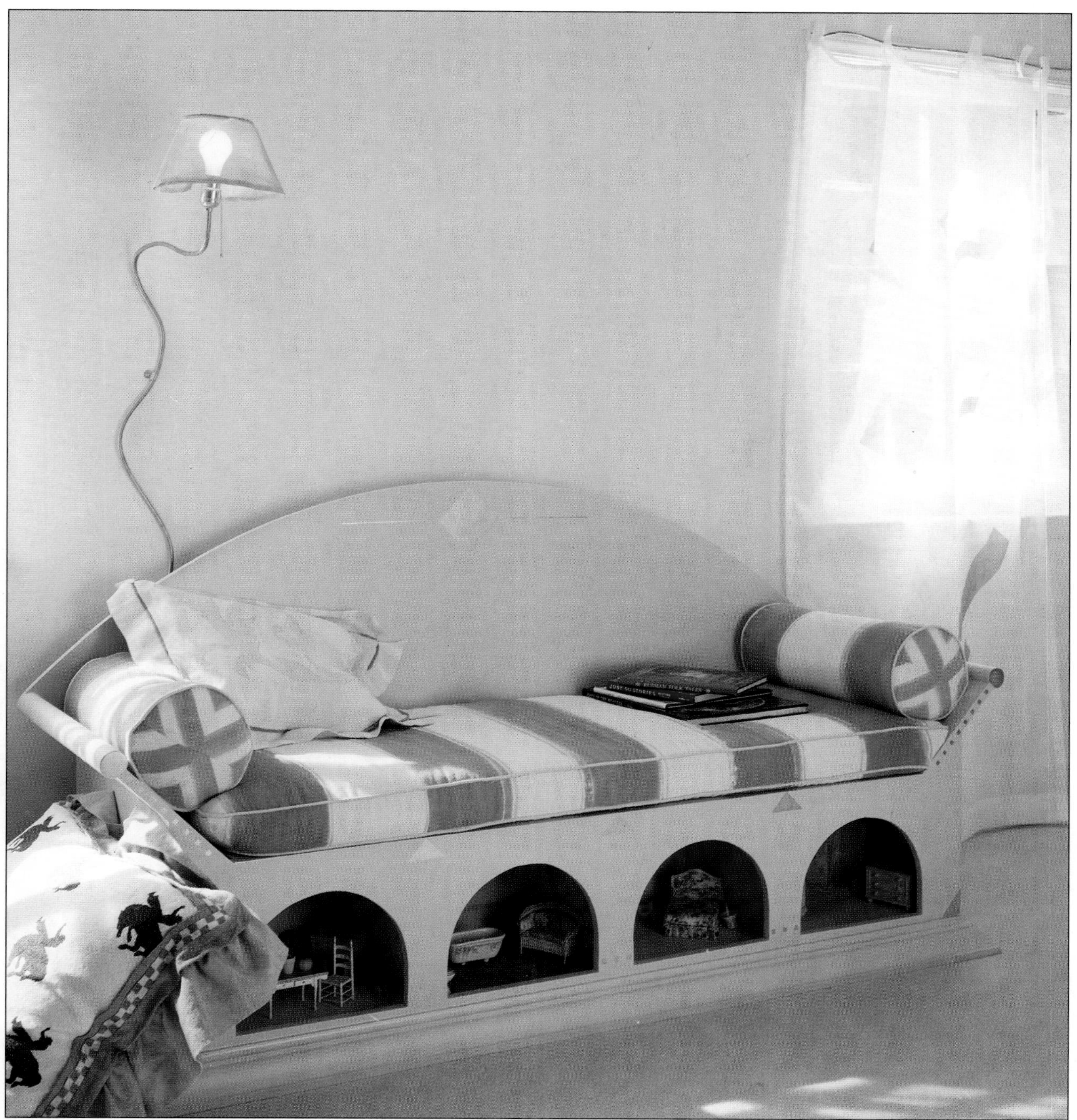

DESIGN: CROWORKS AND JOYCE BOHLMAN DESIGNS

A junior farmhand will love this droll decor paying homage to the colorful holstein. The barn serves double duty as a headboard and storage chest complete with cabinets and drawers.

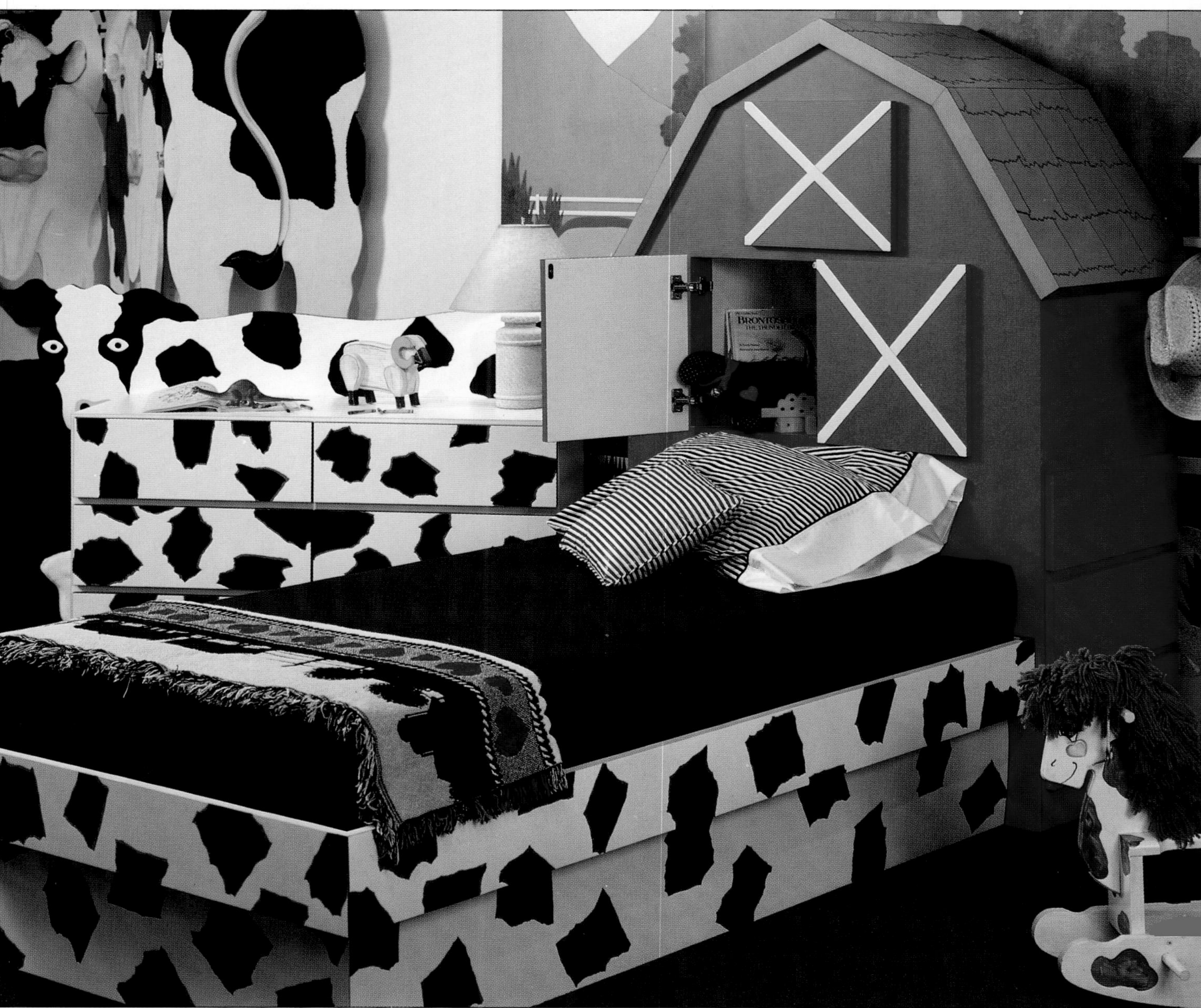

DESIGN: JUVENILE LIFESTYLES, INC.

DESIGN: KATHERINE WALDEN. DECORATIVE PAINTING: AUDREY P. RABY

Panels slide to reveal storage space beneath the built-in window seat. The seat cushion is covered in a pretty yellow and blue fabric complementing the hand-painted design on the panels.

DESIGN: ARLENE ORLANSKY OF DANIELS INTERIORS

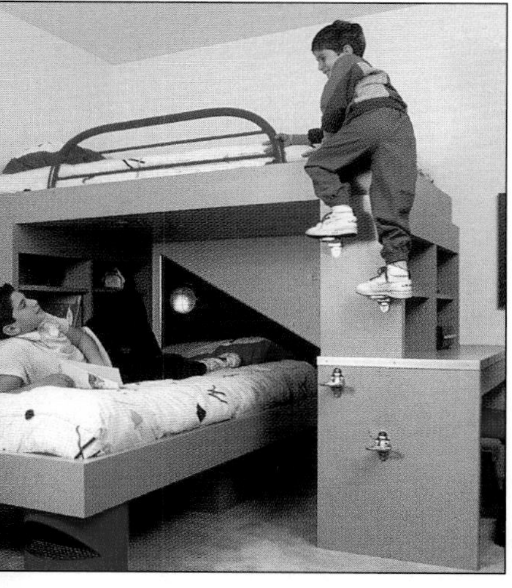

verlapping bunk unit has a n desk and two bookcases— er the desk and the other in the r wall accessible to the occu- f the lower bunk. Folding steps p less room than a ladder.

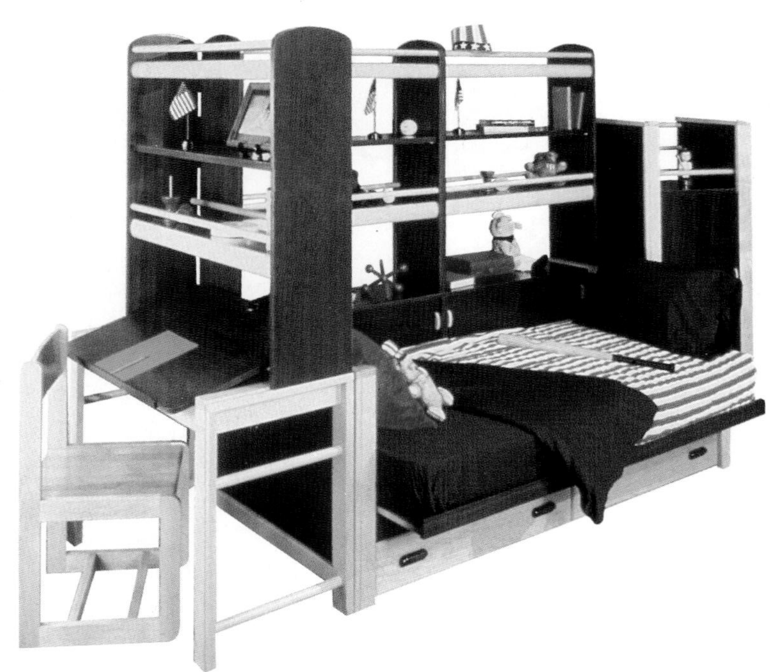

This bedroom grouping fits a lot of features into a little space. A drafting table with multiple tilt positions easily handles homework. Hutches border the chest bed, which slides in slightly to couch depth. A wardrobe at the foot of the bed provides additional storage.

DESIGN: LITTLE ONE'S HAND PAINTED FURNITURE

A symmetrical arrangement keeps peace between sisters sharing a pink, floral-motif bedroom. The morning-glory design on the headboards and bedside table is hand-painted.

Bunk pillars and a panel beneath the tabletop define each child's space at a two-sided desk. Two rolling drawers, one for each resident, are tucked away under the lower bunk.

DESIGN: JUVENILE LIFESTYLES, INC.

SHARED SPACE

DESIGN: JUVENILE LIFESTYLES, INC.

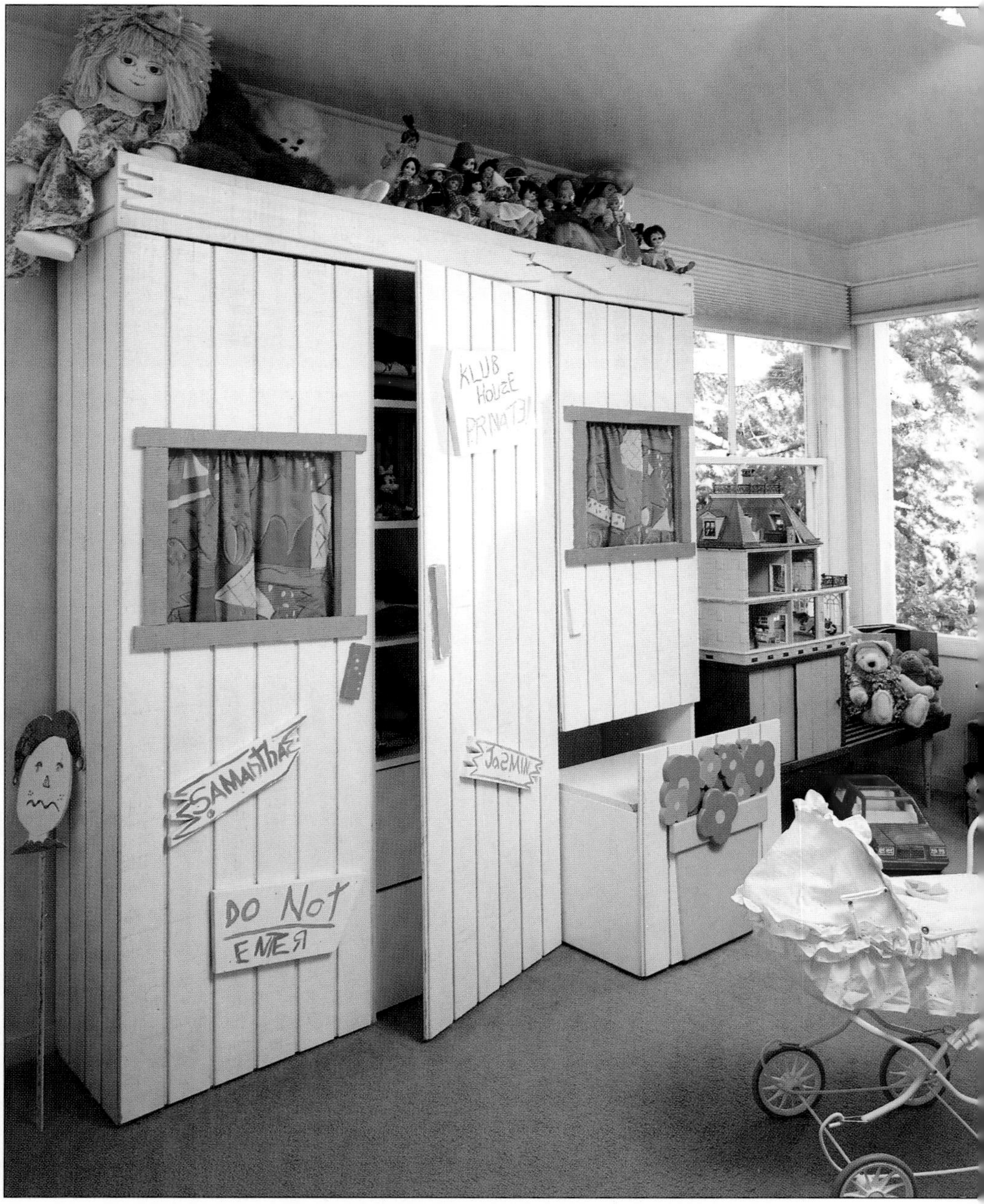

Sisters share a spacious storage unit concealed by a clubhouse facade. A combination bench and toy box, decorated with a flowerpot, pulls out from the unit. Cutouts in the doors, one for each child, serve as puppet theaters.

SHARED SPACE

DESIGN: JAN TETZLAFF/ARABESQUE

A wall unit acts as a room divider, creating two spaces that seem like separate rooms. They're furnished quite differently to suit the dissimilar ages of the two residents.

There's room for two regular occupants in the bunks, plus an overnight guest in the trundle. The twin desks are set at either end of the bunks for maximum privacy.

DESIGN: TECHLINE BY MARSHALL ERDMAN & ASSOCIATES, INC.

SHOW & TELL

The type of collection determines the best method of display. A colorful grouping of buoys hangs from the ceiling in the room at right. Below, bookcases hold a bevy of dolls and stuffed animals.

A young fan displays sports memorabilia atop a cabinet and on the wall. Several peg racks hold caps from favorite teams. Punctuating the theme is a wallpaper border displaying sports graphics.

A model train chugs along on a track set on a high shelf circling the room. Background scenery was cut from plywood, painted, and screwed to the wall. Trees cut from medium density fiberboard were painted and glued in place in front of the track.

DESIGN: FUN FURNITURE

Side-by-side cases contain open shelves for books and knickknacks, plus tiny glass-fronted cabinets to protect delicate figurines. A hand-painted floral design decorates the cabinet doors and top molding.

THEMES & FANTASIES

Life's a day at the beach for the shore-loving resident of this sunny room. Jaunty beach balls abound on the wallpaper and furniture, and stuffed fabric balls decorate the desk, hang from the wall, and adorn the ties atop the window treatment. Sand pails and a picnic at the beach are the subjects of framed pictures on the desk and wall.

DESIGN: DAWN KEARNEY, DESIGN LINE INTERIORS, INC.

A magical rocking horse cabine inspired by a contemporary myth, paired with a mirror frame mad from baby blocks, seashells, marble and model car

Each moment is a call to adventure,
a new possibility
of a new wonder witnessed.
Ask
Receive

DESIGN: TAD TAYLOR'S FANTASY FURNTIURE

DESIGN: DEE THELAN INTERIORS.
DECORATIVE PAINTING: SUZANNE STRACHAN, ARTISTIC EFFECTS

The Old West comes to life in a shared room containing thematic bedding, Native American-style bedspreads and rugs, an intricately tooled saddle, lassos, and models of horses, covered wagons, stagecoaches, and tepees.

Fantasy bunk beds in the form of a medieval castle (at left) are decorated in ice-cream colors suitable for boys or girls. A young boy's field of dreams (below) is filled with baseball paraphernalia—baseballs for bedpost finials, and bats for drawer pulls and balusters on the bed and nightstand.

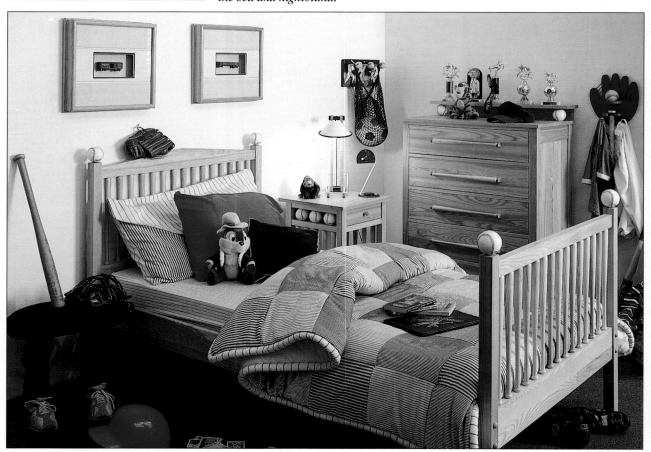

DESIGN: JUVENILE LIFESTYLES, INC.

DESIGN: CAROL SILVERMAN & ASSOCIATES ENVIRONMENTAL DESIGN.
DECORATIVE PAINTING: SUZANNE STRACHAN, ARTISTIC EFFECTS.

A hand-painted mural of exotic wildlife and lush vegetation transports the human occupant of this room to the inner reaches of an African jungle. The bedspread simulates animal skin.

DESIGN: CYNTHIA BRIAN OF STARSTYLE INTERIORS

In this little girl's floral fantasy, delicate blossoms and bows bedeck the walls, window treatment, bedding, canopy, and furniture. Stuffed animals conduct their own tea party at the child-size wicker table and chairs.

DESIGN: TAD TAYLOR'S FANTASY FURNITURE

A fantasy bed resembling a little cottage is set against rolling hills. Bright colors and simple lines make the room look as if it popped out of a cartoon or comic book.

DESIGN: EURODESIGN, LTD.

This efficient wall unit (at left) incorporates open shelving, cabinets, drawers, and a corner desk. The chest bed drawers provide additional storage. A built-in wall unit (below) contains plentiful open and concealed storage. A library ladder securely attached to a track invites kids to use high shelves.

A PLACE FOR EVERYTHING

ARCHITECTS: HRIBAR & WHIPPLE

DESIGN: FUN FURNITURE

A whimsical high-rise building and little house serve as both playthings and storage units. The front of the building opens up and the house roof pops off to divulge stowage space.

Hooks, wall racks, and coat racks are often sufficient to accommodate the few toddler clothes that require hanging. Here, a decorative wall rack holds a little girl's Sunday-best wardrobe.

DESIGN: SUNDAY HENDRICKSON

Constructing an open-back bookcase around and below the window created generous storage and display space in this small room.

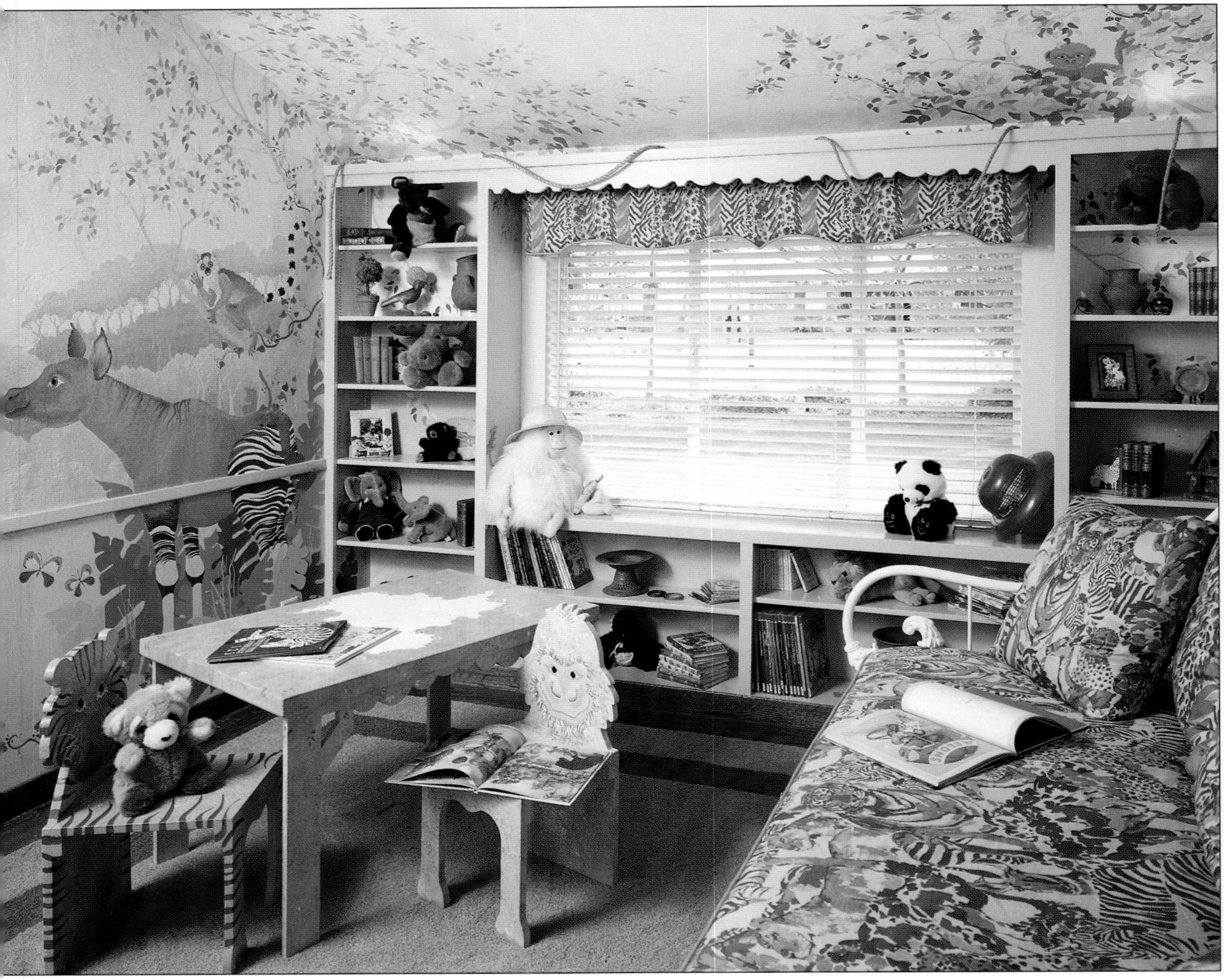

DESIGN: NICOLE PATTEN. DECORATIVE PAINTING: EMILY OCAMPO DESIGNS

DESIGN: HELEN KROEGER, INTERIORS BY DESIGN

To clean up the clutter, this closet was fitted with adjustable shelving, vinyl-coated wire bins, and two levels of rods. The youngster responsible for maintaining order can easily see at a glance where everything belongs.

An antique wardrobe to which shelves have been added holds books, toys, games, and stuffed animals. The doors can be closed when company comes.

READING & WRITING

This sleek white laminate desk with overhead shelving makes a shipshape study center. The thick shelves are actually laminate-covered plywood boxes.

DESIGN: CALVIN L. SMITH ASSOCIATES, INC.

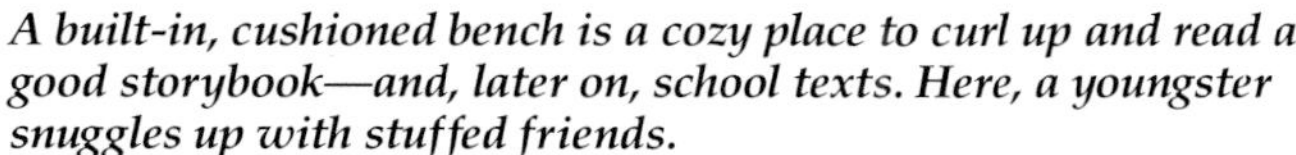

A built-in, cushioned bench is a cozy place to curl up and read a good storybook—and, later on, school texts. Here, a youngster snuggles up with stuffed friends.

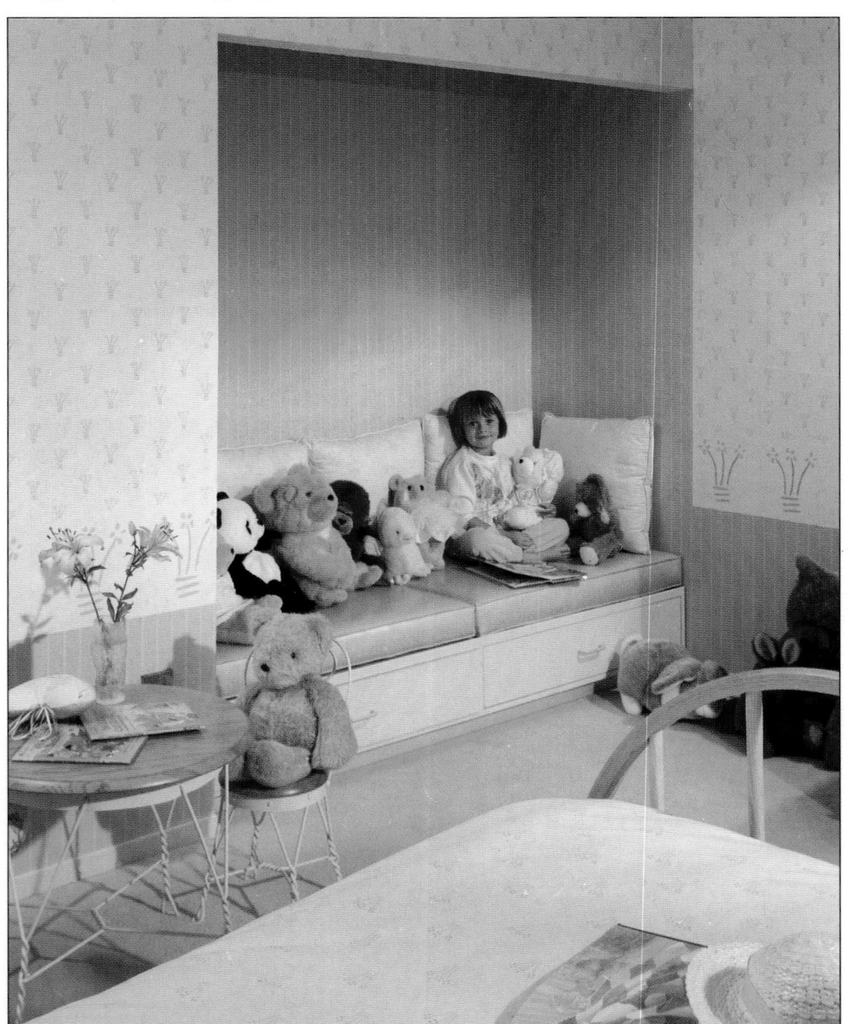

DESIGN: CAROL SPONG, ASID

This drop-front desk swings do reveal cubby holes and a surfac the right size for penning le When closed, it maintains a slim profile. The desk was painted to the adjacent wall unit incorpora wardrobe, chest of drawer entertainment

DESIGN: PALMER/PLETSCH ASSOCIATES

An authentic-looking tepee (at left) is the perfect hideout for a youngster seeking solitude, and a great place to hold pow-wows with friends. This beguiling fantasy (below) beckons kids to climb a magical tree, explore a troll's cave, and slide down the back of a friendly dragon.

DESIGN: M. ENID ARCKLESS, ASID, MEA DESIGNS

HIDEOUTS

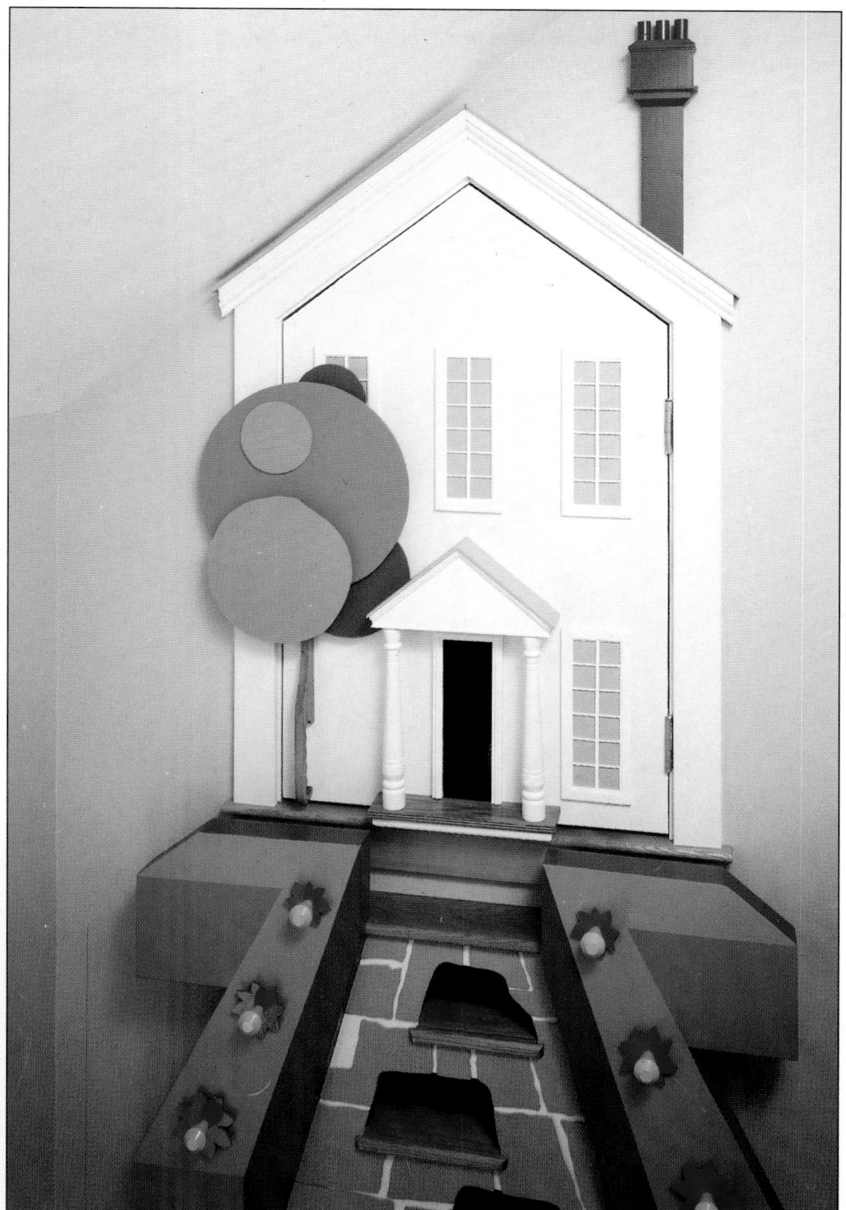

ARCHITECTS: STEVEN FOOTE, PERRY DEAN ROGERS & PARTNERS

Stair treads poking through a faux stone walkway lead to what looks like a house facade attached to the upper wall in a room corner. It's no fake—the front swings opens to a cozy, cushioned hideaway (detail at top).

A colorful circus-motif tent canopy and flaps attach to bunk beds, allowing kids to play and sleep under the big top.

DESIGN: PALMER/PLETSCH ASSOCIATES

Little kids love climbing into snug spaces, such as the crannies in this carpeted climbing structure. The nooks and ledges are also great places to display toys.

ARCHITECTS: COORDT & CO. ARCHITECTURE • PLANNING

Solitude is only a ladder's climb away for the kids who share these high-ceilinged sleeping quarters. As shown in the detail at right, a visitor to the loft can pull down the window shade for extra privacy.

ARCHITECTS: RIVKIN WEISMAN

SWEET DREAMS

DESIGN: SARA OLESKER LTD

An overhead shelf and wallpaper border help define the sleeping area in a bedroom (at right) made serene by an imaginative use of soft colors. The cleverly designed loft bed (below) is actually half of an inverted Victorian four-poster positioned over modular cabinetry and shelving.

DESIGN: ALEXANDER & BYRD, INTERIOR DESIGN ASSOCIATES

DESIGN: DAVID RIVERA DESIGNS, INC.

Built on an irregularly shaped platform, this young musician's custom bed is close to all the action—drums, stereo system, and books. The carpeted lower step is an inviting place to lounge and visit with friends.

DESIGN: AMERICAN WOOD COUNCIL

A built-in captain's bed makes a snug sleeping nook for a child. Shelves at the head and foot hold all the nighttime necessities.

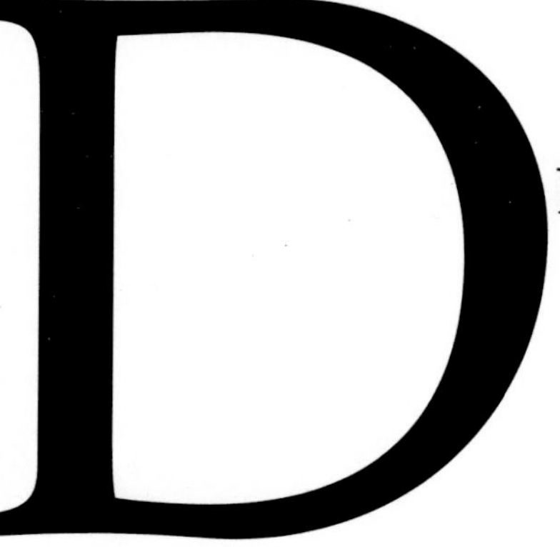

DECORATING DETAILS

A flower-lined path leads to a turreted castle occupied by storybook characters. Who would guess that such an enchanting facade conceals a wall bed?

DESIGN: M. ENID ARCKLESS, ASID, MEA DESIGNS

DESIGN: KATHERINE WALDEN; DECORATIVE PAINTING: AUDREY P. RABY

The area rug and furniture were hand-painted to create a rich, ornate look in a little girl's Victorian-style room.

A skirted, glass-top dressing table and upholstered footstool set against a winsome mural lend old-fashioned charm to this room. The picture frames, lamps, and knickknacks were chosen for their intricate detailing.

The picket fence (at right) frames the view from the nursery window, merging indoors and outdoors. Careful attention was paid to color in this attic bedroom (below): yellows, magentas, and blues in various tints and shades are repeated throughout the room.

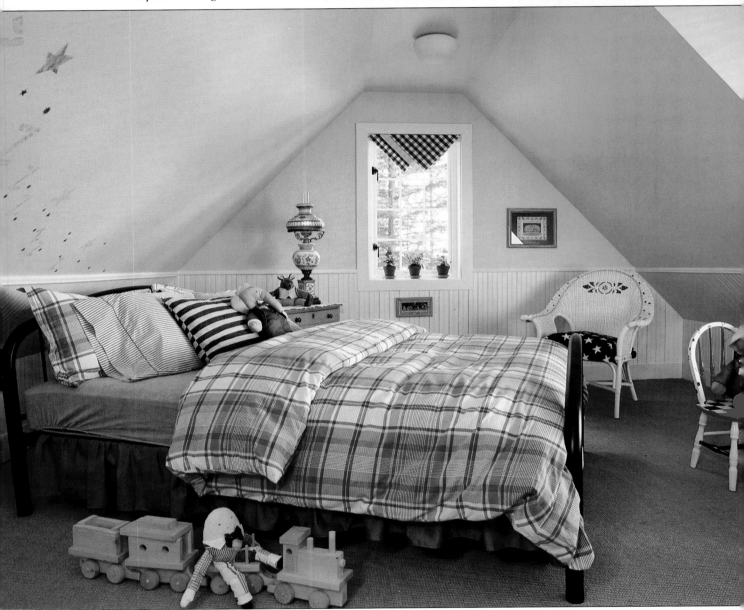

DESIGN: HEIDI EMMETT

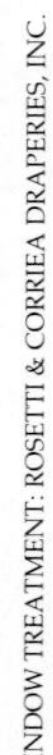

WINDOW TREATMENT: ROSETTI & CORRIEA DRAPERIES, INC.

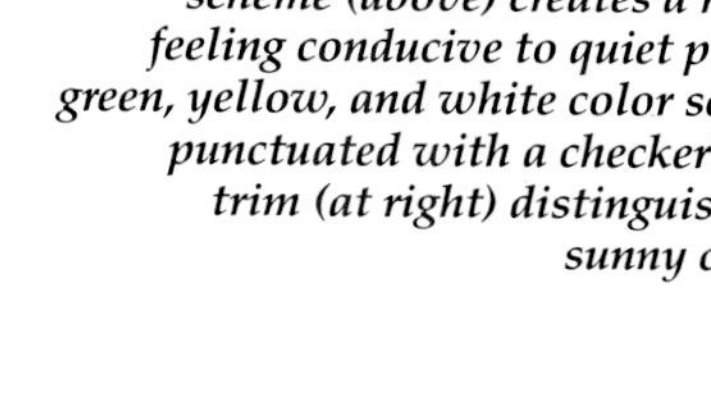

A predominantly pastel color scheme (above) creates a restful feeling conducive to quiet play. A green, yellow, and white color scheme punctuated with a checkerboard trim (at right) distinguish this sunny closet.

Fancifully painted scenes make magic in an attic nursery. A faux skylight brings cheer to the room, even during gloomy weather. The lamp and books atop the dresser aren't real, since the chest is recessed into the wall. Adding to the air of enchantment are rabbits disappearing into a warren (really just a door leading to a storage area).

DESIGN: ANN CARTER

DESIGN: ICKEN ASSOCIATES, INC.

A SHOPPER'S GUIDE

Look at the fanciful, colorful furnishings available for children today, and you'll wish you were a kid again! The options include loft beds that look like castles, chest beds with built-in storage bins, whimsical wardrobes, kid-size chairs and sofas, game-board rugs, cushiony three-dimensional wall hangings, and decorating kits with repositionable borders and appliqués in kid-pleasing motifs. And that's just the beginning.

This chapter tells you what products are available and where to find many of them. It will help you to transform your child's room into a special refuge for dreaming, lounging, studying, playing, and entertaining friends.

An antique brass headboard and a quilted comforter with a colorful undersea motif are the starting points for a young girl's room decor. Now various wallpaper, paint, fabric, and carpet samples are being considered for suitability.

BEDS

Most babies start out in a crib or, for the first few months, in the cozier confines of a cradle or bassinet. A youngster is ready for a bed, either intermediate or adult-size, when he or she attains a height of about 35 inches or repeatedly climbs out of the crib.

Choose carefully. Children spend a lot of time sleeping, so it's important to provide a safe, comfortable sleep surface that supports their growing bodies in a healthful way. Also remember that to a child a bed is more than just a place for slumber. It's a gymnasium, where infants develop motor skills and young kids release pent-up energy. Later on, it's a place for lounging, reading, and seating friends.

The most common beds sold for kids' rooms are described here. Usually, you purchase the mattress separately; see page 433 for tips on choosing a good one.

INFANT BEDS

Safety is the most important consideration in buying this type of bed. You're sure to find something in your budget, since prices start from under $100 (as low as $40 for a no-frills bassinet) and range upward to several hundred dollars, depending on style, materials, and other options. Infants grow so fast that secondhand bedding can give excellent value.

As all but the most starry-eyed first-time parents know, all materials should be washable. And on an older piece of furniture, be sure any paint is lead-free.

Cradles & Bassinets

These tiny beds are popular alternatives to cribs for the first two or three months of life. Their snug size is supposedly comforting to newborns. But once your infant is ready to roll over, such restricted sleeping quarters are no longer safe. Also, these little beds are equipped with only a pad (it should be at least 2 inches thick), and a baby soon needs the firmer support of a mattress.

Since neither cradles nor bassinets are completely regulated, you'll have to take on the responsibility of checking safety features.

Choose a cradle with the highest sides possible to hold the baby securely when the bed is rocked. For safety, the rockers should curve only slightly, moving with a gentle motion. On a suspended cradle, look for a sturdy base, secure pivoting hardware, and a design that lets you lock the cradle in a nonswinging position.

DESIGN: JUVENILE LIFESTYLES, INC.

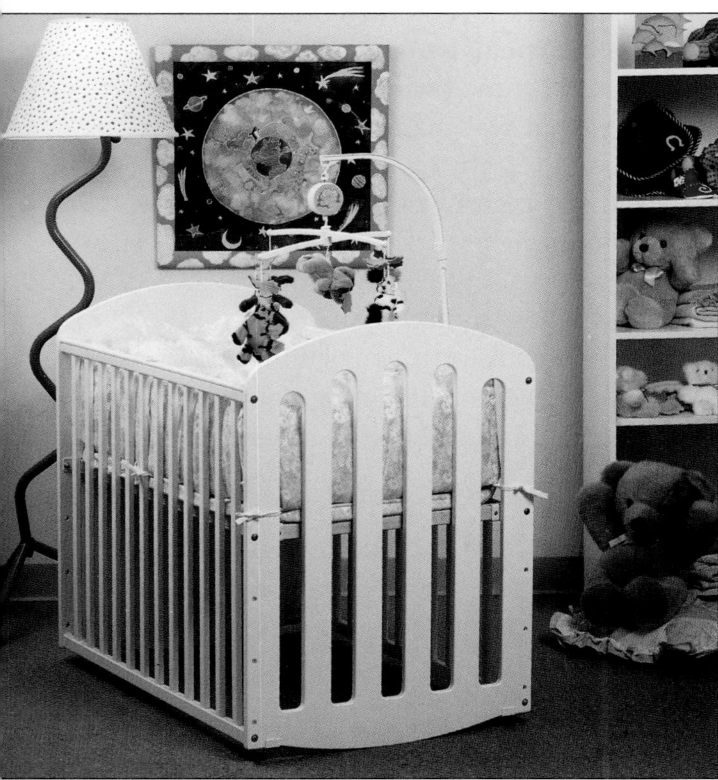

Because of its large size, the European-style cradle at left accommodates babies a few months longer than most cradles would. Pretty wicker bassinet (above) sits securely in its frame and contains ample padding.

A stable base is also critical in a bassinet, which is a basketlike bed (often with a hood at one end) atop a stand that may or may not have wheels. The basket and frame may be a single unit, or the basket may lift off the stand—if it does, make sure the handles are firmly attached to the frame. A wicker model should have no protruding reeds.

Cribs

Most cribs made since 1990 conform to current safety rules; make sure a secondhand or custom-made crib meets these standards before using it.

Slats should be spaced no more than 2⅜ inches apart, corner posts or finials should be no higher than 1/16 inch (canopy and other posts higher than 16 inches don't count), and the mattress should fit snugly with less than two fingers' width between the crib sides and mattress. Any cutouts in the headboard or footboard should be small enough so no part of the baby's body can be trapped in them.

The latching mechanisms that release the drop side should be well out of the baby's reach and require dual action or at least 10 pounds of pressure for release.

Check for tight supports, screws, and bolts. A toddler can be very active, jumping up and down in the crib, so solid construction is especially important.

To discourage a baby from climbing out, the distance between the mattress and the top of the rails should be as great as possible. Methods for lowering mattresses vary. Some cribs have only two levels, while others have three or four. With some, you simply move levers, while others necessitate unbolting, repositioning the bottom support, and rebolting.

An intermediate bed, such as this one with a detachable guardrail, will sleep a youngster from about age 2 to 5.

You can buy a crib with built-in storage or a convertible type. On some models, the rail on one side can be removed to create a day bed, or both side rails can be detached to make a toddler bed. On other models, you can remove the rails and add a mattress extender to lengthen the sleeping area by about 16 inches; the extender covers an area previously occupied by a chest of drawers, which you now move to the side.

The disadvantages of a convertible crib are that it costs more, you may need the crib for another baby, and the lengthened bed is soon outgrown—especially if your youngster refuses to sleep in a "baby bed" and demands an adult bed.

INTERMEDIATE BEDS

Sometimes called toddler, junior, or youth beds, these units are suitable for a relatively short time, usually between the ages of 2 and 5. The

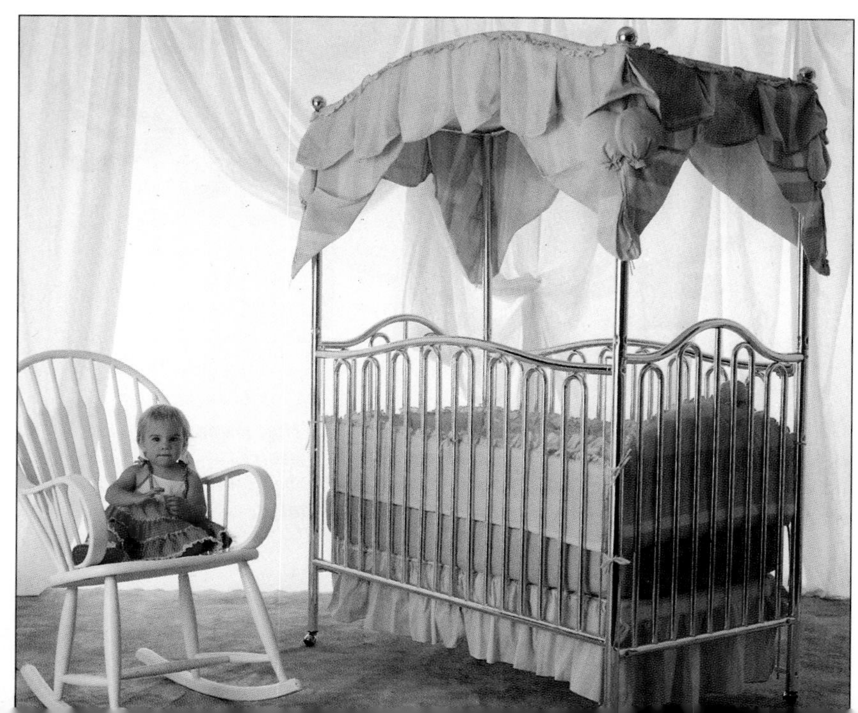

Cribs are available in many styles and materials. This brass model features a colorful canopy and matching bedding and bumpers.

bed may not even last that long if your child thinks it's too babyish and wants a "real bed."

Many parents view intermediate beds as wasteful because of their short life span. Doting relatives sometimes buy one to keep for a visiting child.

In addition to beds that convert from cribs, many types are sold solely as intermediate beds. Some are fantasy beds (see page 435), while others look like miniature versions of adult beds, except that the mattress sits directly on slats and guardrails may be attached to the frame.

There is no standard size: some of these beds can take a crib mattress (though you may need your old one for another baby), and some require a slightly larger mattress. You may have a hard time finding a mattress and bedding for an odd-size model.

You can buy a simple, tubular steel bed frame for about $50, a fantasy race car frame for about $150.

ADULT-SIZE BEDS

A standard adult bed consists of a frame, mattress, and box spring or other support. The frame may be just a plain metal support on casters or may include a headboard and/or footboard. Some beds are categorized by their frame's design—for example, a four-poster bed. Standard beds come in twin, full, queen, and king sizes, although twin is most often used in kids' rooms. If your child is destined to be tall, you may want to purchase an extra-long model, if available, or invest in a custom bed.

When moving a toddler from a crib to an adult bed, use a guardrail to keep the child from falling out. You'll find detachable models made of metal, plastic, or nylon mesh.

On the following pages, we review common types of adult-size beds sold for kids' rooms. What you'll pay depends on design, quality, materials, and other options. Because of the number of components involved, loft beds are usually the priciest. You can get a sturdy loft setup with a bed, guardrail, ladder, armoire, bookcase, and desk for a little under $1,000—or you can spend several times that amount. A wall bed can cost more than $1,000, but most other styles are priced from about $200 to $800. In most cases, the mattress (and box spring, if needed) are extra.

Bunk Beds

These are classic space savers when you're doubling up kids in a room—and even if there's only one child, a second bunk can provide extra play space and accommodation for an overnight guest. Keep in mind that the

DESIGN: PALMER/PLETSCH ASSOCIATES

DESIGN: AMISCO INDUSTRIES, INC.

The sturdy wood-frame bunks (at left), with end rails that serve as a ladder, can be unstacked and used as twin beds if desired. The metal-frame pyramid bunk (above), with a double bed on bottom and a twin bed on top, is designed for stacking mode only.

top bunk will be awkward to make, and that its occupant could swelter on hot nights if the room does not have good ventilation. Also realize that some kids aren't happy about heights.

Conventional bunks stack directly on top of each other, and the most practical models can be unstacked and used as twin beds. A less common configuration consists of an L-shaped arrangement of freestanding beds, with one placed partially under the other. For the greatest versatility, get a unit that can function as stacking bunks, L-bunks, or twin beds. Some manufacturers sell kits that can convert bunks into loft units.

A relatively recent option is a pyramid or stair-step bunk, consisting of a full bed below and a twin bed above.

Some conventional bunk beds allow you to slip either a mattress or a desktop insert into the top of the lower bunk. Your child can use the bottom unit as a desk most of the time, but by adding the mattress, convert it to a bed for an overnight guest.

Examine bunks carefully before you buy. Look for solid construction, with no wobbling when the beds are stacked. The spacing of rails should be narrow enough so a child's head can't accidentally be caught between them. The upper unit should have a sturdy guardrail—one on each side, if the bed isn't placed against a wall. Be sure the mattress is at least 5 inches below the guardrail's upper edge. The ladder, if not integral, should attach securely to the top bunk and be easy for children to climb.

Usually, the mattress rests over slats; in many cases, you can get a thin wooden panel to lay over the slats, so the child in the lower bunk can't kick or poke the mattress of the upper unit.

Not all bunk beds are the same height. Be certain there's adequate headroom for both occupants.

Loft Beds

These elevated beds maximize floor space. Types for young children often incorporate a fantasy motif, such as a castle, and feature a play area underneath. Models intended to see kids into adulthood usually include a desk, with drawers and other storage below. Some manufacturers offer a matching twin bed that goes under the loft to form an L-shaped bunk.

BUYING A MATTRESS

Even though kids may not weigh as much as adults, they need good, firm sleep support just as much as adults do. The technical information provided here can help you select a good mattress. But remember, the deciding factor should be comfort. If your child is too young to make the decision about an adult-size mattress, stretch out on the various models yourself. That's better than relying on product labels, since one manufacturer's "firm" may feel harder than another's "extra-firm."

Innerspring mattresses are the type most commonly sold. Look for more than 100 coils in a crib mattress, more than 200 in a twin mattress, and more than 300 in a full-size model. A high coil count isn't the whole story, though. Wire gauge is also important—the lower the number, the stronger the wire, with 13 the heaviest gauge and 21 the lightest. Also, the more layers of quality cushioning and insulation provided, the more comfortable the mattress will prove.

A high-quality foam mattress is just as good as a well-constructed innerspring mattress. Foam mattresses can consist of a solid core of foam or of several layers of different types of foam laminated together. The traditional latex (synthetic rubber) and the newer high-resilience polyurethanes are among the highest-performance foams. Generally, the higher the density, the better the foam. Be sure to get a minimum density of at least 1.15 pounds per cubic foot in a crib mattress or 2 pounds per cubic foot in an adult-size mattress.

Most beds intended for adults accommodate a box spring to support the mattress and add more comfort. However, the majority of adult-size beds sold in kids' shops are designed for the mattress to rest directly over slats or a wood panel; using a box spring on these beds would make them too high for the frame and wouldn't permit trundle or drawer options under the bed. You can expect a mattress on a rigid support to wear out faster than one on a box spring.

The average cost for good-quality mattresses is as follows: crib mattresses about $90; twin mattresses $150 to $190; and full-size mattresses $250 to $275, plus about a third again as much for a box spring.

STANDARD MATTRESS DIMENSIONS

Bed Size	Width		Length
Crib	28"	X	52"
Twin	39"	X	75"
Extra-long twin	39"	X	80"
Full	54"	X	75"

Most loft beds are best used where ceilings are higher than 8 feet, so be sure there will be enough room for the child to study or play under the loft as well as adequate headroom above. Lower lofts are usually intended for young kids. They often have a slide or a tented area underneath that looks like a playhouse or fort. Some short lofts have a pull-out desk that stores below.

The standard loft has a twin bed, but you can also find models with extra-long twin, full, or queen beds. Most lofts are made of wood. Better-made fantasy types have steel frames, while less expensive ones are made entirely of particleboard.

DESIGN: EURODESIGN, LTD.

Trundle Beds

This space-saving unit pulls out from underneath another bed to accommodate a sibling or an overnight guest. The standard size is twin.

Some trundles are freestanding units on casters, while others sit on attached frames. Many modular furniture lines feature beds with matching trundle units. You can even get trundles for some bunk beds.

Be sure the trundle draws out smoothly, and that your child can handle it alone—unless you want to do the pulling every time it's used.

Captain's & Chest Beds

As the term implies, a captain's bed is named for the built-in units used by ships' captains. It usually contains at least two rows of drawers. Some models have shallow cabinets flanked by sets of double drawers. An authentic-looking captain's bed has high sides—on a ship, they prevent the occupant from being tossed out during rough weather.

A chest bed may feature built-in drawers or a trundle, or both. Models designed for younger children have compartments for toys. The configuration of storage areas varies from one manufacturer to another.

Captain's and chest beds sleep a little higher than standard beds because they incorporate storage below. To make room for this, the mattress sits on slats or a wood panel.

Canopy Beds

Marketed primarily for girls, canopy beds have an overhead framework and often a roof-like covering. Some come with drawers or a trundle below.

Rustic loft (top) leaves plenty of space for play below. Sleek chest bed (bottom) contains two drawers for clothes or toy storage and a trundle bed for overnight guests.

Although many canopy beds can be assembled on site, some can't—so be sure the bed will fit through the doorway before you buy. Also make sure the ceiling is high enough so the bed doesn't overpower the space.

Wall Beds

These disappearing beds swing up into a cabinet or wall unit, freeing floor space for play or hobbies. The mattress and bedding are secured with straps so they stay put when the bed is raised.

Although this type of bed opens up a small room during the daytime, it's difficult for young children to operate on their own, and may make a child's quarters seem less personal.

Fantasy Beds

These whimsical beds come in such shapes as racing cars, airplanes, sailboats, and teddy bears. Although some fantasy beds take a crib mattress, those accommodating a twin size have a longer life. You can even get a fantasy bed in the form of a bunk or loft.

The beds range from fairly inexpensive plastic types to more costly and elaborate models made from wood or steel upholstered with foam and canvas. If the motif you want isn't available ready-made, you can order a custom design.

If you want a bed to serve your child longer, consider getting a standard bed with a fantasy facade bolted to the frame. The facade can be removed when the child outgrows the fantasy. If you're handy, you can make the facade yourself by cutting a sheet of plywood in the shape of the desired motif and painting it or covering it with fabric.

DESIGN: LANDS' END

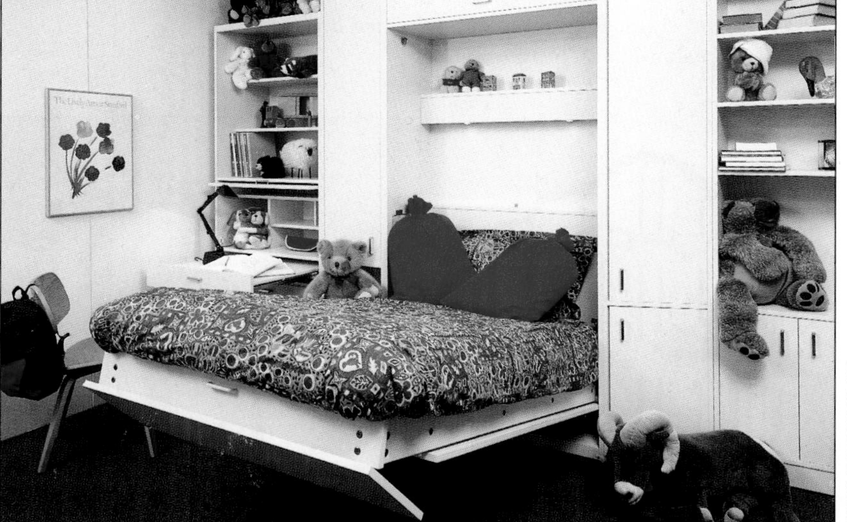

DESIGN: EURODESIGN, LTD.

DESIGN: CLOCKWORK INTERIORS

The decorative canopy bed (top) creates a dainty milieu; the wall bed (middle) saves space in a small room; and the fantasy bed (bottom) appeals to a young rail fan.

TABLES, DESKS & SEATING

Adults work, play, and lounge in other rooms of the house, but kids do all of that in their bedrooms, and they need furniture to accommodate these activities. This section describes work surfaces—from changing tables to computer desks—and seating that kids' rooms need.

Make sure the table or desk you choose is the right height for your child; its top should reach mid-thigh level when the child is standing. See the chart on page 384.

Chairs used for long periods for crafts projects or homework should provide good back support. Your child's feet should rest flat on the floor, and there should be a gap of several inches between young knees and the underside of the table or desk.

Changing Tables

You can change a baby on any stable surface with raised sides and, preferably, a safety strap. Changing tables range from about $50 to several hundred dollars.

The most common design resembles a small shelving unit. The baby goes in the top enclosure, and supplies are stored in shelves underneath. Depending on the model, the table may or may not be able to work as a bookcase or storage unit later on.

Some manufacturers incorporate changing tables as part of wardrobes and dressers. The most versatile ones can be converted to shelving for toys or some other use as the child grows. Some companies sell the flip-top separately. Be wary of any that sits too close to the edge of a dresser; although heavy, it still can be accidentally knocked off.

DESIGN: COSCO

DESIGN: JUVENILE LIFESTYLES, INC.

DESIGN: SAMSON McCANN

Changing table (top left) features a safety rail and restraint belt for baby's protection. The top surface and interior of bedside table (lower left) are spacious enough to hold all the items a youngster needs at bedtime. Benches and base of the adjustable table (above) rotate to three different heights to accommodate youngsters until about age 11.

It isn't really necessary to invest in a separate piece of furniture. If you prefer, you can just buy a mat or portable changing tray to fit on top of an existing piece of furniture.

Bedside Tables

Unless storage is built into the bed's headboard, your child will need some kind of table to hold a lamp, clock, tissues, and other necessities. It's useful to have a shelf or two for books or toys.

You don't have to get a unit sold specifically as a bedside table or nightstand. A low bookcase can work just as well, and even a large storage cube will do. Whatever your choice, just be sure that your child can reach the top surface easily from the bed.

A bedside table isn't practical in some cases, as with a loft bed or the top level of bunk beds. A clip-on light clamped to the headboard or post is one way to provide illumination for these, and lamps, clock radios, and tissue boxes are all available in wall-mounted models; just hang a pocket for a bedtime book. You could also affix a narrow shelf to the wall.

Low Tables & Chairs

Little kids love tables and chairs their own size that they can snuggle into. A diminutive set, available plain or in whimsical designs, will last until your child is about 6 years old. You can pay as little as $50 for molded plastic or as much as several hundred dollars for fancifully painted wood.

Sturdiness is a major consideration, since kids are sure to use the set in ways you never dreamed of, jumping on the tabletop and playing underneath inverted chairs. Children sometimes want their parents to sit with them, so be sure the chairs will bear your weight.

The safest sets have smooth, rounded edges, not sharp ones. Washability is also key, since your child is likely to get crayon marks and paint smears on the surface.

Tables and chairs are available in various heights. If you buy a set, the chairs will be scaled to the table's height—not necessarily the case when you buy them separately. You can replace the legs of some tables with longer ones as your child grows. You can't do the same with chairs, however.

Study Desks

Many types of desks and tables, available in a wide price range, are suitable for schoolwork. Most are stationary, but some fold away or adjust in height as the child grows. Others are incorporated into bunk and loft structures.

Most feature drawers, which are handy for storing little items. Some offer desktop hutches as an option. Surfaces vary in size, so be sure you choose one big enough so your child can spread books and papers out comfortably.

You can make your own desk by fixing a piece of painted plywood or even an old flat door on top of low bookcases or stackable drawers or bins. Or attach a work surface directly to wall studs with sturdy hardware.

DESIGN: DESIGN HORIZONS BY LADD FURNITURE, INC.

Tucked under the white melamine drafting desk (at left) is a rolling cabinet with a drawer front that reverses to white. The height and back support of the chair are adjustable. The modular study center (below), featuring a black melamine surface and wood-veneer drawer fronts, has a computer desk with a pull-out keyboard tray. Hand-painting has transformed a simple wood folding chair into an accent piece.

DESIGN: JUVENILE LIFESTYLES, INC.

SHOPPING FOR FURNITURE

Children's furniture comes in a variety of styles, materials, and quality levels. Prices run a gamut, too. Don't expect good furniture to cost less just because it's for kids.

Even if your budget can accommodate pricey items, you may want to avoid them. If your child is rough with belongings, don't buy the best and expect a sudden change in behavior. Get sturdy but less costly items, and you won't feel as disappointed if they're treated roughly.

To stretch a budget, look for furniture that can be raised, added onto, or reconfigured as a child grows. Other practical choices are pieces that convert to other uses when the child outgrows the original plan.

For the best selection, check kids' shops, general furniture stores, department stores, home-improvement centers, and specialty catalogs. Many high-end and custom items are available through interior designers.

For tips on buying specific types of furniture, refer to the rest of this chapter. Generally, look for solid construction, since kids can use furniture in unpredictable ways. There shouldn't be any splinters, ragged edges, or exposed nails or other hardware to harm children. Rounded corners are a good safety feature. Check drawers, doors, and other moving parts for smooth, safe operation.

Materials

The quality, life expectancy, and cost of a piece of furniture are related to the material of which it is made. The following are some commonly used materials. You'll also find wicker, metal, and molded plastic items.

Wood. A piece of furniture can be made of solid wood, wood veneer over plywood panels, or a combination. Solid wood is more durable, richer looking, and costlier than veneer, although veneered panels are less apt to warp.

Woods are either hardwood (from deciduous trees) or softwood (from conifers). Common hardwoods used for furniture include oak, ash, beech, birch, maple, cherry, and walnut. Hardwoods make more precise joints, hold fasteners better, are more resistant to wear, and generally cost more than softwoods. Common softwoods are pine and fir, used primarily in unfinished furniture.

Composition Board. The two main types used for kids' furniture are particleboard and medium-density fiberboard (MDF)—both are less expensive than solid wood or good-quality plywood, but are also weaker and more likely to chip.

Particleboard is made from very small pieces of wood bonded together, while MDF is a stiffer material made from compressed wood fibers. Both are used as a substrate for laminates. MDF also takes paint well.

MDF costs more than particleboard; its uniform texture allows it to be milled like wood. It's popular with makers of juvenile furniture because it can be cut into fanciful shapes that are smooth all over, even at cut ends. By contrast, particleboard's pocked ends must usually be laminated or hidden in some other way.

Laminates. These popular surfacing materials for kids' furniture are tough, easy to clean, and available in a wide range of colors.

Of the three major surfacing materials, high-pressure plastic laminate is by far the most durable, and also the costliest. Melamine, a surface layer of resin-impregnated paper, is less expensive but very serviceable. The lowest grade is vinyl or paper surface film, which is thin and can peel away.

Computer Desks

Desks designed to hold a home computer system usually feature a hutch top with shelves and ledges to hold components. The desk may be a single unit, or the pedestal and hutch may be sold separately. Prices range from under $100 to several times that amount. Such a desk is of limited use for other tasks, since the computer equipment and supplies take up most of the available space.

Make sure that the position of the monitor and keyboard is suitable for your child. The monitor should be at eye level, and the keyboard lower than standard desk level to avoid stress on the wrists. If the desk top isn't slightly lower than a standard desk, there should be a slide-out keyboard tray at a lower height.

You can set up computer equipment on a regular desk. Some makers of modular furniture offer a keyboard tray that you can affix to the underside of the desk.

Desk Chairs

Some of the most common types are secretarial chairs, folding metal chairs, and straight-back chairs.

Some options for scaled-down seating are shown here. Clockwise from top left they include miniature reproduction of a Queen Anne chair, aniline-dyed wood chair, tubular metal and fabric rocker, dinosaur-motif combination stool and chair, wicker rocker, convertible sofa, small director's chair, rush and wood chair, hickory rocker, and larger director's chair resting on a bean bag.

The one that will last your child the longest is the secretarial chair, since both the seat height and back support are adjustable. Most secretarial chairs roll on casters and are easy to move; the five-footed pedestal gives greatest stability. Generally, the better the upholstery and the more adjustable the chair, the higher the price. A caution: some kids prefer swiveling to studying, so keep that in mind if your child is easily distracted.

Folding metal chairs and straight-back chairs aren't likely to offer as much comfort for long-term sitting or support the back as well.

Folding chairs come in many colors, while straight-back types are most often wood. The seats of either may be hard or padded. Depending on its heft, a straight-back chair may be difficult for a young child to move. Prices range from about $10 for a simple folding chair to several hundred dollars for a fine wooden piece.

Occasional Seating

Adult-size chairs are fine for older kids, but younger ones find the scale overwhelming. They're happier in seating their own size.

Many manufacturers of kids' furniture make scaled-down seating suitable for children until about age 5. You'll find little stools, director's chairs, folding wood chairs, and rockers priced between $10 and $70 at shops selling children's furniture. Pint-size, foam-filled easy chairs and couches, some of which convert into sleeping space for young guests, retail for $50 to $150. Inexpensive bean bags and floor pillows are other options, appealing to kids of all ages.

High-end furniture showrooms sometimes stock such items as bantam-size reproductions of Queen Anne chairs and diminutive wicker chairs and loveseats. These pricey pieces are often available only through designers, and may not be the most practical choices even where budgets permit.

STORAGE

The burgeoning world of storage containers includes plastic bins, tubs, crates, boxes, and jars, plus mesh hammocks, string bags, cardboard boxes, canvas toy chests, wall racks, hanging pockets, hatboxes, and metal lockers. Many storage items intended for other uses can go to work in a kid's room.

Unlike adults' bedrooms, kids' rooms need places to stow not just clothes but also toys, games, puzzles, books, stuffed animals, cherished collections, and other assorted treasures.

Storage units come in myriad forms, from large pieces of furniture to little boxes and bins. They're made of various materials, including wood, composition board, wicker, metal, plastic, and fabric. Prices are just as wide-ranging.

Shop for storage units as you would for any kind of furniture (see page 80). Look for solid construction and durability, and for surfaces that can easily be cleaned. Also make sure that there are no sharp edges that could hurt young users.

Closet Systems

Not only do most bedroom closets waste space, but they're not intended for little kids—the pole and shelf are too high. Luckily, there are easy ways to modify closets to make them more useful.

The best solution is a modular system that will meet the changing needs of a developing child. Poles can be raised, shelves rearranged, and more drawers or hanging space added as the child grows.

You can organize the closet yourself. Home-improvement centers and specialty shops sell components, including poles, shelves, cabinets, stacking drawers, wire baskets, and hooks. Most closet shops also design and install custom systems.

Another option is to hire an independent contractor who specializes in organizing closets. Look for one who has done children's closets before and shows some understanding of a child's storage needs.

A fully developed system can cost from under $100 to thousands of dollars, depending on the closet size, the number and variety of components (generally, drawers are the most expensive units), and the quality of the materials. Price systems carefully: you may find that some custom systems are nearly as economical as do-it-yourself arrangements, and a whole lot easier if you're not especially handy with tools.

Wardrobes

A wardrobe offers convenient clothes storage if the room has no closet or an inadequate one, or if the closet is being used for another purpose.

Since young children don't have many clothes that need hanging, child-size armoires are usually fitted with more drawers or shelves than hanging space. Although they can be charming, these armoires are quickly outgrown—and may cost more than you want to spend.

An adult wardrobe will last longer, but may contain too much hanging space to suit your child's needs. You could modify the interior by adding shelves along one side. Move the pole down to your child's eye level, and gradually raise it as the child grows. Add appeal to an inexpensive, plain unit by painting or wallpapering it inside or out.

Dressers

A chest of drawers stores clothes that can be folded, but it can also hold toys and other items. You can pay less than $100 for a no-frills but functional unit or several times that for a decorative piece of fine furniture.

If you want a young child to be in charge of the dresser, make sure he or she is capable of using it. The child should be able to reach the top draw-

DESIGN: VISADOR COMPANY

A closet system maximizes storage space in a child's room. This slatted shelving system, available through many closet shops and storage contractors, is made of handsome hardwood.

er without standing on a stool or other prop, and to grasp pulls easily to open and close the drawers.

Look for sturdy construction and stability. The dresser shouldn't be so top-heavy that it tips over when the upper drawer is pulled out. For safety, each drawer should move on glides equipped with stops to keep it from coming all the way out.

If the closet is large enough, you could place the dresser inside, or even plan one into a closet system (see page 441).

For a very young child, consider a modular system with stacking drawers; you can add more units as the child grows.

Under-bed Drawers

Easy for a child to reach, drawers under the bed frame provide handy storage for clothing and toys. They're the perfect solution for kids who like to tidy up by throwing everything under the bed.

Some beds, such as chest types, feature built-in drawers. The number and dimensions of drawers vary among manufacturers.

Many modular furniture lines offer freestanding drawers on casters that slide under the bed. Usually two drawers, sitting side by side, fit under a bed. Or you can opt for a trundle frame on casters and use it as one gigantic drawer. You'll pay anywhere from about $100 to $400 for a set of drawers or a trundle frame.

Some mail-order catalogs sell rolling drawers, approximately 2 feet square, made of laminated composition board—some with open tops, some with lids—or wire mesh. A set of two costs about $30 to $60.

Clothes Hampers

For a couple of hundred dollars, you can buy a kids' clothes hamper in the shape of a house or other fanciful form. If that seems too extravagant, one or more large wicker baskets with lids will do the same job for a fraction of the cost.

Another relatively inexpensive choice is a basketball hoop with a long net that can be closed at the bottom. Although not the most attractive solution, it does encourage kids to pick up dirty clothes, if only so they can toss them into the hoop. Just make sure the hoop is emptied frequently.

Bookcases & Shelving Units

Available in all sizes, from small decorative ledges to large wall systems, these units are great for storing or displaying books, toys, collectibles, and other items. Prices depend on size, style, and materials.

Modular pieces let you increase storage or display space as needed. Adjustable shelves make it easy to keep pace with a growing child. Be sure shelves are sturdy enough to bear the weight of their expected load; the lighter the weight, the wider the span you can get away with.

DESIGN: BOSTON AND WINTHROP

DESIGN: FISHER-PRICE

Under-bed drawers (at left) roll out for easy access to clothes, toys, or extra bedding. Chest of drawers (above) is customized with painted pulls and stenciled pinwheels.

Open shelving lets children see where things belong and encourages them to return things to their rightful places. Cabinet doors at the bottom of a unit that rests on the floor will discourage little kids from climbing up—and can also store some odds and ends out of sight.

For safety's sake, don't put a glass-fronted case in a young child's room. Anchor any freestanding unit to the wall if it's the least bit unsteady.

Toy Chests

Some boxes are designed especially to hold toys. Many also can serve as child-size benches or low tables.

Look for one with safety hinges that prevent the lid from falling shut. Another desirable safety feature is an air opening just under the closed lid (in case the child gets trapped inside). Some manufacturers are abandoning lids altogether and making uncovered toy boxes.

Most lidded boxes are priced between $50 and $150. An uncovered chest can cost as little as $30.

Bins, Boxes & Baskets

An easy, economical way to organize toys and games is to sort them in plastic, laminated, cardboard, wire-mesh, or wicker containers. You'll find them in assorted sizes, shapes, colors, and prices in home-improvement centers, hardware stores, specialty shops, and mail-order catalogs.

Look for storage units that have smooth edges, are easy for your child to handle, and will stand up to abuse. Many units are stackable and can be added to as your child's storage needs increase.

Color-coding the bins, boxes, and baskets will help children remember where things go. For example, you can wrap plain cardboard boxes in brightly colored self-adhesive paper.

This folding cabinet is designed as classroom furniture, but most manufacturers will sell such items directly to parents. The unit features adjustable shelves and sturdy casters for easy rolling.

DESIGN: WHITNEY BROTHERS

DESIGN: FUN FURNITURE

The toy chest in the shape of a house has a safety hinge to keep the lid from slamming shut. The one in the form of a yellow taxi is an open chest that doubles as a toy car that toddlers can wheel around the room.

FLOORING

Flooring in kids' rooms, especially those of young children, should break a fall without breaking bones, provide a good surface for play and other activities, and clean up easily.

Resilient Floors

This category includes floors made from vinyl, rubber, and cork—materials that have supplanted linoleum, a type of resilient flooring no longer manufactured in the United States.

Available in many colors, textures, patterns, and styles, resilient floors are flexible underfoot, yet firm, durable, sound-absorbing, and easy to maintain. A protective finish applied at the factory eliminates the need for waxing. A textured material can hide dust and guard against slipping, but doesn't provide a smooth surface for play.

Sheet goods are sold in rolls up to 12 feet wide; most tiles are 12 inches square. Resilient flooring requires a smooth underlayment, since it molds to any irregularities in the subfloor.

Vinyl. Most resilient flooring is made of vinyl. Sheet goods come with an inlaid or printed pattern (inlaid wears better), with or without a cushioned backing (cushioning is more comfortable underfoot but dents more easily).

Vinyl tiles don't generally wear as well as sheet goods, but they offer certain advantages: you can mix different tiles to form custom patterns or provide color accents; you can install them yourself quite easily (if you get self-stick tiles); and you can replace tiles in damaged areas without replacing the whole floor.

Commercial vinyl composition tiles are a good choice for kids' rooms. They're nearly indestructible, and the

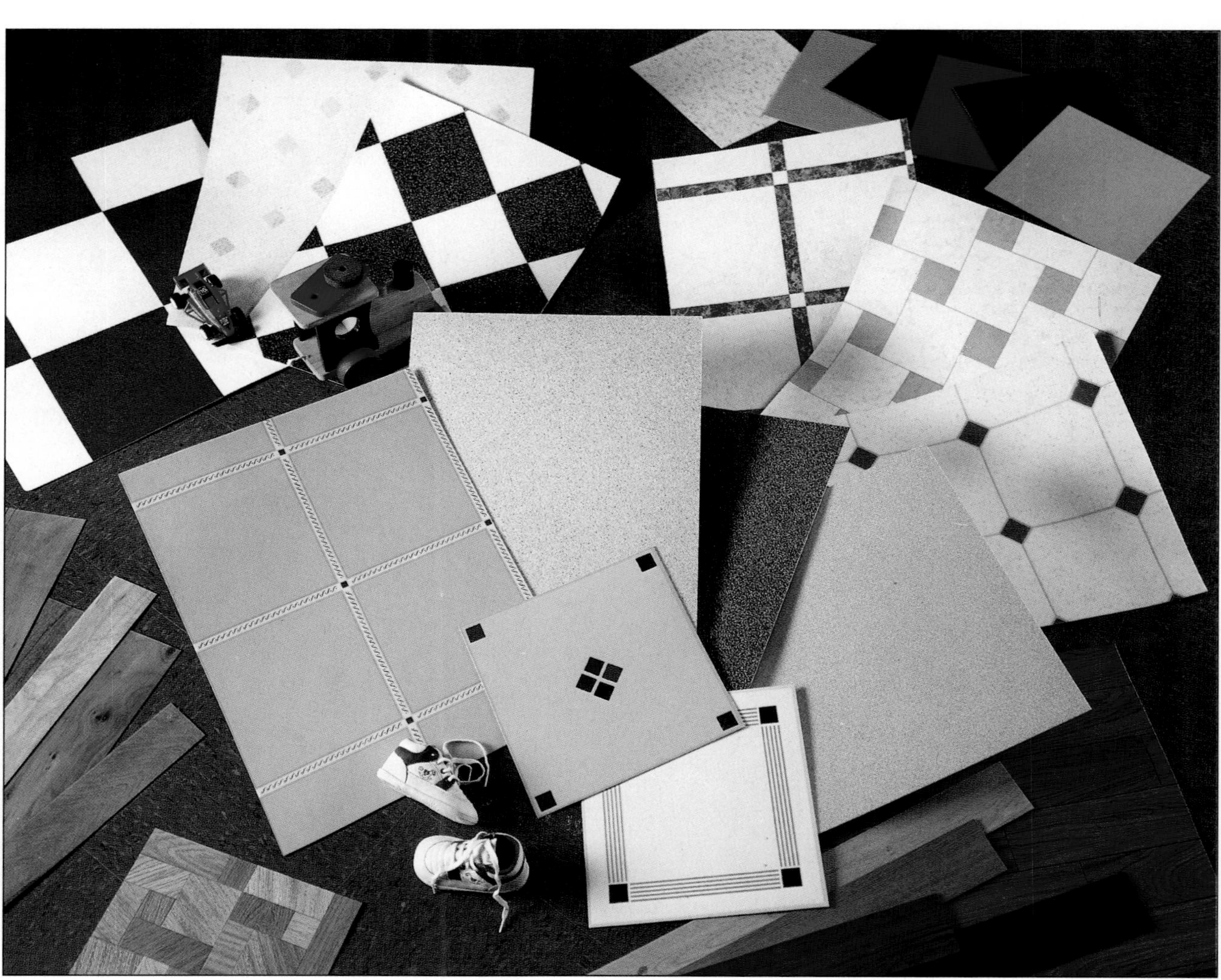

color goes all the way through, masking scrapes and scratches. They're also economical, ranging from less than $1 to about $2 per square foot. On the down side, these tiles don't have a no-wax surface, and patterns are limited. However, they come in a wide range of solid colors, allowing you to create intriguing designs of your own.

There's no need to buy the considerably more expensive solid vinyl or luxury vinyl tiles unless you want a particular pattern—many of which simulate other materials, such as hardwood, slate, or marble. Color goes all the way through a solid vinyl tile, but the pattern is either printed on the surface and protected with a no-wax finish or is molded into the tile surface during the production process and doesn't have a protective finish. Luxury vinyl isn't necessary solid; the term just denotes a high-priced product.

Rubber. Sold in large tiles (approximately 18 inches square), rubber flooring is more often used commercially than in homes. The choice of colors and patterns is much more limited than for vinyl tiles. You'll also pay more for rubber than for vinyl composition tiles—$5 per square foot and up.

Although popular in kitchens, rubber floors with studs or other raised patterns aren't the most practical choice for kids' rooms. The resulting surface is too bumpy for some activities, and dirt tends to build up around the studs.

Cork. Also used on walls and ceilings, cork tiles are made from the granulated bark of the cork oak tree. Naturally sound-insulating, they're sold in various thicknesses, densities, and finishes—plain, waxed, polyurethane-sealed, and vinyl-bonded. You can get vinylized cork with veined patterns, stripes, and other designs.

An active youngster can give a cork floor a beating, so choose tiles with a hard protective finish. Expect to pay about $5 to $8 per square foot.

Wood Floors

A wood floor adds warmth and beauty to a room. But it doesn't absorb sound well and isn't very comfortable to sit on, although adding a rug or two can alleviate both problems.

Most wood flooring comes in narrow strips of random lengths, or in planks of various widths and random lengths. It's milled in several thicknesses and comes in two forms: tongue and groove, which creates a strong interlocking joint, and square-edge, which is nailed through the top. You can also get wood tiles.

Wood flooring may be factory-finished or left unfinished, to be sanded and finished in place. A new wood floor, installed, costs about $7.50 to $15 per square foot, depending on wood type, quality, and finish.

An existing wood floor can be refinished to make it stain and water resistant; professionals usually charge from $2 to $5 per square foot.

Another option is to paint the floor. Your creativity is the only limit —you may decide on a solid color, use

DESIGN: SUNDAY HENDRICKSON

Resilient flooring (opposite page) is a sensible choice for a young child's room. Here is a sampling of vinyl tiles and sheet goods, including some simulating wood. Genuine wood (at right) is another good option for youngsters. The pretty cotton throw rug provides a counterpoint to the rich-looking hardwood—as well as a soft place to sit.

a geometric or freeform design, reproduce a hopscotch grid or other game pattern, or stencil on a design. Protect the paint with polyurethane or another sealer.

Wall-to-wall Carpet

Carpeting makes a nice soft surface for rough play and helps deaden sound, but it's not as practical as hard flooring for young kids. It's more difficult to keep clean, and it won't let blocks be stacked as easily or wheeled toys be rolled as smoothly as on a resilient or wood floor. One type of carpet is designed to promote activity—it comes imprinted with patterns for games such as hopscotch, Chinese checkers, or tick-tack-toe.

Wall-to-wall carpeting is more appropriate in an older child's room, but only you will know whether it's right for your child. You'll be throwing your money away unless your child treats the carpet with some respect.

Generally, man-made carpeting causes fewer allergies than do natural materials (see section on allergies on page 370). Because of its wearability, 100-percent nylon is a good choice. Spills wipe up more easily if the carpet is treated with a stain repellent. Most nylon carpets have a built-in static resistance. By law, all carpets are fire retardant.

A low-pile or short-loop, densely woven carpet is best if it's going into a nursery or toddler's room. A deep shag can conceal objects that a small child might swallow. Plush carpets also hold a lot of dust, which is unhealthy for infants to breathe. A medium color shows less dirt than a very light or dark color, and a variegated texture or pattern will camouflage stains.

Expect to pay from about $5 to $15 per square yard for carpeting a kid's room; remnants, commercial grades, and indoor-outdoor carpeting can save you money. Carpeting printed with game-board designs ranges from about $11 to $18 per square yard.

Rugs

Large area rugs or small throw rugs can be placed strategically on a resilient or wood floor to create soft, comfortable places to sit or play.

While forming cozy islands in a room, throw rugs still allow space for activities that need a flat surface. The most practical throw rugs have a nonslip backing and are machine washable. Throw rugs created for kids come in whimsical shapes and storybook designs. Fluffy bathroom mats, sold in a wide range of colors, are an inexpensive option.

Area rugs cover more territory than throw rugs, making them more expensive and harder to keep clean. Purely decorative rugs (ones designed as area rugs or wall-to-wall carpet remnants with the edges bound) may be more appropriate for older children, since they leave less smooth floor space for games. For young kids, you can opt for a game-board rug produced by a manufacturer who prints games on wall-to-wall carpeting (see at left).

Instead of just sitting on the floor, some rugs educate, entertain, or engage kids in activities. Clockwise from top left: a play rug with roadways along which kids can wheel little wooden cars; a sports-theme rug designed to spark a young one's imagination; and a hopscotch board that comes with beanbag markers. All are fire resistant and have nonskid backing.

WALL TREATMENTS

The ideal wall treatment in a kid's room is not only pleasing to the eye, but also durable and easy to clean. Some treatments serve additional functions—for example, a bulletin board can keep your child organized, and a chalkboard can encourage creativity.

Paint

Painting is one of the simplest, most economical ways to decorate a room. Repaint every few years for a fresh look or to keep pace with your child's changing color preferences. You can change the whole look of the space by investing as little as $10 in painting the trim, or spend several hundred dollars on a mural.

Latex paint has a water base, making it practically odorless, easy to apply, and fast-drying—and tools wash up quickly with soap and water. A flat or eggshell finish is the usual choice for walls and ceilings. For trim and areas that get heavy wear, choose a semigloss enamel. Glossy finishes are more washable and durable, but any nick or bump is highlighted by their sheen.

You can select a single color or use several to complement the furnishings. Or you can choose something fancier: murals and stenciling are decorative paint techniques that work especially well in children's rooms.

If you don't want to tackle an elaborate finish yourself and don't have the budget for a professional, try something simple and playful. For example, you could dip your hands into paint and cover the wall with palm prints.

Chalkboards

Almost any smooth surface can be transformed into a chalkboard by covering it with special chalkboard paint, available at most paint stores. The paint is a flat alkyd that comes in green or black.

Apply it directly to the wall, or coat a piece of hardboard that you attach to the wall. Use two or three coats; and if the surface to be painted is wood, seal it with a primer first.

The chalkboard can be a simple rectangle or a more elaborate shape—for example, an animal silhouette. Consider placing a strip of concave picture molding at the lower edge of the board to hold the chalk and eraser and to catch chalk dust.

Wallpaper

You'll find choosing is easier if you bring along paint chips, samples of upholstery fabrics, and other colors and patterns you plan to use. Also have with you a diagram of the room with the dimensions clearly marked (and with placement and sizes of doors and windows shown) so the sales staff can calculate how much wallpaper you need to buy.

The back of a wallpaper sample usually contains information on the wallpaper's content and says whether or not the material is prepasted, washable, or able to be stripped easily.

Vinyl coverings are practical in a child's room. Fabric-backed vinyl and scrubbable solid vinyl are most durable and easy to clean (even crayon marks come off); expect to pay around $15 to $30 a roll. Vinyl-coated and expanded-vinyl products, costing $8 to $15 a roll, aren't as cleanable. If the walls are bumpy or poorly finished, choose a wallpaper with a textured finish to hide the imperfections.

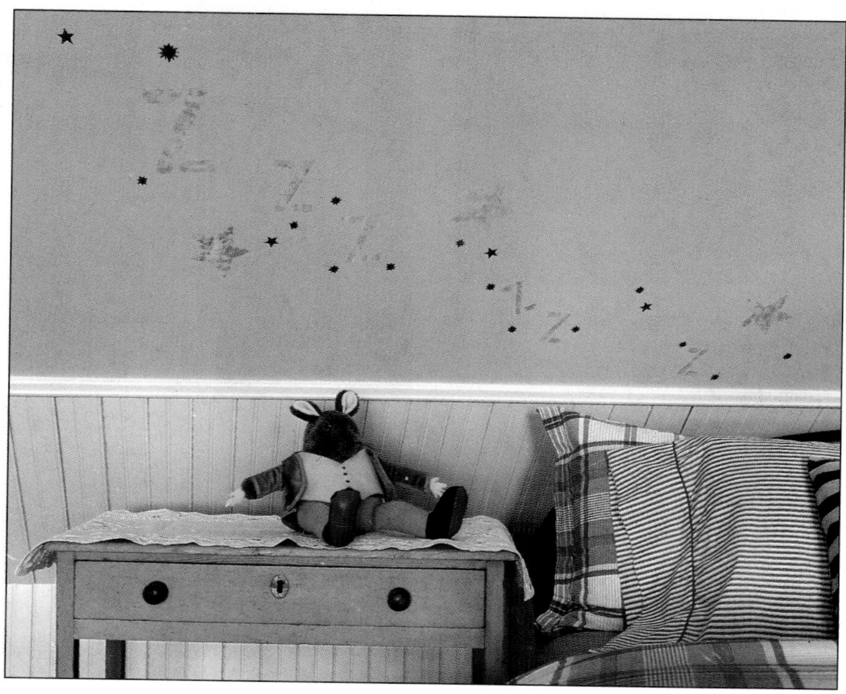

Fuchsia Zs and black and blue stars stenciled on the wall over the bed are designed to lull the occupant of this room to sleep. The bedding picks up the colors of the stencils as well as of the golden backdrop.

Abstract patterns, especially ones with bold colors, are usually better choices for kids' rooms than juvenile themes that will soon be outgrown. If you can't deny your child a faddish design he or she craves, put it on a single wall so that replacing it later won't require too much effort or money.

Ask for patterns that come with matching fabrics and bedding if you want a coordinated look. Also make sure that pictures and other wall-mounted items will work with the wallpaper pattern.

A border—used alone or to complement a wallpaper—is a relatively inexpensive way to jazz up a child's room. Since borders can be changed easily, you can indulge a young child in a juvenile motif—such as dinosaurs, cowboys, trains, or letters of the alphabet—without committing the room permanently to the look.

Borders don't have to go at the top of the wall—they can be applied lower down, where youngsters can see them without craning their necks. A chair-rail border divides the room horizontally: you could paint the walls different colors or use different wallpaper patterns above and below the border, or you could wallpaper one part and paint the other. Some borders look effective placed just above the baseboard, giving toddlers a close-up view of the design. Another option is to use a border around doors and windows.

Paneling

Solid boards or sheet paneling add a decorative touch while protecting the walls. For example, paneling 3 or 4 feet high near the bed defines the sleeping area and guards against soil marks.

The most expensive choice, solid boards are pieces of lumber milled to overlap or interlock. Boards come in a wide range of widths, thicknesses, and lengths. To keep costs down, choose materials stocked locally.

The main types of sheet paneling are plywood and hardboard, both commonly sold in 4- by 8-foot pieces. Plywood consists of thin layers of wood peeled from lumber and glued together; hardboard is made from wood fibers bonded under pressure.

You can get just about any kind of wood laminated to plywood panels. Hardboard paneling comes with imitation wood finishes, or it can be embossed with a pattern. Plywood is more expensive than hardboard, but it's also more durable and less subject to warping and moisture damage.

Sold rolled up like a poster, this specially coated sheet of paper works just like a chalkboard (above). After being purchased, it was cut into the shape of a whale to suit its young owner.

DESIGN: CYNTHIA BRIAN OF STARSTYLE INTERIORS

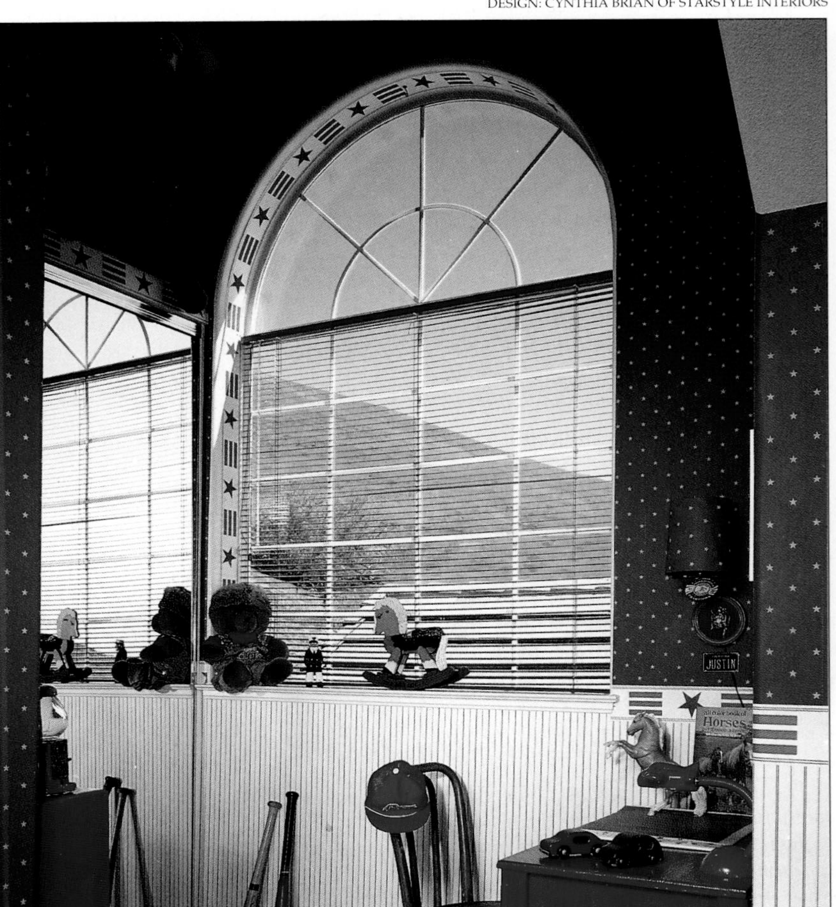

A stars-and-stripes wallpaper border (right) applied to the window recess frames the arch and carries through the patriotic theme.

Bulletin Boards

You can buy a ready-made bulletin board to hang on the wall, or you can make your own by covering an entire wall with cork or fabric-wrapped fiberboard.

Cork is sold in tiles at some floor-covering stores and in sheets at home-improvement centers. Sheet cork, sold by the linear foot from rolls, is much less expensive than tiles. You can get a linear foot of 4-foot-wide cork (equivalent to four tiles) for not much more than you'd pay for one or two tiles. Sheet goods come in up to ¼-inch thickness, while the most substantial tiles are only ⅛ inch thick.

If you don't want pinholes in the wall underneath the cork, glue the cork to soft fiberboard panels (available in 4- by 8-foot rectangles) and screw the panels to wall studs.

You can skip the cork altogether, and use fabric-wrapped fiberboard as a bulletin-board surface. Any coarse fabric that is strong and won't easily ravel will do. Burlap is a practical choice, since its weave will hide the pinholes.

Decorative Moldings

Wood moldings are an inexpensive way to add character to a room. They come in many standard patterns and sizes. You can get them natural, prefinished (painted or stained), or wrapped in vinyl. You can also buy plastic, vinyl, and aluminum moldings that look like wood. Molding systems come with corner pieces that eliminate the need for tricky cuts and joints.

One way to use molding is to divide a wall horizontally. Paint or wallpaper the sections differently for extra interest. You can also put hooks on a chair-rail molding or hang pictures from it.

Other Wall Decor

Pictures are a popular decoration in kids' rooms, just as in other areas of the house. Hang them framed or, if you can tolerate a more casual approach, let your child tack up posters of favorite sports heroes, rock stars, or other celebrities.

For young kids, try the colorful, cushiony wall hangings sold at many children's stores. Priced from about $20 to $80, they come in the shape of airplanes, clouds, balloons, and many other objects.

Borders and decals that are repositionable are another good choice for younger children. Kids' stores and catalogs sell room-decorating kits (about $25 to about $55) containing a continuous border and precut, peel-off appliqués. Designs include dinosaur, circus, football, and undersea motifs that even very young kids can stick on the wall and rearrange by themselves.

DESIGN: DRESCO DESIGN

DESIGN: RUTH LIVINGSTON INTERIOR DESIGN

Denim makes a handsome bulletin board surface in this Western-theme room (top). A cushiony wall hanging (bottom) adds three-dimensional interest to a nursery or toddler's room.

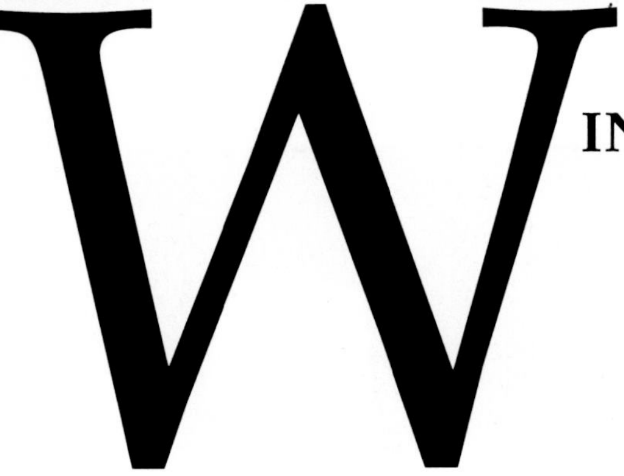

WINDOW TREATMENTS

A cute or cleverly designed window covering will quickly lose its charm unless it's sturdy, easy to clean, and simple for your child to operate. It should also control light the way you intend. A room-darkening treatment can help a small child who takes daytime naps settle down more easily.

The most common window coverings are curtains, blinds, shades, and shutters. There's no need to restrict yourself to a single treatment; you can combine two or more.

Curtains

Choose ready-to-hang or custom curtains, or make them yourself. Specialty bedding shops and catalogs offer ready-made curtains as a standard element in many of their coordinated bed-linen sets. For a custom job, look for fabrics designed especially for kids' rooms—many of them come with matching wallpaper.

Washable, medium-weight cotton and cotton-polyester blends are the most practical curtain fabrics for kids' rooms. Fabric of 100-percent cotton holds bright colors particularly well, although it will fade and rot in the sun unless the curtains are lined. Polyester blended with cotton makes the fabric more lightfast, rot resistant, and wrinkle-proof.

Curtains should be lined with a blackout material if you want the room dark in early morning and on summer evenings. Sheer curtains are fine if you use them in conjunction with a light-blocking shade or blind.

If your child is very young, do yourself a favor by ending the curtains at the bottom of the window frame. Little kids like to tug on floor-length treatments or hide behind them.

Blinds

Available with metal, vinyl, or wood slats, blinds offer the best way to control light. Lowering the blind and closing the slats dims the room, opening the slats lets in some light, and raising the blind floods the room with light.

Stock blinds are fine if you can get ones that fit the window opening exactly. Otherwise, get made-to-measure blinds, especially for an inside mount. Even at custom prices, most blinds are economical. Don't get the most expensive ones for a kid's room, though—the slats are bound to be dented or broken, and the operating mechanism may prove to be an irresistible toy.

Miniblinds with 1-inch metal or vinyl slats are the most common type of blind sold. You can get them in solid colors or in several colors to form horizontal stripes. Vinyl minis are appealing for kids' rooms because they're much less expensive than

DESIGN: JEANESE ROWELL INTERIORS. DECORATIVE PAINTING: KAREN SICKLE

Bows and flounces fill this little girl's room. Adding to the feminine appeal are ruffled valances over light-filtering dotted-swiss sheer curtains. Using the same fabric for valances, bedding, and upholstery establishes a coordinated look.

metal ones—although they're flimsier, come in fewer colors, don't close as tightly, and can warp in a hot spot.

Wood blinds, especially ones with wide slats, are often used as a substitute for shutters. Although twice as expensive as good-quality miniblinds, they're about half the price of custom shutters. Because of their cost, you want to feel fairly confident that your child won't mistreat them. Their weight may make them too heavy for a young child to use.

Shades

The many styles include roller, pleated, Roman, and balloon shades. They range from sheer to opaque, so make sure the shade will control light the way you want. Also keep in mind that most shades allow little ventilation once they're lowered. Costs vary widely, depending on design, materials, workmanship, and the operating mechanism.

Roller shades are a good choice for kids' rooms—although some youngsters find them fascinating playthings. You can trim costs but still get a custom product by sewing or gluing a design onto an inexpensive ready-made shade. Another option is to embellish the shade with fabric paints matching the room's decor.

Shutters

You can adjust shutters to let in a little or a lot of light. They can also cut drafts when closed.

Custom shutters are an investment that will still be there when your child is in college and you've turned the room into a den or spare bedroom. Expect to pay several hundred dollars for a top-quality shutter to fit a standard double-hung window.

For a small fraction of the price, you can get stock shutters from a home-improvement center or lumber yard—but they may not last as long, especially if your child is particularly rough on furnishings.

This window shade (top) serves a dual purpose when it's pulled down: darkening the room and teaching arithmetic. Such a design can be stenciled onto a plain, ready-made shade with acrylic paints. Miniblinds framed by an envelope curtain (bottom) allow great flexibility in controlling light.

DESIGN: COURLAND DESIGN, INC.

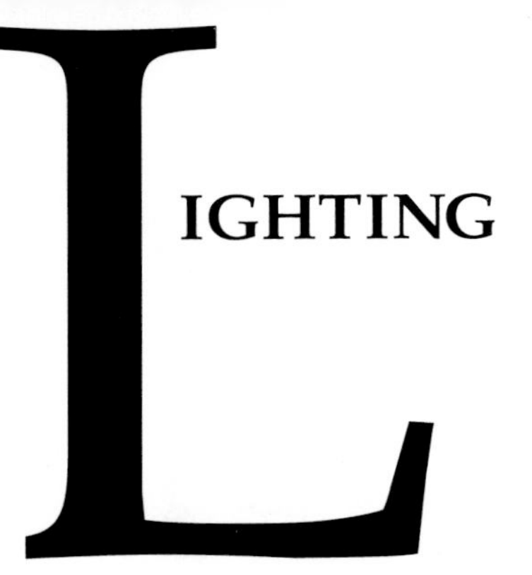

IGHTING

Good lighting results when you use the appropriate fixture and light source (bulb or tube) for the situation. Keep in mind that safety is the key consideration when choosing lighting for young children. Fixtures that are out of reach or won't easily tip over are the best. Those within reach should contain a low-wattage light source that won't burn curious fingers. Other safety features include covers or caps on unused electrical outlets and wire reels to store excess lamp cord.

LIGHTING FIXTURES

You'll find plenty of fixtures to fit most budgets at lighting stores and home-improvement centers, as well as through decorators and lighting designers. But the choice of fixtures with juvenile themes is limited, even at stores catering to kids. If you can't find exactly what you want, consult local electrical supply stores. Many such shops will build fixtures from toys or other items that you provide.

Here are the types of fixtures most commonly used in kids' rooms.

Ceiling Fixtures

A single overhead fixture is usually the main source of general lighting in a child's room. For very young children, an overhead light makes the

Fixtures with kid appeal include these table lamps, clip-ons, floor lamps, and night-lights. The coat-rack lamp not only provides light but also shoe storage and a place to hang clothes.

room less scary and provides enough illumination for play. It's also the safest, since kids can't knock it over or burn themselves. Putting the fixture on a dimmer helps regulate the amount of light in the room.

Track fixtures are widely used to light specific task areas. They make it easy to redirect light to keep pace with a child's changing needs.

Wall Fixtures

Lighting designers who favor wall fixtures in children's rooms say that kids can't tip them over. Those dead-set against the fixtures say that kids sometimes like to hang from them. You'll have to be the one to decide if such a fixture is appropriate in your situation.

To provide general lighting, a wall fixture should be positioned high enough to bounce light off the ceiling. If the room isn't hard-wired for a wall fixture, you can surface-mount the fixture and plug it into an electrical outlet. Try to hide the cord behind heavy furniture such as a dresser, bookcase, or bed.

Table Lamps

These are the fixtures most commonly available with juvenile themes. Usually the motif is restricted to the base, which may appear in the shape of a crayon, boat, airplane, or storybook character. Other types have plain bases and brightly colored or patterned shades. Others sold for the nursery have built-in baby monitors or music boxes.

Of course, a table lamp doesn't have to have an upright base and removable shade. It can be a gooseneck or other type with a movable arm that allows your child to adjust the light to the proper height.

A table lamp should be weighted so that it doesn't tip over easily. For added safety, you can screw the base to the furniture, just as hotels do. Reduce danger further by buying a wire reel to store excess lamp cord.

A bedside lamp should have an on/off switch that your child can easily reach and operate. Avoid "touch lamps," which turn on or off when lightly tapped. They're easily knocked over at night, and young children can frighten themselves by accidentally operating the lamp.

Floor Lamps

These sometimes look like play equipment to a toddler and can tip over easily, so reserve them for older ages.

The many floor styles include jointed types that allow you to move the light closer for reading or other activities; pole lamps containing several lights; and torchères, which bounce light off the ceiling to provide general illumination without glare.

Clip-on Lights

These fixtures, which come in both swivel and gooseneck styles, can go where table lamps don't fit—such as on a headboard or attached to the top bunk of a bunk bed. They're space savers on a crowded desk. Clip-ons can also be clamped to shelves to focus light on collections. Test the fixture before buying to make sure it fastens securely to a surface.

Night-lights

Some types plug into an electrical outlet and automatically glow when the room is dark. Others have tiny bulbs and have to be switched on. You'll even find types that attach to cribs.

Juvenile themes are common. For example, you can get night-lights in the shape of cartoon characters or large glowing crayons.

LIGHT SOURCES

The quality and intensity of light depend on the type of bulb or tube you use. Some fixtures are manufactured to accept a certain type.

Keep in mind that using the proper wattage is essential to protect your child's eyes. Too much light is as bad as too little. You may have to experiment to find the right level for different tasks.

Incandescent

Most widely used in homes, incandescent light is produced by a tungsten thread burning slowly inside a glass bulb. Since the majority of wavelengths are in the red and yellow portion of the color spectrum, incandescent light has a warm quality. On the minus side, incandescent light creates glare and shadows, and is the least energy-efficient light source.

Fluorescent

Produced when electricity causes the phosphor coating inside a tube to glow, fluorescent light is unrivaled for energy efficiency. It also minimizes glare and shadows. Manufacturers have now developed fluorescents in a wide spectrum of colors, so there's no longer any need to put up with a harsh bluish or greenish quality.

In addition to the standard long tubes, you can now buy U-shaped compact tubes, which can replace incandescent bulbs in some fixtures. Miniature tubes in round and cylindrical shapes fit standard lamps.

Halogen

These small, long-lasting bulbs operate much like incandescent bulbs, except that halogen gas surrounding the filament produces an intensely bright light. The bulbs are used in special fixtures with built-in transformers.

Because of their extreme heat, halogens aren't recommended for areas where youngsters can get at them and possibly be burned. Also, touching a bulb with a finger leaves oil on it, which damages the surface and can cause the bulb to explode.

Sunset

ideas for great FLOORS

By the Editors of
Sunset Books

Sunset Books ■ Menlo Park, California

contents

456
On Which We Stand

459
A Planning Primer

481
Great Floor Ideas

555
A Shopper's Guide

712
Index

special features

Comparing Flooring **464**
Warming Your Toes **467**
A Flooring Questionnaire **469**
Pick Your Pattern **475**
Time and Space **479**

on which we stand

WITH MOST THINGS in life, it's the basics that count. And a floor is basic not only to the structure of any room but also to its design. Your floor has to look beautiful and it has to work.

After the walls, the floor is the next largest surface in a room, and you'll want to give it the same careful attention that you give to any other design element. When choosing flooring, you'll probably think first about your options. You'll want to learn about stone, tile, wood, resilient, carpet, laminate, and concrete. You may even want to think outside the box, as they say, and consider such specialty flooring materials as leather or metal.

Take a look at what's out there. There is a new attitude toward flooring materials. No longer is tile necessary for the kitchen and wood a must for the living room. Today a living room floor can be tiled, a bathroom looks great in stone, and a kitchen is warmed by a wood floor. Stay open to new ideas and find out about new materials. To see what your choices are, look at the photographs in this book, visit your local home center, and learn from what friends and neighbors have done.

As you look at these choices, you'll find that each type of material is rich in color, texture, and pattern. Will a light color floor that exudes spaciousness capture your attention? Or will you choose a dark floor that anchors a room's furnishings and allows them to take center stage? Do you want the floor to have a pattern that takes command in the room, or will you

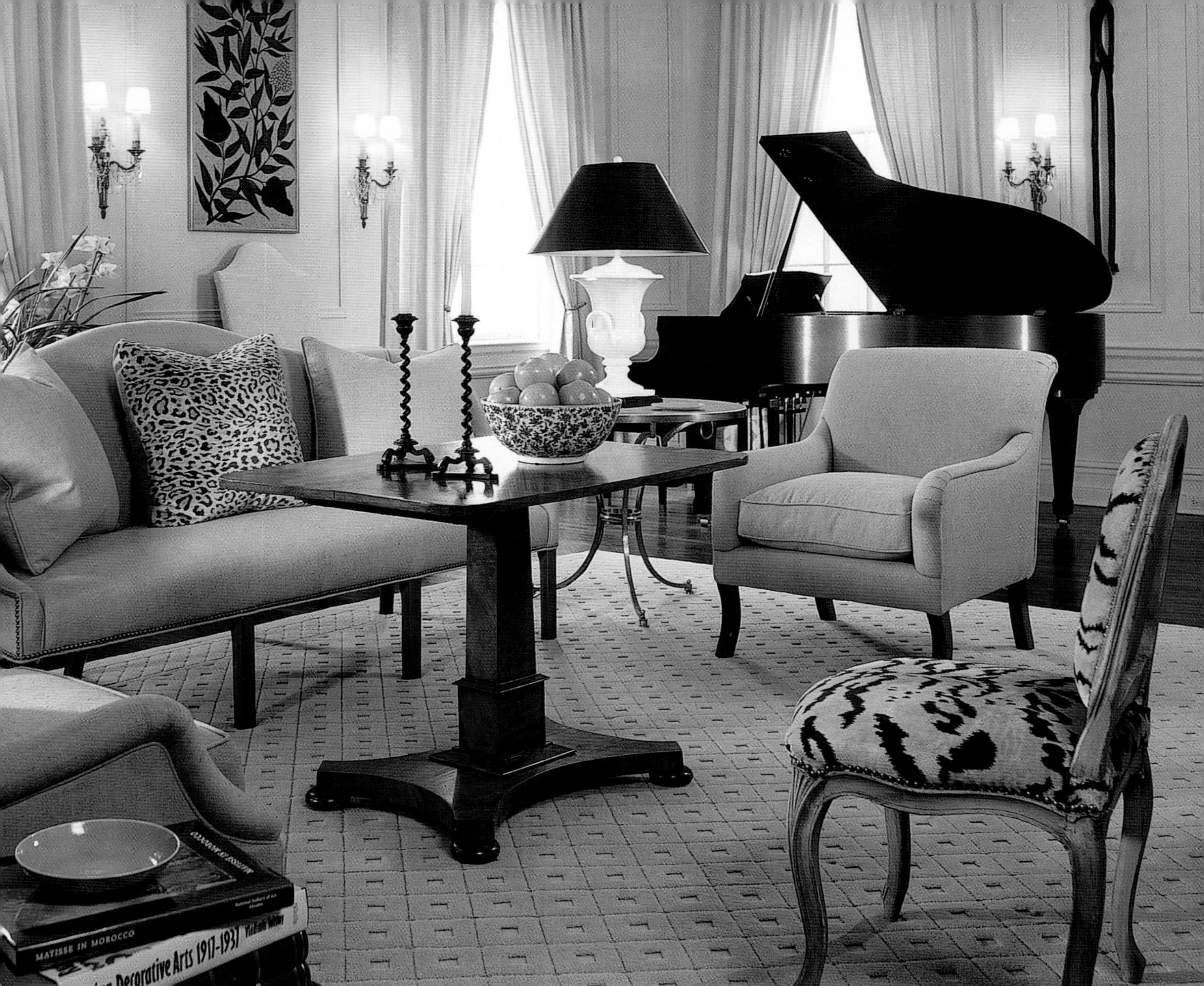

choose a floor that fits an existing design scheme? Are there special features you want to highlight—in a foyer, a dining room, or around a fireplace?

Keeping all these design options in mind, you'll want to focus on the room's function. Think about how your family uses the room. What activities happen there? Who spends time in the room—and how much foot traffic will there be? Where will the furniture be placed? And how much time are you willing to spend maintaining the floor?

The flooring choices you make now will affect the way your house works for you and your family. With a little planning, you'll find that there's a flooring choice that's right for you—one that is beautiful and complements the design of your home while it meets all your practical needs, and that everyone loves to walk on!

A PLANNING PRIMER

FLOORS. You walk on them daily, hardly ever giving a second thought to what's underfoot until the day you realize it's time to make a change. Suddenly there are countless decisions to be made. First, you need to select the right type of flooring for the specific area in your home. What will look best in the space? What will work best over time? What will be practical, easy to keep clean? **USE THIS CHAPTER** to guide you through all the steps you'll need to consider before making the right choice of floor covering. The more you know about flooring, the more satisfied you'll be with your choice. For a quick overview of what's available, go to the chart "Comparing Flooring" on pages 464–465. By the end of this chapter, you'll be able to comfortably decide which direction to take and whether to install the flooring yourself or hire a professional. Now's the time to start exploring new ideas for flooring.

exploring your options

TODAY *it's virtually impossible to say one type of flooring is appropriate to a specific room. Whether it's tile, stone, wood, resilient, carpeting, or laminate, new technologies have made most flooring adaptable to all kinds of situations. Still, there are plenty of practicalities to consider when you are planning to install a new floor. Take the time to decide on a floor that both inspires you now and fits all your practical needs.*

What's available?

Centuries ago fabulous floors belonged only to royalty and could be created only by the most talented craftsmen. Today we have many incredible flooring materials available. Each material possesses its own inherent qualities and when skillfully installed can evoke any feeling or achieve any look. Better yet, some of the least expensive materials can have the most powerful impact for your floor.

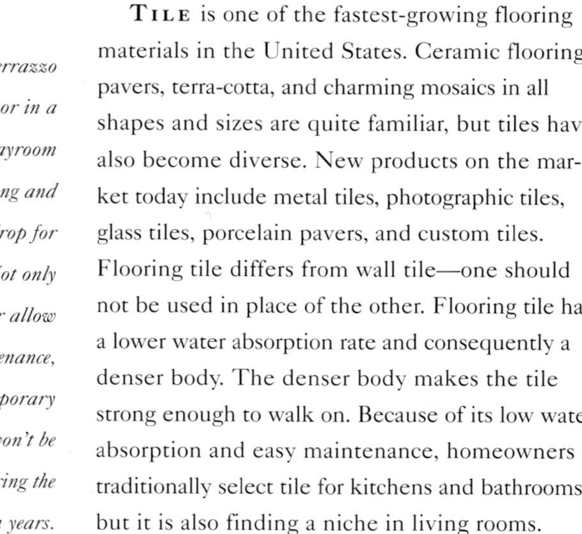

TILE is one of the fastest-growing flooring materials in the United States. Ceramic flooring pavers, terra-cotta, and charming mosaics in all shapes and sizes are quite familiar, but tiles have also become diverse. New products on the market today include metal tiles, photographic tiles, glass tiles, porcelain pavers, and custom tiles. Flooring tile differs from wall tile—one should not be used in place of the other. Flooring tile has a lower water absorption rate and consequently a denser body. The denser body makes the tile strong enough to walk on. Because of its low water absorption and easy maintenance, homeowners traditionally select tile for kitchens and bathrooms, but it is also finding a niche in living rooms.

STONE flooring comes from quarries mostly in Italy, Spain, Turkey, and the United States. Each type of natural stone, from marble to granite to slate, features a unique color, pattern, and hardness. Natural stone is available both as smoothly cut tiles and irregular slabs. Either can be finished to be smooth as glass or tumbled for a timeworn appearance.

A colorful terrazzo tiled floor in a children's playroom serves as a strong and forgiving backdrop for playtime fun. Not only does the floor allow for easy maintenance, but its contemporary styling won't be outgrown during the teen years.

Choosing a variety of flooring materials for one room is a creative option. In this modern home, neutral limestone tiles underscore the living area while hardwood flooring covers the common areas nearby, including an open staircase.

The color choices of stone are endless. You'll find marble in black, cream, red, white, green, gold, gray, and even pink. Some types of marble are heavily veined, such as Nero Marquina, with its ebony color and white veining, while others, such as Golden Spider, are lightly veined. Still others, such as Yellow Desert, look somewhat dappled, as if they were sponge finished. There are also creamy soft and classic types, like Crema Marfil.

If you prefer this softer appearance, you also may like limestone, which is usually light-colored, with a speckled surface. Granite, while having the same breadth of colors as marble, looks more mottled. If you like more irregular stones, you should consider flagstone, which can be reminiscent of medieval castle floors.

Stone can be costly, so you'll want to use it where it makes the most impact in your home. A stone floor in a foyer or entryway, for instance, makes a great first impression on guests.

Wood is warm and inviting and feels good underfoot. Wood flooring is available in a variety of species, from pine and bamboo to maple and oak. It comes prefinished, unfinished, solid, engineered, reclaimed, in parquet and in planks, and in varying grades and cuts. Wood planks range from a narrow 3 inches to a wide 20 inches and can be finished with a penetrating seal or a surface seal. In addition, there are a number of

ABOVE: Sometimes, a little texture can make all the difference. A practical choice, richly textured vinyl looks right at home running across the entire floor of a southwestern kitchen and dining room. RIGHT: In a subtle blend of two textures, tumbled limestone tiles and decorative metal inserts, are used to create a border design.

prefabricated decorative borders and medallions that can be inlaid into a wood floor as a unit.

Throughout history, wood flooring has been used in residential living areas. If you love the look of wood flooring but think something more insulating would perform better, consider a wood floor complemented by an area rug. You might also consider wood for less-used bathrooms, such as a powder room or a guest bath.

Resilient flooring consists of vinyl and linoleum, as well as rubber and cork. Most popular today is vinyl. The focus for resilient vinyl flooring has been on increasing its durability and performance while also developing more natural-looking materials, and the result is a variety of great-looking and long-lasting products. Linoleum came on the scene about 50 years ago. Made from a mixture of ground wood, cork, linseed oil, and resin, it fell out of favor but is now enjoying a resurgence. The resilient category also encompasses rubber and cork flooring. Available in sheets or tiles (cork is also made as a floating floor system), resilient flooring is easy to install and can be cut in a variety of imaginative shapes.

Resilient flooring performs well in hard-working areas such as kitchens, mudrooms, and laundry rooms. And with its imaginative new designs and patterns, resilient flooring can be terrific in a playroom.

Laminate flooring debuted in the early 1980s in Sweden. A high-pressure melamine that is installed as a floating floor, a laminate consists of a base of several layers of paper impregnated with resins. A top layer of decorative paper determines the design, which means if something can be photographed, it can be laminated. The first laminates emulated hardwood floors, but now you can find laminates that look like marble, granite, and ceramic tile. Early laminates had a tendency to chip or delaminate, but durability has been significantly improved and warrantees have been extended accordingly. Glueless laminates that click into place are now available.

Use a laminate wherever you want versatility in performance and a clean, unfettered look.

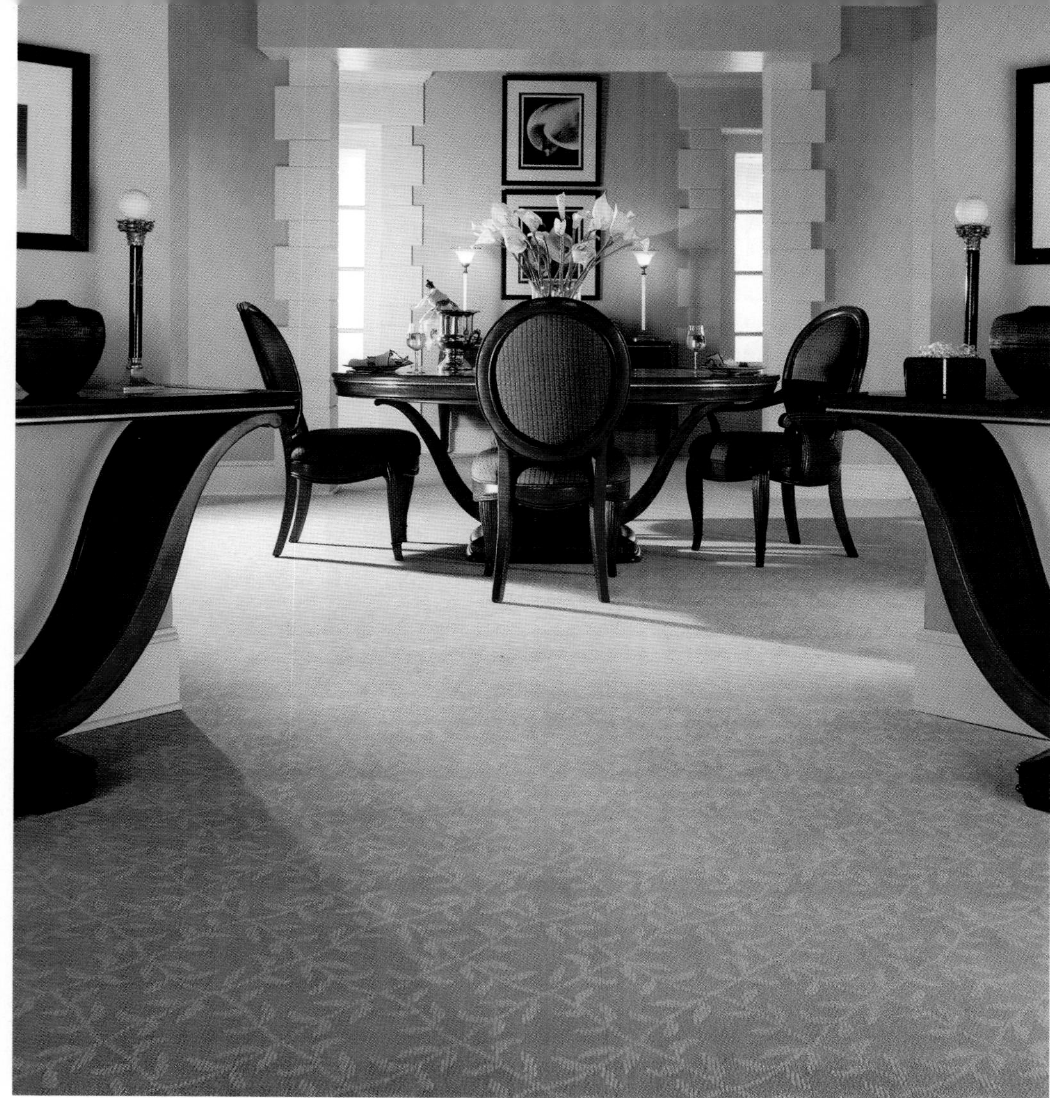

New stain-resistant options allow broadloom carpeting to be used in places where it was previously discouraged, such as dining rooms. Even red wine doesn't pose a threat to light-colored carpets anymore, provided that the carpet has been treated.

It runs beautifully across wide-open great rooms flowing from kitchen to dining to living areas.

Carpeting today is much more than the traditional loop pile we know so well. New technologies have allowed for more texture and surface interest, as well as multiple colors and overall patterns. Loop styles include level loop, multilevel, cut pile, and cut-and-loop patterns. Designs can be sculpted so they appear to pop out. Synthetic fibers are more pleasant to the touch. Custom carpet installers expand design options further, and for carpet padding, manufacturers are working with postconsumer waste to introduce environmentally friendly products. With its cushioning comfort and ability to absorb sound, carpeting is often the first choice for bedrooms.

Specialty flooring uses materials commonly found in industrial and commercial structures, such as concrete, leather, and steel, but are now coming into vogue for high-end residential flooring. Concrete has received the most field testing to date. Appreciated for its ability to take on shape and color, concrete has been embraced by interior designers and architects. It is especially favored for kitchens and dining areas. Leather tiles have typically been used as a novelty to accent a room. Because leather is a natural material, no two tiles are alike and the floor will develop a patina as it ages. Leather should be used only in areas of the home that have little traffic, such as formal living rooms. Steel flooring is available as sleek oversized tiles or industrial grating. It makes a stylish complement to industrial-style kitchens outfitted with stainless steel appliances. Decorative metal pieces are also available as accents for concrete or tile floors.

Comparing Flooring

Each type of flooring material has its intrinsic properties. Since a variety of materials will work in each room of the house, you can use this chart to compare the properties of the flooring materials you're considering.

CERAMIC TILE

ADVANTAGES. Made from hard-fired slabs of clay, ceramic tile is available in hundreds of patterns, colors, shapes, and finishes. Its durability, easy upkeep, and attractiveness are definite advantages. Tiles are usually classified as quarry tiles, commonly unglazed red-clay tiles that are rough and water resistant; terra-cotta, unglazed tiles in earth-tone shades; porcelain pavers, rugged tiles in stonelike shades and textures; and glazed floor tiles, available in glossy, matte, and textured finishes. Floor tiles run the gamut of widths, lengths, and thicknesses. Most popular are 8-inch and 12-inch squares. Costs range from inexpensive to moderate; in general, porcelain is most expensive. Tiles made of purer clays and fired at higher temperatures are generally costlier but better wearing.

DISADVANTAGES. Tile can be cold, noisy, and depending on its "coefficient of friction," slippery underfoot. Porous tiles become stained and harbor bacteria unless properly sealed. Grout can be tough to keep clean, though mildew-resistant and epoxy types are easier.

EXPECTED LIFESPAN. Lifetime

MOST APPROPRIATE LOCATIONS. Kitchens, baths, foyers, mudrooms

APPROXIMATE COST PER SQUARE FOOT. $2.50 to $8.00

STONE

ADVANTAGES. Natural stone (such as slate, marble, limestone, and granite) has been used as flooring for centuries. Today its use is even more practical, thanks to the development of efficient sealers and better surfacing techniques. Stone can be used in its natural shape, known as flagstone, or cut into rectangular blocks or tiles. Generally, pieces are butted tightly together; irregular flagstones require wider grout joints.

DISADVANTAGES. The cost of masonry flooring can be quite high, though recent diamond-saw technology has lowered it considerably. Moreover, the weight of the materials requires a very strong, well-supported subfloor. Some stone is cold and slippery underfoot, though new honed and etched surfaces are safer, subtler alternatives to polished surfaces. Certain stones, such as marble and limestone, absorb stains and dirt readily. Careful sealing is essential.

EXPECTED LIFESPAN. Lifetime

MOST APPROPRIATE LOCATIONS. Kitchens, bathrooms, foyers

APPROXIMATE COST PER SQUARE FOOT. $3.00 to $10.00

HARDWOOD

ADVANTAGES. A classic hardwood floor is warm, feels good underfoot, and can be refinished. Oak is most common, with maple, birch, pine, bamboo, and other woods also available. The three basic types of flooring are narrow strips in random lengths; planks in various widths and random lengths; and tiles laid in blocks or squares. Wood flooring may be factory prefinished or unfinished, to be sanded and finished in place. "Floating" floor systems have several veneered strips atop each backing board. In addition, premanufactured hardwood medallions can be purchased separately and incorporated into the floor design. Engineered wood flooring is more dimensionally stable and may be more compatible than solid wood in moisture-prone areas.

DISADVANTAGES. Moisture damage and inadequate floor substructure are two potential problems to consider. Maintenance is another issue; some surfaces can be mopped or waxed while others cannot. Bleaching and some staining processes may wear unevenly and are difficult to repair. Costs are moderate to high, depending on wood species, grade, and finish.

EXPECTED LIFESPAN. Lifetime

MOST APPROPRIATE LOCATIONS. Living rooms, dining rooms, bedrooms, foyers

APPROXIMATE COST PER SQUARE FOOT. $2.50 to $8.50

RESILIENT

ADVANTAGES. Generally made from solid vinyl or polyurethane, resilients are flexible, moisture and stain resistant, easy to install, and simple to maintain. Available in a great variety of colors, textures, patterns, and styles, tiles can be mixed to form custom patterns or provide color accents. Sheets run up to 12 feet wide, eliminating the need for seaming; tiles are generally 12 inches square. Vinyl, cork, and rubber are comfortable to walk on. A polyurethane finish may eliminate the need for waxing. Costs are generally modest, but expect to pay a premium for custom or imported products.

DISADVANTAGES. Resilients are relatively soft, making them vulnerable to dents and tears; often, though, such damage can be repaired. Tiles may collect moisture between seams if improperly installed. Some vinyl still comes with a photographically applied pattern, but most is inlaid; the latter is more expensive but wears much better.

EXPECTED LIFESPAN. 20 to 30 years

MOST APPROPRIATE LOCATIONS. Kitchens, baths, work and play areas

APPROXIMATE COST PER SQUARE FOOT. $1.00 to $5.00

LAMINATE

ADVANTAGES. Available in many looks from hardwood to stone and ceramic, laminate flooring is similar to countertop laminate but 20 times stronger. Laminate flooring consists of layers of paper impregnated with resins and compressed into a wear-resistant composite on top of a synthetic backing. It can be laid, or "floated," over an existing floor without being glued to the surface. A floating floor is easy to install using a tongue-and-groove system. When installed properly, it creates a single unit impervious to normal household spills and wear. Costs range from inexpensive for glueless laminates to moderate for higher-end and professionally installed laminates.

DISADVANTAGES. Early products had a tendency to chip or delaminate and were not the best choice near water. Because the floor is floated, it can sound a bit hollow. Underlayments of padding are needed to deaden the sound. Laminate flooring cannot be refinished.

EXPECTED LIFESPAN. 10 to 25 years

MOST APPROPRIATE LOCATIONS. Kitchens, baths, work areas, playrooms

APPROXIMATE COST PER SQUARE FOOT. $2.00 to $5.00

CARPETING

ADVANTAGES. Carpeting cushions feet, provides firm traction, and helps deaden sound. It's especially useful to define smaller areas within multiuse layouts or master suites. New tightly woven commercial products are making carpeting more practical. Like resilient flooring, carpeting is available in an array of styles and materials, with prices that vary widely.

DISADVANTAGES. Usually, the more elaborate the material and weave, the greater the problems from moisture absorption, staining, and mildew. Carpeting used in moisture-prone areas should be short-pile and unsculptured, preferably fabricated of nylon or other synthetics; these are washable and hold up better in moist conditions.

EXPECTED LIFESPAN. 10 to 15 years

MOST APPROPRIATE LOCATIONS. Living rooms, bedrooms, playrooms

APPROXIMATE COST PER SQUARE FOOT. $.50 to $5.00

SPECIALTY

ADVANTAGES. For the most part, concrete, leather, and steel have proven their durability in both commercial and industrial applications and are surprisingly malleable in design. A great variety of colors and patterns can be stamped or embedded into concrete. Leather flooring can be sculpted into unique forms. A grated steel floor allows for air flow, which could be beneficial in many areas.

DISADVANTAGES. While leather maintains great acoustics, a material such as steel does not. Leather requires frequent buffing and waxing. Cost of installation can be high for specialty floors. Every 18 to 36 months, concrete installations should be inspected, cleaned, and resealed as required by volume and intensity of traffic. All these materials require a forward-thinking flooring professional.

EXPECTED LIFESPAN.

- Concrete: Lifetime
- Leather: 15 to 25 years
- Steel: Lifetime, with care

MOST APPROPRIATE LOCATIONS.

- Concrete: Kitchens, baths
- Leather: Dens, home offices
- Steel: Kitchens, work areas

APPROXIMATE COST PER SQUARE FOOT.

- Concrete: $5.00 to $7.00
- Leather: $30.00 to $35.00
- Steel: $15.00 to $25.00

Narrowing the field

There is a flooring material for every location, be it wet, highly trafficked, or noisy. You'll want to consider what you need in a floor before you make a choice. Sometimes a material can be adapted to an environment, but that will increase the costs. Most often the best choice for flooring is the material that meets all your needs.

Location, location, location. One of the most important factors to consider is location. Where is your flooring going? How frequently will it be used? Who will be spending most of their time in that room? Floors need to be tailored to the people who use them. A family room should be examined differently than a bedroom, and a family bathroom needs a more hardworking floor than a powder room for guests. Also consider the furniture and other objects that will be used in the room. The wheels of a rolling chair in a home office, for instance, could damage the floor if it's not durable enough for that type of wear.

Safety. If your household includes children, the elderly, or a handicapped person, you will want to choose a flooring that accommodates a range of individual preferences and abilities. Here are some factors that affect the safety of a floor.

Slip resistance. You may want to look into slip-resistant flooring or finishes. A number of flooring materials feature slip-resistant qualities built right into their design. Naturally, carpeting and vinyl are more slip resistant than stone and tile. And a roughly finished stone is more slip resistant than a highly polished one. On the other hand, ceramic tiles vary in slip resistance and are rated by a coefficient of friction (COF) (see page 559 for more information on COF).

Traffic patterns. Think about how many family members and friends walk in and out of the room to be refloored. Each type of

Sheet vinyl flooring is a natural choice for a kitchen. It's affordable, easy to install, soft underfoot, easy to clean, and it comes in a wider range of colors and designs than ever before.

flooring is rated for durability, usually by its affiliated trade association (the Tile Institute of America or the Southern Pine Council, to name two). You'll want to match the ratings to your own flooring requirements. Also, take note of traffic patterns. How do people cross the room? You may consider installing stronger materials to parallel the foot traffic. With some materials, a designer can plan a floor so a stronger path is incorporated in the overall design of the floor.

Sound reduction. The advent of in-home entertainment systems has increased the need for sound reduction and better acoustics. If the room you are reflooring will be used for home entertainment, you can add a layer of cork, rubber, or acoustic flooring beneath the floor. These underlayments isolate and absorb sound and can be especially helpful in reducing it in a hallway or from a second floor. They also soften the tone of footsteps on laminate floors.

Abundant light in this living room puts a spotlight on a luxurious floor made from hardwood planks and cork tiles. The grid on the floor is echoed in the mullions of the French doors.

Warming Your Toes

In-floor, or "radiant," heating might seem like a modern indulgence, but the Romans enjoyed the comfort of warm floors long ago. With an in-floor heating system, the entire floor functions as a silent oversized radiator. And it's clean—no air passes through ducts or fins before reaching the room. The room heats up from the bottom up, warming the feet and body first. The bonus? Not only will your toes appreciate radiant heating, but your wallet will too. A radiant system can save at least 25 percent of your energy costs, and it can run on a variety of energy sources.

Currently the two most common types of radiant heating are hydronic and electric. Hydronic radiant floor systems pump heated water from a boiler through polyethylene, rubber, or copper tubing laid in a pattern underneath the floor. The temperature in each room is controlled by regulating the flow of hot water through the tubing.

Electric in-floor heating systems are made of heat-resistant wire that serpentines over a supporting material. Manufacturers offer rolls and mats of these wires in different sizes to fit the shape of each room. Both types of radiant-heat flooring are typically heated to 85 degrees Fahrenheit.

Radiant heating can be installed under all types of floors, although some materials perform better than others. Check with the manufacturer of your radiant heating system for material guidelines. Installing a radiant floor can easily add more than $5 per square foot to the price of your flooring project. However, if you amortize the energy cost savings, it could prove well worth it. A radiant heating system usually pays for itself in about six years.

Do you like the look of a stone floor but don't have the subfloor to support it? Here the look of stone tiles has been replicated in laminate flooring in a kitchen. It looks impressive, cleans up well, and is comfortable underfoot.

Life span of materials. A number of factors contribute to the life expectancy of flooring materials, including the quality of installation and the level of maintenance during use. A general rule of thumb: Flooring made of natural materials, such as wood or stone, lasts longer than synthetic flooring, such as vinyl. For instance, oak and pine flooring last as long as the home; marble usually lasts beyond the lifetime of the home; and vinyl tiles and vinyl sheet flooring last an average of 20 to 30 years.

Most floors are meant to take a beating with constant use, but if you have children or pets, you'll want to choose flooring that can withstand scratches, spills, and dropped toys to stay good-looking as well as safe.

Consider how long you'll want your flooring to last and compare that to your budget. It may be cost-effective to install flooring that will endure 50 years, rather than using a less-expensive flooring material that will need to be replaced every 10 years. However, if you like change or plan on moving in the near future, you can choose an attractive but inexpensive flooring that you'll be able to change on whim or leave behind if necessary.

Indoor air quality. Indoor air pollution can damage health just as outdoor air pollution does. Air quality has become an issue in relation to flooring because of the adhesives used for installation and claims that certain flooring materials emit chemicals or volatile organic compounds (VOCs) into the air. As a result, low-emitting adhesives are now available that greatly reduce overall installation emissions. They perform as well as their predecessors while adhering to EPA guidelines for improved air quality; ask your installer to use them. You should also be certain that you ventilate your home well during the installation and for at least 48 to 72 hours after. Presently, no floor covering materials are VOC-free; all contain some amount of VOCs for effective performance.

Maintenance. Long after your flooring has been installed, it will continue to need your attention. Depending on the type of flooring you choose, that attention could be minimal or intensive. Know yourself and what routine or periodic maintenance you're willing and able to accept. A leather floor requires buffing every few weeks, a laminate floor needs just a quick wipe with a damp mop, and some wood floors need periodic waxing. Usually the person who purchases the flooring is the one who will clean it. If that's not the case, make sure whoever will be cleaning your floor knows what maintenance is required.

It's also important to recognize that some materials, such as stone and concrete, weather with time. Some people enjoy seeing their floors age gracefully. Others prefer their flooring to remain shiny and new-looking. Take care to choose flooring that suits your preference.

A Flooring Questionnaire

If you've decided you want to redo that floor, it's a good idea to get all your thoughts down on paper before you start rolling up the rugs. This questionnaire can help you analyze your current flooring situation and point you toward ideas for your new floor. Write your answers on a separate sheet of paper, and take that paper with you when meeting with architects, designers, or showroom personnel. The better prepared you are, the smoother the project will go.

1. Why do you want to change the floor? Does it need to be more hardworking? More glamorous?
2. What material(s) would you like to use? Have you considered both traditional and newer materials?
3. How much square footage will be refloored? Does it invlove more than one room?
4. Where is the floor located? In a public or private space?
5. Will moisture be an issue?
7. What is the traffic pattern in the room? Do you have children? Pets?
8. What is your budget?
9. What material covers the floor now? Can it be removed easily?
10. Is the existing subfloor structurally sound?
11. How long do you expect the new floor to last? Do you plan to replace it again?
12. When do you need the floor finished? What is your time framework?
13. For how long can you manage without the new floor?
14. Where are the transitions into other rooms? Are there stairs?
15. What kind of heat do you have? Radiant? Forced air? Baseboard?
16. Will you need outlets and GFIs installed in the floor? Where?
17. Have you considered accessibility and handicap issues?
18. Does anyone in your household suffer from allergies?
19. How will sound in the room be affected by a change in the flooring material?
20. What's your style? Country? Contemporary? Traditional? Eclectic?
21. Do you prefer neutral, bright, or pastel colors?
22. Do you prefer matte or polished finishes? Or a combination?
23. Do you like patterns? Geometrics? Florals? Animal prints?
24. What kind of base trim are you thinking about?
25. How often do you expect to clean and maintain the floor?

designing your floor

While considering *the type of flooring material you want, you'll find you have a few other decisions to make as well. What kind of texture do you prefer? Have you thought of mixing different kinds of flooring? Is the size of your flooring pattern in scale with the dimensions of your room? How will the flooring be laid? Here are some basic design concepts for you to consider. Remember, these are helpful guidelines, not set-in-stone rules.*

BELOW: Pattern takes the ordinary and turns it into the extraordinary. A plain hardwood floor is stained with a sunburst pattern to create a unique focal point in a home office. A urethane coating safely seals the pattern.

OPPOSITE: A black-and-white checked ceramic tile floor inspires the overall design of a spunky bathroom. The floor holds the room's busiest mix of pattern, while a more subtle pattern is used at eye level.

Focus or backdrop?

Your new floor will literally underscore the design of the room in which it sits, as well as the adjacent rooms. It should be harmonious with its surroundings while it performs its crucial task of providing a firm foundation to stand on.

You'll be living with your floor every day. Do you want it to be the first thing noticed in the room, or would you prefer it to be a quiet backdrop? Whether focus or backdrop, your flooring should complement the décor of the room. If you haven't begun to decorate the room, the flooring will serve as a blank canvas. In fact, many people select their flooring first because it covers such a large expanse. It's a lot easier to decide on your flooring and then coordinate the decorative elements, furnishings, and window treatments in the room around the flooring material and style.

Public and private spaces

You'll make different decisions about the new flooring depending on whether it is going into a public area of the house or into a private space. You may want to make the biggest flooring statement in rooms that are frequented by guests. A center medallion of stone or inlaid wood placed in your home's entrance foyer, for example, will serve as a welcome greeting. Placing such a design in a bedroom or in a room where it might be partially covered by furniture would lessen its impact.

In private rooms you'll want to make design choices based on comfort and safety. Thick carpeting may give you the luxurious feel you would like in a master bedroom, while for safety

reasons the choice for the floor in a family bathroom might be slip-resistant tiles.

Elements of design

Designing a room is a way of giving it personality and a look that best expresses your lifestyle. If that sounds daunting, you can break the design down into its components, like style, scale, texture, and those extras that add glamour. Look at each element separately to help you decide how it will affect your flooring choice.

Style. The flooring you choose should reflect the style of your house, whether it's contemporary, country, colonial, or eclectic, as well as your personal style. Hardwood floors are a good choice in a turn-of-the-century kitchen, for example, while laminate would work well in a contemporary family room. And slate could be stunning as it leads guests from a modern foyer right into the great room. Regional design also comes into play. In a southwestern-style home, you might consider terra-cotta tiles for the floor. In an Old World–style villa, handpainted Italian floor tiles might punctuate a dining room.

Scale. A rule of thumb says oversized flooring belongs in large rooms and small-scale flooring belongs in small rooms. Yet breaking this rule may help you get the look you want. Scale is an important but negotiable element in floor design; it really depends on the room and its environment. In a large room that is bright and airy, it could be fun to install a whimsical mosaic floor. A small bathroom with an oversized checkerboard floor can be effective. One rule that does hold true is that a lengthwise floor pattern adds depth to a room, while a pattern

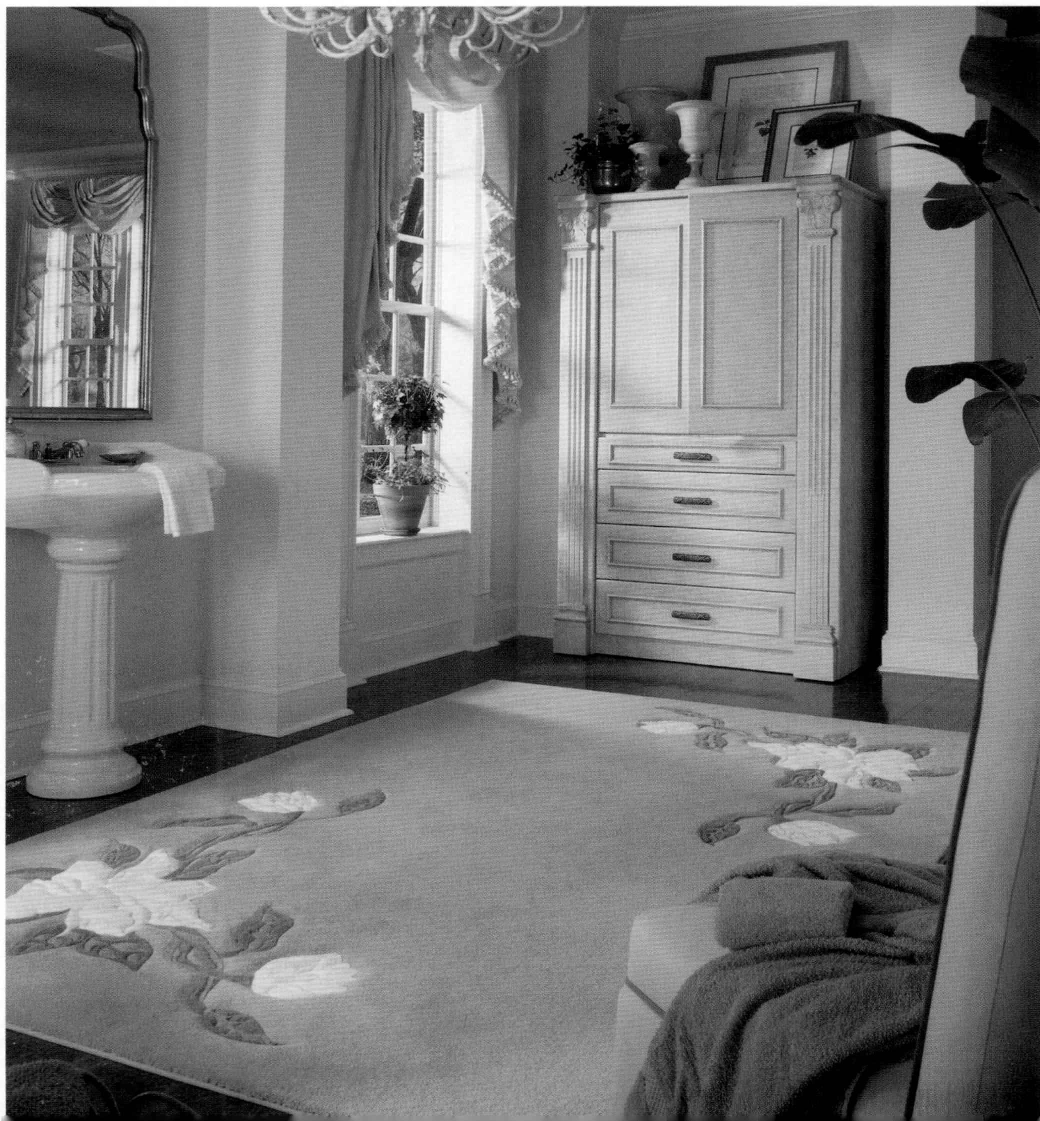

A roomy master bath with a hardwood floor called for softness both visually and underfoot. A velvety area rug provides the comfort factor. Elegant floral elements are custom-sculpted into the carpet's cut-pile construction.

running the width of a room makes it look shorter and wider.

Texture. A variety of textures adds interest to a room. In flooring, texture can be expressed through glazes and finishes. These finishes can even be combined on one floor for dramatic effect. Some tiles today feature varying textures on the same tile, as if the tile, once polished, had been worn down by time in random places. Stone can be honed, tumbled, or polished for varied appeal. And carpets also offer a choice of texture: closed or cut loops, sheared or carved pile. Looped Berber-style carpeting is one of the most popular carpet textures.

Design extras. Each type of flooring material comes with its own set of coordinating design accoutrements. Borders, medallions, and inlays now come premade for wood, tile, and stone floors. And the grout that lies between stone or ceramic tiles is very much a design element. Grout joints can be narrow or wide, plain or colored, depending on the look you want.

A woven wool carpet, inspired by sisal carpeting, is used two ways in one home. In the living/dining area, the carpet is laid wall to wall; in the adjacent foyer, it serves as an area rug on a hardwood floor.

They don't make it like they used to. There are times when only reclaimed lumber will achieve the right effect in a room. In the case of this great room, the vintage flooring came from the same source as the beams in this woodsy home.

Design elements can be used to break up the expanse of a large floor, to highlight a focal point, or to define one area of a room. In a multipurpose room, a good design plan can use different types of floor covering to effectively define two or more areas in a single space. For instance, porcelain tile can emphasize the dining area of a carpeted great room, and leather flooring can underscore a home office nestled in a bedroom suite.

Mixed media. Playing with a variety of materials is a designer's dream. It fosters creativity and allows for infinite design options. Wood can be paired with stone. Ceramic tile can be paired with metal. And concrete flooring can look very sophisticated when embedded with small stones or fossils.

The main concern with a mixed-media floor is how to clean it. Typically, you clean according to the material requiring the most care. Discuss the questions unique to your situation with your flooring professional.

Keeping a visual flow

You'll want visual harmony in your floor so that, in spite of physical interruptions or obstacles like furniture, your eyes will be able to gaze easily across the new floor. Take a look at each of the places where there may be such an interruption and plan for it.

Transitions and junctions. Think about places where the floor meets the walls, the junction between different types of flooring, and the transition from room to room or level to level. How would you like to finish these edges: Will you choose a baseboard molding to edge the perimeter of the floor? Will you have tile run up the toe-kick of your kitchen cabinets? Will you want a marble saddle to make the transition from your wood floor to a marble floor? Or do you prefer all the flooring—carpet, wood, and stone—to be on a level plane? This can be done, but it requires a bit of preplanning with your contractor.

Stairs. If you have a staircase that is affected by your flooring project, you'll want to work it into the theme of your floor. Trimming the risers with the same material as the floor will help to coordinate the stairs with the room. It will also make the stairway safer by providing a visual cue for the elevation.

Grilles, registers, and outlets. Not usually thought of as attractive, grilles, registers, and outlets perform necessary functions in your home. Grilles and registers allow heat to come into a room. New designs now available include unique cutwork patterns as well as colors and materials that coordinate with your new floor.

In-floor outlets allow for more flexibility in the arrangement of furniture. You can place a lamp next to a sofa in the middle of a living room, for example, without having an electrical cord running all the way across the floor to a wall outlet. You'll need to plan ahead and decide where you would like your in-floor outlets to go.

Pick Your Pattern

Most flooring that is composed of squares or pavers can be laid out in a number of ways. Choosing the right pattern for your floor can have a strong impact on its final design. A simple turn or shift of a square will liven up even the most basic flooring. Patterns can also be used to direct the eye to a room's focal point.

Typically, larger patterns are reserved for large rooms and smaller patterns for smaller rooms. As you're deciding what you want, keep in mind that large patterns don't always make a room look smaller. Sometimes they actually open up a room, while small patterns, such as tiny checkerboards, make a space feel cozier.

While choosing your floor, consider other patterns in the room. If your walls are covered in large-scale stripes, you may want your floor to be more subtle. A simple pattern can also help tie together large spaces and produce a feeling of calm.

These patterns are commonly found in flooring design. They each feature countless variations on their theme.

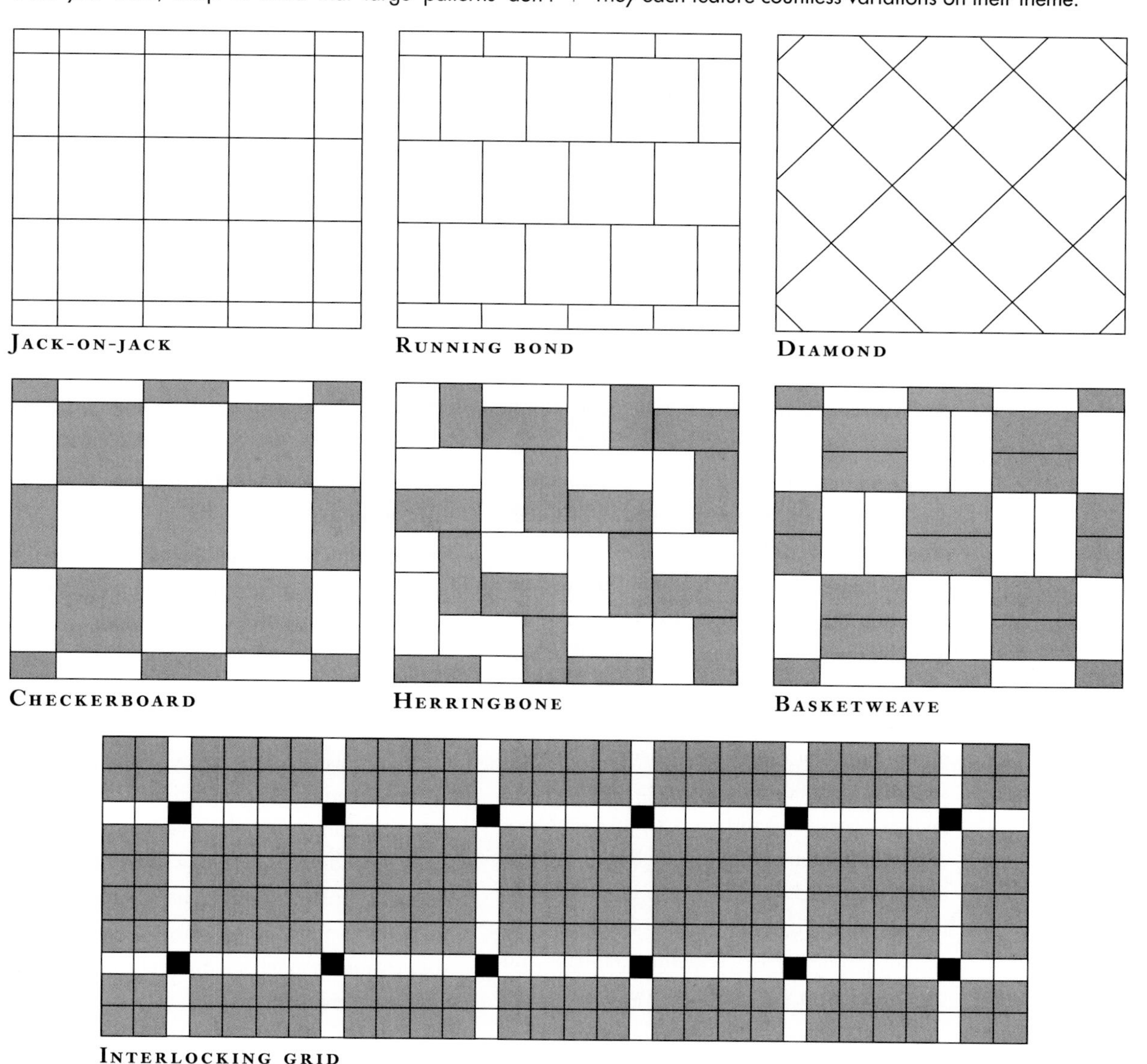

Jack-on-jack

Running bond

Diamond

Checkerboard

Herringbone

Basketweave

Interlocking grid

gearing up

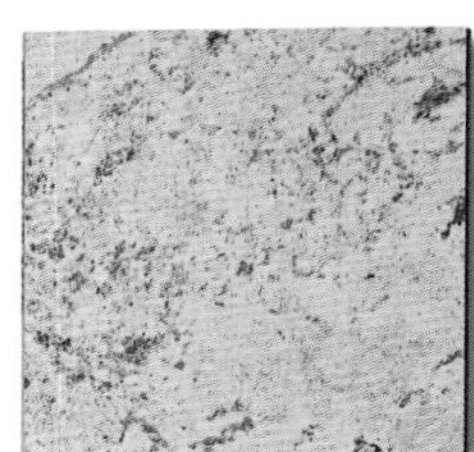

INSTALLING A NEW FLOOR *can be a simple one-day task or a major home improvement. Before you begin, be aware of what your project entails. Your home will be disrupted for a while, so look at a variety of options and ask lots of questions. Survey showrooms and home centers and interview flooring professionals. And don't hesitate to ask for help when you need it.*

Be prepared

A well-stocked flooring showroom or a large home center can be overwhelming in the sheer number of choices it offers, so it's best to do some homework before you visit one. You'll be better able to consider a showroom's professional recommendations and evaluate the choices if you have some ideas in mind.

GATHER YOUR IDEAS. Your inspirations can come from a variety of places. Browse through magazines and books (like this one) and print on-line images. If you're redoing a great room floor, don't confine yourself to finding great room pictures. Take a look at images of other rooms as well. Who knows? You might find the perfect great room floor in a master bathroom photo. For color ideas, gather paint chips, swatches from fabrics used in the room, or favorite vacation snapshots. Create a scrapbook of possibilities and include rough measurements of the room and an outline of your floor. Make note of where light enters the room and where adjoining rooms exist. Take the scrapbook and your notes with you on your showroom outings.

MONEY-SAVING TIPS. Stretch your dollars as far as they will go. There are lots of ways to get a great-looking floor on a limited budget. Here are some hints:

- Choose a less expensive material that emulates a costlier one.
- Work with an inexpensive material like resilient flooring and lay it out in an interesting pattern.
- Have a local artist detail your wood flooring with faux techniques to look like inlaid mahogany.
- Use costlier stones and tiles as a border or accents in a field of stock tile.
- Watch for flooring closeouts or shop for seconds. Some retailers keep their closeouts and seconds available in a separate room.

Planning ahead counts for a lot. Once you have decided on the design and layout, you'll find that installing a cork floor like the one shown opposite is a relatively speedy peel-and-stick or glue-down process.

Where to go

Flooring can be purchased from a variety of sources. Distributors usually specialize in one type of product. Tile and stone distributors are the most familiar. Floor-covering retailers carry a range of different types of flooring materials. Home centers also offer a broad range of materials, often at good prices. Visit several places and shop where you feel comfortable. Imported materials used to take a long time to ship, but that's not so true today because large distributors often maintain a warehouse.

You can call on professionals to help you plan creatively. One inspired designer specified a contrasting shade of ceramic tile to form a "carpet" beneath a dining table. The inset in the floor coordinates with the wall tile.

Ask your flooring installer for samples. Most contractors carry a limited number of samples for you to peruse at home. Requesting flooring samples from retailers is a good idea too. You may be charged a small fee, but you'll get to view the sample in its destined environment.

Need help?

For help in installing flooring, you'll want to contact an architect, interior designer, or installer. Ask friends and family for referrals. Retailers can also refer you to flooring professionals; in fact, larger retailers often subcontract installations. Architects can help you analyze your particular needs and find solutions to tricky problems. Designers are more attuned to style and know about the latest materials.

It's a good idea to get about three estimates for your floor. Ask for references and check to see if the contractor is licensed to perform the intended work. Estimates should include all subfloor preparation, all installation costs, the removal of the existing flooring, the moving of furniture and appliances, and all the necessary flooring materials.

Practical matters

Once you've set a date for installing your new floor, be sure you know when and where your materials will be arriving. In order to acclimate to new surroundings, your flooring material may need to sit in your home for a while before the job begins. Let your contractor know where materials should be left. Stone may simply be left in your driveway, but wood flooring will need to be stored inside and kept dry.

Installing a floor often takes longer than you think. That can be especially frustrating if you're getting your home ready for a holiday or family event. Plan ahead and allow the right amount of time for the floor to settle in its new surroundings before you have a house full of guests. The grout and mortar in a new tile floor require curing time. New carpeting has an odor that needs time to fade a bit.

Removing your old floor. You don't always need to remove your existing flooring. However, if it is truly in bad shape or if adding a new floor on top of it will increase the height of your flooring significantly or will block in appliances, you'll want to remove it.

If the existing floor is resilient and manufactured before 1986, it should be tested for asbestos at a private laboratory. A positive test result means you have to take special precautions to remove the material safely. Check with your local Environmental Protection Agency office. If you choose not to remove the resilient flooring, you can lay most types of flooring right over it.

Subfloors. Before you visit flooring retailers, see if you can tell what's underneath your existing floor. Your contractor will also take a look. Make sure the subfloor is in good condition. This is not the place to skimp. Your flooring installation will only be as good as the subfloor underneath it. A springy or sagging floor is not a good sign. An imperfect subfloor can cause cracked ceramic tiles or allow for moisture to gather, which causes wood planks to cup and joists to squeak. Serious structural problems call for further expertise.

When to refinish. All types of flooring can be patched, repaired, or refinished. Perhaps your old floor just needs sprucing up. A new color grout for a tiled floor? A different finish for a wood floor? If the imperfections on your wood floor are shallow, it can be stripped and given a fresh finish rather than sanded. If your floor has heavier damage and does need to be sanded, sanding will remove only a small percentage of the depth, so you can safely resand a solid wood floor every 15 to 20 years.

Time and Space

Numbers are important in replacing flooring, both to determine the amount of space you'll be covering and to estimate the length of time you'll need to allow to complete the job.

The timing of your project will depend on the material you choose. A resilient, laminate, or carpeted floor can be installed in less than one day, plus 24 hours for glues and adhesives to set. A tile, stone, or wood floor will take longer and could require an extra three to four days for finishing, sealing, curing, and drying. In addition, leveling out an imperfect subfloor can add even more time, depending on the extent of the work.

To determine how much flooring you'll need, measure the longest length and the widest width of your room. Divide odd-shaped rooms, and figure each section separately. Ceramic tile, stone, resilient tile, wood, and laminate are measured by the square foot. Sheets of resilient flooring and carpeting are measured by the square yard. For these materials, measure in square feet and divide by 9 to determine square yardage. For good measure, on all materials add 10 percent to allow for errors and pattern matching. You'll also want to keep some extra materials on hand for future repairs.

GREAT FLOOR IDEAS

Now that you've explored your options, it's time to be inspired! In this chapter you'll find that ideas for great floors are many and varied. As you start your search, you'll come across floors that you think are terrific. You can mark those photographs and then go back later to pare down your favorites. As you revisit the photographs, you'll begin to discover your flooring preferences. **Once you've narrowed** down your choices, ask yourself some questions about each one. Is it practical for your lifestyle? Will it fit in with the décor of your home? Be sure to share these flooring photographs with your designer or contractor. The more they see what you like, the more likely you'll get the floor you want. Take your time and consider your choices carefully. **Making the right choice** for your home is a big decision. Your new floor needs to be both practical and beautiful to be a real success!

tile

THE APPEAL OF ceramic tile cannot be understated. Encompassing ceramic, porcelain, quarry tile, and mosaics, ceramic tile in all its shapes and forms presents one of the widest ranges of flooring available in any one category. In addition, glistening glass tiles, though technically not ceramic, appear in this chapter. Some floors feature the timeless look of tile set with wide grout lines, as in popular terra-cotta tile floors, while other floors, such as those with large-format porcelain tiles set with tight or no-grout joints, provide a seamless appearance. Today ceramic tile has become a virtual chameleon and has been designed to mimic other materials, most notably replicating large slabs of marble or granite. Even photographic images are finding their way onto tiles. How about photos of water on the floor of a guest bathroom? Or lush green grass tiles for a garden room?

Another aspect of ceramic tile that might surprise you is its use throughout the house. On these pages you will see ceramic tile flooring move outside the kitchen and bath into other areas of the home. Many American designers are taking their cue from European homes, which often use ceramic tile flooring in living rooms and bedrooms. The concept works exceptionally well in homes with open floor plans or loftlike spaces where you can see several rooms from one vantage point.

Ceramic tile can be new and exciting, as well as old and traditional. You may be inspired by a tile idea that you never thought of before or become enamored with a classic tiled floor.

Unusually shaped and creatively set ceramic mosaics form a rug design in the center of a mosaic-tiled room. The "rug" provides color, while the rest of the floor remains neutral.

Contrasting with bright yellow walls, a highly polished black-and-white porcelain checkerboard floor is an unexpected greeting for visitors to a traditional home. Tightly butted joints let the glossy look continue uninterrupted through the hallway.

Sturdy porcelain tiles mimic the texture and shadings of stone on the floor of a cozy sitting room. An "area rug" created with tiles placed on the diagonal and finished with a border of smaller tiles covers the main activity center of the room.

Simple, timeless squares of ceramic tile in neutral shades of gray and taupe are randomly arranged on the floor of a sitting alcove. Not only are the tile shades mixed, but the tiles themselves are set off-center from one another.

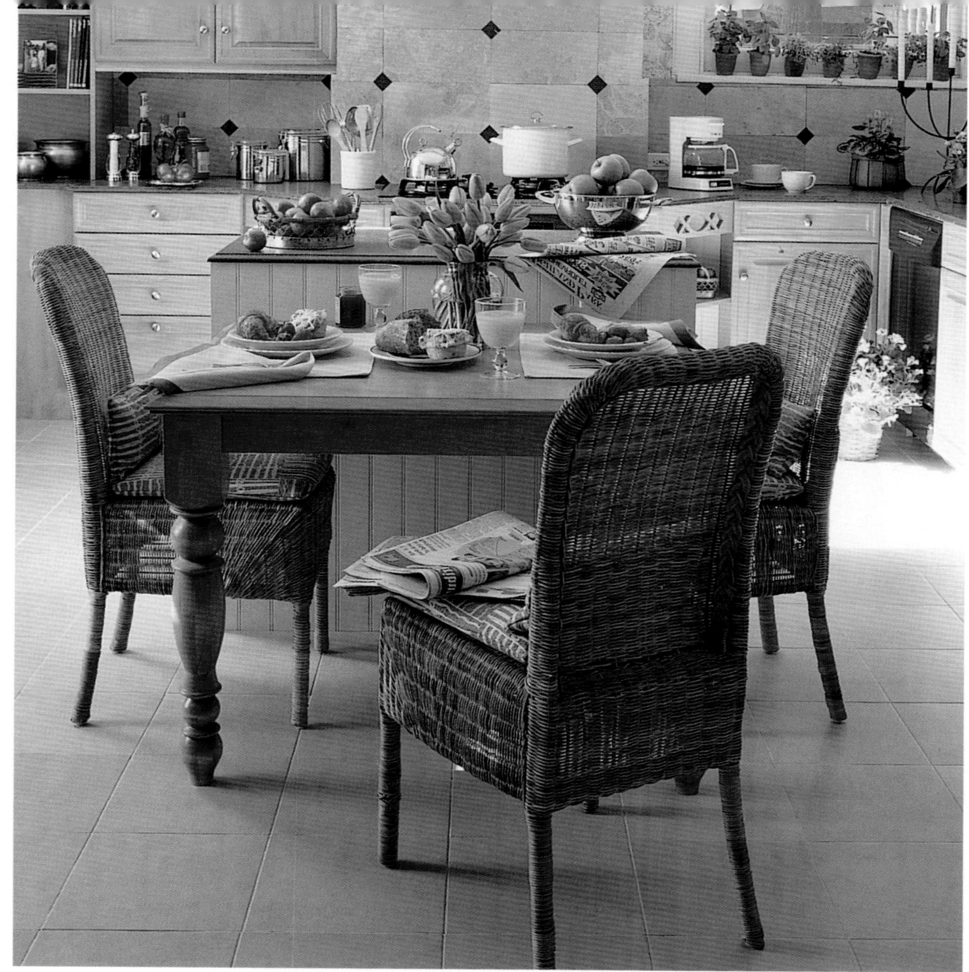

A bisque-colored ceramic tile floor complements a large, sunny kitchen. The light color is repeated in the wall tiles covering the kitchen's backsplash.

Set on an angle and featuring a very traditional grout line, gray ceramic tile covers the floor of a kitchen and dining area. The lines of the floor lead directly to an outdoor patio.

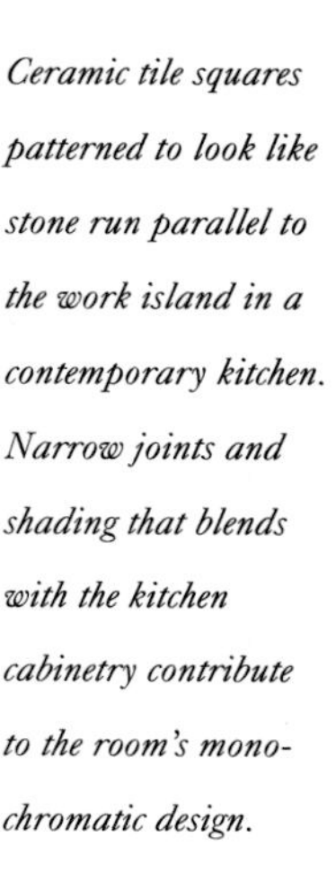

Ceramic tile squares patterned to look like stone run parallel to the work island in a contemporary kitchen. Narrow joints and shading that blends with the kitchen cabinetry contribute to the room's monochromatic design.

Not typically thought of for expansive open spaces today, translucent glass mosaic tiles on the floor bring an air of serenity to a busy eat-in kitchen. The floor's soft neutral shades look custom-made but were chosen from standard glass mosaic colors.

Traditional porcelain mosaic tiles are set in a classic interlocking grid pattern on this kitchen floor. The use of black tiles at each intersection visually breaks up the predominant use of white in the room.

Colorful glass mosaic tiles replicate a vintage Persian carpet complete with fringe. The carpet was prefabricated for easy installation and set in a frame of neutral-colored oversized stone tiles that allow the "carpet" to take center stage.

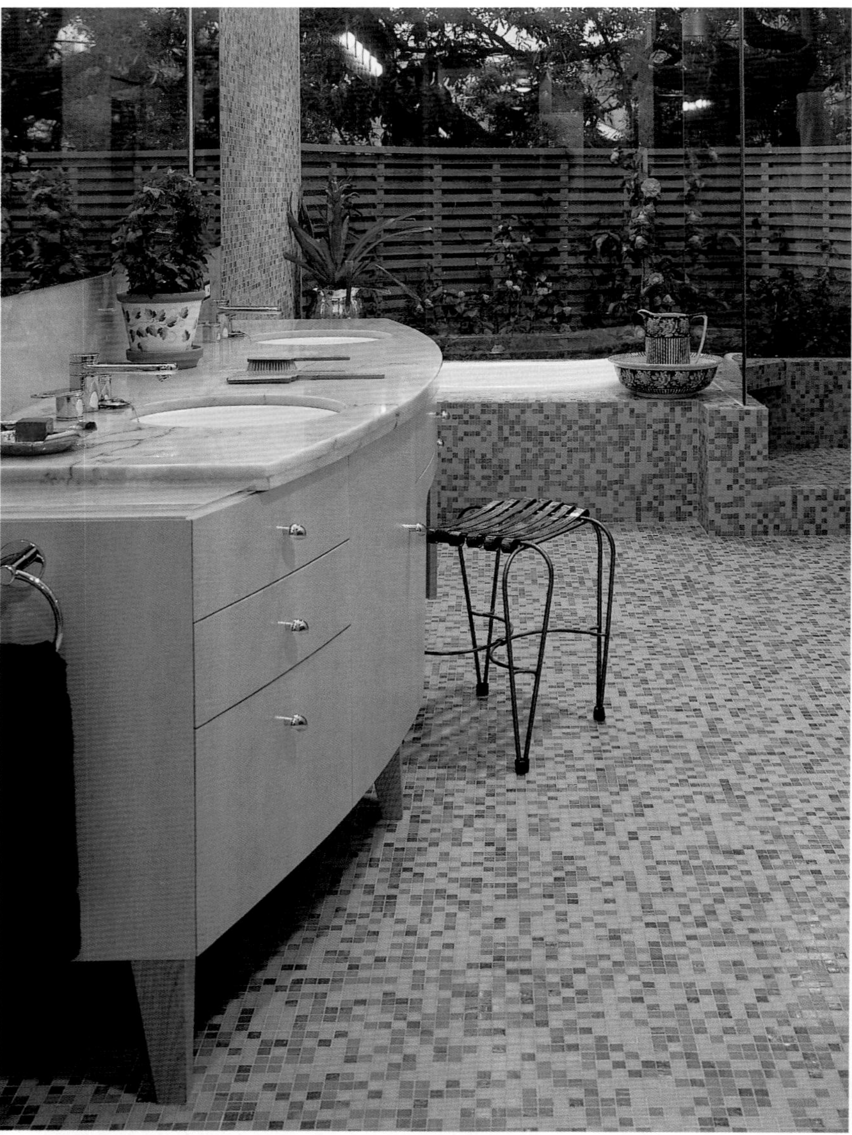

Glass mosaics cover virtually all the surfaces in a contemporary master bath. Visually opening up the narrow space, the mosaics run from floor to ceiling and bath to shower, interrupted only by a vanity mirror and picture window.

A combination of square and rectangular ceramic tiles forms an interlocking grid on the floor of an elegant master bath. Matching tiles run up the wall and outfit the shower, while copper-colored marble mosaics accenting the floor grid are repeated on the backsplash.

Handcrafted ceramic leaves are set free-form within a border and field of preset pebble mosaic tiles to create a focal point in a guest bath. The wide mortar joints and deep texture provide some slip resistance to bathers stepping out of the tub.

Reproduced on large-format ceramic tiles, modular images of manhole covers, crosswalks, and asphalt combine to create a vivid urban streetscape inside a novel bath. The colorful crosswalk tiles follow the entire border of the room.

A simple shower floor features images of river rocks photo-transferred onto ceramic tile. The sharp-focus photography used on the tiles brings a sense of depth to the floor. A slightly abrasive surface makes the floor safer when wet.

A field of glazed porcelain mosaics covers the floor and makes the transition into the shower of a half-bath. Small boxes of black mosaics line the perimeter of the room and run up the center of the shower. A painted wood baseboard completes the floor, and simple black-and-white accessories accentuate the design.

Pillowed terra-cotta flooring paired with tall paned windows makes a dining room look like a garden room. Hand-molded ceramic accent tiles are inset throughout the diagonally set floor, while multiple intersecting lines call attention away from the room's baseboard heating.

Sealed terra-cotta tiles cover the floor of a small guest bedroom, more often used as a den. The randomly mixed colors of the tiles can be attributed to the ceramic clay's natural unglazed state. A wide grout line filled with neutral mortar emphasizes the handcrafted appeal.

Obtuse angles of the cabinetry in an Old World kitchen called for uniquely shaped tiles. A combination of octagonal and square terra-cotta floor tiles complements the space, while decorative glazed accent tiles provide contrast.

stone

Insets of unglazed terra-cotta mosaics repeat the theme of a tiled wall frieze across a yellow marble floor. A geometric strip of the marble tile marks the transition into an adjacent room, where solid terra-cotta insets take the place of the mosaics.

Natural stone is among the oldest types of flooring available. Stone can be imported from exotic faraway places or quarried from your own backyard, if you're lucky enough to have such an indigenous treasure. The following pages are filled with fabulous examples, both traditional and contemporary, of granite, limestone, marble, flagstone, and slate from both near and far. If there is an overriding theme, it's that most of the stone floors shown here embody a sense of history. Even the whimsical terrazzo floors you'll see have origins that can be traced back centuries, when masons would actually hand-place chips of marble and other stones into mortar to form a terrazzo slab.

These floors belong in their environments. The distinguishing characteristic of a stone floor—whether it's the depth of color in a highly polished glamorous marble or the softly rounded edges of an earthy limestone—should fit within the room. The floor should complement its surroundings and provide foundation, but it should not overpower or compete.

Take note as you look at various types of stone flooring. What is it about these floors that engages you? Is it the charm of weathered and tumbled edges that you like? Or is it the sleekness of highly polished slabs with undetectable joints? What colors interest you? You might begin your search with a strong predisposition for a uniform pattern of granite and end up falling in love with a variegated red slate. Keep your mind open and consider the options.

Tightly jointed squares of polished white Carrara marble carry the serene vintage feel of a 1930s-style bathroom. A simple baseboard of painted wood molding neatly finishes the outer edges of the floor.

Speckled granite tiles contrast with a living room's sleek white marble fireplace. Complemented by black grout lines, the speckled pattern camouflages footprints and dust, letting the homeowners enjoy the beauty of the room's monochromatic design.

A black-and-white granite floor runs all the way through a contemporary loft-style space, cutting across expansive living, dining, and entertaining areas. Tightly butted slabs give the appearance of a seamless floor, while geometric area rugs and partitioning walls provide definition and warmth.

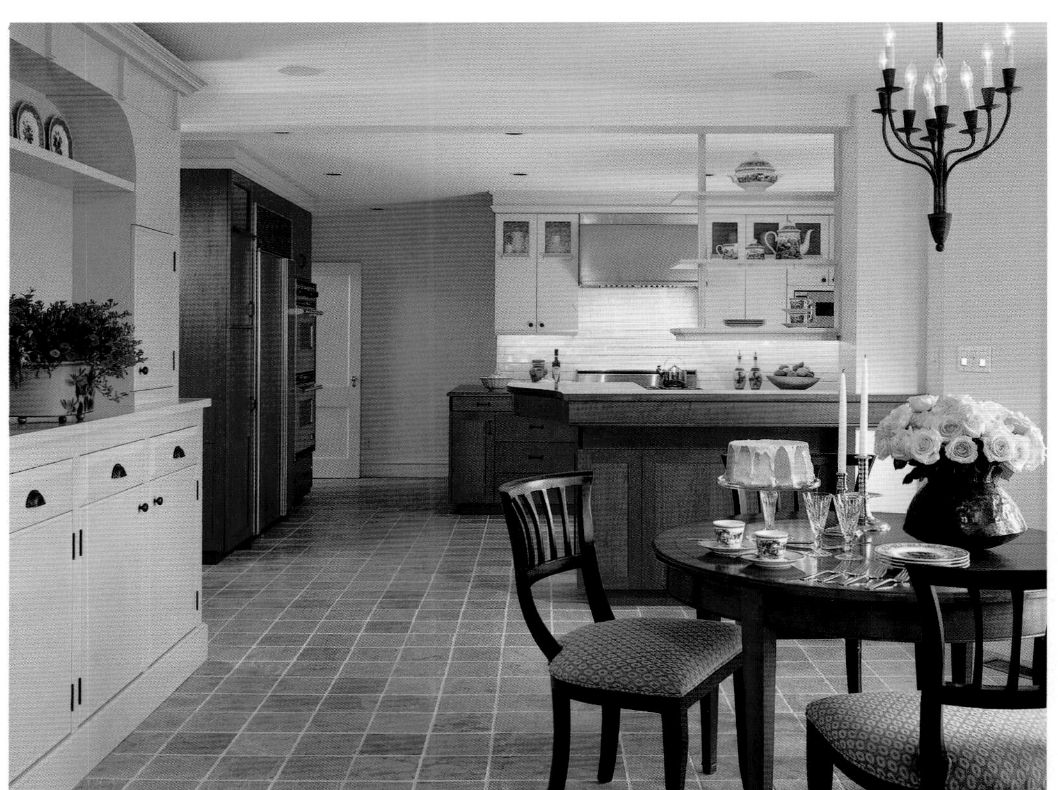

Varying patchworks of tumbled limestone emerge as a hallway progresses from one room to the next. A limestone medallion defines the library, while diagonally set squares lead into a home office. Borders of highly polished striated marble frame each section.

Tumbled limestone tiles set in linear rows softly underscore a simple white kitchen with a touch of color and texture. The floor's white grout lines pick up the white of the cabinets. The gridded floor unites the dining area, the kitchen, and the entry.

Alternating sizes, shapes, and shades of limestone floor tiles carry the eclectic theme of a country kitchen. The earthy tiles and white grout provide a neutral foundation.

KNIGHT'S CROSS
DAVID FRASER
GRAND SLAM GOLF
GOLF IN AMERICA

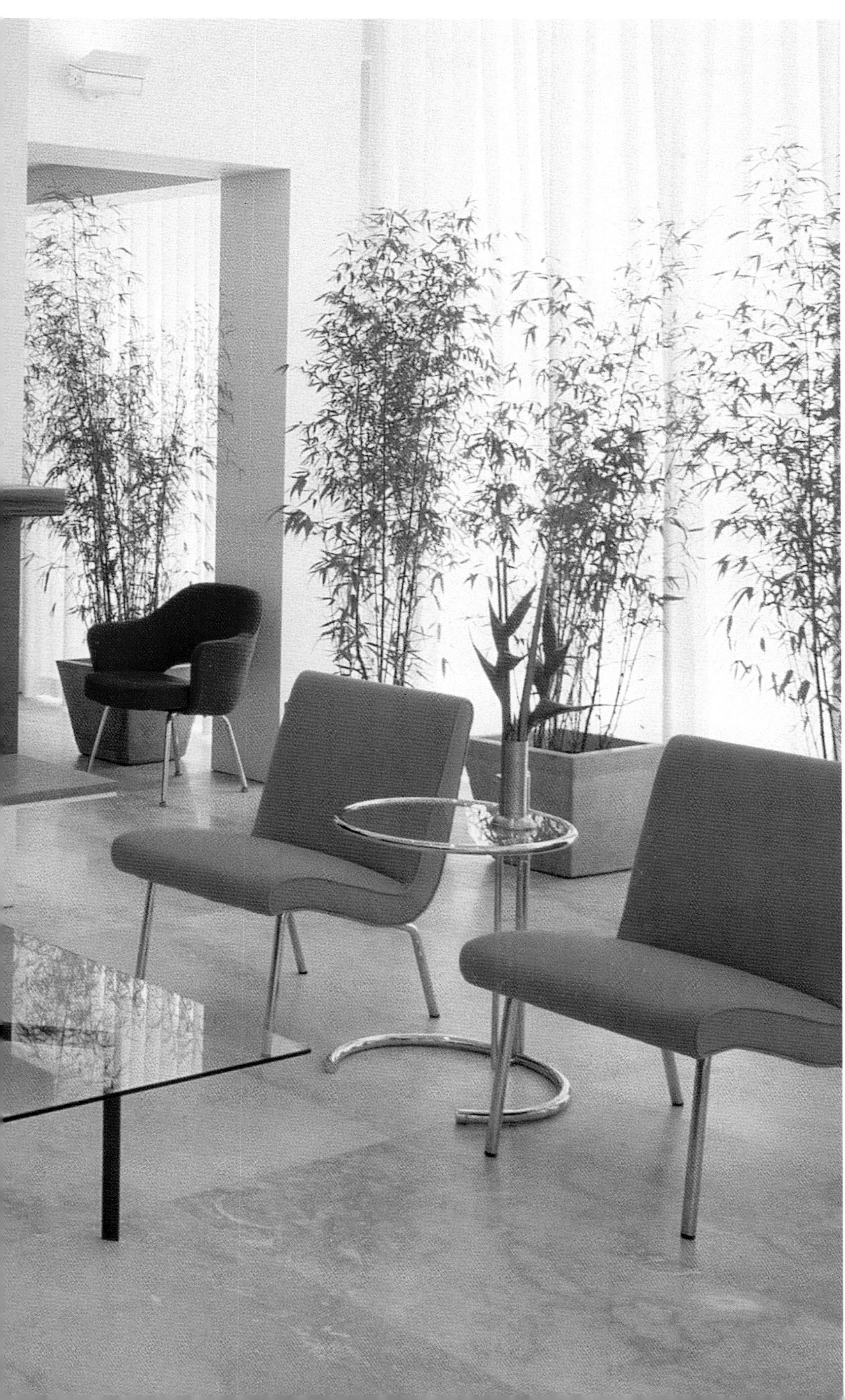

Oversized limestone slab flooring in a color called Princess Yellow has been cut to fit the dimensions of a sparely decorated modern living area. The seamless surface enhances the room's open design while anchoring the entire space with subtle tones of color and texture.

Narrow slate tiles finish the whirlpool tub surround in a master bath and also form the room's baseboard. The use of the same material over several surfaces visually opens the space. Interest is achieved by offsetting the placement of tiles on the floor.

A tightly jointed polished limestone floor begins in the open kitchen and runs through a main hallway, helping to create continuity between the work and entertainment areas of the house. Field tiles are set on a diagonal within a border of the same limestone. The limestone is also used for the baseboard.

A very straightforward gray slate floor contrasts with unfettered light wood cabinetry in a contemporary kitchen. The room's great dimension is emphasized and pattern is achieved by the simple use of white grout lines.

Varied shades of slate tiles fill a rustic great room with hues from yellow to purple. A reclaimed oak saddle beneath a pair of French doors creates a warm transition from outside to in, and a bamboo doormat adds visual interest while helping to keep debris from the outdoors to a minimum.

A combination of traditional gray slate and stainless steel cool down a hardworking kitchen and provide surfaces that perform as well as they look. The floor's mix of sizes and patterns adds visual interest where it's least expected and contributes to the geometry of the room.

Mixed neutral shades of desert slate tiles run right up to the wood wainscoting in a den, continuing the room's refined Mission style. The floor's tight joints and linear setting further emphasize a restrained quality.

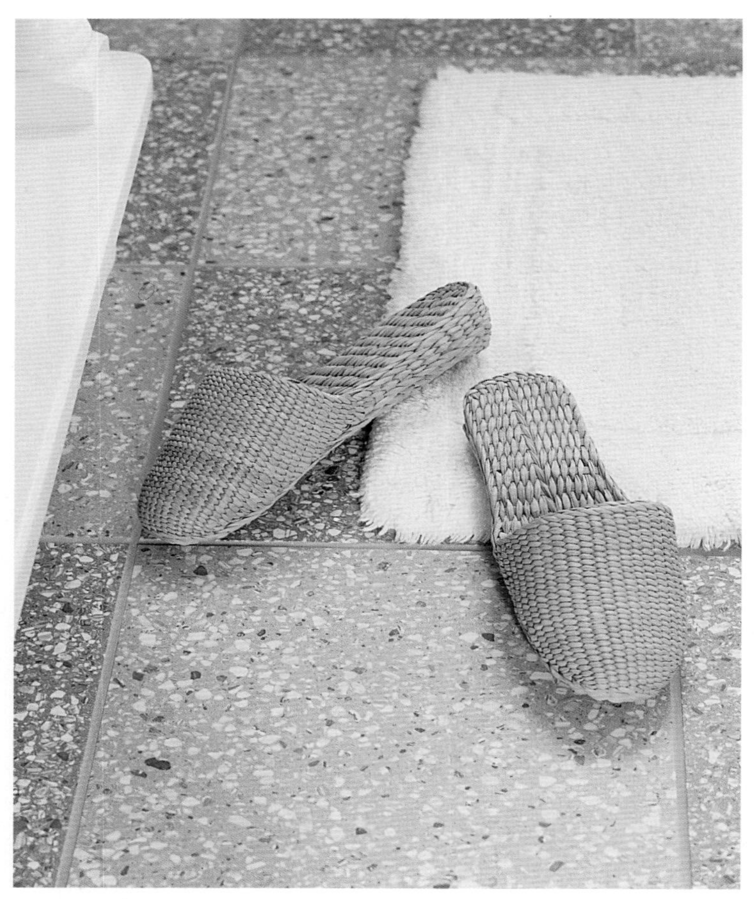

Vintage cobblestones were reclaimed for use in a garden-facing kitchen. The offset placement of the stones follows the pattern of the exterior stone and leads the eye into the garden. A row of short cobblestones finishes the outer edge of the floor where it abuts the French doors.

Classic terrazzo tiles enliven the ultramodern look in a master bath. Alternating brown and yellow hues were used to achieve a checkerboard effect that enlivens an otherwise all-white room.

Although each pebble looks as though it were painstakingly hand-laid centuries ago, Arabesque tiles of natural river pebbles, used here in the sunlit foyer of a new home, come preconfigured. Even the mortar is preworked into the tiles.

wood

IT SEEMS AS IF wood floors are everywhere. A maple floor gives warmth to a vintage kitchen; pine blends almost effortlessly into the living room of an older home; an oak floor lends an air of timelessness to the great room in a new home. Deciding on a new wood floor is the first step. You'll want to choose a particular type of wood, then a board size and a finish to get the desired effect from a wood floor. Will it be a deep, rich mahogany that starkly contrasts with white walls, or a lighter honey shade that makes a room cozy? Do you want to recapture the timeworn characteristics and markings that make wood special? Today you can install vintage floors resurrected from former estates or use boards from age-old logs recovered from riverbeds. There are also alternative new woods, such as bamboo, that have been embraced for their sustainable harvests and for the unique elongated patterns found in their planks.

A warm nutmeg stain finishes a white oak strip floor in a comfortable living room. The grain of the wood floor provides an interesting contrast to the carved stone fireplace and decorative iron fire screen. Running parallel to the fireplace, the floor features a floating wood installation.

In keeping with the simplicity of a colonial theme, a wide-plank hardwood floor is given a wax finish. The low luster of the floor blends well with the room's trim.

Wood floors can serve as the ultimate canvas in a room. Beyond their intrinsic color and texture, they can be intricately painted, washed with shades of color, or inset with creative geometrics. They can be the focus of a room or become a backdrop for the furnishings. What should you look for in wood floors? Most important will be your preference for color, but also note the width of the planks that interest you and the texture of the boards. Wood floors look good in every room of the house—which type of wood is up to you.

Wide bleached planks cover the floor of a rustic great room, serving as a light backdrop to heavy furnishings and upholstery. The floor's light color makes the expanse of the floor look even greater, while the wood's random knots add to the appeal of the room's eclectic interior.

Providing a satiny smooth surface against contrasting dark furnishings, clear maple planking in shades of toast covers the floor of a sophisticated modern bedroom. The bed's headboard and the area rug, set perpendicular to the direction of the flooring, place an emphasis on the long planks.

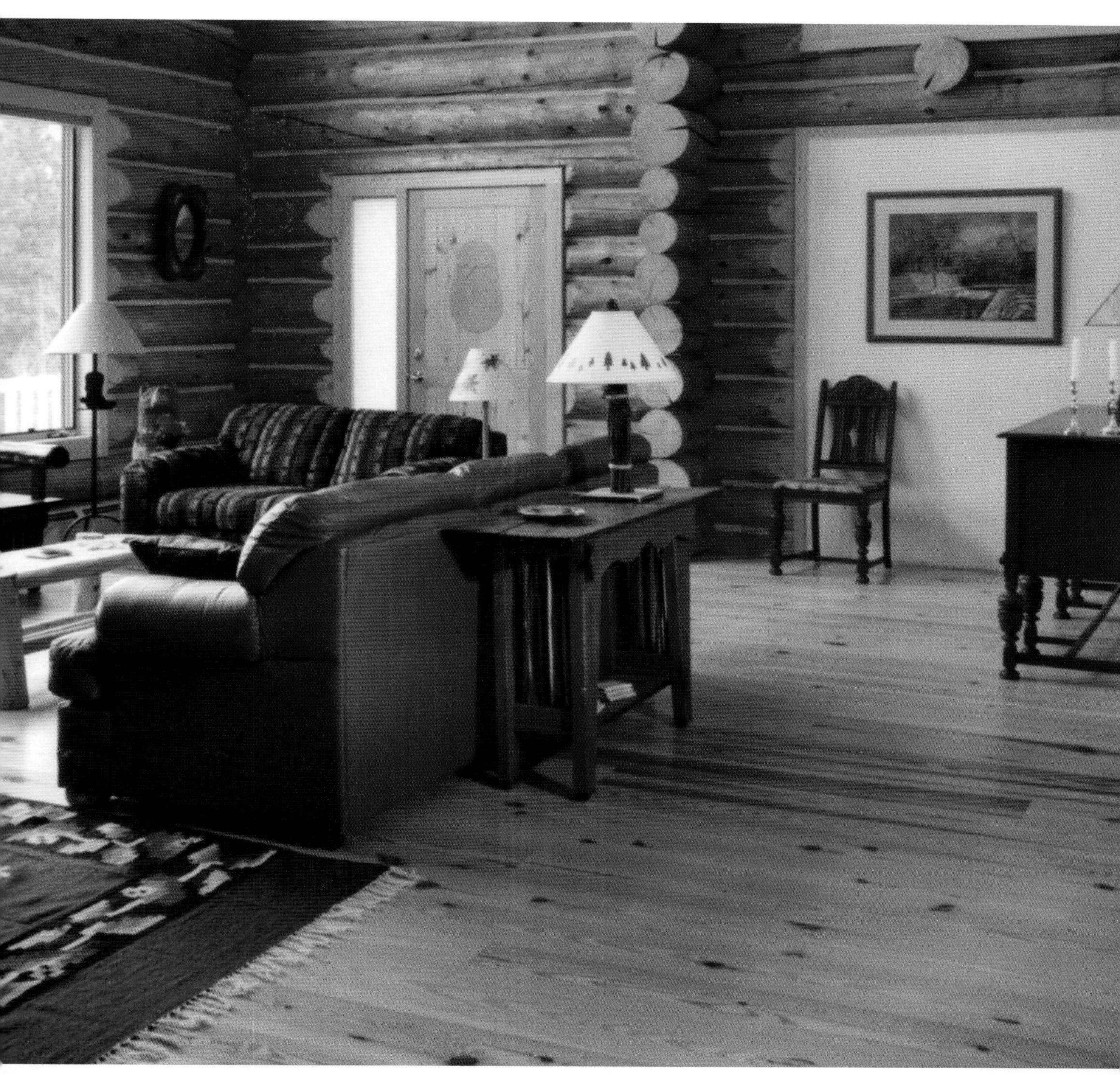

Knotty pine floors in the great room of a log home repeat the pine used in the construction of the home itself, creating an all-enveloping natural environment for homeowners who appreciate the respite of down-home character. The judicious placement of the furniture leaves visible great expanses of the beautiful floor.

Alternating hues of birch flooring run fluidly through an open kitchen and throughout the common areas of a contemporary home. The direction of the planks follows the path of the main hallway.

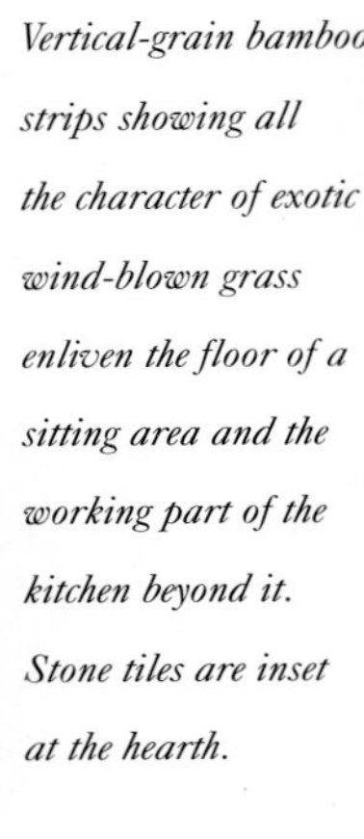

Vertical-grain bamboo strips showing all the character of exotic wind-blown grass enliven the floor of a sitting area and the working part of the kitchen beyond it. Stone tiles are inset at the hearth.

Flat-grain bamboo flooring covers the kitchen area of a great room with abundant light. A contrasting baseboard runs along the base of the cabinetry. In the adjacent living area, a handsome concrete floor was poured in place to the same level as the bamboo floor.

Aged wide-plank hardwoods salvaged from old warehouses are strategically mixed and matched on the floor of an adobe-style southwestern living room. The planks run at an angle to the room's overhead beams, creating a sweeping effect out to panoramic views.

A simple combination of standard hardwood strip flooring in contrasting colors creates a custom look in a formal dining room. A wide band of dark-stained planks serves as the transition from dining to living room, where clear light wood flooring is used.

In a small dining room, a floor of understated clear oak is accented simply by a narrow strip of contrasting wood along the perimeter of the room. A painted white baseboard is incorporated into faux wainscoting rather than blended with the floor.

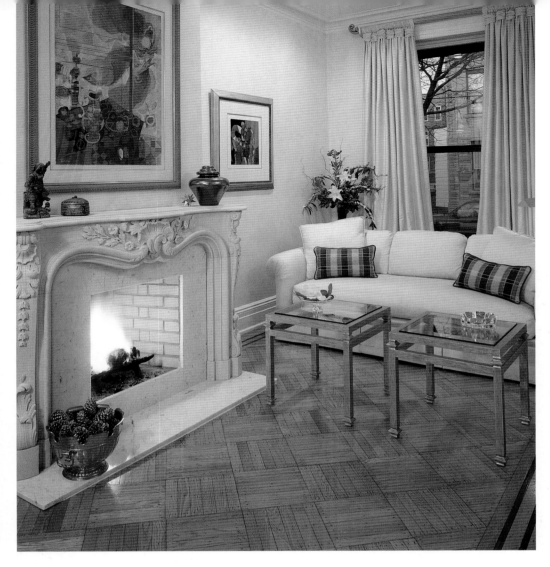

In a diminutive sitting area, a parquet floor is installed on a diagonal to the room's walls. A double row of contrasting wood strips outlines the space, while a painted baseboard finishes the floor. A marble slab is used at the hearth.

A subtle parquet floor features a single wide band of contrasting parquet, giving needed line and angularity to a lush bedroom with soft, rounded forms. Situated in the center of the room, the band takes on a life of its own, not following the shape of the bed or the room's perimeter.

A border of parquet wood flooring curves around the landing of a main staircase. The mix of woods highlights the shadings of the turn-of-the-century stair banister.

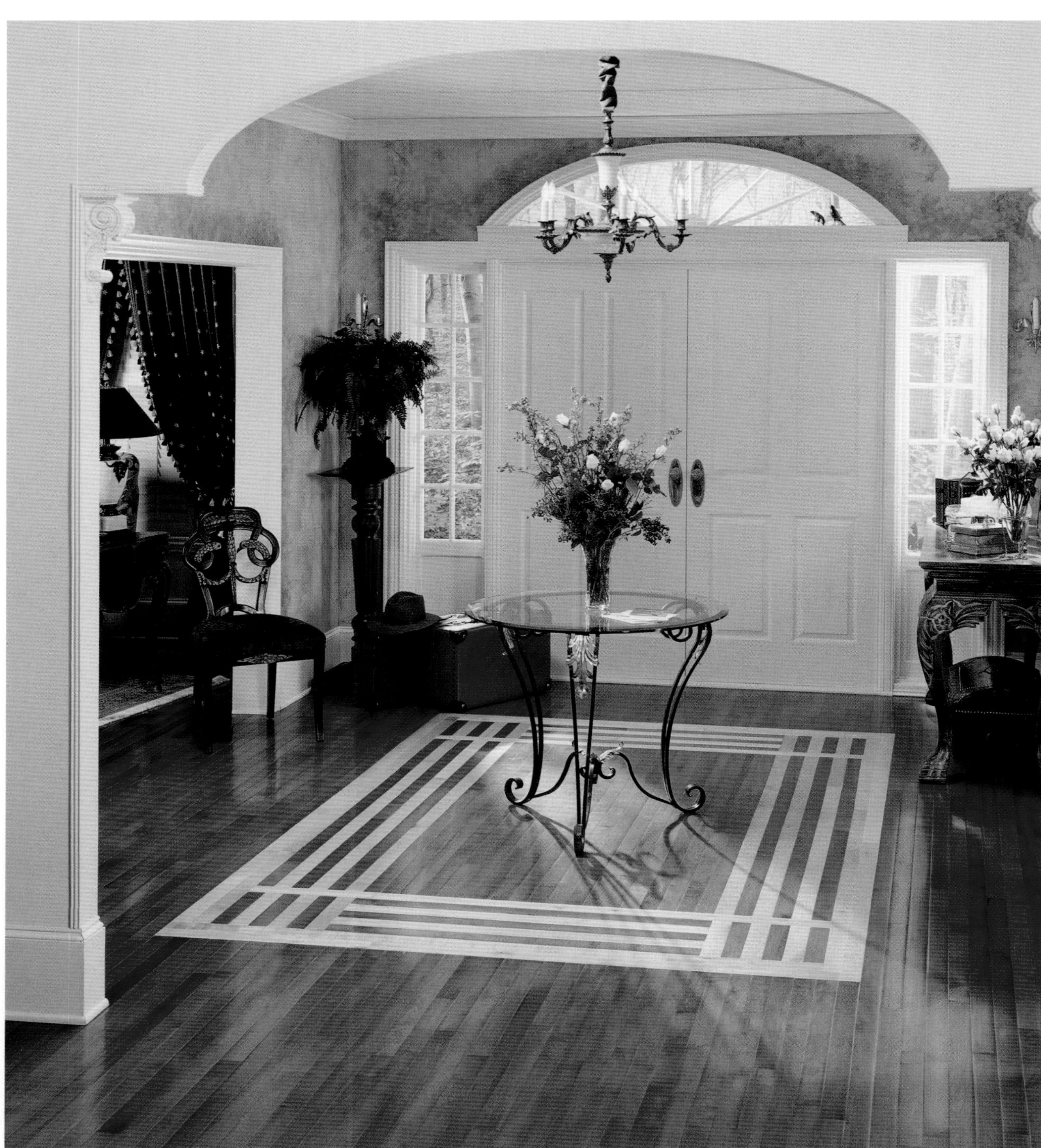

A strategically designed pattern in maple strip wood set against a background of pine flooring underscores the formal entrance of a traditional home. The pattern, as wide as the double entry doors, adds a welcoming brightness to the floor in this sunlit foyer. The pine flooring continues seamlessly into the adjacent room.

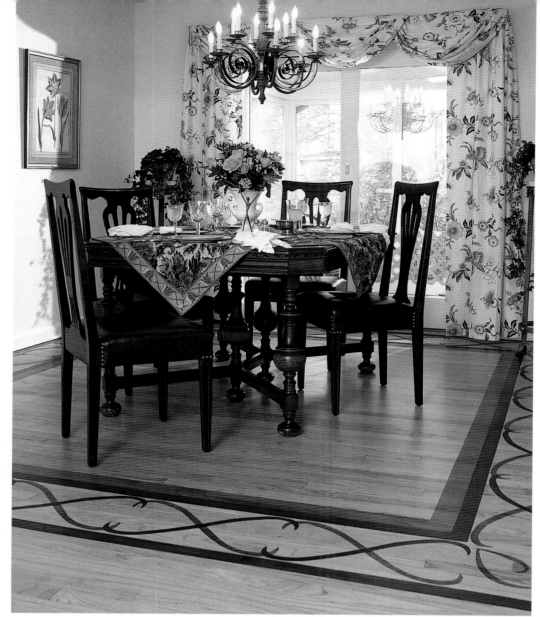

Undulating lines form a romantic hand-painted border around a dining room table. The sheer stains used to create the effect allow the grain of the flooring to show through and blend with the room's décor.

Faux painting gives an old hardwood floor new life. Rather than install a new floor, the vintage oak floor was hand-painted to look like rich, heavily veined marble. Even border tiles are painted around the edge of the room and the staircase.

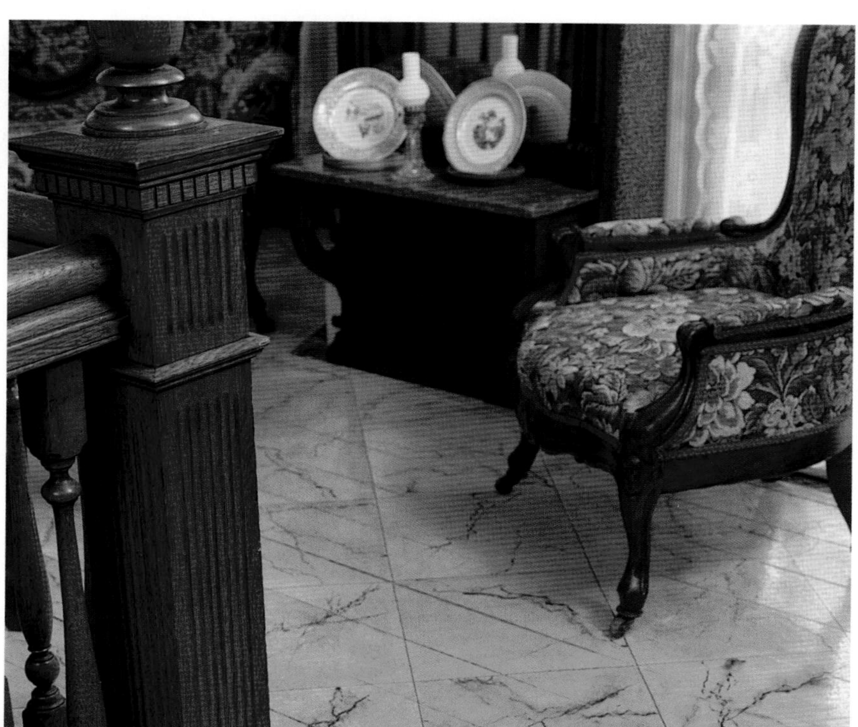

In a child's room a painted finish softens hardwood strip flooring. The floor's pattern of interlocking pastel diamonds is charming, yet sophisticated enough to grow with the child. A painted border follows the room's built-in cabinetry.

Lacework from antique linens inspired the intricate hand-painted hardwood floor in a nursery. Coats of gray-blue paint, the only color in the room, were used to cover the floor first. Then a delicate coat of white "lace" was applied.

Vivid blue paint is washed over the hardwood strip flooring of a living room and extends onto the saddles beneath the exterior doors, bringing the eye to the glorious view outside. No surface of the hardwood floor is left untouched by the wash. A slightly raised area of white ceramic tiles forms a semicircle at the hearth.

resilient

RESILIENT FLOORING is a material you can have fun with. Because it is relatively inexpensive, easy to install, and simple to maintain, resilient flooring invites playful design. Imagine creating an amusing checkerboard with basic red and black vinyl tiles in a children's playroom, or livening up a laundry room with vividly speckled vinyl sheeting. Or imagine mixing varying shades and sizes of stone-colored vinyl in an entryway. The new stone designs in vinyl look surprisingly authentic, as do some of the wood-patterned vinyls.

Although vinyl comes first to mind, resilient flooring encompasses a range of malleable materials—vinyl, linoleum, cork, and rubber—each with its own unique characteristics. Linoleum can take on a retro look that would be wonderful in a renovated mid-century kitchen, or it can be sophisticated enough for use in a living room. Cork can add a touch of nature while helping to mute sound in a media room rich with technology or in a kid's playroom. Rubber flooring has a contemporary look and holds up to rugged use.

It's a given that all resilient flooring is comfortable underfoot. But resilients are also available in the broadest spectrum of colors of any flooring material, which leads to creative ways to use them. Take a look at the range of patterns in each type of resilient flooring, how they're laid out, and how they work visually within a room. From simple mixing and matching of colors to custom inlaid designs, there's a resilient floor for every style and for every room.

A vividly striped linoleum runner that follows the length of an entry hall contrasts starkly with the hall's cool gray concrete surface. Used in place of carpeting, linoleum provides a colorfast covering for the southern-exposed space.

Green linoleum provides a hard-working surface for three well-used rooms: a living/dining area, a galley kitchen, and a laundry room. Whimsical linoleum cutouts capture the color of each area as the floor pattern ebbs and flows, defining each room yet emphasizing the continuity of the space.

THE ART BOOK
Music
HEBRIDES
BRYSON

Easy-care vinyl sheet flooring in a mosaic pattern that evokes garden paths of long ago brings the outdoors into a sunny family room. The wicker furniture and potted plants further the outdoor look.

Linoleum tiles in soft shades of beige and ecru give an earthly grounding to a starkly modern white living room. Baskets for firewood and plants on the coffee table pick up the natural feel of the floor.

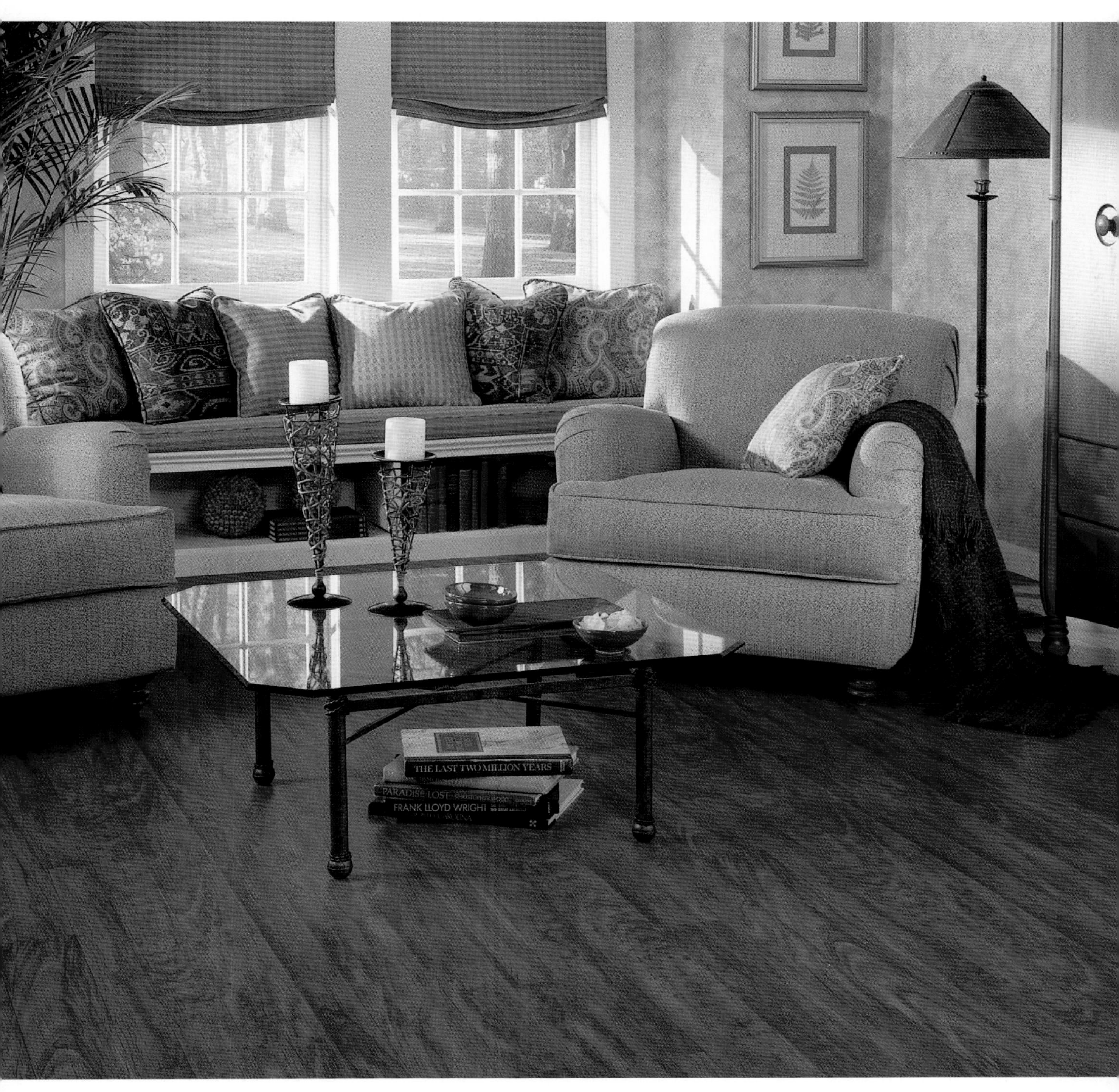

Sheet vinyl that looks like hardwood planking runs wall to wall in a classically styled living room. The plank pattern runs across the room toward the focal point on the far wall—a picturesque window seat. A painted white baseboard anchors the easy-to-maintain yet warmly inviting flooring.

Alternating colors of vinyl tiles in a traditional kitchen give the illusion of a ceramic-tiled floor complete with grout lines. An oversized sculpted baseboard molding is paired with the large checkerboard pattern, which flows from the kitchen to the dining area.

A play of mixed media is achieved by the use of sheet vinyl in a living room. The floor looks like artfully installed hardwood flooring inset with slate tiles, an effect that only a skilled installer could achieve.

Patterned sheet vinyl in an open kitchen only looks like individually laid tiles. Its sophisticated design continues the room's neutral tones but also adds a texture that seems to ground the columned high-ceilinged space.

An unanticipated patchwork of brightly colored cork tiles underscores a frequently used dining room in a landmark home. For the family who enjoys entertaining, the cork provides a soft surface underfoot and minimizes the sound of footsteps in the room. The multicolored tiles provide a springboard for the simple furnishings, including the large wood trestle table.

Standard gray, black, and white cork tiles are playfully positioned in a kitchen inspired by industrial elements. The pattern picks up colors from the space and continues all the way through to a butler's pantry.

Cork flooring outfits a stair landing, providing an attractive surface, as well as traction for safe footing. The area is bordered by geometric black-and-white tiles that serve as a guide to the home's other rooms.

laminate

LAMINATE IS one of the newest types of flooring. Introduced in Sweden as an alternative to hardwood, it became a flooring favorite almost immediately. It's a natural choice when you want to combine goods looks, easy maintenance, and quick installation.

Laminate mimics a vintage wide-plank floor in a turn-of-the-century styled kitchen filled with freestanding appliances. The black-grained pattern of the wide planks leads the eye toward a large window with a garden view.

A wall of cheery turquoise cabinets is anchored by a light pine laminate floor. A slim dark molding defines the line where the two meet. The pattern of the narrow laminate planks runs parallel to a main wall, visually expanding the kitchen's width.

Most laminates replicate wood flooring. But wood-patterned laminate is definitely not one-dimensional. Just like solid wood, wood-patterned laminate comes in a range of styles—from elegant to rustic to contemporary. You can also find precious and exotic woods, like chestnut or teak, emulated in laminate.

Many intricate and sophisticated wood designs, such as weaves and herringbones, are also available in laminate. In real wood such designs would be costly because of the labor-intensive handwork they require. In laminate, however, designs are possible that might not even be considered in wood.

In addition to wood, ceramic- and stone-patterned laminate tiles are also available. Cut into squares rather than planks, these laminates allow for some creative applications. Marble colors can be mixed for innovative checkered floors. Similar colors can be placed on the floor and along the perimeter to create a subtle border. The look of seamless flooring can be created by using laminate tiles in one color, such as a single shade of granite-patterned laminate.

By viewing laminate floors in actual rooms, you'll see how wood and stone patterns and their variations accommodate a variety of styles. Keep an eye out for designs and colors that interest you to help narrow down your choices.

MARCEL DUCHAMP
modern primitives
CANALETTO

Laminate provides a splinter-free, easy-to-maintain surface in a child's nursery. The baby can crawl, drop toys, and spill foods without getting hurt or harming the floor. The molded hardwood baseboard is painted the same color as the room's walls.

Golden bamboo laminate flooring captures the multicultural theme of a family room while providing a neutral background for the room's dark furnishings. The simple flat baseboard molding is stained to match a pair of carved wood doors.

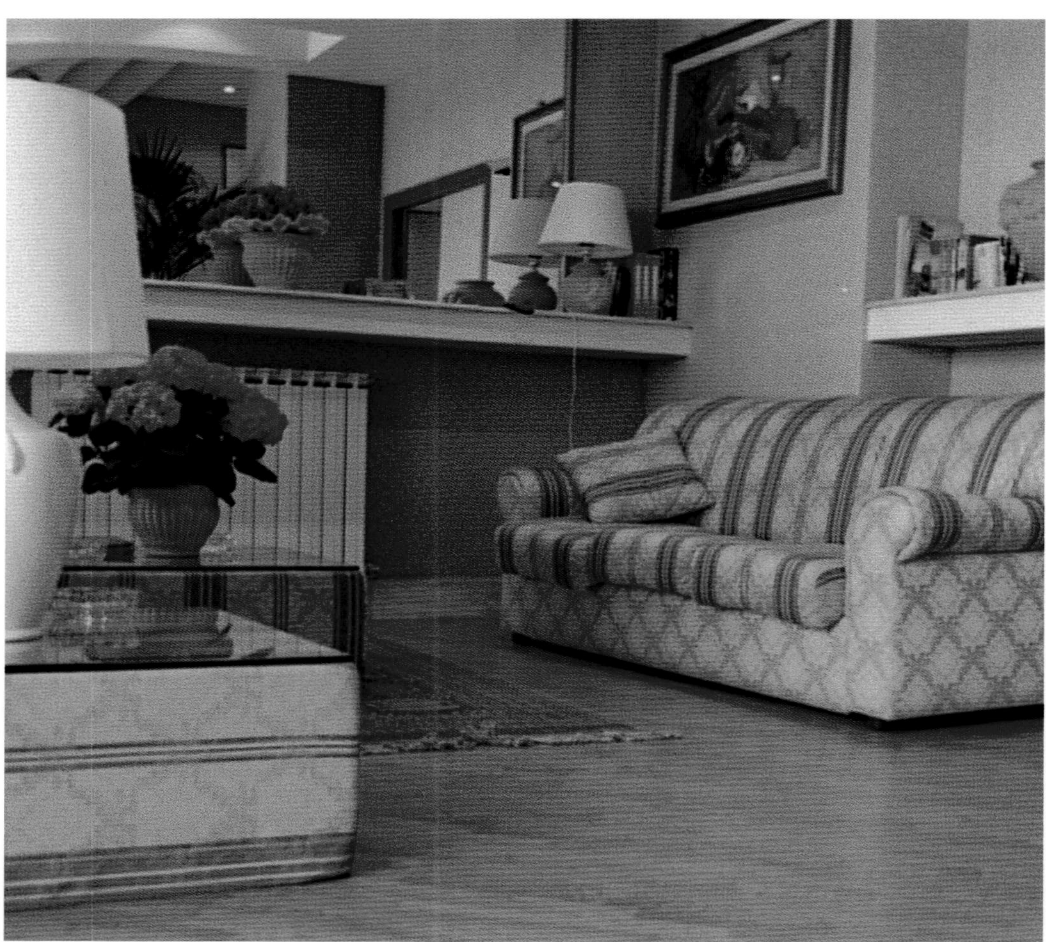

An understated laminate floor runs the depth of a reading nook off a formal living room. Outside the nook the laminate flooring runs diagonally, drawing the eye in. An Oriental carpet softens any echoes in the space and helps keep this home library a quiet place to read.

A natural laminate floor performs well in the highly trafficked entrance and living area off the kitchen of a small apartment. The floor's color anchors the room's splash of lavender-hued walls.

A light wood laminate floor brings color and texture to an otherwise unadorned white kitchen. The grain pattern in the floor hides footprints and spills until they can be swept away.

A cost-effective flooring alternative, laminate emulates a ceramic tile surface in this old-fashioned bath. The modular tile units fit together along simulated "grout lines," giving the look that usually comes only from master craftsmen.

A minimalist bedroom receives its visual interest from an artfully laid laminate floor. The floor's muted shades are defined by a contrasting baseboard. An underlayment of felted material softens the sound of footsteps across the floor.

carpet

THERE'S NO DENYING the warmth and security that a lush carpet can bring to a room. It's the kind of comfort underfoot you want for your family. And if your family includes children, there is no need to be concerned about the high maintenance of carpeting. Today's stain-resistant finishes mean easy care and less worry in choosing carpeting.

On the following pages you will see wall-to-wall carpeting and a range of area rugs. You'll notice that area rugs can work well in certain circumstances. If you have an existing wood floor, you can let the wood show in all its glory from beneath an area rug cut smaller than the room. Or you can use a simple area rug to delineate one area of a floor, like a dining space. In a bedroom suite you may prefer wall-to-wall carpeting. Installing it from the bedroom through the dressing area and into the bathroom means that in the morning your feet never have to touch a cold floor.

Soft lavender carpeting with a velvety cut pile runs wall to wall in a living room, bringing a hint of color to the Asian-style furnishings.

Once you've decided whether an area rug or wall-to-wall carpeting is best for your room, take a look at color and weave and fiber. Do you want your carpet to make a statement or create a subtle background? Do you want the look and maintenance of a shag carpet or the easy care of tightly woven level loop? Would you like carpeting made of woven plants and grasses, such as sisal, or traditional wools and familiar manufactured fibers? When you choose carpets as your flooring, you'll have myriad choices in color, texture, and fiber.

Ceramic tile flooring cleverly frames the white cut-pile carpeting in a highly styled living room. The carpet itself follows the lines of a custom sectional sofa in the room. Painstaking efforts were taken in installing the flooring to assure that the carpet was level with the tile, a look that adds to the luxurious feel of the room.

A cut-and-loop pile creates a textured trellis pattern for wall-to-wall carpeting in a comfortable living room. The carpeting's soft color functions as a neutral that allows for a great deal of flexibility in design.

The natural-color loop pile of a berber carpet blends into a living room by mimicking the nubby texture of the room's sofa, yet it contrasts with its adjacent design elements—the sofa's long silk fringe and the sinuously shaped table legs.

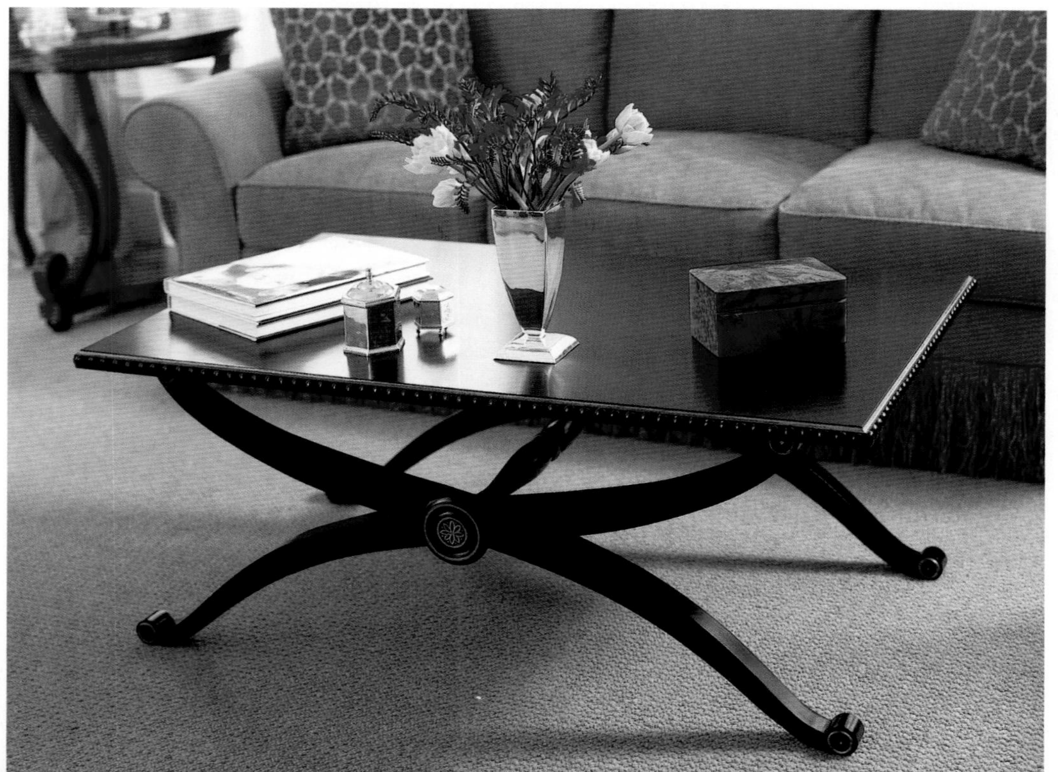

An allover Persian-inspired pattern and an intricate floral border are the hallmarks of this colorful, closely clipped Oriental rug. Not only does the carpet provide a design focus in the foyer; it also protects the wide-plank hardwood floor.

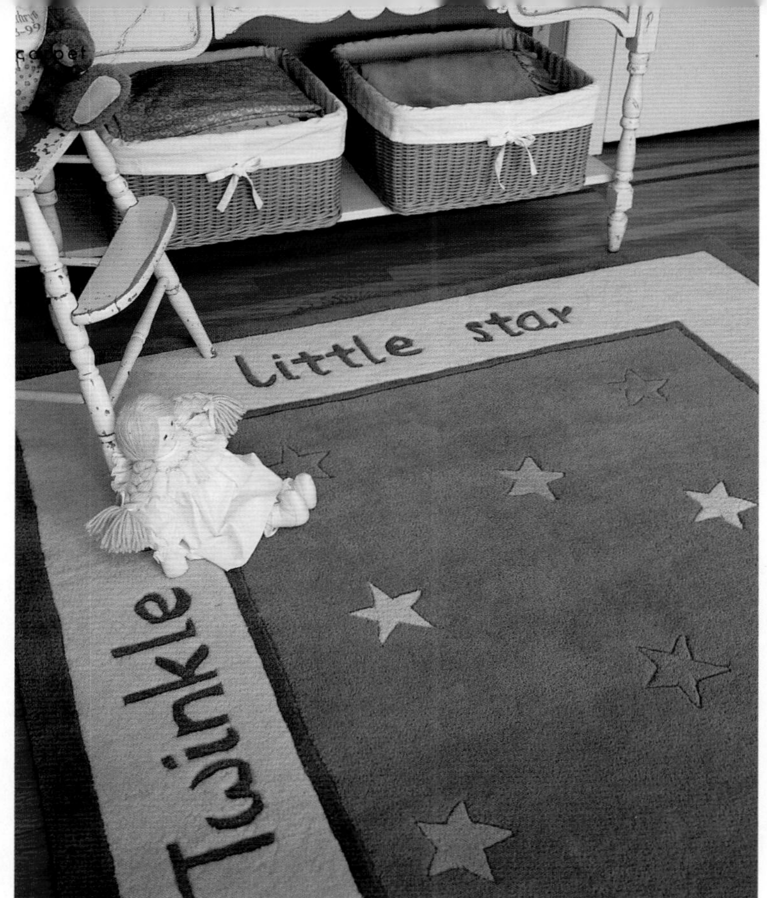

The conversation area of a sunlit blue-and-yellow living room is centered around a floral needlepoint rug with diagonally shaped corners. The rug, designed to echo the patterns in the upholstery, protects the room's hardwood floor under the furniture but does not conceal the wood in the rest of the room.

The words to a familiar childhood nursery rhyme are sculpted into the border of a custom-made area rug for a baby's room. The rug's plush cut pile provides a cushiony platform for baby's first steps.

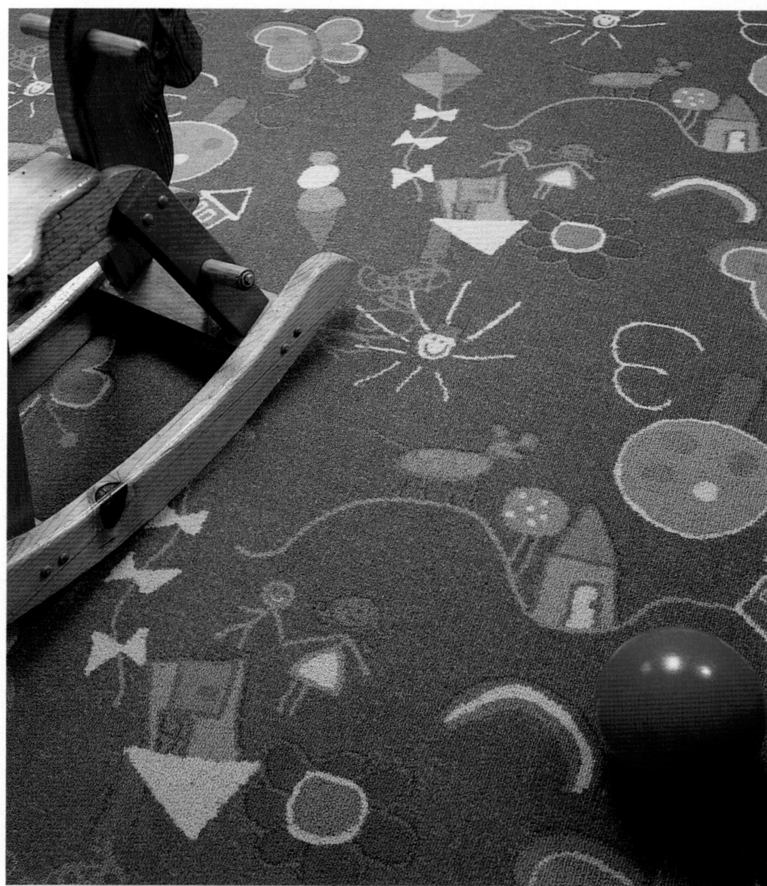

A charming broadloom carpet designed with primitive childlike imagery covers the floor of a toddler's playroom. The dense short-loop pile allows the carpet's vivid colors to pop and provides an easy-to-clean surface.

CARPE
DIEM!

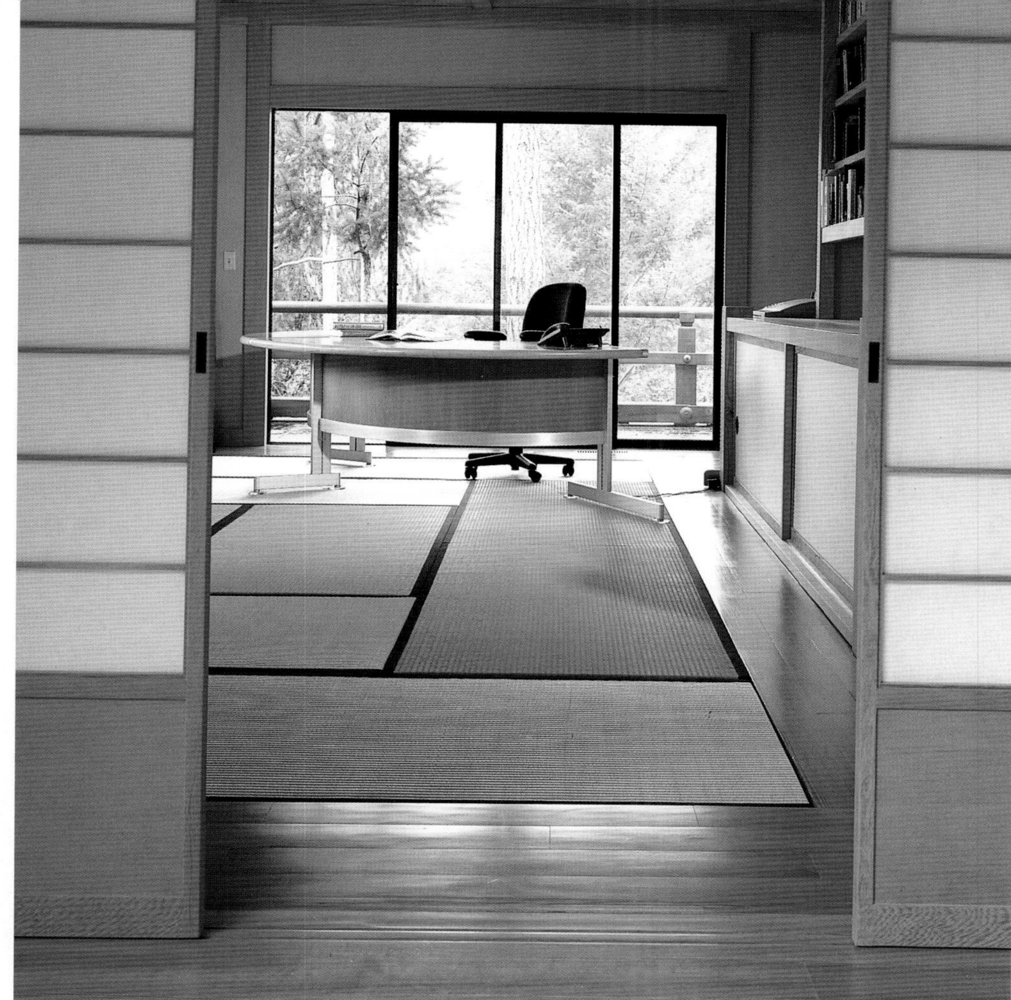

An imaginative area rug in a home office gives the illusion of overlapping tatami mats beneath a desk, a look reinforced by the Shoji-screen-like doors. Yet the rug's two colors add a whole new dimension to the cleanly styled space.

Complementing breezy wicker furniture with white cotton cushions, wall-to-wall natural sisal seems to bring the outdoors into a garden room. Because the natural sisal won't fade, it performs well in the room's unforgiving sunlight.

An oversized sisal rug warms the slate floor of a very organically designed great room. A smaller, colorful Oriental rug that matches the room's pillows is layered on top of the sisal between the sofas, further emphasizing the sitting area.

specialties

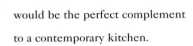

IF YOU'RE LOOKING for an inspired floor, consider the materials highlighted in this section—including concrete, leather, and steel— which are exemplary models of forward-thinking choices. They are relatively new to residential flooring, but you've probably seen these flooring materials in offices, shopping centers, and other commercial spaces. The materials take on a fresh look when used in the home.

Of all the specialties, concrete is the most prevalent material for new home floors. Although not inexpensive, concrete is relatively less costly than leather or steel and packs a powerful design punch. It also lends itself to experimentation. You can have seashells embedded in the concrete flooring of a beach house, for example, or small pebbles added in a home that looks out on a mountain stream. Leather can be quite luxurious and a bit indulgent when used as flooring. Envision a leather-floored den complete with a comfortable chair and your favorite books. A stainless floor, on the other hand, would be the perfect complement to a contemporary kitchen.

For a more budget-conscious approach, you might consider using a touch of one of these materials to accent your floor. For instance, if you like the look of metal, you could use a metallic border with a ceramic tiled floor. Or if you have your eye on leather tiles for a home library, you could create a leather-floored reading nook and use wood flooring for the rest of the room. Specialty flooring materials can now play a unique role in home flooring design.

Bands of amber-colored concrete cut across the eating area in front of a kitchen peninsula. A lighted toe-kick beneath the peninsula cabinetry illuminates the perimeter of the floor, highlighting its mottled texture.

Cast in place, wedges of neutrally colored concrete fluidly follow the unusually curved walls of a great room.

A cast-concrete floor in a sun-drenched room mimics the look of vintage terra-cotta tiles—from pillowed surfaces to wide contrasting grout lines—while providing a more forgiving floor.

A floor of naturally shaped leather lends an air of timeworn elegance to a living room filled with Mediterranean antiques. Each piece of leather is a slightly different shade from the adjacent one, emphasizing each individual shape.

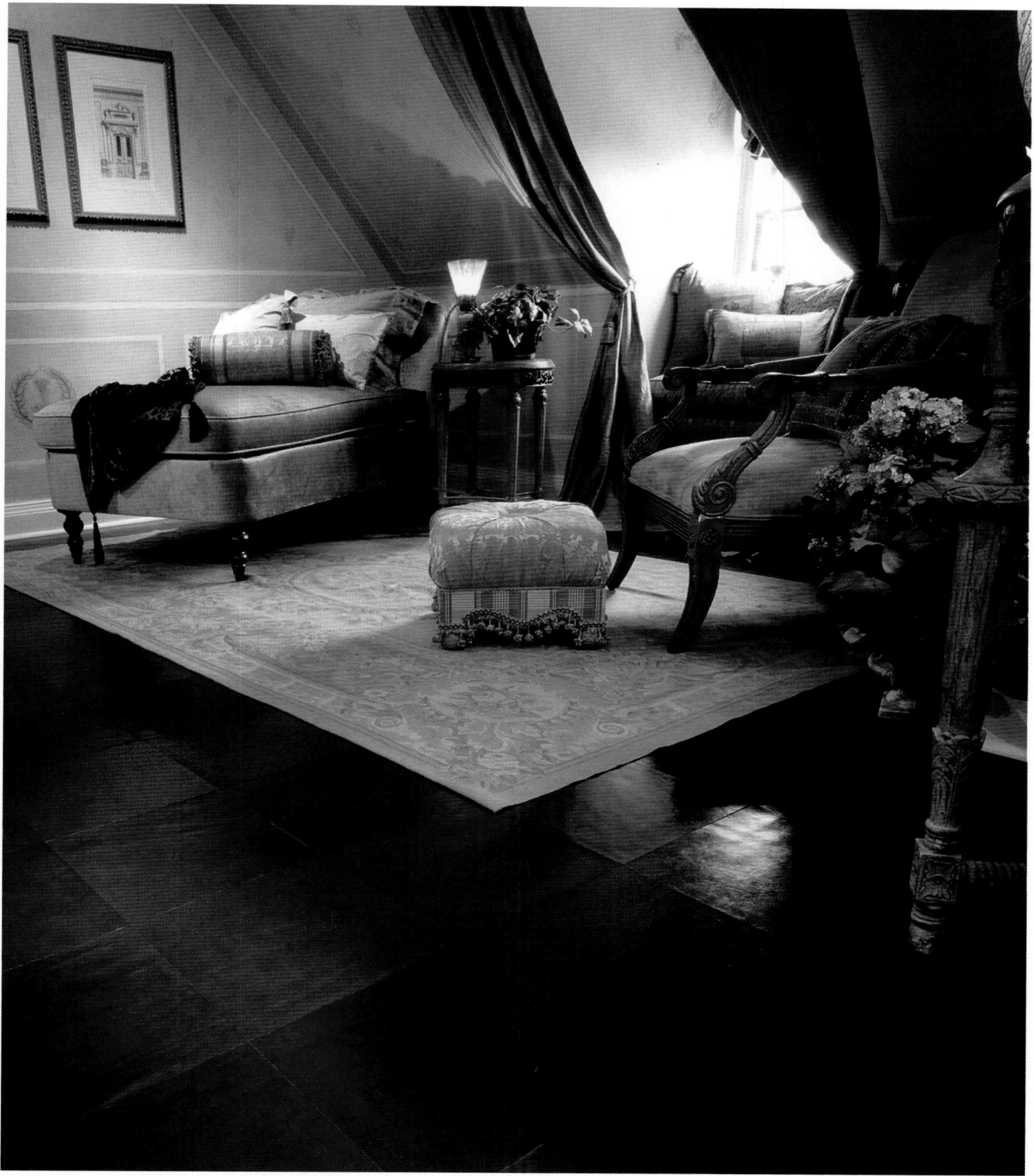

Square leather tiles bring a richness to the sitting area of an under-the-eaves bedroom. The floor's deep brown shading complements the room's creamy upholstered furniture. A wool area rug protects the floor from both direct sunlight and scuff marks.

Varied shades of natural leather floor tiles set the tone for an Asian-inspired living room filled with modern furniture. The leather floor abuts an interior rock garden. An area rug protects the room's main gathering place.

Triangular shapes of red leather form a uniquely creative floor for a loft dining room. Beyond the canvas that separates the dining space, hardwood floors run through the more highly trafficked areas of the loft.

A double row of textured metallic floor tiles follows the perimeter of a porcelain tile–covered living room floor. Metallic diamonds inset between the porcelain field tiles repeat the theme across the entire surface.

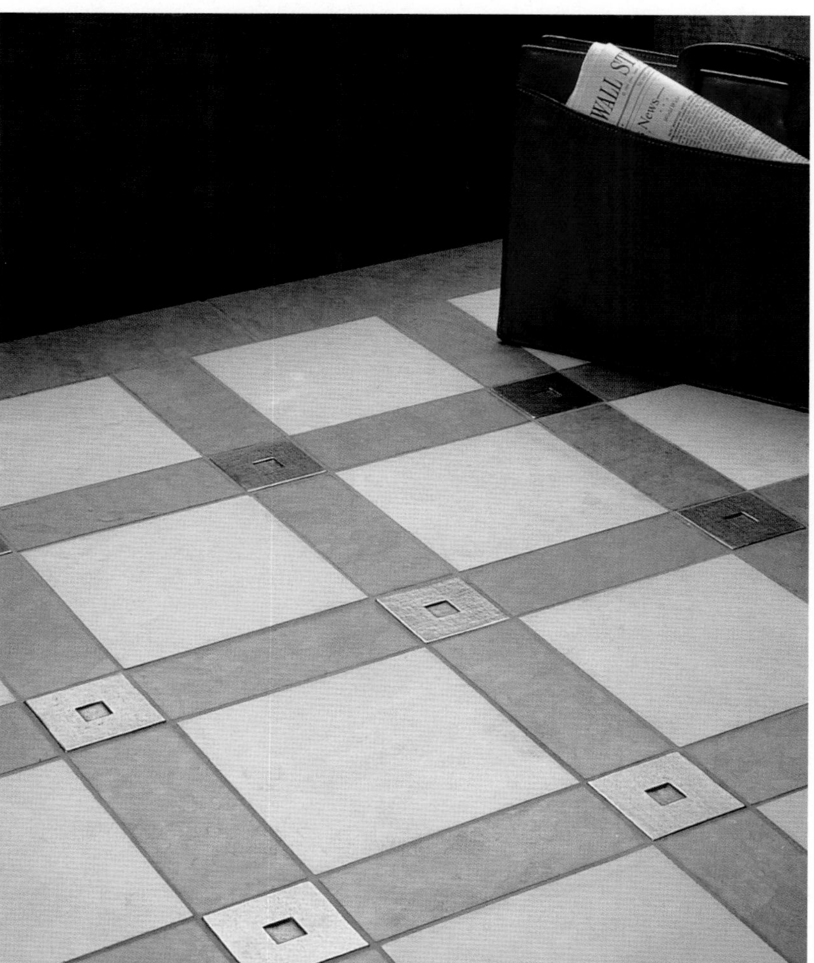

Steel foundry art tiles bring renewed interest to a traditional tiled floor. The art tiles are strategically placed in the center of the floor, where they provide the most impact. As a cost-saving measure, no steel pieces are used at the perimeter.

A SHOPPER'S GUIDE

CHOOSING FLOORING MATERIAL isn't necessarily easy. Not only is there a tremendous range of types of materials to choose from, but each type of flooring material also has its own subset of choices. The daunting task of choosing one (or maybe a mix of two or three types) might leave even a seasoned flooring expert a bit bewildered, especially if it was the expert's personal residence that was under renovation. But don't be overwhelmed by the fact that this is *your* home. Find the look that you like, and there is certain to be an appropriate solution for your floor. **THIS CHAPTER** is designed to help you make sense of all the options available for your floor. Now that you've browsed through the flooring images shown in the Great Ideas section, you probably have an idea of the flooring materials you like. Read on for more specific information on the flooring you're considering.

Ceramic Tile

A COOL-TO-THE-TOUCH CHAMELEON

There are two major types of ceramic floor tiles (also known as pavers): quarry tile, which is extruded from natural clay or shale, and tile made by the "pressed-dust" method, which includes ceramic and porcelain pavers.

Is it possible to tell which is which just by looking at a tile? Actually, yes. Since quarry tiles are made by an extrusion process, you can identify them by the grooves on their backs. Pressed tiles, on the other hand, have raised points or grids on the back.

Both types of ceramic tile are very strong, and both can be glazed or unglazed. In fact, glazed tiles can present a great number of design options. Some factories apply 15 or more layers of glaze material to a tile simply to make the tile look more natural.

Keep in mind that although you can use glazed tile on your floor, you need to check its glaze-wear rating. You don't want to place glazed tile in a high-traffic area where the glaze will wear down too quickly. On a scale from 0 to 5, a floor tile's glaze-wear rating can range from 2 for light traffic to a high-traffic 5.

Diagonally set sand-colored ceramic tiles designate the cooking area in a family kitchen. A pebbled mosaic border of stone separates the diagonal tiles from straight-on field tiles.

Quarry tile

Extruded to provide uniform density, rugged quarry tiles perform extremely well in high-traffic areas. Available in a range of earthy colors, sizes, and shapes, quarry tile can be glazed or unglazed, though unglazed is more popular.

Quarry tile

Most quarry tile comes unglazed in the clay colors of yellow, brown, rust, or red. It can be made very thick and therefore very strong. When it is extruded, a dense surface forms that reduces the staining and porosity of the unglazed surface. The resulting tile has a water absorption rate of less than 5 percent, which makes quarry tile a good candidate for high-traffic areas and hardworking kitchens. Unglazed quarry tile will last much longer than a glazed tile whose thin glazed surface will wear off eventually.

Ceramic pavers

Ceramic pavers made by the pressed-dust method can have a waterabsorption rate from 0 to 5 percent, but generally manufacturers make them with 2 to 3 percent absorption to improve bonding and to make cutting somewhat easier.

Glazed ceramic pavers can have textured, matte, painted, or photographic finishes. Unglazed pavers, such as earthy terra-cotta or saltillo tiles, will be more absorbent than their glazed cousins and should be sealed for protection against surface water and stains.

Porcelain pavers

One of the most misunderstood tiles, porcelain tiles have a water absorption rate of less than 0.5 percent. They are so dense they can be left unglazed and will last a very long time. Until recently, the color ranges and finishes of unglazed porcelain pavers were limited and considered more institutional, but that's no longer true.

CERAMIC TILE

The popularity of stone has resulted in glazed ceramic pavers taking on its texture. A great variety of shapes and sizes is available in ceramic pavers, which usually have matching wall tiles.

PORCELAIN TILE

Because of its durability, easy maintenance, and through-body color, porcelain is an ideal choice for a floor that replicates stone. Tiles can be finished with simple sanding, so chips are less likely to show.

PHOTOGRAPHY ON CERAMIC TILE

Porcelain pavers come in a wide range of styles and colors, emulating natural materials from terra-cotta to slate. The oversized formats of recently introduced porcelain pavers are also gaining favor.

So what's the catch? There are consequences to making a tile with a near-zero water absorption rate. Because of its density, porcelain tile needs to be physically supported while the adhesive sets. Also, porcelain tile is much harder to cut. You'll need a diamond wet-saw.

There is also a slight chance of staining with unglazed porcelains. Manufacturers are solving this by adding a clear glaze to the surface of the "unglazed" tile.

Mosaics

Mosaic tiles, once popular in prewar residences, are small porcelain tiles that measure about 2¼ by 2¼ inches at the maximum. They are generally sheet-mounted at the factory to save time in installation. They, too, are strong and have low water absorption.

Because they are small, mosaics can follow a contour, as in a shower floor. Mosaic tiles also allow for multiple drainage channels in wet areas to improve slip resistance. They recently have become quite popular as accents to larger tiles.

Glass

Often used as an accent to a ceramic tiled floor, glass is another material being constructed into tiles. Glass tiles are impervious to moisture, making them useful for kitchens and baths. And they can be eco-friendly too. Many companies are manufacturing glass tiles from recycled bottles and other glass products.

Trim units

Although not as ornamental as wall tile trims, paver trims are available to coordinate with tile flooring. Paver trims, such as bullnoses and cove bases, serve a functional purpose. They typically round out hard edges on stair treads. Or they can be used as a finish molding rising a few inches up the wall around the perimeter of the floor and along cabinet toe-kicks.

Many intricate mosaic designs and color combinations are available as pre-mounted sheets. It's rare today to see a hand-laid mosaic design. Some ceramic mosaics set in grout are available as large tiles.

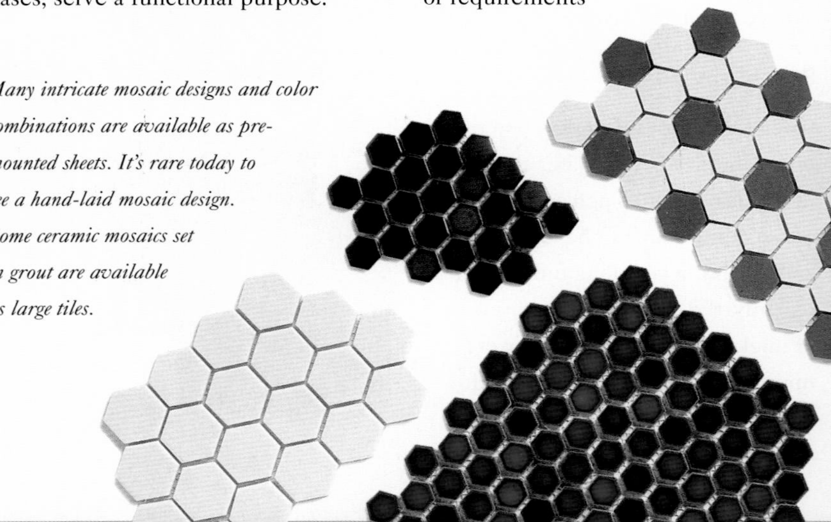

Color and shade variation

Because of the handcrafted nature of ceramic tiles, the Ceramic Tile Distributors Association (CTDA) has implemented a color/shade variation program. The CTDA found that some customers were disappointed when their tiles arrived in varying colors. Although these random variations are part of the beauty of a handcrafted tile, you might not want the diversity. Check the CTDA color/shade designation for your tile. It can range from V1 (uniform appearance) to V4 (substantial variation). If there is no CTDA designation, ask your dealer about the variations you can expect.

Also, when installing tile, it's good practice to blend the tiles from several boxes to avoid any shade shifts from lot to lot.

Slip resistance

There's no question—some ceramic tiles are slippery. Yet there are no national standards or requirements for slip resistance or coefficient of friction (COF). For practical purposes, however, the COF for floor tile is measured. Knowing the COF of your tile can help you make a sound choice at the beginning. For instance, the Americans with Disabilities Act (ADA) recommends a COF of 0.6 or greater on flat surfaces and 0.8 on ramps and inclines. If you have seniors or disabled persons in your household, you may want to take the COF into consideration.

There are also other ways to ensure a safe floor, such as choosing a tile that allows for well-placed grout lines or increasing the size of your grout joints.

A tiled floor can be made more slip resistant by applying slip-resistant coatings. The down side to having a no-slip floor? The more slip resistant a tile is, the harder it is to clean.

Care and cleaning

Because floor tile is water-resistant, spills and dirt stay on its surface. That makes tile pretty easy to clean. The best approach is first to sweep away or vacuum debris and scrape off any thick substances. You can use nylon scrubbing pads to remove stains from both tile and grout, but never use steel wool. Once the debris has been cleared, then damp-mop using a pH-neutral cleaner with no abrasives. One trick of the trade is to add glass cleaner or rubbing alcohol to your bucket of cleaning water to prevent streaks after it has dried.

To further protect your investment, you may need to seal certain types of tile, including some quarry tile, terra-cotta tile, and others. Grout sealers may be recommended for cement-based grouts. Ask your dealer if your floor requires sealing. Sealers need to be stripped and resealed periodically.

Installation

Because a ceramic tiled floor calls for a flat and rigid subfloor, it's likely that your contractor will begin by removing all your original flooring material. The contractor then will cover an uneven or damaged floor with an underlayment, typically cement backer board. Next, the contractor might assemble a few rows of tile to get an idea of how the overall pattern will fall. The next step is to comb out adhesive or pour a bed of mortar and set your tiles in it. The contractor will trim tiles as necessary. After all the tiles have been set, the contractor will grout the joints with a cement-based grout (or an epoxy grout when setting tile in areas that will be subject to temperatures in excess of 100°F, such as shower stalls or on floors with radiant heating).

There should be a soft joint (or control joint) that is caulked, not grouted, when tile abuts another plane (or material), such as between a tub and the floor, in corners, or between wood and metal or tile. Control joints control where cracks may occur in your flooring system. Overall, it takes grout about a week to cure. Once the grout has cured, a grout sealer can be applied if needed.

Reflecting the brilliance of gemstones, glass tiles can bring a translucent or iridescent quality to a room. They come in all sizes, shapes, and finishes, from glistening mosaics to opaque brick-shaped pavers. A few lines are crafted from recycled glass.

Stone

NATURALLY REFINED AND SOPHISTICATED

For the most part, natural stone can be used anywhere that ceramic tile can be used. It can be left in its natural rough-hewn state or cut into geometric shapes, including mosaics. And thanks to new technologies, stone is now more competitively priced than ever before. Color and veining patterns are the major distinctions among natural stone. Limestone, marble, granite, slate, and terrazzo are the most common types of stone used for flooring. The one caveat is that the heavy weight of a masonry floor requires a well-supported subfloor.

RIGHT: Randomly set tumbled limestone tiles in two sizes cover the floor and tub facing of a master bath.
BELOW: Limestone tiles are available in a range of soft colors. Etched tiles and mosaic designs can be used as accents.

LIMESTONE

Limestone

Limestone does not show much graining. It has a smooth, granular surface and varies in hardness. Although limestone is most often seen in creamy white or yellow tones, it also comes in black, gray, and brown. Limestone is more likely to stain than marble.

Marble

Marble, with its veining, is one of the most elegant stones, but susceptible to staining. Featuring one of the widest color ranges in natural stone, marble is available in black, cream, red, white, green, gold, gray, and pink. Some marbles are heavily veined, such as Nero Marquina with its ebony color and white veining, while others, such as Golden Spider, are lightly

TUMBLED MARBLE

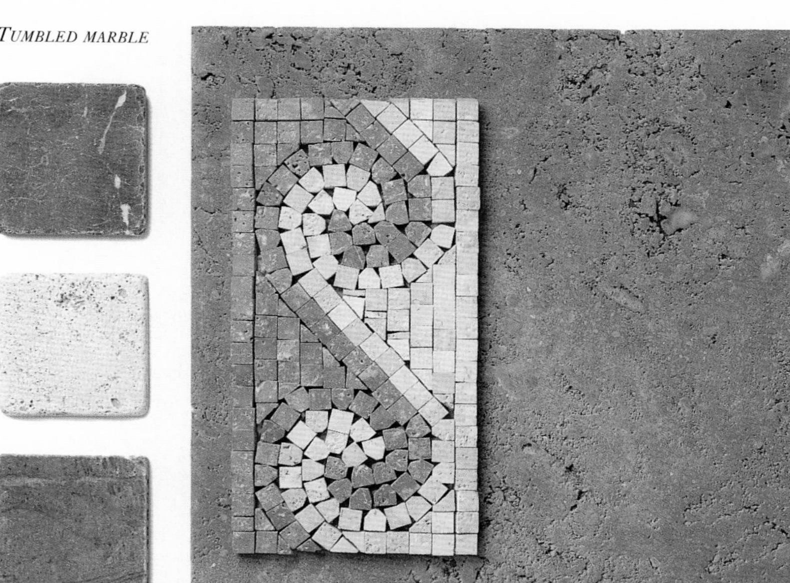

Perceived as one of the most formal flooring materials, marble has two distinct looks. As shown above, marble that has been either tumbled or antiqued has a soft texture. Polished marble in all its true color and veining, as shown below, looks luxurious.

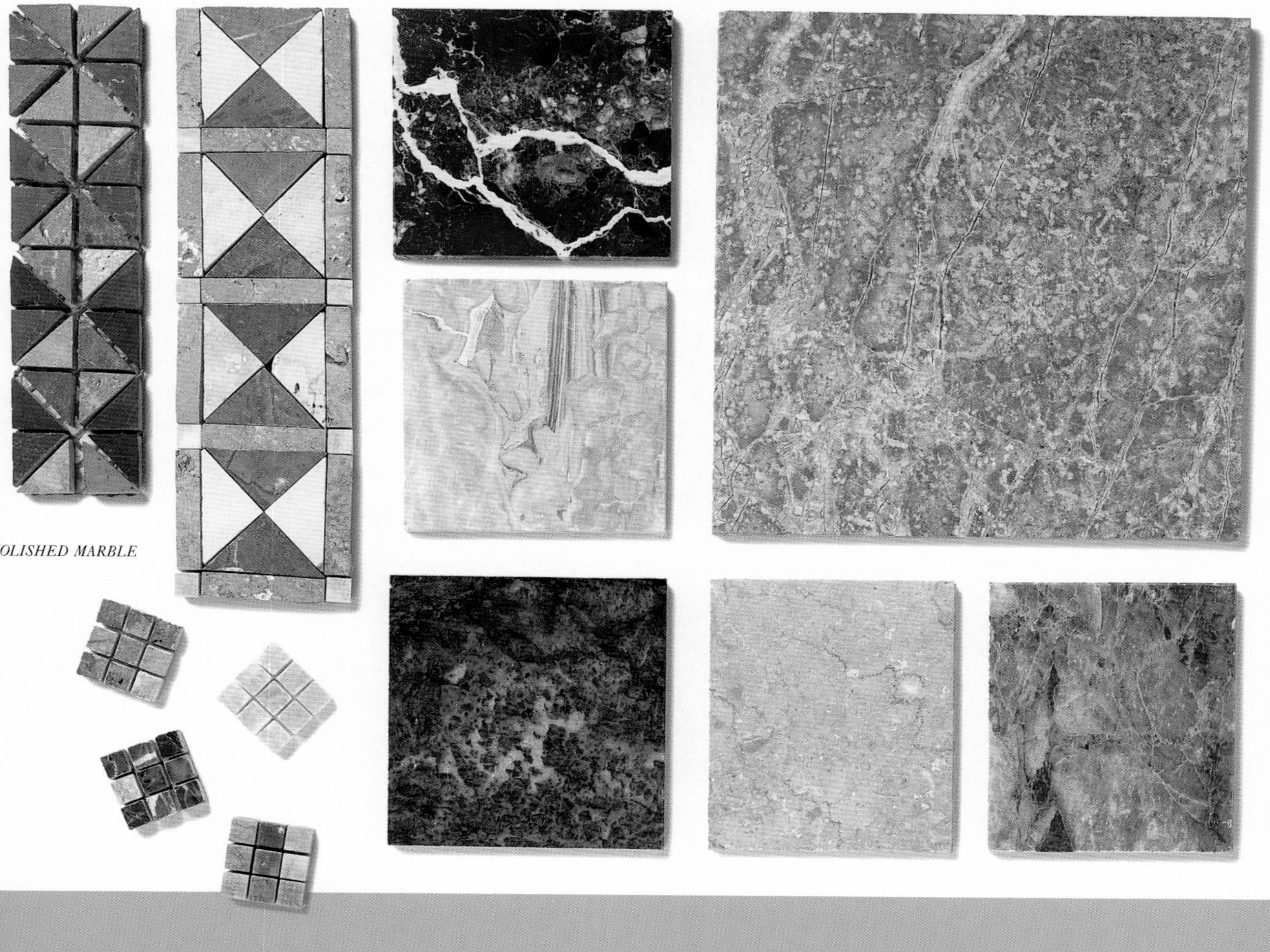

POLISHED MARBLE

veined. Still others, such as Yellow Desert, look somewhat mottled, as if they were sponge finished. And there are also creamy soft classics, like Crema Marfil.

Slate

Slate, a fine-grained stone, tends to be thin and splits along natural grains and fissures, creating a rustic textured surface. Slate usually comes in black, gray, or green, but many interesting variations exist.

Granite

Granite is a close-grained rock with a mottled pattern often combining two or more colors and comes in hues from salt-and-pepper to rich rust tones to black. A very hard material, it is easier than marble to maintain. However, it is porous and will stain.

Terrazzo

Terrazzo, also known as agglomerate stone, is a man-made stone that features marble, granite, onyx, or glass chips anchored in a binder of cement or nonporous resin. Terrazzo can be poured in place or precast.

Flagstone

You might hear the term *flagstone* used in reference to stone paving. Flagstone is simply a generic term for flat slabs of paving stone, usually slate or limestone. These slabs often feature irregular edges and frequently are used outdoors for patios and pool decks, although many flooring

Often seen in shades of gray, slate tiles (above) are available in marvelous colors from reds to yellows to greens. Eye-catching patterns of granite (below) are favored in slab format, presenting a seamless floor.

Slate

Granite

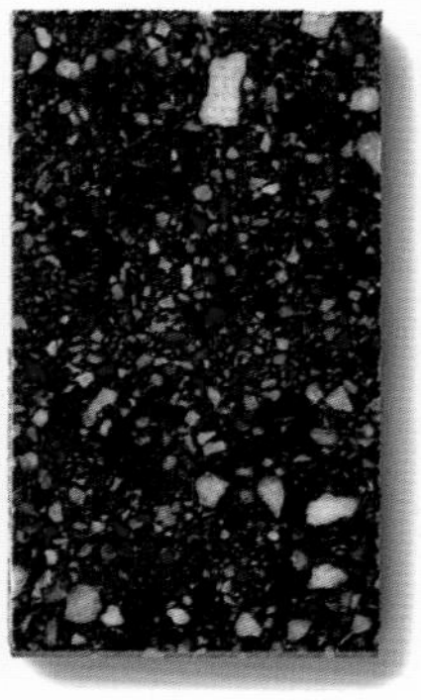
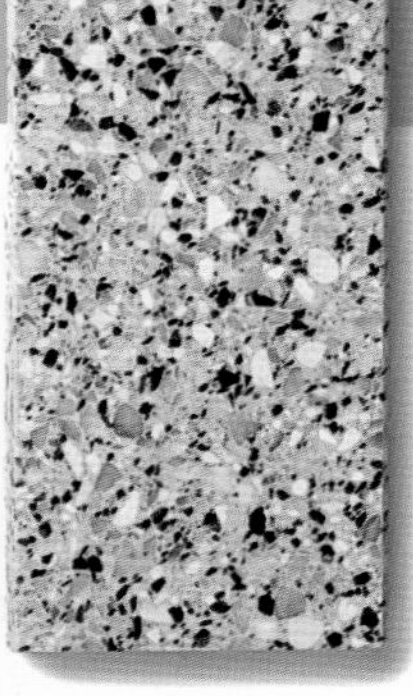

Terrazzo

The irregularly shaped chips in terrazzo, small or large, one color or multicolored, create a wealth of patterns and textures in this man-made stone.

designers are bringing this rustic look indoors to garden and sunrooms.

Surface finishes

Not only does a variety of natural stones exist, but there are six main types of surface finishes that you can choose from. More textured finishes are being favored today, as opposed to the high shine from past decades. Their gain can be attributed in part to better slip resistance, but it's due mainly to their matte appearance.

A honed finish has a flat to low sheen and appears very smooth, although it may be porous. A polished finish creates a glossy surface that brings out the color of a stone. A polished surface is very smooth and not very porous but will wear with time. A flamed finish creates a rough surface developed through intense heat. The surface is very porous. A tumbled finish, created by tumbling pieces of stone, results in a slightly rough, worn texture. A sandblasted finish results from blasting stone with a pressurized flow of water and sand. It creates a textured surface with a matte gloss. A sawn finish shows the rough, circular path of a diamond-tipped saw blade. A bash-hammered finish is a textured surface created by a pounding action.

Water-jet options

You might see precut stone medallions, borders, or inlays when shopping for flooring. These look fabulous and will add a custom touch to your floor. New water-jet cutting techniques allow these special pieces to be crafted quickly and affordably. Usually designs are created first on computer. Then the design is used to guide the water jets through the stone cutting.

Care and cleaning

Dust-mop your stone floor frequently with a clean, untreated, dry dust mop, and it will last for many years. Dirt and grit do the most damage to a stone floor. Area rugs inside and outside an entrance will help keep abrasives to a minimum. Blot up spills immediately, and use a pH-neutral detergent or stone soap to clean your floor. Do not use vinegar or lemon juice.

Sealants

To protect against staining and acid damage, you should apply a sealant on porous stones and finishes. You can choose to seal minimally with a stone soap or more intently with a penetrating sealer and a hard wax. Whatever sealer you select, test its appearance on a sample of your stone before applying it to the floor.

Installation

The irregularity of natural stone calls for a thick cushion of mortar to compensate for varying thickness. If working with a wood subfloor, your contractor may want to protect it with felt and possibly a layer of wire mesh to prevent the mortar from cracking. Your contractor will likely work in sections, spreading the mortar in stages. The mortar should set for 24 hours. Then the joints will be filled with similar mortar. A sealer can be applied once the mortared joints have dried.

Wood

AN AGE-OLD CLASSIC WITHSTANDS THE TEST OF TIME

When you choose wood, you're choosing one of the warmest, most time-tested, and versatile flooring materials. And one that looks better with time.

Types of wood

Many wood species are used for flooring. Each one has its own natural color, markings, and advantages.

Oak flooring comes in either white or red. The color of white oak runs from a creamy white or light brown to medium brown. It's a bit harder than red oak, has smaller markings, and has a more uniform appearance. Red oak is reddish brown, and its open grain makes it somewhat porous.

Maple flooring runs from pale white to light reddish brown. It has a uniform texture and closed grain and is very hard, harder than red oak.

Pine, considered a softwood rather than a hardwood like oak or maple, was commonly used in early American flooring because of its natural stability. Longleaf heart pine (on a par with red oak) and southern yellow pine are the hardest of all pines. Minor dents and dings will happen over time but tend to enhance a floor's character.

Bamboo flooring is similar to oak in dent resistance and is much more dimensionally stable than most wood flooring. Because bamboo is harvested from grass and rejuvenates itself to maturity in three to five years, it is environmentally friendly. It comes in both vertical and flat-grain patterns and in a light natural and a darker amber color.

Strips of reddish-brown Bankirai, a smooth and very durable tropical wood from Indonesia, on the floor of a living room will ultimately weather to an even richer shade.

Cherry is appreciated for its warm reddish coloring, straight grain, and smooth texture. It looks sleek when sanded and finished and is frequently used for cabinetry. Of medium density, it is dimensionally stable upon kiln drying.

Mahogany, an extremely durable high-density wood, has a deep reddish brown color and very fine graining. Mahogany encompasses a few different timber species. It was first discovered in the West Indies but now, due to sustainable harvesting, comes from Mexico, and Central and South America.

Teak, similar in strength to oak, is naturally resistant to insects, fungus, termites, and temperature shifts. Recently brought back into vogue through sustainable sources, it has a distinct shading that varies from yellowish brown to dark golden brown. Its grain runs straight, although its texture can be uneven.

Types of construction

Wood floors can be made from solid wood, from engineered wood, or from reclaimed wood.

Solid wood is any wood that is one piece from top to bottom. It performs best in a moisture-controlled environment. Engineered wood flooring is made of cross-stacked layers of base wood with a veneer top layer of your choice of wood. Engineered wood flooring is more dimensionally stable and can be installed where solid wood cannot because of moisture. Reclaimed or recycled woods are made from boards salvaged from old buildings or river bottoms. The salvaged pieces can be 60 to 70 years old and sometimes come with a history. Since this wood usually comes from old-growth forests, it is harder and denser than new-growth wood. Typical reclaimed species include chestnut, hickory, cherry, and oak.

Sizes

Wood flooring started as planks or wide boards; then the standard moved to 2¼-inch-wide strips and later to 1½-inch strips. Now there's a broad range available. Strip flooring still ranges from 1½ to 2¼ inches wide. Plank flooring ranges from 3 to 8 inches wide. Parquet is another form of wood flooring that involves decorative cuts of wood pieced together to

Many popular wood species are being used for floors today. Each one shown here is its natural color—no stains were used—and has its own particular markings. Wood can be chosen by color or level of hardness.

Oak

Maple

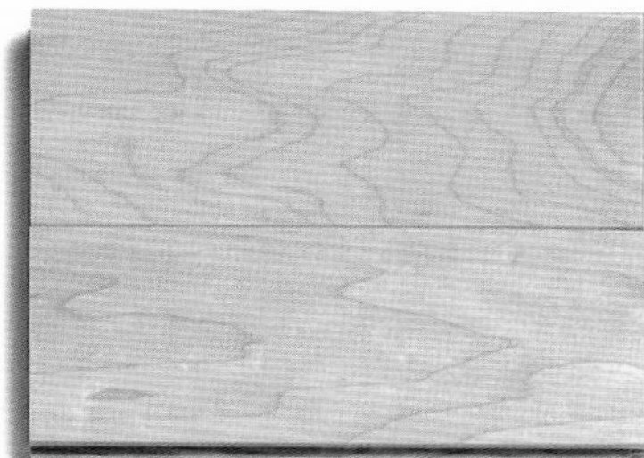

Mahogany

Teak

Vertical bamboo

Horizontal bamboo

Brazilian cherry

American cherry

Rustic hickory pecan

Fumed white oak

Geometric field patterns and corner designs

create a geometric design. The pieces are usually held in place by nails or with adhesives or with both.

Grade

Different species of woods have different standards. The higher the grade, the clearer the wood. Oak has three basic grades. Select oak is mostly clear, but shows some natural characteristics, such as knots and color variations. No. 1 Common oak shows light and dark colors, knots, flags, and wormholes. No. 2 Common oak is even more rustic. Maple has three grades ranging from Clear, with limited character marks, to No. 1 Common and No. 2 Common, with more characteristics of the species. There are various grades as well as hardnesses of pine flooring. Within each type of pine—yellow, white, or heart, the grades range from a rustic country look with all of the wood's characteristics to a clear wood.

Cut

The angle that a saw cuts a piece of wood determines its cut. The three standard hardwood cuts include plainsawn, quartersawn, and riftsawn. Plainsawn, which shows growth ring patterns, is the most common.

Quartersawn wood is more refined and less susceptible to moisture, but it's also more costly. Riftsawn wood is cut at an angle slightly different from quartersawn wood.

Finishes and treatments

To finish a wood floor, you can choose a surface finish made of synthetic resin or use a penetrating stain or wax. Surface finishes are available in high-gloss, semigloss, satin, and matte. But your choices don't end there. Surface finishes include oil-modified urethane, moisture-cured urethane, conversion varnish, and water-based urethane. Moisture-cured urethane is the most durable of these finishes, yet it's the hardest to apply. With a two- to three-hour drying time, water-based urethane dries the fastest.

Penetrating stains and waxes will soak into the pores of your wood floor and harden to form a protective seal. If you wax your floor, you should only use cleaning products specifically made for wax finishes. Also recognize that these same stains can be used to mimic the inlays of exotic woods.

As wood floors grow more popular, many homeowners are turning to faux finishes for cost-effective custom looks. You can paint hardwood floors of any type, whether they are old or new and whether the finish was applied on-site or in the factory. Paint professionals recommend water-based paints for best results.

Although experts caution you may weaken your floor, wood flooring can be bleached for effect too. Bleaching wood involves brushing the wood with caustic soda or ammonia and applying hydrogen peroxide.

If you're looking for a whitish finish, pickling may be a better choice. By rubbing white paint into your wood flooring, pickling will highlight its markings.

Inlays

Ready-to-install, prefabricated wood tiles with medallions, starbursts, and borders are available through most wood flooring dealers. Most of these off-the-shelf designs are laser-cut creations. At one time, such designs needed to be hand-cut and so were quite costly. These prefabricated pieces let you affordably mix and match to create your own patterns. Preplanning your floor design is crucial if you decide to use an inlay.

Care and cleaning

Dirt, grit, and sand pose the main threat to a hardwood floor. They act like sandpaper on a floor's finish, resulting in scratches, dents, and dulling. Placing floor mats or area rugs at your home's entrances will help trap dirt and prevent damage. It's also important that you wipe up spills right away, and when you vacuum be sure to use a vacuum with a brush attachment, not a beater bar. After vacuuming or sweeping, you may damp-mop your floor using a neutral-pH wood cleaner. If your floor is sealed properly, water won't damage it.

Installation

To allow your wood flooring to acclimate, it will probably be delivered to you about four days before installation. The most popular way to install a solid wood floor is to nail down unfinished solid wood flooring to a wood subfloor (usually 3/4-inch plywood) or joists (or glue parquet tiles directly to a concrete slab), then sand it and apply a finish. If you can bear the dust and fumes, this method provides the most design options. Wood flooring can be made to lie end to end, or it can have a tongue-and-groove construction that fits together like a puzzle. Prefinished flooring is sanded and finished in the factory, cutting on-site job time by at least half. Floating installations, in which planks are joined to one another rather than a subfloor, are used for engineered wood floors. Some engineered wood flooring can be nailed down, which requires a wood subfloor.

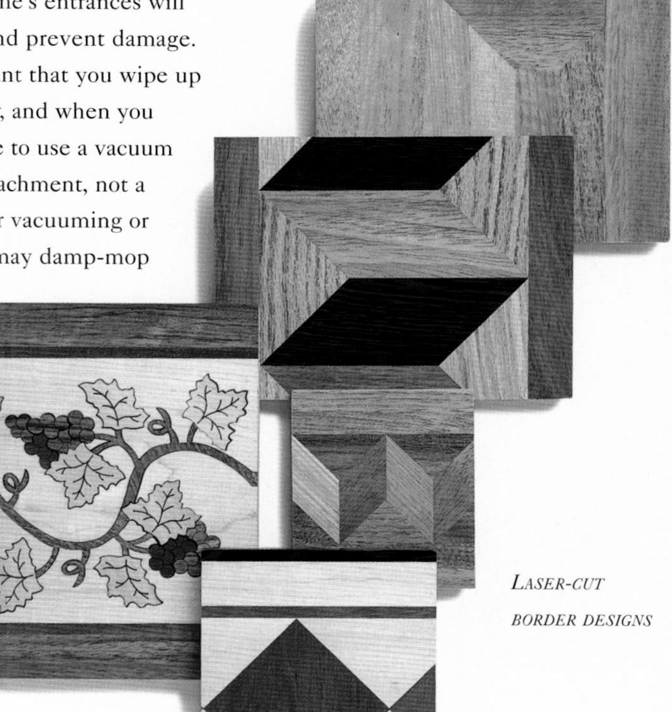

Laser-cut border designs

Resilient

EASY CARE AND GOOD LOOKS, TOO!

New advances have made resilient flooring more appealing than ever. Not only have protective finishes been developed that make resilient flooring more durable, but manufacturers are employing new technologies to replicate traditional flooring materials, including stone, slate, and tile. At the same time they are enhancing the unique properties of resilient flooring. Embossing and luminescence give dimension to resilient flooring, while metallic finishes are being used as accents. The most popular resilient flooring is vinyl, but linoleum has recently made a comeback in its full retro glory. Cork and rubber also fall under the resilient flooring category. More custom design options are available if you choose a commercial resilient. For a custom design, you'll need the help of a designer.

Vinyl

Vinyl flooring comes in tiles or sheets, features a foam or vinyl core layered on a backing, and is finished with a design layer protected by a wear surface. Or vinyl flooring can be inlaid with vinyl granules fused on a backing of vinyl or felt. A vinyl backing will offer more resilience.

There are three types of vinyl surfaces: no-wax, urethane, and enhanced urethane. No-wax resists scuffs, scrapes, and some stains but requires occasional polishing.

Urethane surfaces will stand up better to scuffs, scrapes, and stains. They hold their polished finish longer than a no-wax finish.

Enhanced urethane outperforms both no-wax and urethane surfaces.

Linoleum

Linoleum was invented in the late nineteenth century and extensively used as flooring in tiles and sheets until the 1960s. This durable material, being made from flax, is ecologically sound. The name *linoleum* comes from *linum* (Latin for flax) and *oleum* (which means oil). Linseed oil, which is derived from flax and rosin, is oxidized to create linoleum cement. This cement is then mixed with wood flour and limestone and poured over sheets of jute backing material. It is allowed to cure to reach the desired flexibility and resilience.

Cork

Cork, which comes from the outer bark of oak trees, has been used as a flooring material for more than a century.

Cork flooring is durable, provides acoustical and thermal insulation, and is resistant to moisture and decay. It is harvested from trees in a sustainable manner and comes either as cork floor tiles or most recently as tongue-and-groove cork flooring.

Vinyl

Linoleum

Rubber

The inherent properties of rubber flooring tiles are durability, natural resiliency, and low maintenance. Like cork, rubber is dimensionally stable, sound absorbent, and recyclable. As its styling improves and the number of design profiles grows, rubber flooring is gaining favor in homes. It's great for wet areas and recreation rooms. Some rubber flooring claims to self-heal from scratches and abrasions.

Care and cleaning

The trick to keeping resilient flooring in good shape is good preventive care. You need to protect your floor against indentations and furniture damage. Make sure your furniture legs have large-surface, nonstaining floor protectors. Glides should be covered with felt pads. Also check to see that rubber wheels are nonstaining.

You will need to protect a resilient floor from dirt. Using mats at your home's entrances will help keep grit to a minimum. You'll need to be sure that your mats feature latex backing rather than rubber, which may stain your floor. Because extreme heat and sun pose a threat to a resilient floor, you need to draw your window coverings during strong sunlight to minimize fading. On a regular basis, you'll need only to sweep or vacuum your floor and then mop it with a pH-neutral cleaner.

Installation

Resilient flooring needs 24 hours to acclimate before it's cut. Afterward, an installer will either trim resilient sheet flooring in place or cut from a template of the room, allowing for expansion due to changes in humidity. There's usually no need to remove existing flooring if it's in good condition. In fact, if your existing floor is an old resilient floor, it might be advisable not to remove it because some old resilient products contain asbestos (today's resilient flooring does not contain asbestos).

Most resilient tile is self-adhesive, basically peel and stick. If your new sheet flooring requires a seam and is being applied over an old floor, the installer will offset the two seams. The installer will then either apply adhesive to the entire surface area or to the perimeter of the floor, and use a roller to tightly bond the flooring to the subfloor, and a seam sealer to bond the seams.

Rubber

Cork

Laminate

EUROPEAN STYLING MEETS EASY MAINTENANCE

Laminate flooring was originally developed in Sweden during the early 1980s, making it one of the newest flooring materials available. Constructed of a sturdy core made of recycled materials, laminated with several layers of paper, topped by a design layer, and finished with a protective coating, it is valued for its durability, ease of installation, and ease of maintenance. Some early concerns arose regarding laminate flooring that chipped or delaminated and about the hollow sound produced when laminates were walked on. In response to those complaints, laminate flooring has improved significantly over the last 20 years. Today's laminate amazingly resists dents, burns, and stains. Pads have been developed to place beneath laminate flooring to absorb the sound of footsteps. Best of all, laminate

A laminate floor looks like smooth hardwood planking. Laminate panels are laid perpendicular to one another to designate a transition into an adjacent room. Base trim conceals the expansion areas.

Stone laminate

Wood laminate

flooring now can be used in any room, including kitchens and baths.

With these and other improvements, warranties have been extended from 10 years to 15, then to triple 15 (warranty against stains, wear, and water damage), then to 25 years, and now to lifetime. Some manufacturers have divided their lines into different grades to reflect warranty length.

Styling

Laminate styling also has improved greatly. At first, all laminated floors emulated wood flooring, simply because that was the material in demand at the time. Since it's the top design layer that features the image of your desired flooring, almost any type of material can be replicated. Now you can choose many variations of wood looks, from birch to maple to walnut, including patterns such as herringbone and checks, and blocked and plank floors. Imitation stone laminates mimic varying shades of marble, granite, limestone, and more.

Trim pieces

Laminate floor systems include all the accoutrements you'll need to finish your floor. Laminate wall bases and quarter rounds come in colors and finishes that complement the floor. There are also transition moldings for use where a laminate floor meets a different flooring material, such as carpet, tile, stone, or wood. Laminate threshold moldings are available to use in doorways, as are step moldings for staircases.

Care and cleaning

To protect a laminate floor, it's important that you place area rugs or mats at the entrances to your home and use felt protectors and rubber casters on furniture. Other than that, a laminate floor will require only sweeping or vacuuming and damp-mopping. For tough stains, such as ink, it's safe to use nail polish remover or alcohol on laminate. There is no need for stripping or waxing a laminate floor.

Installation

Laminate flooring can be installed over almost any existing flooring, so long as it is smooth and well bonded. Unlike traditional wood floors, laminate floors are installed as "floating floors." Simply put, the floor is not physically attached to the subfloor. Adhesive attaches the laminate boards to one another only. There are also tongue-and-groove laminates that don't require adhesives. They just click into place. Expansion areas are left along the perimeter of the finished floor, allowing it to expand and contract as necessary with temperature and humidity changes. The expansion areas are concealed by the wall base trim.

Carpet

NOT YOUR TYPICAL WALL-TO-WALL ANYMORE

Carpeting is available in a greater variety of patterns, color combinations, and constructions than ever before. In addition to providing design, carpeting enhances your home by absorbing sound, insulating against cold, cushioning your feet, and helping to prevent slips and falls. Carpets come either as broadloom for wall-to-wall applications or prebound as area rugs.

When shopping for carpet, look for performance rating guidelines. These ratings are based on traffic performance. Typically, they are based on a 5-point scale, with 4 or 5 being best for the highest-traffic areas.

Fiber

Fiber is carpet's basic ingredient. There are five basic types of carpet pile fibers: nylon, olefin, polyester, acrylic, and wool. Plant fibers such as sisal offer another choice. Fibers can be blended to combine the best characteristics of each in one carpet. For instance, sisal can be blended with wool for optimal feel and wear resistance. Most carpeting in the United States is made of nylon, and for good reason: It is wear resistant and resilient, withstands the weight and movement of furniture, and comes in many colors. It also resists soils and stains.

Leather trims the border of a natural-color wool area rug featuring dual-level loop construction, a design that replicates the look of sisal carpeting.

SISAL

Natural-fiber sisal is a great neutral floor covering but should be used only in dry areas because it is susceptible to moisture and staining. It can get slippery and is not recommended for stairs.

Olefin (or polypropylene) is also a strong fiber. It, too, resists wear and stains and static electricity. It holds up well against moisture, which makes it suitable for indoor/outdoor rooms.

Polyester maintains its color and looks the most lush when used in thick, cut-pile textures. Polyester is also easy to clean and resistant to water-soluble stains.

Acrylic looks like wool and costs much less. It has a low static level and is moisture and mildew resistant.

Wool has been touted through the ages for its overall performance. It is soft, has high bulk, and comes in many colors. However, it can be more expensive than synthetic fibers.

Pile

The construction of a carpet's pile gives it a distinct texture and pattern. There are three main construction techniques: level loop, multilevel loop, and cut pile. Sometimes, in much the same way fibers are blended in a carpet, these techniques are combined to add even more dimension.

Level-loop pile features loops at the same height. It is informal and includes the popular Berber carpets. It doesn't show footprints, so it works in high-traffic areas. In general, the tighter the loop, the more durable the carpet.

Multilevel-loop pile, with loop heights at two or three different levels, creates interesting patterns. It, too, is durable and has a casual look.

Cut-pile carpet means that the loops are cut, creating tufts of yarn. It has a more formal look. The type of fiber, density of tufts, and amount of twist in the yarn all play a role in the durability of a cut-pile carpet.

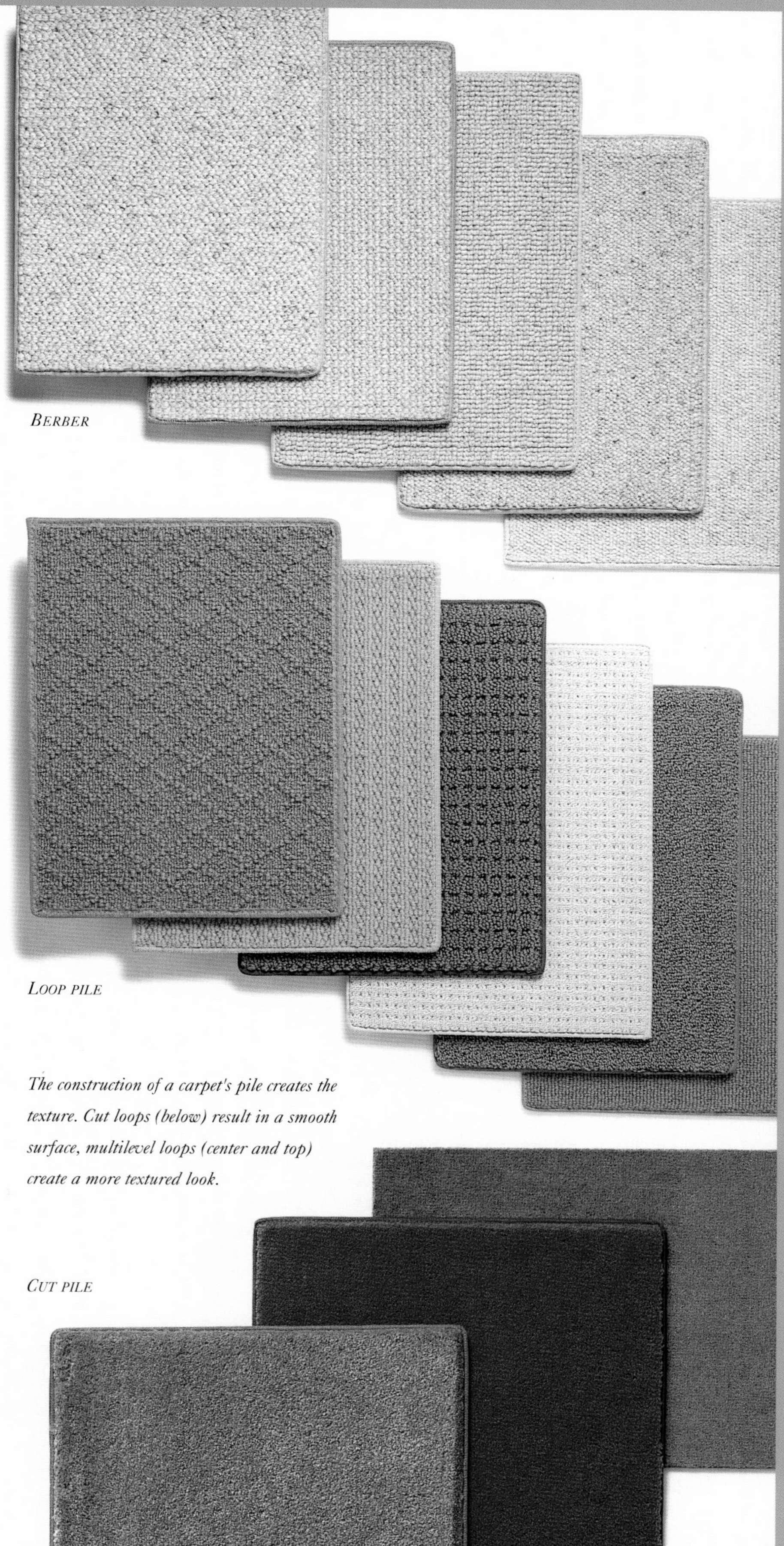

Berber

Loop pile

The construction of a carpet's pile creates the texture. Cut loops (below) result in a smooth surface, multilevel loops (center and top) create a more textured look.

Cut pile

Care and cleaning

Many carpets today come with stain protection, soil protection, and static resistance. New stain- and soil-resistant technology makes carpeting and rugs much easier to clean, but it's still important to remove stains as quickly as possible. Always absorb wet spills by blotting, not rubbing. Most homeowners steam-clean their carpets once a year. In between, regular vacuuming is recommended.

Custom options

To further broaden your options, some carpeting manufacturers are offering custom work for both area rugs and broadloom (wall-to-wall). That means you can virtually create your own design using such elements as borders or have your carpet dyed to match whatever color you like. You can also ask for custom binding to finish the edges of your carpet. Carpeting can be bound to any size you need, whether you're looking for an area rug or a wall-to-wall carpet that can be easily removed as necessary. You can also choose a binding material to match or contrast with the carpet, depending on your preference.

Carpet cushion

Using carpet cushion under a carpet makes it feel and look better longer and helps improve insulation. Carpet cushion is made from polyurethane foam, fiber, or rubber, or from recycled materials. The type and thickness of the cushion you'll need varies according to traffic patterns. Bedrooms, dens, lounge areas, and other rooms with light or moderate traffic can use thicker and softer cushion, while living rooms, hallways, stairs, and other heavy-traffic areas require thinner cushion. A quality sisal, however, will be backed with thick latex and won't require cushioning.

Installation

Carpeting can be installed over wood or concrete. First, the installer fastens tackless strips around the room's perimeter. If carpet cushion is desired, it is put down and stretched to fit. Then the carpet is cut to a manageable size. After rolling out the carpet for the majority of the room, the installer cuts additional pieces for

ABOVE: Available in both neutrals and colorful shades, a basic blend of loop and cut-pile construction can be used to execute unique patterns on broadloom carpeting.
RIGHT: Geometric patterns in broadloom carpet in a range of colors create a subtle design on which the décor of the room can rest.

curves and niches. Seams are created where pieces of carpet meet. Using a knee kicker, the installer attaches the carpet to one wall of tackless strips. Using a power stretcher, the carpet is stretched to fit the room. Finally, the installer trims the carpet more closely and cuts out obstacles. In some cases, such as sisal, a direct glue-down installation is recommended in place of tackless strips.

RIGHT: *The shag carpet is back. Shading is more subtle than before, but now there are choices in the lengths of shaggy cut pile, ranging from short and conservative, called frieze, to long and adventurous, called rya.*

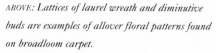

ABOVE: *Lattices of laurel wreath and diminutive buds are examples of allover floral patterns found on broadloom carpet.*

RIGHT: *A closed-loop area rug combining a floral border with a geometric field could be the focal point in a room. Keep in mind that as long as colors coordinate, carpeting patterns need not match other fabrics in the room.*

Specialties

FOR THE FASHION-FORWARD SET

If you're feeling adventurous when it comes to your floor, specialty flooring offers interesting options. While these specialties may seem new to you, they've been used commercially for years. Think of your favorite boutique store or funky downtown restaurant. You're sure to see great examples of specialty flooring there. They come with some outstanding properties. So if your budget permits experimentation, don't hesitate to check out these alternatives.

Poured-in-place concrete covers the floor of a creatively designed kitchen. Natural concrete is inset with wedges of colored concrete in shades of amber, taupe, and green. The colors pick up the brushed steel from the kitchen island and the warm honeyed hues of the maple cabinetry.

Concrete

Concrete's not just for your ordinary gray driveway anymore. Because of its flexibility, it can take on color, texture, and shape, mimicking other, more costly flooring materials. And it offers long-term performance.

Concrete flooring comes precast, cast-in-place, or in the form of concrete floor tiles. It can be poured right over a concrete slab structure. Portland cement, water, sand, and coarse aggregate are proportioned and mixed to produce concrete flooring. Because its hardening process continues for years, concrete gets stronger as it gets older.

Concrete may be colored by adding pigments before or after it is in place, by using chemical stains, or by exposing aggregates, such as marble, granite chips, or pebbles, at the surface. Textured finishes can vary from rough to polished. Patterns can be scored, stamped, rolled, or inlaid into the concrete. Some designers have been known to use divider strips (most commonly redwood) to form panels of various sizes and shapes.

The best way to maintain a concrete floor is to have it sealed. Urethane, epoxy, or water-based sealers are your typical choices. Once the sealer is applied, cleaning is as simple as sweeping and damp-mopping.

Leather

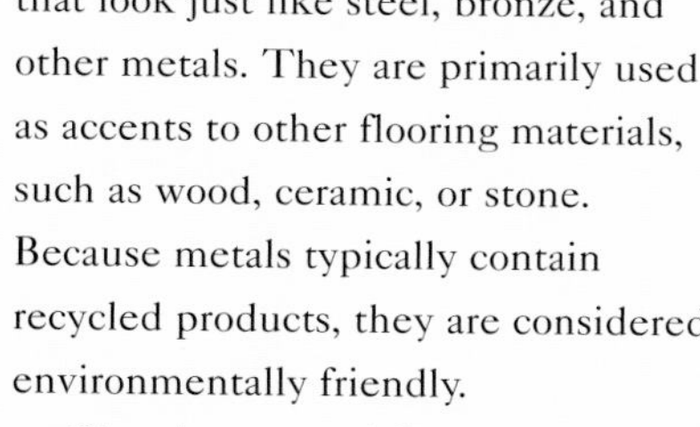

Leather

Leather floor tile is made from the same material as leather-soled shoes. Just like its apparel counterpart, the leather for flooring is tanned and dyed with aniline dye. Well-made leather flooring features a waxed finish that is heated into the material. Available in numerous colors and sizes, leather flooring will develop a patina over time. It possesses great sound-insulating properties and is warm to the touch. It can be used throughout the home but is not recommended for high-moisture areas, including kitchens and baths, or high-traffic areas, such as entrances. You'll probably also want to install a leather floor in areas out of direct sunlight.

It's easier than you'd expect to keep a leather floor clean. You'll need to vacuum your leather floor with a soft brush attachment weekly. Once a month, you can damp-mop your floor. Annual waxing is recommended.

Metal

Metal flooring runs the gamut from sleek stainless steel tiles to industrial-type grated floors. Steel is frequently used for open staircases because of its structural superiority. In addition, metallic composite materials have evolved into tiles that look just like steel, bronze, and other metals. They are primarily used as accents to other flooring materials, such as wood, ceramic, or stone. Because metals typically contain recycled products, they are considered environmentally friendly.

Cleaning a metal floor calls for sweeping with a soft-bristled broom or dust-mopping to remove any loose particles, then damp-mopping with a nonabrasive pH-neutral cleaner.

Metal

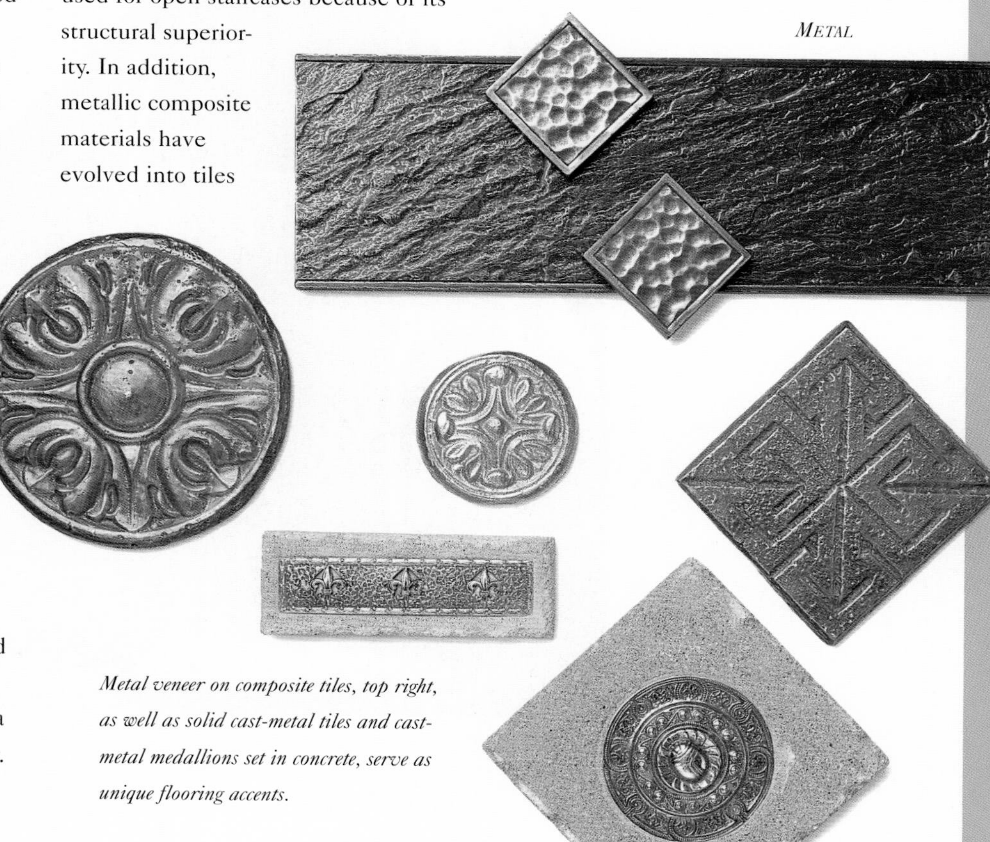

Metal veneer on composite tiles, top right, as well as solid cast-metal tiles and cast-metal medallions set in concrete, serve as unique flooring accents.

Sunset

ideas for great BACKYARD COTTAGES

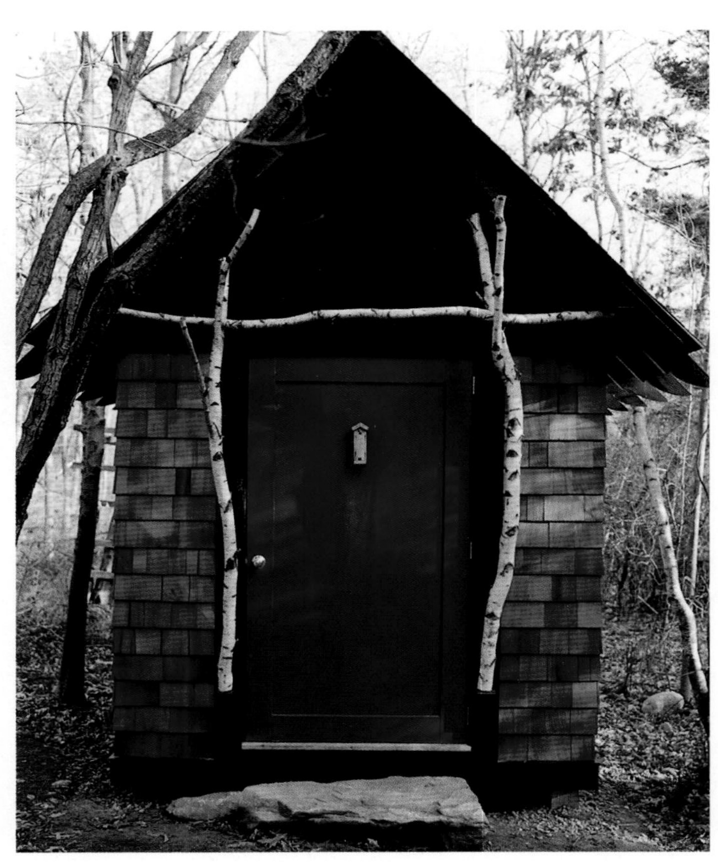

By Cynthia Bix and
the Editors of Sunset Books

Sunset Books ■ Menlo Park, California

contents

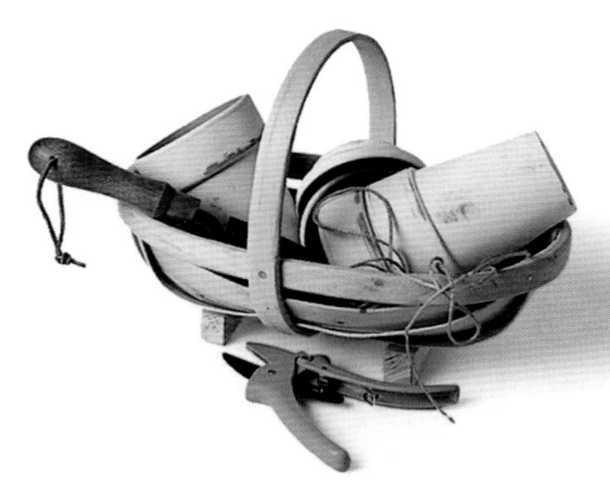

580 Cottage Pleasures

583 Planning Your Cottage

609 A Gallery of Cottages

675 Cottage Elements

712 Index

special features

Professional Profiles **600**

Understanding Architectural Drawings **603**

Roof Roundup **676**

Overhead Options **677**

Paint and Stain Portfolio **678**

Fooling the Eye **679**

Energy-Efficient Windows **680**

Windows Defined **681**

Path and Patio Pavings **685**

Flooring Sampler **689**

cottage pleasures

IMAGINE AN INTIMATE SPACE, beautifully furnished and outfitted with all your favorite things, where you can go to read, work, putter, sketch, drink tea with a friend, or even take a long, uninterrupted snooze. The beauties of the garden—leaves fluttering in the breeze, warm sunshine, birdsong—are all around you.

Now picture that room or space out in your backyard, completely separate from the house. Perhaps it's a one-room hideaway tucked in among the garden foliage, or a bathhouse poised at the edge of a pool, or a dining pavilion set in an expanse of lawn. Such a retreat offers one of life's great delights—the opportunity to enjoy private time, to play, or to entertain your friends in a setting apart from the everyday. It's almost like being on vacation in your own backyard.

Small buildings separate from the main house are a venerable architectural tradition. From the timbered "secret houses" of Elizabethan England to the elegant teahouses of classical Japan, from Victorian summerhouses to enclosed gazebos alongside Dutch canals, such buildings have provided places for contemplation, entertainment, and ceremony for centuries.

For most people, the word "cottage" conjures up a compelling picture. Cottages are the stuff of fairy tales and country villages, of seaside, lake, and woodland—unassuming structures tucked cozily into their surroundings.

Cottages are where generations have dwelt in modest comfort and where, today, people go to leave behind the cares (and often the pretensions) of modern living.

Today, the style we call "cottage" is defined as much by mood as by architecture. Contemporary backyard buildings display a wide variety of forms and serve many functions. A playhouse may look like a little log cabin or an antebellum mansion in miniature. A guest house could be anything from a storybook cottage to a tent cabin. Perhaps your dream potting shed is a small version of a Victorian glass house, or your ideal dining space is an ornate pavilion in the style of an ancient Greek temple. Your cottage can be a unique expression of your own highly individual taste and your most cherished dreams.

The first section of this book, "Planning Your Cottage," introduces you to practical concerns involved in realizing your dreams. For a tantalizing look at an array of design possibilities, turn to "A Gallery of Cottages," beginning on page 609. Finally, for an overview of essential cottage components, see "Cottage Elements" on pages 675–701. Read, absorb, dream, and—begin!

PLANNING YOUR COTTAGE

BE IT A RUSTIC POTTING SHED or a gingerbread-trimmed guest house, a pool house or a home office, a backyard cottage has irresistible charm for many of us because it embodies our dream of a place that's truly our own. This chapter is designed to help you make that dream a reality—guiding you along the journey that leads from your first impressionistic visions to an actual finished cottage in your backyard. YOU'LL BEGIN by thinking about how you want to use your cottage and by taking a comprehensive look at your property—your main house as well as your neighbor's, your yard, and your street. Next, we take you through the steps involved in working with your local planning and building departments, in seeking help from professionals, and in considering feasibility and costs. FINALLY, you'll get a short course in the most exciting and creative aspect of planning your cottage: developing its style and design, both inside and out.

making basic decisions

DECIDING HOW *your cottage will be used is the starting point for nearly all of the choices you'll need to make about siting, structure, design—every aspect of your backyard addition. This is the fun part of the project, when you visualize yourself, your family, and friends using and enjoying your new space.*

How will you use it?

When you dream about your cottage, what do you envision? If you're an avid reader, it may be a tranquil garden hideaway open to gentle breezes. For a painter or a quilter, it's likely to be a colorful, light-filled space with tools and materials close at hand—a place where work can go on uninterrupted without ever having to be stashed away at five o'clock. For a busy working parent, it's an office that provides needed separation from the concerns of the main house; for someone else, it's a gathering place for friends and neighbors amid the beauties of the garden.

As you'll see in more detail later in this chapter, the use you'll make of your cottage will affect everything from its design details to the building regulations that govern its construction. Here are just a few possible ways you might want to use your backyard cottage:

- Mini-retreat
- Guest quarters
- Entertaining/dining space
- Children's playhouse
- Home office
- Arts and crafts studio
- Woodshop
- Potting or tool shed
- Pool house

Of course, you may put a backyard building to more than one use. A craft studio with cupboards for supplies and works-in-progress could double as a casual guesthouse, or a prettily decorated potting shed could also be a hideaway for relaxing in a rocking chair with a good book. It's all up to you.

A charmingly civilized garden shed is a pleasant retreat as well as a practical place for potting plants and arranging flowers.

Where will it go?

The uses you envision for your cottage greatly affect its siting: that is, where on your property it will be placed. This is a matter of simple common sense. A potting shed should be close to garden areas; a hideaway or retreat may be best tucked away along the property edge. An entertainment pavilion benefits from proximity to the main house, while a home office might be best farther away. For more about siting, see "Part of the landscape," page 588.

A crucial aspect of siting your cottage is determining your need for utilities (electricity, gas, water, sewer, telephone). If you envision a

At the end of a garden path, a guest cottage draped with roses and wisteria nestles beneath shade trees, extending an invitation to come and stay awhile.

SAME SPACE, DIFFERENT USES

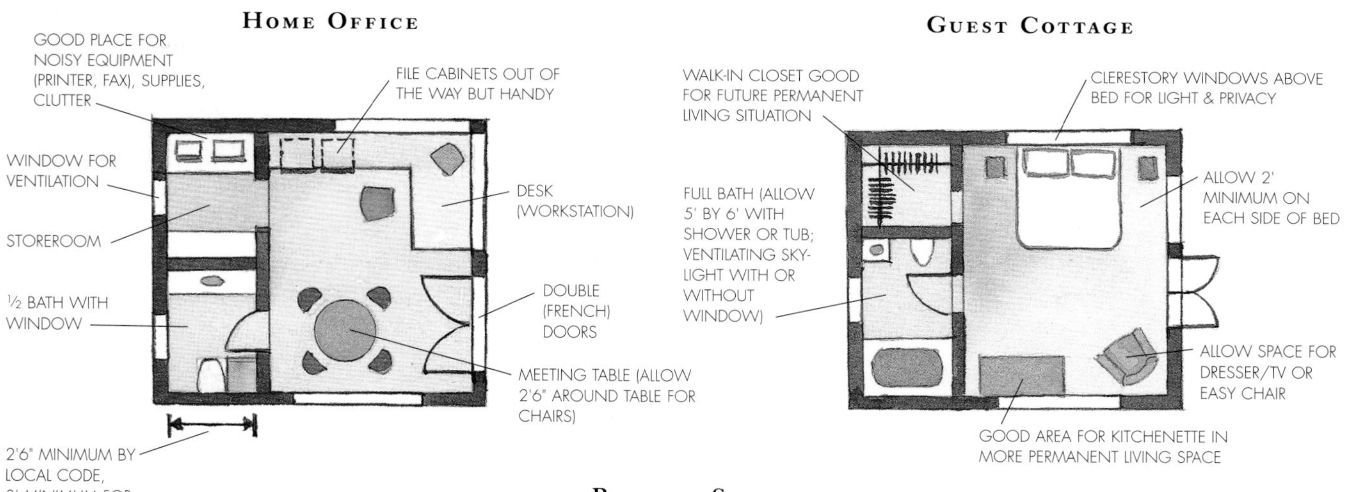

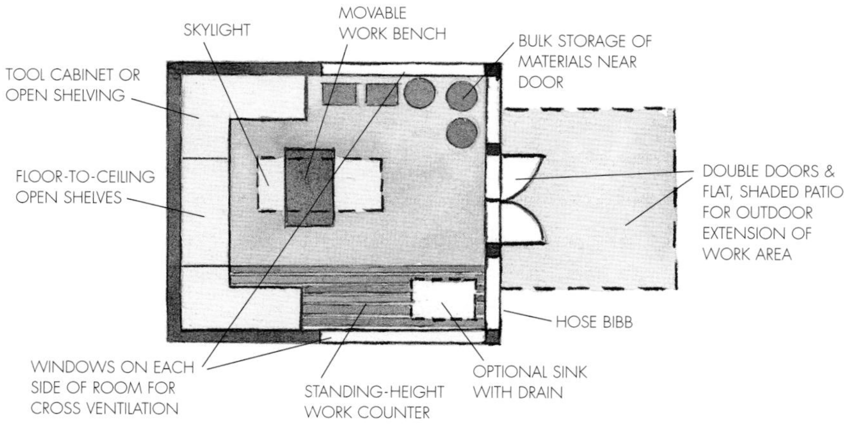

Constructed with Spanish cedar siding and trim of recycled redwood, a classic cottage blends gracefully into its woodsy surroundings. Equipped with kitchenette and bath, it can function as a guesthouse or an office.

very simple space—a freestanding screened retreat, for example—in which to relax during the daytime, this probably isn't an issue. But if you want water and electricity, your plans become more complicated.

You'll want to find out right away where utility lines and pipes are located on your property and whether you can hook up to them (see page 593), and you'll need to pay a visit early in the game to your local planning/zoning department (see page 597) in order to get an idea of your project's feasibility.

How big should it be?

How much room do you need? This is a case in which "small" really is "beautiful," since much of the charm of a cottage lies in its miniaturized quality. That simple getaway space could be quite small—say, 10 by 10 feet. A guest cottage could be as small as 12 by 14 feet or as generous as 20 by 30 feet.

A tape measure is your best tool for getting a rough idea of the space you need. Go through your home, or that of a friend whose rooms you like, and take down the dimensions of various rooms. How big is a comfortable bedroom or a small playroom? How much counter or desk space does a home office require? Looking through books about remodeling specific rooms can also be helpful in determining dimensions. Don't forget that a tiny cottage can also gain a feeling of expansion with the addition of a small porch, a deck, or even a bay window.

Your tape measure will also help when you're considering the furnishings and equipment you want to include. Will you want to do yoga in your cottage? Measure the length of your yoga mat. Are you going to use the space for weaving or designing with fabrics? Measure your loom or your cutting table and sewing machine table.

Of course, storage is important, too. You'll need shelves and/or cupboards for those fabrics, that yarn, or your dishes. How many books do you want on the shelves of your reading lair? If you're planning a shed for potting and puttering, gather your tools, a typical assortment of pots, and other necessities to see how much space they take. Plan for more storage space than you think you need, if at all possible.

Looking ahead

No matter how you intend to use your cottage now, it's wise to think ahead to different ways you might use it in the future. Circumstances change: children grow up and move out, parents move in, or a home office becomes necessary. It's a good idea to make your space as flexible as possible. A children's playhouse can be made to a scale that will suit the little ones now but also accommodate a home office when the kids are grown. Conversely, your poolside cabana may be a perfect space to transform into a separate dwelling for your child-become-teenager. Your summerhouse (perhaps with some special adjustments) may make way for an elderly parent.

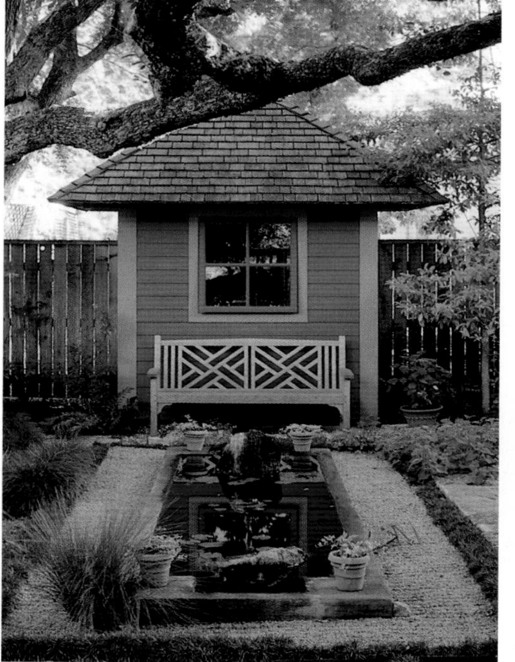

The elegance of this little shed belies its humble function as a storehouse for garden gear. Its handsome roof line and accompanying Chippendale-style bench make it a focal point in the carefully designed landscape.

To allow for such eventualities, it's a good idea to include utilities in your cottage from the start or make sure that they will be relatively easy to add later.

It could be a children's playhouse, but the tiny structure at right, just 6 feet across, is used as a potting shed. Inside, a potting bench holds bedding plants and gardening paraphernalia (above). A spirited color scheme—created with tung-oil stains—and decorative trim create one-of-a-kind appeal.

site specific

WHERE YOU PLACE *your cottage will be determined partly by your own desires and aesthetic leanings, partly by local regulations governing the building of any structure, and partly by the nature of the property itself. For an overview of these important considerations, read on.*

Fitted perfectly into the landscape, a handsome pavilion is a focal point at the apex of converging beds of perennials.

New or remodeled?

Will your backyard cottage be entirely new construction or a replacement or renovation of an existing outbuilding? Many properties already have a storage shed, an unused detached garage, or even an old barn. To create a livable new space out of such a building, begin by evaluating its condition, location, and good and bad points. It's a good idea to consult an architect or a contractor for a realistic evaluation.

A new structure built from the ground up on a new site usually must fulfill numerous code and zoning requirements (see pages 596–597). But an existing building that you remodel—or even a new but same-size structure on the same site as an old one—may not be subject to the same requirements. Check before proceeding.

Part of the landscape

When deciding where to place a new cottage, consider both how it will look in your landscape and what you want to see when you are inside the structure, looking out. Do you want to be able to see your cottage from the house or from particular places on your property? You might want to be able to observe a children's playhouse from your kitchen window, but you might want a potting shed or a guesthouse to be largely concealed. Privacy might be called for in a writer's space, but an area for entertaining might benefit from a closer connection with the main house and the garden at large. Also consider access; a potting shed should be near the garden areas it will serve, and a dining area should not require a long walk from your kitchen.

What was once a garage has been transformed into a dazzling poolside guest house. Zoning ordinances dictated that the original 20- by 24-foot size be maintained, but adding a windowed roof monitor and a porch was allowed—to dramatic effect.

No matter what its function, a well-designed cottage can be an attractive feature of your landscape. It can serve as a focal point, drawing your eye to an especially pretty corner of the property or distracting the eye from a not-so-attractive neighboring house. Or it can be a delightful surprise waiting to be discovered around a bend.

Wherever you place your cottage, you will want it to relate comfortably to its surroundings. Perhaps you would like it to be surrounded by trees and foliage so that it looks like an integral part of the landscape. If you can, place it where there are already mature plantings. If that's not possible, find out what fast-growing trees, shrubs, and vines would be good choices for your climate and exposure. And don't forget that flowering plants, in beds and borders or in containers and even window boxes, can add charm and color. In fact, creative landscaping

Flowering plants spilling over and around a structure are the essence of cottage charm. Allow roses to clamber up walls (below and right), or plant a window box with a generous helping of flowering plants and vines (below right).

will help ensure a graceful transition between cottage and garden that will enhance both.

To determine how to orient your cottage, look in all directions from the proposed site to get an idea of available views. You may want to look back at your house or garden from the cottage, or you may want to get a sense of complete detachment, either by partially screening the view with plants or a trellis or by tucking the structure out of sight. If you have a beautiful view toward mountains, a meadow, or a lake, you may want to look out on that. And, of course, you want a "good-neighbor" cottage, one that will not encroach on your neighbors' views, sunlight, or privacy—or be subjected to unwanted sights or sounds from next door.

Consider your climate

In addition to aesthetic considerations, think about your cottage's placement in relation to weather conditions. Is it hot much of the time where you live? Is there a high average annual rainfall? Do you live in an area with dramatic seasonal changes, or in a climate that's relatively mild year-round? These factors affect how your cottage will need to be sited.

THE SUN'S PATH

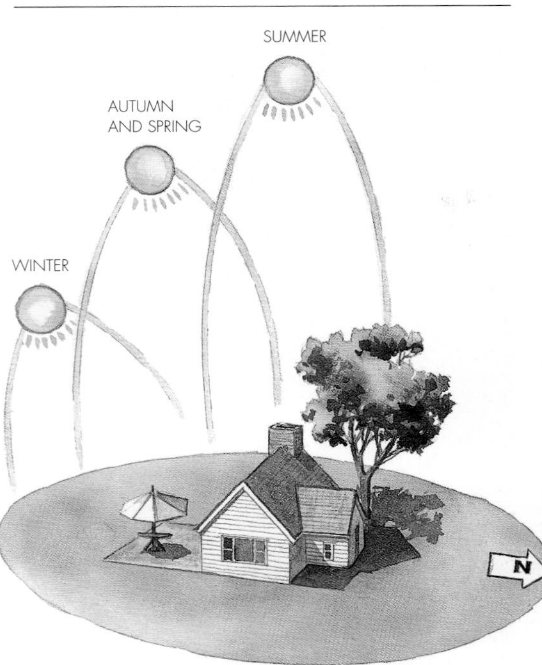

Sunlight strikes your property at predictable angles, depending on the time of year and where you live. The sun's arc is higher in summer and lower in winter.

Tucked away at the end of a garden path, this cottage stays cool on even the warmest afternoons, thanks to abundant shade provided by surrounding trees and mature shrubs.

Do you want a sunny spot or a shaded, sheltered one? In a hot climate—or on especially warm days anywhere—shade is welcome, but most spaces benefit from the sun's warmth and light at least some of the time. Still, you don't want to be trapped in a space that feels like a sauna! Sheltering trees can help, as can shutters, curtains, and nearby water— a fountain or a small pond—to cool the surrounding air. Deciduous trees, shrubs, and vines planted around a structure will afford shade in the summer and let in light and warmth in the winter, when the branches are bare.

Observe the sun's position at various times of the day and, if possible, different times of the year. Generally, a northern exposure is cool because it rarely receives sun. An exposed south-facing location is warmer because, from sunrise to sunset, the sun never leaves it. An east-facing property is cooler, as it receives only morning sun, while a structure that faces west is often hot because it receives the full force of the sun's afternoon rays. These factors will affect where on your property you place your cottage as well as how you orient the building itself. For example, a building with south-facing windows will benefit from an overhang on that side; this will partially shade it from summer sun but let in light in winter, when the sun is lower.

Looking at practicalities

Many other practical considerations will also affect where you site your cottage. These include the configuration of the ground (is it level or sloping?), soil conditions and drainage, other structures and paved areas on your property, zoning restrictions (see page 597), established plantings and trees, and your cottage's relationship to neighboring houses and lots as well as to the street.

You'll also need to consider the locations of utilities—gas, electric, television cable, water, and sewer. In the simplest of scenarios, a potting shed may require water but not electricity; in that case you can either make use of a nearby hose bibb or plumb in a sink, the latter calling for some kind of drainage as well as water pipes. A home office will require electricity and telephone lines but not necessarily plumbing. In the most complex scenario, a fully equipped guest cabin with bath requires a sewer connection, water lines, and electrical hookups.

Seasonal use is another important consideration in determining what utilities you'll need. Will this be a summertime-only retreat, or an all-season one? In all but the balmiest climates, three- or four-season cottages require a heat source (see page 690).

SLOPING SITES

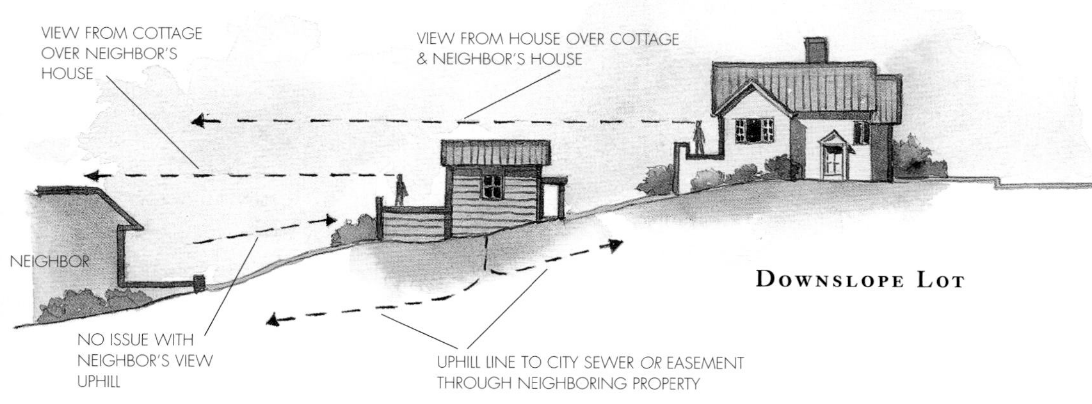

On a sloping lot, you must consider such factors as water runoff and drainage, sewer lines (flowing downhill or helped uphill by means of a pump), and sight lines in relation to neighboring structures.

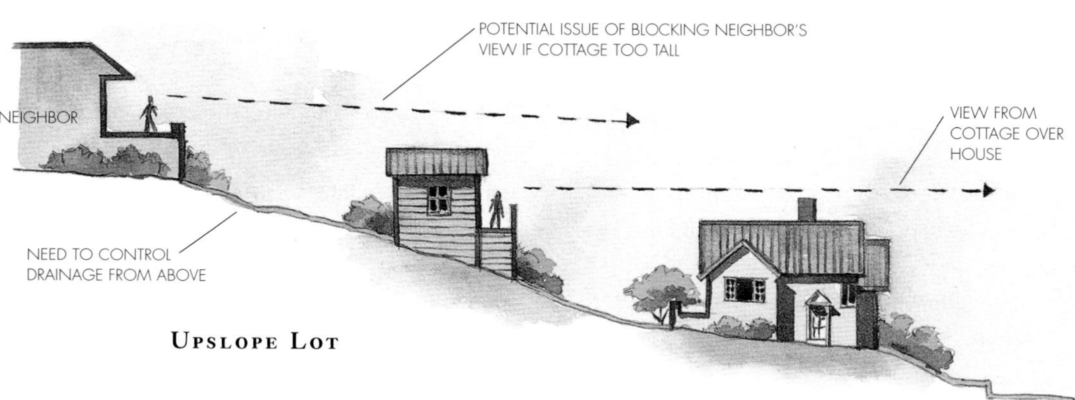

creating a site plan

BEGIN WITH WHAT ARCHITECTS CALL *the "broad brush" approach. The easiest, quickest way to get a general idea of where your cottage should go is to do a small-scale sketch of your property showing the relationships among its various elements—property lines, existing structures, plantings, pavings, and so forth.*

This simple drawing doesn't have to be of professional quality, but it should be neat enough and sufficiently accurate in scale to serve as a preliminary plan to show to your local planning department, your banker if necessary, and perhaps your neighbors. It will also provide a starting point for discussion if you work with an architect or designer and/or a contractor.

With the help of a partner, take rough measurements of your lot and its various features, using a tape measure at least 50 feet long. (Sometimes you can save time and effort by obtaining dimensions and gradients from your deed map, house plans, or a topographical map of your lot. Or they may be available through your city hall, county office, title company, bank, or mortgage company.)

For your rough sketch, use plain paper or a sheet of graph paper with ¼-inch squares. (A common scale for site plans is ⅛ inch = 1 foot.) At this stage, you want to keep your drawing small and simple so that you can focus on the big picture and work through a lot of ideas quickly.

The following information should appear in one form or another on the site plan. Some details, such as the locations of utilities and easements, can be left until later if obtaining the information is problematic at this stage. However, if your property is on a slope, it's important to indicate that on this first sketch.

- **PROPERTY LINES AND DIMENSIONS.** Outline your property accurately and to scale (to within a foot or so), and write its dimensions on the site map. Note the locations of fences and walls, streets and sidewalks, property lines, and neighbors' houses. Right now all of this is still fairly inexact; you may need to obtain more precise surveys when you're further along in the planning process.
- **BUILDINGS.** Show your house and any other structures on your property, to scale. Show relevant doors or windows, such as a door that leads to where your cottage might go or a window that looks out on your backyard.
- **PAVED AREAS.** Show all driveways, paths, steps, patios, and decks.
- **EXPOSURE.** Draw an arrow to indicate north; then note shaded and sunlit areas of your landscape. Indicate the direction of the prevailing wind and note any microclimates, such as hot spots or deeply shaded areas that stay damp and cool all the time.

- **Easements.** Easements give utility companies, local municipalities, or sometimes neighbors the right to enter your property, usually to run electric lines, sewers, and so on. You usually cannot build within an easement.
- **Utilities.** If you're planning amenities that call for installing utilities, you'll need to map sewer, water, gas, and electric and cable television lines. You can do this now or wait until later. But keep in mind that any plumbing requires a sewer connection or a septic tank. (Sewers depend on gravity and must run downhill; otherwise they require a pump.) Utilities for a cottage will almost always be run from the main house and use the same meters.
- **Gradient and drainage.** If applicable, indicate the general slope and any significant high and low points on your property. (A professional topographic survey may be required later, during the design phase.)
- **Existing plantings.** Note established trees, shrubs, planting beds, and borders.
- **Views.** Note all views, attractive or unattractive. If appropriate, you can use a ladder to check views from different elevations. Consider how a backyard building might be viewed from inside the house, from various positions on the property, and from nearby houses or streets.
- **Neighborhood.** Unless you live on a very large property or out in the country, you will probably find it useful to make a rough sketch of your immediate neighborhood as shown on page 18. Evaluating the positions of streets and neighboring houses will help you decide on the best location for your cottage and will also be useful to your local planning department in evaluating the site.

Trying out possibilities

Once you have drawn your plan, you can begin to play with different possible sites for your cottage and with differing configurations for the footprint, or ground floor area, of the building itself. For each scheme, place a separate sheet of

A SAMPLE SITE PLAN

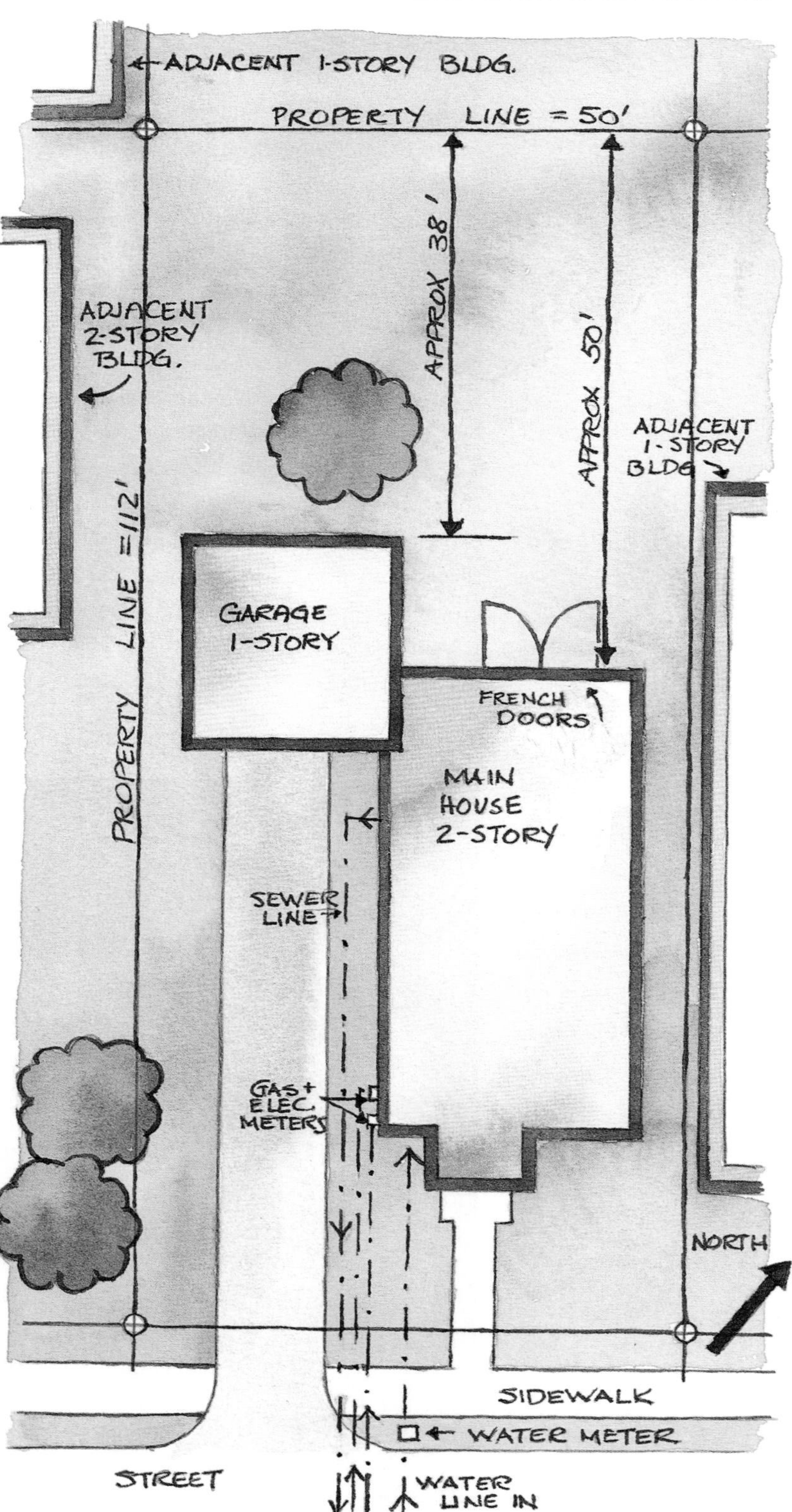

tracing paper over your site plan and sketch in a rough shape to represent the location and approximate footprint of your proposed building. Then you can study how it relates to surrounding foliage, the house, and the neighborhood. To enhance your cottage, you can experiment with paths, patios or decks, and planting areas—elements that provide a transition between cottage and garden.

There's a "flow" among areas in your yard, just as there's a certain "flow" among rooms in your house. Can you create an easy, natural pathway from the house to the cottage? Can you tuck the cottage among established trees, so that it becomes a private retreat? How can you orient cottage windows toward the sun without feeling exposed to the sight lines from your neighbor's second-story deck? Using tracing-paper overlays on your site map lets you try out many solutions to your particular issues until you come up with one that you like.

NEIGHBORHOOD PLAN

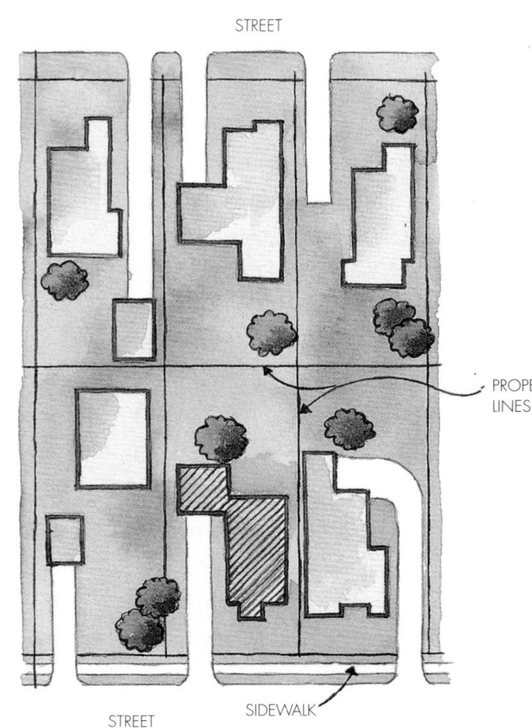

Set above the garage on a hillside lot, this artist's studio required special attention to foundation and drainage issues as well as its relationship to neighboring structures.

ONE SITE, THREE VARIATIONS

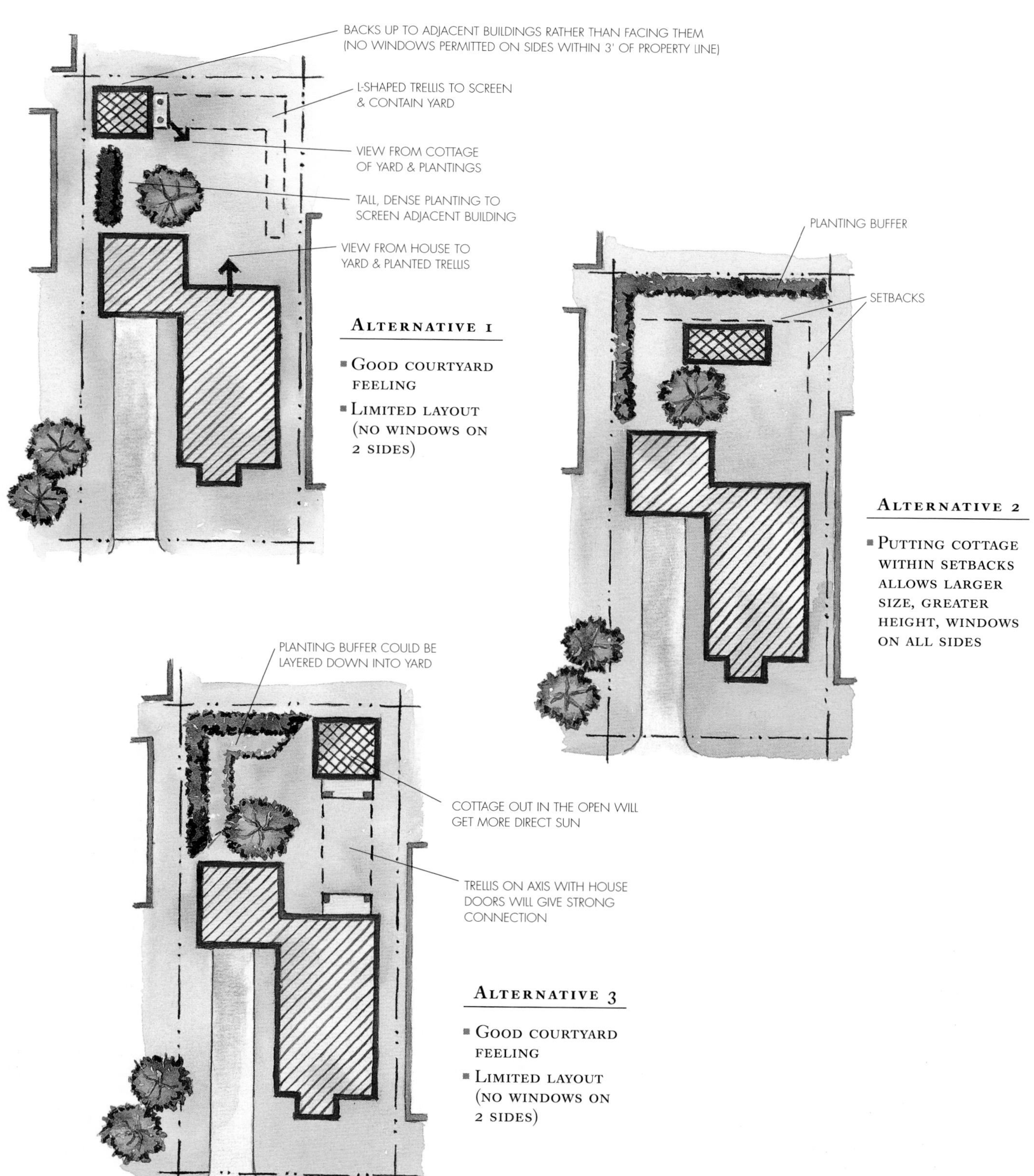
BACKS UP TO ADJACENT BUILDINGS RATHER THAN FACING THEM (NO WINDOWS PERMITTED ON SIDES WITHIN 3' OF PROPERTY LINE)
L-SHAPED TRELLIS TO SCREEN & CONTAIN YARD
VIEW FROM COTTAGE OF YARD & PLANTINGS
TALL, DENSE PLANTING TO SCREEN ADJACENT BUILDING
VIEW FROM HOUSE TO YARD & PLANTED TRELLIS
ALTERNATIVE 1
GOOD COURTYARD FEELING
LIMITED LAYOUT (NO WINDOWS ON 2 SIDES)
PLANTING BUFFER
SETBACKS
ALTERNATIVE 2
PUTTING COTTAGE WITHIN SETBACKS ALLOWS LARGER SIZE, GREATER HEIGHT, WINDOWS ON ALL SIDES
PLANTING BUFFER COULD BE LAYERED DOWN INTO YARD
COTTAGE OUT IN THE OPEN WILL GET MORE DIRECT SUN
TRELLIS ON AXIS WITH HOUSE DOORS WILL GIVE STRONG CONNECTION
ALTERNATIVE 3
GOOD COURTYARD FEELING
LIMITED LAYOUT (NO WINDOWS ON 2 SIDES)

getting down to business

Now that you *have something on paper, it's time to determine whether your project is feasible. This depends on two important factors: your budget and approval from your local planning and building departments. Below, we guide you through these crucial preliminary steps.*

Dollars and sense

Before you proceed too far along with your plans and dreams, it's crucial to take a cold, hard look at budget. Many planned projects never get built because of inadequate attention to this aspect of building a cottage.

For a rough idea of expenses without involving architects or contractors at this stage, use basic square-foot costs in your calculations. The square-foot figure will vary according to where you live, what utilities you want, and other factors. Call around to general contractors in your area (get names from the phone book or from friends and neighbors). Describe your site, how you plan to use your cottage, and access for building equipment and supplies. Ask what a range of square-foot costs might be for such a project, and multiply these figures by the proposed square footage of your cottage. Then you must add building and permit fees, fees for an

This trim-looking office is just a few feet from the fenced property in a corner of the yard. By code, windows are not allowed on the two back walls.

architect or designer if you will use one, and fees for surveys, soil reports, utility hookups, and other requirements.

Once you know what you can realistically expect, you can scale down or expand your ideas according to your own budgetary constraints. Maybe you'll decide you can paint or sculpt perfectly well in a smaller space; or maybe you'll be delighted to find that you can afford to plumb in a small sink in your potting shed.

A visit to your planning department

If you're putting up a simple garden shed on a large country lot, you can most likely go ahead with whatever site and design you choose. But in most places, you must follow specific guidelines governing construction of what's sometimes called an "accessory building."

Your site plan sketch will be your most helpful tool in determining whether your project is feasible. Begin by taking it to your local planning department officials. Usually they can tell you right away about any restrictions. These might include how many square feet your cottage can be, how far from your property line it must sit, how tall it can be, and whether you can build a structure for use as an office to which clients will come. If regulations limit your plans, you may be able to get a variance through the planning department.

You will probably need to deal with two city or county departments, each with its own set of codes or ordinances.

THE PLANNING/ZONING DEPARTMENT oversees the broad picture. Zoning regulates what building uses are allowed—commercial, industrial, or residential. (This may affect a home office, which may require client parking, for example.) The planning/zoning department determines how high your building can be, how much of your lot it can cover, and where it can be placed on the property—specifically with regard to setback, or distance from lot lines. In some circumstances, the planning department may require you to obtain a survey of your lot.

BUILDING RESTRICTIONS

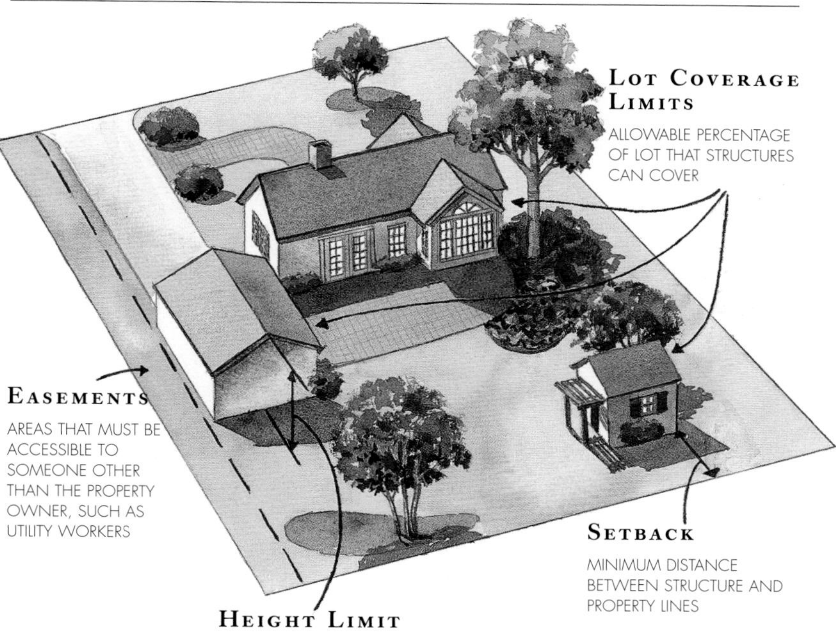

You may be asked to erect "story poles"—a rough framework of vertical 2 by 4s that outlines the cottage's proposed "envelope" (its three-dimensional outline) and shows whether it will block neighbors' views, shade their sunny yard areas, and so forth.

Sometimes the planning department will require a *design review* to decide if certain architectural design standards have been met. In a development community or historic neighborhood, for example, your design, site, and building details—even your choice of trees—may be subject to review by a homeowners' or historical preservation committee.

THE BUILDING DEPARTMENT is concerned with specifications for the building itself—with its safety and structural integrity. The Uniform Building Code, which is similar from place to place, sets standards for materials and construction, addressing safety issues, structural elements, utilities, sewers, and so forth. You must get a permit from this department before you can do any work. An inspector will visit the site periodically during construction and must sign off on the job when it is finished.

launching the process

ONCE YOU'VE DONE *the preliminary legwork, it's time to get down to details. Let's assume your general idea and site for the cottage have been given preliminary approval by the planning department. This is the point at which you begin to make decisions about whether to hire professional help and how much of the work to do yourself.*

Professional help or DIY?

Deciding whether to do it yourself or to use the services of professionals should come early in the planning process, whether you're remodeling or building from the ground up. It's vital to be realistic about your skills and your available time. Building a backyard cottage is basically the same as building a house, except on a smaller scale. It may require everything from laying a foundation to framing and roofing to plumbing and electrical work.

If you are an experienced builder or designer, or if your cottage will be a simple affair on level ground, you may consider designing and building it yourself, either from "scratch" or from a kit or mail-order plan (see facing page). Or you may want to use professionals for some aspects of the project and do some parts yourself.

If you do build it yourself, you can always subcontract jobs you don't feel comfortable doing—pouring a foundation, for example, or doing the electrical work (see "Subcontractors" on page 600). Work on a detached backyard structure usually doesn't greatly disrupt daily life, so the slower pace of a weekend do-it-yourselfer isn't necessarily a problem.

Designed and built by the owner, this shed is roofed and faced with pressure-treated pine plank pieces.

If you decide to hire an architect or designer, you can expect a creative professional approach and a unique and attractive design. You'll usually save time and money by involving these professionals early in the process, probably soon after you've taken your initial site plan sketch to the city building department. Besides creating the design, an architect or designer can help you evaluate your budget realistically, deal with codes and permits, and generally move the project along through construction to completion. To learn more about the work of architects and other professionals, see page 600.

Alternative approaches

If you want an original design created especially for you, your best choice is to hire an architect or a building designer. But two other options—a kit or prefabricated structure and mail-order plans—can work well if you don't require a site-specific building design. Another option is to select a prefab or mail-order cottage or shed but get help from a builder in putting it together. You can also hire an architect to help set it artfully into your landscape or customize details.

Kits and prefabs. Prefabricated cottages and sheds are available in a variety of styles, from canvas-sided bungalows that you erect on site-built wooden platforms to fanciful playhouses or elegant glass summerhouses. Some can be ordered in kit form that an experienced do-it-yourselfer can put together; others require consultation with a company representative, who tailors the design to your needs, then installs the prefabricated components or works with your architect or builder to install them.

Do-it-yourself projects often offer great flexibility, because you can add your own personal touches to the basic prefabricated elements. Approaches vary with the manufacturer.

Look for advertisements for prefabricated buildings in home and design magazines, or do research on the Internet. As with any building put up on your property, you must comply with local planning and building department requirements, which will probably include filing for a building permit. Ask before you order!

Mail-order plans. Garden and building magazines, and some books, offer plans you can send away for. Some books include the plans themselves. Depending on your building expertise, you can use such plans to build a structure yourself or to guide a professional contractor,

On the facing page, a bold two-story structure features a striking combination of barrel and shed roofs—the work of an architect's imagination and expertise. Below, an 8-foot-square enclosed workshop with covered, lattice-screened storage area was built from mail-order plans.

Professional Profiles

Building professionals can help you in a variety of ways, as summarized in the following brief overview. Sometimes a range of services is offered within a single design-build firm, including the work of architects, designers, and contractors.

- **Architects.** These state-licensed professionals have a bachelor's or master's degree in architecture. When you hire an architect, you're hiring a highly trained imagination capable of creating a livable space that's beautiful as well as structurally sound. Architects' fees may be a percentage of construction costs (ranging roughly from 10% to 15%), a lump sum, an hourly rate, or a combination.
- **Building designers.** A building designer may be licensed (by the American Institute of Building Designers or, sometimes, as a contractor) or unlicensed. If you know exactly what you want, these professionals can translate your ideas directly into plans. Hiring an unlicensed building designer gives you less legal protection in the event of trouble, but his or her fees may be lower. Note that even a building designer with a contractor's license may need to subcontract to an architect or engineer for some structural details and calculations.
- **Draftpersons.** Drafters may be members of a skilled trade or unlicensed architects' apprentices. From a design done by you or your architect, they can produce working drawings (from which you or your contractor can work) needed for building permits.
- **Landscape architects and designers.** The integration of your cottage with your landscape is usually an important issue, and landscape professionals can help you create a satisfying relationship between indoors and outdoors, building and garden. Sometimes an architect or building designer will perform this function. But landscape professionals usually have a greater knowledge of plants—how to choose and install them.
- **Structural and soils engineers.** If you're planning to build on an unstable or steep lot or use an unusual structural design, you should consult an engineer. A soils engineer evaluates soil conditions and establishes design specifications for foundations. A structural engineer, often working with the calculations a soils engineer provides, designs the building structure, including foundation piers and footings to suit the site. Engineers also provide wind- and load-stress calculations as required.
- **General contractors.** Licensed general contractors specialize in construction, though some of them have design experience as well. They may do all the work themselves or hire qualified subcontractors while still assuming responsibility for ordering materials, coordinating subcontractors, and seeing that the job is completed according to contract.
- **Subcontractors.** If you act as your own general contractor, it's up to you to hire, coordinate, and supervise whatever subcontractors the job requires—such as carpenters, plumbers, and electricians. You'll be responsible for permits, insurance, and any payroll taxes. Besides doing the work according to your drawings, subcontractors can often supply you with product information and pick up materials for you.

Choosing a professional

To find an architect or designer, begin with the best source of all—personal referrals. Ask friends and neighbors for their recommendations, and look for architects' or designers' signs on job sites. You can also check with local and state chapters of professional organizations such as the AIA (American Institute of Architects).

Once you have collected a few names, interview the professionals to get a sense of what it would be like to work with them. Look at photographs or visit the sites of similar projects with which they've been involved, and talk with the homeowners. Try to find a professional with whom you can communicate easily and whose opinion and taste you trust.

Built from mail-order plans, a cooking cabana has an extra-wide opening for moving patio furniture inside for dining. The window box is the owner's personal touch.

builder, or carpenter. Often, you can use a basic shed plan to construct a structure, then individualize it by adding special design details.

Photographs or drawings of completed structures show you their general look, although details are usually available only with the plans. In addition to specifications for the basic exterior structure, the architectural blueprints offered often include construction details for siding, flooring, roofing, windows, skylights, doors, and extras such as interior shelving, decorative cupolas, and lattices.

Packages usually contain two sets of detailed plans. You'll probably need multiple sets—for obtaining bids and permits, for reference at the building site, and, if applicable, for your lender. Some subcontractors—foundation, plumbing, electrical, and HVAC (heating, ventilation, and air-conditioning)—may need partial sets.

Most mail-order plans are authorized for use on the condition that you comply with all local codes, ordinances, regulations, and requirements, including permits and inspections at the time of construction. Many cities and states now require that an architect or engineer review, stamp, and sign a plan for a large structure prior to construction. To find out if this is true in your area, contact your local building department.

Project phases

Whether you do some or all of the planning and work yourself or hire professionals all the way, the process of designing and building your cottage will probably follow the same basic pattern.

- **Programming phase.** This architect's phrase refers to the stage during which you and/or your architect or designer gather all basic information relevant to your project. Here's where you review your collection of clippings and photos, talk about your ideas and dreams, and collect hard data such as boundary and topographical surveys, utilities information, and planning department regulations. You also become

Tucked beneath the intriguing roof of this summerhouse is a stylish workspace, complete with computer. The elegant octagonal structure, built to custom specifications, was fabricated in sections and shipped to the site for assembly.

practical about budget, getting a clear idea of how much the project is likely to cost and what's affordable for you.

- **Design phase.** This is both the most challenging and the most exciting phase of your project. You and/or your architect will explore design concepts as well as siting options (based on what you've learned from your local planning department). Through a series of rough sketches, both the exterior shape and the interior design will evolve. You might want to experiment right on your proposed site with "story poles" (see page 597) to help you visualize how your proposed building relates to its surroundings.

  Now is also the time to have surveys made by licensed surveyors, if that hasn't already been done and the building department requests them. One kind is a survey of your property's boundaries. The other, a topographic survey showing land contours, is important if your land isn't flat.

  Of course, you will also develop the building's style and design, from the outer "skin" to each interior detail. When it all finally comes together, your architect or designer (or a drafter) will create drawings for submission to the planning/zoning department. These may include a neighborhood plan, the site plan, floor and roof plans, and exterior elevations (see facing page). Once these are approved, final construction documents, or working drawings, can be created from them, specifying materials, products, and finishes as well as all building details. The working drawings will be submitted to the building department for a plan check and a building permit (which may take several weeks) and to any builders or contractors for bidding purposes. They will also serve as guides for the actual construction.

  Now is the time to select a contractor. This may be someone the architect has previously worked with or someone recommended through a personal referral. Get three bids on the job, if at all possible. Research the contractor's previous work, and select someone with whom you feel you can work comfortably.

  When you choose your contractor, you will work out a contract that spells out starting and estimated completion dates, cost (a lump sum or time-and-materials), payment schedule, site access, hours of construction, policies regarding change orders during construction, cleanup, and other factors.

- **Construction phase.** Your dreams are about to become reality! Once permits have been obtained and you've selected your contractor or builder (if applicable), it's time for actual construction to begin. This can be an involved process unless the project is very simple, but if you keep on top of it at all stages, the results will be well worth it.

  If you're doing the work yourself, you'll be responsible for ordering and buying materials, hiring any subcontractors, setting schedules, and arranging for inspections. Otherwise, the general contractor will take care of these aspects, and you (and your architect, if there is one) will work with the contractor on making decisions and handling the problems that inevitably crop up. A final inspection by the building department will be required on completion.

Exterior design details such as this cottage's storybook roof and fascia help to establish a structure's character.

Understanding Architectural Drawings

Architects commonly work with and produce three basic types of drawings. Sometimes additional 3-D drawings may be created.

Plans are the basic tool for planning. A plan may show anything from an entire neighborhood to a single built-in bench; it may be a site plan, a floor plan, an enlarged plan of a single room, and so forth. Essentially, it's a bird's-eye view—a flattened view seen from above. Plans include the horizontal dimensions of the building and its rooms.

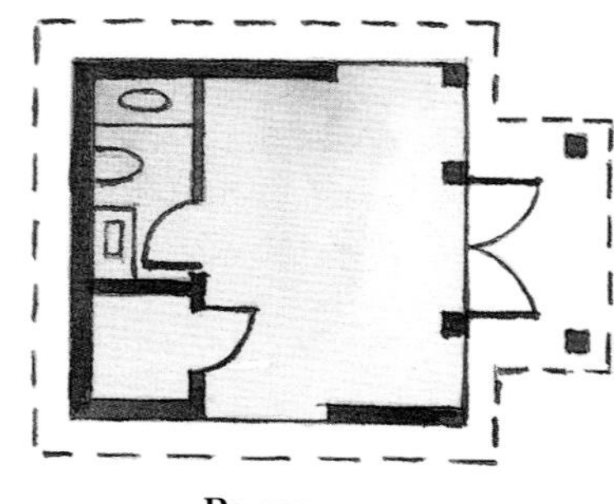

PLAN

Sections show a profile of a building or a detail of a building; they make a visual "cut" vertically through the building or detail. (Similarly, a site section shows a cut through the earth, especially a hill, as shown on page 591.) Sections are a good tool for understanding the interior spaces and construction system of a building. They may include cross sections and lengthwise sections of the entire building as well as wall sections and sections of details such as built-in cabinets. These drawings include vertical dimensions, or heights and changes in level, explaining visually how spaces relate to one another.

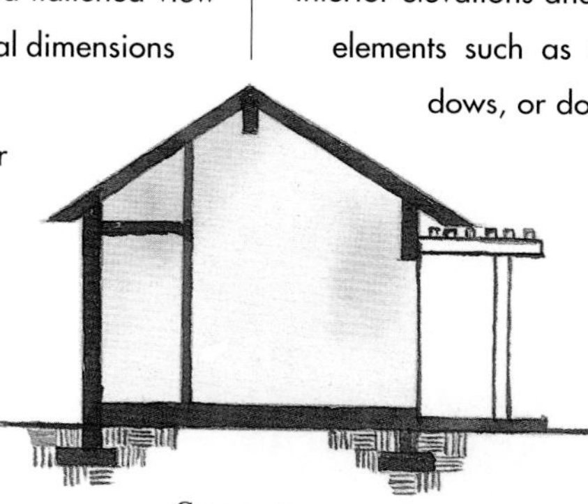

SECTION

ELEVATION

Elevations show you a building or a room as if you are standing directly back and looking at it; they may include views from different directions, conveying the building's general appearance and scale. There are exterior and interior elevations and enlarged detail elevations showing elements such as roofing, moldings, fireplaces, windows, or doors.

3-D views, which are less common, are sometimes used for preliminary design work. They help you visualize what an interior or exterior will look like by representing it in perspective—from above, from a distance, or from an angle. More difficult and time-consuming to produce, they are not usually provided with working drawings.

3-D VIEWS

ISOMETRIC DRAWING

1-POINT PERSPECTIVE DRAWING

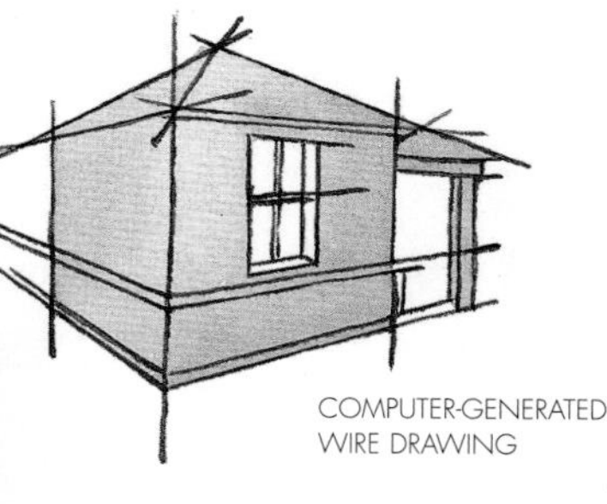

COMPUTER-GENERATED WIRE DRAWING

a matter of style

COTTAGE STYLE, *for one person, might mean the picture of old-fashioned charm associated with cottages of bygone times. For someone else, it might be something quite different. A quick look at some style considerations is presented here to inspire you as you think about your own cottage.*

Style grab bag

Traditionally cottages have been unassuming little dwellings. Many older cottages were built as vacation homes or even as outbuildings on large estates. But historically cottages have also been main residences for people of modest means. In the past they were often constructed of local materials—stone from the rocky countryside, logs from surrounding forests—although they also might be built with wood shingles or other conventional materials. Reflecting their traditional position outside the mainstream of fashion and design, cottages tend to be casually furnished—even a bit quirky—with a friendly mix of hand-me-downs and inexpensive furniture, memorabilia and flea market finds.

These days, the cottage in your backyard can be any style you choose. It will naturally have the small scale and possibly the easy, casual approach common to traditional cottages, but there the resemblance may end. Your cottage may be built in the image of a tiny Greek tem-

The ageless simplicity of Japanese architecture inspired this small teahouse. Hallmarks of its style are the open sides, shoji screens, sloping roofline, and natural-finish wood.

ple, or it may be a rustic-looking log cabin or a gingerbread Victorian mansion in miniature. You may opt for the look of a Japanese teahouse or for a small but sleek contemporary structure.

In fact, because a backyard cottage can be less "serious" than a main dwelling, you may want to have a little fun with its design—to create something you would love but feel you can't do with your main residence. Perhaps you've always harbored a secret desire for a Hansel and Gretel fairytale cottage—or a wildly contemporary, all-glass studio. Unless you think you'll run into problems with your neighbors or your local design review board, you can let yourself go when it comes to style.

To match or not to match?

You may want your cottage to echo the lines, colors, and style of your house, especially if the two are close together. Some styles are more flexible than others. A shingled Cape Cod house might call for a cottage in the same style, whereas a stucco ranch house might blend with a wider range of cottage styles.

Sometimes you can suggest a connection between your main and accessory buildings by using a unifying element, such as similar roof lines, window styles, siding, or trim colors.

You probably don't want to build a rustic potting shed a stone's throw from an elegant Georgian-style home, or a formal-looking cabana across the pool from a cabin-style home. But with enough separation between cottage and main house, you can build something that is a departure in design. Skillful handling and design will make the difference between a successful marriage of styles and an awkward one.

Foundations of style

All the components you choose for constructing your cottage—from the framing and roofing to the flooring and siding—carry out a certain kind of style. Deciding on the basic construction technique will be an important step toward firming up the general style of your cottage. The

The many-windowed summerhouse above has an unmistakable air of elegance, thanks to its shape as well as its decorative trim, hardware, and stained glass. At left, the inimitable style of a free spirit is expressed in a hideaway approached through a colorful archway. The artist owner displays original work and found objects on the cottage door.

basic framing component of a cottage, like that of a house, can be any of these:

- Conventional wood stud framing
- Masonry (brick, stone, concrete block, adobe)
- Alternative construction (rammed earth, straw bale, metal stud)

Wood-frame houses are the most common and most versatile; they may be finished with a cladding, or siding, of various materials. Wood siding—such as shingles or boards—is most widely chosen. But decorative brick or stone, stucco, metal, or even glass can be used on wood frame construction.

A masonry structure of stone, brick, or adobe has its own unique character, while alternative construction techniques such as rammed earth might give a quite different look.

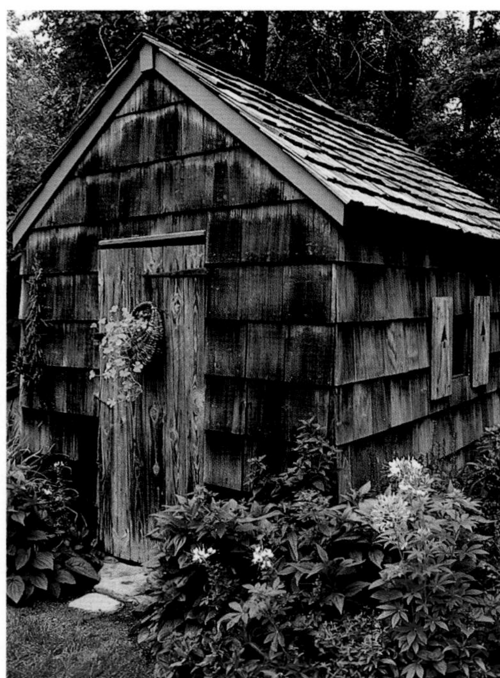

Weathered wood shakes and shingles, recycled wood shutters and door, a simple stone for a doorstep—all contribute to a rustic look, set off by a basket of blooms.

Materials and finishes

You'll face myriad choices among elements such as roof styles and roofing materials, siding, doors, windows, skylights, paint, trim, hardware, and embellishments (cupolas, shutters, and weathervanes, for example). Although making these choices can be bewildering, it's also fun, since this is what creates the character of your cottage.

The spirit of the Carpenter Gothic wooden house, which evolved in the mid-1800s from Methodist campground cottages, is expressed in this little gem, festooned with gingerbread trim and brightened with a creative paint scheme.

A traditional peaked-roof structure clad in wooden shingles, with shutters at the windows and a vine-covered trellis alongside the front door, is the essence of the old-fashioned cottage. A shed-roofed mini-tower painted in primary colors makes another statement, a classic Monticello-style brick cottage yet another. For a look at many choices, turn to the section beginning on page 675.

Interior style

No matter what activities you plan to pursue in your cottage, you undoubtedly want the indoor space to be beautiful and pleasant as well as practical. In an art or crafts studio, for example, clarity of light may be of paramount importance. Skylights and lots of windows may be called for to let in maximum light.

The charm of a Swedish log dwelling inhabits an artfully framed sleeping enclosure (left). Below, bold use of color imparts a sense of fun, while a work-room's creative clutter (bottom) provides inspiration for its artist owner.

No doubt you also want your cottage to be a place where you can really express yourself. Perhaps you've always wanted a room painted bright yellow, but no one in your family wants that color in the main house. You can have your sunny walls in this special cottage. Or if your main house is a friendly but sometimes over-whelming hodgepodge of family clutter, you might want a retreat that's perfectly serene—no furniture at all, just some Japanese-style matting on a polished wood floor and light streaming in the open door. Or maybe you want to create a little bit of Provence in a summerhouse meant for dining and entertaining, complete with an old wooden hutch to hold dishes and a long, scrubbed wood dining table. For a look at many options, turn to the following two chapters.

A GALLERY OF COTTAGES

Getting inspired is one of the first—and most enjoyable—steps on the path toward creating a cottage in your backyard. You may already be focused about the style and design you want, or you may still be in the early stages of dreaming and idea gathering. Either way, you'll find plenty to spark your imagination in the array of photos offered in this chapter. **Arranged according to the uses they serve,** the cottages we show you in these pages range from delightful hideaways for reading and relaxing to pretty playhouses for children and charming guest quarters that will have your friends clamoring for a visit. Just for fun, we also feature some lighthearted approaches—out-of-the-ordinary designs, for example, and little backyard homes for pets. **As you browse,** consider both the use you envision for your own space and the designs that especially appeal to you. Who knows? One of the ideas you find here may set you on your way to making your cottage dream come true.

relaxing retreats

A COTTAGE DESIGNED just for relaxation makes "getting away from it all" as easy as going out into your own backyard. Whether it's a tiny room just big enough for one person or a gracious space large enough for a gathering of friends or family, such a retreat feels like pure indulgence.

You have your choice when it comes to complexity of construction. You may opt for a simple enclosure to be used mostly for lounging and reading during the daytime, with only a comfortable chair and windows open to the breeze and no need for electricity or running water. Or you may want something a little more elaborate—a spacious, comfortable "living room" complete with lights, a fireplace, and perhaps a wet bar.

Here's your chance to exercise your creativity, since the whole point is to design a special space that appeals to your sense of aesthetics as well as comfort. As you'll see on the following pages, your personal retreat can resemble a fishing cabin or an old-fashioned screened porch, a garden pavilion or an elegant great room. The choice is all yours.

An old pump house in a neglected back corner of the owner's property has been transformed into an elegantly simple retreat, now a welcoming destination in the garden—especially in the evening, when its lights beckon. The cottage is set close to boundary fences, but setback requirements were not an issue because this was a remodel of an existing structure.

Craftsman-style French doors open into a serene space handsomely floored in mahogany and furnished in utter simplicity.

A unique ceiling treatment that follows the roof peak was created with bamboo poles, conferring architectural distinction and evoking the feeling of a quieter time and place.

Perched on a dock at the edge of a duck pond, this buoyant little boathouse measures just 10 by 10 feet yet packs in miles of style. The interior, featuring paddles, a carved wood salmon, and a collection of lures, reflects the owner-builders' love of fishing; the cheery color palette adds to the sense of fun and relaxation.

A bell-shaped roof, custom-made from copper, lends distinctive European style to the handsome octagonal garden house below. Cooling breezes and garden fragrances waft in through the many doors and windows.

A charming reading retreat (facing page) began with an old well, over which the owner built a wood floor and an arbor (its beams and rafters are still visible inside). Walls, a gabled roof, and a brick floor came later. Materials are a delightful hodgepodge of recycled lumber, shingles, and windows, including vintage glass block. For an interior view, see page 674.

Its creator dubbed this breezy retreat a "folly"—a whimsical little structure. The freestanding screened "porch" rises from a native-stone foundation in a tree-shaded field. Wicker furnishings, bamboo shades, and antiqued board cupboards reinforce the friendly style.

Constructed of weather-resistant natural cedar inside and out, this modest little house blends effortlessly with its surroundings. Designed for relaxing before or after a swim in the nearby pool (not visible), it offers comfy wicker furnishings that invite chatting, plus a tiny adjacent kitchen and changing room.

An old tractor shed, built circa 1790, is now an airy gathering place. Its sculptor-owner concocted the "relief" on the original roll-back barn doors from lumber scraps; the big table was made from old attic floorboards. A clear polycarbonate plastic overhang shields the doorway from rain. In winter, the owner simply packs up the furniture and lets the snow blow through.

in the treetops

For the child in us, there's probably nothing more appealing than the idea of a secret hideout nestled among the branches of a beloved tree. From the Swiss Family Robinson to contemporary creators of treetop home offices, adventurous spirits just naturally take to the trees.

A treehouse can be literally up a tree, supported by a system of beams and cables, or it can be closer to the ground yet framed and even partially supported by tree trunks or limbs. It may be a simple roofed platform with safety railings all around or a multiroom dwelling complete with heat, light, and all the comforts of home—or something in between. Access can be rough-and-ready (a simple ladder) or more "civilized" (a flight of stairs complete with landings at various levels).

Before embarking on construction, you'll need to do some basic fact-finding. Although a simple, close-to-the-ground treehouse may not be subject to the same regulations as a conventional structure, it's a good idea to check with your local building department for guidance. You should also be aware of such crucial considerations as the choice and treatment of the "host" tree, the safety and stability of the structure itself, and safe access from the ground. And if children will be using the treehouse, adequate supervision must be provided. You can find help in the many books and articles available about treehouses.

Massive redwood trunks are essential to the character, if not the actual structure, of the rustic sleeping pavilion at right. It began as a gazebo, accessible over decking in a wooded lakefront garden; now it houses a bed designed to be taken apart and stored in winter. At left, a simple house was built above the stump when the main part of an old bay tree died. Nestled among the suckers that grew up around it, the house is reached by steps in back.

This handsome treehouse, dubbed "Reynolds' Folly," wraps right around a backyard tree. The owner's son climbs a rope ladder to the porch; a wire trolley lets him zip over to another tree.

gardeners' hideaways

An air of friendly charm imbues many gardeners' hideaways, whether they function as working garden sheds or as informal garden rooms meant for relaxation, too. Those that house all the gritty elements of gardening—pots, bags of soil, garden tools and equipment, flats of seedlings—must be practical, down-to-earth structures that can take some hard knocks. Yet many garden cottages are also havens for garden putterers—places where their owners love to spend their leisure time. As such, they often express the unique personality and style of their inhabitants.

A working potting shed requires an ample counter or workbench for potting; storage shelves or cupboards for pots, tools, and other equipment; and perhaps containers for soil, fertilizer, and so on. If you'll start seedlings or winter plants in your shed, you'll need windows that let in adequate light. An important requirement is running water, either from a nearby hose bibb or from a sink plumbed into the shed. The floor must be practical, too; a simple on-grade floor of loose-laid bricks or pavers or of pea gravel will generally give secure footing yet allow for water runoff.

A garden cottage meant for relaxation (at least some of the time) can take a variety of aesthetic directions. Lots of windows can make the space light and pleasant, as long as there's also provision for shade on hot days. Decorative touches might include bright paint, decorative garden accessories, and even the pots themselves.

Seen through the frame of a rose arbor behind the main house, this potting shed appears as a delightful surprise in the landscape. It's usefully situated directly across from the vegetable garden.

Built from recycled wood and wire screening, a roomy potting bench offers plenty of counter space as well as open shelves above and below for storage. A brightly stenciled paint job gives it personality. Note the creative storage and decorative details, including hanging tiered baskets, a grocer's scale, and whimsical garden ornaments.

The bright yellow doors, with their surrounding molding of electric blue, extend a cheery welcome into the shed's light-filled interior. Except for the weatherproof metal doors and the acrylic roofing, only recycled construction materials were used. The "floor" is a crunchy layer of practical pea gravel.

Here's a working garden shed that's also a wonderful private place to take a break. The big window (salvaged from a construction project) looks out onto a "secret garden" and stone obelisk. The sliding barn door (below) allows easy access for garden equipment—and for the children who love to play inside.

This appealing shed is the busy center from which the owner maintains a six-acre garden. Built-in counters and shelves and a big wooden table provide plenty of work surfaces. A century-old chicken-ranch workers' house, the cottage has been given a face-lift inside and out yet retains its rustic character. Besides providing storage space for garden equipment, it's a mini-gallery for seed packet art.

Perspective belies the true scale of this little white garden house and storage shed. It started life as a duck house; the Dutch door (originally a window) is barely people-size. Remodeling the shed was a family project for the owners, as is the garden of ornamental vegetables and cutting flowers.

Created from recycled materials—old wooden storm windows, used fence posts, salvaged nursery potting tables, even white birch for beams—this light, bright retreat-cum-potting shed is a haven for its owner, an avid gardener. In winter, she heats the space with a portable plug-in radiator and snuggles up with seed catalogs. In summer, the trees shade the space and open doors admit cooling breezes.

home at work

THE HOME OFFICE, it seems, is here to stay. For many of us, working at home is our best option; we can be near our families, avoid long commutes, and work in a peaceful, semi-secluded environment. Even those whose jobs take them away during the day may find a home office a necessity for work overflow in the evenings and on weekends.

A backyard cottage can be the perfect solution. Be it a converted garage or a brand-new structure, a detached home office gives just the right degree of separation between your home life and your work life. Whether you're a writer, a marketing consultant, or an entrepreneur running a small business, you can set up an office that meets your particular needs while also functioning as an attractive part of your landscape. On these pages you'll see examples of both simple and elaborate structural design, with varying interior styles.

Aesthetics aside, essential elements are electricity, heat (in most climates), phone and Internet connections, and adequate work surfaces and storage. (It's nice to have a bathroom and a place to make a cup of coffee or tea, but these may not be necessities.) Measure the things you'll need and use on a regular basis, from computer and fax machine to chair and file cabinets, and plan on plenty of space for office supplies.

A two-story plan multiplies the usable area of this backyard structure. The owner-architect's studio is upstairs (facing page); below are a small bath, kitchenette, and bedroom.

Tucked under the gable roof, this architect's work space receives lots of natural light through a skylight and windows at both ends, augmented by good-looking light fixtures. A built-in desk and a broad ledge running around the room offer maximum work surface in a tiny space. Light washes of color on pine and spruce board paneling echo the color of sky and trees, giving this serene space the feeling of a nest among the trees.

Outdoors it's cold and snowy, but inside this backyard cottage office the atmosphere is cozy. Although furnishings are spare, as befits the serious working space of this writer and editor, the natural wood paneling, rug, and shelves of books create a warm feeling. The design makes efficient use of the tiny area by utilizing built-ins—a wrap-around work surface, bookshelves, and compartments sized for computer components.

The simple wood-shingled cottage fits naturally into its woodsy setting. Large awning windows on facing walls let in winter light when surrounding tree branches are bare; in summer leafy boughs will shade the little cottage and help keep it cool, especially when the windows are propped open to admit breezes.

Coming upon this writer's haven is meant to feel like discovering a hidden workshop deep in the woods. You enter by stages: past the trellised pavilion into an open space, then into the studio itself. With their barrel roofs, office and pavilion give a mirror-image impression; the trellised pavilion wall echoes the office's divided-light doors and windows. Sophisticated simplicity characterizes the interior space. French doors and generous window area allow forest light to play in pleasing patterns over natural fir flooring.

Rather than lose planting space on her small urban lot, the owner of this architect's studio moved her garden upward. Flowers and grasses grow on the roof in 5 inches of soil over a waterproof membrane. Drip irrigation waters the drought-tolerant plants. Floor-to-ceiling windows and a Dutch door are among recycled construction materials; shingles are sustainably harvested redwood.

Inside the compact office space, work surfaces and storage cabinets are neatly organized for maximum efficiency. An original take on recycling is the countertop, made from a salvaged wood bowling alley surface.

just for fun

Lucky the child who has a playhouse of his or her own. Though even an empty refrigerator box can be a fun hideaway, a playhouse built to order is a dream come true.

The dream of a playhouse at right is enhanced by a wealth of decorative play-yard accents, from birdhouse to railroad-car planter. Note how the exterior details—dormer windows, porch railing, lanterns, windows, and trim—are perfectly scaled to playhouse size.

Options range from designing and building a playhouse yourself to ordering one premade (finished or in kit form) or having it custom-designed. Adding details is part of the fun. Playhouses are perfect candidates for fanciful little porches, decorative trim, Dutch doors, and window boxes.

Sporting all the architectural details of a full-size country cottage, this playhouse was purchased ready-made. Inside, a child-size ladder leads to a loft with its own window on the world.

Follow the same safety guidelines you would follow for any room in which children will be playing. Provide plenty of ventilation, and make sure doors and windows can't lock shut, trapping children inside. If there are windows, use tempered glass or plastic. And there's no substitute for adult supervision—you will probably want to site your playhouse where you can easily watch it from the house.

Built to an adequate scale, your playhouse can become a home office or a guest cottage when the kids are grown. It's important to think through possible future uses during the planning stage so that you can either install necessary utilities when you build the playhouse or make it easy to hook them up later. Keep in mind, too, that an office or guest cottage may require a more permanent foundation than a playhouse meant to last only a few years.

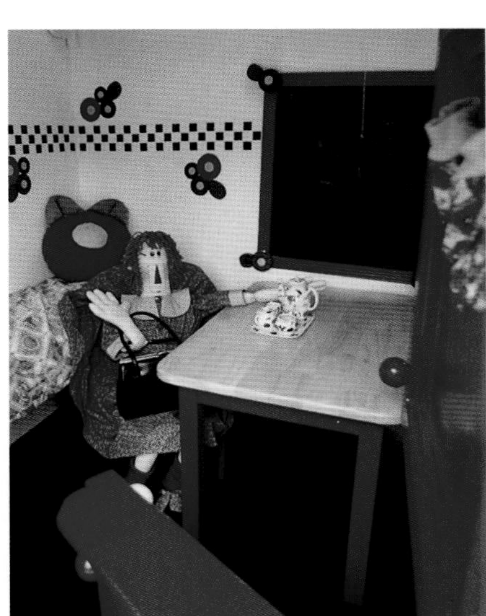

Upstairs is for kids, downstairs for dogs! Go through a crayon-bright Dutch door and you're greeted by a cozy play space complete with a table set for tea. The playhouse "basement" is ready for a real canine occupant or a plush pet.

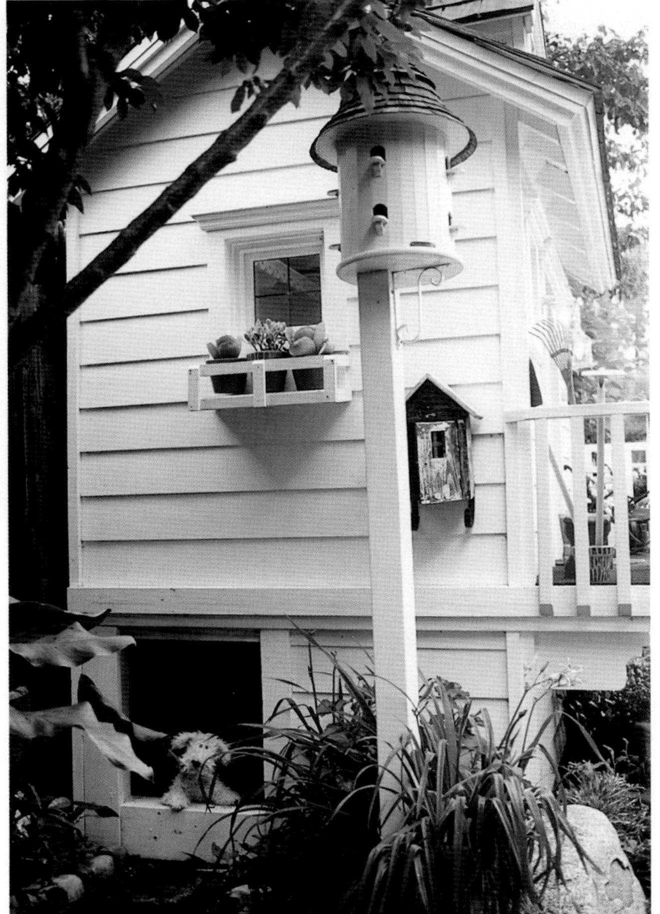

a style tour

Regional styles of architecture are powerful icons that allow us to instantly conjure up an image of a particular place. Think of Tuscany, and you see clay-tiled roofs above the faded gold of peeling, sun-washed stucco walls; rural Midwest America brings to mind images of red barns in an agricultural sea of green. Building a backyard cottage gives you the opportunity to re-create a particular regional style that appeals to you, whether it evokes childhood memories, recalls a memorable travel destination, or reflects the distinctive style of the area in which you live.

Often people feel freer to play with regional style when building a small backyard structure than they would in building a main residence. You'll find cottages with echoes of regional styles throughout this book—see, for example, the Asian-inspired shelter on page 604. And on these four pages we've assembled a small sampling of cottages that come right out and make bold reference to distinctive geographic influences in the United States and Europe.

Since the earliest European settlements in North America, the log cabin has been a symbol of this country's frontier spirit. This version shares the compact size and essential simplicity of its forerunners; its decor is a lighthearted take on classic country and folk elements that includes rustic handcrafted furniture, a Native American rug, "homespun" textiles—even a "trophy" chandelier.

Designed as a playhouse, this little log cabin is pure fun for kids and grown-ups alike.

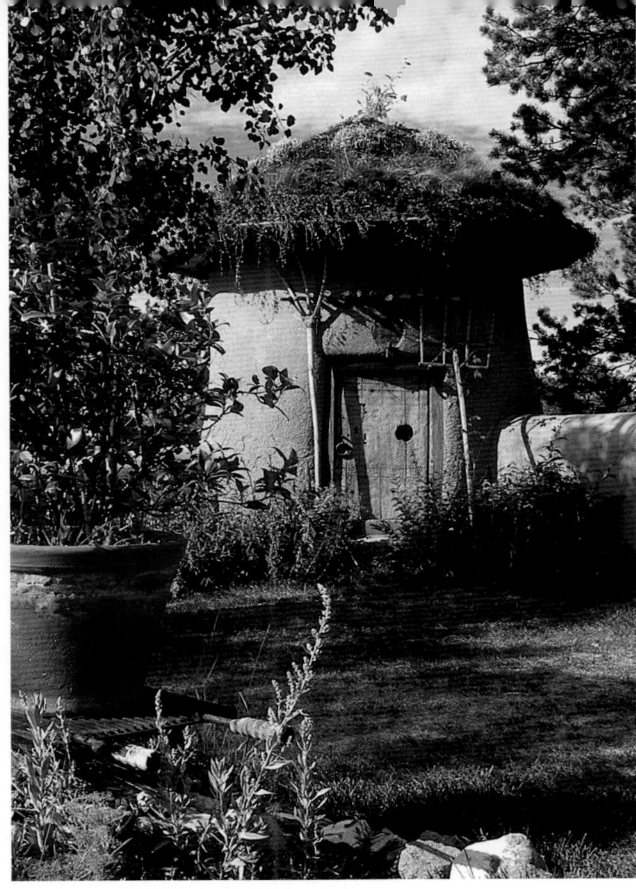

A tiny adobe shelter set into a Santa Fe garden wall pays homage to architectural traditions of the American Southwest. Vegetation sprouts at its feet and on its roof, emphasizing the connection between the clay-and-sand building material and the earth from which it "grows."

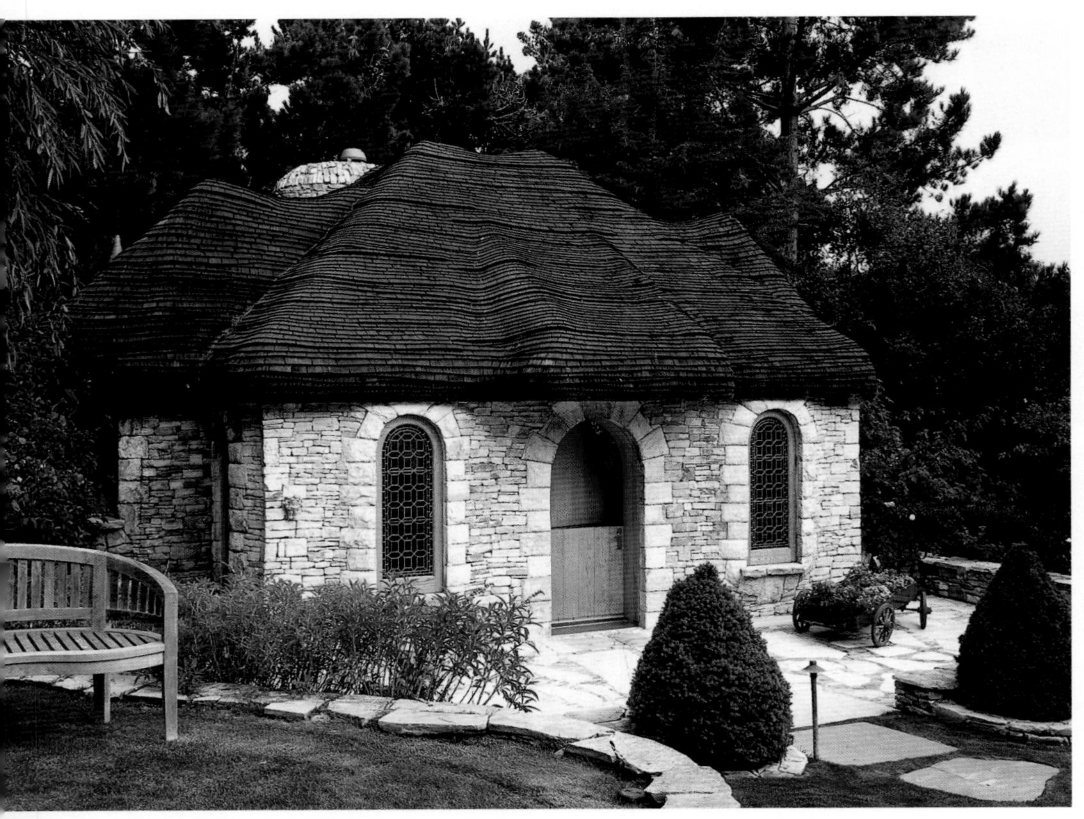

It could be in England's Cotswolds, but this evocative guest cottage is actually in California. Like its English models, it's constructed of local stone; the shingled roof, with its rounded contours and deep eaves, has the look of thatching. Arched leaded glass windows set into thick stone walls are also typical of the traditional English stone cottage.

Enter the cobbled courtyard of this vine-covered garden cottage and you might think you were in Tuscany (though it's really the northeastern United States). Inside and out, the owner-designer's passion for antique architectural fragments and garden ornaments creates a flavor of bygone romance combined with contemporary flair.

creature comforts

For dedicated dog lovers, that special backyard cottage just might be a doghouse. After all, don't our canine companions deserve the best? Its size makes this a good do-it-yourself project—if every scrap of lumber isn't sawed perfectly, will your dog complain? And since the inherent nature of doghouses is a bit on the whimsical side in the first place, this is the perfect opportunity to have fun with design. Want a Wild West town in miniature? A pooch-size lighthouse? Or how about a miniature Southwestern-style adobe?

If you don't want to build an elaborate structure, you might enlist your creativity to make use of alternative materials or structures. Outgrown children's playhouses have been converted into generous-size kennels. One inventive soul turned a clean wooden wine barrel on its side, added supports at the bottom, and thereby created the serviceable and good-looking doghouse shown on the facing page. Here we show you a few ideas to inspire you to design your own doggy digs.

On the fancy side of doghouse design, inventive approaches abound. At left, a small-scale lighthouse replica is one pooch's haven; below, Franny and Zoey share an elegant patio "lean-to" complete with topiary accents.

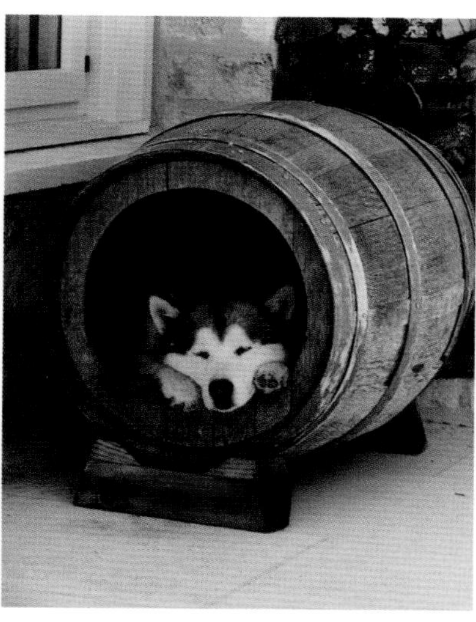

A humble wine barrel, "remodeled" as a canine cottage, is a comfy spot for a snooze.

An entire Wild West street scene offers doggone fine accommodations for two canine pardners.

People love this fanciful dwelling—dubbed the "Bowhaus" by its designer—as much as its occupant does! With its perky contours, decorative trim, and bold color created with weather-resistant tung-oil stains, it really brightens up the landscape.

art in process

A PAINTER, A SCULPTOR, a potter, a fabric artist—anyone who works with the visual arts—longs at some point for a special place for germinating the seeds of creative ideas and bringing them to fruition. It's probably not just the space and solitude you crave, either—it's the chance to make free with all of your "stuff." Bags of clay and jars of brushes, piles of fabric, canvases on stretchers, kilns, easels, soldering irons—all the delightful clutter necessary for making art—take up room. You need the freedom to leave these things out instead of stashing them away every time a room is needed for more mundane pursuits.

The refined potting studio at right—a renovated barn—welcomes visitors with a handsome façade draped in potato vine. Its symmetry, along with the spare gravel courtyard, gives a slightly formal feeling. The studio's 100-year-old redwood siding came from another building on the property; the old barn door has been installed above the new French doors.

Whether your studio is a reclaimed garage or a custom-built artist's cottage, practical requirements depend on how you will use the space. A watercolorist might need little more than room for an easel, paints, and paper, whereas a potter requires a kiln, a potter's wheel, and generous work and storage surfaces. Take stock of your needs: the size and type of work surface (a long table for cutting fabrics, a counter for framing pictures), storage, and display space (if you'll use your studio as a mini-gallery, too).

In its wooded Maine setting, this rustic potter's studio looks like a natural part of the landscape. Peeled tree trunks support the roof of the porch, where shelves display the artist's wares.

Interior surfaces—especially flooring—most likely will need to be able to withstand hard use, spills, and splatters. As for utilities, you may or may not need running water, but you will almost certainly want a generous helping of light, natural and artificial. Be judicious in placing windows and skylights so that you will have light where you want it, not glaring onto your work.

Inside the serene work space, bathed in cool light, a potter's kiln gleams in one corner; shelves hold completed pieces. Work surfaces and storage are combined tidily in units like the one pictured at left.

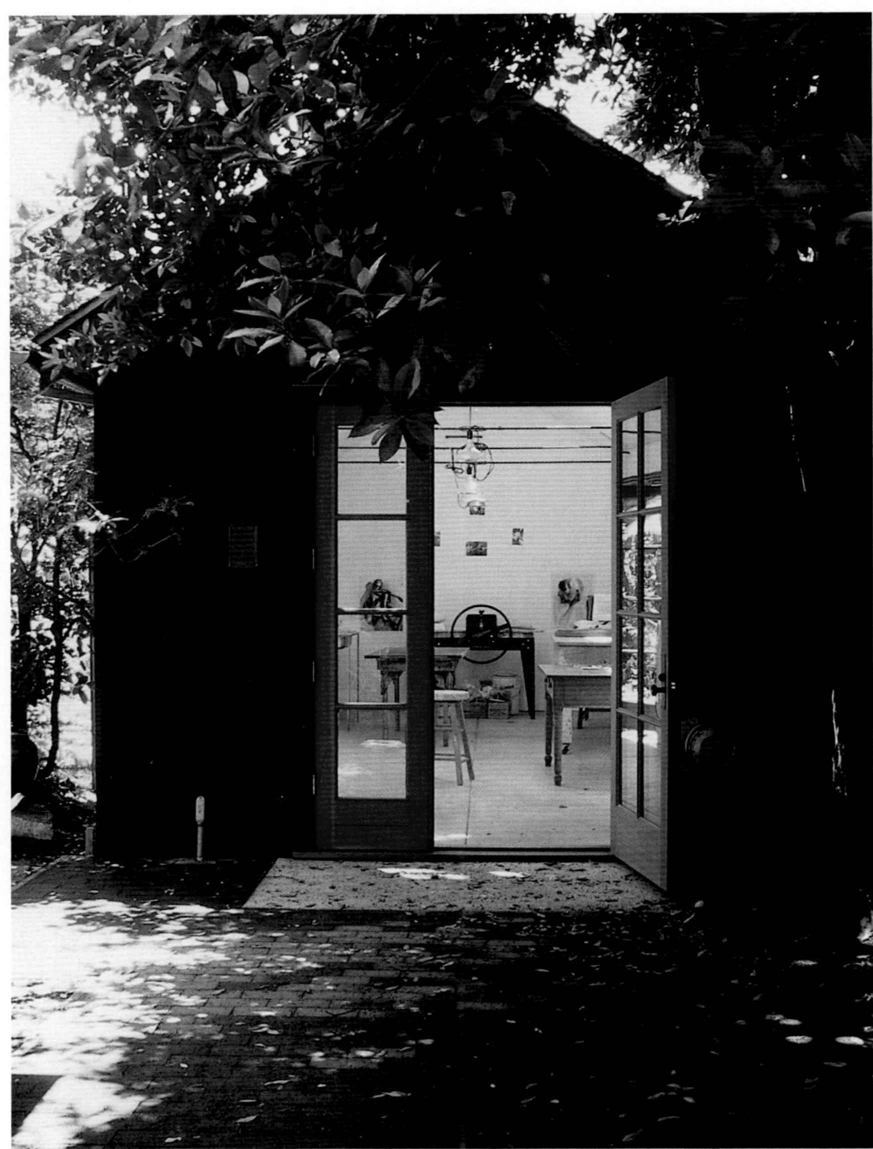

Tall French doors swing wide to reveal an airy, light-filled studio within this rustic wood building. The spare interior houses a potter's kiln and equipment; the white walls also make a good place to tack up photos for critiquing.

Cement floors can take the hard knocks that are sometimes a product of the artistic process. Skylights bathe the space in light; cables support utilitarian artificial lighting. A stainless steel sink is a practical addition.

Step through an arched courtyard door and you've entered the artist-owner's special universe. Enveloped in blooming plants, the stucco cottage has the clay-tile roof typical of Mediterranean buildings. Inside, the studio features a fireplace and a bed, so it can double as a guest cottage.

SONOMA COUNTY

At the end of a winding path from the main house, a studio is both painter's work space and gallery. Inside (left), the northern exposure affords clear, nonglaring light from skylights, windows, and glass doors; track lights spotlight works on display. A loft (out of view) affords storage; an adjoining finished garage adds more display space.

In the South, a screened porch is de rigueur, letting summer breezes in and keeping pesky mosquitoes out—so a screened cottage makes perfect sense. Here at a bend in a path between the main house and a creek, the artist-owner is often at work with a small easel and paints. Railings around the screen walls are perfect for displaying her miniature canvases.

taking the plunge

IF YOU HAVE A SWIMMING POOL on your property, your enjoyment—and that of your guests—will be greatly enhanced by having a pool house close at hand. Such a building adds a whole extra level of comfort and convenience, usually in the form of a bathroom and shower and a changing room—lots better than running in and out the back door, trailing water and wet towels through the house. A pool house can be a wonderful asset for entertaining, too, whether you simply install a fridge for cold drinks and snacks or (space and budget permitting) add a small kitchen, a barbecue, and perhaps an indoor or outdoor dining area.

Practicalities aside, a pool house can also be lovely to look at. A handsome cottage at one end of a pool provides a focal point in the landscape; an appealing reflection in the pool waters often is a bonus. Hiding equipment away within the pool house contributes to making the area attractive, too. Good-looking paving, fencing, and plantings extending to and around the pool house can effectively link main house, pool house, pool, and landscape elements into one unified picture.

Like the prow of a liner about to set sail, the tiny porch of this two-story pool house juts forward toward the water. Climbing the stairway suggests embarking up a ship's gangplank. Shingled in classic Cape Cod style, the structure is screened upstairs to make a cool and comfortable summer guest room. Tucked below are a bathroom and handy storage space for pool paraphernalia.

At the edge of a free-form pool, this gem of a pool house immediately draws the eye with its bright white trim and unusual roof line. The rippled mirror image of the structure doubles its appeal.

Surrounded by a sea of gardens and shrubbery, the pool area is bounded by a rustic wood fence that perfectly complements the style of the house. Perennial borders bloom at its feet; copper post caps repeat the shape of the cottage's hip roof, seen above.

In the changing room, clean white walls and a slatted wood bench provide practical surfaces for dripping swimmers and their gear. The space is pleasantly sunny and bright; hopper windows ventilate the room without directing chilling breezes downward.

A safety feature can also contribute style to the landscape, as evidenced by the picket fence. The arbor above the entry gate adds a welcoming grace note and encourages flowering vines to climb up its latticed sides.

The style of the main house—an 18th-century saltbox—is echoed in the dormer windows, white-painted shingles and siding, and handsome pergola of the pool house. A central portal leads toward tennis courts. On one side are bathroom, changing room, and kitchenette; the other side holds pool equipment, games, and, in winter, the patio furniture.

ready-made style

THANKS TO THE MANY mail-order plans and even prefabricated buildings available today, a backyard cottage may be easier to own than you think. You have a broad array of choices, from elegant prefabricated glass conservatories to simple sheds sold as kits or guest cottage plans that you send away for.

If you choose one of the more elaborate prefabricated shelters, you may begin by consulting with a design professional associated with the manufacturer. This person may help with everything from obtaining building permits to adapting the design to your specifics, then building and installing the structure on site.

At the other end of the spectrum, you may order plans for a shed or cottage from a home improvement book or magazine, then build it yourself or with professional help. Or you may purchase a kit—complete with precut wood, hardware, and instructions—from a building or home improvement center or through the Internet, a catalog, or a book. Some structures, such as children's playhouses, can be ordered ready-made. They'll be shipped in prefabricated parts to be unloaded and set up on a foundation by the company or by you.

Whatever route you take, you must still do your homework regarding siting considerations and code requirements, as described on pages 596–597. And don't forget that every cottage needs a foundation; together with any utilities you want, this adds to the expense and complexity of the project.

This prefab garden shed was trucked to its site already assembled. Note the double doors and ramp for wheeling large and heavy items in and out. The owners' own charming touches include a birdhouse tucked below the roof.

The interior of the kit-built tent bungalow at right has a unique ornithological theme, thanks to a talented decorative artist. Furnishings bring to mind 19th-century naturalists' field expeditions, during which the comforts of home—even Oriental rugs—lent a feeling of permanence to temporary dwellings.

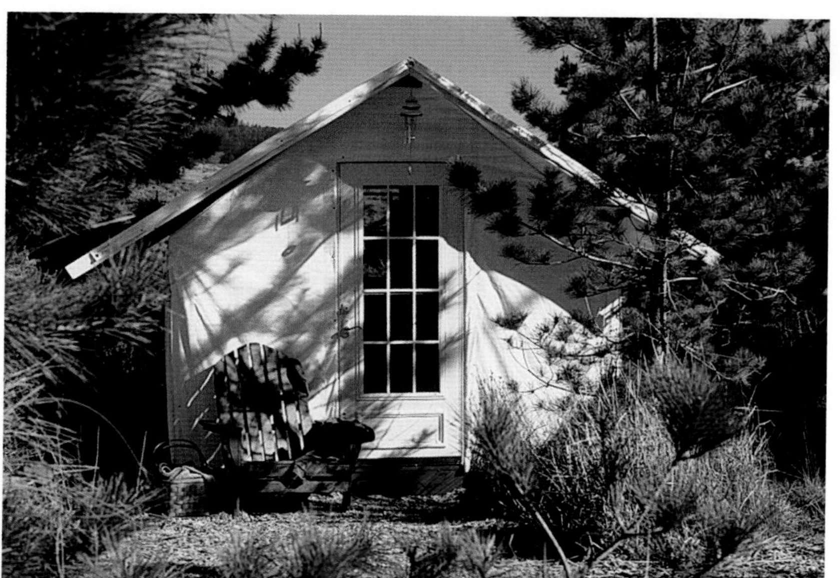

Combining the fun of camping with the comfort of a cottage, a good-looking prefab tent bungalow sits securely atop a wooden platform. Waterproof laminated vinyl walls are supported on a wood or metal frame. "Civilized" components include wood-frame windows and door.

Built from mail-order plans, this jewel of a cottage is an irresistible spot for relaxing. Only 9 by 12 feet, it's made of stock materials purchased at a home center. Key to the design are standard oak French doors, installed upside down and hinged on top to be used as windows; dowels prop them open to let in breezes. One-of-a-kind furnishings and collectibles give the interior its unique character.

An elegant prefabricated glass house recalls its Victorian ancestors in details like ornamental ridge cresting on the roof. Surrounded by white roses and lemon trees, it's a striking garden destination.

The owners customized the interior space for use as a potting shed, adding a wooden work counter complete with sink and an old stone trough to hold potting soil. On a sunny day, it's a particular pleasure to work in this light-filled room.

pure whimsy

SOMETIMES IT'S GOOD FOR THE SOUL to abandon practicality and have a little old-fashioned fun. What better way to express the spirit of fun than to create a backyard fantasy all your own? That's what the cottages pictured here are all about. Whether you like your dose of whimsy on the subtle side or over the top, you can find creative ways to express it with siding, paint, and doodads, as these homeowners have done. Perhaps your cottage style will be an expression of a passionate interest (such as trains or boats), or maybe it will represent in miniature a beloved locale (real or imaginary, from a favorite book or movie). As long as you don't transgress neighborhood rules (written and unwritten), you can feel free to go ahead and have a good time!

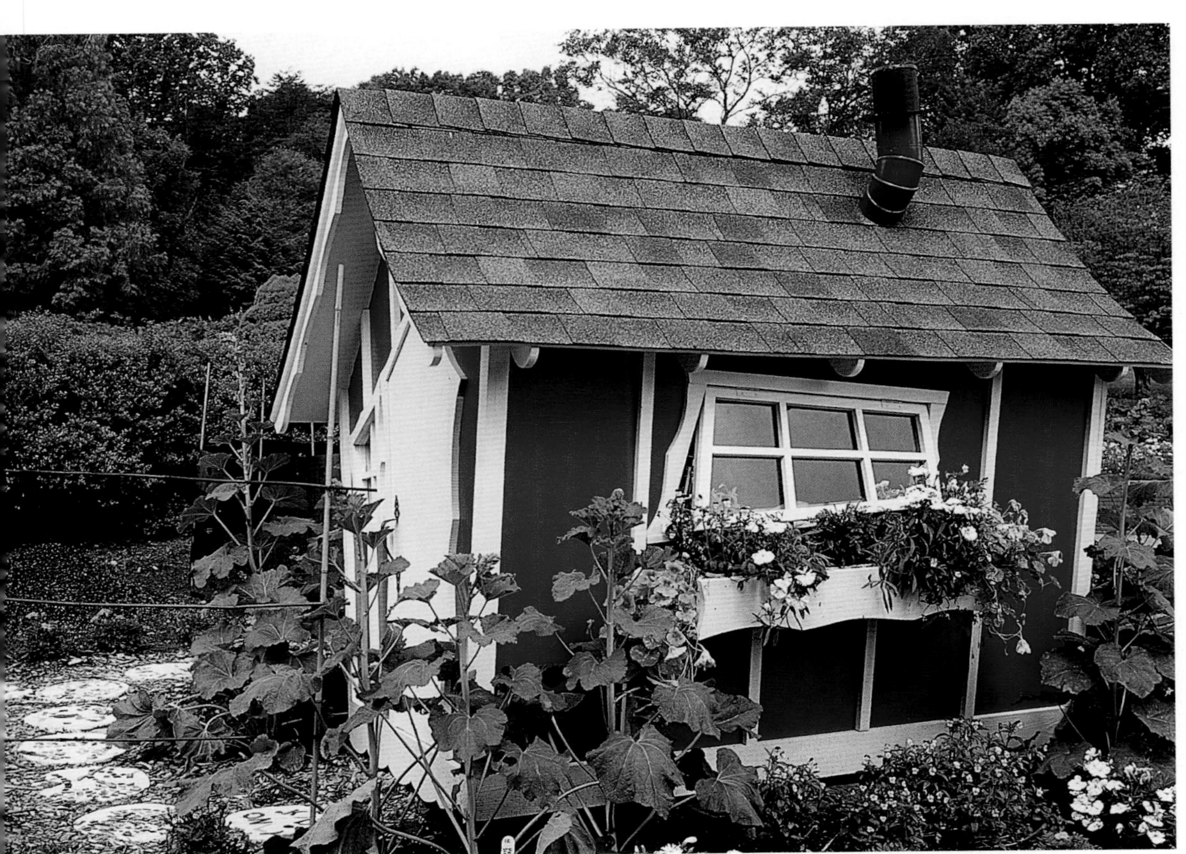

This slightly off-kilter version of a storybook cottage is just plain fun. (Its playful exterior belies its practical function as a garden shed.) While some elements—like the crooked chimney pipe and skewed windows—are clearly goofy, the basic structure is just regular enough to keep it from looking like a mistake. The surrounding flowers are just the right scale.

A train station in the garden? Or how about a tugboat? A love of railroad lore inspired the decor for the cottage at right, reminiscent of an old-time rural train depot. Below right, an actual cabin from an old tug has been outfitted as a potting shed. And a real chicken coop, decked out with vintage signs and mini-windmill, adds a playful touch to the landscape below left.

come to stay

From a cozy cabin in the woods to an elegant poolside getaway, guest cottages of every stripe say "Welcome!" These little homes-away-from-home can range from the most basic of shelters to fully equipped small houses. You can erect a simple sleeping cottage just big enough for a bed and a chair, or you can pull out all the stops and offer your guests a dwelling complete with living room, bedroom, bath, and even a small kitchen.

Designed as an artist's studio and guest quarters, this cottage inhabits its setting with natural grace. Clapboard siding and roof shingles of untreated Western red cedar will weather to a soft silver. The tall chimney and the small, square windows under the eaves give the structure timeless cottage appeal. On the opposite side, large windows face out on a harbor.

Obviously, a "full-service" guest cottage is a large project—akin to building a house, on a smaller scale. In addition to requiring a generous amount of property, it calls for a complete complement of utilities and indoor accoutrements—fixtures, appliances, furnishings. But the beauty of such a cottage is its versatility. Sometime in the future, it might become a dwelling for an older child or an aging relative, or it could bring in income as a rental unit if local zoning ordinances allow that. When you apply for permits and building department approval (see pages 596–597), you'll want to plan ahead regarding any such possibilities.

A modest entrance conveys a cozy feeling the minute you step inside. Tongue-and-groove paneling, Shaker-style pegs for hanging jackets, and firewood stacked under a simple bench all bespeak casual warmth.

Whether your accommodations are to be simple or elaborate, think of the fun you'll have decorating for your guests! Make clever use of an overflow of furniture and decor from your main house, or put together a collection of new or flea-market finds. Go elegant or go zany; pick up on a theme, be it tropical island or Old Mexico; or go for an intriguing color palette. And have fun with accessories—playful signs, perhaps, or your collection of souvenir plates or teddy bears. The things that charm you are bound to charm your guests, too.

The main living area centers on a fireplace of local granite. Among the simple, comfortable furnishings are a daybed handcrafted by the owner's son and a built-in desk and storage unit. Bedroom, bath, and kitchenette are around the corner.

It's a slice of the tropics—on an urban lot in Northern California! Everything about this retreat is designed to make guests smile, from the diminutive front porch to the banana-yellow paint to the funky galvanized roof, reminiscent of a Pacific island beach hut. The cabana was created using redwood from a derelict shed; the banana tree, growing in a tangle of shrubbery, inspired the style.

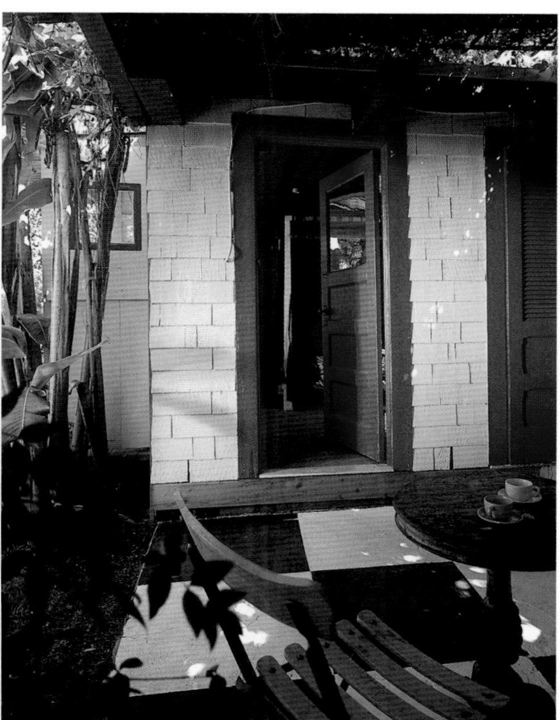

Out the side door, a tiny patio offers a shaded spot to relax with a cup of tea—or perhaps a rum punch. In keeping with the beach feeling, the structure's design encourages ready movement between indoors and outdoors.

Iridescent netting—a colorful take on tropical mosquito netting—surrounds the handmade camp-style bed. The bare floor is cool underfoot and easy to clean.

Offering all the comforts of home, this Craftsman-style bungalow has a bedroom tucked under the dormer and a living area with pocket doors that can open the entire wall to the outdoors.

The bungalow's focal point is the generously proportioned Colorado bluestone fireplace, with its built-in display niche. Guests can cozy up to the hearth in the cool of the evening, then fling open the doors when a warm day dawns.

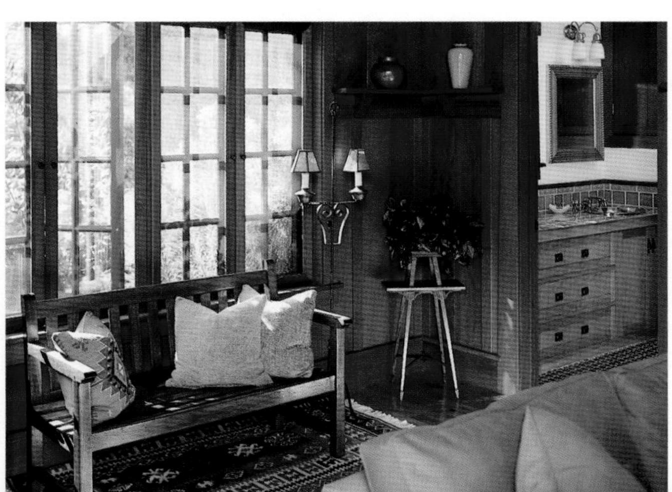

Warm and welcoming, the interior packs a lot into a small space. A tiny dining area adjoins the living room (above), connecting with the compact kitchen through French windows that can be left open or closed to set off the space. Paneling and woodwork in rich natural redwood pull it all together. At one end of the living area, a bank of casement windows (left) opens onto the garden. A bathroom is tucked to one side.

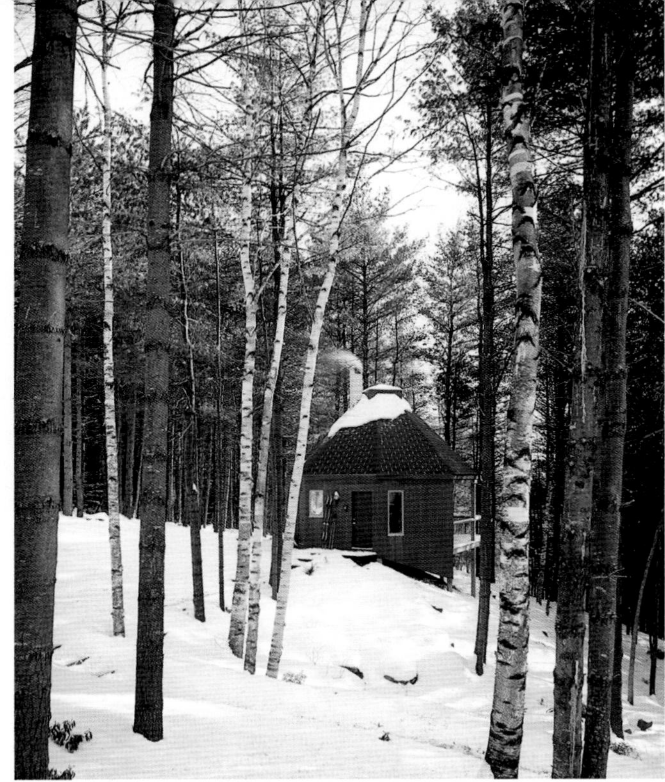

With wood smoke curling from its chimney pipe, a tiny cabin in the woods beckons invitingly across the snowy expanse. The pavilion roof, practical for shedding snow, accommodates a skylit sleeping loft (below). Doors slide open to a deck. A wood stove keeps the entire space toasty even when the mercury drops at night.

The cozy bedroom, like the rest of the interior, is paneled in classic knotty pine; traditional bedding and a braided rug add warm color. The furnishings are spare, as befits a casual ski cabin, and the simplicity of the interior allows the eye to focus on the winterscape outside the windows.

Interiors depicted in the works of Swedish painter Carl Larsson inspired the decor. The painted floral motifs, as well as the cream-and-soft-green color scheme, are hallmarks of Larsson's visual world. Curling up on the window seat at right, with its built-in bookshelves, is an experience every guest anticipates.

This tree-shaded cottage invites lucky guests to wander at will, in through the wide sliding pocket doors or out onto the brick patio. A low roof line, overhanging eaves, and small-paned windows create classic cottage appeal.

Elements from beloved bygone eras enliven the interior. In the tiny kitchen (left), a restored Wedgwood stove and 1930s-style cabinetry set the tone. In the living-dining area (above), the vintage jukebox and neon clock from the 1950s bestow a lighthearted atmosphere. Tongue-and-groove paneling is used throughout.

made for entertaining

CANDLELIGHT DINNERS under the stars, pool house barbecues, cozy fireside gatherings—any kind of get-together feels special in a backyard-cottage setting. Backyard entertaining places may be fully enclosed dwellings that double as pool houses, retreats, or guest cottages, or they may be more informal, partially roofed and walled structures—or even enclosures within patio walls that become defined as entertainment areas.

Some entertainment spaces have cooking facilities—full kitchens or outdoor barbecue areas. Others may simply be pleasant places to sit for drinks and snacks, or for a luncheon or supper prepared in the main house. Still others may gather folks around a fireplace for intimate talk and relaxation.

Because they are often situated in a lovely garden or poolside setting, backyard entertaining venues offer an atmosphere where everybody feels relaxed. And if an occasion calls for a large guest list, a backyard cottage often allows for free movement between indoors and out.

Whatever form your entertaining structure takes, be sure to provide protection from daytime heat and evening chill as well as a source of light for evening entertaining—candlelight, electric light, or both. You'll want plenty of comfortable seating, along with tables for plates and glasses. And don't be surprised if your guests decide to linger.

Situated next to a vineyard, this handsome structure is at one with its sunwashed surroundings. Spanish influences are clear in the clay-tile roofing, adobe-like golden stucco, peeled-wood posts ("vigas") and ceiling beams, and adobe-style fireplaces indoors and out.

Inside, warm tones create a mellowed look. The floor is stained concrete (see page 689 for a closeup). Mixing several stains produced the woodwork color.

For a unique textured effect, interior walls were plastered with taping compound mixed with straw, then faux-painted.

The roof of this little dining pavilion seems to float lightly above the "room" below it. Trusses of red cedar support the curved copper; the open space beneath receives natural light from overhead through a strip of translucent plastic at the roof's center. The 8- by 12-foot space is just large enough for a small table and chairs.

Here's the perfect setting for outdoor entertaining—a stone-pillared pavilion with handsome built-in barbecue and hearth. Close at hand inside the multipurpose structure are a kitchenette, a bathroom, and—for sheer luxury—a sauna. In inclement weather, custom-crafted wooden "storm" doors close over the glazed French doors.

Tucked into an intimate courtyard and roofed with an open arbor, this outdoor dining "room" is a gracious setting in which to share a meal with friends. In the evening, candles flicker in the chandelier above the table, while strings of outdoor lights lend sparkle. Close proximity to the house makes serving a breeze.

As stunningly decorated and furnished as any living room in a principal dwelling, an area designed for entertaining features a soaring vaulted ceiling, rugged slate tile flooring, and an entire wall of windows and French doors. Guests can pull chairs up to the island counter to chat while drinks and snacks are being prepared in the kitchen.

In the evening with lights aglow, this entertainment cottage is a vision of gracious elegance. The sweeping landscape of mature trees is in keeping with the grandeur of the Palladian façade and the graceful roof line.

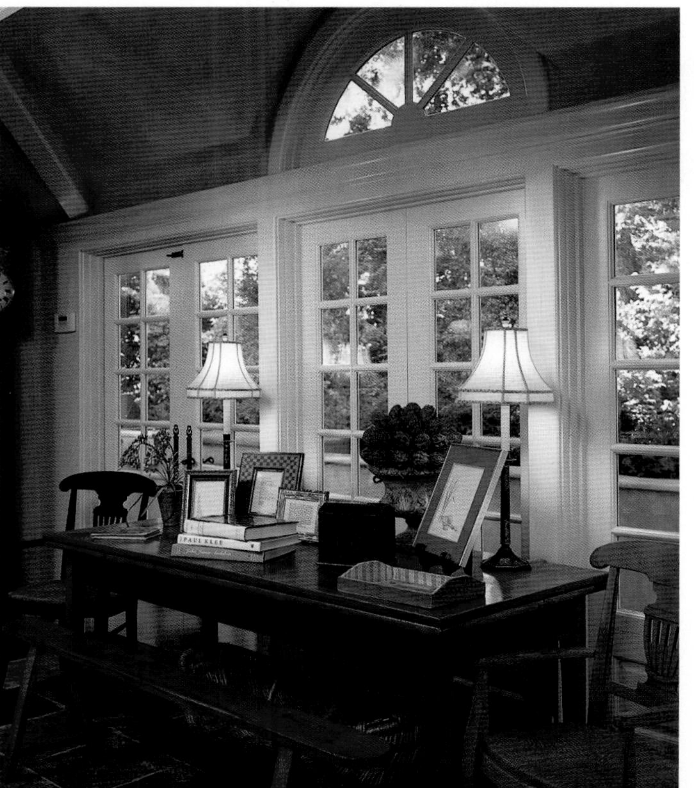

Furnishings strike a balance between formality and casual comfort. This table, with its rustic bench, matched lamps, and simple tableau of books and pictures, is a perfect example. It's a natural spot for guests to sit and chat while enjoying the view.

sleeping under the stars

SOME OF US NEVER OUTGROW our delight in sleeping out under the stars. As adults, though, we usually want a little more comfort than the lumpy sleeping bags we dragged out into the backyard as kids. Build a simple sleeping shelter, and you can have your cake and eat it, too.

As the examples on these pages show, you can be protected from dewdrops and insects yet still be able to fall asleep with the breezes wafting over your face and the stars visible overhead in the night sky. Not only that, but if you opt for a creative design you will have a structure that adds interest to your landscape as well as providing an extra place to accommodate overnight guests.

It's a unique experience to sleep out in this highly original pavilion fashioned of clear acrylic and screening atop a simple 8- by 10-foot wood platform. The transparent walls let dreamers take in the white pines, the stars, and often even deer passing quietly on their way to drink from a nearby pond.

This shelter takes the old-fashioned sleeping porch and moves it into the woods, where the sound of breezes in the trees lulls guests to sleep. The Victorian-style door and wood-framed screen "walls" reinforce the feeling of having turned back the clock to a simpler time. Visitors pass through a vine-hung portal formed by a set of iron doors reclaimed from a local mine.

COTTAGE ELEMENTS

From its sheltering roof to the flowers blooming at its feet, from the curtains at its windows to the furnishings that make it feel like home, each facet of your backyard cottage contributes to its overall look as well as to your own comfort and enjoyment. While this chapter can't examine every detail involved in putting a cottage together, it does aim to provide an overview of options. **For your cottage exterior**, we review what's available today in roofing and siding styles and materials, windows and doors—even trim and embellishments. In addition, we give you a short course on landscaping to help you make your cottage a beautiful and integral feature of your property. **Moving indoors**, we acquaint you with creative wall, floor, and window treatments and provide tips on how to make the most of your space. From this starting point, you can go on to find and install the particular elements that will make your backyard cottage a one-of-a-kind treasure.

Exterior Style

ROOFING, SIDING, WINDOWS, DOORS—AND ALL THE TRIMMINGS

The exterior envelope or "skin" of your cottage serves both essential practical purposes and aesthetic ones. It consists of the basic components of any building—roof, siding, windows and doors, and hardware such as door handles—as well as an almost infinite variety of embellishments. The choices you make among all these elements will help set the style of your cottage as well as make it a solid, weathertight building.

Roofs

The essential part of even the most primitive structure, a roof over our heads is so basic that many of us don't really stop to consider how many forms it can take or what a variety of materials can be used for roofing.

Almost all roofs require a sheathing, or roof deck (usually of plywood or boards), over which the finish material is applied. But beyond this, choices abound. Depending on its design, a roof can give your structure the look of a medieval English cottage, a Southwest desert adobe, or a space-age greenhouse. And as the chart on the facing page illustrates, materials can range from nothing-fancy asphalt shingles to storybook thatching.

Roof Roundup

Roofs come in many shapes—some traditional, others "invented" by contemporary architects. These are some of the styles commonly used for backyard cottages.

Barrel. Semicylindrical, or curved (see the photo on page 598).

Bell. A roof that has a bell-shaped cross-section (see page 613).

Flat. A roof that has no slope, only a slight pitch to allow for water drainage.

Gable. The classic peaked roof, with two sides sloping downward from a central ridge to form a gable at each end.

Gambrel. Also called *Dutch gable*, a roof with two pitches on each side—as seen on the classic American barn and at right.

Hip. Four sloping sides connected by "hip" joints and meeting in a ridge on top or forming a pyramid-shaped *pavilion* roof (see photo below).

Shed. A roof with only one pitched plane (see example on page 625).

This handsome shed has an asphalt-shingled roof that overhangs the entire structure for unbroken protection. Coupled with ship-lap siding and multipaned door and windows, it's an attractive backyard addition.

Overhead Options

Asphalt shingles

Asphalt shingle

Made from asphalt-saturated fiberglass or paper mat.
Advantages. One of the least expensive options, readily available in many colors and types.
Disadvantages. Deteriorates more quickly than some materials. As a petroleum by-product, it's not the most environmentally friendly choice.

Wood shakes

Wood shingle/shake

A classic choice either as smooth, uniformly shaped shingles or as more unevenly textured shakes.
Advantages. Contributes natural-style good looks, insulates well.
Disadvantages. Requires diligent maintenance, vulnerable to fire and insects.

Clay or concrete tile

Elongated, curved tiles traditionally shaped from clay, now mostly concrete made to mimic the originals. The classic choice for Southwestern style.
Advantages. Noncombustible, distinctive in style.
Disadvantages. Heavy, expensive, and unsuitable for climates with freeze/thaw cycles.

Metal

Either sheets or shingles that mimic such materials as slate and wood.
Advantages. Noncombustible, durable, and, if made from recycled materials, environmentally friendly.
Disadvantages. Can be complicated and expensive to install.

Copper

Slate

Time-honored and beautiful, but not always widely available.
Advantages. Durable and noncombustible, with a classic beauty.
Disadvantages. Expensive, heavy; requires maintenance to remain weathertight.

Glass or plastic

Safety glass, acrylic, or the newer clear polycarbonate plastic. Familiar in conservatories and greenhouses, also used in creative contemporary structures (see page 672).

Glass

Advantages. Gives a bright, open look. Insulates well if double glazed, can facilitate passive solar heating.
Disadvantages. Special framing required to support large expanses of glass safely.

Sod

Sod

Unusual today but once common on the American prairie and in rural Scandinavia, with grass-planted turf atop a normal roof (see page 630).
Advantages. Fun, unique; can have good insulating qualities.
Disadvantages. Tricky to construct, requires vigilant maintenance.

Thatching

Thatched

An old technique featuring straw, reed, or similar materials fastened together.
Advantages. Has a quaint, traditional cottage look; can be waterproof, provide good insulation.
Disadvantages. Not an option for most people—few artisans know the technique. Vulnerable to fire and insects.

Three types of wood siding—board and batten (top), shingles (center), and clapboard (bottom)—can give cottages very different looks.

Siding

The outer layer of your walls is every bit as important as the roof in protecting your backyard structure from the weather. But siding offers much more than protection. The materials you choose do much to create the "look" of your structure.

Wood. By far the most common choice is solid board siding. Among possible variations are *board and batten* (wide boards nailed vertically, their joints covered by narrow strips of wood); *clapboard* (overlapping beveled horizontal boards); and *wood shingles or shakes*. All can be left natural (with sealants applied), stained, or painted.

Wood siding has the great advantage of design flexibility; it can lend your backyard structure the look of a rustic barn, a Japanese teahouse, or a sleek contemporary dwelling. Wood siding is almost always applied to a wood-frame structure, which is first covered with a sheathing of exterior plywood, fiberboard, or gypsum board and often with an additional layer of building paper or the newer "house wrap" material for extra weather protection.

Paint and Stain Portfolio

Exterior paint. Oil-based or water-based (latex), exterior paint can be flat, low-luster, semigloss, or high-gloss. Usually siding is painted with a flat finish and trim is painted in low-luster or semigloss for durability. In most cases, latex is the paint of choice—it's fast-drying and easy to clean up with soap and water.

Paints can be custom-mixed to any color, or you can choose from a wide array of standard colors. Paint companies often offer preselected palettes to help coordinate trim and siding. Wood must always be painted with a coat of primer before the finish coat is applied.

If insects and spiders are a problem in your yard, ask at your paint store or home improvement center about repellent additives that can be mixed into the paint.

Exterior stain. Stains may be semitransparent or solid-color (opaque). The former contain enough pigment to tint the wood surface but not enough to mask the natural grain completely; they produce a natural, informal look. Solid-color stains are essentially paints; their heavy pigments cover the wood grain completely.

Under most conditions, semitransparent stain has a shorter life span than either paint or solid-color stain.

Water sealer. Applied to unfinished wood, clear sealers won't color the wood but will darken it slightly. You can buy them in oil- or water-based versions. Many formulations include both UV-blockers and mildewcides to protect wood; some come in slightly tinted versions. Like semitransparent stains, sealers need to be renewed every few years, but they allow you to show off wood that has a beautiful grain and color.

Set into a hillside, this cottage built of rustic stone and roofed with wood shakes has become an almost integral element in the landscape.

Masonry. A completely different look is presented by homes constructed of *stucco* (often associated with Mediterranean or Spanish architecture), *stone* (rustic and natural), *brick* (new or old), *cement block*, or *adobe* (a mixture of sand, clay, water, and sometimes straw). New, environmentally friendly techniques developed for building with rammed or cast earth or straw bales result in houses that have the look of adobe.

Some masonry materials, such as stucco, are applied to wood framing and sheathing. Others, like true adobe or rammed earth, actually form the walls.

Other choices. *Vinyl and aluminum sidings*, with factory-applied enamel coating in a variety of colors and textures, mimic the look of horizontal board siding. They are generally durable and low-maintenance, although some vinyl siding can become stiff and crack in extreme cold. *Corrugated aluminum sheet siding* is sometimes used to convey an up-to-date industrial look.

Walls of *safety glass or plastic*—nowadays, usually clear polycarbonate—let in maximum sunlight and trap heat inside; venting is important to prevent moisture buildup.

Yet another possibility is the traditional *log cabin* with the logs forming the walls and no additional siding applied.

Fooling the Eye

One creative way to dress up the wall of a shed or cottage is to fool the eye with *trompe l'oeil* painting. An entire scene or a fragment of one can bring a Parisian street corner to your backyard or create a blooming vine on a wall where in reality nothing will grow.

Using shadowing and perspective, trompe l'oeil gives the illusion of three dimensions. The painted scene can even be cleverly mixed with actual objects—a real pot of flowers hanging on the painted wall, for example.

Painters who achieve such effects can be found through interior decorators and paint stores. Ask to see the artist's portfolio or, if possible, on-site work.

A contemporary summerhouse makes its design statement via elegant leaded-glass French doors and casement windows on all sides.

Windows and doors

You can select new windows and doors in a variety of standard sizes, shapes, and materials from specialty manufacturers, home improvement centers, or lumberyards. Recycled windows and doors offer another possibility; just keep in mind that extra attention must be paid to fitting your finds into new construction and making them weathertight.

The way you finish your windows and doors will go a long way toward setting your cottage style. A rustic unfinished Dutch door creates one impression, a door with a bright coat of high-gloss paint another. Similarly, window frames may be natural-finish wood or colorfully painted. Consider whether you want your window and door frames to blend into the total picture or to stand out as decorative elements in themselves.

Additional embellishments help set your style. Windows may be flanked by shutters, overhung with awnings, or underscored with window boxes. Doors may sport decorative hardware and other ornaments. And don't overlook the effect of curtains or shades when viewed from outside.

If insects—or larger critters—are a potential problem, you may want to install screen doors and windows that accept screens.

Door choices. Doors suitable for backyard cottages may be basic exterior wood doors (with or without glass windows), patio doors (French or sliding), Dutch doors (with independent upper and lower sections), barn doors on overhead tracks, or roll-up garage-style doors.

Will your structure be used for storage of garden equipment or large items? Calculate whether you might need an extra-wide, double, or garage-style door to facilitate moving large items in and out.

Energy-Efficient Windows

Most windows are rated with a "U value" to indicate the rate of heat flow through them. The lower the U value, the more energy-efficient the window; a low value (0.2 to 0.3) is preferable in a cold climate, while an average U value (0.4 to 0.6) is fine in a warm climate. Look for the rating on the manufacturer's label. In general, old-fashioned double-hung windows tend to have higher U values than casement and awning windows, which seal better.

Double-glazing, or insulating glass made of two panes of glass sealed together with space between, can go a long way toward preventing heat loss. The newer low-e (low-emissivity) glass adds a coating that reduces indoor heat loss in cold weather and keeps ultraviolet rays out—which helps prevent fading of furnishings. Tinted glass can also block solar heat gain to help keep your cottage cool in hot weather.

Don't overlook the old-fashioned canvas awning or the vine-covered "eyebrow" or overhead trellis—naturals for keeping out hot sun. In addition, caulking and weather-stripping doors and windows is an easy, inexpensive way to increase energy efficiency.

Window options. Windows come in almost unlimited shapes, or you can gang various shapes and sizes to create a window wall. Most basic shapes are available as standard orders from home improvement centers or companies that specialize in windows, or you can custom-order special shapes, sizes, and kinds of glass—at a price, of course.

Besides regular window glass, you can choose decorative treatments such as beveled glass, stained glass, diamond-pane windows, bull's-eyes or roundels (resembling the bottoms of glass bottles), or contemporary-looking glass block (see photo on page 674).

Frames may be of wood, wood with aluminum or vinyl cladding, aluminum, vinyl, steel, or fiberglass. Wood has the advantage of being paintable in any color, but cladding (available in a range of colors) eliminates most exterior maintenance problems. Aluminum—the least expensive alternative—is low-maintenance but stylistically more limited. Vinyl is virtually maintenance-free, though it lacks the natural feel and look of wood; fiberglass is similar but varies in quality. Durable steel, the most expensive choice, is excellent for clean, contemporary styling. Aluminum and steel windows generally do not insulate as well as other types.

Skylights. Available in a wide range of sizes and styles, fixed and operable, with or without screens, a skylight may be the answer if you have privacy issues or want extra light and ventilation. Consider placement carefully; a south-facing skylight can offer dramatic shifting light throughout the day but may let in too much light and heat, whereas a north-facing skylight usually provides soft, uniform light rather than high drama.

Windows Defined

Windows can be operable or fixed, or you can combine the two—a fixed square window directly above or below an awning window, for example. Here is a brief survey of the types most commonly used for cottages.

Awning. A good choice because of its small size and simplicity, this window is hinged on top to open out from the bottom; when open, it acts like an awning to keep out rain.

Casement. Hinged on one side to be cranked or pushed open, this style provides maximum ventilation—and the tight seals on today's casement windows make them especially energy-efficient.

Clerestory. Usually small and fixed, these high windows let in light while maintaining privacy. Practical only in buildings with relatively high ceilings, they can be useful in a larger cottage where privacy is an issue.

Decorative. Small decorative windows may be round—called *ox-eye*—as well as hexagonal, triangular, or other shapes; they're usually fixed rather than operable.

Double-hung. This traditional window has upper and lower sashes that slide up and down by means of springs, weights, or friction devices. With or without divided glass panes, it gives any dwelling a classic look.

Picture. This large fixed pane of glass, sometimes flanked by operable windows, might be considered to emphasize an expansive view. Otherwise, it's less appropriate in scale than other windows for most cottages.

Sliding-sash. This window moves horizontally, like a sliding Japanese screen, in grooves or between runners at the top and bottom of the window frame.

Casement (top right)

Double-hung (middle right)

Awning (bottom right)

Octagonal (above)

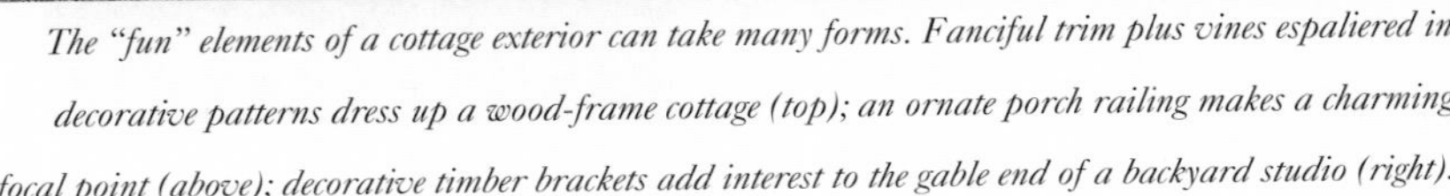

The "fun" elements of a cottage exterior can take many forms. Fanciful trim plus vines espaliered in decorative patterns dress up a wood-frame cottage (top); an ornate porch railing makes a charming focal point (above); decorative timber brackets add interest to the gable end of a backyard studio (right).

Trim and embellishments

Here's the fun part of cottage building—the opportunity to put a personal stamp on your backyard creation. You can take the most basic structure, be it a revamped garage or a shed built from a kit, and give it color, life, and individuality by adding your own decorative details.

Elements like rafters, trim, and such embellishments as cupolas are integral to a building. (The practical purpose of trim is to cover or protect joints, edges, or ends of siding or other materials.) Over the centuries, architectural styles have been defined as much by their trim—or lack of it—as by their general forms. One obvious example is the highly decorative woodwork associated with the Victorian "gingerbread" style.

The hardware on your cottage—doorknobs, hinges, and so on—provides another opportunity for expression. While hardware can be purely functional and almost invisible, it can also be decorative and even whimsical.

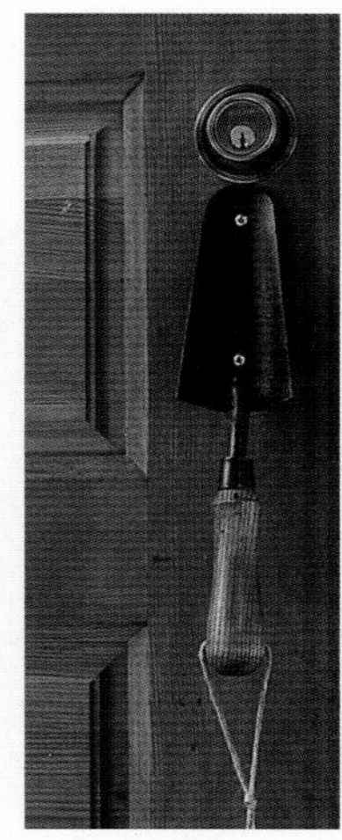

Unlike integral decorations, a host of purely decorative objects—signs, objets d'art, and other ornaments—can be tacked onto cottage walls with a hammer and nails.

Here are a few ideas for adding decorative touches to your cottage exterior:

- Decorative tiles on walls, across steps, around windows or doors—grouted in or hung on hooks
- Signs, plaques, and small art pieces, hung singly or in groups
- Lattices and trellises, fixed to the cottage or anchored in large pots or planting boxes set against the walls
- Lanterns or sconces, decorative or functional
- Mirrors on exterior walls
- Window and door shutters, working or strictly decorative
- Baskets and buckets hung on walls or set on a porch
- Antique tools or other objects mounted on walls in rows or patterns

It's all in the details: a sign and found objects personalize a gardener's shed (left), a weathervane tops a steeply pitched roof (above), and a garden trowel becomes a door handle (top).

Beautiful Surroundings

ENHANCING YOUR COTTAGE'S APPEAL WITH ARTFUL LANDSCAPING

What could be more appealing than a cottage set at the end of a curving garden path, nestled among the trees as if it's always been there—or at the edge of a backyard patio, knee-deep in a bed of flowers? Whatever its size and style, your backyard cottage is part and parcel of a larger picture that includes your private landscape (your yard and garden), your main house, and perhaps even your neighborhood. Ideally, everything should blend harmoniously.

How you incorporate your backyard structure into your landscape is partly governed by the size of your property. A large lot obviously gives you the widest range of options: you can tuck a cottage or shed out of sight among the trees, place it as a focal point to be viewed across a rolling green lawn or even a pond, or incorporate it into a more formal complex that includes house, patio, garden beds, and perhaps a swimming pool. On a smaller lot, your challenge is to integrate the cottage into the landscape while keeping it in proportion to the property and garden as a whole.

This cottage courtyard has it all—a fountain splashes gently; container plantings clamber up walls and bloom in corners; and brick paving, tiled stucco walls, and rustic wood accents create no-fuss style.

Landscape features are generally divided into "hardscape" (pathways, patios, decks, fences, and walls) and plantings. Both can play a role in connecting your cottage to the main house and creating a pleasing outdoor environment.

Pathways, patios, and decks

Patios and decks form the "floor" of your landscape, while pathways are like hallways—they connect your cottage with your house and with the rest of your property.

PATIOS AND DECKS. Outdoor "floors" may surround your cottage or be situated on just one or two sides. They can function as extensions of your cottage, expanding perceived and actual usable space. In good weather, a patio or deck can be a dining room, a sunroom—even a dance floor!

You may be able to design a landscape in which the patio is a widening of the path to your cottage, with both made of the same materials. The deck or patio itself need not be a square or rectangle; curved and irregular shapes are graceful and can accommodate unusual property configurations.

Generally, patios are installed on flat sites, whereas wood decks, which usually rest on vertical posts set in concrete, have the flexibility to span sloping ground. Decks are usually built of decay-resistant woods such as redwood or cedar, of pressure-treated lumber, or of the newer, environmentally friendly wood products such as synthetic wood-polymer composites. Patios, like paths, can be constructed of a variety of materials. Proper grading and preparation of the bed on which a patio surface will be installed are essential; consult your supplier for details, or see the Sunset book *Ideas for Great Patios & Decks.*

PATHWAYS. A path might be straight and true, leading directly from, say, the back patio of your main house to your cottage; or it might meander in curves through your property.

Straight paths could be flanked by beds of flowers or by low hedges. Such paths—and geometric or symmetrical garden layouts—usually convey an air of formality. A quite different feeling is created by a path that is winding and enshrouded by plantings so that its destination isn't obvious at first, allowing visitors to "discover" the cottage at path's end.

Any path, straight or meandering, will be most comfortable for walking if it is at least 4 feet wide.

Walls, fences, and overheads

Perhaps your backyard cottage is uncomfortably close to the neighbors, or maybe you want a sense of enclosure even if privacy isn't an issue. Or perhaps

Path and Patio Pavings

Choices in path and patio surfaces abound; each has its own particular look as well as practical attributes.

Bark and chips. Shredded bark, wood chips, and other loose materials are soft and springy, inexpensive, and easy to install (they do require a header or edging to contain them). They drain well and create a casual look. Clearing off fallen leaves can be difficult, because the bark tends to get raked up with the leaves.

Brick. Classic brick pavers can be set in a variety of patterns, in sand or in mortar. Mortar-set bricks can give a formal or contemporary look, while bricks in sand tend to look more casual, less uniform. A mortared surface is smoother and easier to maintain, but sand affords better drainage. Either surface can be slippery when wet.

Concrete. As a poured slab or individual pavers, concrete is durable and versatile. You can have poured concrete in a host of tints and textures, stamped to look like stone tile or flagstone, or in irregularly shaped pads with planting spaces between.

Individual square pavers, laid in sand, can be butted together or separated by gravel or a ground cover. Or you can choose circles, rectangles, irregular shapes, or interlocking pavers (see examples on facing page). Inexpensive and simple to use, most concrete pavers are ideal for do-it-yourselfers.

Gravel. Available in a variety of textures and tones (white and red as well as grays), gravel can be raked into patterns or used as a decorative element with other paving materials. It must be confined inside edgings or headers.

Relatively inexpensive and quick-draining, gravel does have two drawbacks: it can be hard to keep clear of fallen leaves, and it can scratch flooring when tracked indoors.

Stone. Durable and beautiful, stone has timeless appeal. Natural flagstones or cut tiles come in a wide range of subtle colors and textures (see examples below right). This is one of the more expensive paving options, though cost varies according to where you live in relation to where the stone originates.

Stones thicker than about 1 inch can be set in sand, with gravel or plantings in between; with time they will settle into the garden almost as if nature had placed them there. Thinner stones need to be set in mortar, resulting in a smoother surface with a more formal look.

Some stone can be slippery when wet, and some porous types stain easily.

Tile. Ceramic paving tiles in natural-colored terra-cotta or brightly colored patterns can add style and beauty to any patio. The stablest bed for outdoor tile is mortar over a concrete slab, though sometimes heavy tiles can be laid in sand; ask your supplier. Glazed tiles are extremely slippery when wet; unglazed tiles are best for paths and patios, with perhaps a few fancy glazed ones as accents. If you live in a cold climate, select tile that is freeze-thaw stable, identified as impervious or vitreous.

Tile should be sealed for protection against surface water and stains; if your tile isn't factory sealed, ask your supplier for recommendations.

Certain elements—a white picket fence paired with a perennial border, a rose-covered arbor entrance—are classic expressions of cottage charm.

you want to visually define the boundaries of an area around your cottage. A fence or wall—one constructed of wood or masonry or a "living" fence of foliage—may be just what you need.

You may have a situation like that shown on pages 610–611, with a cottage near the property line benefiting from a fairly high fence. Or you may have a setting in which a private courtyard could extend a cottage's livable space. For just the suggestion of a boundary, you may simply want to partially surround your structure with something low and open—an old-fashioned picket fence, perhaps, or a split-rail or Japanese tied-bamboo fence.

As with any structure you build on your property, you will need to consult local zoning and building codes (see pages 596–597).

In choosing materials, consider the look and style of the structures on your property. Usually it's best to match or at least coordinate materials for a unified look. And don't overlook the softening effect of vines; they can add an attractive layer of color and texture. In fact, often you can save money by using less solid barriers such as lattice panels or wood-and-wire fencing in combination with climbing plants to achieve privacy and a sense of separation.

Of course, you can also use plants alone. Trees, shrubs, or even bamboo (where its roots can be controlled) can make terrific screens, though they will take time to become established.

To create a garden "room" adjacent to your backyard cottage or to extend its roofed area, consider adding an overhead in the form of an arbor, either freestanding or attached to the cottage wall or roof. In addition to offering a frame for flowering or leafy plantings, an arbor adds a pleasing vertical dimension to the landscape and provides filtered shade where needed. Sometimes a small arbor—with or without an attached fence and gate—can be used to create an entry area in front of a cottage.

This welcoming entrance to a cottage courtyard is distinguished by a simple overhead structure that can support climbing vines.

Plantings

Unless you're landscaping your property from scratch, you'll probably be fitting your cottage into a landscape that already features established trees, shrubs, and planting beds. You'll need to decide what you want to keep and what you want to modify or add to the present garden.

If you want a clean, open look that emphasizes the building and makes it appear larger, you might opt for paving the area around your cottage, then adding a narrow strip of foundation plantings, container plants, or a combination.

For the opposite effect, and to give the cottage a settled-in look, surround it closely with lush, massed plantings. Trees and shrubs immediately surrounding the cottage will tend to make it appear smaller and less dominating in your landscape. Foundation plantings or many containers massed close to the foundation will help anchor your cottage to the site. A double row of plantings (taller ones in back) will create a sense of depth; in fact, layering plants is one surefire way to create depth on a small lot.

If you have a tight space that does not allow for much in-ground planting, or if you want to enhance and soften your cottage's appearance, wood or metal trellises can be placed against walls, around windows, and over doorways to encourage leafy and flowering vines to clamber up the sides and even over the roof. The vines can be planted in the ground at the base of the walls or in containers.

In addition, you might consider installing window boxes and filling them with flowers as well as spilling and trailing plants. Or you can add color and greenery in pots attached to walls with metal hangers and in hanging pots suspended from eaves or overhangs.

Any new trees and shrubs that you plant should be appropriately scaled to the size of your cottage. Be sure to check how tall and wide they will eventually grow.

Outdoor lighting

If you plan to use your garden and cottage at night, you'll need to light the way to it. Landscape lighting is an art in itself, transforming outdoor spaces into magical and often dramatic scenes as well as addressing safety concerns.

Lighting pathways is a must, and many low-voltage systems now available feature fixtures designed to be placed at intervals along paths. You can purchase kits to install yourself or have a system custom-designed and installed. In addition, lights mounted on trees and on cottage or house walls and eaves can cast light down onto steps and paths, while strategically positioned upward-facing lights can be used to dramatically illuminate trees and shrubbery. For an easy and delightful addition to permanent lighting, use strings of mini-lights along steps, railings, and walkways. Other decorative lighting can include hanging or wall-mounted lanterns.

Ask at your local home improvement center, lighting store, or hardware store for information about specific outdoor lighting needs. For a professional-quality overall lighting plan, consult a lighting designer.

A Southwest-style courtyard gives an impression of lavish color and pattern, thanks to containers brimming with blooms.

Handcrafted low-voltage copper lanterns light a garden path (right). A decorative garden lantern of cast metal can hold a candle (far right).

Inside Story

FLOOR, WALL, AND WINDOW TREATMENTS CREATE ATMOSPHERE AND STYLE

The interior of your cottage may be plain or fancy, sparely furnished or filled with friendly clutter. The way you will use your cottage and its basic construction style are the two factors that most affect how you "do" its indoor space.

A rustic structure that's partly open to the elements will most likely be one you'll furnish simply—with minimal decoration and with wall and floor treatments and furniture that can withstand exposure to temperature variations, even blowing rain or snow. A working potting shed or a sculpture studio calls for unfussy flooring and wall treatments that can take some hard knocks. At the other end of the spectrum, a house-in-miniature guest cottage allows you to pull out all the stops when it comes to flooring and wall treatments, furnishings and decorative elements.

Consider the role that textures play in setting a tone. Rough wood or stone, nubby fabrics, and earthenware or basketry tend to give a rustic, comfortable feeling. Smooth, finished textures—polished wood or metal, some ceramic tile, glass or acrylic, and silky fabrics—convey an air of refinement and perhaps modernity. (Of course, you will mix these elements to some extent, and that can add interest to any interior.)

Color, too, plays an important role. Natural wood tones are often associated with warmth and coziness. White or soft pastels can give a room a light, airy, or romantic feeling; bright primary colors liven up the atmosphere instantly. One versatile approach is to let walls and flooring be fairly neutral, or natural wood, and add interest with color accents—on woodwork or in decorative accessories.

Flooring

Even in a fully furnished guest cottage, flooring should be of practical, long-wearing material that demands little upkeep and can withstand comings and goings from pool, garden, or patio. Generally, it's wise to stay away from wall-to-wall carpeting, which can suffer from dampness in a cottage that sits unheated for periods of time and can be hard to keep clean. If soft floor coverings are called for, choose area rugs and smaller throw rugs—perhaps hooked or braided rugs or matting such as seagrass or sisal.

Cottage flooring can be light and fanciful, like the painted wood at top, or elegant and enduring, like the slate tiles above. At left are examples of unglazed terra-cotta floor tiles and decorative glazed tiles.

Flooring Sampler

Here's a guide to flooring choices that are both practical and attractive for a backyard cottage.

Ceramic tile

Ceramic tile. A practical choice, ceramic tile is available in a vast array of colors and patterns. For a rustic look, you can choose unglazed quarry or terra-cotta tiles (be aware that these are porous and can get stained unless properly sealed). Rough, water-resistant red-clay tiles, rugged, stone-like porcelain pavers, and glazed floor tiles are all good choices but can be slippery when wet.

Stone with mosaic tile inset

Stone tile. Natural stone (such as slate or limestone) cut into tiles makes beautiful and durable flooring that's especially attractive in a building that has close connections with the outdoors. Although the cost can be high, stone is long-lasting and classic in design.

Concrete. No longer confined to slabs of gray, concrete flooring can now look stylish and interesting, thanks to tinting and etching techniques that give it color and pattern. Although a bare concrete floor can be cold underfoot, it's also extremely durable and easy to care for—and you can always add area rugs to warm it up. Of course, a plain concrete slab can also be the base for almost any other kind of flooring.

Tinted concrete

Brick. Suitable for on-grade structures that have no raised foundations, such as potting sheds and rustic retreats, brick is durable and can be either laid in sand or installed with mortared joints.

Wood. A classic hardwood floor is hard to beat for warmth, versatility, and good looks. If your cottage has a raised floor (subflooring laid over wood joists), you can nail wood flooring onto the subfloor. If you're on a concrete slab foundation that's level and in good condition, you can install a "floating" floor of prefinished wood veneer or one of the plastic laminates that looks like wood.

Red fir

Hardwood floors can be sanded and refinished as they age; prefinished floors are particularly durable, and the thicker veneers can be sanded and refinished once or twice. Some creative souls have used vintage recycled wood flooring with success; its mellow character is unrivaled.

Resilient flooring. A low-maintenance, practical choice, this category includes solid vinyl or polyurethane sheet flooring or tiles and old-fashioned linoleum and cork—natural products available with updated looks.

Linoleum

Warming Up

Unless you live in a tropical climate, your winter weather probably ranges from chilly and damp to freezing cold. To use your backyard cottage during the cold months, you'll need some kind of insulation and heating.

If you are building a new structure, you have the opportunity to add insulation in the ceiling (the most important), in the walls, and—if there's a raised floor rather than, say, an on-grade concrete slab—under the flooring. Your architect or contractor can advise you about what kind of insulation to use.

You can also raise the temperature inside your cottage by choosing the right windows—preferably insulating double-glazed ones as described on page 680. South-facing windows and skylights will make the most of the sun's warmth during the day. A tile, concrete, or brick floor warmed by the sun can act as passive solar heating as it absorbs warmth and radiates it back.

As for heating, you have several options. While gas heat is the most efficient, you'll need to have a gas line run to your cottage—practical only for a fairly large-scale project. A delightful and practical option is a wood stove, now available in a wide range of styles and sizes; new models, including pellet-burning stoves, are designed to burn fuel cleanly. Check with your local building department to find out if a stove is permissible and how it must be installed. Consult local dealers and Internet web sites for general information about wood stoves.

The easiest option of all is a plug-in electric heater such as the radiator types widely available. Although electric heating is expensive, it's an instant way to make your space toasty—but check with your local utility company or consult an electrician to make sure the power supply to your cottage is adequate to handle the demands of a plug-in heater.

A wood stove warms this cozy space; thick cast-earth walls provide extra insulation as well as sculptured good looks.

Creative ways with paint and stenciling—including a stenciled message above the windows—make this cottage interior a delight.

Wall treatments

Unless you have a rustic structure with interior walls left unfinished (like the one shown on page 674), the walls of your cottage will probably be finished with wood paneling or sheetrock nailed onto the wall studs.

Wood paneling can be either solid-board or sheet paneling. Generally, solid boards have edges specially milled to overlap or interlock. They may be narrow tongue-and-groove (a quintessential vintage cottage look), or wider boards installed vertically or horizontally. As with flooring, a handy builder can recycle vintage interior paneling to create walls with a unique aged beauty.

Sheet paneling is a catchall term for wall paneling that comes in large, machine-made panels; it's less expensive than solid board paneling but less durable, and it doesn't have the same classic good looks.

Good-quality solid-board paneling may be left natural (unfinished) and sealed, or be stained and sealed. In fact, wood paneling such as knotty pine is practically synonymous with cabin and cottage style. Wood paneling of any type can also be painted, of course—as can sheetrock. Latex paint in flat, eggshell, and satin finishes is available in every color of the rainbow, premixed or custom-mixed. Preselected coordinated palettes for walls, ceilings, and trim are sometimes offered by paint companies. But remember that out in your backyard cottage you have the freedom to exercise your imagination and creativity without making the same level of commitment to style and formality that your main house might require.

Particularly popular today are faux paint finishes that feature techniques such as pickling, sponging, ragging, and color washing. These can be used to create all kinds of effects, from the illusion of an antique, peeling surface to a wall that glows with rich layers of subtly mixed colors. For more information about faux finishes, see the Sunset book *Decorative Paint & Faux Finishes*. Other decorative ways with paint, such as stenciling or trompe l'oeil painting (see page 679), are a wonderful way to dress up your space and put a personal stamp on its decor.

Generally speaking, wallpaper is less practical for a backyard structure—unless it's a fairly elaborate, heated cottage. Wallpaper is subject to mildew when dampness is present, and, except for the wipeable vinyl type, it's vulnerable to dirt. It usually requires an even wall surface for proper installation.

Artful stenciling (top left) can transform a simple architectural element into a focal point. Old-fashioned beadboard gains panache with a faux-painting process known as pickling (top right), while solid board paneling takes on a whole new look when applied horizontally and washed with a striking stain (left). Below, traditional knotty-pine paneling looks clean and contemporary around a tiled zero-clearance fireplace.

Window treatments

If your cottage is in a secluded setting, or if you're using it for entertaining or other pursuits that don't require privacy, it's often best to leave windows uncovered—the better to admit sunlight and garden views. Style-wise, many windows are so attractive in their own right that it's a shame to cover them up.

But if privacy is an issue, if windows feel bare or cold, or if you will be using your cottage at night and don't want the "black hole" effect of uncovered windows, you will want window treatments that complement and carry out the style of your cottage. Most backyard cottages call for something fairly casual and unstructured rather than formal draperies or fancy shades. But here again, your cottage is the place to indulge your stylistic whims and fantasies—and if that calls for elegant balloon shades or Victorian velvet drapes, so be it.

Most window treatments fall into two main categories: "soft" treatments such as curtains and fabric shades, and "hard" treatments such as shutters and blinds. The following is a brief survey of options.

Curtains. Fabric curtains are the most versatile and may be the least expensive choice. Informal curtains can be gathered on a rod or attached to a rod by tabs, rings, or ties. They can be made to any length, either with or without a valance—an abbreviated "curtain" at the top of a window. Or you can opt for unstructured swags of fabric simply draped around the window frame.

Seen from the outside, an inexpensive bamboo shade contributes casual good looks to a cottage window as well as providing daytime privacy.

The range of fabrics available allows you to vary the look, from country-style gingham to romantic gauze. If you like to sew, you can whip up simple curtains in a jiffy; other options include having them custom-made or buying ready-made curtains from home furnishing stores, specialty shops, and mail-order or Internet outlets.

Washable curtains are most practical in a cottage subject to mildew from dampness or temperature extremes.

Hardware for curtains—rods, finials, and holdbacks—is available in many styles and materials. These elements can help set the style of your cottage interior.

Shades. One popular and practical choice for a backyard cottage is the familiar bamboo shade, along with its cousins made of woven natural grasses and reeds. You can choose anything from inexpensive roll-ups from import stores to custom-made woven shades.

Among fabric shades, the simpler, tailored types—such as roller and Roman shades or the contemporary honeycomb type—are generally the most appropriate for a cottage. These can be made up in almost as wide a variety of fabrics as can curtains—even canvas or special indoor-outdoor fabrics. Some types—especially the newer pleated shades with an insulating honeycomb design—help to conserve energy.

Shades may be lined or unlined. Again, you can make them yourself (see

Curtain rod finials and holdbacks in floral or abstract designs add that extra decorative touch to cottage window treatments.

the Sunset book *Simply Window Treatments*) or have them custom-made. If dampness and mildew are an issue, keep in mind that fabric shades can be more difficult to take down than curtains, and most require dry-cleaning.

Shutters and screens. Louvered wood or wood-look interior shutters are unrivaled for durability and style. Available in natural-finish wood, painted, or unpainted (for you to finish), they can be found with the traditional 1¼-inch louvers or with wider louvers ("plantation shutters"). While shutters are one of the more expensive window treatment options, with good care they will look attractive for years. You may be able to find ready-made shutters to fit your windows (the least costly); otherwise, you'll need to have them made.

One interesting option is the traditional Japanese shoji screen, which features a wood frame with a special paper or fiberglass insert that lets soft light enter the room while maintaining privacy. Shoji screens may either slide in a track or be hinged to fold open like shutters.

Blinds. This "hard" window treatment is perfect in a cottage with a contemporary look, whether you choose traditional Venetian blinds with 2-inch slats or miniblinds with 1-inch slats. Blinds can be wood, painted aluminum, or polycarbonate plastic, in a rainbow of colors and patterns; Venetion blinds also come with fabric slats. Blinds are a practical choice when you want clean good looks along with privacy and light control.

A graceful fabric swag (top left) is all you need to dress up a window that looks out on a pretty view; ruffle-trimmed cotton curtains with simple tiebacks say "country cabin" (top right); for a tailored, contemporary treatment, choose miniblinds (above).

Feathering the Nest

SPACE-SAVING FURNISHINGS, STORAGE IDEAS, AND LIGHTING

Almost by definition, space in a backyard cottage is at a premium. That miniaturized quality is part of the charm of such a structure, but if you also want the space to feel comfortably cozy without being crowded—and if you have things you need to store in your cottage—it's important to use your space efficiently.

Try to suit the scale and amount of furnishings and accessories to both the scale and the function of your cottage. For example, a tiny reading retreat may need only a chair or two and perhaps a bookshelf and some plants—much more would ruin its atmosphere of repose. A potting shed, on the other hand, is meant for storage as well as work—and sometimes it's also a place to sit and relax. It may feature shelving and bins, a work surface that can double as storage, and perhaps a chair or bench. At the other end of the spectrum, a guest cottage might include sleeping, dining, and food preparation areas, all on a small scale. Here, clever use must be made of space to provide for sleeping, seating, and storage.

Storage units and space-saving, multipurpose furniture will be your best tools for creating a workable, livable space. For storage pieces, visit specialty storage stores, home improvement

The friendly clutter of a working artist's private space speaks volumes about the owner's interests and passions. Every surface is used for display, from windowsills and high ledges to countertops and the shelves beneath them.

A quilter's idea of heaven might be an at-a-glance display like this one, which groups fabrics by color in a generous system of built-in shelves.

Supplementing shelves and bins in a potting shed, a wire grid with S hooks makes a handy storage wall that also shows off favorite objects. (For more views of this space, see pages 620–621.)

centers, and even hardware stores, and study catalogs—there's lots to choose from! For space-saving furniture, look at home furnishing catalogs and magazines, especially those that feature living in small spaces.

In plain sight

In the small, casual setting of a backyard cottage, storing things in plain sight helps conserve space and contributes to a lived-in feeling. Here are a few ideas for doing so in an attractive, organized way. Be sure that anything mounted on the wall is firmly anchored, preferably on a backing board that is screwed into the wall studs.

Open shelving. Fasten wood, wire, coated-wire, or glass shelving to the walls—use traditional shelves with brackets or the newer, keyhole-mounted "floating" shelves. Or purchase small wall-hung drawer units, display cupboards, or racks.

If you have exposed studs in unfinished walls, install shelves between the studs to take advantage of the space. (Recessed shelving and wall niches are also constructed this way, but the framing is usually hidden behind the sheetrock or paneling.) Of course, you can always make use of modular freestanding units.

A roll-around shelf unit backed with fabric-covered panels stores and displays things wherever you want them at the moment.

Good old Peg-Board is a practical, inexpensive, and good-looking "canvas" for storing and displaying everything from garden tools to cooking utensils. Paint it for a dressier look.

Stacking bins and baskets. You can purchase sets or mix and match components, or you can buy individual plastic or metal bins or wicker baskets to organize items on a bookshelf or other ready-made shelving unit. For maximum flexibility, consider units that can be rolled around.

Peg racks and hooks. For a quick and easy storage solution, mount a Shaker wooden peg rack or a row of coat hooks—or even vintage doorknobs—along a wall to hang just about anything: jackets and hats, gardener's tote bags, even (as the Shakers did) ladder-back chairs. Or mount a curtain rod along a wall at waist height or above a work counter to hang items individually or in baskets or canvas bags, using the kind of hooks designed for pot racks.

A classic cottage entryway features a row of hooks on which to sling jackets, hats, and bags; a bench beneath provides a place to sit and pull off boots. Baskets, lined (like those below) or unlined, are available at stores specializing in storage; use them alone or tuck them into shelves.

Peg-Board and grids. Traditionally the handyman's best friend, a perforated storage surface takes up almost no room and is both inexpensive and practical; for a more finished look, you can paint the board. Both perforated-board and wire-grid systems accept a variety of hooks, brackets for small shelves, and little bins or drawers.

Ledges. Whether they are part of your cottage's construction (as shown on page 627) or added later, ledges running around your walls are great places to park small items, both useful and decorative.

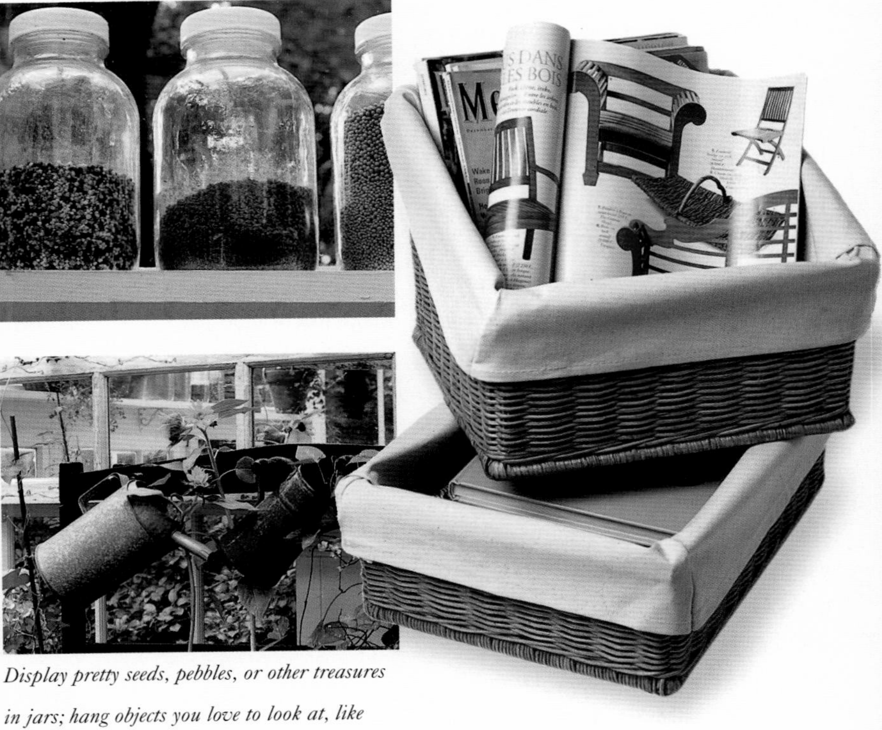

Display pretty seeds, pebbles, or other treasures in jars; hang objects you love to look at, like these watering cans, on a row of hooks.

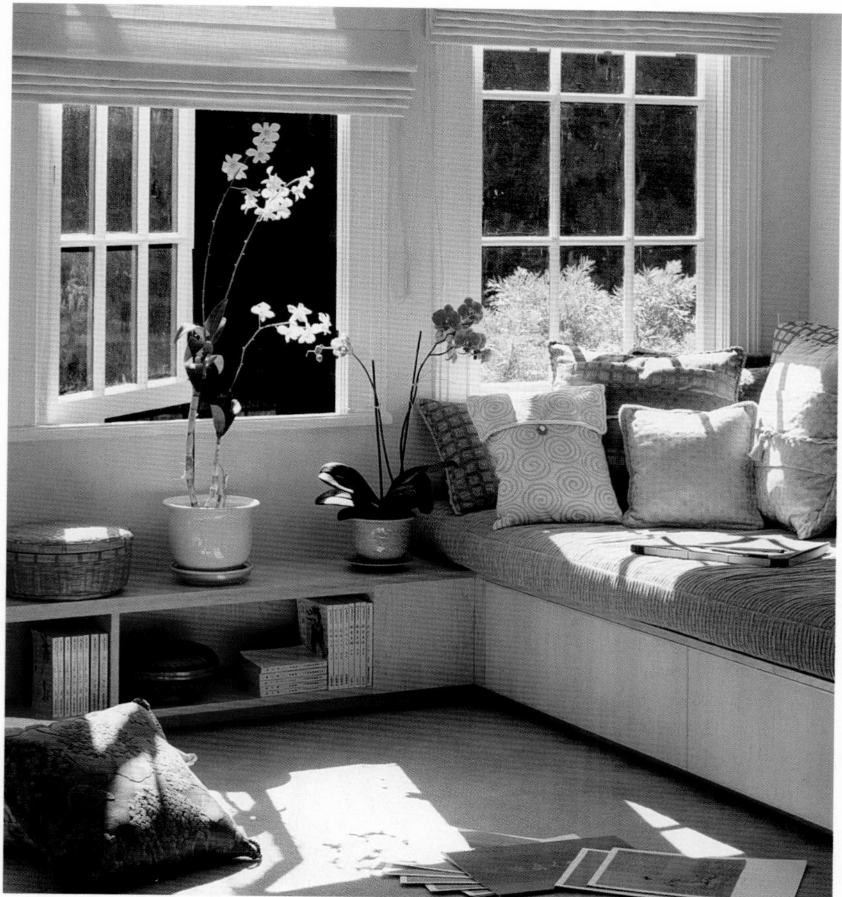

Carefully designed built-in furniture can do more than double duty. Beneath this couch are pull-out storage compartments, and a low bookcase extends from one end. The cushion is mattress-size, providing a spare bed.

Clever furnishings

Furnishing a small space gives you the opportunity to use your creativity and imagination. Here are a few ideas for compact approaches to using furniture.

VINTAGE AND VINTAGE-STYLE. Don't overlook such pieces as armoires, Hoosier cabinets, washstands, buffets, hutches, and chests that can make great storage and work areas. You can even convert an armoire into a self-contained "mini-office," sewing center, or potting workbench by modifying its interior with hooks, additional shelves, and so on.

Older furniture doesn't have to be in perfect shape; in fact, you can create a wonderful one-of-a-kind piece with creative use of paint and such decorative techniques as stenciling.

Cabinets, countertops, drawers, and shelving offer storage and work space galore in this fabric artist's garage-size studio. You can create a space like this with ready-made cabinets and countertops.

Updated with a contemporary plumbed-in sink and faucet, an antique washstand is now a compact, all-in-one vanity, sink, and towel rack.

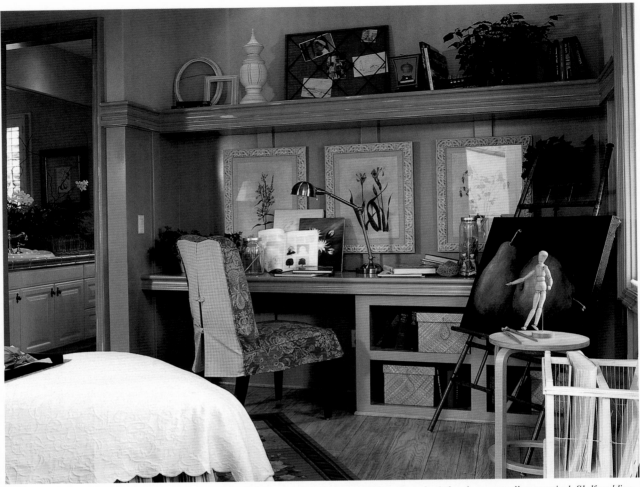

A built-in system of shelf, counter, and storage cubes is handsome as well as practical. Shelf molding and board paneling, as well as framed botanical prints, plants, and decorative bric-a-brac, lend style to this hard-working arrangement.

Built-in. Time-honored built-ins like Murphy beds that fold down from the wall, benches with lids that lift to reveal storage compartments, and built-in buffet/china cabinets are being updated in keeping with today's trend toward smaller houses. If you are handy yourself or can afford to hire a carpenter, you can equip your cottage with built-in furniture that fulfills several functions at once.

Handcrafted for a tiny guest house, a pull-out table allows a custom wall unit to double as a surface for working, eating, or serving. The 22-inch-deep tabletop retracts into a bookcase.

A drawer built under a window seat provides clever camouflaged storage for files in a small-space cottage office.

Ample windows above a cottage sink bathe the room in natural light during the daytime; soft recessed lighting and track lights turn up the wattage when natural light wanes.

A contemporary wall fixture is a work of art as well as a source of light.

Indoor lighting

By day, natural light is often all you need to brighten your cottage. Leave a French door open so light and air stream in; leave windows (especially south-facing ones) uncurtained to admit maximum sunlight. On overcast days or in a cottage that doesn't receive bright light, supplement natural light with light fixtures. And if you will be using your cottage at night, of course you'll need to plan for some form of lighting. Light fixtures can do much to set the style of your cottage decor.

Part of the charm of a simple cottage without electricity is the cozy, camping-out atmosphere created by the flickering light of candles and lanterns. (Just be sure to use them safely and to never leave them unattended.) If your cottage does have wiring, you may use anything from simple table lamps to beautiful wired-in ceiling and wall fixtures.

For the most effective lighting, use a combination of *ambient lighting* (soft light from overhead sources) and *task and accent lighting* (track lights and freestanding lamps that focus light for reading and other pursuits or that illuminate objects for display).

The soft glow of an old-fashioned oil lamp (left) or a contemporary electric lamp like the one at right, with a rustic twig base, should inspire convivial evenings in any backyard cottage.

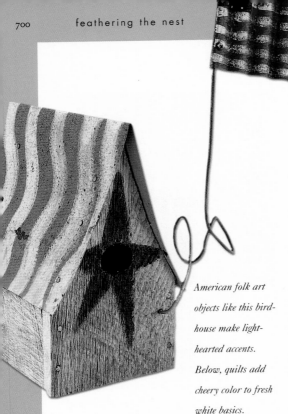

Decorative touches

Whether you've built your dream cottage from the ground up or are dressing up an existing shed, adding your own touches will give your backyard getaway a unique personal style. It's with these details that you really get to have fun—in large part because this is a private, informal environment where anything goes.

You can go for a particular style you love—be it classic American country, tropical island, or French Provençal—and assemble everything in keeping with that style, from curtains to drinking glasses. You can focus on a color scheme—all white, perhaps, or brilliant primaries—and carry it out with

American folk art objects like this birdhouse make lighthearted accents. Below, quilts add cheery color to fresh white basics.

Gather flowers from your own garden to bring brightness and fragrance into your cottage.

It's all in how you look at it; why not use a stepladder as a display rack?

If you own dishes you love, you needn't hide them away in cabinets. Displayed on open shelves, they can become part of your cottage decor.

vases of flowers, baskets, fabrics, lampshades, even knickknacks. Or you can simply fill your cottage with everything you love—vintage gardening tools, botanical prints bought on a trip to Europe, or all those mismatched fabric samples you've been collecting, sewn into a delightful hodgepodge of throw pillows for a built-in bench.

Think of your cottage's wall, floor, and window treatments as a backdrop for your "gallery" of beloved things. Hang prints and posters, mirrors, interesting signs, quilts, and related decorative objects or plates arranged in interesting patterns. Line up pretty bottles, dishes and cups, figurines, small potted plants or vases of flowers, and other small objects on shelves, ledges, and windowsills. Hang baskets or even antique tools from rafters.

Grouping art pieces like these colorful hand-painted "calendar" plaques, can have a big design impact.

IDEAS FOR GREAT WALL SYSTEMS design & photography credits

design

FRONT MATTER

4 Design: Freddy Moran and Carlene Anderson Kitchen Design **7** Interior design: EJ Interior Design, Inc.

A PLANNING PRIMER

8 Architect: Obie Bowman. Styling: Julie Atwood **13 (upper left)** Design: Jane Walter and Robert Adams/Summer-House **13 (upper right)** Ikea **21 (both)** Interior design: Sandy Bacon/Sandy Bacon Design Group. Home theater: John Maxon/Integrated System Design. Cabinets: Heartwood Studio **23 (upper left three and bottom right)** Ikea **24** Interior design: David Ramey/David Ramey Interior Design **25 (top)** Interior design: Ann Jones Interiors **26 (bottom left)** Architect: Scott Johnson **27 (top right)** Architect: Mui Ho **27 (bottom left)** Architect: Dave Davis/Dixon Weinstein Architects **27 (bottom right)** Organized Living

GREAT WALL SYSTEMS

28 Architect: Jarvis Architects **30** Architect: David Stark Wilson/ Wilson Architects **31** Interior design: Sasha Emerson Design Studio **32 (bottom)** Design: Holly Opfelt Design **33 (top left)** Interior design: City Studios **33 (top right)** The Container Store **33 (bottom)** Pottery Barn **34 (top)** Interior design: Bauer Interior Design **34 (bottom right)** Interior design: Wayne Palmer **35** Design: Nina Bookbinder **36 (top)** Architect: Colleen Mahoney/Mahoney Architects. General contractor: Cove Construction **37** Design: Cheng Design **39** Building design: William Gottlieb. Interior design: Markie Nelson **40** Interior design: Mel Lowrance **41** Design: Terri Taylor **42 (top)** Architect: Steven Goldstein **42 (bottom)** Interior design: EJ Interior design, Inc. **43** Architect: Mark Becker Inc. **44 (top)** Design: Jacobson, Silverstein & Winslow Architects/Paul Winans Construction Inc. **44 (bottom)** Architect/designer: Donald Clement. Cabinet fabrication: Apple Woodworks **45 (top)** Architect/designer: Donald Clement. Cabinet fabrication: Apple Woodworks **45 (bottom)** Interior design: Kit Parmentier/Allison Rose **46** Design: Daniel and Christine Hale/DMH The Art of Furniture **47** Design: Nancy Gilbert/San Anselmo Country Store **48 (top)** Interior design: Janice Olson/ JD–Just Design by Janice **48 (bottom)** Interior design: Sasha Emerson Design Studio **49 (bottom right)** Architect: Mark Becker, Interior design: Tami Becker **50** Interior design: Linda Applewhite **51** Architect: Charles Rose. General contractor: Dennis Jones. Lighting designer: Linda Ferry **52 (top)** Architect: Remick Associates Architects-Builders, Inc. Leaded glass window: Masaoka Glass Design **52 (bottom)** Architect: Edward Buchanan/Jarvis Architects **54** Architect: Charles Rose. General contractor: Dennis Jones. Lighting designer: Linda Ferry **55** Architect: Mark Becker, Inc. **56** Architect: J. Allen Sayles. Interior design: Sue Kahn **57** Design Group. Interior design: Judith Owens Interiors. Custom home builder: The Owen Companies. Lighting design: Catherine Ng/Lightsmiths **58 (top)** Interior design: Denise Foley Design and David Brewster **59** Architect: Steven Goldstein Architect **60 (left)** Design: Nancy Cowall Cutler **61 (top)** Lighting Design: Randall Whitehead Lighting, Inc. Architect: Erikson Zebroski Design Group **61 (bottom)** Interior design: Greg Mewbourne. Architect: David Gillespie **62** Interior design: Jeanese Rowell Design **63** Interior design: Pamela Pennington/Tsun Yen Tang Wahab/Pamela Pennington Studios **64 (all)** Design: Gordana Pavlovic/Design Studio Gordana LLC **65** Interior design: Renne Prudhomme, Vicki Saxton/Flegels. LCO flat screen television: Sound Perfection. Wall system fabrication: Segale Bros. **66 (top)** Design: Sandra C. Watkins. Paint color and fabrics: Joan Osburn/Osburn Design **66 (bottom)** Interior design: Sandy Crawford. Architect: Steve Feller **67 (top)** Architect: Thomas Bateman Hood **67 (bottom)** Interior design: Molly McGowan Interiors. Cabinetry: Rutt of Lafayette **68** Architect: Mark Becker Inc. **69** Architect: Steven Goldstein **70 (both)** Design: Aleks

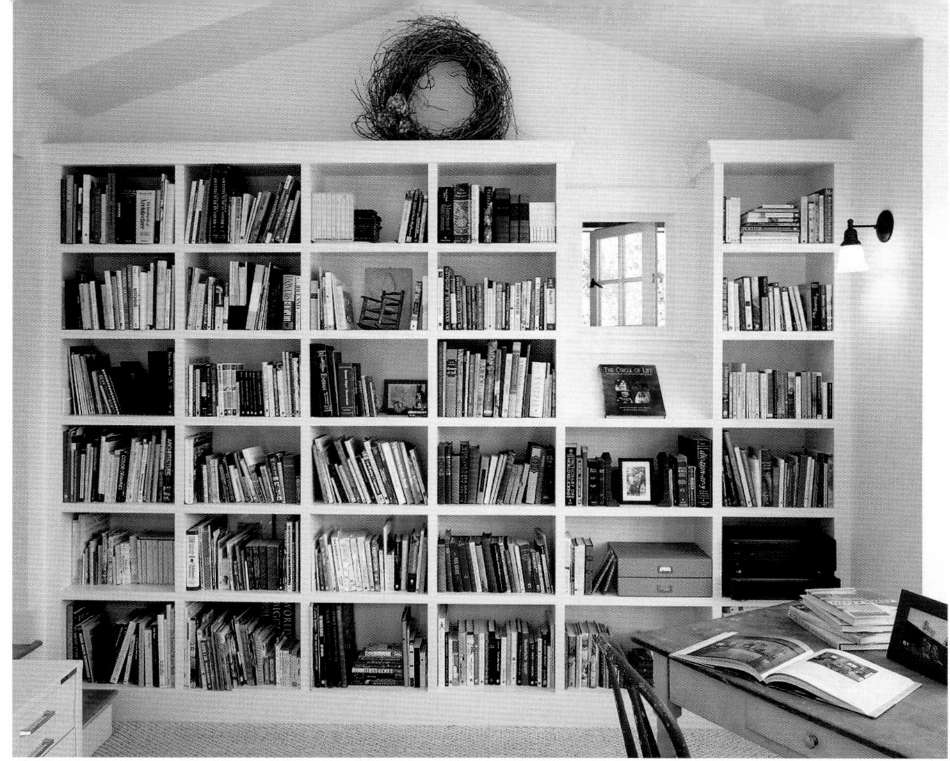

Istanbullu Architects **71 (top)** Design: Kent and Pam Greene **71 (bottom)** Architect: Mark Becker Inc. **72** Design: Bret Hancock/Thacher & Thompson Architects **73** Interior design: Barbara Jacobs. Cabinetry fabrication: Dana Karren **74 (top)** Interior design: Lisa Malloy/ Interior Inspirations **74 (bottom)** Architect/designer: Donald Clement. Cabinet fabrication: Apple Woodworks **75 (top)** Architect: Remick Associates Architects-Builders, Inc. **75 (bottom)** Architect: David Trachtenberg Architects **76 (top)** Architect: Gary Earl Parsons **76 (bottom left)** Design: Andre Rothblatt Architecture **76 (bottom right)** Design: Mercedes Corbell Design + Architecture **77 (top)** Architect: Jarvis Architects **77 (bottom)** Architect: Sanborn Designs Incorporated **79** Architect: Luther M. Hintz. Interior design: Pamela Pearce Design **80** Design: Celeste Lewis Architect **81 (bottom left)** Architect: Bassenian/Lagoni Architects. Interior design: Pacific Dimensions, Inc. **81 (bottom right)** Design: Charles Wooldridge **82 (both)** Design: W. David Martin, Architect **85** Studio Becker **86 (top)** Interior design: Lisa Malloy/ Interior Inspirations **87 (top left)** California Closets **87 (bottom left)** Whirlpool

A SHOPPER'S GUIDE

88 Interior design: Mark Mack **92 (bottom)** Ikea **94 (top left)** Ikea **94 (top right)** Zinc Details **95 (top right)** Studio Becker **96 (upper left)** Studio Becker **96 (upper right)** The Kitchen Source/The Bath & Beyond **96 (bottom left)** Häfele America Co. **96 (bottom right)** Eurodesign Ltd. **101 (top right)** Rev-A-Shelf **101 (bottom right)** Interior design: Kremer Design Group **102 (both)** Fenton MacLaren Home Furnishings **103 (top left)** Design: Debra S. Weiss **103 (bottom left)** Interior design: Barbara Jacobs/ Barbara Jacobs Interior Design. Cabinets: Al Orozco **103 (bottom right)** San Anselmo Country Store **104 (both)** Galvins Workspace Furniture **105** Interior design: Claudia Fleury/Claudia's Designs **106 (top)** Ikea **106 (bottom)** Galvins Workspace Furniture **107 (top right)** Ikea **108 (both)** Eurodesign Ltd. **109** House of European Design **111 (bottom left)** Ikea **111 (bottom right)** Eurodesign Ltd. **112** Interior design: Gigi Rogers Design **113 (top all)** Ikea **115 (bottom all)** The Kitchen Source/The Bath & Beyond **116** Organized Living **117 (top and bottom right)** Organized Living **117 (bottom left)** Ikea **118 (both)** House of European Design **119 (bottom)** Organized Living **120 (center left)** Häfele America Co. **121 (top and bottom left)** Eurodesign Ltd. **121 (bottom right)** Häfele America Co. **122 (top left)** Eurodesign Ltd. **122 (bottom left)** Häfele America Co. **122 (top right)** Interior design: Steven W. Sanborn **123 (top and center right)** Eurodesign Ltd. **123 (bottom left)** Galvins Workspace Furniture

BACK MATTER

702 Architect/designer: Donald Clement. Cabinet fabrication: Apple Woodworks **703** Architect: Edward Buchanan/Jarvis Architects

photography

Jean Allsopp: 27 bottom left, 66 bottom; **Ron Anderson/ Gloria Gale:** 81 top; **Michael Bruk:** 67 top; **Grey Crawford:** 70 all; **Tria Giovan:** 38 bottom, 49 left; **John Granen:** 39; **Ken Gutmaker:** 25 top left, 50 bottom, 76 bottom left, 96 top right, 105; **Jamie Hadley:** 7, 13 top left and right, 14–15 all, 23 bottom left and top three, 24 bottom, 25 bottom left, 26 top right, 27 bottom right, 28, 30 bottom, 31, 35, 42 all, 43, 44 bottom, 45 all, 46 bottom, 47, 49 bottom right, 52 bottom, 55 right, 59, 64 all, 66 top, 68 bottom, 69, 71 bottom, 73, 74 all, 75 bottom, 77 top, 85, 86 top, 90–95 all, 96 left top and bottom, 98–99 all, 101 bottom left, 102 all, 103 bottom right, 104 all, 106–110 all, 111 bottom left and right, 112 bottom, 113 top three, 116 left, 117–119 all, 120 left, 121 top and bottom left and right, 122 left top and bottom, 123–124 all, 126 left and bottom, 127 all, 702, 703; **Philip Harvey:** 27 top right, 34 top, 36 top, 44 top, 51, 52 top, 54, 57, 61 top, 75 top, 76 top, 77 bottom, 79, 96 bottom right, 97, 100, 101 bottom right, 113 bottom, 114–115 all, 121 middle right, 122 right top and bottom; **Alex Hayden:** 71 top, 80; **Muffy Kibbey:** 87 bottom left; **Sylvia Martin:** 61 bottom; **E. Andrew McKinney:** 4, 21, 32 bottom, 33 top left, 40, 48 top, 56 bottom, 58 top, 62 bottom, 65, 67 bottom, 81 bottom left, 103 left top and bottom, 112 top; **Kit Morris:** 49 top, 60 left; **Bradley Olman:** 86 bottom; **Heather Reid:** 76 bottom right; **Tom Rider:** 9; **Mark Rutherford:** 126 top right; **Michael Shopenn:** 81 bottom right; **Michael Skott:** 32 top, 34 bottom left, 36 bottom, 48 bottom, 111 top; **Robin Stancliff:** 41 right; **Thomas J. Story:** 37, 72 bottom, 82 all, 116 right, 120 right top and bottom; **Tim Street-Porter:** 26 bottom left, 83 bottom left, 87 bottom right, 88; **Roger Turk:** 83 top; **Brian Vanden Brink:** 13 bottom, 23 bottom right, 25 bottom right, 53, 58 bottom, 60 right, 78 bottom, 84 bottom, 103 top right; **Michael Venera/Pottery Barn:** 33 bottom; **David Wakely:** 34 bottom right; **Jessie Walker:** 83 bottom right; **Eric Zepeda:** 63

IDEAS FOR GREAT HOME LIGHTING design and photography credits

design

FRONT MATTER

128 Architect: Remick Associates Architects-Builders, Inc.; Interior designer: Donna White Interiors **130** Lighting designer: Catherine Ng/Lightsmiths Design Group; Architect: Steve MacCracken **131** Lighting designer: Catherine Ng/Lightsmiths Design Group; Architect: The Bradley Group; Designer: Eckhard Evers

A PLANNING PRIMER

132 Lighting designer: Linda Ferry; Architect: Charles Rose; General contractor: Dennis Jones **134** Interior design: Jennifer Bevans Interiors **135 top left** Lighting designer: Catherine Ng/Lightsmiths Design Group; Architect/engineer: Roger Hartley; Interior architecture and design: Jessica Hall Associates; Interior finishes: Melinda Field Carwile/Field Studio **135 center** Design: Brian A. Murphy and Fro Vakili, BAM Construction/Design **135 bottom** Lighting designer: Catherine Ng/Lightsmiths Design Group; Architect/engineer: Roger Hartley; Interior architecture and design: Jessica Hall Associates; Interior finishes: Melinda Field Carwile/Field Studio **136–137** Lighting designer: Randall Whitehead Lighting Inc.; Architect: Erikson Zebroski Design Group **146 top right** LIMN **147 left** Architect: Remick Associates Architects-Builders, Inc.; Interior designer: Gary Hutton Designs **149** Lighting design and installation: Berghoff Design Group; Technical support: Jonathan Hille

GREAT LIGHTING IDEAS

152 Designer: John Malick and Associates **154** Interior design: McWhorter/Ross Design Group **155** Lighting designer: Catherine Ng/Lightsmiths Design Group; Architect/engineer: Roger Hartley; Interior architecture and design: Jessica Hall Associates; Interior finishes: Melinda Field Carwile/Field Studio **156 top** Lighting designer: Catherine Ng/Lightsmiths Design Group; Architect: Steve MacCracken; Interior designer: Ron Smith **156 bottom** Lighting designer: Randall Whitehead Lighting Inc.; Architect: Erikson Zebroski Design Group **157** Lighting designer: Linda Ferry; Architect: Charles Rose; General contractor: Dennis Jones **158** Lighting designer: Catherine Ng/Lightsmiths Design Group; Interior designer: Judith Owen Interiors; Custom home builder: The Owen Companies **159** Interior designer: Marilyn Riding; Neon artist: Brian Coleman/Tercera Gallery **160 left** Design: Idea House at San Francisco Design Center **160–161** Lighting designer: Linda Ferry; Architect: Lee Von Hasseln **162** Lighting designer: Catherine Ng/Lightsmiths Design Group; Interior designer: Barbara Jacobs Interior Design **163 top** Lighting designer: Randall Whitehead Lighting Inc.; Architect: Erikson Zebroski Design Group **163 bottom** Architect: Brian Murphy **164** Lighting designer: Linda Ferry; Design: Pat & Bob Grace **165 top** Interior design: Richard Witzel & Associates **165 bottom** Product supplier: The Gardener **166** Lighting designer: Bryan Burkhart/California Architectural Lighting **167 bottom** Design: Brian A. Murphy and Fro Vakili/BAM Construction/Design **168** Lighting designer: Linda Ferry; Architect: Charles Rose; General contractor: Dennis Jones **169 bottom** Interior design: Sanborn Design, Inc. and Courtyard Collections **170** Lighting designer: Becca Foster Lighting Design; Architect: Michael Harris Architecture; Contractor: Pete Moffat Construction **171** Lighting designer: Melinda Morrison; Architect: Kuth/Ranieri **172** Lighting designer: Linda Ferry; Design: Pat & Bob Grace **174 top** Light-ing designer: Linda Ferry; Interior designer: Alissa Lillie/Marie Fisher Interiors; Architect: Brian Peters; Cabinet design: Sheron Bailey Curutchet **174 bottom** Lighting designer: Bryan Burkhart/California Architectural Lighting **175** Design: Josh Schweitzer/Schweitzer BIM **176** Lighting designer: Linda Ferry; Architect: Charles Rose; Interior designer: Michelle Pheasant Design **177 top** Lighting designer: Epifanio Juarez/Juarez Design; Architect: Marc Randall Robinson; Interior architecture and design: Scott Design **177 bottom** Interior designer: Eugenia Erskine Esberg/EJ Interior Design **178** Lighting designer: Linda Ferry; Architect: Eric Miller Architects, Inc.; Glass artist: Ahnalisa Miller **179** Architect: Marc Randall Robinson; Lighting designer: Epifanio Juarez/Juarez Design; Interior architecture and design: Scott Design **180** Architect: Backen, Arragoni & Ross **181 top** Architect: James Gillam Architects; Design: Jan Nissen Laidley **181 bottom** Lighting designer: Linda Ferry; Interior designer: Edward Perrault Design Associates, Inc. **182 top and bottom** Lighting designer: Linda Ferry; Architect: Eric Miller Architects, Inc.; Candle ring and sconce: Carl Olsen **182–183** Lighting designer: Catherine Ng/Lightsmiths Design Group; Architect: Steve MacCracken; Interior designer: Ron Smith **184** Architect: Kuth/Ranieri Architects **185** Lighting designer: Terry Ohm; Interior designer: Ann Maurice Interior Design **186** Design: Nick Cann/Graphics + Design **187 top** Lighting designer: Epifanio Juarez/Juarez Design **187 bottom** Lighting designer: Becca Foster Lighting Design; Architect: Michael Harris Architecture; Contractor: Pete Moffat Construction **188** Lighting designer: Linda Ferry; Architect: Lee Von Hasseln **189** Lighting designer: Linda Ferry; Architect: Brian Peters; Interior designer: Alissa Lillie/Marie Fisher Interiors; Cabinet design: Sheron Bailey Curutchet **190** Lighting designer: Linda Ferry; Architect: Charles Rose; General contractor: Dennis Jones **191 bottom** Interior and lighting design: Kenton Knapp **192** Architect: Kuth/Ranieri Architects **193 top** Lighting designer: Becca Foster Lighting Design; Architect: Michael Harris Architecture; Contractor: Pete Moffat Construction **193 bottom** Lighting designer: Randall Whitehead Lighting Inc.; Architect:

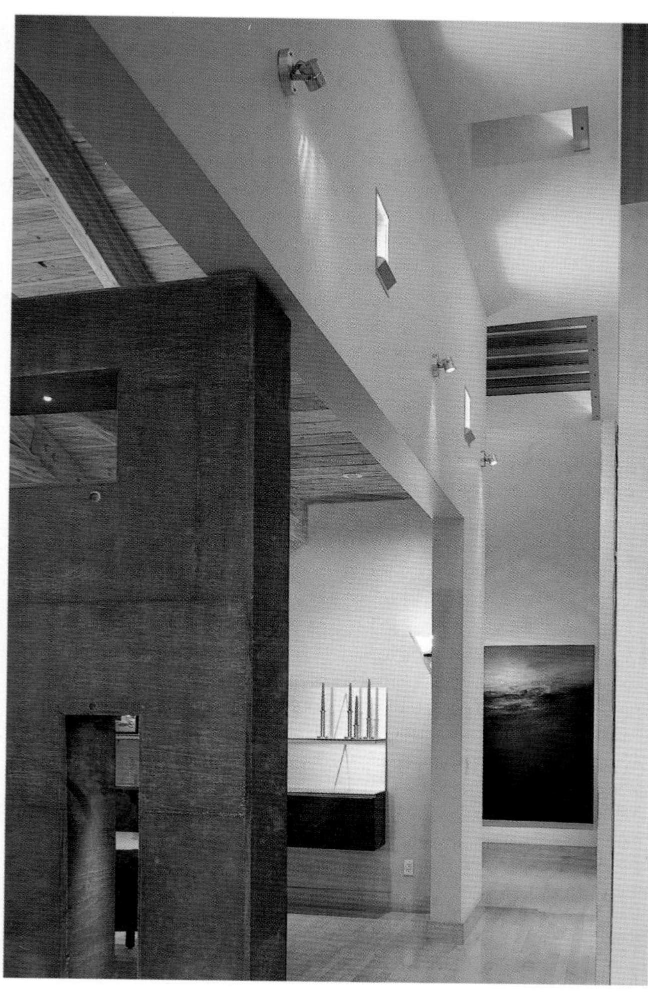

Erikson Zebroski Design Group **194 bottom** Architect: Nancy Schenholtz/Schenholtz Associates **195** Light-ing designer: Linda Ferry; Architect: Charles Rose; Glass artist: Masaoka Glass Design **196** Architects: Backen, Arragoni & Ross **197 bottom** Lighting designer: Melinda Morrison; Architect: Kuth/Ranieri **198 top** Architect: Peter Bohlin **198 bottom** Interior design: Osburn Design **199** Lighting designer: Randall Whitehead Lighting Inc.; Architect: Erikson Zebroski Design Group **200** Interior design: Jennie Gisslow/ Design Source **201** Lighting designer: Catherine Ng/Lightsmiths Design Group; Interior designer: Barbara Jacobs Interior Design **202 top** Cabinets: Kevin Coy; Contractor/builder: Peter Kyle **202 bottom** Lighting designer: Melinda Morrison; Architect: Kuth/Ranieri **203** Interior designer: Mary Ann McEwan/ Reviresco Design **204 top left** Lighting designer: Linda Ferry; Architect: Charles Rose; General contractor: Dennis Jones **204–205** Architect: Abraham Rothenberg **206** Landscape designer: Scott Cohen/The Green Scene **207** Lighting designer: Linda Ferry; Architect: Charles Rose; Glass artist: Masaoka Glass Design **208** Fence light: Artistic Cedar Post Company **209 top** Lighting designer: Linda Ferry; Original architect: Marcel Sedletzky; Remodel architect: Brian Peters; Contractor: Dennis L. Jones **209 bottom** Lighting designer: Becca Foster Lighting Design; Architect: Michael Harris Architecture; Contractor: Pete Moffat Construction **210** Architect: Backen, Arragoni & Ross **211 bottom** Lighting designer: Linda Ferry; Architect: Charles Rose **212 bottom right** Design: Yugi Koide **214** Lighting designer: Randall Whitehead Lighting Inc. **215 top** Design: Topher Delaney **215 bottom** Architect: Steven Erlich Architects **216 top** Lighting designer: Linda Ferry; Architect: Charles Rose **216 bottom** Lighting designer: Catherine Ng/Lightsmiths Design Group **217** Landscape architect: Robert W. Chittock

A SHOPPER'S GUIDE

218 Lighting designer: Linda Ferry; Design: Pat & Bob Grace **226** Neon artist: Alan Masaoka **226–227** Fiber optics: Fiberstars, Inc. **230 bottom left, 231 center left and bottom right, 233 top center and top right, 234 center** LIMN

BACK MATTER

705 Lighting designer: Catherine Ng/Lightsmiths Design Group; Architect: Steve MacCracken; Interior designer: Ron Smith

photography

Scott Atkinson: 130 top, 138–139 all, 142, 143 bottom, 170 top, 221 top right, 222 all, 223 bottom right, 230 bottom right, 231 bottom left, 233 top left and bottom grouping, 234 left, 243 top left, center, and bottom left, 244 bottom right grouping, 245 top left, 246 center, 247 top right grouping, 250 bottom grouping, 251 center left, top right, and bottom right; **Karen Bussolini:** 205; **Jared Chandler/www.beateworks.com:** 200 bottom; **Tria Giovan:** 173, 212 top; **Laurey W. Glenn:** 169 top; **Jamie Hadley:** 154 bottom; **Philip Harvey:** 128, 129 top, 130 bottom, 131, 132, 133, 134 bottom, 135 all, 13, 147 left, top right, and center right, 153, 155, 156 both, 157, 158 bottom, 159, 161, 162, 163 top, 164, 165 bottom, 166, 167 bottom, 168, 169 bottom, 170 bottom, 171, 172, 174 both,175, 176, 177 top, 178 bottom, 179, 180, 181 both, 182 both, 183, 184 bottom, 185, 186, 187 bottom, 188 bottom, 189, 190, 191, 192, 193 both, 194 top, 195, 196, 197, 198 bottom, 199, 201, 202 bottom, 203, 204 top, 206 bottom, 207, 209 both, 210, 211, 214, 215 bottom, 216 both, 217, 218, 245 bottom right, 705; **James Frederick Housel:** 208; **Muffy Kibbey:** 167 top; **davidduncan livingston.com:** 204 bottom, 215 top; **Renee Lynn:** 212 bottom left; **Peter Malinowski/In Site:** 149 both; **Stephen Marley:** 187 top; **McDonald/PhotoGarden, Inc.:** 212 bottom right; **E. Andrew McKinney:** 129 second, third, and fifth from top, 134 top, 140 top, 143 top, 144 top, 146 all, 147 bottom right, 148, 154 top, 160 left, 165 top, 177 bottom, 178 top, 184 top, 188 top, 200 top, 202 top, 219 all, 220 all, 221 top left four and bottom three, 223 top all and bottom left both, 224 all, 225 all, 226 both, 227 both, 229 all, 230 top and bottom left, 231 right four, 232 all, 233 top right three, 234 top center and bottom, 235 all, 236 all, 237 all, 238 all, 239 top all and bottom right, 241 top left two and bottom all, 244 top two, 245 top right two, 246 bottom left and right, 247 bottom left, 248 top two and bottom right, 249 top and bottom left two; **Ellen Pearlson:** 194 bottom; **Norman A. Plate:** 247 bottom right grouping, 248 bottom left; **Mark Rutherford:** 150 right, 151 all, 239 bottom left, 240 all, 241 top right two, 242 all, 243 top right and bottom right, 244 center left, 245 bottom left, 247 top left grouping, 249 center and bottom right, 250 top, 251 bottom left; **Jim Sadlon:** 213; **Michael Skott:** 129 fourth from top, 158 top; **Tim Street-Porter/www.beateworks.com:** 163 bottom; **Brian Vanden Brink:** 198 top; **David Wakely:** 152; **Suzanne Woodard:** 129 bottom, 150 left, 206 top

IDEAS FOR GREAT BABY ROOMS design credits

FRONT MATTER

252. Muralist: Roxane Murphy Smith. 254 (bottom). Design: Bellini, Butera. Decorative Artist: Audrey Busby. 255. Interior Design: Elizabeth Benefield.

CHAPTER ONE/ A PLANNING PRIMER

256. Design: Bridget Baskett-Stone and Steve Stone. 257. Hearthsong

The Master Plan

258 (tape measure) Rockridge Kids. 258. Interior Design: Claire L. Sommers/McCabe & Sommers Interiors. 259. Interior Design: Lynz Designs & Associates/Lynda Pratt Notaro. 260–261. Design by Heija Tabb Nunn. 263. Go to Your Room. 264–265. Interior Design: Juvenile Lifestyles, Inc./ Norm Claybaugh. Muralist: Rebecca. 267. Interior Design: David Weatherford Antiques and Interiors/Lori Broznowski. 268. Interior Design: Barbara McQueen Interior Design. 269. Muralist: Betts Art/ Todd Betts.

A Safe Haven

270 (monitor). Rockridge Kids. 270 (gate). Design and fabrication: Paul La Bruna. 271 (bottom right). Muralist: Sherrill Hull. 271 (top right). Window Treatment: Mara Rigel.

A Look That Will Last

272–273. Interior Design and Design Collage: David Weatherford Antiques and Interiors/ Lori Broznowski. 274. Muralist: Quinn Art/Jeannie Lovell. 275. Interior Design: David Dalton Associates. 276. Interior Design: Juvenile Lifestyles, Inc/ Norm Claybaugh .

CHAPTER TWO/ GREAT BABY ROOM IDEAS

278. Interior Design: Little Folk Art/Susan Salzman

Tying it all Together

280 (top). Bear: Goodnight Room. Blocks: Rockridge Kids. 280–281. Artisan: Heidi Favour. 282–283. Design: Cathleen Waronker and Melissa Dietz with Susan Salzman/ Little Folk Art. Upholsterer: Lillian Leygerer. 284–285. Design: Little Folk Art/ Susan Salzman. 286–287. Interior Design: Mary Engelbreit's Studio. 288–289. Artist: Catherine Richards.

Murals and Color

290 (top). Rockridge Kids. 290–291. Interior Design: Juvenile Lifestyles, Inc./Norm Claybaugh. 292–293. Decorative Artist: Cheryl Mussman Smith. 294. Interior Design: City Studios. 295. Design: Sasha Emerson Levin. 296–297. Muralist: Betts Art/ Todd Betts. 298–299. Interior Design: Juvenile Lifestyles, Inc./Norm Claybaugh. Muralist: Debbra. 300–301. Muralist: Betts Art/ Todd Betts. 302–303. Muralist: Betts Art/ Todd Betts. 304. Muralist: Quinn Art/Jeannie Lovell. 305. Muralists: Art 4 Architecture/ Constance Scott and Sara Winchester. 306–307. Muralist: Janet White.

Small Wonders

308 (top). Dollhouse furniture: Sweet Dreams. Teapot: Rockridge Kids. 308. Interior Design: Erin Blake. 309. Design: Laurie McCartney for www.babystyle.com. 310. Design: Victoria Havlish. 311. Interior Design by Kathryn Hill Interiors. 312 (top). Goodnight Moon Furniture and Accessories for A Child's Home. 312 (bottom). Design: Rosetree Cottage Interiors/Furnishings. Muralist: Roxane Murphy Smith. 313. Interior Designer: Jennifer Morgan Peterson.

Peas in a Pod

314 (top). Goodnight Room. 314–315. Design: Valerie Rostek. 316. Design and fabrication of changing units: Paul La Bruna. 317. Stenciling: Susan Griffin. 318. Muralist: Jennifer Carrasco. 319. Melissa Beyeler with design consultant Heather Stone for Imagine That.

Comfort Counts

320 (top). Bellini. 321. Goodnight Moon Furniture and Accessories for A Child's Home. 322. Muralist: Demar Feldman Studios/Miriam Feldman. Furniture from Imagine That. 323. Little Folk Art/ Susan Salzman. 324 (top). Design: Cindy Lorensen. 324 (bottom). Design: Rosetree Cottage Interiors/ Furnishings. Muralist: Roxane Murphy Smith. 325. Design: Viola Lee Icken and Bill Icken/Icken Associates Inc.

Clutter Control

326 (top). Hearthsong, Rockridge Kids, Goodnight Room, Cotton and Co. 326. Melissa Beyeler with design consultant Heather Stone for Imagine That. 327. Goodnight Moon Furniture and Accessories for A Child's Home. 328–329. Design and fabrication: Holly Opfelt. Chenille stacking pillows: Baby Rose. 330. Design: Bridget Baskett-Stone and Steve Stone. 331 (top). Interior Design: McCabe & Sommers Interiors/ Claire L. Sommers. 331 (bottom). Melissa Beyeler with design consultant Heather Stone for Imagine That.

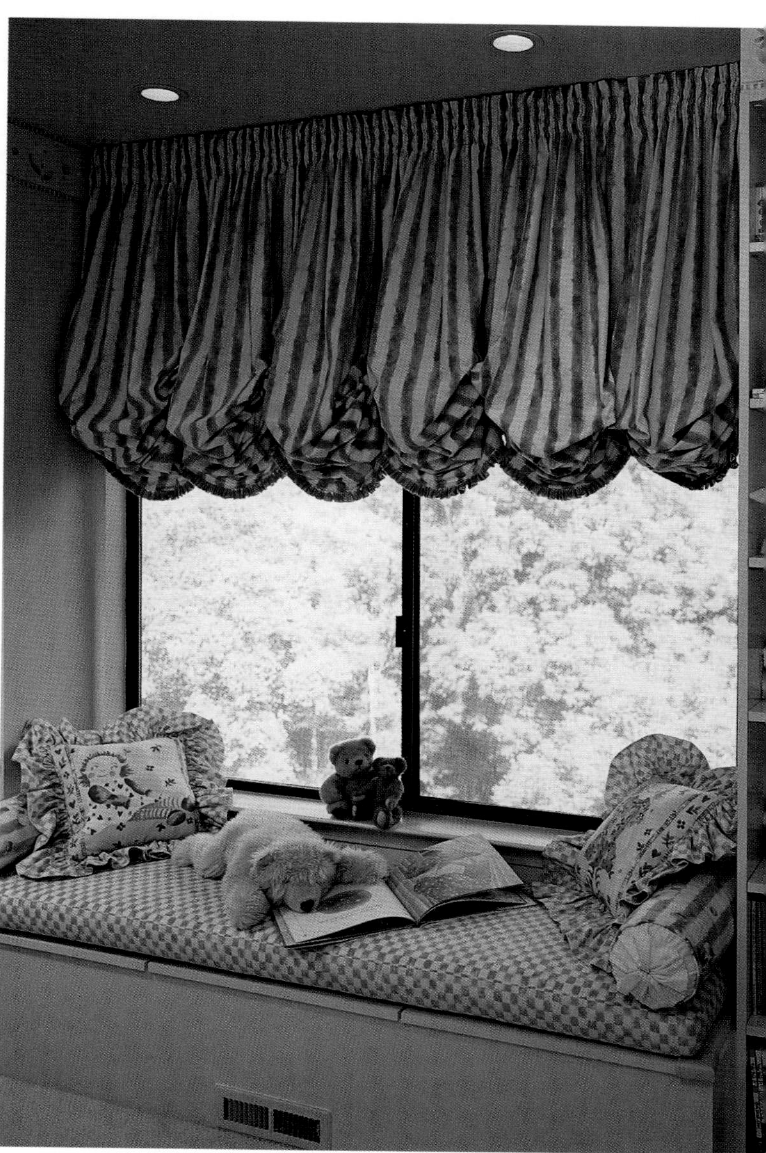

CHAPTER THREE/ A SHOPPER'S GUIDE

332. Muralist: Demar Feldman Studios/Miriam Feldman. Furniture from Imagine That. 333. Land of Nod.

Cribs and Cradles

334. Go To Your Room. 335. Bellini of Bellevue. 336 (top). Baby Rose. 336 (bottom). Arm's Reach Concepts. 337. Bellini of Bellevue.

Dressers and Changing Tables

338. Go to Your Room. 339, 340. Bellini of Bellevue. 341. IKEA.

Rocking Chairs

342 (top right). Chicago Textiles. 342 (bottom). Eddie Bauer, Inc.

Storage

344. Interior Design: Ann Davies Interiors. 345 (top and bottom). IKEA. 346 (top and right). IKEA. 346 (bottom). Cartan's Kids Stuff.

Crib Bedding

347 Mobile: IKEA. 347 (bottom). Go To Your Room. 348 Mobile: Land of Nod. 348 Cushion: Camp Kazoo. 349 (top left, center left). Bellini of Bellevue. 349 (top right, bottom right and left). Land of Nod. 349 (center right). Eddie Bauer, Inc.

Wall Treatments

351 (top). Muralist: Rebecca/ Juvenile Lifestyles. Wallpapers: Laura Ashley.

Flooring

352 (top and bottom right). Barbara McQueen Interior Design. 352 (bottom left). Westling Design/Christopher Stearns. 353 (top). Carpet Sculpture Studio/Joyce Harris. 353 (bottom left, clockwise from top left). Associated Warehouses Inc.; M.G. Whitney; M.G. Whitney; Textures, Inc.; Textures, Inc. 353 (bottom right) L. Greenberg and Associates. Flooring sourced by Barbara McQueen Interior Design.

Window Treatments

354. Hand-painted fabric: Katherina Powell. Fabrication: Jean-Marie Adams. 355 (top). Barbara McQueen Interior Design. 355 (middle). Design and fabrication: Holly Opfelt.

Lighting

356 (from left to right). Shades of Light. Goodnight Moon Furniture and Accessories for A Child's Home. Go to Your Room. 357 (clockwise from top left). Bellini of Bellevue; Shades of Light; IKEA; IKEA; Shades of Light.

Safety

358–359. Safetyproofing by Safety for Toddlers of Kirkland, Washington. 359. Muralist: Sherrill Hull.

Credits

707. Interior Design: Ann Davies Interiors.

PHOTOGRAPHERS

Unless noted, all photographs are by E. Andrew McKinney.
Brad Bartholomew: 348 (bottom).
Larry Hawley: 336 (bottom).
Oleg March: 325.
Barbara Elliot Martin, courtesy of Mary Engelbreit's Children's Companion: 286–287.
Sibila Savage: 254 (top), 257, 258 (top), 270 (top), 277 (bottom), 280 (top), 290 (top), 308 (top), 314 (top), 326 (top), 333, 343.

IDEAS FOR GREAT BACKYARD COTTAGES design and photography credits

design

FRONT MATTER

580 bottom Design: LeAnna Olson

PLANNING YOUR COTTAGE

582 Garden Design: Bob Dash **586** Design: Bob Dal Bon/ Structure 1 **587 top** Landscape Design: James David **587 bottom left and right** Design: Barbara Butler Artist-Builder, Inc. **588 bottom** Architect: Carol A. Wilson **589 top** Architect: Charles M. Moore/Moore-Poe Architects; Construction: Charles Mize/The Wilson-Mize Company **594** Architect: Barbara Chambers/ Chambers and Chambers; Construction: Dougall Construction **596 bottom** Design/Construction: Matt Erwin and Tamsen McCracken **598 bottom** Architect: Roc Caivano **599 top** Design/ Construction: Sam Eskildsen **599 bottom** Architect: George Israel for Southern Living Plans **601 top** Architect: Robert C. Chestnut for Southern Living Plans **601 bottom** Design: Amdega Limited **604 bottom** Design: Van-Martin Rowe Design of Pasadena **605 bottom** Design: Grant Liere and Nixie Barton **606 top** Design: Leonna Duff **607 top right** Decorative Painting: Pam Snell **607 bottom** Design: Sheri Sayre

A GALLERY OF COTTAGES

608 Architect: Lee H. Skolnick **610 bottom–611** Architect: David Trachtenberg/Trachtenberg Architects; Landscape Architect: Robert Trachtenberg/Garden Architecture; Contractor: Mueller Nicholls, Inc. **612–613 top** Design: Kim and Debie Stuart **613 bottom** Architect/Builder: Bill Galli; Landscape Designer: Peter Koenig **614** Interior Design: Michael D. Trapp **615** Design: Laura Courtney **616** Architect: Roc Caivano **617** Design: Tim Prentice **618 bottom** Design: Barbara and Gary Greensweig **619 top** Design: Ronald Lee Fleming/The Townscape Institute; Housewright: Tom Curtis **619 bottom** Design: Stephanie and Larry Feeney **620 bottom–621** Design: Robert and Nancy Tiner **623** Design: Janet Tiffany **624** Garden Design: Jacqueline Heriteau and Holly B. Hunter **625** Design: Penny Michels **626 bottom–627** Architect: Mark A. Hutker/Mark Hutker Associates & Architects Inc.; Landscape Architect: Steve Stimson/Stephen Stimson Associates **628** Architect: Charles Myer/Charles R. Myer & Co.; Builder: Michael Pollen **629** Architect: Tom Cullins/Truex Cullins & Partners Architects **630–631** Architect: Kathryn Rogers/Sogno Design Group **633** Design: Alicia and Bill Hitchcock **634 bottom–635** Design: Josef H. Maison/Custom Log, Ltd.; Interior Design: Nancy Maison/A Great Find **636 top** Design: Carol Anthony **636 bottom** Design: Diane Stevenson Design; Stonework: Michael Murphy; Leaded Glass: Alan Masaoka **637** Interior Design: Michael D. Trapp **638 bottom left** Design: Hap and Barbara Arnold **638 bottom right** Design: Sharon Fisher **639 top left** Design: Carol Biel **639 top right** Design: Brian and Debrah Nelson **639 bottom** Design: Barbara Butler Artist-Builder, Inc. **641** Design: David Phillips **642** Architect: Michael Keller **643** Courtyard Design: Carlos Mora; Garden Design: Yvonne Axene, assisted by Saul Velsquez **644–645 top** Design: Barbara Greensweig; Design/ Construction: Jim Tranchina **645 bottom** Design: Harriet Adams/The Potager **647** Architect: Mark A. Hutker/Mark Hutker Associates & Architects, Inc.; Landscape Architect: Steve Stimson/ Stephen Stimson Associates **648–649 all** Architect: McKee Patterson/Austin Patterson Disston Architects **650 bottom** Design: Gardensheds; Garden Design: Paula Mancester **651 top** Design: Charles de Lisle/The Charles de Lisle Program; Decorative Painting: Willem Racké/Willem Racké Studios **651 bottom** Design: Sweetwater Bungalows **652** Design: Hal Ainsworth for Southern Living Plans **653** Design: Amdega Limited; Interior Design: Vic and Carolyn Riches **655 top** Design: Ray Hugenberger, and Bob Dal Bon/Structure 1 **656 bottom–657** Architect: Roc Caivano **658–659** Design: Ene Osteraas-Constable/WOWHAUS, www.thewowhaus.com **660–661** Architect: Robert Remiker; Interior Design: Sarita Patel; Landscape Design: Angela and Tom Campbell **662–663** Architect: Rob Whitten **664–665** Architect: Jarvis Architects **666 bottom–667** Architect: Adrian Martinez; Construction: Doug Earl Construction and Marshall Vincent Construction; Interior Design: Ken and Noni Kahn and David Phillips; Garden Design: Geared for Growing **668** Architect: T. Scott Teas/TFH Architects **669 top** Architectural and Interior Design: Pamela Dreyfuss Interior Design; Millwork and Doors: Creative Cabinets **669 bottom** Courtyard Design: Carlos Mora; Garden Design: Yvonne Axene assisted by Saul Velsquez **670–671** Architect: Dennis O'Conner/The O'Conner Company; Landscape Architect: Marta Fry Landscape; Interior Design: Elizabeth Hill/Selby House **672 bottom** Design: Tim Prentice **673** Design/Construction: Jim Knott

COTTAGE ELEMENTS

674 Design: Laura Courtney; Chair Artist: Tim Whyard **676 top** Design: Elizabeth Lair Design **676 bottom** Design: Summerwood Products, www.summerwood.com **677 top left** Architect: Scott Design Associates **677 top center** Architects: Richard Bernhard and John Priestly/ Bernhard & Priestly Architects; Builder: Jay Fischer/Cold Mountain Builders **678 bottom right** Garden Design: Bob Dash **679 bottom** Design: Linda Hoffman/Guided Imagery Productions **682 bottom right** Architects: Bill Curtis and Russell Windham/Curtis & Windham Architects; Builder: Temple Pace/ Pace Development, Inc. **683 bottom left** Design: Elaine Shreve **684 top** Courtyard Design: Carlos Mora; Garden Design: Yvonne Axene assisted by

Saul Velsquez **685 top** Fireclay Tile **686 bottom** Design: Conni Cross **687 bottom center** Hadco Lighting **688 top right** Interior Design: Drysdale Associates Interior Design **688 bottom right** Interior Design: Elizabeth Hill/Selby House; Architect: Dennis O'Conner/The O'Conner Company **689 top left** Architect: Roc Caivano **689 bottom left** Interior Design: Pamela Dreyfuss Interior Design **689 center** Interior Design: Ken and Noni Kahn and David Phillips **689 top right** Architect: Roc Caivano **689 bottom right** Design: Georgie Kajer/Kajer Architects **690 left** Design: Brad Tito/Lazok Tito Consulting **690 right** Decorative Painting: Pam Snell **691 top left** Architect: Jarvis Architects **691 top right** Decorative Painting: Justina Jorrin Barnard **691 center** Architect: Mark A. Hutker/Mark Hutker Associates & Architects, Inc. **691 bottom** Design: Paul Zsafen **693 top right** Interior Design: Nancy Maison/A Great Find **694** Design: Sheri Sayre **695 top left** Design: Freddy Moran, and Carlene Anderson Kitchen Design **695 top right** Design: Robert and Nancy Tiner **695 bottom** Design: Mary Jo Bowling **696 top left** Design: Barbara Baker **696 top right** Design: Dirk Stennick, Architect **696 top and bottom center** Design: Penny Michels **697 top** Design: Dan Phipps & Associates Architects; Cabinets: Detail A Studios **697 bottom left** Design: Mark Adolph/Creative Concepts Design & Construction, and Sandy Hogan **697 bottom right** Design: Carolyn and Russ Walker; Sink and Faucet: Kohler **698 top** Architect: Bassenian/Lagoni Architects; Interior Design: Pacific Dimensions, Inc. **698 bottom left** Architect: Charles M. Moore/Moore-Poe Architects; Cabinetmaker: James Jennings **698 bottom right** Interior Design: Janice Stone for Sunset's California Idea House **699 top left** Interior Design: Kremer Design Group **699 top right** Architect: Mark A. Hutker/Mark Hutker Associates & Architects, Inc. **699 bottom right** GardenHome **700 bottom** Interior Design: Roberta Brown Root **701 top left** Design: Claire and Jamie Wright

photography

If not otherwise credited, photographs are by **Jamie Hadley**.

Jean Allsopp: 645 bottom left and right, 682 bottom right; **Frank Balthis:** 651 bottom; **Karen Bussolini:** 581, 587 top, 625 all, 696 top and bottom center; **Brian Carter/The Garden Picture Library:** 683 bottom right; **Crandall & Crandall:** 696 top left; **Eric Crichton/The Garden Picture Library:** 680 top; **Robin Cushman:** 580 bottom; **Ken Druse:** 700 top right; **Derek Fell:** 602, 677 left center, 682 top; **Jay Graham:** 612, 613 top left and right; **Ken Gutmaker:** 613 bottom, 701 bottom; **Lynne Harrison:** 655 bottom right, 676 top, 677 top right, 678 bottom left, 683 top, 709; **Margot Hartford:** 696 top right; **Philip Harvey:** 592, 596 top, 604 bottom, 610 top, 633 all, 684 bottom left, 685 both, 688 bottom left, 699 top left and bottom right; **Douglas Johnson Photography:** 607 top right, 690 top right; **Muffy Kibbey:** 594; **Lamontagne/The Garden Picture Library:** 605 top; **David McDonald:** 619 bottom; **E. Andrew McKinney:** 579 third from bottom, 580 top, 586, 604 top, 610 bottom, 611 both, 620 bottom, 621 both, 653 both, 655 top and bottom left, 658, 659 both, 670, 671 both, 673 both, 675, 677 top left, 687 bottom right, 688 bottom right, 692 bottom, 693 bottom right, 695 top left and right, 696 bottom right, 698 top, 700 top left; **Allan Mandell:** 605 bottom, 607 bottom, 677 bottom center, 683 bottom left, 694, 701 top left; **Charles Mann:** 636 top, 677 bottom right, 687 top right; **Sylvia Martin:** 599 top, 681 bottom right; **Stephanie Massey:** 585; **Steven Mays:** 691 top right; **Emily Minton:** 589 top, 652 both, 698 bottom left; **Terrence Moore:** 690 left; **Jerry Pavia:** 582, 589 bottom center and right, 590, 654 bottom, 678 left center and bottom right, 679 top, 681 top and center right, 682 bottom left, 692 top; **John Peden:** 628 both; **Robert Perron:** 646 bottom; **David Phelps:** 689 bottom right; **Norman A. Plate:** 679 bottom; **Susan A. Roth:** 606 top, 650 bottom, 686 both; **James R. Salomon:** 588 bottom; **Sibila Savage:** 642 both; **Michael Skott:** 578, 678 top left, 681 center, 699 bottom left, 700 bottom, 701 top right; **Robin Stancliff:** 697 bottom left; **John Sutton:** 697 top; **Tim Street-Porter/www.beateworks.com:** 691 bottom; **Thomas J. Story:** 695 bottom; **Courtesy of Summerwood Products, www.summerwood.com:** 676 bottom; **Van Chaplin:** 599 bottom, 601 top; **Brian Vanden Brink:** 606 bottom, 607 top left, 662, 663 both, 688 top right; **David Wakely:** 697 bottom right, 698 bottom right; **Jessie Walker:** 584 bottom

IDEAS FOR GREAT FLOORS photo credits

Abet Laminati: 536 top
Aged Woods, Inc.: 517
American Olean: 478; 493
Ann Sacks: 464 top right; 482; 488 bottom; 494; 502–503; 507 bottom; 553 bottom
Armstrong World Industries, Inc.: 533; 534–535
Artistic Tile, Inc. (1-800-260-8646; www.artistictile.com): 462 bottom; 508 bottom
Bisazza Glass Tile: 488 top
Blackstock Leather, Inc. (1-800-663-6657; www.blackstockleather.com): 551 (Photograph by Doug Hall); 552 top (Photograph by David Lee) and bottom (Photograph by Paul Warchol)
Bomanite Corporation: 465 bottom right; 548; 549; 550 top; 576
Bruce hardwood floors: title page; 464 bottom; 469; 479; 511; 512 bottom; 516 top; 518; 520; 564; 710
Congoleum Corporation: 462 top; 466; 526 top; 527; 529 top
Crossville Porcelain Stone/USA: 484
Engelmann, Inc. Contractors, Sun Valley, Idaho: 514 top; 560
Phillip Ennis: 490 bottom (Nicholas Calder); 497 (Terra Designs/Anna Salibelo); 498–499 (IDT/Stuart Narofsky); 500 top (Angela Grande Associates with Claus, Architect); 501 (Nicholas Calder); 504 bottom (Dineen Nealy Architects); 509; 545 (Denise Balaser); 556 (John Buscarello)
Forbo Linoleum, Inc.: 525; 526 bottom
Formica Corporation: 468; 512; 532; 535; 536 bottom; 538; 539
Tria Giovan: 508 top
Ken Gutmaker: 537
Jamie Hadley: 575 bottom right
Imagine Tile, Inc.: 492 top and bottom
Dennis Krukowski: 485 (Siskin Valls, Inc.); 512 top (George Constant, Inc.)
Masland Carpets & Rugs: 463; 472; 473; 543
E. Andrew McKinney: 465 bottom left; 496; 516 bottom; 524; 542 bottom; 544 top and bottom; 547 top and bottom; 550 bottom; 572 top; 570 top
Melabee M Miller: 458 (Fentell Housing Corp., Vorhees, NJ); 465 top right and (Deborah Leamann Interiors, Pennington, NJ); 505 (Sharon Draznin, Short Hills, NJ); 519 top (Lisa Melone, Summit, NJ); 542 top (Deborah Leamann Interiors, Pennington, NJ)
Nafco, by Domco Tarkett: 528; 529 bottom
National Wood Flooring Association: 510; 513
Bradley Olman: 521 top and bottom
Questech® Metals from Crossville Porcelain Stone/USA: 553 top
Kenneth Rice Photography/ www.kenricephoto.com: 459 bottom
Mark Samu: 486 (Len Kurkowski A.I.A.); 487 bottom (Eileen Boyd Design); 491 (The Tile Studio); 495 top (Courtesy Hearst Publications); 504 top (Anne Tarasoff Design); 519 bottom (Courtesy Hearst Publications); 522 top (Courtesy Hearst Publications); 541 (Lee Najman)
Seneca Tiles, Inc. (1-800-426-4335; www.SenecaTiles.com): 554 (T.A. Etter Photography)
Alan Shortall 2001: 460; 461; 464 top left; 471; 474; 487 top; 500 bottom; 506; 507 top and bottom; 546
Tim Street-Porter/beateworks.com: 490 top (Scott Johnson Architect); 523 (Brian Murphy Architect)
Tarkett, Inc.: 456; 465 top left
Through the Lens Management/ R. Greg Hursley: 480
TimberGrass Fine Bamboo Flooring & Panels, Bainbridge Island, WA: 514 bottom; 515 (Photographs by Art Grice)
Jessie Walker Associates: 457 (David Smith, Designer); 470 (Michael Muha of M.G. Michael & Associates, Inc., Birmingham, MI); 483 and back cover; 489 (Steve Knutson of Knutson Designs, Evanston, IL); 495 bottom (Past Basket, Dave McFadden, Designer, Geneva, IL); 499 (Allen Portnoy, ASID, Chicago, IL); 540 (Kay McCarthy, Designer; Jim Thorp, Architect, Burr Ridge, IL)
Wicanders Cork Flooring: 467; 477; 530–531; 531 top and bottom

IDEAS FOR GREAT KIDS' ROOMS
photo credits

Peter Aaron/Esto, 383 bottom, 421
Amisco Industries, Inc., 432 right
Lea Babcock, 423 bottom
Laurie Black, 426 bottom, 447
Andrew Bordwin, 371, 372 top, 380, 383 right, 385 bottom, 386 top, 396 top, 398, 402 top, 410 top left, 411 bottom, 413, 415 bottom, 427 bottom right, 442 right, 451 bottom
Child Craft, 376 middle left and bottom left, 401 bottom right
Cosco, 436 top left
Crandall & Crandall, 410 top, 411 top, 416 top
Stephen Cridland, 418 bottom, 420 top, 432 left
Mark Darley/Esto, 412 bottom
Design Horizons by Ladd Furniture, Inc., 437 top
eurodesign, Ltd., 373, 412 top, 434 bottom
Richard Fish, 401 left
Fisher-Price, 442 left
Scott Frances/Esto, 367 top, 368, 393, 422 top
Fun Furniture, 407 bottom, 443 bottom
Michael Garland, 367 bottom, 382 bottom, 388 left, 414 bottom, 417, 445
Shelley Gazin, 449 top
Jeff Goldberg/Esto, 379
Philip Harvey, 360, 362, 363 bottom, 364, 366, 378, 381 bottom, 382 top, 390, 391, 394, 396 bottom, 397, 399, 400, 402 bottom, 403, 406, 409, 410 bottom, 411 top left, 414 top, 836 bottom, 423 top, 424, 426 top, 427 top, 428, 430, 431 top, 435 middle, 436 bottom left and right, 437 bottom, 439, 440, 444, 446, 448, 450, 452, 454
Lands' End, 363 top, 435 top
Stephen Marley, 404 top
Norman McGrath, 381 top
Norman A. Plate, 451 top
Kenneth Rice, 435 bottom
Southern Living Magazine, 372 bottom, 387, 401 top right, 425 left, 427 bottom left
Techline by Marshall Erdman & Associates, Inc., 385 middle, 404 bottom
3M, 361
Brian Vanden Brink, 405 top, 419
VanderSchuit Studio, 376 top, 386 bottom, 388 right, 408, 416 bottom, 418 top, 420 bottom, 425 right, 431 bottom, 434 top
John Vaughan, 449 bottom
Visador Company, 441
Darrow M. Watt, 385 top
Whitney Brothers, 443 top
Doug Wilson, 407 top
Tom Wyatt, 415 top

cover and front matter credits

Front cover:
Main image: John Granen
Bottom 1: Thomas J. Story
Bottom 2: George Ross
Bottom 3: Thomas J. Story
Bottom 4: John Granen

Back cover:
Top left: Congoleum Corporation
Top right: Ann Sacks
Bottom left: Thomas J. Story
Bottom right: John Granen

Page 1: Thomas J. Story
Page 3: James Carrier

index

A

A-bulbs, 220, 228–229, 234
Accent lighting, 134, **135,** 136, 145, 158, 178, 224, 240
Accessories, specialized, 120–123
Acoustic flooring, **461,** 467, 524, **530,** 568
Acrylic roofs, **621, 672**
Activities, planned 367
Adhesive(s)
  air quality and, 468
  for laminate, 571
  for parquet flooring, 566
  for porcelain pavers, 558
  for tiles, 559
  time for setting of, 479
Adjustable furnishings, 378
Adobe, 606, **636,** 679
Ages and stages, 371–373, 377
Aluminum siding, 679
Ambient lighting, 134–135, 136, 143, 158, 200, 222, 234, 240
Americans with Disabilities Act (ADA), 559
Appliqués, wall, **389**
Arbors, **620, 648, 669,** 686
Architects, working with, 599, 600
Architectural drawings, 603
Armoires, 340
Art, lighting for, **136,** 139, **156, 157, 169,** 184, **185, 186,** 232, **233**
Art studios, **594, 640–645, 694**
Asbestos, 479, 569
Audio tapes, 23
  sizes of, 17

B

Baby gates. *See* Safety gates
Baby monitor, 263, 359
Backlighting, **138,** 139, **149, 158,** 208
Ballasts, 144, 145, 222, 229, 244
Bamboo, 461, 464, 510, **514, 515,** 564, **565**
Bark, shredded, 685
Baskets, storage, 443
Bassinets, 334. *See also* Beds
  and safety, 270
Bathrooms, 26, **37, 45**
  lighting, 147, 194, **194–199,** 236–237
Battery-operated lights, 233
Beam pattern, 146
Bedding for cribs, 347–349
Bedrooms, 25, **44, 54, 82**
  lighting, 188, **188–193**
Beds and daybeds, **320, 322, 323, 324, 422–423,** 430–435. *See also* Cradles; Cribs
  adult-size, 432
  bassinets, 430
  built-in, **380, 423**
  bunk, **401, 402, 404, 410, 420,** 432
  canopy, **380, 390, 411,** 434–435
  captain's, **423,** 434
  chest, **401, 412**
  cradles, 430
  cribs, **371, 376, 383, 396,** 431
  and safety, 369
  fantasy, **411,** 435
  fold-down, **82, 123**
  intermediate, 431, **442**
  loft, **365, 368, 398, 422,** 433, **434**
  platform, **423**
  sleigh, **363**
  wall, **425,** 435
Bedside tables, **363, 383, 388, 410, 436,** 437
Benches, **34**
Bins, boxes and baskets, 117, 120, 443
Birch, 464, **514**
Bleaching, 567
Blinds, 354, 693. *See also* Window treatments
Bookcases, 345–346, 442. *See also* Storage
Books, typical sizes of, 17
Bookshelves, 10, 16–17, **30, 34, 36, 38, 39, 47, 48, 52, 55, 73, 78,** 102, 106
Book walls, **27, 38, 40–41**
Border(s), 476
  of area rug, **544**
  of carpeting, 574
  ceramic tile, 473, **492**
  cork, **531**
  limestone, **462, 504**
  marble, **501**
  metallic, 548
  mosaic, **490**
  porcelain, **484**
  stone, 473, 563
  wood, 473, **516, 519, 521, 522, 566,** 567
Bounce lighting, **139,** 194. *See also* Indirect lighting
Brackets, 19, **33, 60,** 92–93
Brick, **664,** 679, **684,** 685, 689
Broadloom. *See* carpeting
Budget, 260, 468, 476, 596–597
Building department, 597, 599, 602, 619
Built-in furniture, 698
Built-in lighting, 135, 146, **147,** 154, 158, 178, 188, 225
Built-ins, **7,** 12–**13, 25, 39, 40–41, 42, 43, 44, 45, 50–55, 58, 59, 66, 68–71, 72, 73, 74, 75, 76, 77, 78,** 79, **80, 81, 82, 86, 87, 88**
Bulbs, *see* Light bulbs
Bulletin boards, 449
Bunk Beds. *See* Beds
Buying a mattress, 433

C

Cabinets, **7,** 10, 11, **39, 41, 42, 43, 44, 45, 51, 52, 57, 59, 66, 67, 68–71, 72, 73, 77, 78, 79, 80, 81, 86, 87, 88**
  for children, **26, 32, 48**
  inserts, 120
  shopping for stock, 114–115
Cable, electrical, 148, 150–151, 246, **247,** 248–259
Cable lights, **147,** 158, **167, 186, 201, 202,** 239
Canopy beds. *See* Beds
Captain's beds. *See* Beds
Carbon monoxide alarm, 358
Carpeting, 446, 463, 465, **473,** 540, **540–547**
  for acoustics, **461**
  installation of, 479
  for luxurious feel, 470
  measuring for, 479
  odor of new, 479
  shopping for, 572–575
  slip resistance of, 466
  texture of, 473
Cast-earth construction, 679, **690**
Caulking, 559
Ceiling fixutres, 452–453
Ceilings, lighting, 138, 154
Ceramic tile, 460, 464, **471, 478, 482–495,** 685, **688,** 689. *See also* Terra-cotta; Tile(s)
  around carpeting, **541**
  faux, **528**
  at hearth, **523**
  measuring for, 479
  metal and, 474
  replicating in laminate, 465
  shopping for, 556–559
  slip resistance of, 466
  subfloor for, 479
  texture of, 473
Ceramic Tile Distributors Association (CTDA), 558
Chairs
  desk, **364–365, 368, 380, 383,** 438
  low tables and, 367, 372, 381, 386, 436, 437, 439
  nursing, 263, 320, 342
Chalkboards, **381,** 447, 448
Chandeliers, 135, 137, 178, **181,** 221, 234, 235
Changing tables, **265, 286,** 338, **383, 397, 449**
  and safety, 271
Checkerboard design, **471,** 472, 475, **483,** 524
Cherry, 564, **565**
Chest beds. *See* Beds
Chestnut, 565
Children's rooms, **26, 32, 48**
Circline tubes, 223, 228–229, 234
Circuit mapping, 150–151

Page numbers in **boldface** refer to photographs or illustrations

Cleaning. *See* Maintenance
Climate, 590–591, 690
Clip-on lamps. See Lamps
Closets, 25, **52, 67, 87,** 118, 119, 345–346, **415, 427,** 441
Clothes hampers, 442
Clutter control, **326–331,** 433–349
Cobblestones, **509**
Codes, building, 588, **596,** 597, 599
COF (coefficient of friction), 466, 559
Cohesion in style, **280–289**
Cold cathode light, 145, 226–227
Collection displays, **4, 54, 56, 57, 58, 60, 61, 65, 66, 71, 78, 80, 83,** 391, **405–407**
  lighting, 139, **158**
Color, **276, 290–291, 293, 294–295,** 368, 688. *See also* Murals for boys or girls, 269, 274, **285**
Color rendition, 140–141, 144, 145
Color temperature, 141, 145, 222
Comfort in nursery, providing for parents and baby, **320–325**
Compact discs, 23, **66, 70,** 113
  size of, 17
Compact fluorescent bulbs, 145, 222, 223, 228–229
Components, wall system, 10–11
  shopping for, 90–101
Concrete, 463, 465, **549**
  carpeting over, 574
  cast-in-place, **548, 550**
  design possibilities of, 474, 548, 576
  linoleum runner on, **524**
  poured, **515**
  weathering of, 468
Concrete paving, **684,** 685
Construction phase, 602
Contemporary rooms, 390
Contractors, 600, 602
Contrast, 277
Convertible furnishings, 376
Copper roofs, **613, 668, 677**
Cordless phone, as safety feature, 359
Cork, 462, **467**
  acoustic use of, 467, 524, **530,** 568
  comfort of, 465, **530**
  installation of, **477**
  safety of, **531**
Control panels, 137, 158, 245
Controls, 137, 158, 188, 242–245
  for outdoor lighting, 250–251
Costs, 596–597
Counter extension, 121
Cradles, 334–335. *See also* Beds
  and safety, 270
Crema Marfil marble, 461, 562
Cribs, 335–337. *See also* beds
  bedding for, 347–349
  mattresses for, 337
  and safety, 270
  and stimulation for babies, 277
Cubbyholes, **27, 44, 46, 54–55, 61, 78, 84, 86**
Curtains, 355, 680, 692, **693.** *See also* Window treatments
Cushion, carpet, 574

D

Dark rooms, 267
Daylight sensors, 250
Decks, 684–685
Decorating considerations, 366–370
Decorative fixtures, 135, 137, 158, 178
Decorative moldings, 449
Decorative touches, 700–701
Design, 470–475
Design and style, 12–13, 16–19
Designers, 599, 600
Design phase, 602
Desks, **41, 42, 71, 72–77, 82, 104, 364, 365, 368, 373, 380, 382, 383, 401, 402, 404, 408, 416–418, 436–438**
  built-in, **373, 379, 380, 398, 401, 402**
  computer, **437,** 438
  loft beds and, **364**
Diaper bins, 263, 341
Diaper-changing surfaces, 263. *See also* Changing tables; Dressers
Dimensions
  for seating, 384
  for shelving, 384
Dimmers, 137, 145, 154, 158, 178, 184, 194, 200, 222, 244, 245
Dining area lighting, 178, **178–183**
Dining rooms, 24–25, **47, 49, 58, 68, 69**
Dishes, **4, 47, 50, 55, 56, 58, 120**
Display, **4, 25, 26, 33, 36, 37, 42, 48, 49, 50, 51, 53, 54, 56–61, 65, 68. 71, 78, 80, 83,** 391, **405–407**
Distributors, 476
Doghouses, **638–639**
Doors, 680
Doors, cabinet, 10, 11, 96–99
  drop-down, 96
  folding, **64, 87**
  glass, **45, 48, 58, 74, 75, 77,** 97
  hardware, 98, 99
  hinged, 11, **96**
  knobs, 99
  pulls, 99
  retractable, 11, **96**
  shopping for, 96–99
  sliding, **67, 76, 82, 96**
Downlighting, **138, 149,** 150, 154, 208
Downlights, **147,** 158, 184, 208, 240–241
Drawers, 10, 11, **43, 44, 45, 74, 76, 77, 81, 85, 86, 88,** 100–101
  guides for, 101
  organizers for, 101
  shopping for, 96–99
  under bed, 442
Drawings, 602
  architectural, 603
Drawings, plan 392, 592–595
Dressers, 339–340, **383, 400, 409, 410, 427,** 441
Dressing tables, **373, 424**
DVDs, size of, 17

E

Easements, 593, **597**
Electrical cable, 148, 150–151, 246, **247,** 248–249
Electrical and heating safety, 369
Electricity, 585–586, 591, 690
Electronic equipment, 20–23
  cabinetry for, 20, **21, 23, 42, 62–67, 71, 77, 121**
  shopping for, 110–113
Elements, room, 380–389
Energy efficiency, 144, 145, 147, 170, 220, 222, 680
Energy requirements, 222
Engineers, 600
Entertaining spaces, 666–671
Entryways, 17, **53, 80, 81, 86**
  lighting, 154, **154–157, 207**
EPA (Environmental Protection Agency), 468, 479
ER bulbs, 221
Essentials for new babies' rooms, 263
Exposure, 590–591, 592

F

Fan/light combinations, 234, 235
Fantasy beds. *See* Beds
Fantasy Rooms. *See* Theme rooms
Fences, **647, 648,** 685–686
Fiber optics, 135, 145, **158, 183, 198**
Finishes, 479, 563, 567. *See also* Sealers, Sealants
Finishes for furniture, 124–125
Fireplaces, **39, 42, 51, 54, 63**
Fixtures, 146–147, 230–241, 452–453
  built-in, 135, 146, **147,** 154, 158
  installing, 150–151
  movable, 230–233
  outdoor, 148, **206–217,** 246–249
  recessed, **147,** 240–241
  solar, 251
  surface-mounted, 234–235
  track, **147, 174,** 238–239
Flagstone, 461, 464, 562–563
Floating floor, 462, 464, 465, **511,** 567, 571
Flooring, 352–353, **367, 381,** 386, 444–446, 620, 688–689
Floor lamps, 453
Floor plans, **585**
Fluorescent light, 140, 144–145, 147, **166,** 170, **175,** 194, 200, 222–223, 228–229, 234, 237, 453
  color of, 140, 145, 222
  dimming, 137, 244
Fold-down beds, **82, 123**
Folding screen, **372**
Footcandles, 142–143
Framing, 605–606
Freestanding storage, 12, **13, 46–49, 62, 77, 83**
  shopping for, 102–105
Furnishings, 694–701
Furniture, 263, 334–347, 383. *See also* by individual type
  adjustable, 378
  convertible, 376
  custom- or hand-painted, **360, 372, 383, 386, 396, 401, 402, 407, 409, 413, 442**
  finishes, 124–125
  modular, **373,** 376, **404, 412**
  and safety, 271–271, 369
  storage. *See* Storage furniture
  shopping for, 102–105, 343, 438

G

Garages, **86,** 117
Garden lighting **149,** 208, 251
Garden sheds, **584, 585, 587, 620–625, 650, 654, 655, 683, 695**
GFCI, 194, 242, 248
Glare, 137, 145, 178, 188, 200, 206, 208

Glass, 460, 482, **488, 490,** 558, **559**
insulating, 680, 690
roofs, **653,** 679
walls, **653,** 679
Glass doors, **45, 48, 58, 74, 75, 77,** 95
Glass shelves, **33, 36, 45, 58**
shopping for, 91
Glue. *See* Adhesive(s)
Golden Spider marble, 561
Granite, 460, 461, 464, **498, 499,** 562
replicating, 482
tiles, **499**
Gravel, 620, **621,** 685
Grazing,139, **139, 202, 211**
Grid storage, **695,** 696
Grilles, 474
Grout
ceramic tile with, 479, 482, **487**
curing of, 479
design of, 473
faux, **550**
granite with, **499**
installation of, 559
limestone with, **500**
slate with, **505**
slip resistance of, 559
terra-cotta with, **494**
Guest cottages, **585, 589, 636, 656–665, 672–673**
Guided, drawer, 101
Gussets, 93
Gym, **123**

H

Hallways, **27, 72, 74, 86**
lighting, 184, **184–187**
Halogen light, quartz, 134, 140, 145, 147, 200, 224–225, 228–229, 239, 453
handling, 225
Hampers, clothes, 442
Hardware, 683, 692
for doors, 96–99
for shelves, 19, 92, 93, 94, 95
Hardwood, 464, 472, **480,** 510, **510–523.** *See also* Wood
area rug(s) on, **472, 473, 543, 545**
faux, **527, 529**
in grid design, **467**
shopping for, 564–567
stained with pattern, **470**
staircase, **461**
Hazards, eliminating, 270–271, 358–359
Headboards, **25, 44**
Heating, 591, 690
Heating and electrical safety, 369
Heat, radiant, 467
Heights, shelf, 16, 17
Hickory, 565
HID bulbs, 145, 228–229
Hideouts, **418–421**
Hinges, **64, 96,** 98
Hobby areas, 382
Home offices, **27, 34, 41, 71, 72–77, 82, 104, 107, 585, 596,** 597, **626–631**
Home theaters, 20–23, **64,** 112
Housing boxes, 238, 240, 246

I–J

Incandescent light, 140, 144, 220–221, 222, 228–229, 234, 453
Indirect lighting, 135, **139,** 146, 194. *See also* Lighting
Indoor air quality, 468
Infancy, 371, 377. *See also* Cribs, Nurseries
Infant beds. *See* Beds
Inlays, 473
in concrete, 576
stone, 563
wood, 462, 567
Installation, 478–479
of carpeting, 574–575
of ceramic tile, 479, 559
of laminate, 571
of lighting, 150–151
of resilient flooring, 569
of stone, 563
of wood, 567
Insulating glass, 680, 690
Insulation, 690
Interests, and personalitiy, 366
Intermediate beds. *See* Beds
Ironing boards, **122**
Junctions, 474

K

Kelvin scale, 141
Kitchens, **25, 31, 32, 35, 45, 49, 50, 52, 56, 60, 76, 78, 83, 105**
lighting, 147, 170, **170–177**
Kits, 598–599, 650. *See also* Prefabricated structures

L

Ladders, **34, 71**
library, **38, 64, 79,** 109
Laminate, 462–463, 465, 472, 532
installation of, 479
for wall systems, 14–15, 91
look of ceramic tile, **538, 539**
look of stone, **468**
look of wood, **532–537**
maintenance of, 468
measuring for, 479
shopping for, 570–571
subfloor under, 467
Lamp components, 237
Lamps, 158, 230–233. *See also* Lighting
Landscape, fitting into, 588–590
Landscape professionals, 600
Landscaping, 589–590, 684–687
Large rooms, 267, **275**
Laser discs, sizes of 17
Latches, door 99
Lattices, 683, 686
Laundry areas, **27, 87**
Layering light, 136–137
Layouts, creating, 266–267
Leather, 463, 465
on area rug, 572
in den, 548
in dining room, **552**
in home office, 474
in living room, **550, 552**
maintenance of, 468, 577
Ledges, **33**
Libraries, **38, 64, 79**
Library ladder, **412**
Light bulbs, 144–145. *See also individual types.*
comparisons, 228–229
energy requirements for, 222
silvered-bowl, 137, 221, 228–229
Lighting, **36, 41, 54–55, 57, 58, 61,** 356–357, 388, 452–453, **669,** 687, 699
built-in, **373**
recessed, **388**
shopping for, 126
types of, 134–135
Light levels, 142–143, 154
outdoor, 148
Light ratios, 136–137, 143
Limestone, 461, 464, 496
oversized slabs of, **502–503**
polished, **504,** 560, 561
tumbled, **462, 500, 501**
Linoleum, 462, 524, **524, 525, 526,** 568, 689
Living areas, **7, 24, 34, 36, 38, 39, 40–41, 42, 43, 51, 57, 58, 59, 60, 61, 63, 66, 67, 70, 71**
Living room lighting, 158, **158–169, 210–211**
Loads, circuit, 150–151
Loft beds. *See* Beds
Log cabins, **634, 635,** 679
Low-voltage lighting, 135, 145, 147, 148, 184, 208, 224, 240, 241, 244, 246, 248–249
Lumens, 142

M

Magazine rack, **34**
Mahogany, 564, **565**
Mail-order plans, 599–601, 650, **652**
Maintenance, 370
of carpeting, 574
of concrete, 576
of laminate, 468, 571
of leather, 468, 577
of metal, 577
of resilient flooring, 569
of stone, 563
of tile, 559
of wood, 468, 567
Makeup lights, 194, **194–199,** 236–237
Maple, 461, 464, **512, 520,** 564, **565,** 566
Marble, 460, 464, **497,** 560, 561–562
Carrara, **496**
faux, 482, **521**
at hearth, **519**
life span of, 468
mosaics, **491**
saddle, 474
striated, **501**
types of, 461
Masonry, 606, 679
Materials, for shelving, 14–15
shopping for, 90–101
Mattress, buying, 433
Measurements, 479
Medallions, 567
metal, **577**
stone, 470, 473, **501,** 563
tile, 473
wood, 462, 464, 470, 473
Media centers, 20–23, **24, 62–67,** 110–112
Melamine, 21, 91, 462–463
Mercury vapot lights, 145, 228–229
Metal, 577. *See also* Steel
ceramic and, 474
decorative, 463
halide lights, 228–229
inserts, **462**
Mobiles, 263, 348
Modular furnishings, 376
Modular systems, 10, 12, **13, 32, 35, 41, 48, 85, 86, 117, 119**
shopping for, 106–109, 122–123
Moldings, 52, 74, 127, 449
Moonlights, 233
Mortar, 479, **490, 494, 508,** 559, 563

Mosaic(s), 460
glass, **488, 490**
marble, **491**
porcelain, **493,** 558
in rug design, **482, 488**
stone, **556,** 560, **561**
terra-cotta, **497**
Moses basket, 335, 336
Motion sensors, 150, 243, 250–251
Murals, 273, 274, **292–293, 296–307, 317,** 350

N

Neighbors, 590, 593, **594**
Neon, 135, 145, **159,** 226
Nero Marquina marble, 461, 561
Night lights, 233, 357, 453
Nursery plans
basics of, 258–263
choosing a room, 264–269
clutter control, **326–331,** 344–349
comfort in, providing for parents and baby, **320–325**
layouts for, creating 266–267
look and feel, creating, 272–277, **279–331**
safety in, 270–271, 358–359
sharing rooms, 268–269, **314–319**
Nurseries, **371, 376, 383, 385, 396–397.** *See also* Cribs

O

Oak, 461, 464, 564, **565**
clear, **516**
grades of, 566
life span of, 468
marble faux painting on, **521**
with nutmeg stain, **511**
saddle, 474, **506**
Occasional seating, 439. *See also* Chairs, Seating
Odd-shaped rooms, 267
Office lighting, 200, **200–204**
Office space, **585, 596,** 597, **626–631**
Organizers
cabinet, 120
drawer, 101
office, 121
wire, 121
Outdoor lighting, 148–151, 206, **206–217,** 246–249
controls for, 250–251
Outlet covers, 271, 358
Outlets, 474
electrical, 150, 242–243
Overheads, 680, 686

P

Paint, 447, 678, 691
faux finishes, 691
trompe d'oeil, 679
Painted furniture, custom- or hand-, **360, 372, 383, 386, 396, 401, 402, 407, 409, 413, 442**
Painting, **290–307, 521, 522, 523,** 567. *See also* Murals
risks to pregnant women, 269
Paneling, 448, **627, 656, 661, 662, 664,** 690–691
PAR bulbs, 220, 225, 228–229
Partners in planning, 374–375
Parquet, 461, **518–519,** 565–566, 567
Particleboard, 14, 91
Paths, 684–685, 687
Patios, 684–685
Pattern, 475, 479, **520, 525**
Pavers, 460, 464, 475, 556–559. *See also* Ceramic tile; Tile(s)
Paving, 685
Pecan, **565**
Peg-Board, 696
Peg racks, 696
Pendants, 135, **146,** 170, **234,** 235
Period rooms, 390. *See also* Theme rooms
Personality and interests, 366
Photocells, 150, 233, 250, 251
Pickling, 567
Picture lights, 139, **169,** 232, **233**
Picture shelves, **33**
Pine, 461, 464, 468, **513, 520,** 564, 566
Planks, wood, 461, **510, 516, 517,** 565
Planning department, 586, 592, 597, 599, 602
Planning, guidelines for, 365–393, 459–479, 583–607
activities, spaces for, 367
drawings, 392
for future uses, 587, 656
partners in, 374–375
Plans, mail-order, 599–601, 650, **652**
Plans, site, 592–595
Plantings, 589, 590, **630,** 686, 687
Plants, lighting for, 139, **149,** 208
Plastic, 677, 679. *See also* Acrylic roofs
Play areas, **362, 367, 372,** 381, **382, 383, 385, 398, 418–421**
Playhouses, **632–633, 634–635**
Play tables. *See* Tables, desks and seating
Plywood, 14, 15, 90–91
Polyurethane, 465
Pool houses, **589, 646–649**
Pool lighting, 208, **216, 217, 247**
Porcelain
pavers, 460, 464, 557–558
tiles, 474, 482, **484, 489, 493, 553**
Potters' studios, **640–642**
Potting sheds, **584, 585, 587, 620–625, 650, 654, 655, 683, 695**
Prefabricated structures, 599, **601,** 650, **651, 653**
Professional help, 598–599, 600, 602
Programming phase, 601–602
Pullout shelves, 11, **49, 85, 120**
Pulls, door, 99
Puppet theaters, **362, 372, 403**

Q, R

Quartz halogen. *See* Halogen
Questionnaire, flooring, 469
Ratios of light, 136–137, 143
Ready-to-assemble systems, 12
Receptacles, 242–243
Recessed fixtures, **147,** 240–241
Records, 17, 23, **77**
Refinishing, 479
Reflectance, 141
Reflector bulbs, 220, 228–229
Registers, 474
Removal, of old floor, 479
Resilient flooring, 462, 465, 476, 524, **524–531,** 689. *See also* Flooring
installation of, 479
measuring for, 479
shopping for, 568–569
Retreats, **610–617**
Rheostats. *See* Dimmers
Rocking chairs, 342
Roofs, 676–677. *See also* Acrylic, Copper, Glass, Sod, Tile, Wood
Room-by-room wall systems solutions, 24–27
Room dividers, **23, 44, 67, 68–71, 118**
Room elements, 380–389
Room for two or more. *See* Shared rooms
Rooms to grow, 376–378
Room types and styles, 389–391. *See also* Theme rooms
Rope lights, 150, **236,** 237
Rubber, 462, 465, 467, 524, 569
Rug(s), area, 446
with border, **544**
custom options for, 574
on granite, **498**
on hardwood, 567
on laminate, **537,** 540, 571
on leather, **551, 552**
Oriental, **537, 543**
prebound, 572
replicating, **484, 488**
sisal, **546**
tatami-like, **547**
on wood, 462, **472, 473, 512, 575**

S

Saddle, 474, **506, 523**
Safety, 270–271, 358–359, 466, 470. *See also* Slip resistance
Safety gates, 358
Safety latches and locks, 358
Safety tips, 369
Saltillo, 557
Samples, 478
Scale, 367, 472
Sconces, **146,** 154, 158, 235, 237
Scrapbook, 476
Screen
folding, **372**
shoji, **604,** 693
Sealers, sealants, 479, 678
for concrete, 576
for grout, 559
for stone, 563
for wood, 567
Seating, 436–439
dimensions for, 384
occasional, **367, 381, 399, 416,** 439
Security lighting, 150, 206, 246, 250–251
Setbacks, **597, 611**
Sewing center, **122**
Shades, 355, 680, 692–693. *See also* Window treatments
Sharing rooms, 268–269, **314–319, 368, 378,** 379–380, **381, 386, 402–424, 410, 421**
Sheet products, 14, 15, 90–91
Shelves, **4, 7, 8,** 10, 11, **28, 30–37, 49, 50, 51, 53, 55, 56, 58, 60, 61, 65, 67, 72, 73, 74, 75, 76, 77, 78, 79, 81, 86,** 345–346, 442, 586–587, 695
dimensions, 16, 17, 18, 384
finishes, 124–125
folding, **120**
glass, **33, 36, 45, 58,** 91
hardware, 19, 92–95
materials, 14–15, 90–93

shopping for, 90–95
utility, **116,** 117
Shingles, 677, 678
Shutters, 693. *See also* Window treatments
Sidecar sleepers, 335, 336
Siding, 678–679. *See also* Adobe, Stone, Stucco, Wood
Silhouetting, **138**
Silvered-bowl bulbs, 137, 221, 228–229
Sisal, 540, **546, 547,** 572, 574, 575
Site plans, 592–595
Siting, 585–586, 588–591
Size of cottage, 586–587
Skylights, 681, 690
Slate, 464, 472, 560, 562, **670,** 677, **688,** 689
in bathroom, **504**
in den, **507**
faux, **529**
in great room, **506, 546**
in kitchen, **505, 507**
Sleeping places for babies and parents, 258, 263, **320–325.** *See also* Cradles; Cribs
Sleeping shelters, **672–673**
Sleeping spaces, 380
Slides, drawer, 101
Slip resistance, 466, **490, 492,** 558–559, 563
Sloping sites, **591,** 593, **594**
Small rooms, 265, **308–313**
Smoke detectors, 358
Sod roofs, **630–631,** 677
Solar lighting, 251
Sound reduction, 467
Southern Pine Council, 467
Space savers, 387, 399–402
Spans, shelf, 18
Specialty flooring, 463, 465, **548–553,** 576–577
Stains, exterior, **587, 639,** 678
Stairs, **461,** 474
lighting for, 184, **184, 186–187**
Stairways, **27, 61, 79, 80, 81**
Steel, 463, 465, 548, **553,** 577
Stenciling, **621, 690, 691**
Stock cabinets, shopping for, 114–115
Stone, 460–461, 464, 496, **496–509, 514, 614, 636, 669,** 679, 685, 689
distributors, 476
faux, **486, 570,** 571
glass mosaic "area rug" in, **488**
grout and, 473
installation of, 479
life span of, 468
measuring for, 479
medallion, 470
replicating, **484**
shopping for, 560–563
slip resistance of, 466, **490,** 563
storage of, 478
texture of, 473
wood and, 474
Storage, 263, **326–331,** 344–349, 385, **399–401, 403, 412–415, 422, 423, 427,** 440–443, 586–587, 694–698
baskets, 443
bins, **385,** 443
boxes, 443
built-in, **372, 376, 380, 381, 383, 385, 386, 405**
closed, **393, 394, 400, 401, 403, 413**
loft bed and, **365, 422**
modular, **373, 385, 412**
safety, 369
toy boxes, **381,** 443
under-bed, **402, 431,** 442
wardrobes, **366, 401, 415, 416,** 441
Storage furniture, 12, **13, 46, 47, 48, 49, 50, 51**
Storage walls, **38, 39–45, 70, 71, 108, 109**
Story poles, 597, 602
Strip lights, 135, 170, 208, 225, 237
Stucco, **643, 667,** 679, **684**
Studios, **594, 640–645, 694**
Study areas, **380,** 382, **393, 404, 408, 416–417, 437–439**
built-in, **373, 398, 401, 402**
computer, **437,** 438
loft bed and, **364–365**
Style, 12–13, 16–19, 389–391, 472
planning, 604–607
regional, **634–637**
Subfloor, 464, 479, 559, 560, 563, 567
Sun exposure, 590–591, 592
Surface wiring, 151
Surveyors, 602
Swags, 692, **693**
Swimming pool lighting, 208, **216, 217, 247**
Switches, 158, 184, 188, 242–245

T

Table, fold-down, **121**
Table lamps. *See* Lighting
Tables, desks and seating, 436–439
low, **367, 372, 381, 386, 436, 439**
Task lighting, 134, 136, **146,** 200, 222, 224, 232, 236–237
recommended levels, 142–143
T-bulbs, 221, 228–229
Teak, 564, **565**
Teenagers, 373, 377
Temperature, Kelvin, 141
Tent cabins, **651**
Tents, **394, 418, 420**
Terra-cotta, 460, 464, 472, 482
with ceramic accent tiles, **495**
faux, **550**
mosaics, **497**
sealed, **494,** 557, 559
Terrazzo, **460, 508,** 560, 562, **563**
Testing light levels, 143
Texture, 473, **490, 500, 502–503, 529**
of carpeting, 540, **542**
of ceramic pavers, 557
of concrete, **549,** 576
of metal, **553**
of stone, 563
of teak, 564
of terrazzo, **563**
Thatched roofs, 677
Theme rooms, **363, 367,** 389, **400, 408–411, 418, 425**
Tile(s), 460, 482, **482–495,** 685, **688,** 689. *See also* Ceramic tile
as accents, 476
Arabesque, **508**
concrete, 576
cork, **467, 477, 530, 531,** 568
distributors of, 476
installation of, 479, 559
Italian, 472
laminate, 532
leather, 463, 548, **551, 552**
limestone, **462, 500, 504, 560**
linoleum, **526**
metallic, **553,** 577
parquet, 567
porcelain, 474, 482, **484, 489, 493, 553**
quarry, 482, 556, 557, 559
resilient, 465, 479, 569
roofs, **643, 667,** 677
rubber, 569
slate, **504, 562**
slip-resistant, 466, 472
steel, 463, **553,** 577
stone, 464, 473, **488, 514**
terra-cotta, 472, **494**
terrazzo, **508**
textures of, 473
at transitions, 474
vinyl, 468, **528,** 568
wall, 460
wood, 464
Tile Institute of America, 467
Time, as factor in planning, 262
Timers, 150, 243, 251
Torchères, **146,** 158, 231
Toy boxes. *See* Storage
Toy chests, 346
Track lighting, **147, 174,** 220, 238–239. *See also* Cable lights
Tracks and brackets, 19, **33,** 92
Traction. *See* Slip resistance
Traffic patterns, 466–467
Transformers, 148, 225, 238, 239, 240, 241, 244, 248
Transitions, 474, **506**
Treehouses, **618–619**
Trellises, 680, 683, 687
Trim, exterior, **682,** 683
Trim units, 558, 571
Trompe d'oeil painting, 679
Trundle beds. *See* Beds
Tubes, fluorescent, 144–145, 222–223, 228–229, 237
Tubes, incandescent, **196,** 221, 228–229, 237
Turntables, **77**
Types and styles of rooms, 389–391. *See also* Theme rooms

U

Under-bed drawers. *See* Storage
Unfitted furnishings, 12, **13, 46–49, 62, 77, 83**
shopping for, 102–105
Uniform Building Code, 597
Uplighting, **139,** 150, 154, 208
Uplights, **169,** 232, **233, 248**
Utilities, 585–586, 587, 591, 593, 640, 656, 690
Utility areas, **27, 84–87**
shopping for, 116–119
U-value, 680

V

Veneer tape, 91
Videotapes, 17, 23
Vinyl, 462, 465, 524, 568
life span of, 468
in sheets, **462, 466, 526, 527, 529**
slip resistance of, 466
in tiles, **528**
Vinyl flooring, 689
Vinyl siding, 679
Visual flow, 474
VOCs (volatile organic compounds), 468

W

Wall appliqués, **389**
Wall beds. *See* Beds
Wall fixtures. *See* Lighting
Wallpaper, 691

Wall sconces, **146,** 154, 158, 235
Wall system components, 10–11
Wall-to-wall carpet, 446
Wall treatments, 350–351, 447–449, 690–691. *See also* Murals
  borders, **363, 367, 368, 372, 378, 386, 389, 393, 396, 422, 426, 448**
  canvas, **396**
  and ceiling, **386**
  custom painted, **363, 388, 390, 391, 411, 414, 426, 427, 447**
  fabric, **386, 449**
  other, **389**
  wallpaper, **372, 377, 378, 379, 383, 387, 394, 402, 406, 408, 416, 417,** 447, **448, 449**
Wall washing, 139, **149,** 158, **161**
Wardrobes. *See* Storage
Water, 590, 591
Window boxes, 589, 687
Windows and doors, 388, 680–681, 690, 699
  and safety, 271, 359, 369
  treatments, 354–355, 450–451
    blinds, **367, 394, 410, 412, 414, 427, 448**
    curtains, **362, 363, 366, 379, 380, 390, 410, 411, 450**
    shades, **367, 372, 378, 380, 381, 387, 410, 451**
    shutters, 451
Window seats, **372, 418**
Window treatments, 354–355, 450–451, 680, 692–693
Wine storage, **87**
Wire grids, **695,** 696
Wireless controls, 245
Wire management, 113
Wiring, 150–151, 245
  track, 239
Wood, 15, 461–462, 464, 510, **510–523.** *See also* Hardwood
  borders, 473
  carpeting over, 574
  chips, 685
  decks, 685
  faux techniques on, 476
  finishes, 124–125
  flooring, **610, 688,** 689
  framing, 606
  installation of, 479
  life span of, 468
  maintenance of, 468
  measuring for, 479
  medallion, 462, 470, 473
  paneling, **627, 656, 661, 662, 664,** 690–691
  reclaimed, **474**
  refinishing, 479
  roofing, **599, 676,** 677
  shopping for, 90–91, 564–567
  siding, **586, 599, 616, 631, 641, 676,** 678
  stone and, 474
  storage of, 478
  subfloor for, 479
  treatments for, 678
Wood floors. *See* Flooring
Work space lighting, 200, **200–205**

X–Z

Xenon bulbs, 225
Yellow Desert marble, 461, 562
Zoning, 586, 588, **589,** 591, 597, 602